Lawyer Negotiation

ASPEN CASEBOOK SERIES

Lawyer Negotiation
Theory, Practice, and Law

Second Edition

Jay Folberg

University of San Francisco

Dwight Golann

Suffolk University

Wolters Kluwer

Law & Business

AUSTIN   BOSTON   CHICAGO   NEW YORK   THE NETHERLANDS

Aspen Publishers
Attn: Permissions Department
76 Ninth Avenue, 7th Floor
New York, NY 10011-5201

To contact Customer Care, e-mail customer.service@aspenpublishers.com, call 1-800-234-1660, fax 1-800-901-9075, or mail correspondence to:

Aspen Publishers
Attn: Order Department
PO Box 990
Frederick, MD 21705

Printed in the United States of America.

1 2 3 4 5 6 7 8 9 0

ISBN 978-0-7355-9970-3

Library of Congress Cataloging-in-Publication Data

Folberg, Jay, 1941.
  Lawyer negotiation : theory, practice, and law / Jay Folberg, Dwight Golann.—2nd ed.
    p. cm.
  Includes bibliographical references and index.
  ISBN 978-0-7355-9970-3 (alk. paper)
    1. Negotiation—United States. 2. Dispute resolution (Law)—United States. I. Golann, Dwight. II. Title.

KF9084.F65 2011
347.73'9—dc22

2010046587

About Wolters Kluwer Law & Business

Wolters Kluwer Law & Business is a leading provider of research information and workflow solutions in key specialty areas. The strengths of the individual brands of Aspen Publishers, CCH, Kluwer Law International and Loislaw are aligned within Wolters Kluwer Law & Business to provide comprehensive, in-depth solutions and expert-authored content for the legal, professional and education markets.

CCH was founded in 1913 and has served more than four generations of business professionals and their clients. The CCH products in the Wolters Kluwer Law & Business group are highly regarded electronic and print resources for legal, securities, antitrust and trade regulation, government contracting, banking, pension, payroll, employment and labor, and healthcare reimbursement and compliance professionals.

Aspen Publishers is a leading information provider for attorneys, business professionals and law students. Written by preeminent authorities, Aspen products offer analytical and practical information in a range of specialty practice areas from securities law and intellectual property to mergers and acquisitions and pension/ benefits. Aspen's trusted legal education resources provide professors and students with high-quality, up-to-date and effective resources for successful instruction and study in all areas of the law.

Kluwer Law International supplies the global business community with comprehensive English-language international legal information. Legal practitioners, corporate counsel and business executives around the world rely on the Kluwer Law International journals, loose-leafs, books and electronic products for authoritative information in many areas of international legal practice.

Loislaw is a premier provider of digitized legal content to small law firm practitioners of various specializations. Loislaw provides attorneys with the ability to quickly and efficiently find the necessary legal information they need, when and where they need it, by facilitating access to primary law as well as state-specific law, records, forms and treatises.

Wolters Kluwer Law & Business, a unit of Wolters Kluwer, is headquartered in New York and Riverwoods, Illinois. Wolters Kluwer is a leading multinational publisher and information services company.

To my father, Lew Folberg, the pawn broker who taught me the art of negotiation

—*J.F.*

To my father, Herbert Goldberg, whose inventiveness in other fields has inspired my work

—*D.G.*

SUMMARY OF CONTENTS

CONTENTS

CHAPTER 13
MEDIATING FOR NEGOTIATION ADVANTAGE   317

CHAPTER 14
NEGOTIATED SETTLEMENT POLICY AND LIMITS   355

PREFACE

This book is based on three key assumptions: First, to represent clients effectively, lawyers must be skilled negotiators. Second, lawyer negotiation differs from direct negotiation between parties because lawyers are professional agents for clients and therefore have unique responsibilities and potential conflicts. Finally, a negotiation textbook should be interesting to read; bring together the latest, best, and most provocative writing on negotiation; and lend itself to interactive teaching.

Our book, therefore, has a different perspective from most other texts on negotiation. It focuses on legal negotiation — the settling of substantial legal claims in which the disputants are represented by attorneys. Although the emphasis is on negotiating settlements of disputes, negotiation of deals and transactions is also fully covered. This book includes a chapter on obstacles to reaching agreements and assisted negotiation. Another chapter covers mediating for negotiation advantage. The reality is that lawyers now regularly use mediation to conclude difficult negotiations of litigated disputes and need to understand how mediation works and how to use it as a creative negotiation tool to best meet their clients' needs. Most students enrolling in a negotiation course will not take a separate mediation course, and if they do it is more likely to focus on how to be a mediator rather than an advocate in the process, as emphasized here.

The text is practical while grounded in theory, and lawyer-focused but also enriched by interdisciplinary material. This book asks many questions and poses problems designed to provoke critical thinking about the readings and stimulate class discussion. Accompanying role-plays and exercises provided in the Teacher's Manual allow students to apply the readings and bring the text material to life. These role-plays again center on the types of disputes in which students are likely to find themselves as practicing lawyers — cases with legal claims or issues, rather than neighborhood quarrels or purely personal conflicts. There is also a comprehensive bibliography to give students access to a wide variety of writings on negotiation and mediation by scholars and practitioners in the field.

This second edition of *Lawyer Negotiation* follows the same organization as the first edition and contains the same core elements. We have updated some of our narrative and included excerpts from the most recent writings on negotiation, so that teachers will not need to prepare supplements in order to assign entirely up-to-date material. Readings have been carefully edited to keep the material interesting and lively. Additional notes extend the topic coverage, including game theory, perceptions, psychological traps, emotional intelligence, decision analysis, use of computer software, apologies, and collaborative law practice. We also take advantage of technology, and of students' increasing preference for electronic and video formats. Items that have traditionally gone into a paper appendix now appear on the book's Web site. This makes this book easier to carry without sacrificing depth, allows readers to download specific codes or standards for discussion, and permits us to update the book's appendix between editions when new rules or laws pertaining to negotiation are promulgated. A DVD is also available to professors to illustrate some of the points and enhance the role-play discussions.

The book's fourteen chapters are designed for a semester course with readings assigned before class so that class time can be devoted to exercises, role-plays, and discussion. The first chapter explores the nature of conflict and the second the role of perceptions and settlement psychology. We then analyze in chapter 3 both competitive and cooperative bargaining, and in chapter 4 provide help in combining the approaches and choosing a comfortable style. After setting out an analytic structure to help students make sense of negotiation and understand styles, we offer in chapters 5 through 7 a step-by-step explanation and comparison. The negotiation process and outcome-enhancing skills are covered in these three chapters, which provide instruction from preparation through writing the agreement. Following a chapter on telephone and cyber negotiation, students are guided in chapter 9 to explore issues of gender, culture, and race. Chapters 10 and 11 then examine negotiation ethics and the law of negotiation. Obstacles to negotiation are reviewed in chapter 12, and the use of mediation to fill client needs advantageously is then presented in chapter 13. Finally, in chapter 14, there is an exploration of negotiation policy and limits.

A note about form: To focus discussion and conserve space, we have substantially edited the readings and have deleted most footnotes, references, and case citations. Deletions of material are shown by three dots or ellipses, but omitted footnotes and other references are not indicated. Cited authority in the text usually appears only by author name and year of publication, with a full reference in the bibliography.

This book is the culmination of our combined decades of teaching and negotiating in legal contexts. Although our acknowledgments follow, we are particularly grateful to the many students and lawyers whom we have had the pleasure of teaching negotiation and from whom we have learned much about what works in a negotiation class. We are also thankful to the professors who have suggested corrections and improvements for this new edition.

December 2010

J.F.
D.G.

ACKNOWLEDGMENTS

This negotiation book has evolved from our comprehensive coursebook, Resolving Disputes: Theory, Practice, and Law, which we wrote with Lisa Kloppenberg and Thomas Stipanowich. Although this book has grown to become a text of its own with multiple editions, it would not exist without Lisa and Tom's collaboration in creating the survey text, from which this volume had its genesis. We are grateful for their continuing encouragement and friendship. We benefited from their enthusiasm for this project, and we look forward to partnering with them in the future.

We are thankful for the support and assistance we have each received from the staffs and librarians of the law schools at the University of San Francisco and Suffolk University. Special thanks go to the professors who suggested corrections and improvements for this second edition. We are most grateful to the students and lawyers whom we have trained and worked with in negotiation and mediation. They have inspired us and guided what we have selected here to present to the next generation of lawyers.

Finally, we are indebted to the many authors and publishers who have granted their permission for us to edit and include parts of their publications. More specifically, we thank the following sources for permission to publish excerpts of their work:

Abramson, Harold, Mediation Representation: Advocating in a Problem-Solving Process. Copyright © 2004 by the National Institute for Trial Advocacy (NITA). Reprinted with permission from the National Institute for Trial Advocacy. Further reproduction is prohibited.

Adair, Wendy, L. and Jeanne M. Brett, "Culture and Negotiation Process" in *The Handbook of Negotiation and Culture* by M. Gelfand and J. Brett (eds.) 158-176. Copyright © 2004. Reprinted by permission.

Adler, Robert S., and Elliot M. Silverstein, "When David Meets Goliath: Dealing with Power Differentials in Negotiations," 5 Harvard Negotiation Law Review 1. Copyright © 2000. Reprinted with permission.

Adler, Warren, Excerpt from The War of the Roses. Copyright © 1951. Reprinted by permission.

Arnold, Tom, "20 Common Errors in Mediation Advocacy," 13 Alternatives 69 (1995). Copyright © 1995. Reprinted with permission of John Wiley & Sons, Inc.

Bazerman, Max H., and Malhorta, Deepax, "Negotiation Genius: How to Overcome Obstacles and Achieve Brilliant Results at the Bargaining Table and Beyond." From Negotiation Genius: How to Overcome Obstacles and Achieve Brilliant Results at the Bargaining Table and Beyond Copyright © 2007 by Deepak Malhotra and Max H. Bazerman. Used by permission of Bantam Books, a division of Random House, Inc.

Benjamin, Robert, "Terry Waite: A Study in Authenticity" Adapted from http://www.mediate.com. Summer, 2002. Copyright © 2002. Reprinted with permission.

Birke, Richard, "Decision Trees — Made Easy." Copyright © 2004 by Richard Birke. Reprinted with permission.

Brazil, Wayne D., "A Judge's Perspective on Lawyering and ADR," 19, Alternatives 44 (January 2001). Copyright © 2001. Reprinted with permission of John Wiley & Sons, Inc.

Bryan, Kathy, A., "Why Should Businesses Hire Settlement Counsel" Journal of Dispute Resolution 195. Copyright © 2008. Reprinted with permission.

Cohen, Amy, "Gender: An (Un) Useful Category of Prescriptive Negotiation Analysis" Texas Journal of Women and Law 13, 69. Copyright © 2003. Reprinted with permission.

Condlin, Robert, J., "Bargaining in the Dark: The Normative Incoherence of lawyer Dispute Bargaining Profile" Maryland Law Review 51(1), 71-72, 75-82, 84-85. Copyright © 1992. Reprinted with permission.

Craver, Charles B., "Effective Legal Negotiation and Settlement," excerpted from Effective Legal Negotiation and Settlement. Copyright ©2001 Matthew Bender & Company, Inc., a member of the LexisNexis Group. All rights reserved.

Craver, Charles, "Race and Negotiation Performance: Does Race Predict Success as a Negotiator?" 2001, Dispute Resolution, 8:1, p. 22-27. Copyright © 2001 by the American Bar Association. Reprinted with permission.

Epstein, Lynn, A., "Cyber E-Mail Negotiations vs. Traditional Negotiation: Will Cyber Technology Supplant Traditional Means of Settling Negotiation?" Tulsa Law Journal 36, 839 Copyright © 2001. Reprinted with permission.

Epstein, Lynn A., "Post-Settlement Malpractice: Undoing the Done Deal," 46 Cath. U. L. Rev. 453. Copyright © 1997. Reprinted with permission.

Fisher, Roger, "Negotiating Powers: Getting and Using Influence," From J. William Breslin and Jeffrey Rubin, eds., Negotiation American Behavioral Scientist (Vol. 27, No. 2), pp. 149-166, Copyright © 1983 by Sage Publications. Reprinted by permission of Sage Publications.

Fiss, Owen M., "Against Settlement." From Yale Law Journal, Vol. 93, pp. 1073. Reprinted by permission of the Yale Law Journal Company, Inc.

Goodpaster, Gary, "A Primer on Competitive Bargaining," 1996 Journal of Dispute Resolution 325. Copyright © 1996 by Journal of Dispute Resolution. Reprinted with permission.

Harr, Jonathan. From A Civil Action by Jonathan Harr. Copyright © 1995 by Jonathan Harr. Used by permission of Random House, Inc.

Heen, Sheila, and John Richardson, "I See a Pattern Here and the Pattern is You," Personality and Dispute Resolution in the Handbook of Dispute Resolution by M. I. Moffitt and R.C. Bordone, eds. Copyright © 2005 John Wiley & Sons, Inc. Reprinted with permission.

Hetherington, H., Lee, "The Wizard and Dorothy, Patton and Rommel: Negotiation Parables in Fiction and Fact" Pepperdine Law Review, 289(28) 311-315. Copyright © 2001. Reprinted with permission.

Katsh, Ethan, "Online Dispute Resolution" The Handbook of Dispute Resolution by M. Moffitt and R. Bardone (eds.) 425, 428-437. Copyright © 2005. Reprinted with permission.

Kichaven, Jeffrey, G. "How Advocacy Fits in Effective Mediation," Alternatives 16, 60 Copyright © 1999. Reprinted with permission.

Kolb, Deborah M., and Judith Williams, "Introduction: Recognizing the Shadow Negotiation." Reprinted with permission of Simon & Schuster Adult Publishing Group. From The Shadow Negotiation: How Women Can Master the Hidden Agendas That Determine Bargaining Success by Deborah M. Kolb, Ph.D., and Judith Williams, Ph.D. Copyright © 2000 by Deborah M. Kolb, Ph.D., and Judith Williams, Ph.D.

Korobkin, Russell, "A Positive Theory of Legal Negotiation," 88 Georgetown Law Review 1789. Copyright © 2000. Reprinted with permission.

Korobkin, Russell, Michael Moffit, and Nancy Welsh, "The Law of Bargaining," 87 Marquette Law Review 4, 839-842 (2004). Reprinted with permission.

Lax, David A., and James K. Sebenius. "The Manager as Negotiator: Bargaining For Cooperation and Competitive Gain," Copyright © 1986 by David A. Lax and James K. Sebenius. All rights reserved.

Longan, Patrick, "Ethics in Settlement Negotiations: Foreword," 52 Mercer Law Review 810-816. Copyright © 2001. Reprinted with permission.

Malan, Douglas, S., "A Numbers Game," Connecticut Law Tribune 36(4). Copyright © 2010. Reprinted with permission.

Menkel-Meadow, Carrie, "Toward Another View of Legal Negotiation: The Structure of Problem Solving" UCLA Law Review, 31, 754. Copyright © 1984 Reprinted by permission.

Miller, Lee E., and Jessica Miller, "A Woman's Guide to Successful Negotiating," pp. 66-73 (2002). Reproduced with permission of the McGraw-Hill Companies.

Mnookin, Robert H., Excerpt from Bargaining with the Devil: When to Negotiate, When to Fight. Copyright © 2010 Simon & Schuster. Reprinted with permission.

Mnookin, Robert H, "Why Negotiations Fail: An Exploration of Barriers to the Resolution of Conflict" Ohio State Journal of Dispute and Resolution 8, 235-443, 238-249. Copyright © 1993. Reprinted with permission.

Mnookin, Robert H., Scott R. Peppet, and Andrew S. Tulumello. Reprinted by permission of the publisher from Beyond Winning: Negotiation to Create Value in Deals and Disputes by Robert H. Mnookin, Scott R. Peppet, and Andrew S. Tulumello, pp. 37-42, 282-286, Cambridge, MA: The Belknap Press of Harvard University Press. Copyright © 2000 by the President and Fellows of Harvard College.

Moffitt, Michael, "Contingent Agreements: Agreeing to Disagree About the Future," Marquette Law Review (87) 691. Copyright © 2004. Reprinted with permission.

Moffitt, Michael, "Three Things to Be Against (Settlement, Not Included)," Fordham Law Review 78, 1203 Copyright © 2009. Reprinted with permission.

Nadler, Janice, "Rapport in Legal Negotiation: How Small Talk Can Facilitate E-Mail Deal Making," Harvard Negotiation Law Review 223, 225. Copyright © 2004. Reprinted with permission.

Nelken, Melissa, Reprinted from Understanding Negotiation with permission. Copyright © 2007 Matthew Bender & Company, Inc., a member of the LexisNexis Group. All rights reserved.

O'Connor, Theron, "Planning and Executing an Effective Concession Strategy." Reprinted with permission of the author.

Spolter, Jerry, "A Mediator's Tip: Talk to Me!" The Recorder 4, March 8, 2000. Copyright © 2000. Reprinted with permission.

Sumner, Anna, Aven, "Is the Gummy Rule of Today Truly Better Than The toothy Rule of Tomorrow? How Federal Rule 68 Should Be Modified," Duke University Law Journal 852, 1055. Copyright © 2003. Reprinted by permission.

Welsh, Nancy, and Barbara McAdoo, "Alternative Dispute Resolution in Minnesota—An Update on Rule 114," in Edward J. Bergman and John C. Bickerman, eds., Court-Annexed Mediation: Critical Perspectives on State and Federal Programs 203 (1998). Printed by permission of Pike & Fischer, Inc.

Wetlaufer, Gerald, "The Limits of Integrative Bargaining," 85 Georgetown Law Journal 369. Copyright © 1996. Reprinted with permission.

White, James J., "Pros and Cons of 'Getting to YES'; Roger Fisher, Comments on White's Review," 34 Journal of Legal Education. Copyright © 1984. Reprinted with permission.

Williams, Gerald R., "Negotiation as a Healing Process," 1996 Journal of Dispute Resolution 1-65 (1996). Reprinted with permission.

Wood, Robert, W., "Taxing Matters in Settling Cases," California Lawyer 41. Copyright © 2007. Reprinted with permission.

Zitrin, Richard A., and Carol M. Langford, "The Moral Compass of the American Lawyer." From The Moral Compass of the American Lawyer, Copyright © 1999 by Richard Zitrin and Carol M. Langford. Used by permission of Ballantine Books, a division of Random House, Inc.

Lawyer Negotiation

CHAPTER

1

Negotiation and Conflict

A. Introduction to Negotiation

Negotiation is the process of communication used to get something we want when another person has control over whether or how we can get it. If we could have everything we wanted, materially and emotionally, without the concurrence of anyone else, there would be no need to negotiate. Because of our interdependence, the need to negotiate is pervasive.

Everyone negotiates as part of modern life. However, because lawyers are paid to negotiate for others, we are considered professionals. A law student reading only casebooks might not know that the vast majority of disputes in which lawyers are involved are negotiated to a settlement without trial. Many major transactions are also the result of lawyer-negotiated agreements. Negotiation is at the core of what lawyers do in representing clients.

Most lawyers think they are skilled negotiators because they negotiate frequently. Negotiating frequently does not necessarily result in negotiating effectively. Unlike trial practice, negotiation is usually done in private without the opportunity to compare results or benefit from a critique. Those with whom you negotiate rarely give an honest assessment of how you did, and it is most often in their interest for you to believe you did well. Regardless of our intuitive ability, negotiation skills and results can be improved with analysis and understanding, as well as practice.

Lawyer negotiation takes place within the dynamics of settling a dispute or shaping a deal. It is not always a tidy process that tracks a textbook diagram. In this book we use a seven-stage model of negotiation, recognizing that all negotiations do not follow the same lineal staging and each stage will not necessarily be completed. The negotiation dance can be improvised to fit the situation. For example, we list initial interactions and offers as part of Stage 2 before exchanging information; however, the initial offer or demand may often follow an exchange of information. The seven stages are:

1. Preparation and Setting Goals
2. Initial Interaction and Offers
3. Exchanging and Refining Information
4. Bargaining
5. Moving Toward Closure
6. Reaching Impasse or Agreement
7. Finalizing the Agreement

Negotiation occurs because there are differences between what parties want or how they perceive a situation. As a professional negotiator you have an edge if you understand the nature of the conflict to be resolved, the psychology of negotiation, and contrasting styles of bargaining. So, we begin with the nature of conflict and the role of perceptions, as well as emotional dimensions and psychological traps. Next we look at the advantages and disadvantages of using a more competitive or cooperative bargaining style. We then examine the stages of negotiation and the activities associated with each step. Subsequent chapters look at gender and culture, ethics, and the role of law in negotiations.

B. Conflict Is What We Make It

Although conflict can cause distress and is usually viewed negatively, it can function in positive ways. Conflict may motivate you to take action and change your situation in ways that improve your life and better fulfill your self-interests. Conflict can, however, also create a crisis mentality that becomes destructive. Lawyers can help create more constructive outcomes from conflicts or they can make a difficult situation worse. The ability to help clients better understand the conflict, reframe the issues, and realistically analyze their interests and how they can be negotiated is an important lawyering skill.

Conflict is divided into two categories: interpersonal (differences that arise between individuals or groups) and intrapersonal (conflicts within ourselves). Interpersonal conflict is a situation in which the parties each want something that they perceive as incompatible with what the other wants. Because the parties in an interpersonal conflict cannot both have all that they want, their interests or goals are divergent. Lawyers are retained to help resolve interpersonal conflicts between our clients and others. A client may also be conflicted internally about what it is they really want from an opponent. For example, does your client really want to return to the job from which she was fired, or does she want only to restore her self-respect and get compensation? Does the father you represent in a divorce really want custody of the children, or is he internally conflicted about the decision to divorce and trying to hold onto the marital relationship? Recognizing these two different types of conflict can be critical in achieving client goals.

Another distinction that can be useful in negotiation and mediation is between the manifest conflict, which is overt or expressed, and the underlying conflict, which is hidden or denied. Lawyers most often deal with manifest conflicts, which we refer to as disputes. A conflict may not become a dispute if it is not communicated in the form of a complaint or claim. However, what is communicated may be only a part of or symbol of the underlying conflict. The dispute between brothers over control of a family business seems safer to contest than the underlying conflict of who was the favored son or a better child. Indian tribes may actively dispute government fishing quotas, while the underlying conflict involves the more fundamental issue of outside control and alteration of Native American traditions. Residential development disputes may focus in court on specific environmental regulations or traffic issues, but the underlying conflict is about the changing character of the community. This dichotomy between the overt dispute and the hidden conflict can be viewed for purposes of negotiation as the presenting problem and the hidden agenda.

If the agreements reached in negotiation resolve only the presenting problems, they are less likely to last unless legally enforced. Surfacing the underlying conflict can clarify issues, focus objectives, generate new possibilities for settlement, and ultimately improve relationships. Dealing with the underlying conflicts, however, may be emotionally difficult for clients and can stimulate internal conflict. Many lawyers are not comfortable with opening emotional issues and may not have the capacity to address them. We look more into the emotional aspects of conflict and settlements shortly.

Professor Rubin, in the excerpt that follows, emphasizes "building relationships in negotiations," and explains the concepts of "enlightened self-interest" and "ripeness."

❖ **Jeffrey Z. Rubin,** SOME WISE AND MISTAKEN ASSUMPTIONS
ABOUT CONFLICT AND NEGOTIATION

Negotiation Theory and Practice 3, Program on Negotiation Books
(J.Z. Rubin & W. Breslin eds., 1991)

For many years the attention of conflict researchers and theorists was directed to the laudable objective of conflict resolution. This term denotes as an outcome a state of attitude change that effectively brings an end to the conflict in question. In contrast, conflict settlement denotes outcomes in which the overt conflict has been brought to an end, even though the underlying bases may or may not have been addressed. . . . The gradual shift over the last years from a focus on resolution to a focus on settlement has had an important implication for the conflict field: It has increased the importance of understanding negotiation — which, after all, is a method of settling conflict rather than resolving it. The focus of negotiation is not attitude change per se, but an agreement to change behavior in ways that make settlement possible. Two people with underlying differences of beliefs or values (for example, over the issue of a woman's right to abortion or the existence of a higher deity) may come to change their views through discussion and an exchange of views, but it would be inappropriate and inaccurate to describe such an exchange as "negotiation." . . .

Cooperation, Competition, and Enlightened Self-Interest

Required for effective conflict settlement is neither cooperation nor competition, but what may be referred to as "enlightened self interest." By this I simply mean a variation on what several conflict theorists have previously described as an "individualistic orientation" — an outlook in which the disputant is simply interested in doing well for himself or herself, without regard for anyone else, out neither to help nor hinder the other's efforts to obtain his or her goal. The added word "enlightened" refers to the acknowledgment by each side that the other is also likely to be pursuing a path of self interest — and that it may be possible for both to do well in the exchange. If there are ways in which I can move toward my objective in negotiation, while at the same time making it

Enlightened self-interest is the key to negotiation

possible for you to approach your goal, then why not behave in ways that make both possible?

Notice that what I am describing here is neither pure individualism (where one side does not care at all about how the other is doing) nor pure cooperation (where each side cares deeply about helping the other to do well, likes and values the other side, etc.) — but an amalgam of the two. . . . I do not have to like or trust you in order to negotiate wisely with you. Nor do I have to be driven by the passion of a competitive desire to beat you. All that is necessary is for me to find some way of getting what I want — perhaps even more than I considered possible — by leaving the door open for you too to do well. "Trust" and "trustworthiness," concepts central to the development of cooperation, are no longer necessary — only the understanding of what the other person may want or need.

A number of anecdotes have emerged to make this point . . . Jack Sprat and his wife — one preferring lean, the other fat — can lick the platter clean if they understand their respective interests. The interesting thing about this conjugal pair is that, married though they may be, when it comes to dining preferences they are hardly interdependent at all. For Jack and his wife to "lick the platter clean" requires neither that the two love each other nor care about helping each other in every way possible; nor does it require that each be determined to get more of the platter's contents than the other. Instead, it is enlightened self interest that makes possible an optimal solution to the problem of resource distribution. . . .

The Importance of "Relationship" in Negotiation

Much of the negotiation analysis that has taken place over the last 25 years has focused on the "bottom line": who gets how much once an agreement has been reached. The emphasis has thus largely been an economic one, and this emphasis has been strengthened by the significant role of game theory and other mathematical or economic formulations.

This economic focus is being supplanted by a richer, and more accurate, portrayal of negotiation in terms not only of economic, but also of relational, considerations. As any visitor to the Turkish Bazaar in Istanbul will tell you, the purchase of an oriental carpet involves a great deal more than the exchange of money for an old rug. The emerging relationship between shopkeeper and customer is far more significant, weaving ever so naturally into the economic aspects of the transaction. . . .

Psychologists, sociologists, and anthropologists have long understood the importance of "relationship" in any interpersonal transaction, but only recently have conflict analysts begun to take this as seriously as it deserves. Although it seems convenient to distinguish negotiation in one time only exchanges (ones where you have no history of contact with the other party, come together for a "quickie," and then expect never to see the other again) from negotiation in ongoing relationships, this distinction is more illusory than real. Rarely does one negotiate in the absence of future consequences. Even if you and I meet once and once only, our reputations have a way of surviving the exchange, coloring the expectations that others will have of us in the future. . . .

The Role of "Ripeness"

Although it is comforting to assume people can start negotiating any time they want, such is not the case. First of all, just as it takes two hands to clap, it takes two to negotiate. You may be ready to come to the table for serious discussion, but your counterpart may not. Unless you are both at the table (or connected by a telephone line or cable link), no agreement is possible.

Second, even if both of you are present at the same place, at the same time, one or both of you may not be sufficiently motivated to take the conflict seriously. It is tempting to sit back, do nothing, and hope that the mere passage of time will turn events to your advantage. People typically do not sit down to negotiate unless and until they have reached a point of "stalemate," where each no longer believes it possible to obtain what he or she wants through efforts at domination or coercion. It is only at this point, when the two sides grudgingly acknowledge the need for joint work if any agreement is to be reached, that negotiation can take place.

By "ripeness," then, I mean a stage of conflict in which all parties are ready to take their conflict seriously, and are willing to do whatever may be necessary to bring the conflict to a close. To pluck fruit from a tree before it is ripe is as problematic as waiting too long. There is a right time to negotiate, and the wise negotiator will attempt to seek out this point.

It is also possible, of course, to help "create" such a right time. One way of doing so entails the use of threat and coercion, as the two sides (either with or without the assistance of an outside intervenor) walk (or are led) to the edge of "lover's leap," stare into the abyss below, and contemplate the consequences of failing to reach agreement. The farther the drop — that is, the more terrible the consequences of failing to settle — the greater the pressure on each side to take the conflict seriously. There are at least two serious problems with such "coercive" means of creating a ripe conflict: First, as can be seen in the history of the arms race between the United States and the Soviet Union, it encourages further conflict escalation, as each side tries to "motivate" the other to settle by upping the ante a little bit at a time. Second, such escalatory moves invite a game of "chicken," in which each hopes that the other will be the first to succumb to coercion.

[handwritten margin note: Coercion usually doesn't work too well]

There is a second — and far better — way to create a situation that is ripe for settlement: namely, through the introduction of new opportunities for joint gain. If each side can be persuaded that there is more to gain than to lose through collaboration — that by working jointly, rewards can be harvested that stand to advance each side's respective agenda — then a basis for agreement can be established. . . .

Notes and Questions

1. Morton Deutsch, who pioneered the modern study of conflict resolution, distinguished manifest conflict from underlying conflict, as summarized in our introductory comments (see Deutsch 1973). Rubin, a former student of Deutsch, separates settlement of the manifest conflict behaviors from the attitude changes necessary to bring an end to the underlying base of conflict. We noted a similar distinction between the presenting problem and the hidden agenda. Do you agree that settlement only of the manifest problem is unlikely to last? Why or why not? Is litigation limited only to the manifest or presenting issues? Is Rubin correct in indicating that negotiation is only a method of settling conflict rather than resolving it?

2. Professor Rubin in his excerpt introduces the concept of "enlightened self-interest," which is related to the "utility" theory that began with Jeremy Bentham in the late 1700s and underlies much of the current analysis of negotiation. How does enlightened self-interest, or utility theory, explain Rubin's conclusion that Mr. and Mrs. Sprat could reach an "optimal solution" and "lick the platter clean?" Is he correct in indicating that "trust" and "trustworthiness" are not relevant to reaching optimal solutions? Why or why not?

3. Just as it takes two or more people to have a conflict, so it takes two or more people to reach agreement. Ripeness of the conflict is critical for those involved to begin serious negotiation toward resolution. What do you think Rubin means when he suggests that new opportunities for joint gain create ripeness? How might this concept help lawyers get disputes resolved?

4. How do lawyers most often create "ripeness" to seriously negotiate and settle disputes?

C. The Triangle of Conflict and Negotiation

Rubin discusses bottom-line negotiation and the limits of focusing only on the economic aspects of a conflict. There is increasing recognition that to negotiate a satisfactory resolution of a conflict there must be an understanding of and attention to the emotional and relationship components, or what Rubin refers to as the underlying bases of the conflict. Even though the dominant focus in most lawyer negotiations is on the trade-offs involving legal claims or economic considerations measured in money damages, neglecting the nonmonetary components resulting from conflicts can lead to an impasse or a settlement that does not hold.

There are three sets of factors at work in most conflicts. They can be thought of as the three "Es": economic, emotional, and extrinsic. These form the three sides of the negotiation triangle, which relate to needs and interests that are discussed in Chapter 3.

NEGOTIATION TRIANGLE

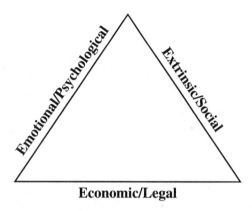

Economic/Legal

Legal issues and rights are what often bring lawyers to the negotiation table to bargain over economic damages. Once there, the other two sides of the triangle that impact clients enclose and influence the negotiation process and outcome. The emotional component refers to the internal pushes and pulls on parties created by the conflict that affect how they feel about themselves. The extrinsic elements are the setting and social considerations, including how others will view what is going on and how the resolution will appear to third parties. "Face saving" is frequently referred to in the negotiation literature; it is an extrinsic social factor that also has an emotional impact. The three sides of the triangle are interrelated and have an impact on one another. The mix of what matters for purposes of resolving a conflict will vary depending on the subject and the sensitivities and history between the parties, as well as their attorneys. A purely commercial case will most heavily involve economic considerations. However, all three elements are involved to some extent in every type of dispute. A business person sued for breach of contract has feelings about accusations from a longtime supplier and concerns about his reputation in the business community. A divorce or employment dispute, although focused on legal rights and money, will invoke more emotional and extrinsic factors. For example, in a divorce, what will children, grandparents, and neighbors think about new parenting arrangements? In a wrongful termination case, how will acceptance of the economic offer appear to co-workers who remain friends with the terminated worker? Attention to the non-economic factors can help prevent or end a negotiation impasse and move the matter to resolution.

It can be difficult to quantify the emotional and extrinsic factors, but there might be ways to satisfy the internal-emotional and external-social factors in a manner that both settles the case and helps resolve the conflict. As you read the following fact situation and resulting lawsuit, settled a year and a half after the incident, consider what roles both emotional and social factors might have played in negotiating a settlement agreement.

Problem — Tiger Attack

On December 25, 2007, Tatiana, a 250-pound Siberian tiger in the San Francisco Zoo, leapt out of her enclosure, killed 17-year-old Carlos Sousa, Jr., and injured two of his friends, brothers Amritpal Dhaliwal, then 19, and Kulbir Dhaliwal, then 23. The tiger was shot dead by police. The media coverage was extensive. Zoo spokesman Sam Singer, hired by the zoo for damage control, seemed to blame the brothers for the incident, suggesting that they taunted the tiger. Animal rights advocates protested the shooting of the tiger. Zoo attendance and donations dropped.

A claim for the death of Carlos Sousa, Jr. was settled. The Dhaliwal brothers sued the San Francisco Zoological Society, the City of San Francisco, and Sam Singer. Their federal lawsuit alleged that the zoo was negligent in maintaining a tiger enclosure several feet below recommended standards, claimed their civil rights were violated because their car was improperly seized, and accused Singer of libel and slander for comments he made to media implying that they might have been taunting the tiger. They also alleged that police officials had ordered officers to issue warrants for their arrest, accusing them of manslaughter in the death of their deceased friend, Carlos Sousa, Jr., even though an investigation could not substantiate any basis for bringing charges against them. Substantial damages were sought by the brothers, well beyond the relatively modest amounts for physical injuries and medical expenses.

1. If you were advising the zoo, would you recommend that it negotiate a settlement? Is there any downside for the zoo in negotiating? Would your answers be different if you were representing the Dhaliwal brothers?
2. What are the non-economic factors in this conflict, and how might they be addressed in negotiation?
3. What might the Dhaliwal brothers obtain in a negotiated settlement that they could not win at trial?

The emotional side of the triangle of conflict might be the most difficult for you to deal with if you are not trained in psychology. You might negotiate what you think is a great resolution of a dispute, only to have it rejected by your client, who must agree before a settlement or deal is finalized. Understanding the emotional stages experienced by a client in a conflict can help you better represent your client in negotiations. Professor Gerald Williams identifies the emotional stages a client might follow to move out of a conflict and get on with his life or business. The last phase of renewal or transformation may be more an inspirational hope than a realized reality.

❖ **Gerald R. Williams,** *NEGOTIATION AS A HEALING PROCESS*
J. Disp. Resol. 1 (1996)

The Five Steps for Recovering from Conflict

. . . Just as researchers have found that getting *into* a conflict is a multi-step process that typically involves naming, blaming, claiming, rejection, and a decision to go public, even so, the task of getting *out of* a conflict requires the disputants to work their way through a multistage process.

A. Denial

As a preliminary model of the process of recovering from conflict, the first stage is typically a condition of *denial*. As James Hall explains, there is in each of us "a deep-seated human desire *not* to be the one at fault, *not* to be the one who must change." This resistance to being the one at fault, to being the one who must change, is part of what makes conflict so painful and its resolution so difficult. Most conflicts are a story of two parties, both of whom contributed to the problem, and neither of whom wants to admit his or her role in it. In the literature on grieving we gain a broader sense of what is meant by the term *denial* and some of the risks it poses to the parties and others: "The person will strongly deny the reality of what has happened, or search for reasons why it has happened, and take revenge on themselves and others.". . . From this perspective, we might even say that, in most instances, conflicts are meaningful; they have a purpose. Their purpose is to hold up a mirror so disputants may see themselves in a new light, an experience as painful as it is valuable. . . .

Properly understood, then, conflicts serve as such a mirror. They expose the disputants' weaknesses; the areas in which they have been too much the victim, or too much the exploiter; their complexes, their unresolved angers, and their feelings of specialness and entitlement. Because it is so painful for disputants to see these parts of themselves exposed by their own involvement in the conflict, they need the protection and reinforcement, the containment and channeling, that the lawyer-client relationship provides, and they need the benefit of the full play of the negotiation process to help them gradually face what they see in the mirror and to come to terms with it. . . .

B. Acceptance

The next step is *acceptance*. It may take time, but at some point the parties need to move beyond denial and to *accept the possibility that they themselves are part of the problem.* They do not yet need to *do* anything about it, just to accept the possibility that the problem does not begin and end with the other side, that they themselves may have some complicity in the problem. In some cases, however, it may be that one side actually is wholly innocent and the other wholly to blame for the problem. But even when parties are wholly innocent, they still need to accept the possibility there is *something they could do now to move the situation in the direction of an appropriate resolution.* Again, they don't need to actually take action, they simply need to register a change in attitude that opens them to the possibility of movement in the direction of an appropriate solution.

C. Sacrifice

Assuming the parties have accepted the possibility they are part of the problem, or the possibility there is something they could do now to move in the direction of a resolution, the next step is to consider what they might be willing to do about it. In its starkest form, the principle is that, for the conflict to be resolved, the parties must be willing to make a sacrifice. From a judge's point of view, the minimum sacrifice required for a valid settlement agreement is a *compromise* by each side, meaning that both parties must make some concession, must move from their original position. But as a general matter, mere concessions or compromises do not require a change of heart. It has been observed that people usually are not willing to make a sacrifice until they have been brought to a more humble attitude. . . . Assuming that sacrifices need to be made, what should they be? This is an extremely delicate question. We know, for example, that some people have a history of being *too compliant*, of giving away too much, whether motivated by a need for affection and approval, by fear of reprisals, or for some other reason. For those who are too compliant, the sacrifice called for would probably *not* be to make more concessions to their antagonist, but rather to forebear from giving, to reverse themselves, to give up the part of themselves that always wants to please others. For other people, the problem may be just the opposite. They may be exploiters who are too good at looking out for themselves at others' expense. For them, the sacrifice may be to recognize their exploitive patterns and become more conscious of the interests and needs of other people. There are many other possibilities. The answer will depend on the personalities involved and the particularities of their situations. In some situations, parties may need to sacrifice — to let go of — such things as a desire for a total victory, or an impulse for revenge, a mistaken belief that they themselves are faultless and the other side totally to blame, their pride, their unwillingness to acknowledge or appreciate another's point of view, or their unwillingness to forgive another for his or her mistake. In other situations, parties may need to give up the belief that they can get away with exploiting others, their belief that they are better or more deserving than others, or their excessive opinions of their own abilities, worth, privileged status, etc. There may be situations in which parties need to give up their hope of obtaining a windfall or other unearned benefit, or give up their envy or spite or jealousy with respect to possessions, luck, and social position.

Before proceeding to the fourth step, there is one final consideration. Is it mandatory that parties make a sacrifice? The answer is a firm "no." There can be no *requirement* that the client have a change of heart. It is fundamental that, as lawyers, we implicitly and explicitly declare to our clients that they can stay just the way they are, and so long as they do not expect us to do that which is illegal or unethical, we will stand by them. Our willingness to represent our clients should not depend upon their willingness to change, much less to move in directions *we* think right. As Shaffer and Elkins remind us, "the client has to be free to be wrong." The negotiation process, then, is not intended for lawyers to impose our values upon our clients, but for us to help contain and channel our clients' energies in appropriate ways until they have had enough time to see their own situations more clearly and to discover for themselves what steps they may be willing to make.

D. Leap of Faith

The fourth stage refers to action or movement, what might be called the *leap of faith*. It is a leap of faith, for example, to admit to the other side that you might be *willing* to make a sacrifice to resolve the case. Practicing lawyers recognize it as the moment when their client looks them in the eye and asks, "If I do this, can you guarantee it will work?" And the lawyer has to reply, "No, I can't guarantee that, because I don't know that. But the trial is coming up really soon, and we haven't thought of anything better to do, but you decide." And the client must decide. . . .

E. Renewal or Healing from Conflict

If the process works well enough, and both parties are willing to move by incremental leaps of faith in the direction of agreement, and if they seek in the process to fathom the underlying problems and address them along the way, the effect can be two-fold: they may reach a mutually acceptable solution and, in the best of circumstances, they may also experience a change of heart, be reconciled to one another and healed and feel renewed as human beings. This is the transformation objective; it is the goal or purpose of all ritual processes, whether it be theater or court trial or graduation exercise or religious rite or negotiated settlement. Rituals are to help prepare the participants, those on whose behalf the ceremony is enacted, to move forward in a new condition, to a new phase of life. *Renewal* or transformation in this context means not simply they are as good as they were before the conflict, but they are better — they are more whole, or more compassionate, or less greedy, or otherwise changed in an important way from their attitude or condition before the crisis began. Certainly, when people experience such a fundamental change through the process of conflict resolution, they will be far less likely to find themselves in a similar conflict again. On the other hand, if they fail at this process, then to the extent the conflict was a product of their own developmental shortcomings, it is likely they will find themselves in similar conflicts in the future, returning again and again until the party acknowledges and addresses the underlying developmental need. . . .

Notes and Questions

5. Elizabeth Kubler-Ross, in her 1969 book *On Death and Dying*, introduced a model known as the five stages of grief, by which people deal with grief and tragedy, specifically when diagnosed with a terminal illness. Kubler-Ross's five stages are denial, anger, bargaining, depression, and acceptance. This five-stage model, or some variation, has since been applied by authors to every type of personal loss, including divorce and bankruptcy. How does Professor Williams's five-stage model differ from Kubler-Ross's five stages of dealing with death? Do you agree with Williams's five-stage analysis as applied to conflict?

6. Many people have a negative view of conflict and try to avoid it. Do you? Was conflict viewed as negative in your family? During your childhood, how did your family deal with conflict? Will you try to model the same conflict process for your children?

7. As a lawyer, will you welcome representing clients who seek your help to resolve their conflicts with others? Why or why not?

CHAPTER
2

Perception, Fairness, Psychological Traps, and Emotions

A. The Role of Perceptions

The key to understanding and mastering negotiation is to be aware that those in conflict and who want something from one another see the situation differently. It is these differences that give root to conflict and to the need to negotiate, as well as to the possibility of agreement. We assess conflict and evaluate a case or the worth of an item differently because of differing perceptions. Our individual perceptions determine how we view ourselves, others, and the world. No two views are exactly the same. For example, we may selectively perceive or differ in our perceptions of the following:

- facts
- people
- interests
- history
- fairness
- priorities
- relative power

- abilities
- available resources
- scarcity
- timing
- costs
- applicable law or rules
- likely outcomes

Our view of each of these elements, as well as our perceptions of other variables, shape how we see the world and how we form differences. It is because of such differences in perceptions that people bet on horse races, wage war, and pursue lawsuits.

A classic Japanese story, on which the film *Rashomon* is based, illustrates the role of perceptions and how the truth through one person's eyes may be very different from another's, as seen through the prism of the individuals' own perceptions. Through divergent narratives, the story and the film explore how perceptions distort or enhance different people's memories of a single event, in this case, the death of a Samurai warrior. Each tells the "truth" but perceives it very differently. The film, like the story, is unsettling because, as in much of life, no single truth emerges.

A popular book and film, *The War of the Roses*, by Warren Adler, and its 2004 sequel, *The Children of the Roses*, capture different truths as perceived by divorcing couples. Early in the original story, Oliver and Barbara Rose reveal to their

13

separate lawyers their perspectives on the marriage and how their family home should be divided. Each sees the marriage relationship and what's fair differently, as filtered through his or her own experience, values, and selective vision. Is there any doubt, based on such different perceptions, that the war between the Roses would follow?

❖ **Warren Adler, THE WAR OF THE ROSES**

51 (Stonehouse Press, 1981)

[Oliver Rose's perception:] "She just upped and said, 'No more marriage.' Like her whole persona had been transformed. Maybe it's something chemical that happens as forty gets closer."

He had . . . been a good and loving husband. He had nearly offered "faithful" to complete the triad but that would have discounted his two episodes with hookers during conventions in San Francisco and Las Vegas when the children were small. My God, she had everything she could possibly want. . . .

What confused him most was that he had not been warned. Not a sign. He hated to be taken by surprise.

"And the house?" Goldstein asked.

"I don't know. Say half the value. After all, we did it together. Half of everything is okay with me. . . ."

[Barbara Rose's perception:] "He's like some kind of animal. Almost invisible. He leaves early, before we get up, and comes home late, long after we've gone to bed. He doesn't take his meals at home. . . ."

"You think it's fair for me to have devoted nearly twenty years to his career, his needs, his wants, his desires, his security. I gave up my schooling for him. I had his children. And I devoted a hell of a lot more time to that house than he did. Besides, the house is all I have to show for it. I can't match his earning power. Hell, in a few years he'll be able to replace its value. I'll just have cash. Well, that's not good enough. I want the house. I want all of it. It's not only a house. It's a symbol of a life-style. And I intend to keep it that way. That's fair. . . ."

"It's my house. I worked my ass off for it," she said.

The following reading further develops the theme that conflict is subjective and flows from different perceptions in people's minds. Rummel's "subjectivity principle" may help to explain the *War of the Roses* and many other conflicts that would otherwise defy understanding and resolution.

❖ **R.J. Rummel, THE CONFLICT HELIX**

13 (Transaction Publishers, 1991)

The Subjectivity Principle

Perceived reality is your painting. You are the artist. You mix the colors, draw the lines, fix the focus, achieve the artistic balance. Reality disciplines your painting; it is your starting point. As the artist, you add here, leave out there; substitute color, simplify; and provide this reality with a point, a theme, a center of interest. You produce a thousand such paintings every moment. With unconscious artistry. Each a personal statement. Individualistic.

Now, most people realize that their perception of things can be wrong, that they may be mistaken. No doubt you have had disagreements with others on what you all saw or heard. And probably you have heard of eyewitnesses who widely disagree over the facts of a crime or accident. Some teachers who wish to dramatically illustrate such disagreement have staged mock fights or holdups in a classroom. A masked man rushes in, pointing some weapon at the teacher; demands his wallet; and with it hastily exits, leaving the class stunned. Then each member of the class is asked to write down what he saw and heard. Their versions usually differ widely.

But, of course, such are rapidly changing situations in which careful observation is difficult. Surely, you might think, if there were time to study a situation or event you would perceive it as others do. This is easy enough to test. Ask two people to describe in writing a furnished room, say your living room, or a car you may own. Then compare. You will find many similarities, but you should also find some important and interesting differences. Sometimes such differences result from error, inattentiveness. However, there is something more fundamental. Even attentive observers often will see things differently. And each can be correct.

There are a number of reasons for this. First, people may have different vantage points and their visual perspectives thus will differ. A round, flat object viewed from above will appear round, from an angle it will appear an ellipse, from the side a rectangle. This problem of perspective is acute in active, contact sports such as football or basketball. From the referee's line of sight there is no foul, but many spectators (especially the television audiences who see multiple angles and instant replays) know they saw an obvious violation.

But people can compare or change perspectives. Were this all, perception would not be a basic problem. The second reason for different perceptions is more fundamental. You endow what you sense with meaning. The outside world is an amorphous blend of a multitude of interwoven colors, lights, sounds, smells, tastes and material. You make sense of this complex by carving it into different concepts, such as table, chair, or boy. Learning a language is part of learning to perceive the world.

You also endow this reality with value. Thus what you perceive becomes good or bad, repulsive or attractive, dangerous or safe. You see a man running toward you with a knife as dangerous; a calm lake as peaceful; a child murderer as bad; a contribution to charity as good. And so on.

Cultures are systems of meanings laid onto reality; to become acculturated is to learn the language through which a culture gives the world unique shape and evaluation. A clear example of this is a cross, which to a Christian signifies the death of Jesus for mankind as well as the whole complex of values and beliefs bound up in the religion. Yet, to non-Christian cultures a cross may be meaningless: simply two pieces of wood connected at right angles. . . .

Besides varying perspectives and meanings, a third reason for different perceptions is that people have unique experiences and learning capacities, even when they share the same culture. Each person has his own background. No two people learn alike. Moreover, people have different occupations, and each occupation emphasizes and ignores different aspects of reality. Simply by virtue of their separate occupational interests, the world will be perceived dissimilarly by a philosopher, priest, engineer, union worker, or lawyer.

Two people may perceive the same thing from the same perspective, therefore, but each through their diverse languages, evaluations, experience, and occupations, may perceive it differently and endow it with personal meaning. Dissimilar perspective, meaning, and experience together explain why your perception will often differ radically from others.

There is yet an even more basic reason: what you sense is unconsciously transformed within your mental field in order to maintain a psychological balance. This mental process is familiar to you. People often perceive what they want to perceive, what they ardently hope to see. Their minds go to great pains to extract from the world that which they put there. People tend to see things consistent with their beliefs. If you believe businesspeople, politicians, or bureaucrats are bad, you will tend to see their failings. If you like a person, you tend to see the good; hate him and you tend to see the worst. Some people are optimists, usually seeing a bottle half full; others are pessimists, seeing the same bottle half empty.

Your perception is thus the result of a complex transformation of amorphous sensory stimuli. At various stages your personal experience, beliefs, and character affect what you perceive. . . . Independent of the outside world's powers to force your perception, you have power to impose a perception on reality. You can hallucinate. You can magnify some things to fill your perception in spite of what else is happening. Think of the whisper of one's name.

What you perceive in reality is a balance between these two sets of powers: the outside world's powers to make you perceive specific things and your powers to impose a certain perception on the world. This is the most basic opposition, the most basic conflict. Its outcome is what you perceive reality to be . . . . The elements of the subjectivity principle are perception, mental field, and balance: your perception is a balance between the powers of your mental field and the outside world. It is a balance between the perception you tend to impose on the outside world and the strength of what is out there to force its own reality on you. It is a balance between what you unconsciously want to perceive and what you cannot help but perceive . . . .

This balance that envelopes your mental field changes with your interest and concentration. Its shape and extension will depend on your personality and experience. And, of course, your culture. No wonder, then, that you are likely to perceive things differently from others. Your perception is subjective and personal. Reality does not draw its picture on a clean slate — your mind. Nor is your mind a passive movie screen on which sensory stimuli impact, to create a moving picture of the world. Rather, your mind is an active agent of perception, creating and transforming reality, while at the same time being disciplined and sometimes dominated by it. . . .

You and I may perceive reality differently and we both may be right. We are simply viewing the same thing from different perspectives and each emphasizing a deferent aspect. Blind men feeling different parts of an elephant may each believe they are correct and the others wrong about their perception. Yet, all can be correct; all can have a different part of the truth.

Notes and Questions

Rummel's subjectivity principle explains how we process the information and stimuli around us through the filters of our experience, needs, and biases. The complexity of our environment and our minds prevents us from taking it all in whole, so we focus selectively on some stimuli and ignore others. We develop shortcuts in our perceptual systems that allow us to function and process information more quickly and make timely decisions. These shortcuts, known as heuristics, can serve us well. However, mental shortcuts create the risk that our selectivity will distort reality as seen by others. The different ways we process information can lead to conflict based on our different realities.

A key concept in understanding the cause of disputes is *selective perception*. Jeffrey Rubin describes this phenomenon and its offspring, *self-fulfilling prophecies*:

> Let us begin with selective perception. . . . In an escalating conflict, we tend to see what we want to see and to distort information to support our expectations. One way we do this is by selectively testing hypotheses. We form a hypothesis about the adversary such as, this person is nasty. Then we gather information to confirm our hypothesis and ignore information that does not support it. In selective perception we have only dealt with perceptions. When behavior is introduced, we have self-fulfilling prophecy, which connects attitudes and behaviors. I have an expectation of you that leads me to behave in a way that produces a response in you that confirms my expectation. My prophecy about the kind of person that you are is fulfilled. (Rubin 1993)

1. Is the subjectivity principle, as explained by Rummel, the same concept as selective perception and self-fulfilling prophecies, as described by Rubin?

2. Can you recall a conflict you have experienced that might be better understood in light of the subjectivity principle?

3. John Milton, in *Paradise Lost,* poetically stated: "The mind is its own place, and in itself can make a heaven of Hell, a hell of Heaven" (Milton 1909). In explaining his subjectivity principle, is Rummel just restating Milton?

4. If a conflict between people is the result of different perceptions, what might be of help in resolving the conflict?

5. Is there a connection between Rummel's subjectivity principle and the distinction made in Chapter 1 between the manifest conflict and the underlying conflict? Can you articulate an explanation of manifest conflict or underlying conflict based on Rummel's subjectivity principle?

6. Is the conflict between Barbara and Oliver Rose really over their house, or something else? If the division or ownership of the house is the manifest or presenting conflict, what is the underlying conflict or "hidden agenda?" Can lawyers negotiate what may be the underlying conflict regarding gender roles? Can they do something about each Rose's need for recognition of his or her contribution to the house and the marriage?

B. The Impact of Fairness

Our list of selective perceptions at the beginning of this chapter included "fairness." Differing views of fairness are at the heart of many litigated conflicts and failed negotiations. Fairness, like other perceptions, is in the mind of the beholder. A client may hire you to negotiate on her behalf because she feels she has been treated unfairly and that you, as a lawyer, can help her obtain what is fair. Fairness, as perceived by clients, can also become central in assessing whether to accept or reject a negotiated settlement or deal.

An outcome that appears fair can be more important than winning or losing. Fairness may define for some whether they won or lost. Offers may be rejected even though they are economically advantageous because in the client's mind the result is not fair.

Classroom experiments with "ultimatum games" illustrate the importance of perceived fairness in negotiation. In these games, Player 1 is given a fixed sum of money or chips (for example, $100) as a windfall that she might have found on the street and is asked to propose a division of that sum with Player 2 (e.g., $75 to Player 1 and $25 to Player 2). Player 1 has complete discretion to divide the money as she wishes; Player 2 can choose only whether to accept or reject Player 1's proposal. If Player 2 accepts the offer, both players will keep the money as allocated. If Player 2 rejects the offer, neither player will receive anything.

Economic theory dictates that Player 1 should offer only a little more than zero to Player 2, and that Player 2 should accept this amount as better than nothing. In fact, in classroom experiments Player 1 generally offers 30 to 50 percent of the sum to Player 2, and when less than 50 percent is offered, many recipients will reject the offer, preferring to walk away with nothing rather than accept what they perceive to be an unfair result. The results of this game reflect the importance of our innate value of being treated fairly (see Brams & Taylor 1996).

Perceptions of fairness consist of two components. Distributional fairness is a quantitative notion of material outcome—what you get as the result of a negotiation. Procedural fairness relates to the process used to reach the outcome—how you were treated during the negotiation. Both of these components shape people's willingness to accept settlements and their feelings of how well attorneys represented them in the negotiation process.

Problem — The Home-Run Ball Catch

More than 40,000 fans were at the ballpark to see the San Francisco Giants' last game of the 2001 season. Most had come to see Barry Bonds add another home run to his already record-breaking total of 72. Alex Popov and Patrick Hayashi were two fans in the right field arcade standing-room section, hoping to catch a Bonds home-run ball. Sure enough, Bonds's 73rd home-run ball came sailing over the right field bleachers into Popov's outstretched glove. Within seconds, Popov fell to the ground as a rush of people converged on him and the ball. Madness followed before security officers arrived. When Popov was pulled from the pile of fans, the ball was no longer in his glove. Patrick Hayashi emerged with the ball in hand.

Both men claimed ownership of the valuable home-run ball, temporarily in Hayashi's possession. Both thought the ball was worth more than $1 million, based on the sale of Mark McGwire's 70th home-run ball in 1998 for more than $3 million. Each man offered the other less than $100,000 to relinquish any claim on the ball. Each expressed strong public views that he was entitled to complete ownership and was making a generous offer to the other. Both Popov and Hayashi cited principles of fairness and baseball fan culture entitling them to the ball. Popov argued that first possession controls, and Hayashi believed the fan who ended up in possession owned the ball. They insulted one another as liars and thieves. They both hired lawyers and filed suit in the California superior court.

Newspaper editorials, letters, talk show hosts, Barry Bonds, and several mediators all suggested that the ball be sold and the proceeds be split by the men or that the money be given to charity. Neither Popov nor Hayashi thought that evenly splitting what they were individually entitled to was fair, nor did they feel that they could concede anything in light of the insults cast on them by the other. Following 18 months of public bickering and litigation about what was fair, the judge ordered that the ball be sold and the proceeds evenly split. On June 25, 2003, the ball, seated on black velvet and encased in glass, was sold at auction to a comic book impresario for a final bid of $450,000. Popov and Hayashi each received $225,000, minus auction expenses, and each incurred attorneys' fees exceeding that amount. Popov was sued by his attorney for fees and expenses of $473,530, and also for $19,000 by a law professor who served as an expert witness. (The whole sorry story and background is captured in the 2004 film *Up for Grabs*.)

1. Neither Popov nor Hayashi appeared to be guided by rational self-interest in making decisions about how to maximize their ultimate economic outcome. What do you think got in the way? Might the negotiation result have been different if they had been friends or at least had not have publicly insulted one another?
2. After reading the article by Professor Welsh, which follows, can you explain why both men might not have attributed their contact with the home-run ball to luck, and why they were not happy to evenly divide the economic windfall?
3. Did the fact that the entire home-run ball melee was televised and that both men made boastful and insulting public statements influence the negotiation? How might you explain this in terms of the conflict/negotiation triangle presented in Chapter 1?
4. If you were representing Popov, how might you have approached the negotiation in terms of the fairness issues? Did both men suffer from the litigation curse of being in a lawsuit in which they were absolutely convinced fairness was on their side?

Fairness perceptions are significant in understanding negotiation behaviors of participants in negotiating deals and litigation settlements. Because perceptions of fairness are so important in attorney-conducted negotiations, we consider this element separately from the other factors that influence negotiations. The following reading examines the criteria that people use to judge fairness and the variables that determine perceptions of fairness.

❖ **Nancy A. Welsh,** *PERCEPTIONS OF FAIRNESS IN NEGOTIATION*
87 Marq. L. Rev. 753 (2004)

Distributive Fairness Perceptions

The concept of distributive fairness focuses on the criteria that lead people to feel that they have received their fair share of available benefits — i.e., that the outcome of a negotiation or other decision making process is fair. People often disagree, however, regarding the criteria that should be applied in order to determine whether an outcome is fair. As is obvious from reading judicial opinions in appellate cases, even impartial and educated people can review the identical record and reach widely disparate yet equally principled conclusions regarding what constitutes a fair outcome. The definition of distributive fairness is, therefore, inevitably subjective. This realization leads to the following questions: What criteria do people — including negotiators — use to guide their judgments regarding distributive fairness? What variables influence people's selection among different criteria, and why do people find it difficult to reach agreement even when they share a commitment to achieving an equitable outcome?

A. Competing Criteria for Judging Distributive Fairness

The various criteria for judging outcomes' fairness can be distilled into four basic, competing principles or rules — equality, need, generosity, and equity. The equality principle provides that everyone in a group should share its benefits equally. According to the need principle, "those who need more of a benefit should get more than those who need it less." The generosity principle decrees that one person's outcome should not exceed the outcomes achieved by others. Finally, the equity principle ties the distribution of benefits to people's relative contribution. Those who have — contributed more should receive more than those who have contributed less. The closer that the actual outcome of a negotiation is to the outcome a negotiator anticipated based on the application of one of these principles, the greater the likelihood that the negotiator will perceive the outcome as fair.

Imagine the application of the four principles described supra to a negotiation between two individuals who are establishing a joint venture and negotiating the distribution of income. The first negotiator, who has little capital, is contributing the idea and the time and energy to implement the idea. The other negotiator is supplying the needed funds for the development and marketing of the idea. If these individuals are guided by the equality principle, they will distribute the income from the joint venture equally. If they use the need principle, the poorer negotiator who is contributing "sweat equity" will receive a greater share of the income. Under the generosity principle, neither negotiator would want his income to exceed the income of the other. Last, and perhaps most difficult, is the application of the equity principle. Both contributions are needed. Whose is more valuable? . . .

B. Variables Affecting Negotiators' Selection Among Competing Fair Allocation Principles

Research has shown that several variables influence negotiators' selections among the various fair allocation principles that could apply to a particular negotiation. These variables include self-interest, social relationships, and the interaction between cultural norms and situational needs.

1. The Influence of Self-Interest and Relationships Between Negotiators

If no relationship exists between negotiators, self-interest will guide their choice of the appropriate allocation principle to use in negotiation. A negotiator who does not expect future interactions with the other person will use whatever principle — need, generosity, equality, or equity — produces the better result for her. When a negotiator has a negative relationship with the other person, she will aim to gain more than the other negotiator, even if this requires undertaking a risky strategy. She certainly will not worry about achieving an outcome that is fair for that other, despised negotiator. Thus, "[n]egative affect within the context of potential relationships can remove fairness barriers."

On the other hand, the existence of a positive relationship with another negotiator makes the attainment of a fair outcome relevant. Further, positive social relationships influence negotiators' selection of the particular fair allocation principle that will anchor their negotiations. If a negotiator is dividing a resource with someone else and expects future, positive interactions with that person, the negotiator tends to use the equality principle to define distributive fairness. . . . Relationships obviously matter in negotiators' definitions of fair outcomes.

2. The Influence of Situational Needs and Cultural Norms

As commerce has become increasingly global, cross-cultural negotiation has also become more commonplace. Some cultures are known for placing greater emphasis upon maintaining social relationships than attaining individual objectives. Many believe, therefore, that the cultural dimension of collectivism-individualism should have great salience in the negotiation context. Simply, "individualism refers to a tendency to put a stronger emphasis on one's personal interest and goals, whereas collectivism refers to a stronger emphasis on the interests and goals of one's in-group members." Collectivist negotiators ought to be more likely than individualists to choose harmony-enhancing principles for the distribution of benefits (e.g., equality, need, or generosity principles).

Research indicates, however, that negotiators' choices among the various allocation principles are not so predictable. First, and consistent with the importance of relationships noted above, it is only when collectivists are negotiating with other in-group members that they are more likely to use a harmony-enhancing principle. If they are not closely related to the other negotiators, collectivists behave like individualists and tie fair allocation to contribution, thus leading to their use of the equitable principle. Second, collectivists' choice among allocation principles depends upon the extent to which they anticipate receiving some portion of the benefits being allocated. If a collectivist will not be a recipient (e.g., a supervisor allocating rewards to employees), the collectivist is less likely to be concerned about fostering harmony and more likely to use the equitable principle that will enhance value creation (e.g., productivity). . . .

Procedural Fairness Perceptions

Definition and Effects of Procedural Fairness

Procedural fairness is concerned with people's perceptions of the fairness of the procedures or processes used to arrive at outcomes. Researchers have found that people's perceptions of procedural justice have profound effects. First, people who believe that they have been treated in a procedurally fair manner are more likely to conclude that the resulting outcome is substantively fair. In effect, a person's perception of procedural fairness anchors general fairness impressions or serves as a fairness heuristic. Second, people who believe that they were treated fairly in a dispute resolution or decision-making procedure are more likely to comply with the outcome of the procedure. This effect will occur even if the outcomes are not favorable or produce unhappiness . . .

Conclusion

Lawyers and clients rely upon their assessments of fairness to make all sorts of decisions during negotiation: What offer shall we make? How should we respond to the other side's demand? Should we settle or make a counteroffer? Is the other side being so ridiculous that it is time to call an impasse?

Each one of these questions requires consideration of fairness, and it should now be quite clear that fairness is largely a matter of perception. Perhaps what is most interesting about the research that has been done regarding fairness perceptions is the extent to which it undermines the iconic image of two rational negotiators locked in a battle of logic, economics, and will. Rather, the research reveals that negotiators' aspirations and moves will be significantly influenced by the culture and context within which they are negotiating, their own self-interest, and most intriguing of all, their sense of connection to each other. Ironically, as negotiations become increasingly global and virtual, it is the development of those old-fashioned relationships that may matter most.

C. Psychological Traps and Professional Objectivity

Studying the perceptions and distortions of reasoning that immerse people in conflict helps us better understand clients' disputes. Although lawyers advocate and negotiate on behalf of clients, we are less subject to the partisan perspectives that can skew our client's perceptions. This is because although we, as lawyers, may be professional adversaries, we do not have a direct stake in the outcomes, so we can think more clearly and rationally. This is the common wisdom, but is it true?

We can often recognize our clients' partisan perceptions, but we are easily fooled by our own biases and distortions. By definition, what we believe, even if selective, is our reality. The longer we work with a client on a case or a deal, the more we share the same reality — distorted or not. We might be no more able than our clients to objectively analyze the weaknesses of their case or the strengths of the other side's arguments. It can be very helpful for you to understand some of the psychological factors likely to affect not only your client's thinking, but also your own assessment of case value and the attractiveness of offers to settle. Psychological traps and biases often lead us into disputes and influence how we negotiate.

Much of what we know about the hidden forces that create conflict and shape our decisions is attributable to work done in the 1970s and 1980s by cognitive psychologists Amos Tversky and Daniel Kahneman, whose work was recognized with a Nobel Prize in 2002 (see Tversky & Kahneman, 1981; Kahneman, Slovic & Tversky, 1982). They found that there are consistent biases in perceptions and decision making that can be traced to mental shortcuts, or what they labeled *heuristics*. More recently, experiments have been conducted with law students and lawyers that confirm that these cognitive traps apply to our bargaining decisions and advice.

> Problem
>
> Students at your school, who had expected to attend a required lecture without charge, are told after they arrive that they will each have to pay $20 to cover unexpected expenses. They can, however, spin a roulette wheel with four chances in five of paying nothing and one chance of having to pay $100. Which will most choose and why? (Hint: The answer is within the list below.)

Top Ten Psychological Traps

The following is an alphabetical list of the top ten common mental traps that can create disputes or make them more difficult to resolve. Some are interrelated. We return to these cognitive shortcuts and expand the list later when we examine why negotiations fail. They also come into play in the next section on how mediators can move negotiations through an impasse to settlement.

- *Anchoring*: A dispute over the value of an item often arises because we form an estimate of an unsure value by comparing it to something we know or to a number to which we are exposed that is then planted in our brain. The number you are exposed to as a value anchors your calculation and influences your thinking. When a client is burnt by hot soup at a restaurant, she may think the restaurant is to blame and her claim is worth millions because she heard about a multimillion-dollar verdict against McDonald's for coffee that was served too hot. You, as a sophisticated lawyer, understand that this case is distinguishable from the McDonald's case, which was reduced on appeal as excessive, and that this client's case is much weaker and worth less than that one, so you adjust from the McDonald's verdict downward. The question is whether you adjust far enough. Research suggests that you will not adjust sufficiently because of the anchoring effect, which could also distort your analysis and expectation.

- *Confirmation bias*: We tend to give credit to information that is consistent with our preexisting beliefs and wishes rather than information that challenges or contradicts them. This can dig us deeper into conflict when dealing with those who have different beliefs or values. We read and believe articles that confirm dark chocolate and red wine are good for us, and skim past articles that question the studies.

- *Consensus error (projection)*: We tend to falsely believe that others think the way we do or have values similar to ours. We also believe that others like what we like and want what we want. Those who enjoy loud music presume everyone wants to hear their amplified radio selections. Conflict can be created when we find out we were wrong.

- *Framing*: Our thinking about an issue and our answer to a question are affected by how the question is presented. Asking a priest if you can smoke while you pray is likely to result in a different answer than asking if you can pray while you smoke.

- *Loss aversion (Status quo bias)*: Losses tend to be felt more painfully than equivalent gains are relished, so that a dollar loss is felt greater than a dollar gain. We don't value equal trades from a neutral perspective. We tend to overvalue what we have to give up relative to what we get, making us often regret what we have done. Also, negotiating parties are more likely to view their own concessions (losses) as more valuable than equivalent concessions they get from the other side (gains).

- *Naive realism*: We tend to think that the way we see the world is the way it really is and anyone seeing it differently is naive. This bias is in play when your idea or offer is rejected with the preface that in the "real world" things are different.

- *Overconfidence*: We tend to rate our abilities, chance of being right, and good luck more highly than is warranted. Because we can't always be right, disputes happen. We are also overconfident about our ability to assess uncertain data and tend to give more weight to what we know than what we don't know. As a matter of fact, we are overconfident about ourselves in general. As examples, surveys have found that 70 percent of all drivers believe that they are more competent than the average driver, and 80 percent of lawyers think that they are more ethical than the average attorney (Fox & Birke 2000). In negotiation, overconfidence can be compounded by positive illusions we have about the relative righteousness of our case or cause.

- *Reactive devaluation*: Whatever proposal comes from the other side cannot be good for us. Anything done or suggested by them is suspect. For example, if Democrats propose legislation, Republicans are likely to reject it, and vice versa. Also, any information or offer received is perceived as less valuable than what might be withheld. This tends to escalate conflict.

- *Selective perception*: Whenever we encounter a new situation, we must interpret a universe of unfamiliar, often conflicting data that is more than we can process. We respond by instinctively forming a hypothesis about the situation in the time available, then organizing what we see and hear with the help of that premise. Our hypothesis also operates as a filter, by automatically screening out what doesn't support it — which in turn reinforces the belief that our initial view was correct. Henry David Thoreau was probably thinking about this when he said, "We see only the world we look for." Selective perception is also the basis of self-fulfilling prophesies and stereotyping. For example, if you are negotiating with a lawyer you believe is hostile and not to be trusted, you may dismiss his initial friendly greeting as manipulative and selectively see him scrutinizing you with suspicion. Your stilted behavior toward him will likely result in him seeing you as antagonistic. Mutually reinforced surly behavior will be selectively observed and remembered to the exclusion of overtures of civility. You will feel that your own insight and keen ability to "read" others is confirmed, and your self-fulfilling prophecy will be realized.

- *Self-serving biases*: We are our own best friend in justifying our actions while seeing the same behavior in someone else as a shortcoming. We know that we are personally responsible for our successes, but our failures are the result of bad luck or circumstances beyond our control. When we are late it is for good reason; others keep us waiting because of their bad planning and insensitivity. Our miscalculation or misstatement is a simple mistake, but our opponent's similar error is the result of deception.

Some of the psychological factors and biases described above may work against one another when making tactical decisions driving a negotiation. For example, as will be discussed later, there are differing views about the advantages and disadvantages of making the first offer in a negotiation. Making the first offer, particularly if the values involved are uncertain or without ready comparisons, could take advantage of the anchoring bias set by your offer. However, reactive devaluation, which may be at a peak near the beginning of negotiations, could cause the other side to radically discount your first offer because of their suspicion.

Questions

7. Does knowing about the potential of these perceptual biases and cognitive errors result in not being affected by them? How can you best guard against them or overcome your own cognitive errors?

8. What is your role if you are aware of your client's perception biases and cognitive distortions? Must you agree to a desired goal or an outcome acceptable to your client if you are aware that the goal or acceptance is the result of a misperception or cognitive error?

9. How might you counter cognitive error and perceptual distortion that may result in your negotiating opponent rejecting a settlement that is otherwise acceptable? For example, how would you handle the anchoring problem, where your opponent is fixed on what you regard as an unrealistic outcome in another case, or the tendency of your opponent to reject your truly generous offer because of suspicion of any offer coming from you?

D. The Role of Emotions and Emotional Intelligence

Many of us are attracted to the study of law because we value a rational approach to issues rather than emotional responses that seem to get in the way of logic and problem solving. The conventional wisdom is that lawyers should leave their emotions behind in their professional roles, including negotiating. This is easier said than done, and might not always be wise.

None of us are automatons, even when we try to appear so. Nor are those with whom we negotiate without emotional content that helps shape their conduct. We all have emotional needs and reactions that contribute to the creation of conflicts and are part of how we interact and deal with others. Recognizing and mastering these emotions is usually more helpful than denying and ignoring them.

More important, our clients have emotional needs that they might not readily express to us. As you learned from the readings in Chapter 1, emotional concerns, as well as substantive needs, may be critical factors that have to be satisfied to reach a settlement. Learning to recognize emotions as part of disputes and understanding their role can be an important key to negotiation success.

Negotiation effectiveness depends on interpersonal competency and a type of emotional intelligence. Emotional intelligence is the capacity to monitor our feelings and read the feelings of those whom we encounter as a guide to our actions and responses. Research (see Mayer 2001) has helped isolate three primary components of emotional intelligence:

- emotional perception,
- emotional understanding, and
- emotional management.

An emotionally intelligent negotiator has an advantage in controlling her own emotions and understanding the emotions of an opponent to better control the negotiating process. Emotional intelligence may contribute to successful negotiator behavior (see Barry, Fulmer & Van Kleef 2004).

The theme of emotional intelligence and its role in success, although not new, was brought to public attention by Daniel Goleman in his popular book *Emotional Intelligence: Why It Can Matter More Than IQ* (1995). Goleman identified 20 emotional intelligence competencies, which he thought "twice as important in contributing to excellence as . . . pure intellect and expertise."

Although there is a benefit in mastering any of these competencies, ability in all 20 emotional competencies would be a tremendous advantage in negotiation and in life. The competencies are interrelated and complement one another. Goleman clustered these emotional skills in four groups:

Self-Awareness	**Social Awareness**
Emotional self-awareness	Empathy
Accurate self-assessment	Organizational awareness
Self-confidence	Service orientation

Self-Management	**Social Skills**
Self-control	Developing others
Trustworthiness	Leadership
Conscientiousness	Influence
Adaptability	Communication
Achievement orientation	Change catalyst
Initiative	Conflict management
	Building bonds
	Teamwork and collaboration

Joshua Rosenberg, a law professor and a psychologist, weaves together our previous readings on perception and self-fulfilling prophecies with emotional intelligence.

❖ **Joshua D. Rosenberg,** *INTERPERSONAL DYNAMICS: HELPING LAWYERS LEARN THE SKILLS, AND THE IMPORTANCE, OF HUMAN RELATIONSHIPS IN THE PRACTICE OF LAW*

55 U. of Miami L. Rev. 1225 (2004)

Basically, most lawyers and academics vastly overestimate the importance of reason and logic. We tend to view them as both the primary motivator of our own behavior and the primary tool to change the thinking and behavior of others. Although they are important, they are only one part of the puzzle. There are important differences between the kind of dispassionate reasoning and analysis in which lawyers and law students engage while sitting at desks at home, in the office, or in the library, and the kind of activities in which we engage when we are dealing in real time with real people. Real time, real life interactions implicate emotions, learned patterns of behavior, habituated perspectives and frames of reference, and other human, but not reasoned, responses.

The reactions to emotions occur whether or not the person is aware of either the reaction or the emotion, and they significantly impact the outcome of most negotiations and most other interpersonal interactions. People who become anxious may tend to over-accommodate the other by inappropriately giving in on the substance of the discussion, or may tend to talk too much (or too little) in an unconscious effort to forestall that anxiety. People who become irritated may tend to become slightly belligerent or withdrawn in ways that can harm their interactions. Any feelings are likely to trigger unconscious patterns of thought and behavior that will inevitably influence an interaction. . . .

It is not just how we think about what we perceive that is tainted by our feelings. Our very perceptions themselves are determined, in part, by our feelings (and thoughts). As an initial matter, emotions precipitate changes in the autonomic nervous system. These changes include increasing the heart rate, changing breathing patterns, skin changes such as perspiration or blushing, and redirecting blood flow (anger has been found to direct blood to the hands, presumably for combat; fear has been shown to redirect blood to the legs, presumably for running). At a micro level, these changes in the autonomic nervous system change not only our ability to think, but also our ability to act and perceive. Along with our thoughts, our blood flow, and our energy, the focus of our attention and our ability to take in data are significantly changed by our emotional state. Not only our behavior, but also our perceptions become both differently focused and less accurate. . . .

The Result: Interacting Systems and Self-Fulfilling Prophecies

Basically, our thoughts, feelings, behaviors and perceptions influence each other. We react to our perceptions of the world around us while our own behavior impacts on the world. Of course, the patterns of our behavior, thoughts, perceptions and feelings are far from random. We tend to learn patterns of thought, feeling, and behavioral reactions in childhood. In adulthood we tend to engage in those patterns we learned as children, often resulting in "self-fulfilling prophecies" that tend to reinforce those same old patterns. Basically, because of our particular frame of reference (thoughts, feelings, etc.), we expect people to act in certain ways, and we act toward them in ways that tend to precipitate the behaviors we expect. When people do act in the ways we expected, we interpret that behavior in line with our expectations, and we react in certain predictable ways (which tend to confirm to us the validity of our earlier expectations).

Negotiation experts are aware of the significant impact of self-fulfilling prophecies on negotiations, but the actual impact of these patterns extends well beyond "negotiations," to encompass most of our interactions in life. . . . [S]elf-fulfilling prophecies and other generally unconscious learned responses significantly impact the outcome of most negotiations and most other interpersonal interactions.

Human Communication: Colliding Systems

As all of the above suggests, despite our typical estimation to the contrary, we are often unaware of the actual causes (and unintentional consequences) of our own behavior, thinking, emotions, and perceptions. We are not sufficiently self-aware to realize how many of our patterns of acting and thinking are ingrained, unconscious or triggered by our autonomic nervous system rather than by reason. Communication, of course, is a two-way street, and much of the time we are even more misguided about what is headed toward us than we are about where we ourselves are going. Just as we incorrectly believe that we understand our own behavior better than we do, we also (and to a much greater degree) wrongly believe that we understand others much better than we actually do. . . .

As an initial matter, researchers have concluded that the single greatest weakness of most negotiators is that they too often fail to even consider the thinking and emotions of others. Perhaps even more significantly, when we do attempt to consider the thinking and feelings of others, we usually get it wrong. We often attribute to them moods, goals or motivations that simply are not there, or we exaggerate the significance of one of many reactions they may be having and forget that, like our own, their reactions might be both dynamic and complex.

While we tend to be accepting of situational factors that impact our own behavior, we tend to be unaware of, and inattentive to, the impact of such situational factors on others. As a result, we tend to think of ourselves as more sympathetic, as having a better case, or as being a better person than the one with whom we are dealing. In turn, this often leads us to devalue the other's case and proposals, and to fail to reach agreements that are available and would have been in our client's (or our own, as the case may be) best interest.

Basically, we tend to assume, too often inaccurately, that the message we take from the other is actually the message they intended to send. We vastly underestimate not only the impact of our own perspectives, feelings and thinking on the message we take in, but also the role of simple miscommunication.

Compounding the problem of our misperceptions of others is the fact that we are basically unaware that the problem even exists. Research clearly shows that more than 98% of us are unable to tell when others are lying or telling the truth. We are essentially equally likely to believe those who are lying as we are to believe those who are telling the truth, and we are equally likely to disbelieve those who are actually telling the truth as we are to disbelieve those who are actually lying. Interestingly, and typically, I have never met a person who believes that she is a part of that 98% majority.

All of this obviously makes for significant misunderstandings and unnecessary conflict. Even worse, it is often self-perpetuating. Because we believe that we already understand others, we rarely take the time to try to understand them better. If they do not act as we want or hope, we tend to attribute their "failure" to act "properly" to some personality defect on their part. Rather than seek to learn more about them, we tend to dismiss them or negatively characterize them. We will in turn likely act in ways that may ultimately alienate them, and they will likely react in ways that will confirm, in our minds, our initial understanding. Human communication is then the interaction of two individuals, each of whom believes that she alone understands both herself and the other, while in fact neither really understands either herself or the other, and neither seeks to gain understanding (because each thinks she already has it). Perhaps more surprising than the amount of miscommunication and conflict in the world is the fact that, at least occasionally, accurate communication does take place. . . .

Questions

10. Do you agree that we vastly overestimate the importance of reason and logic?
11. How would you describe the connection between emotional intelligence and successful negotiation?
12. Can emotional intelligence be taught?

CHAPTER
3

Competitive and Cooperative
Negotiation

We each have our own approach of how to get what we want. So it is with negotiation. Our negotiation approach or style is rooted in our values, assumptions, experiences, goals, and the situation. Even though you may have a general style, you may change your approach to a negotiation based on the specifics and the needs of your client. Many terms are used to describe different negotiating styles in a range from hard to soft. For purposes of introducing the approaches and distinguishing them, we use here two basic categories: competitive and cooperative.

Problem — Microsoft v. Stac

Bill Gates became the richest man in the world by being smart, diligent, and keenly competitive. As a negotiator, he was known for being aggressive and competitive, although there are accounts of him using his considerable creative skills to negotiate value-added cooperative outcomes. Consider the following example where Gates used two different approaches to an intellectual property claim at different stages in the dispute.

Stac Electronics was an engineering company founded in 1983 by seven friends at Caltech. The company developed its "Stacker" disc compression software in 1990. Bill Gates, CEO of Microsoft, wanted Stac's data compression technology and met personally with Stac's president, Gary Clow, to discuss licensing of Stac's software. The negotiations were turned over to other Microsoft executives and lawyers to negotiate. Although willing to pay Stac a modest gross license fee, Microsoft refused to pay Stac any per-user royalty for its patented compression technology. Microsoft took a hard line, saying that it could have other sources develop reliable data compression technology that could be incorporated into the MS-DOS operating system, which would have an immediate and adverse effect on the viability of Stacker and threaten Stac's continued economic viability. Microsoft had a reputation of using its huge market share and resources to negotiate in a hard fashion and favorably license software that it incorporated into its products. Negotiations broke off, and in 1993, Microsoft released MS-DOS 6.0, which included a disk compression program called Double Space. Stac was outraged, as Microsoft had previously examined the Stacker code as part of the due diligence process in their earlier negotiations and Stac believed that Microsoft infringed its patent.

Microsoft would not budge on Stac's claim, and Stac filed a patent infringement suit against Microsoft. Microsoft counterclaimed that Stac had misappropriated the Microsoft trade secret of a preloading feature that was included in Stacker 3.1. In 1994, a federal court jury in California awarded Stac $120 million in compensatory damages, coming to about $5.50 per copy of MS-DOS 6.0 that had been sold. The jury also concluded that Stac misappropriated Microsoft's trade secret and simultaneously awarded Microsoft $13.6 million on the counterclaim.

Feelings on both sides were negative and intense. Mr. Clow appeared on CBS's *Eye to Eye with Connie Chung* and described his negotiations against Microsoft Chairman Bill Gates as "like a knife fight." Bill Gates, the subject of a profile on the show, walked out of an interview when Ms. Chung asked him about Mr. Clow's charges.

A new round of negotiations commenced in the changed circumstances of the jury verdict. Both sides had the option of legal appeals over the jury verdicts. Instead, their lawyers negotiated in a more cooperative manner and created a deal that caught Wall Street off guard, favorably affecting the share price of both companies. Each side agreed to drop its claims in exchange for cross-licensing all of their existing patents, as well as future ones over the next five years. The pact called for Microsoft to pay Stac license royalties totaling $43 million over 43 months, while also investing $39.9 million for a 15-percent equity stake in Stac. The total $82.9 million outlay represented a gain for Microsoft, which had already charged off $120 million for the jury award in its fiscal third quarter and now was able to credit much of the difference in the current period. Stac also came out ahead, by getting a significant cash infusion without a long appeals process to collect money from Microsoft. Mr. Clow said that $82.9 million being turned over by Microsoft represented more than Stac would have gotten had the $120 million been paid, because income taxes and Stac's own $13.6-million penalty would have whittled the final amount to about $64 million. In addition, Stac formed an alliance with the most powerful player in the software industry. Mr. Clow stated that, "this is not personal. This makes good business sense going forward. . . . This demonstrates it is possible to do win-win deals." Microsoft's executives concurred. "This is a lot more fun than disagreeing," said Michael Brown, Microsoft's vice president of finance, referring to the more cooperative final round of negotiation.

1. Why might Gates have played hardball when he first negotiated with Stac's Clow?
2. Why did Gates then change his approach and have his lawyers negotiate a more cooperative deal going forward?
3. What are the advantages and disadvantages of each approach to negotiation?
4. How do you decide when to use a competitive or cooperative negotiation style?

The *competitive* approach assumes that the purpose of bargaining is to obtain the best possible economic result for your client, usually at the expense of the other side. A competitive bargainer is likely to think that negotiation involves a limited resource or fund that must be distributed between competing parties — in effect, a fixed economic "pie." In a competitive approach, the parties' relationships and other intangibles are not of primary importance. The competitive bargainer's goal is to pay as little as possible (if a buyer or defendant) or obtain as much as possible (if a seller or plaintiff), as a dollar more for your opponent is necessarily a dollar less for you. A competitive bargainer, in other words, sees negotiation much as a litigator sees a trial: Someone must win and someone must lose, and her central mission is to win. This approach is also known as "distributive" or "zero-sum" bargaining, because the negotiators see their task as distributing a fixed, limited resource between them.

A simple example of where competitive bargaining is likely to occur is when a lawyer negotiates with an insurance adjuster in a distant city to settle a client's claim for property damage to a car caused by a falling tree limb. The client, we will assume, has since changed insurance companies, and the lawyer does not expect to do business with this adjuster again, so neither sees any interest in nurturing a relationship. In this situation both sides have a limited joint interest in conducting the bargaining process efficiently. Both the lawyer and the adjuster are likely to see their sole goal as agreeing on a dollar amount that the company will pay the insured to give up his claim, and to assume that a better settlement for one will necessarily be worse for the other.

In this negotiation, each side may posture about the dimensions of the issue or conflict, initiate a demand or offer (a specific proposal for resolving the dispute), and bargain over that proposal or present a counterproposal. A competitive negotiator will attempt to change the other side's perception to persuade them that their case is weaker and worth less than they thought and that her case is stronger and more valuable than her opponent previously recognized. Incremental concessions are usually made that narrow the bargaining range. Finally, a compromise settlement may be agreed upon. This approach to negotiation centers on predetermined positions and maximizing individual gain.

A *cooperative* bargainer, by contrast, does not view negotiation "pies" as fixed. Cooperative bargainers work to identify interests and examine differences in how the parties value items. They then search jointly with the other negotiator — viewed more as a partner rather than an opponent — for options and a solution that will best satisfy both parties' interests. Cooperative negotiation is marked by an effort to understand one another's perceptions and reexamine them together to arrive at a shared picture or a mutually acceptable valuation. This cooperative approach is frequently called "integrative" bargaining, because it emphasizes integrating the parties' needs to find the best joint solution. It is also referred to as "interest-based" negotiation because it sees the goal of bargaining as satisfying people's underlying interests.

Rather than moving from positions to counter-positions to a compromise settlement, cooperative negotiators search for a variety of alternatives that optimize the interests that they have prioritized. The parties can then create an outcome from a combination of generated options so that a joint decision, with more benefits to all, can be achieved. This more collaborative approach does not necessarily produce a simple compromise between competing positions. It seeks a creative settlement not bound by predetermined positions.

A classic situation that calls for cooperative bargaining is an effort by two businesses to form a joint venture. Cooperative bargainers would first ask what special resources and capabilities each partner could bring to the deal (for example, does Partner A have special expertise in marketing, whereas Partner B has more strength in design? Does one have good access to financing, whereas the other has open office space?). The negotiators would also ask whether either partner had particular needs, for example, one for an assured stream of income and the other for cutting-edge technology. Cooperative bargainers would focus on finding terms that best exploit each partner's abilities and minimize weaknesses, creating the strongest possible future partnership.

Cooperative and competitive bargaining are not mutually exclusive. Working to "bake" the biggest possible "pie" does not, in itself, say anything about how the final pie will be divided. Savvy competitive negotiators, for example, will look earnestly for ways to "expand the pie." Competitors, however, are likely to see expanding the pie as less important than getting the largest possible piece for their clients. Cooperative bargainers must also face the pie-dividing problem, but tend to give it less significance than competitors. In the joint venture example described above, cooperatives would emphasize creating the best possible deal. They would then look for a principle for dividing the benefits (that is, the "pie") that both partners saw as fair, rather than trying to outfox their partner to get the lion's share.

In practice, cooperative and competitive approaches may be mixed or sequenced, depending on the setting, subject matter, and personalities of the negotiators. However, descriptions of cooperative and competitive styles, as well as distinctions between these two approaches, provide a paradigm for understanding the dynamics of negotiation.

There are styles of negotiating that go beyond either cooperative or competitive, which might be seen as more intense versions of each approach. Those competitive negotiators that we label *adversarial* bargainers view negotiation as a kind of war and believe that all is fair in winning it. Extreme adversarial bargainers may be willing to renege on tentative agreements, misrepresent their authority, make empty threats, and distort facts that cannot easily be checked or challenged, if such tactics seem likely to win them a better outcome.

By contrast, *problem-solving* bargainers employ intensely cooperative, interest-based tactics. Problem solvers focus almost exclusively on finding solutions that will maximize the value of the deal for both parties. Problem solvers are extremely reluctant to obtain a better outcome for their client at the expense of their counterpart and insist on using genuinely neutral principles to accomplish the task of allocating benefits.

For simplicity, we follow the convention of generally referring to bargaining styles in terms of *competitive* and *cooperative*, but we also separately discuss adversarial and problem-solving techniques. The distinctions between adversarial and competitive styles (often used interchangeably), on the one hand, and cooperative and problem-solving styles (also used interchangeably), on the other hand, are not always clear.

Note: Game Theory and the Prisoners' Dilemma

To illustrate the distinction and tension between competitive and cooperative negotiation behavior, some teachers introduce game theory and use variations of a scored game known as the prisoners' dilemma. (A prisoners' dilemma-type exercise may have been assigned prior to reading this chapter.) Chess players and lawyers make strategic decisions based on what they anticipate will be the response of others. Game theory combines mathematical and economic concepts to calculate and quantify what others are likely to do in response to what you do. It can provide valuable knowledge about the likely payoffs and risks of being cooperative or competitive. Classic game theory models assume that the players are economically rational and will behave in ways that maximize their quantifiable interests. It is more difficult to factor in psychological and emotional motivations, although newer theories at the intersection of economics and psychology have had some success with the combination.

The discipline of game theory was refined during World War II and applied to military tactics. Game theory was made more accessible for use by negotiators through the writing of a Harvard mathematician, Howard Raiffa, in his classic book *The Art and Science of Negotiation* (1982). Professor Raiffa's most recent negotiation book, which includes application of game theory, is *Negotiation Analysis: The Science of Art and Collaborative Decision Making* (2002). A book specifically applying game theory to negotiation of legal disputes is Baird, Gertner, and Picker's *Game Theory and the Law* (1994). A short handbook for lawyers is by Louis Kaplow and Steven Shavell, *Decision Analysis, Game Theory, and Information* (2004).

The prisoners' dilemma game demonstrates the potential benefits of cooperation, as well as the risk of getting sucked in and clobbered by the other side, who may not reciprocate your cooperation. References to prisoners' dilemma situations and the possibility of defection from past patterns of cooperation are common in negotiation literature and are referenced in some of the readings in this book, so we briefly explain the concept here.

The original prisoners' dilemma is a multiple-round exercise in which players are instructed that two co-conspirators in crime have been caught and placed in separate rooms without being allowed to communicate with one another. They are separately told by the police that they will each be convicted of a lesser offense and serve one year in prison unless one of them testifies to help convict the other of a greater offense, which carries a penalty of five years. The testifying prisoner will then be released without serving time. However, if each testifies against the other, their five-year sentences will be reduced by one year, so each will then serve four years. They must each choose without knowing what the other prisoner will decide to do. Then, after finding out the result of their first-round choices, they will each choose again until seven rounds are completed. Their cumulative years of incarceration for seven rounds will be their individual game score, with the lowest number being the best. If they are both silent for seven rounds, in effect cooperating with one another, each receives a total of 7 years (1×7). If they each agree to testify in all seven rounds, they will each receive 28 years (4×7). If one testifies in each round and the other is silent, the testifier gets off free and the silent one receives 35 years in prison (5×7). If each is silent for six rounds and then one testifies, or defects, in the seventh round, the defector receives a seventh round score of zero, or 6 years total for all rounds, and the other gets 5 years for the last round, for a seven-round total of 11 years $(6 \times 1 + 5)$. In other words, it pays to obtain cooperation from the other player while you defect. The more times you defect, the better for you, unless the other player also defects and testifies, in which event you both end up with many years served. The paradox is that each player might optimize her individual outcome by defecting, but both are better off if they cooperate in silence than if they *both* defect.

The prisoners' dilemma game can serve as a metaphor for negotiation and life. Cooperation can be risky if you are not sure of the cooperation of others. If there is just one round to play, you are probably better off defecting. In multiple rounds, cooperation is safer than defecting, but defecting can provide quantitative rewards if only one person defects while others cooperate. Correct anticipation or prediction of the moves from others is one key to success. Gaining trust and then using that trust to your advantage when you betray it can score points. However, if defection and self-serving competition become the norm, all are worse off. Competitive negotiation tends to occur when the interaction is viewed as a single round and winning is valued more than an ongoing relationship. The more rounds with the same players, the more complex the decisions and the greater the opportunity for retaliation. Repeated interaction with anticipation of future dealings tends to produce more cooperation, as does concern about retaliation and your reputation among others with whom you might later negotiate. However, there is temptation to defect if you know it is the last round because the other player(s) cannot retaliate. (All of this may help explain why negotiation among attorneys who regularly interact together in a small town tends to be more cooperative than negotiation among attorneys in a big city who have less-frequent contact.)

The game does not directly factor in questions about the moral value or satisfaction of cooperation over competition (or vice versa), or the societal costs of rewarding defection or promoting crime. International tournaments have been structured around repetitive prisoners' dilemma games, and books have been written about the results, with analogous lessons for real-life negotiation (see Axelrod 1984).

———————————

We now examine the underpinnings of the contrasting negotiation approaches and some of the strategies and tactics associated with each.

A. Competitive/Adversarial Approach

❖ Gary Goodpaster, *A PRIMER ON COMPETITIVE BARGAINING*

J. Disp. Resol. 325 (1996)

One cannot understand negotiation without understanding competitive behavior in negotiation. It is not that competing is a good way to negotiate; it may or may not be, depending on the circumstances. Understanding competition in negotiation is important simply because many people do compete when they negotiate, either by choice or happenstance. . . .

Competitive Negotiation Strategy

In competitive negotiation or distributive bargaining, the parties' actual or perceived respective aims or goals conflict. In this context, the negotiator's aim is to maximize the realization of its goals. Since the goals conflict, either in fact or supposition, one party's gains are the other party's losses. Therefore, a negotiator's goal is to win by gaining as much value as possible from the other party . . . . Not only is the competitive negotiator out to gain as much as he or she can, but he or she will take risks, even the risk of non-agreement, to secure a significant gain.

The competitive negotiator adopts a risky strategy which involves the taking of firm, almost extreme positions, making few and small concessions, and withholding information that may be useful to the other party. The intention, and hoped-for effect, behind this basic strategy is to persuade the other party that it must make concessions if it is to get an agreement. In addition to this basic strategy, competitive negotiators may also use various ploys or tactics aimed at pressuring, unsettling, unbalancing or even misleading the other party to secure an agreement with its demands.

In an important sense, the competitive negotiator plays negotiation as an information game. In this game, the object is to get as much information from the other party as possible while disclosing as little information as possible. Alternatively, a competitive negotiator sometimes provides the other party with misleading clues, bluffs, and ambiguous assertions with multiple meanings, which are not actually false, but nevertheless mislead the other party into drawing incorrect conclusions that are beneficial to the competitor.

The information the competitive negotiator seeks is the other party's bottom line. How much he will maximally give or minimally accept to make a deal. On the other hand, the competitive negotiator wants to persuade the other side about the firmness of the negotiator's own asserted bottom line. The competitive negotiator works to convince the other party that it will settle only at some point that is higher (or lower, as the case may be) than its actual and unrevealed bottom line.

In skillful hands the bargaining position performs a double function. It conceals, and it reveals. The bargaining position is used to indicate — to unfold gradually, step by step — the maximum expectation of the negotiator, while at the same time concealing, for as long as necessary, his minimum expectation.

By indirect means, such as the manner and timing of the changes in your bargaining position, you, as a negotiator, try to convince the other side that your maximum expectation is really your minimum breaking-off point. . . . Since you have taken an appropriate bargaining position at the start of negotiations, each change in your position should give ever-clearer indications of your maximum expectation. Also, each change should be designed to encourage or pressure the other side to reciprocate with at least as much information as you give them, if not more.

Taking a firm position and conceding little will incline the other party to think the competitor has little to give. Thus, if there is to be a deal, then the other party must give or concede more.

1. Pure Bargaining, Haggling, and Just Trading Figures

When the parties are apart and have no reason, other than their mutual choice, to settle at any particular point between them, they are in a "pure bargaining" situation. It is easy to see how the simple negotiation game . . . can degenerate into a contest of haggling or just trading figures. The parties' positions — the particular dollar figures they are offering — are not connected to any reason or rationale. Basically, both buyer and seller are seeking to maximize gains. Each attempts to accomplish this by seeing how far the other party can be pushed.

Often this happens in competitive bargaining, particularly with unsophisticated competitive bargainers and usually in the late and ending stages of a negotiation. When it occurs, the "take as much as you can" grab is transparent and signals that the parties, or at least one party, is bargaining just to win as much as possible. Automobile dealers' sales practices exemplify this phenomenon. A new car dealer usually pegs an asking price to a manufacturer's suggested retail sticker price and to items the dealer adds to the car. Once those starting prices are left behind, the dealer and buyer usually just trade dollar figures until they reach one they are both comfortable with. Similarly, travelers who visit native markets or bazaars, or those who visit flea markets or garage sales in this country, sometimes experience much the same kind of trading. Offers and counteroffers are thrown back and forth, each party testing the other party's resolve to stick with a figure by refusing to budge further or threatening to walk away. In essence, bargaining in this fashion is really nothing but a contest of firmness or a game of chicken.

2.   Focal Points or Mutually Prominent Alternatives

It is revealing to analyze a pure bargaining situation where two equally competitive negotiators bargain with each other. Once the bargaining parties have assured their bottom lines or reservation values and have staked out their respective positions on the bargaining range, nothing inherently seems to impel settlement at any particular point between the positions, except each party's expectations regarding what the other side in fact will accept. This is problematic, however, for with each guided by expectations and knowing that the other is too, expectations become compounded. A bargain is struck when somebody makes a final, sufficient concession. Why does he concede? Because he thinks the other will not. "I must concede because he won't. He won't because he thinks I will. He thinks I will because he thinks I think he thinks so. . . ." There is some range of alternative outcomes in which any point is better for both sides than no agreement at all. To insist on any such point is pure bargaining, since one always would take less rather than reach no agreement at all, and since one always can recede if retreat proves necessary to agreement. Yet if both parties are aware of the limits to this range, any outcome is a point from which at least one party would have been willing to retreat and the other knows it! . . .

Because people bargain competitively for various reasons, negotiators and mediators need to understand competition in negotiation in order to respond appropriately. Some people bargain competitively without giving much conscious attention to the matter. Others compete in response to the other party's competitive behavior. In this response, they follow the common pattern that a particular kind of behavior elicits a similar behavior in response. In other words, one party frames the negotiation as a contest, and the other party picks up the competitive cues and behaves accordingly. Further, people naturally incline to competitive bargaining when they are non-trusting. In such situations, in order to avoid putting themselves at risk, non-trusting people act guardedly and adopt elements of the competitive strategy, for example, withholding information or misrepresenting a position. Finally, one can readily imagine ambiguous bargaining situations, in which at least one party is non-trusting, quickly devolving into a competitive negotiation between both parties. The non-trusting party acts defensively, and the other party senses this as competitive behavior and, therefore, acts in a similar fashion.

Negotiators, however, can also consciously adopt a competitive strategy. Negotiators are most likely to compete purposefully when:

- the parties have an adversarial relationship;
- a negotiator has a bargaining power advantage and can dominate the situation;
- a negotiator perceives an opportunity for gain at the expense of the other party;
- the other party appears susceptible to competitive tactics;
- the negotiator is defending against competitive moves; or
- there is no concern for the future relationship between the parties.

This list suggests that competitive bargaining most likely occurs in situations such as labor and lawsuit negotiations, insurance and similar claims type settlements, and in one-time transactions between a relatively experienced party and a relatively inexperienced party. One would, for example, expect to see it in sales transactions where the parties will probably not see each other again.

Representative bargaining or bargaining for a constituency may also prompt competitive bargaining even when there will be future negotiations between equally sophisticated parties. The negotiator's accountability may override relationship concerns and reasons for cooperation. The concerned audience, consisting of a client, constituency, coalition partner, or other phantom party at the table, is, in effect, looking over the negotiator's shoulder. The negotiator, therefore, takes positions and makes moves she believes her client either expects or would approve. International negotiations between countries, union-management, lawsuit negotiations, and negotiations between different parties in interest-group coalition negotiations sometimes evidence this pattern.

Aside from circumstantial or situational pressures, there are some parties who bargain competitively because they believe that is the way to conduct business. There are also parties who are simply predisposed to bargain competitively and will incline to do so opportunistically in any bargaining situation if possible.

Finally, it is important to note that one can bargain competitively in a negotiation on some issues and cooperatively on others. In other words, a negotiator can selectively use competitive strategy or tactics on particular issues, while using a cooperative or problem-solving strategy on other issues. In such a case, extracting gain competitively may not greatly endanger future relationships. . . .

Obviously, competitive bargaining covers a continuum of behaviors from the simplest, unreflective adversarial actions to highly conscious and virtually scripted contests. As such, competitive bargaining moves are natural responses in some negotiation situations and advantageous or profitable actions in others. . . .

Questions

1. What are the advantages of adopting a competitive approach to bargaining?
2. What are the downsides of competitive bargaining?
3. Have you experienced competitive negotiation? What were the circumstances?

Competitive Variation — Adversarial   We turn now to a more aggressive form of competitive negotiation, which we refer to as *adversarial*. There is no shortage of advice about how to be a tough bargainer and how to get what you want in a negotiation. Check the self-help and business advice sections of large booksellers for an array of titles on this subject, including *Guerrilla Negotiating* (1999). Although adversarial negotiation may at times be advantageous, many of these guides appear to assume that the opposing side is ignorant or gullible and will have no future opportunity to retaliate. Other books and articles catalog "hardball" tactics to warn you of what you might encounter. These writings are premised on the theory that to be "forewarned is forearmed." Roger Dawson, the author of *Secrets of Power Negotiating* (2001), challenges the myth of cooperative "win-win" negotiation before sharing his adversarial secrets and what you need to watch out for so you do not become the victim of others' hardball tactics. His list of power negotiating gambits includes the following:

- *Ask for more than you expect to get*: You can get away with an outrageous opening position if you imply some flexibility.
- *Never say yes to the first offer*: Saying yes triggers two thoughts in the other person's mind: "I could have done better," and "something must be wrong."
- *Flinch at proposals*: The other side may not expect to get what is asked for; however, if you do not show surprise you're communicating that it is a possibility.
- *Always play reluctant seller*: This is a great way to squeeze the other side's negotiating range before the negotiation even starts.
- *Use the vise technique*: "You'll have to do better than that."
- *Don't let the other side know you have the authority to make a decision*: Don't let the other person trick you into admitting that you have authority.
- *Don't fall into the trap of thinking that splitting the difference is the fair thing to do*: Splitting the difference doesn't mean down the middle, because you can do it more than once.
- *Always ask for a trade-off*: Any time the other side asks you for a concession, ask for something in return.
- *Good guy/bad guy*: It's an effective way of putting more pressure on the other person without creating confrontation.
- *Nibbling*: Using the nibbling gambit, you can get a little bit more even after you have agreed on everything.
- *Taper concessions*: Taper concessions to communicate that the other side is getting the best possible deal.
- *Withdrawing an offer*: You can do it by backing off your last price concession or by withdrawing an offer to include freight, installation, and so on.

- *The decoy*: Use a decoy to take attention away from the real issue in the negotiation.
- *Red herring*: This is a phony demand that can be withdrawn, but only in exchange for a concession.
- *Cherry picking*: Ask for alternatives and then pick the best parts from multiple choices.
- *Escalation*: Raising demands after both sides reach an agreement.
- *Time pressure*: The rule in negotiating is that 80 percent of the concessions occur in the last 20 percent of time available.
- *Being prepared to walk away*: Project to the other side that you will walk away from the negotiations if you can't get what you want.
- *The fait accompli*: This occurs when one negotiator simply assumes the other will accept an assumed settlement rather than go to the trouble of reopening the negotiations.
- *Ultimatums*: Ultimatums are very high-profile statements that tend to strike fear into inexperienced negotiators.

Questions

4. Do any of these tactics seem unethical? Negotiation presents a fertile area for ethical transgressions, with relatively little guidance as to ethical limits. The ethics of negotiation are addressed in Chapter 10.
5. Is there a difference between hard, competitive negotiation and "dirty" bargaining tricks? If so, how would you distinguish them?
6. Are there any gambits or techniques that you could add to Dawson's list?
7. If the tactics listed by Dawson were used against you, what would you do? If any of these behaviors did produce an adverse result for your client, what would be your approach the next time you found yourself matched against this opponent?

Note: Responses to Competitive Hardball and Difficult People

Some of the books and articles cataloging competitive negotiation tactics also prescribe competitive antidotes that could be used in response. Most of these reactive "hardball" tactics are either responses in kind or intended to notch up the positioning in a dance of "one-upmanship." The most effective counter-move or response to sharp competitive tactics will depend on the context of the negotiation, your relationship with the other negotiators, your alternatives to continued negotiations, the strength of your own position, your goals in the negotiation, and the information available to you. The key to any effective response is being able to recognize aggressive and deceptive tactics and under-standing their potential effect in distorting your perspective and masking the opposition's weaknesses.

There are alternatives to responding in kind to hardball tactics or ending the negotiation. The behavior can be recognized and labeled for what it is and then dismissed by making light of it, or you can just ignore it. You can be direct by making it clear that the tactic is not working and is interfering with either of you getting what you want out of a possible deal or settlement, and that it will not be tolerated. In effect, you can discuss and set ground rules for further negotiations. Hardball tactics are most commonly used in the absence of an ongoing relationship or friendship. Taking time to become friendlier before the bargaining begins or emphasizing the likely continuing contact or repeat plays following this negotiation might discourage hardball tactics — or it might not.

The subject of responding to aggressive moves is related more generally to how we can best negotiate with people we consider difficult. Seminars and training programs are frequently offered to help us deal with "difficult people." The proliferation of these programs, including ones offered for attorneys, reflects the commonly experienced frustration most of us have had in trying to work or negotiate with others whom we perceive as being insensitive, obstinate, selfish, overly competitive, or generally unreasonable. It is an interesting paradox that experience with difficult people should be so common when few, if any, of us view ourselves as being difficult. Do you think the people you consider difficult believe themselves to be so? Studies show that opponents usually see us as more demanding and less reasonable than we view ourselves (Thomas & Pondy 1977).

William Ury, in his book *Getting Past No: Negotiating with Difficult People* (1991), outlines problem behavior from difficult people in negotiations and offers five easy-to-remember counter-tactics, to which we have added our summary of his advice:

> **Stage One: Don't React — Go to the Balcony.** This means controlling your own behavior and distancing yourself from your natural impulses and emotions. Become an observer to an opponent's bad behavior rather than getting sucked into the game.
> **Stage Two: Disarm Them — Step to Their Side.** Don't fight your opponent, join him. Defuse anger, fear, and suspicion. Feel his pain and empathize, without agreeing to his demands or conceding.
> **Stage Three: Change the Game — Don't Reject . . . Reframe.** Ask questions to figure out what motivates the difficult behavior. Reshape the negotiation to address the issue you want to resolve and in the direction you want it to move.
> **Stage Four: Make It Easy to Say Yes — Build Them a Golden Bridge.** Make your devised outcome the opponent's idea, involve him in the solution, and help him "save face" and look good. Act more like a mediator than an adversary.
> **Stage Five: Make It Hard to Say No — Bring Them to Their Senses, Not Their Knees.** Now that you have made it easy for the opponent to say yes, educate him so it is difficult to say no. Make it clear that his alternatives are worse than what you are offering.

B. Cooperative/Problem Solving Approach

Cooperative or collaborative negotiation involves parties in an effort to jointly meet each others' needs and satisfy interests. In their best-selling book *Getting to YES* (1991), which popularized non-adversarial negotiation, Roger Fisher, William Ury, and Bruce Patton suggest that "you can change the game," so that negotiation need not be positional or competitive. They prescribe an interest-based approach with suggested tactics and the use of objective criteria for joint decisions that they refer to as "principled" negotiation or "negotiation on the merits." *Getting to Yes* is recommended reading in many courses and training classes, so you may be familiar with it. The five basic elements of principled negotiation as listed by Fisher, Ury, and Patton are:

1. *Separate the people from the problem.* The negotiators should focus on attacking the problem posed by the negotiations, not each other.
2. *Focus on interests, not positions.* Distinguish positions, which are what you want, from interests, which are why you want them. Look for mutual or complementary interests that will make agreement possible.
3. *Invent options for mutual gain.* Even if the parties' interests differ, there might be bargaining outcomes that will advance the interests of both. The story is told of two sisters who are trying to decide which of them should get the only orange in the house. Once they realize that one sister wants to squeeze the orange for its juice, and the other wants to grate the rind to flavor a cake, a "win-win" agreement that furthers the interests of each becomes apparent.
4. *Insist on objective criteria.* Not all disputes and negotiations lend themselves to a "win-win" outcome. An insurance claim for damage to a car may create such a dispute, as each dollar paid by the insurance company is one dollar less for it. (Bargaining about issues of this nature is generally referred to as "zero-sum" bargaining.) Fisher, Ury, and Patton suggest that the parties first attempt to agree on objective criteria to determine the outcome. Thus, instead of negotiating over the value of a destroyed car, both parties might agree that the standard "blue book" price will determine the settlement amount. "Commit yourself to reaching a solution based on principle, not pressure."
5. *Know your Best Alternative to a Negotiated Agreement (BATNA).* The reason you negotiate with someone is to produce better results than you could obtain without negotiating. If you do not know the best you are likely to obtain without negotiating, you might accept an offer you should reject or might reject an offer better than you can otherwise get. Your BATNA is the measure to decide if you are better off agreeing to a negotiated outcome or pursuing your alternatives, whether it be a trial or a deal with someone else. Your BATNA is the basis of comparison to protect you from bad negotiating decisions and permits the exploration of imaginative solutions to satisfy your interests.

Note: Positions vs. Interests

The central theme of cooperative negotiation is that the negotiators focus on the parties' underlying interests rather than on the positions they take. Interest-based bargainers begin with the assumption that a party's position is simply one way (and often not the most efficient or effective one) to satisfy a need or interest. In most disputes parties have multiple interests of varying intensities. In Chapter 1 we looked at the triangle of conflict and presented the three components of satisfactory settlements as the three "Es": economic, emotional, and extrinsic. These relate to the interests that cooperative negotiators attempt to meet in working toward an integrative resolution. Similarly, *Getting to Yes* explains interests in terms of "basic human needs," including security, economic well-being, a sense of belonging, recognition, and control over one's life (1991, 48). These needs or interests can be further explained as follows:

- *Process interests.* People have a "process" interest in having disagreements resolved in a manner they consider fair. This usually includes the opportunity to tell their story and have the feeling that they have been understood. A cooperative negotiator will sometimes address an opponent's process interest by listening quietly while he vents angry emotions or accusations, then demonstrating, for example, by summarizing what has been said, that while the listener does not agree with what the speaker has said, he has heard and made an effort to understand it — so-called active listening ("So if I understand you correctly, you believe that . . ."). Participants may also have an interest in having a negotiation proceed in an orderly and predictable way.
- *Personal interests.* Most people have a personal interest in feeling respected in their work and as human beings, and in being seen as acting consistently with what they have said in the past and in accordance with their moral standards. Negotiators might address these personal interests by treating everyone courteously and attending to "face saving" needs.
- *Relational interests.* The parties might also have an interest in preserving or creating an ongoing relationship. This is particularly true in contractual disputes, because the very existence of a contract indicates that the parties once saw a benefit in working together, but it can also be true in disputes that arise from less formal connections. Examples of situations with relational interests include divorce and child custody disputes, land use controversies between neighbors, workplace disputes, and disagreements between companies and longtime customers.
- *Economic interests.* Disputants usually have economic or substantive interests. This is where most negotiations begin and where many end unsuccessfully because other interests are not addressed. Economic interests are most easy to state in the form of demands and offers, which are statements of positions. These positions may be misleading when viewed only in terms of dollars. People need money to satisfy other needs, whether material, social, or emotional. Finding out how the money will be used or what needs it will satisfy is essential to fashioning an interest-based agreement or integrative outcome.

Fisher, Ury, and Patton recognize that it is not always easy in negotiations to identify interests, as distinguished from positions. The technique they recommend is to ask "Why?" Why do you want a particular outcome, and why does the other side take the position it does? Do not ask the person with whom you are negotiating "Why?" to seek justification of his position or challenge it, "but for an understanding of the needs, hopes, fears, or desires that it serves" (1991, 44). If you understand why the person wants what he is insisting upon, you can better explore how his interests can be met so you can get from him what you need.

———————————

Cooperative Variation — Problem Solving   A variation of the cooperative approach, or perhaps another label for it, is *problem solving*. Problem-solving negotiators employ intensely cooperative, interest-based tactics. Problem solvers focus almost exclusively on finding solutions that will maximize the value of the deal for both parties. Problem solvers do not want to obtain a better outcome for their client at the expense of their counterpart and insist on using genuinely neutral principles to accomplish the task of allocating benefits. Negotiation is viewed as a collaboration to solve the challenge of finding opportunities for creating additional value through complementary interests. An early voice for the problem-solving approach to negotiation, Professor Carrie Menkel-Meadow, explains the process in the next article.

❖ **Carrie Menkel-Meadow,** *Toward Another View of Legal Negotiation: The Structure of Problem Solving*

31 UCLA L. Rev. 754 (1984)

The Structure of Problem Solving

1. Identifying the Parties' Underlying Needs and Objectives

Unlike the adversarial model which makes assumptions about the parties' desires to maximize individual gain, problem solving begins by attempting to determine the actual needs of particular clients. The problem-solving model seeks to avoid a lawyer who acts for a hypothetical, rather than a real, client by creating a "standardized person to whom he attributes standardized ends."

Ascertaining the client's needs will, of course, begin with the initial interview. This is not the place to review the extensive interview literature, but in thinking ahead to the negotiation which might occur, a lawyer might begin by asking the client such general questions as "how would you like to see this all turn out?" or "what would you like to accomplish here?" before channelling the client's objectives in directions the lawyer knows are legally possible. The client may be the best source of ideas that go beyond what the court or the legal system might commonly permit. Once the client's ideas are brought to the surface, the lawyer can explore the needs they are meant to satisfy, and the legal and nonlegal consequences of these and other solutions.

Since so many legal problems are reduced to monetary solutions, consideration of the economic needs and objectives of the client faced with a dispute or transaction is a good place to begin. What are the monetary requirements now — compensation, return on investment, liquidity for payment? What might be the future monetary needs? What is the money needed for? Are any cheaper means available? Are there cash substitutes that are available and acceptable? What are the tax consequences of payment/receipt now? Later? What payment structure is desirable — lump sum, installments? Why? What are the transaction costs or solution costs of negotiation as opposed to litigation?

Next the lawyer might consider that with which she is most familiar — the legal issues. What legal regulations govern the parties' situation? Must there be an admission of liability? Is a legal judgment necessary? Why? Is a formal document evidencing agreement desirable or required? What are the likely future legal consequences of actions taken? What are the parties likely to do if one of them breaches an agreement? What assets will be available in the future for legal action, if necessary?

The negotiator might consider how any solution affects the client's relationship to others. What are the social needs of the parties? How do others feel about this dispute or transaction? Will family members, friends, business associates, employers, employees be affected by actions taken by the parties? If not affected now, how will any of these people feel if things change in the future?

The negotiator might also ask the client to consider the personal feelings generated by the dispute or transaction. What are the psychological needs of the parties? Does one desire vindication, retribution, power? Why? What will be the long-term psychological consequences of satisfying or not satisfying these needs? How risk averse are the parties? What are their motivations for pursuing their aims in the negotiation? How might some of these feelings change if they forego litigation now or if they insist on obtaining some advantage?

Finally, the negotiator might also consider the ethical concerns of the parties. How fair do they desire to be with each other? What are the consequences of acting altruistically or dishonestly now? In the future? Will there be feelings of guilt later for "taking advantage" or the other side?

For each of these basic categories of needs the negotiator should also consider how the needs may change over the long run. There may be additional needs which the client has not articulated and which have as yet unrealized consequences. Frequently, some of the latent needs or concerns can be ascertained by simply following up a client's statement of need with an inquiry as to why that item or thing is desired. For each stated need, the lawyer should engage in a systematic inquiry into long and short run consequences and the latent concerns behind those which are manifest.

Ideally, this framework for determining the parties' needs must be considered from both parties' perspectives. At the very least, it should encourage lawyers and clients to consider whether all the potential needs presented by a negotiation have been canvassed. . . .

In negotiation, as in counseling, the lawyer should be certain that she acts with full knowledge of the client's desires. Within the suggested framework, the lawyer ranks the client's preferences in terms of what is important to the client rather than what the lawyer assumes about the "typical" client.

In order to engage in problem-solving negotiation the lawyer must first ascertain her clients' underlying needs or objectives. In addition, the lawyer may want to explore whether there are unstated objectives, pursue those which she thinks appropriate to the situation, or probe the legitimacy and propriety of particular goals. It should be noted, however, that the lawyer's role in exploring latent concerns or discussing the propriety of objectives can come dangerously close to the role of the lawyer in the adversarial model who imposes his own values or makes assumptions about what the client wants to accomplish. Finally, in order to pursue solutions that will be advantageous for both parties, the lawyer must ascertain the likely underlying needs and objectives of the other party. The client is a primary source for this information, but the lawyer should pursue other sources throughout the negotiation process.

2. Creating solutions

a. Meeting the Parties' Needs

Having identified the parties' needs one can begin the search for solutions with those that are suggested by the parties or that otherwise directly meet the parties' needs.

For example, in a personal injury case the injured plaintiff may have economic needs for compensation and rehabilitation costs that extend into the future. In such cases, structured settlements, paid over time, and according to a variety of formulas, may more closely meet the needs of the parties than a single lump sum payment. . . .

Regardless of how limited the possible solutions may appear to be, they are, in this context, far more likely to satisfy the parties and effectuate a more permanent agreement than would most results achieved in court or in adversarial negotiations. . . .

b. Expanding the Resources Available

Of course, the parties' needs will not be sufficiently complementary in all cases to permit direct solutions. Needs may conflict or there may be conflict over the material required to satisfy the needs. In addition to focusing on the parties' needs as a source of solutions, negotiators can attempt to expand the resources that the parties may eventually have to divide. In essence, this aspect of problem-solving negotiation seeks wherever possible to convert zero-sum games into non-zero-sum or positive-sum games. By expanding resources or the material available for division, more of the parties' total set of needs may be satisfied. Indeed, as the literature on legal transactions and the economic efficiency of such transactions makes clear, the parties come together to transact business precisely because their joint action is likely to increase the wealth available to both. To the extent that principles of wealth creation and resource expansion from transactional negotiation can be assimilated to dispute negotiation, the parties to a negotiation have the opportunity to help each other by looking for ways to expand what is available to them.

Various substantive strategies may increase the material available for distribution. Resources can be expanded by exploring what could be distributed, when it could be distributed, by whom it would be distributed, how it could be distributed and how much of it could be distributed. . . .

c. Just or Fair Solutions

For those who seek the most effective or efficient solutions from a utilitarian perspective, it is enough to settle at a point where no party can gain without hurting the other party. This is the best solution that can be reached when all preferences and needs are taken into account. But legal negotiations leave us with two special non-Pareto optimal problems. First, should the zealous advocate pursue a gain for his client that would cause a loss to the other side? Second, when might the negotiator choose to pursue less gain for his client or actually cause his client to suffer some loss so as to benefit or not hurt the other side? In some sense these questions are on opposite sides of the same coin. Without solving either definitively, the problem-solving model of negotiation may provide some avenues of inquiry.

In the first case the lawyer and client together can consider whether the pursuit of an additional gain at an equivalent or higher cost to the other side is likely to affect the result in an adverse way. The second party may be so hurt, angry or defeated that the solution will be difficult or more expensive to implement. Having answered the utilitarian question, the legal negotiator must then take into account the rules of her profession. . . .

Because problem-solving negotiations are likely to result in a greater number of potential solutions not contemplated in advance, the client in such negotiations is more likely to become involved in evaluating proposals. This will be particularly true where a client's objectives or needs may change over time, or need to be reevaluated as new proposals are forthcoming. Thus, the increased fluidity and emphasis on the parties' underlying interests may result in greater client involvement in the legal negotiation process. One of the key differences between the conventional adversarial model and the problem-solving model is the extent to which the parties and their lawyers engage in a continually interactive negotiation process, using the opportunity to seek new solutions rather than simply moving along a predetermined linear scale of compromise. . . .

Conclusion

This Article has outlined a systematic approach to legal negotiation premised on the notion that agreements will be more effective when the parties conceive of their purposes as solving the problem or planning the transaction, rather than winning or gaining unilateral advantage. The creative problem-solving approach outlined here depends on two structural components: (1) identifying the parties' underlying needs and objectives, and (2) crafting solutions, first by attempting to meet those needs directly, and second, by attempting to meet more of those needs through expanding the resources available. By utilizing such a framework for negotiations, the parties should recognize the synergistic advantage of such an approach over the adversarial and manipulative strategies of zero-sum negotiations. Parties should be able to achieve solutions to disputes that would not have been possible in court-ordered resolutions. . . .

The attraction of the problem-solving approach to negotiations is that it returns the solution of the problem to the client and forces the lawyer to perform her essential role in the legal system — that of solving problems. By using her professional expertise to canvas possible solutions to the problems and by constantly referring back to the client's real needs and objectives, the lawyer can make the negotiation process more responsive, while at the same time reducing the client's desire for potentially destructive unilateral victory. By utilizing a problem-solving approach the lawyer may be able to avoid the analog of iatrogenic illness, refusing to make worse or increase the costs of the legal problem by her intervention. The client will not, then, experience his dispute or transaction as getting worse simply because of his entrance into the legal system. . . .

Questions

8. In what ways does problem-solving negotiation differ from the cooperative techniques of *Getting to Yes*? If the difference is a matter of emphasis, what seems to be the emphasis?
9. Which of the differences you thought of are most likely to be of use in settling legal controversies?
10. Are particular skills required for problem-solving negotiation? Are these skills within the repertoire of most attorneys? Do you have these skills?
11. Do you agree that, "The attraction of the problem-solving approach to negotiations is that it returns the solution of the problem to the client. . . ."? Is this always desirable or wanted by the client? When might this not be an attraction?
12. Can problem-solving negotiation occur if only one side wants to pursue this approach? Please explain your answer.

C. The Tension Between Creating Value and Claiming Value

The negotiation concepts popularized by *Getting to Yes*, whether labeled as cooperative or problem solving, have been widely taught and very influential since the book first appeared in 1981. However, some experienced negotiators believe the underlying theory and tactics espoused by Fisher, Ury, and Patton are naive and could set up adherents to this approach for failure. One frequently-cited critic is James White, a well-respected professor and longtime teacher of negotiation. Professor White's review, excerpted next, is followed by comments from Professor Fisher.

❖ **James J. White,** PROS AND CONS OF "GETTING TO YES"; **and Roger Fisher,** COMMENT ON WHITE'S REVIEW

34 J. Legal Educ. 115 (1984)

Getting to Yes is a puzzling book. On the one hand it offers a forceful and persuasive criticism of much traditional negotiating behavior. It suggests a variety of negotiating techniques that are both clever and likely to facilitate effective negotiation. On the other hand, the authors seem to deny the existence of a significant part of the negotiation process, and to oversimplify or explain away many of the most troublesome problems inherent in the art and practice of negotiation. The book is frequently naive, occasionally self-righteous, but often helpful. . . .

Unfortunately the book's emphasis upon mutually profitable adjustment, on the "problem solving" aspect of bargaining, is also the book's weakness. It is a weakness because emphasis of this aspect of bargaining is done to almost total exclusion of the other aspect of bargaining, "distributional bargaining," where one for me is minus one for you . . . . [S]ome would describe a typical negotiation as one in which the parties initially begin by cooperative or efficiency bargaining in which each gains something with each new adjustment without the other losing any significant benefit. Eventually, however, one comes to bargaining in which added benefits to one impose corresponding significant costs on the other. . . .

One can concede the authors' thesis (that too many negotiators are incapable of engaging in problem solving or in finding adequate options for mutual gain), yet still maintain that the most demanding aspect of nearly every negotiation is the distributional one in which one seeks more at the expense of the other. My principal criticism of the book is that it seems to overlook the ultimate hard bargaining. Had the authors stated that they were dividing the negotiation process in two and were dealing with only part of it, that omission would be excusable. That is not what they have done. Rather they seem to assume that a clever negotiator can make any negotiation into problem solving. . . . To my mind this is naive. By so distorting reality, they detract from their powerful and central thesis.

Chapter 5, entitled "Insist on Objective Criteria," is a particularly naive misperception or rejection of the guts of distributive negotiation. Here, as elsewhere, the authors draw a stark distinction between a negotiator who simply takes a position without explanation and sticks to it as a matter of "will," and the negotiator who is reasonable and insists upon "objective criteria." Of course the world is hardly as simple as the authors suggest. Every party who takes a position will have some rationale for that position; every able negotiator rationalizes every position that he takes. Rarely will an effective negotiator simply assert "X" as his price and insist that the other party meet it.

The suggestion that one can find objective criteria (as opposed to persuasive rationalizations) seems quite inaccurate. . . . To say that there are objective criteria . . . in the case of a personal injury suit for a million dollars or an $800,000 judgment, is to ignore the true dynamics of the situation and to exaggerate the power of objective criteria. Any lawyer who has been involved in a personal injury suit will marvel at the capacity of an effective plaintiff's lawyer . . . to give the superficial appearance of certainty and objectivity to questions that are inherently imponderable. . . . Their suggestion that the parties look to objective criteria to strengthen their cases is a useful technique used by every able negotiator. Occasionally it may do what they suggest: give an obvious answer on which all can agree. Most of the time it will do no more than give the superficial appearance of reasonableness and honesty to one party's position. . . .

The author's consideration of "dirty tricks" in negotiation suffers from more of the same faults found in their treatment of objective criteria. At a superficial level I find their treatment of dirty tricks to be distasteful because it is so thoroughly self-righteous. The chapter is written as though there were one and only one definition of appropriate negotiating behavior. . . . The authors seem not to perceive that between "full disclosure" and "deliberate deception" lies a continuum, not a yawning chasm. They seem to ignore the fact that in one sense the negotiator's role is at least passively to mislead his opponent about his settling point while at the same time to engage in ethical behavior.

Finally, because the book almost totally disregards distributive bargaining, it necessarily ignores a large number of factors that probably have a significant impact on the outcome of negotiations. . . . There is evidence that the level of the first offer, and the pace and form of concessions all affect the outcome of negotiation, yet there is no consideration of those matters. Doubtless the authors can be forgiven for that. No book of 163 pages can be expected to deal with every aspect of negotiation. Yet this one suffers more than most, for implicitly if not explicitly, it seems to suggest that it is presenting the "true method.". . .

Comment by Roger Fisher

. . . White is more concerned with the way the world is, and I am more concerned with what intelligent people ought to do. One task is to teach the truth, to tell students the unpleasant facts of life, including how people typically negotiate. But I want a student to negotiate better than his or her father. I see my task as to give the best possible prescriptive advice, taking into account the way other human beings are likely to behave as well as one's own emotions and psychological state. . . .

The world is a rough place. It is also a place where, taken collectively, we are incompetent at resolving our differences in ways that efficiently and amicably serve our mutual interest. It is important that students learn about bluffing and hard bargaining, because they will certainly encounter it. It is also important that our students become more skillful and wise than most people in dealing with differences. Thus to some extent, White and I are emphasizing different aspects of what needs to be taught. . . .

The most fundamental difference between White's way of thinking and mine seems to concern the negotiation of distributional issues "where one for me is minus one for you.". . . By focusing on the substantive issues (where the parties' interests may be directly opposed), White overlooks the shared interest that the parties continue to have in the process for resolving that substantive difference. How to resolve the substantive difference is a shared problem. Both parties have an interest in identifying quickly and amicably a result acceptable to each, if one is possible. How to do so is a problem. A good solution to that process-problem requires joint action. . . .

The guts of the negotiation problem, in my view, is not who gets the last dollar, but what is the best process for resolving that issue. It is certainly a mistake to assume that the only process available for resolving distributional questions is hard bargaining over positions. In my judgment it is also a mistake to assume that such hard bargaining is the best process for resolving differences efficiently and in the long-term interest of either side. . . .

White seems to find the concept of "raw power" useful for a negotiator. I do not. For a negotiator, the critical questions of power are (1) how to enhance one's ability to influence favorably a negotiator on the other side, and (2) how to use such ability as one has. My ability to exert influence depends upon the cumulative impact of several factors: skill and knowledge, the state of our relationship, the legitimacy of our respective interests, the elegance of a proposed solution, my willingness and ability to commit myself, and the relative attractiveness to each side of its best alternative. In advance of a negotiation I can work to enhance each of those elements. . . .

Without knowing the particular subject matter of a negotiation or the identity of the people on the other side, what is the best advice one can give to a negotiator? People may prefer to ask different questions, but I have not yet heard better answers to the question on which we were and are working. . . .

Questions

13. Are you more persuaded by White or Fisher? Is Professor Fisher naive, or is Professor White too skeptical? Can they both be correct in some ways?

14. Have you experienced situations in which you were open and cooperative initially and then felt that you might have revealed too much or been too accommodating, so that you did not get what you wanted for yourself? If you were in that same situation again, would you behave differently? What are the trade-offs?

15. If a positional negotiator views the person across the table as an opponent, and if an adversarial bargainer views that person as an adversary, then what is the most apt designation for two people negotiating cooperatively?

16. Does an attorney's reputation for openness and cooperation present a particular attraction to a client willing to pay a premium for that attorney to engage in "hard bargaining" or sharp tactics on his behalf? (For an interesting real-life example, see David McKean and Douglas Frantz's *Friends in High Places: The Rise and Fall of Clark Clifford*, 1995.)

17. Can "problem-solving" negotiation occur if only one side wants to pursue this approach?

CHAPTER
4

A Combined Approach and Choosing a Style

A. Combined Approach — Creating Value and Claiming Value

The distributional bargaining to which Professors White and Fisher refer in Chapter 3 occurs when the issue being negotiated is singular or all apparent possibilities of joint gain have been exhausted. Negotiation by a tourist over the cash price of a single item from a transient merchant at a bazaar is a simple example of a zero-sum game, in which a dollar more for the seller is a dollar less for the purchaser and no future relationship is anticipated. Where the possibility exists to go beyond a zero-sum situation and create additional value, such as in the Microsoft-Stac dispute reported in Chapter 3, a dilemma exists for negotiators between pursuing the cooperative moves to enhance the total value available jointly, and competitive behavior to individually claim increased value and gain an advantage. Understanding this dichotomy of opportunities and the choice it presents creates a tension, because after value is created through cooperation and sharing information about interests, value claiming is likely to occur, and the information we shared could haunt us.

The next reading, from an influential book by David Lax and James Sebenius, identifies some of the sources of creating value in negotiation. It also introduces the "negotiator's dilemma," the tension that exists between the behaviors that tend to create value and those that individually claim the value that was jointly created. These two authors, like Professor Menkel-Meadow in Chapter 3, suggest open communication and sharing information to avoid leaving joint gains on the table. The critique by Gerald Wetlaufer, which follows our *Note* on differences and joint gains, is more cautionary about buying into "win-win" negotiation and advises against sharing certain information, at least for the pecuniary reasons offered by Lax and Sebenius.

❖ **David A. Lax & James K. Sebenius,** *THE MANAGER AS NEGOTIATOR: BARGAINING FOR COOPERATION AND COMPETITIVE GAIN*

29 (The Free Press, 1986)

The Negotiator's Dilemma: Creating and Claiming Value

We assume that each negotiator strives to advance his interests, whether they are narrowly conceived or include such concerns as improving the relationship, acting in accord with conceptions of equity, or furthering the welfare of others. Negotiators must learn, in part from each other, what is jointly possible and desirable. To do so requires some degree of cooperation. But, at the same time, they seek to advance their individual interests. This involves some degree of competition.

That negotiation includes cooperation and competition, common and conflicting interests, is nothing new. In fact, it is typically understood that these elements are both present and can be disentangled.

Deep down, however, some people believe that the elements of conflict are illusory, that meaningful communication will erase any such unfortunate misperceptions. Others see mainly competition and take the cooperative pieces to be minimal. Some overtly acknowledge the reality of each aspect but direct all their attention to one of them and wish, pretend, or act as if the other does not exist. Still others hold to a more balanced view that accepts both elements as significant but seeks to treat them separately. . . . [W]e argue that all these approaches are flawed.

A deeper analysis shows that the competitive and cooperative elements are inextricably entwined. In practice, they cannot be separated. This bonding is fundamentally important to the analysis, structuring, and conduct of negotiation. There is a central, inescapable tension between cooperative moves to create value jointly and competitive moves to gain individual advantage. This tension affects virtually all tactical and strategic choice. Analysts must come to grips with it; negotiators must manage it. Neither denial nor discomfort will make it disappear.

Warring Conceptions of Negotiation

Negotiators and analysts tend to fall into two groups that are guided by warring conceptions of the bargaining process. In the left-hand corner are the "value creators" and in the right-hand corner are the "value claimers."

Value Creators

Value creators tend to believe that, above all, successful negotiators must be inventive and cooperative enough to devise an agreement that yields considerable gain to each party, relative to no-agreement possibilities. Some speak about the need for replacing the "win-lose" image of negotiation with "win-win" negotiation, from which all parties presumably derive great value. . . .

Communication and sharing information can help negotiators to create value jointly. Consider the case of a singer negotiating with the owner of an auditorium over payment for a proposed concert. They reached impasse over the size of the fee with the performer's demands exceeding the owner's highest offer. In fact, when the amount of the fixed payment was the issue, no possibility of agreement may have existed at all. The singer, however, based his demand on the expectation that the house would certainly be filled with fans while the owner projected only a half-capacity crowd. Ironically, this difference in their beliefs about attendance provided a way out. They reached a mutually acceptable arrangement in which the performer received a modest fixed fee plus a set percentage of the ticket receipts. The singer, given his beliefs, thus expected an adequate to fairly large payment; the concert hall owner was happy with the agreement because he only expected to pay a moderate fee. This "contingent" arrangement . . . permitted the concert to occur, leaving both parties feeling better off and fully willing to live with the outcome.

In addition to information sharing and honest communication, the drive to create value by discovering joint gains can require ingenuity and may benefit from a variety of techniques and attitudes. The parties can treat the negotiation as solving a joint problem; they can organize brainstorming sessions to invent creative solutions to their problems. They may succeed by putting familiar pieces of the problem together in ways that people had not previously seen, as well as by wholesale reformulations of the problem.

Roger Fisher and Bill Ury give an example that concerns the difficult Egyptian Israeli negotiations over where to draw a boundary in the Sinai. "This appeared to be an absolutely classic example of zero sum bargaining, in which each square mile lost to one party was the other side's gain. For years the negotiations proceeded inconclusively with proposed boundary lines drawn and redrawn on innumerable maps. On probing the real interests of the two sides, however, Egypt was found to care a great deal about sovereignty over the Sinai while Israel was heavily concerned with its security. As such, a creative solution could be devised to "unbundle" these different interests and give to each what it valued most. In the Sinai, this involved creating a demilitarized zone under the Egyptian flag. This had the effect of giving Egypt "sovereignty" and Israel "security." This situation exemplifies extremely common tendencies to assume that negotiators' interests are in direct opposition, a conviction that can sometimes be corrected by communicating, sharing information, and inventing solutions. . . .

We create value by finding joint gains for all negotiating parties. A joint gain represents an improvement from each party's point of view; one's gain need not be another's loss. An extremely simple example makes the point. Say that two young boys each have three pieces of fruit. Willy, who hates bananas and loves pears, has a banana and two oranges. Sam, who hates pears and loves bananas, has a pear and two apples. The first move is easy: they trade banana for pear and are both happier. But after making this deal, they realize that they can do still better. Though each has a taste both for apples and oranges, a second piece of the same fruit is less desirable than the first. So they also swap an apple for an orange. The banana pear exchange represents an improvement over the no trade alternative; the apple orange transaction that leaves each with three different kinds of fruit improves the original agreement — is a joint gain — for both boys.

The economist's analogy is simple: Creativity has expanded the size of the pie under negotiation. Value creators see the essence of negotiating as expanding the pie, as pursuing joint gains. This is aided by openness, clear communication, sharing information, creativity, an attitude of joint problem solving, and cultivating common interests.

Value Claimers

Value claimers, on the other hand, tend to see this drive for joint gain as naive and weak minded. For them, negotiation is hard, tough bargaining. The object of negotiation is to convince the other guy that he wants what you have to offer much more than you want what he has; moreover, you have all the time in the world while he is up against pressing deadlines. To "win" at negotiating — and thus make the other fellow "lose" — one must start high, concede slowly, exaggerate the value of concessions, minimize the benefits of the other's concessions, conceal information, argue forcefully on behalf of principles that imply favorable settlements, make commitments to accept only highly favorable agreements, and be willing to outwait the other fellow.

The hardest of bargainers will threaten to walk away or to retaliate harshly if their one-sided demands are not met; they may ridicule, attack, and intimidate their adversaries. . . . At the heart of this adversarial approach is an image of a negotiation with a winner and a loser: "We are dividing a pie of fixed size and every slice I give to you is a slice I do not get; thus, I need to claim as much of the value as possible by giving you as little as possible."

A Fundamental Tension of Negotiation

Both of these images of negotiation are incomplete and inadequate. Value creating and value claiming are linked parts of negotiation. Both processes are present. No matter how much creative problem solving enlarges the pie, it must still be divided; value that has been created must be claimed. And, if the pie is not enlarged, there will be less to divide; there is more value to be claimed if one has helped create it first. An essential tension in negotiation exists between cooperative moves to create value and competitive moves to claim it.

[T]he concert hall owner may offer the singer a percentage of the gate combined with a fixed fee that is just barely high enough to induce the singer to sign the contract. Even when the parties to a potential agreement share strong common interests, one side may claim the lion's share of the value an agreement creates. . . .

The Tension at the Tactical Level

The tension between cooperative moves to create value and competitive moves to claim it is greatly exacerbated by the interaction of the tactics used either to create or claim value.

First, tactics for claiming value (which we will call "claiming tactics") can impede its creation. Exaggerating the value of concessions and minimizing the benefit of others' concessions presents a distorted picture of one's relative preferences; thus, mutually beneficial trades may not be discovered. Making threats or commitments to highly favorable outcomes surely impedes hearing and understanding others' interests. Concealing information may also cause one to leave joint gains on the table. In fact, excessive use of tactics for claiming value may well sour the parties' relationship and reduce the trust between them. Such tactics may also evoke a variety of unhelpful interests. Conflict may escalate and make joint prospects less appealing and settlement less likely.

Second, approaches to creating value are vulnerable to tactics for claiming value. Revealing information about one's relative preferences is risky. . . . The information that a negotiator would accept position A in return for a favorable resolution on a second issue can be exploited: "So, you'll accept A. Good. Now, let's move on to discuss the merits of the second issue." The willingness to make a new, creative offer can often be taken as a sign that its proposer is able and willing to make further concessions. Thus, such offers sometimes remain undisclosed. Even purely shared interests can be held hostage in exchange for concessions on other issues. Though a divorcing husband and wife may both prefer giving the wife custody of the child, the husband may "suddenly" develop strong parental instincts to extract concessions in alimony in return for giving the wife custody.

In tactical choices, each negotiator thus has reasons not to be open and cooperative. Each also has apparent incentives to try to claim value. Moves to claim value thus tend to drive out moves to create it. Yet, if both choose to claim value, by being dishonest or less than forthcoming about preferences, beliefs, or minimum requirements, they may miss mutually beneficial terms for agreement.

Indeed, the structure of many bargaining situations suggests that negotiators will tend to leave joint gains on the table or even reach impasses when mutually acceptable agreements are available.

Note: Differences Can Create Joint Gains

Lax and Sebenius go on to summarize the differences that can lead to joint gains and creation of value. In an article published in 2002 (19 Negotiation J. 5-28), they elaborate on differences that may be the source of unrealized value. These differences can be summarized as follows:

- Differences in relative valuation or priorities can lead to exchanges, directly or by "unbundling" differently valued interests. The apple and orange fruit exchange noted in the reading is an example of differences in relative valuation that create trading value.
- Differences in tolerance for risk and *risk aversion* suggest insurance-like risk-sharing arrangements in negotiated transactions. A risk-averse litigant may be willing to discount what she will receive or pay more as a certain amount rather than bear the risk of losing at trial. If the opposing side is more risk tolerant, they can be rewarded by paying less or receiving more because they are not so averse to the risk of trial.
- Differences in *time preference* can lead to altered patterns of payments or actions over time. If a claimant needs money immediately and a defendant has a reserve set aside for settlement of the claim, a quick payment can create value for both sides and enhance the chance of an agreement.
- Different *capabilities* can be combined. Companies with complementary capabilities can negotiate deals and mergers to create value that neither could achieve alone. For example, a company with strong production capacity can combine forces with a company that has sophisticated marketing and distribution abilities to collectively enhance profitability and create value between them.
- Differences in *cost/revenue structure* can create cost saving trades. For example, if a butcher, who gets meat wholesale, can trade meat with a shoe merchant, who gets shoes wholesale, they have created value for themselves by each getting what would not otherwise be available to them at wholesale cost.
- Differences in *forecasts* can lead to contingent agreements when the items under negotiation are uncertain and themselves subject to different probability estimates, or when each party feels that it will fare well under, and perhaps can influence, a proposed contingent resolution procedure. In a negotiation over executive compensation where the prospective executive

has a more optimistic view of her abilities to produce revenue than does the company, she may agree to a lower salary with a higher bonus contingent on revenue increases. Both negotiating sides may feel better off because they have structured an employment deal based on their own forecasts and have, in effect, created value for themselves.

- Other differences (evaluation criteria, the importance of precedent, the value of personal reputation, constituency attitudes, the organizational situation, conceptions of fairness, and so on) can also be fashioned into joint gains. For example, a law firm being threatened with a suit by a former clerk for sexual harassment may be willing to settle a claim for much more if it is cast as payment for wrongful termination.

These "differences" relate to the role perceptions play in understanding conflict, as explained in Chapter 2, particularly by Rummel in his excerpt on "The Subjectivity Principle." You will note that we have come full circle in connecting the cause of conflict — different perceptions that are all in our heads — to a suggested approach for constructively resolving conflicts, recognizing the different perceptions and trading on them.

❖ Gerald B. Wetlaufer, *The Limits of Integrative Bargaining*

85 Geo. L.J. 369 (1996)

It is now conventional wisdom that opportunities for integrative bargaining are widely available, that they are often unrecognized and unexploited, and that as a result both parties to negotiations and society as a whole are worse off than would otherwise have been the case. The failure to recognize and exploit these opportunities may reflect a failure of education, curable either by reading or by attending a course or seminar. It may reflect the "I'm right, you're wrong, and I can prove it" style of discourse associated with law school education and historically male modes of moral reasoning. Or it may be the result of the "negotiator's dilemma" in which the open and cooperative tactics thought appropriate to integrative bargaining are systematically exploited and driven out by the more combative tactics generally associated with distributive bargaining — starting high, conceding slowly, concealing and misrepresenting one's own interests, arguing coercively, threatening, and bluffing.

If the problem at hand is our failure to recognize and exploit opportunities for integrative bargaining, the solution, we are told, is to shift away from the tactics of distributive bargaining and toward the tactics appropriate to integrative bargaining: cooperation, openness, and truthtelling. Individual negotiators should embrace these tactics not because they are good or ethical, or because they will help to build a better society, but instead because they will promote the individual's immediate pecuniary self-interest. . . .

The proponents of integrative bargaining usually assert that opportunities for such bargaining are widely, if not universally, available. Lax and Sebenius, in the most important contribution yet made to our understanding of these matters, catalogue the opportunities for integrative bargaining. Their list includes differences between the parties in terms of (1) their interests, (2) their projections concerning possible future events (3) their willingness to accept risks, and (4) their time preferences regarding payment or performance. . . . All four of these circumstances will sometimes, but only under certain further conditions and with certain important qualifications, afford opportunities for the parties to expand the pie through integrative bargaining. . . .

[The author next argues and attempts to demonstrate that the listed differences between negotiating parties rarely provide opportunities to lastingly expand the pie and create joint, integrative gains. He makes reference to the Lax and Sebenius example of a singer negotiating with the owner of an auditorium over payment for a proposed concert.]

A final claim that can now be evaluated is that opportunities for integrative bargaining necessarily imply that it is in a negotiator's immediate pecuniary self-interest to engage in the tactics of cooperation, openness, truthtelling, honesty, and trust. First, I have demonstrated that opportunities for integrative bargaining, especially meaningful opportunities for integrative bargaining (e.g., where the pie may be made to expand and to stay expanded), exist within a narrower range of circumstances than sometimes has been claimed. Some of the differences cited by Lax and Sebenius simply do not create opportunities for integrative bargaining. Others, namely those involving different assessments regarding future events, create opportunities to expand the pie only if the parties are willing to bet on their projections. And even when the parties are willing to bet, there will be opportunities for integrative bargaining only some of the time and only in ways that will sometimes prove self-defeating in the sense that the pie may eventually return to its original size. If the pie shrinks back, one or both of the parties will be worse off than they had expected to be and, potentially worse off than they would have been had they not entered the agreement. Other circumstances named by Lax and Sebenius — multiple issues differently valued, differing projections concerning future events, differing time preferences, differing levels of risk aversion — sometimes offer opportunities for integrative bargaining but sometimes do not. Although the general claim is made that opportunities for integrative bargaining provide a reason, based solely on immediate pecuniary self-interest, to engage in openness and truthtelling, those opportunities are considerably less pervasive than has been announced. Thus, this argument for openness and truthtelling is, in that degree, narrower and less persuasive.

Second, even within the range of circumstances in which there are significant opportunities for integrative bargaining, the bargainer must almost always engage in distributive bargaining as well. Therefore, it is in the bargainer's self-interest not just to adopt the tactics of openness and truthtelling that are said to be appropriate to integrative bargaining, but somehow also to adopt the tactics of truth-hiding and dissimulation that are said to be appropriate in distributive bargaining. However we might manage these incompatible tactics, this situation presents at most a weak and highly qualified argument for openness and truthtelling. Moreover, the argument for openness and truthtelling is not an argument for openness and truthtelling with respect to everything, but instead, is limited to information useful in identifying and exploiting opportunities for integrative bargaining. Thus, an opportunity for integrative bargaining will present an occasion for a certain amount of truthtelling with respect to one's relative interest in various issues (or one's projections about the future or aversion to risk) without also presenting even a weak argument for truthtelling with respect to one's reservation price. . . .

If there is a general case for cooperation, openness, and truthtelling in negotiations, that case is multidimensional and parts of it are expressly ethical. Certainly, because there are opportunities for integrative bargaining, a measure of openness and truthtelling is sometimes warranted as a matter of a negotiator's immediate pecuniary self-interest. Similarly, a negotiator's long-term pecuniary self-interest may sometimes be served by openness and truthtelling because of the costs that may be associated with a reputation for sharp dealing. But it is also true that a negotiator's pecuniary self-interest is, at best, only a portion of his true self-interest. Thus, it may be in his true self- interest to accept some pecuniary costs for the sake of living in a community in which cooperation, truthtelling, and ethical behavior are the norm. Moreover, Plato's Socrates may have been right when he argued that a person who has some combination of wealth and virtue may be happier and better off than a person who has more wealth but less virtue. . . .

We have, in certain respects, allowed ourselves to be dazzled and seduced by the possibilities of integrative or "win-win" bargaining. That, in turn, has led to a certain amount of overclaiming. The reason, I think, is that if we hold these possibilities in a certain light and squint our eyes just hard enough, they look for all the world like the Holy Grail of negotiations. They seem to offer that which we have wanted most to find. What they seem to offer — though in the end it is only an illusion — is the long-sought proof that cooperation, honesty, and good behavior will carry the day not because they are virtuous, not because they will benefit society as a whole, but because they are in everyone's individual and pecuniary self-interest. But however much we may want "honesty" to be "the best policy" in this strong sense, the discovery of integrative bargaining has not, at least so far, provided that long-sought proof.

Perhaps the time has finally come to consider the possibility that this proof will always elude us, for the simple reason that the world in which we live does not, in this particular way, conform to our wishes. Even if there is just the chance that this is so, and it looks much more like a certainty than a chance, it would be appropriate to acknowledge the ultimate insufficiency of understanding self-interest in narrowly pecuniary terms. It would be appropriate to attend in a systematic way to the facts that, even when it is contrary to our pecuniary self-interest, relationships matter; that we care about our reputations, not just for effectiveness but also for decency and good behavior: that we care about living in — and helping to create — communities in which pecuniary self-interest is not the only language that is spoken; and that Plato's Socrates may have gotten it right. And it would be appropriate to acknowledge the central importance of the ethical case against certain forms of competitive and self-interested behavior, especially those forms of behavior, central to the process of negotiations, that involve misrepresentations and other conduct that imposes harm upon others.

Questions

1. Are the suggestions made by Lax and Sebenius for creating value by focusing on differences equally applicable to settlement of legal disputes and to deal-making negotiations? What differences in the above list could be utilized in settling a claim for damages by an injured driver against an insurance company?

2. Do Gerald Wetlaufer's comments reflect the same concerns as those of James White? Is there any fundamental difference in their expressed view of "win-win" negotiation or in how negotiators should behave? If so, how do they differ?

3. Professor Wetlaufer concludes that being open and cooperative in negotiations may not benefit immediate pecuniary interests, but that relationships matter and that Plato may have been correct in teaching that virtue is more important than wealth. Even if we believe this is true when we negotiate for ourselves, as lawyers who negotiate for clients, can we trade off a client's potential gain for our sense of virtue?

4. Do clients have a say in what information is voluntarily revealed and how cooperative they want their attorney to be in negotiating on their behalf?

5. Do the immediate pecuniary interests of the client and the longer-term interests of the attorney in maintaining good working relations with other lawyers or a reputation for "decency" create a conflict of interest between attorney and client?

1. Cooperation vs. Competitiveness — Who Decides?

Problem

Assume that you have established yourself as an effective attorney with a good reputation for your straightforward, cooperative style. You have been a guest lecturer at local law schools about civility in the practice of law and the importance of maintaining a credible professional reputation. Your largest individual client, the president of a regional bank, which your firm also represents, has retained you to represent him in a divorce action initiated by his wife, knowing that you have experience in domestic relations practice. He explains that his highest priority is to retain total control of the bank with no share of the bank stock going to his wife, even though the law might give her a claim to some of it. He wants you to seek for him primary custody of their two middle-school-aged children, for whom he and his wife have both been active parents, so you can use that as a bargaining chip later to assure his retention of the bank stock.

1. What would you tell him?
2. Who should decide negotiation strategies and approaches, you or your client?

2. Ends vs. Means

Generally clients get to choose the objective of negotiation, and lawyers use their professional judgment in selecting the means of obtaining the client's objectives. Of course, it's not quite so simple. In matters of litigation, the lawyer owes the client an ethical obligation of zealous advocacy in pursuit of a client's interests. Some scholars interpret the ethical norms to mean "the final authority on important issues of strategy rests with the client; and the client may discharge his lawyer at will, but the lawyer has only limited ability to withdraw from representation" (Gilson & Mnookin 1995, 550). Mnookin and Gilson believe that a lawyer who wishes to pursue a cooperative approach, with a sensitivity for long-term professional relationships with other attorneys, may not be able to do so in the litigation context, or at least that the client calls the negotiation shots. They also point out that the client can fire the lawyer at will if the lawyer seems more cooperative than the client wishes, but that ethical norms do not always allow the lawyer to quit if the client insists on a more aggressive strategy.

A different perspective is offered by Professor Robert J. Condlin, who points to practical norms that may differ from ethical norms for attorneys. He distinguishes between the reality of what lawyers do in negotiation and what the ethical rules appear to demand. The distinction, according to Condlin, is really between ends and means. Clients have control over the end result desired, and lawyers choose the means. "Lawyers are persons in their own right, with moral and political rights and obligations of their own, and even though they must take direction from their clients, they need not do everything asked. For example, the duty of deference distinguishes between questions of ends and questions of means, and reserves to lawyers the tactical and technical decisions of how best to advance client objectives" (Condlin 1992, 71).

According to Condlin, lawyers must be substantively competitive in negotiating for clients but can choose their own personal style. Competitive attorneys can adopt a cordial and respectful persona in their negotiations, though this can be a fine and difficult distinction. Condlin refers to this tug between a client's wishes for the lawyer to defect from a pattern of cooperation and the lawyer's desire for long-term cooperation as the "bargainer's dilemma." Like the prisoners' dilemma, different negotiation tactics may be called for if the situation is viewed as a single- or multiple-round game. Clients tend to view litigation and some deals as a one-round game. Lawyers usually view their negotiation with other lawyers as unlimited multiple rounds, where any defect will bring future retaliation and a blemished reputation. Thus, the "bargainer's dilemma."

We probe this dilemma in more depth when we examine the ethical constraints on lawyer negotiation in Chapter 10, "Negotiation Ethics." Articles by Professors Condlin and Mnookin (with co-authors Peppet and Tulumello) are presented there. In the meantime, assume that lawyers, when negotiating for clients, do have a choice of being more cooperative or more competitive in their negotiation approach. Also recall that the choice of how to fulfill clients' interests is not completely bipolar. Cooperation may be the best way to fill the needs of all clients in negotiation when an integrative outcome is possible that allows each party to get some of what they want. In such situations, a competitive approach may eliminate the possibility of a win-win outcome that is otherwise available; however, it may produce an outcome most favorable for the client of a successful competitive negotiator.

B. Choosing an Effective Approach

1. *Negotiating Within Your Comfort Zone*

Being cooperative, problem solving, competitive, or adversarial is, at least in part, a matter of choice. The choice you make depends on a number of factors. The subject of the negotiation, the interrelation between issues, the past or anticipated future relationship between the parties and between the attorneys, your counterpart's negotiation approach, the customs and conventions where the negotiation occurs, the amount of time available, and the amount at stake may all influence your approach to negotiation. The biggest factor, however, is your own comfort zone, formed by your personality and values. To the extent that how you negotiate is driven by personality and values, it may be better described as a matter of style rather than approach. Behavioral style is in large part a function of who you are. Choosing a style that does not fit your personality and values, if not a recipe for failure, is likely to make your work as a negotiator difficult and dissatisfying. To succeed as a professional and find satisfaction in what you are doing, you must negotiate within your personal comfort zone.

Defining our negotiating comfort zone is not always an easy task. It is a common desire to be liked rather than disliked. We know that we are more likely to be liked when we are cooperative and giving than when we are adversarial and taking. However, we also know that winners are admired, and we want to be respected for vigorously representing our clients' interests and succeeding when we negotiate on their behalf. Law students without legal experience may share the view of attorneys popularized in movies and television series as hard-charging, aggressive lawyers. The dramatic, adversarial scenes popularly portrayed in dramatized jury trials may be transposed in our minds to all opposing lawyer interactions. As a result, many students have a latent fear that their preference for cooperation and friendliness will not serve them or their clients well in negotiation.

Other students may have thrived on competition and winning in sports and other contests. We know that law students are a self-selected group of achievers who have succeeded, at least academically, and made it into law school through a competitive admissions process. Competition appears to be encouraged by the legal system, where cooperation and generosity may be viewed as a virtuous but less-valued quality. So it is understandable that some students are conflicted about whether negotiation should be approached as a professional game in which their competitive qualities are let loose and rewarded with success.

Those of you who have enjoyed competition know from your experience that good competitors can be friendly, gracious, and ethical. Similarly, not all competitive negotiators manifest an adversarial persona. A pleasant and respectful personal style is not necessarily inconsistent with competitive negotiation, any more than being cordial in competitive sports is inconsistent with wanting to win. The style you choose in negotiation may depend on how you define the game and the relationship you want with your negotiation counterpart.

Your negotiation style may also depend in large measure on your ingrained personality pattern. If personality patterns drive how we and others approach negotiation, can we discern those patterns in ourselves and others, and how can we benefit from the information?

Because personality does matter in how we interact with others, how we deal with conflict, and how we negotiate, researchers have attempted to test and measure personality traits that influence these functions. The *Thomas-Kilmann Conflict Mode Instrument* (or "Thomas-Kilmann test") is one of the best methods available to assess one's tendencies as a negotiator and is administered in some law school negotiation courses. This widely used personality test measures five dimensions of how individuals deal with conflict and negotiation to determine their degree of assertiveness and/or cooperation. The Thomas-Kilmann test asks test takers to respond to 30 statements (for example, "I feel that differences are not always worth worrying about" or "I make some effort to get my way") and self-score their answers. The results give the taker a profile of how strongly she scores in all five categories: Competitor, Accommodator (sometimes also called Cooperator), Avoider, Compromiser, and Collaborator (sometimes called Problem Solver).

One of the strengths of the test is that it provides relative scores rather than a simple yes-no or categorical placement: When you take the test, you receive a score along a continuum from very high to very low as a Competitor, for instance. Test takers receive scores in all five categories. This gives the taker a nuanced portrait of herself as a composite of several, sometimes conflicting, tendencies. Each of the Thomas-Kilmann test categories has advantages and disadvantages in negotiation (See R. Mnookin, S. Peppet & A. Tulumello, *Negotiator's Empathy and Assertiveness*, 14 Alternative 133, 1996.)

The five categories of conflict management styles are:

- *competing* — high on assertiveness and low on cooperation;
- *accommodating* — low on assertiveness and high on cooperation;
- *avoiding* — low on assertiveness and cooperation;
- *compromising* — moderate on assertiveness and cooperation; and
- *collaborating* — high on assertiveness and cooperation.

Another personality test is the *Five-Factor Model* of personality, also known as the "big five" taxonomy. This test is used extensively in experimental psychology to determine the five major categories describing broad personality traits, and it has been applied to negotiation outcomes. (See B. Barry & R. Friedman, *Bargainer Characteristics in Distributive and Integrative Negotiation*, 74 J. Personality & Soc. Psychol. 345, 1998.) The five factors that comprise the test are:

- *extroversion* — sociable, assertive, and talkative;
- *agreeableness* — flexible, cooperative, and trusting;
- *conscientiousness* — responsible, organized, and achievement oriented;
- *emotional stability* — secure and confident; and
- *openness* — imaginative, broad-minded, and curious.

The best known and most widely referred to personality test is the *Myers-Briggs Type Indicator*. You may have taken this test. It is administered over 2 million times a year by large companies, the U.S. government, and academic institutions. It is the subject of countless research studies and articles, including ones that analyze the impact of personality variables on negotiation. (See D. Peters, *Forever Jung: Psychological Type Theory, The Myers-Briggs Type Indicator and Learning Negotiation,* 42 Drake L. Rev. 1, 1993.) Myers-Briggs measures four sets of contrasting personality dimensions:

- *introverted* or *extroverted*;
- *sensing* or *intuitive*;
- *thinking* or *feeling*; and
- *perceiving* or *judging*.

There is now considerable literature on the role of personality in negotiation styles and outcomes, based on studies of personality test results and experimental research. However, the utility of this literature for instructional purposes is limited because of the lack of consensus among the studies and the limitations of their methodology. The following reading recognizes those limitations, but offers answers to the questions most often asked about personality and negotiation.

❖ **Sheila Heen & John Richardson, "*I See a Pattern Here and the Pattern Is You*": Personality and Dispute Resolution**

The Handbook of Dispute Resolution 202
(M.L. Moffitt & R.C. Bordone eds., 2005)

Anyone who has more than one child knows that differences in personality are real. The first born may be quiet, eager to please, and shy in new situations. His sister comes along and is an extrovert — smiling early and befriending strangers as a toddler. These traits may remain constant throughout life as the firstborn becomes a writer and his sister makes friends easily and often as a college student, professional, and retiree.

Intuitively, we know that there are differences between individuals. Your spouse is agreeable, your brother irascible, your coworker weepy, and your neighbor hyperrational.

The hard question is this: are there ways to describe the differences in people's personalities that can be useful in conducting and advising negotiations? After all, negotiation is all about dealing with people, getting along with them, and persuading them. Shouldn't knowing how people are different (and what to do about it) be an integral part of negotiation theory and strategy?

One would think so. And yet, the intersection of dispute resolution and personality is a tangle of confusion and contradiction. It is not unexplored territory — scholars have tried to find answers. And it is interesting — there is fascinating work going on and much speculation about what is being learned. Yet there are few clear, satisfying answers to questions that interest dispute resolution professionals most: Are particular personalities better negotiators? Should I negotiate differently with different personalities? And what about when the people and their problematic personalities really are the problem?

[After reviewing the most widely used personality tests, their limitations, and the literature about the reported results, the authors list and answer six questions asked about personality and negotiation.]

1. *Is there really such a thing as personality differences?* It certainly seems so. Whether hard wired by genes or chemical mix, prompted by experience or influenced by the context, two people in a similar situation will often respond differently. This may be particularly so in the pressurized context of a dispute.

Personality researchers attempt to identify and isolate traits that are consistent across situations and different between individuals. This is where things get tricky. Human beings are complex enough, and adaptable enough, that defining and tracking traits, particularly through the dynamic process of negotiation, has proven very difficult.

2. *Or are there particular personality traits that give better outcomes?* With the exception of cognitive ability (more is better), there is no strong answer in the current research. Although you can find small-scale studies suggesting this or that trait is helpful, you can also find studies that say it does not improve outcomes.

3. *Okay, so should I negotiate differently with different personality types?* The biggest obstacle to setting your negotiation strategy based on the other person's personality is figuring out what it is. Because people act differently in different situations, researchers have found that people consistently misperceive the personality traits of those with whom they negotiate or are in dispute.

The best advice is to be aware of your own tendencies, have a broad repertoire of approaches and strategies, and be able to engage difficulties constructively as they come up. Pay attention to particular behavior you see, rather than trying to globalize how the other person "is." And if one approach doesn't seem to be working, try another.

4. *Isn't it true that some disputes are hopeless because people's personalities just aren't going to change?*

It is certainly true that there are limits to what can change, and that some differences between people are harder to reconcile than others. And there are definitely limits to *your ability to change the other person's personality*.

Yet the impulse to throw up our hands and attribute the problem to the other person's personality flaws is a dangerous one. It blames the other person for the dispute, blinding us to our own contributions to the problem. It may also encourage us to give up on a relationship or dispute too easily or too quickly, when finding a way to work together with less frustration remains possible.

In addition, there are at least three paths forward that personality finger-pointing ignores. Remember that human beings' *behavior* can often change without a grand *personality* change. You might shift the context — offering a private caucus or written channel of communication, for example. You can try to influence the other person's behavior by influencing the story he or she tells about what's going on. Or you might try changing your contribution to the dynamic between you. The other person is reacting both to you and to his or her own experiences, tendencies, and stories, and that's a complex enough set of factors to suggest that progress is possible.

Finally, do not underestimate people's ability to change over time. As a person ages, encounters different life experiences, and makes the transition to new phases in life (where he or she may feel more secure or happier, or have more room for reflection for example), his or her traits and tendencies evolve.

You may find that your personality gradually moves into a different era, one you would not have predicted from where you stand now.

5. *Why is personality profiling so popular, if it's so inconclusive?*

People love to talk about themselves. And they especially love to talk about other people. Personality profiling also fits our interest in simplifying the world and the infinitely complex relationships in it. Researchers have long documented the effects of the fundamental attribution error, where we believe we know why people act the way they do, and tend to attribute especially bad behavior to their problematic personality.

People are so complicated that we can't really describe them with few enough variables to meet our needs for parsimony. People can only keep about seven items in their head at one time, before they go into cognitive overload. So they make up something that they can handle in their heads, whether or not it is accurate.

6. *So why pay attention to personality at all?* The fields of personality and negotiation are both relatively young. Our ability to map interaction in negotiation and dispute resolution, and to recommend paths of influence, is in its infancy. And our ability to isolate traits and trace them through complex interaction is still maturing.

Still, familiarity with common differences between individuals is useful. It reminds us that not every approach to influence works with every person. It can help us generate diagnostic hypotheses about why a negotiation is in trouble ("Ah! We may proceed to closure at different paces"), and come up with prescriptive advice to try out. It may also help us be more forgiving of others' seemingly crazy behavior if we can spot it as a difference in the way the two of us see and respond to the world.

Familiarity with personality differences can also be a self-reflection and coaching tool for yourself. It can help you identify and work on behavior that doesn't come naturally to you. It can also help you explain your behavior to others: "I've learned that I'm not very comfortable making commitments before I have a chance to think things through. Can you give me the weekend and we'll nail this down on Monday?" Becoming familiar with some of the traits that affect your ability to mediate, negotiate, or respond well to disputes can help you become more aware of the situations that bring out these traits, and other choices you might make.

Questions

6. Are the style categories and personality dimensions used by the three test instruments just different ways to label the same personality traits, or do they really measure different aspects of personality?

7. After 18 years or more as a student and as an experienced test taker, if your negotiation course readings and class discussion gave you the impression that your instructor valued collaboration more than avoidance or competition, do you think your responses to the 30 statements on the Thomas-Kilmann test (e.g., "I feel that differences are not always worth worrying about" or "I make some effort to get my way") might be influenced by the instructor's values or not provide a totally accurate measure of your conflict style?

8. Given that all three of the personality tests described above rely on self-assessment answers, do you think the results are likely to match the assessment of your personality by opponents, family, friends, and colleagues?

9. Do you feel that personality testing is helpful as an aid to better understand and improve how you negotiate? Does your answer depend on your view of whether personality traits and behavior can be altered? Do you consciously take stock of the personality type of your counterparts when negotiating? Are there ways you can find out about their personalities before engaging with them?

2. Effectiveness and Style

Problem

You are planning to buy a new car upon graduation. You are living in a metropolitan area and have many dealers to choose from. You plan to have your local mechanic service the vehicle, and don't expect problems with it (if you did, you would look to the manufacturer), so you don't expect to see the dealer much after the sale. You are preoccupied with the bar exam and don't want to do the bargaining yourself. Luckily you have the option of asking either of two relatives to serve as your negotiator in this transaction. Your sister Jill is an avid shopper, who enjoys the give and take of haggling and bargains assertively for the last dollar (to tell the truth, she can be somewhat stubborn and argumentative at times). Your cousin Brian is much more agreeable, personable, and accommodating. He thinks that it is important to meet both sides' needs in a deal, and frankly is more fair-minded than Jill.

1. Which would you ask to negotiate for you to buy the car?
2. Assume that you are still bargaining for a car after graduation but your plans have changed. You will be moving to a small community in which dealers are few and far between. Moreover, you can't afford a new car yet, so you are looking for a vehicle three to five years old. You expect to return to the seller for routine maintenance and servicing. Which relative would you choose for this negotiation?
3. If your choices varied depending on the situation, or the choice was at least a much closer call in one scenario than the other, what does this say about your personal view of whether one bargaining style is more effective than another in all settings?

As you know, negotiation is usually done in private and accompanied by confidentiality, so there is little opportunity to compare results. How lawyers behave in negotiation and what they do is not fully known. Lawyers' tales of negotiations, as well as personality tests, are filtered through the lens of the tellers' perceptions. Unless negotiations can be systematically observed on a grand scale, we will never know what really works best to produce desired negotiated outcomes. Few lawyers ever "lose" a negotiation, or tell about it if they believe they did not do well. Spoken and written "war stories" of successful negotiations are not reliable descriptions of what typically occurs, or even of what occurred in the reported negotiation. (There do not appear to be any books on "How I Failed as a Negotiator.") Obstacles to the study and profiling of negotiations leave new lawyers little reliable guidance on what is successful in negotiation and how to weigh the polar tensions they may feel between competition and cooperation to negotiate effectively within their comfort zone.

Two studies help fill the void of information about how lawyers negotiate and which behaviors and styles are effective. Both studies are necessarily limited because they rely on attorneys responding to questionnaires and reporting their perceptions of effective and ineffective negotiation behavior by their opponents in recent negotiations. Nonetheless, both studies provide sources of information about how lawyers negotiate and what is considered effective, as well as ineffective. Because the studies were similar and conducted more than 20 years apart, we can obtain clues about changes over time in how attorneys negotiate (see Schneider 2000).

The news from the studies is both good and bad. The good news for students struggling with the tension of deciding on their negotiation comfort zone and not knowing if what they are inclined to do is the right way to negotiate is that there is no one right way.

Both competitive and cooperative styles can be effective approaches to negotiation if done well and with integrity. Being an effective competitive negotiator does not require the use of tricks or deceit. Some competitive techniques can be legitimate ways to pursue negotiation goals, provided they are not carried to extremes. Being a cooperative negotiator need not be based on naiveté or being a pushover. Cooperative attorneys, who appear from the studies to predominate in numbers and perceived effectiveness, are most successful when they are mindful of the interests they are pursuing and set limits on their cooperation.

The studies indicate that the percentage of attorneys who are adversarial has increased — only about two-thirds of lawyer negotiators are classified as cooperative. The rating of cooperative negotiators as more effective than adversarial negotiators has also increased. Again, it should be noted that some adversarial attorneys are rated as effective, but in a much lower proportion. Some admirable behaviors of negotiators (like preparation, a focus on the client's interests, and high ethical standards) are shared by effective competitive and effective cooperative attorney negotiators.

The bad news is that the more recent study reported that adversarial negotiators are becoming more extreme and unpleasant. The terms most frequently used to describe them are more negative than 20 years ago. This might not bode well for the legal profession or for clients, if the reports are accurate, because this group as a whole appears less effective as negotiators than previously reported.

❖ **Andrea Kupfer Schneider,** *Perception, Reputation and Reality: An Empirical Study of Negotiation Skills*

6 Disp. Resol. Mag. 24 (Summer 2000)

In 1976, law professor Gerald Williams undertook a study on lawyer negotiation styles by surveying 1,000 lawyers in the Phoenix area about their most recent negotiation experience. . . . Close to 60 percent of all cooperative negotiators were considered effective by their peers. Only 25 percent of competitive negotiators were considered effective.

It has been more than 20 years since Williams conducted his research. In the meantime, much has changed in the legal profession and in legal education. These changes include who is entering the law, the evolution of alternative dispute resolution and the growth of mega-law firms. This period also coincides with the decline in the reputation of the legal profession. How have these changes impacted how lawyers negotiate and how effective they are? To answer this question, I have added to Williams' study in the Milwaukee and Chicago legal communities with twice the number of lawyers. . . .

Of the 690 complete responses, 30 percent were from women. Interestingly, 17.8 percent discussed female negotiators. The ethnicity of respondents was overwhelmingly Caucasian (94.6 percent). The other 5.4 percent of lawyers were divided among African-American (3.1 percent), Asian (0.1 percent), Hispanic (1.3 percent), Native American (0.1 percent), and Other (0.8 percent). Fifty-seven percent of respondents practiced in Milwaukee and 43 percent practiced in Chicago. Finally, respondents came from a wide variety of practice areas: commercial (15.7 percent), corporate (6 percent), criminal (8.3 percent), family (12.3 percent), labor and employment (12.2 percent), personal injury (15.4 percent), property and real estate (11 percent) and other (19.1 percent).

Study Results

I worked with statisticians at the Institute for Survey and Policy Research at the University of Wisconsin-Milwaukee to perform cluster analyses on the results. The first step was to divide negotiators into two groups as the Williams study had originally done. The lawyers divided into two clusters of approximately 64 percent and 36 percent. Given the adjectives listed, I labeled these clusters problem solving and adversarial. I labeled these clusters differently from Williams' original labels of competitive and cooperative for two reasons. First, I believe in the 20 years since the Williams study, the popular understanding of "cooperative" has changed from the positive use by Williams to a more negative definition implying "wimpiness." Someone labeled "cooperative" is more likely to be associated with soft-bargaining (roll-over-and-play-dead) than the positive adjectives actually used by Williams. Second, "problem-solving" and "adversarial" are labels more in current use in the negotiation literature. . . . Problem-solving adjectives encompass several different elements of behavior. First, this negotiator is upstanding (ethical, trustworthy). Second, this negotiator is pleasant (personable, agreeable, sociable) and interested in the other side (fair-minded, communicative, perceptive, helpful). Third, this negotiator is flexible (accommodating, adaptable). Finally, this negotiator is prepared (experienced, rational, confident, realistic, astute, poised). . . .

The adversarial adjectives offer a strong contrast. The adversarial negotiator is inflexible (stubborn, assertive, demanding, firm, tough, forceful) and self-centered (headstrong, arrogant, egotistical). This negotiator likes to fight (irritating, argumentative, quarrelsome, hostile) and the method of fighting is questionable (suspicious, manipulative, evasive). Only two adjectives appear completely positive — confident and experienced — and these are the only two adjectives also cited for problem-solving negotiators. Thus we see very different approaches to negotiation.

The next step is a comparison of groups and effectiveness ratings. The survey asked each respondent to rate the other attorney's effectiveness as a negotiator compared to other attorneys with whom the respondent had negotiated. Lawyers were rated: ineffective, average, or effective (see Table 3).

Table 3
Number of Lawyers Per Group by Perceived Effectiveness (2000)

	Ineffective	Average	Effective
Problem-Solving	14	166	213
Adversarial	120	84	21

Several items should stand out from these results. Respondents rated only 9 percent of their adversarial peers as effective. And only 9 percent of all effective lawyers were described as adversarial. Furthermore, 90 percent of lawyers seen as ineffective fell into the adversarial group. On the flip side of the analysis, 91 percent of lawyers seen as effective chose a problem-solving method of negotiation. More than 50 percent of problem-solving lawyers were perceived as effective and only 4 percent of these problem-solving lawyers were seen as ineffective.

Therefore, contrary to the popular (student) view that problem-solving behavior is risky, it is instead adversarial bargaining that is risky. A lawyer is much more likely to be perceived as effective when engaging in problem-solving behavior.

Comparing the Studies

After looking at the general results for the study, it is important to compare the behavioral traits of those negotiators perceived as effective. Have the characteristics of "effective" lawyers changed over the years? And since the two styles are so clearly different, what are the characteristics of effective problem-solvers and effective adversarials? Recognizing that the problem-solvers are generally perceived as more effective, nevertheless it is useful to understand what makes those attorneys in each style effective. . . .

Much of the list of adjectives remains the same, including the top five from the Williams study. The adjectives describe a negotiator who is both assertive (experienced, realistic, fair, astute, careful, wise) and empathetic (perceptive, communicative, accommodating, agreeable, adaptable). This mirrors what Professor Robert Mnookin and his co-authors have described as effective negotiation behavior. Furthermore, the effective problem-solver is also good (ethical, trustworthy) and offers enjoyable company (personable, sociable, poised). It should be no surprise this negotiator is seen as effective. . . .

The lack of change in the description of effective problem-solving offers some interesting insights. For example, despite the public perception of lawyers, it appears that close to two-thirds of lawyers continue to engage in non-adversarial modes of communication and that these same lawyers are perceived as highly effective compared to their peers. . . .

The competitive negotiator described by Williams was not nearly so unpleasant and negative. The top five adjectives describing the effectiveness competitive negotiator in the Williams study were: (1) convincing, (2) experienced, (3) perceptive, (4) rational, and (5) analytical. None of these adjectives have particularly negative connotations. In fact, perceptive even demonstrates some interest in the other side. Now the top five adjectives describing an effective adversarial negotiator are (1) egotistical, (2) demanding, (3) ambitious, (4) experienced, and (5) confident. Clearly things have changed for the worse when the most important description given to a lawyer is egotistical. The rest of the top 20 list is even more damning. Out of the entire list of adjectives, over half have negative connotations. Even their peers view these adversarial lawyers poorly as people despite their negotiation effectiveness.

Another interesting note is the lack of overlap between adjectives describing effective problem-solving behavior and adjectives describing effective adversarial behavior. In the Williams study, fully 14 of the top adjectives for the cooperative and competitive groups overlapped. This, of course, provided helpful advice to students that, regardless of which style they chose, these were the adjectives that were found to be effective. In this study only two adjectives overlap: experienced and confident. This lack of overlap suggests that the two negotiation styles have clearly diverged even more from one another in the last 24 years and that it has become more unlikely that a negotiator would move between these antithetical types of negotiation styles.

Finally, we can compare the effectiveness rating of Williams' two groups to this study. Compared to the Williams study, the percentage of problem-solving negotiators who were effective has dropped from 59 percent to 54 percent. The changes in the percentage of adversarial bargainers, however, is much more striking. In the Williams study, 25 percent of competitive negotiators were seen as effective, compared to 9 percent in this study. Alternatively, 33 percent of competitive negotiators were seen as ineffective in the Williams study while 53 percent were in this study.

In comparing general effectiveness of the lawyer population, the Williams study stated that 49 percent of the attorneys were considered effective, 38 percent were rated as average, and 12 percent were rated as ineffective. In contrast, only 38 percent of attorneys in this study were rated effective. As the vast majority of those attorneys who were considered ineffective were also adversarial negotiators (90 percent of ineffective lawyers were adversarial), we can hypothesize that the increase in ineffective lawyers (to 22 percent from 12 percent) comes from the increase in adversarial bargainers (to 36 percent from 27 percent).

Lessons to Be Drawn

We can draw a few different lessons from this development in negotiation behavior. First, it looks as if the two predominant styles are growing further apart. While the problem-solving or cooperative group has remained much the same, the adversarial or competitive group is seen as growing more extreme and more negative. Second, as adversarial bargaining has become more extreme, it has also become far less effective. This is a key lesson for those hoping to become effective "Rambo" negotiators.

It appears that the declining public perception of lawyers is mirrored in how lawyers view each other. Fewer lawyers are viewed as effective by their peers and more lawyers are viewed negatively. Lawyers and popular culture are in accord in their perceptions and those perceptions are poor all around, at least as regards a significant minority of attorneys. . . .

What we can see in the preliminary results of this study is some interesting trends in terms of behavior and perceptions. A problem-solving approach to negotiation continues to be seen as effective by the legal community. The importance of developing this kind of reputation, particularly in smaller markets and within a practice area, has already been discussed. Furthermore, contrary to public perceptions, the majority of lawyers do engage in problem-solving behavior during a negotiation. On the other hand, the negative public perception of lawyers is matched by lawyers' own perceptions of the growing number and increased nastiness of adversarial lawyers. The good news is that the bar also increasingly views these adversarial lawyers as ineffective.

Note: A Critique of the Studies

Professor Schneider provides more detail about her study and a more extensive analysis in *Shattering Negotiation Myths: Empirical Evidence on the Effectiveness of Negotiation Style* (2002). Several concerns are raised by the research on the effectiveness of negotiation styles.

First, as Professor Schneider recognizes, her study measured only negotiators' *perceptions* of how they and opponents performed, not actual results. The study is therefore fundamentally different from the prisoners' dilemma studies described in Chapter 3, which examined the results of actual tournament bargaining. These and other studies show that two cooperative bargainers working together do produce the most total value and two competitive bargainers the least, but that a player who uses a competitive strategy can "claim value" from a cooperative player, at least in a one-time encounter.

A fundamental concern in any survey based on perceptions is that human beings consistently overrate their own effectiveness. Recall, for example, the study of ABA members, which found that, "on average lawyers rated themselves in at least the top 80th percentile on such qualities as ability, honesty, negotiation skills and cooperativeness" (Birke 2000, 214).

Another problem in relying on perceptions is the "in group/out group" issue. As we will see, people who see themselves in one group as opposed to another consistently see their group "as more talented, honest, and morally upright while simultaneously vilifying the Other" (Sebenius 2002, 129). If problem-solving respondents in the survey saw themselves as basically different from adversarials — likely, given the negative adjectives that characterized the latter group — they might well rate them lower.

In a variant on the "in/out" effect, studies have found that people rate persons they perceive as being similar to them as likable and effective; those who are thought to be dissimilar are rated less likable and less effective (Birke & Fox 2000, 54-55). Again, this makes it difficult for dissimilar groups to reliably rate each other's effectiveness. Professor Schneider reports that her respondents were subject to the "similarity" effect. Respondents who saw the other bargainers as having goals very similar to their own (whether problem-solving or adversarial) rated them as effective by a ratio of more than 4 to 1 (combining the top categories, 187 rated effective to 43 ineffective). By contrast, negotiators who saw their counterparts as having dissimilar goals rated them as ineffective by a ratio of 30 to 1 (Schneider 2002, 194).

The strong tendency of humans to overrate themselves and underrate people they see as different means the "winner" of a study based on perceptions will usually be the group that predominates in the survey responses. The Schneider survey required lawyers to cooperate in filling out a questionnaire, and only 29 percent of the surveyed lawyers responded (Schneider 2000, 158). Problem solvers (64 percent of responses) greatly outnumbered adversarials (36 percent) among the responders. Given the cognitive forces and self-selection at work in the study, it is not surprising that problem solving prevailed in the "effectiveness" poll.

Finally, the meaning of the categories in the study is not clear. The top seven words assigned to problem solvers are "ethical, experienced, personable, rational, trustworthy, self-controlled and confident." The top seven words for adversarials are "stubborn, headstrong, arrogant, assertive, irritating, argumentative and egotistical." Is it fair to say that honest competitive bargainers should be assigned to the adversarial category, or could the words attributed to problem solvers be applied equally as well to them? Because the words in the "problem-solver" category could also be assigned to competitives, the study does not actually tell us whether honest competitive bargainers are more or less effective than problem solvers.

Questions

10. What do you think accounts for the finding that adversarial negotiators are growing more extreme and negative and that, overall, fewer lawyers are viewed as effective by their peers?

11. Professor Schneider's respondents were over 30 percent women, compared to only 3 percent women in Professor Williams's original study. Do you believe this difference helps account for the significant increase in the percentage of negotiators who were perceived to be cooperative or problem solving?

12. As previously noted, a negotiator who believes and lives by highly competitive values may nevertheless manifest personal empathy, concern, friendliness, and warmth and may appear to engage in problem-solving behavior. These characteristics can build trust for purposes of maximizing individual gain. Because both studies surveyed *perceived* qualities and goals, is it possible that they underreported effective adversarial negotiators who were so successful that they induced opponents to see them as cooperative or problem solving when, in fact, they were not? Have you known anyone who exuded a style you thought to be cooperative turn out to be highly competitive or to have masked her purpose in this way, like a "wolf in sheep's clothing"? (Have you ever tried this?)

CHAPTER
5

Negotiation Step by Step—The Beginning

A. Negotiation Stages and Approaches

Negotiation, whether competitive, cooperative, or a mixed approach, can be viewed as occurring in stages. Even though lawyer negotiation is often not a tidy process, breaking negotiation into stages is a way to help understand and analyze the process. There is, however, no script—all negotiations do not follow the same lineal staging, and each stage will not necessarily be completed in all negotiations.

Listed below are the activities typically occurring in the seven stages of competitive or cooperative negotiation. The activities within each stage can be mixed or alternated between competitive and cooperative, bearing in mind the warning that cooperation is commonly driven out by competitiveness. Of course, the labels "competitive" and "cooperative," like all one-word descriptions, are too simple. Adversarial and problem-solving, positional and interest-based, or distributive and integrative may better capture the behavioral contrast. Although each pair of bipolar negotiation labels may signify nuanced differences, we will use them synonymously. Finally, note that although some of the activities and tasks within the two approaches are similar, the sequence of stages may vary between positional and interest-based approaches. For example, making demands and offers comes earlier in positional negotiation and later in interest negotiation, following the exchange of information, if at all.

Stage	Competitive/adversarial approach	Cooperative/problem-solving approach
1. Preparation and Setting Goals	➤ Planning and research ➤ Counseling client about negotiation ➤ Assessing power of each party ➤ Formulating positions and bottom line ➤ Setting goals	➤ Planning and research ➤ Counseling client about negotiation ➤ Assessing needs of each party ➤ Formulating best alternative to negotiated agreement (BATNA) and reservation point ➤ Setting goals

Stage	Competitive/adversarial approach	Cooperative/problem-solving approach
2. Initial Interactions	➢ Setting tone ➢ Establishing credentials and authority ➢ Making first demand or offer	➢ Setting tone ➢ Establishing rapport and trust ➢ Agreeing on agenda
3. Exchanging and Refining Information	➢ Asking questions ➢ Offering overstated or understated valuations ➢ Informational bargaining ➢ Formal discovery ➢ Stating positions (often exaggerated)	➢ Asking questions ➢ Sharing assessments or appraisals ➢ Information exchange ➢ Informal discovery (I'll show you mine, if you'll show me yours) ➢ Stating needs or interests
4. Bargaining	➢ Argument and persuasion ➢ Making concessions ➢ Forming coalitions and holding out	➢ Proposing principles ➢ Applying principled criteria ➢ Trading off priorities and brainstorming solutions
5. Moving Toward Closure	➢ Using power and threats ➢ Creating time crisis ➢ Evaluating offers	➢ Examining BATNAs ➢ Agreeing on deadlines ➢ Decision analysis
6. Reaching Impasse or Agreement	➢ Possible impasse ➢ Compromising ➢ Adding conditions	➢ Possible, but less likely, impasse ➢ Reaching mutual decisions through joint problem solving ➢ Creating alternative outcomes
7. Finalizing and Writing Agreements	➢ Preparing opposing drafts of agreement ➢ Negotiating over drafts ➢ Approval, ratification, and buy-in (if necessary)	➢ Memorializing terms ➢ Concurring on single text agreement ➢ Approval, ratification, and buy-in (if necessary)

© 2009 Jay Folberg

Note and Questions

Professor Williams, in his article "Negotiation as a Healing Process," part of which is excerpted in Chapter 1, refers to negotiation as a ritual. He goes on to say:

In law school we learn that no two cases are alike, and in our culture we assume that no two people are alike. We might surmise from this that no two negotiations are alike. Fortunately, this is only partially true. One of the defining characteristics of a ritual, including the ritual of negotiation, is that it provides an accepted structure for and sequencing of events. As a general proposition, then, we can say *the ritual of negotiation unfolds in predictable stages over time*. The predictability helps explain why so many lawyers lose patience-with the process; it is highly repetitive, and thus not as stimulating as new adventures would be. This aspect of ritual is well captured by W. John Smith when he says, "*ritual* connotes . . . behavior that is formally organized into repeatable patterns. Perhaps the fundamental and pervasive function of these patterns is to facilitate orderly interactions between individuals." The point could not be more clear. Negotiation is a highly repetitive process. Without predictable patterns, the negotiators could not hope to achieve orderly interaction with each other. As Smith explains: "Ritual behavior facilitates interactions because it makes available information about the nature of events, and about the participants in them, that each participating individual must have to interact without generating chaos." The task now is to develop a working knowledge of the predictable stages of the negotiation process. (Williams 1996, 33)

1. Have you found negotiations in which you were involved to be predictable in process? What types of negotiations are most likely to follow a ritualistic or predictable pattern? Might there be different negotiation rituals depending on what is being negotiated and the setting of the negotiation?
2. How might the stages of negotiation or the activities in each stage differ if the negotiation follows the creating and claiming approach suggested in the excerpt from Lax and Sebenius in Chapter 4?
3. Can you think of how concurring on a single text agreement, listed on the chart as Stage 7 — "Finalizing and Writing Agreements," might be taken up out of order and used in earlier stages to help formulate choices, bargain, and reach decisions? For a fascinating application of the single text procedure in reaching agreement between Israel and Egypt at Camp David, see Jimmy Carter's book *Keeping Faith: Memoirs of a President* (1982).

B. Getting Ready to Negotiate

Watching a good negotiator or hearing about an effective negotiation can give the impression that it comes easily and that success is the result of intuitive ability, cleverness, and quick thinking. However, similar to trial practice, appellate advocacy, or any other disciplined endeavor, success in negotiation is in large part the result of planning, research, and preparation. The famous quote by Antoine de Saint-Exupery that "a goal without a plan is just a wish" is applicable to negotiation.

The following excerpt provides a helpful blueprint for effective negotiation preparation that is likely to maximize results in most bargaining situations by refining your BATNA and reservation point, as well as by anticipating your opponent's bargaining zone.

1. *Preparation*

❖ **Russell Korobkin,** *A POSITIVE THEORY OF LEGAL NEGOTIATION*

88 Geo. L.J. 1789 (2000)

[The author posits two negotiation situations: one a potential transaction for the purchase by Esau of Jacob's catering business, and the other a potential settlement of a suit by Goliath against David for battery.]

All observers of the negotiation process agree that painstaking preparation is critical to success at the bargaining table . . . "Internal" preparation refers to research that the negotiator does to set and adjust his own RP [reservation point or price]. "External" preparation refers to research that the negotiator does to estimate and manipulate the other party's RP.

1. Internal Preparation: Alternatives and BATNAs

A negotiator cannot determine his RP without first understanding his substitutes for and the opportunity costs of reaching a negotiated agreement. This, of course, requires research. Esau cannot determine how much he is willing to pay for Jacob's business without investigating his other options. Most obviously, Esau will want to investigate what other catering companies are for sale in his area, their asking prices, and how they compare in quality and earning potential to Jacob's. He also might consider other types of businesses that are for sale. And he will likely consider the possibility of investing his money passively and working for someone else, rather than investing in a business.

Alternatives to reaching an agreement can be nearly limitless in transactional negotiations, and creativity in generating the list of alternatives is a critical skill to the negotiator. The panoply of alternatives is generally more circumscribed in dispute resolution negotiations. If Goliath fails to reach a settlement of some sort with David, he has the alternative of seeking an adjudicated outcome of the dispute and the alternative of dropping the suit. Most likely, he does not have the choice of suing someone else instead of David, in the same way that Esau has the choice of buying a business other than Jacob's.

After identifying the various alternatives to reaching a negotiated agreement, the negotiator needs to determine which alternative is most desirable. Fisher and his coauthors coined the appropriate term "BATNA" — "best alternative to a negotiated agreement" — to identify this choice. The identity and quality of a negotiator's BATNA is the primary input into his RP.

If the negotiator's BATNA and the subject of the negotiation are perfectly interchangeable, determining the reservation price is quite simple: The reservation price is merely the value of the BATNA. For example, if Esau's BATNA is buying another catering business for $190,000 that is identical to Jacob's in terms of quality, earnings potential, and all other factors that are important to Esau, then his RP is $190,000. If Jacob will sell for some amount less than that, Esau will be better off buying Jacob's company than he would be pursuing his best alternative. If Jacob demands more than $190,000, Esau is better off buying the alternative company and not reaching an agreement with Jacob.

In most circumstances, however, the subject of a negotiation and the negotiator's BATNA are not perfect substitutes. If Jacob's business is of higher quality, has a higher earnings potential, or is located closer to Esau's home, he would probably be willing to pay a premium for it over what he would pay for the alternative choice. For example, if the alternative business is selling for $190,000, Esau might determine he would be willing to pay up to a $10,000 premium over the alternative for Jacob's business and thus set his RP at $200,000. On the other hand, if Esau's BATNA is more desirable to him than Jacob's business, Esau will discount the value of his BATNA by the amount necessary to make the two alternatives equally desirable values for the money; perhaps he will set his RP at $180,000 in recognition that his BATNA is $10,000 more desirable than Jacob's business, and Jacob's business would be equally desirable only at a $10,000 discount.

Assume Goliath determines that his BATNA is proceeding to trial. He will attempt to place a value on his BATNA by researching the facts of the case, the relevant legal precedent, and jury awards in similar cases, all as a means of estimating the expected value of litigating to a jury verdict. If Goliath's research leads to an estimate that he has a 75% chance of winning a jury verdict, and the likely verdict if he does prevail is $100,000, then using a simple expected value calculation ($100,000 × .75) would lead him to value his BATNA at $75,000.

For most plaintiffs, however, a settlement of a specified amount is preferable to a jury verdict with the same expected value, both because litigation entails additional costs and because most individuals are risk averse and therefore prefer a certain payment to a risky probability of payment with the same expected value. Goliath might determine, for example, that a $50,000 settlement would have the equivalent value to him of a jury verdict with an expected value of $75,000, because pursuing a jury verdict would entail greater tangible and intangible costs such as attorneys' fees, emotional strain, inconvenience, and the risk of losing the case altogether. If so, Goliath would set his RP at $50,000. On the other hand, it is possible that Goliath would find a $75,000 verdict more desirable than a $75,000 pretrial settlement. For example, perhaps Goliath would find additional value in having a jury of his peers publicly recognize the validity of his grievance against David. If Goliath believes that such psychic benefits of a jury verdict would make a verdict worth $10,000 more to him than a settlement of the same amount (after taking into account the added risks and costs of litigation), he would set his RP at $85,000. . . .

Internal preparation serves two related purposes. By considering the value of obvious alternatives to reaching a negotiated agreement, the negotiator can accurately estimate his RP. This is of critical importance because without a precise and accurate estimation of his RP the negotiator cannot be sure to avoid the most basic negotiating mistake — agreeing to a deal when he would have been better off walking away from the table with no agreement.

By investigating an even wider range of alternatives to reaching agreement and by more thoroughly investigating the value of obvious alternatives, the negotiator can alter his RP in a way that will shift the bargaining zone to his advantage. Rather than just considering the asking price of other catering companies listed for sale in his town, Esau might contact catering companies that are not for sale to find out if their owners might consider selling under the right conditions. This could lead to the identification of a company similar to Jacob's that could be purchased for $175,000, which would have the effect of reducing Esau's RP to $175,000 and therefore shifting the bargaining zone lower. Goliath's attorney might conduct additional legal research, perhaps exploring other, more novel, theories of liability. If he determines that one or more alternative legal theories has a reasonable chance of success in court, Goliath might adjust upward his estimate of prevailing at trial — and therefore the value of his BATNA of trial — allowing him to adjust upward his RP.

2.   External Preparation: The Opponent's Alternatives and BATNA

Internal preparation enables the negotiator to estimate his RP accurately and favorably. Of course, the bargaining zone is fixed by *both* parties' RPs. External preparation allows the negotiator to estimate his opponent's RP. If Esau is savvy, he will attempt to research Jacob's alternatives to a negotiated agreement as well as his own alternatives. For example, other caterers might know whether Jacob has had other offers for his business, how much the business might bring on the open market, or how anxious Jacob is to sell — all factors that will help Esau to accurately predict Jacob's RP and therefore pinpoint the low end of the bargaining zone. This information will also prepare Esau to attempt to persuade Jacob during the course of negotiations to lower his RP. . . .

It is worth noting that in the litigation context both parties often have the same alternatives and the same BATNA. If plaintiff Goliath determines that his BATNA is going to trial, then defendant David's only alternative — and therefore his BATNA by default — is going to trial as well. In this circumstance, internal preparation and external preparation merge. For example, when Goliath's lawyer conducts legal research, he is attempting to simultaneously estimate the value of both parties' BATNAs. Of course, just because the parties have the same BATNA, they will not necessarily estimate the market value of it identically, much less arrive at identical RPs. Research suggests that an "egocentric bias" is likely to cause litigants to interpret material facts in a light favorable to their legal position, thus causing them to overestimate the expected value of an adjudicated outcome. Consequently, it is likely that, examining the same operative facts and legal precedent, plaintiff Goliath will place a higher value on the BATNA of trial than defendant David. This difference in perception often will be offset, however, by the fact that plaintiff Goliath is likely to set his RP, or the minimum settlement he will accept, below his perceived expected value of trial to account for the higher costs and higher risk associated with trial, while defendant David is likely to set his RP, or the maximum settlement he will agree to pay, above the expected value of trial for the same reasons. As long as the parties' preference for settlement rather than trial outweighs their egocentric biases, a bargaining zone will still exist, although it will be smaller than it would be if the parties agreed on the expected value of trial. Research also suggests that both parties are likely to be more risk averse when they are less confident in their prediction of the expected value of trial. In other words, the less confident the parties are in the value that they place on the BATNA of trial, the larger the bargaining zone between the RPs is likely to be.

---

2. *Setting Goals*

In addition to thinking through the least you can accept, or your reservation point, it is also helpful to formulate goals and set high expectations. High expectations lead to better outcomes, as discussed in this excerpt by Richard Shell.

❖ G. Richard Shell, *Bargaining for Advantage: Negotiation Strategies for Reasonable People*

28 (Penguin, 2006)

Goals: You'll Never Hit the Target if You Don't Aim

In Lewis Carroll's *Alice's Adventures in Wonderland,* Alice finds herself at a crossroads where a Cheshire Cat materializes. Alice asks the Cat, "Would you tell me please, which way I ought to go from here?" The Cat replies, "That depends a good deal on where you want to get to." "I don't much care where — " says Alice. "Then it doesn't matter which way you go," the Cat replies, cutting her off.

To become an effective negotiator, you must find out where you want to go — and why. That means committing yourself to specific, justifiable goals. It also means taking the time to transform your goals from simple targets into genuine — and appropriately high — *expectations.* . . .

Our goals give us direction, but our expectations are what give weight and conviction to our statements at the bargaining table. We are most animated when we are striving to achieve what we feel we justly deserve.

So it is with negotiation. Our goals give us direction, but our expectations are what give weight and conviction to our statements at the bargaining table. We are most animated when we are striving to achieve what we feel we justly deserve. The more time we spend preparing for a particular negotiation and the more information we gather that reinforces our belief that our goal is legitimate and achievable, the firmer the expectations grow. . . .

What you aim for often determines what you get. Why? The first reason is obvious: Your goals set the upper limit of what you will ask for. You mentally concede everything beyond your goal, so you seldom do better than that benchmark.

Second, research on goals reveals that they trigger powerful psychological "striving" mechanisms. Sports psychologists and educators alike confirm that setting specific goals motivates people, focusing and concentrating their attention and psychological powers.

Third, we are more persuasive when we are committed to achieving some specific purpose, in contrast to the occasions when we ask for things half-heartedly or merely react to initiatives proposed by others. Our commitment is infectious. People around us feel drawn toward our goals. . . .

Goals Versus "Bottom Lines"

Most negotiating books and experts emphasize the importance of having a "bottom line," "walkaway," or "reservation price" for negotiation. Indeed, the bottom line is a fundamental bargaining concept on which much of modern negotiation theory is built. It is the *minimum acceptable level* you require to say "yes" in a negotiation. By definition, if you cannot achieve your bottom line, you would rather seek another solution to your problem or wait until another opportunity comes your way. When two parties have bottom lines that permit an agreement at some point between them, theorists speak of there being a "positive bargaining zone." When the two bottom lines do not overlap, they speak of a "negative bargaining zone". . . .

A well-framed goal is quite different from a bottom line. As I use the word, "goal" is your *highest legitimate expectation* of what you should achieve. . . .

Researchers have discovered that humans have a limited capacity for maintaining focus in complex, stressful situations such as negotiations. Consequently, once a negotiation is under way, we gravitate toward the single focal point that has the psychological significance for us. Once most people set a firm bottom line in a negotiation, that becomes their dominant reference point as discussions proceed. They measure success or failure with reference to their bottom line. Having a goal as your reference point, by contrast, prompts you to think you are facing a potential "loss" for any offer you receive below your goal. And we know that avoiding losses is a powerful motivating force. This power is not working as strongly for you when you focus solely on your bottom line.

What is the practical effect of having your bottom line become your dominant reference point in a negotiation? Over a lifetime of negotiating, your results will tend to hover at a point just above this minimum acceptable level. For most reasonable people, the bottom line is the most natural focal point. Disappointment arises if we cannot get the other side to agree to meet our minimum requirements (usually established by our available alternatives or our needs away from the table), and satisfaction arises just above that level. Meanwhile, someone else who is more skilled at orienting himself toward ambitious goals will do much better. Not surprising, research shows that parties with higher (but still realistic) goals outperform those with more modest ones, all else being equal.

To avoid falling into the trap of letting our bottom line become our reference point, be aware of your absolute limits, but do not dwell on them. Instead, work energetically on formulating your goals, . . . [T]est the other side's reaction to your goal. Then, if you must, gradually re-orient toward a bottom line as that becomes necessary to close the deal. With experience, you should be able to keep both your goal and your bottom line in view at the same time without losing your goal focus. Research suggests that the best negotiators have this ability. . . .

If setting goals is so vital to effective preparation, how should you do it? Use the following simple steps:

1. Think carefully about what you really want — and remember that money is often a means, not an end.
2. Set an optimistic — but justifiable — target.
3. Be specific. . . .
4. Get committed. Write down your goal and, if possible, discuss the goal with someone else.
5. Carry your goal with you into the negotiation.

Set an Optimistic, Justifiable Target

When you set goals, think boldly and optimistically about what you would like to see happen. Research has repeatedly shown that people who have higher expectations in negotiations perform better and get more than people who have modest or "I'll do my best" goals, provided they really believe in their targets. . . .

Once you have thought about what an optimistic, challenging goal would look like, spend a few minutes permitting realism to dampen your expectations. *Optimistic goals are effective only if they are feasible; that is, only if you believe in them and they can be justified according to some standard or norm.* . . . [N]egotiation positions must usually be supported by some standard, benchmark, or precedent, or they lose their credibility. . . .

Commit to Your Goal: Write It Down and Talk About It

Your goal is only as effective as your commitment to it. There are several simple things you can do that will increase your level of psychological attachment to your goal. First, as I suggested above, you should make sure it is justified and supported by solid arguments. You must believe in your goal to be committed to it.

Second, it helps if you spend just a few moments vividly imagining the way it would look or feel to achieve your goal. Visualization helps engage our mind more fully in the achievement process and also raises our level of self-confidence and commitment . . .

Third, psychologists and marketing professionals report that the act of *writing a goal down* engages our sense of commitment much more effectively than does the mere act of thinking about it. The act of writing makes a thought more "real" and objective, obligating us to follow up on it — at least in our own eyes.

Questions

4. Can you explain the difference between BATNA and RP?
5. Can you explain the difference between goals and expectations?
6. Does the advice to set high expectations work only if the other side does not follow the same advice? Will setting high expectations, particularly if done by both sides to a negotiation, likely lead to larger "negative bargaining zones," as explained by Shell, and thus more frequent impasse? Is there a way for two optimistic negotiators to deal with this and reach agreement?
7. If expectations in negotiation are, in part, a function of previous success and failure, as Shell suggests, how does a new lawyer set expectations? Would a client be well advised to seek out a lawyer who has had well-known recent success in trials and negotiations on the theory that "success breeds success"?' How might you leverage someone else's success with a similar case to your advantage in a negotiation?

For an in-depth scholarly discussion of the role of aspirations in settlement negotiations, see Korobkin (2002). Korobkin concludes that high aspirations may help negotiators reach better results, but at the cost of a greater risk of impasse and personal dissatisfaction in not fully achieving the expectations created by high aspirations.

3. Negotiation Preparation Checklists

The following checklist expands on the concepts developed in the previous readings and includes some points from the selections that follow. You may want to create a personal, comprehensive checklist to use in preparing for negotiations in both litigation and transactional settings. Using a checklist is a way to discipline your thinking so you may eventually not need the list. This checklist, although longer than one you might create, provides an inventory of helpful questions from which you can choose, depending on the case and the time available.

I. Information and Strategy

1. Information

- ☐ What information will help determine your opponent's needs, interests, and objectives?
- ☐ What questions will you ask to elicit such information?
- ☐ What information is the other side likely to seek?
- ☐ What are you willing to reveal, and how do you plan to disclose it?
- ☐ What should you be careful to protect, and how do you prevent disclosure?
- ☐ Are there any advantageous trades of information?

2. Alternatives

- ☐ What is your best alternative if no agreement is reached (BATNA)?
- ☐ Can you improve your BATNA or the way it is perceived?
- ☐ What is your worst alternative if no agreement is reached?
- ☐ What are your opponent's best and worst alternatives?
- ☐ How can you change how your opponent perceives his alternatives?
- ☐ If an offered settlement is not accepted, are costs and attorneys' fees triggered?

3. Interests

- ☐ What are your client's interests and their relative importance?
- ☐ How does your opponent see your client's interests?
- ☐ What are your opponent's interests?
- ☐ How can you change your opponent's perspective about his and your interests?

4. Solutions and Positions

- ☐ What ideas do you have for a solution (based on what you know now)?
- ☐ Will you assert a position, and if so, what will it be?
- ☐ What is your opponent's current position or proposed solution?

5. *Principles and Standards*

- ☐ What principles can you cite in support of your position?
- ☐ Which are most persuasive?
- ☐ What principles is your opponent likely to cite?

6. *Communication*

- ☐ Should you communicate prior to a negotiation meeting?
- ☐ What theme or story will best present your case?
- ☐ What messages do you want to send?
- ☐ Are there any special communication issues to consider based on culture?

7. *Relationship*

- ☐ Who should be at the table?
- ☐ Are there any relationship problems?
- ☐ Will there be a continuing relationship?
- ☐ Is there trust between you and your opponent?
- ☐ How can you build trust and credibility?

II. Bargaining

1. *Process and Location*

- ☐ Should you establish an agenda?
- ☐ Are there applicable negotiation customs or rituals?
- ☐ Can you negotiate over or influence the process?
- ☐ Where do you want to negotiate?

2. *Expectations and Bottom Lines*

- ☐ What goals and objectives do you hope to achieve?
- ☐ What is the best outcome you can realistically envision?
- ☐ What minimum terms are you willing to accept?
- ☐ What is your reservation or walkaway point?
- ☐ What are your opponent's likely goals and expectations?
- ☐ What value system will your opponent use in assessing his case?

3. *Your Tactics*

- ☐ What negotiation style or approach will you take?
- ☐ Should you insist on any "preconditions"?
- ☐ What should be your first demand or offer?
- ☐ How will you support your demands and offers?
- ☐ How will you move from your starting point to where you would like to end?

4. *Your Opponent's Tactics*

- ☐ What is the style of your opponent?
- ☐ What negotiation techniques do you expect your opponent to use?
- ☐ What pattern or moves do you anticipate? How will you counter those tactics?

5. *Concessions*

- ☐ What early concession will you make, if necessary?
- ☐ Do you have any easy "give-a-ways"?
- ☐ Are there any nonmonetary concessions you can give?
- ☐ Are there low-cost concessions of greater value to your opponent?
- ☐ What messages do you want to send with your concessions? What concessions do you anticipate receiving?

III. Settlement/Deal

- ☐ What terms will you insist upon?
- ☐ Do you have specific language for a final agreement?
- ☐ Are there terms and provisions you anticipate your opponent will insist on?
- ☐ What legal requirements are there for an enforceable settlement or deal?
- ☐ Who must sign or approve the agreement?
- ☐ Will there be time factors to consider?
- ☐ Will you or your opponent insist that the settlement be confidential?
- ☐ Should the settlement/deal be publicized? If so, how?

Note: Web and Computer-Assisted Preparation

The questions to ask yourself in preparation will, in part, depend on your negotiation style and the subject of the negotiation. The purposes of your negotiation preparation are to determine your strategy, BATNA, reservation point, first offer, and management of concession. Similarly, you will use the information generated from your preparation to anticipate what your opponent perceives, values, and will do during the negotiations.

Today's technology makes it possible to obtain on the Web and plug into a computer program the information necessary to prepare, generate options, value trade-offs, and anticipate the moves of a negotiation opponent. If computers can be used to research law, play chess (calculating the probable moves of an opponent and choosing the best move from all available options), engage in sophisticated market research, anticipate terrorist attacks, and plot wars, they should be of help in preparing for negotiations.

Googling or Binging your negotiation counterparts and checking them out on social and professional networking sites is an easy way to learn about their background and experience. You can use the Web to obtain clues about how they might negotiate, the value they might place on items of potential trade, and their interests. Knowing more about an opponent can also aid in establishing trust and rapport. Please don't forget that the people with whom you negotiate will likely use Web searches to learn all they can about you.

Another value of the Web is to help you calculate your BATNAs. What both sides to a negotiation previously had to guess at, and as a result probably perceived differently, can now be determined by a computer search. For example, the cost of replacing equipment or an object of art can quickly be found by a search in a truly worldwide marketplace. Thus, the creation of objective criteria to propose for resolution of an anticipated issue can be easily researched and prepared in advance. You can better research jury awards for similar injuries and court decisions on questions that might have to be decided if your negotiation fails. Diligent electronic research may also reveal the outcome of similar negotiations.

Proprietary software programs can help you analyze the negotiation style that is most comfortable for you and determine the approach likely to be used by your negotiating counterpart, provided some questions can be answered about them. The programs can also assist you in designing concessions and assigning relative values to them. They collect input that is used to suggest the best opening offer and counteroffers. These programs can also formulate questions for you to ask during a negotiation and predict the actions of an opposing negotiator, along with recommended strategies for you to use. Finally, they can help you value and decide on outcomes once proposals emerge.

Although these programs are sophisticated with a type of built-in negotiation intelligence, like with any productivity software, the quality of the result ultimately depends on the input you provide. If nothing else, a good negotiation software program can provide a guide for what you should do to be well prepared to negotiate and what the alternative approaches may be. They can also catalog tactics you might not have considered and organize ideas and data helpful to you before commencing a negotiation. At the time of this writing the most comprehensive and user-friendly negotiation preparation software is Negotiator Pro, available at *www.negotiatorpro.com*. This program assesses negotiator styles based on responses to questions about each negotiator and then offers strategies of how to negotiate with the profiled personality type. A unique feature includes an international negotiation analysis where parties can learn about cultural differences.

C. Initial Interaction

1. Trust and Rapport

How we feel about those with whom we negotiate is a critical element to whether an agreement will be reached. Just as you may feel you can quickly "read" the character and trustworthiness of those you face, so others are forming a quick impression of you. The maxims that "you never get a second chance to make a first impression" and "first impressions matter" need to be considered as you prepare for and commence a negotiation.

The impression you make on an opponent will probably be formed, in part, before you meet. If the negotiation is of significance, you and your opponent will find out what you can about one another. Your reputation will precede you into the negotiation. In addition to informal inquiries among those with whom you have previously negotiated or had other professional contact, the Internet opens your public history, both accomplishments and mistakes, for all to see. So your preparation for a negotiation, in terms of the impression you make and whether you can be trusted, involves your entire professional life. Although a misimpression can be corrected, it is an uphill struggle because of what we know about self-fulfilling prophecies and the selective way we view evidence to support earlier impressions. Trust is more likely to develop between negotiators if they see one another as similar. Similarity of backgrounds, experience, values, tastes, or group identity helps develop rapport and smoothes the way to trust. There is a delicate balance when opening a negotiation session between engaging in "small talk" that might establish a shared interest, affiliation, or acquaintance for the purpose of creating rapport, and getting to the point regarding the issues in dispute. However, taking time to learn enough about your counterpart to find commonalities and the opportunity to establish a personal connection as the basis for trust is usually time well spent.

The flip side of trust — distrust — inhibits negotiation. Distrust tends to be reciprocated and becomes a self-fulfilling prophecy engendering negative behavior and selective perceptions that confirm the reasons for not trusting one another. Distrust is an obstacle to the exchange of information and collaboration or joint problem solving.

Unless negotiators know one another socially or have had positive professional experiences together, mistrust is more the norm at the beginning of a negotiation because you know the other side can prevent you from getting something you want. So, setting a positive tone and early moves to build trust are important. If you can start on a positive note, you can build a momentum of trust that can carry the negotiations through difficult times. Trust initiated through good listening, sincere compliments, or small opening concessions builds upon itself through reciprocity. Consider the following dramatic example of creating trust by paying attention to local custom and the offering of a small gift.

❖ Robert Benjamin, *TERRY WAITE: A STUDY IN AUTHENTICITY*

http://www.mediate.com (Summer 2002)

Terry Waite has been both hostage negotiator and hostage. He was instrumental in gaining the release of two Anglican [p]riests held captive by the Libyan leader Omar Khadafy, and subsequently was himself taken hostage for five years by a militant group associated with the Ayatollah Khomeini in Iran. As a negotiator, Waite had to deal face to face with a man who fit the mold of most negotiators' "worst-fear scenario" when his and other people's lives were on the line.

In 1983, in the course of ongoing hostilities between the United States and the United Kingdom and Libya, Colonel Omar Khadafy lashed out at the West by taking hostages. The conventional wisdom about the Colonel was that he was quite simply a "madman" — the principal "evildoer" of his time. If trust, as it is often stated, is a pre-requisite for negotiation, then Khadafy was a poor prospect. Many cautioned against trying to negotiate with someone so erratic, unpredictable and downright evil. Given the situation, Waite, of course, saw little alternative except to negotiate; Khadafy was the only one who had the authority to order the hostages' release.

After making contact through circuitous sources, Waite's introductory meeting with Khadafy could not have inspired less confidence. Just getting to the meeting was daunting. Without benefit of car, body guard, or protection of any kind, he was required to walk across a sports stadium playing field, where the bodies of those executed or tortured the night before by Khadafy security forces were laid out from one side to the other.

Waite abided by cultural tradition and presented Khadafy with a gift—a book on Islam. Given the circumstances and gravity of the situation, that act seems absurdly silly and out of place, but was not. It served to alter the atmosphere of the discussions and set the stage. Waite knew he could not just "cut to the chase" and any chance he might have of success required awareness and attention to ritual. A delighted Khadafy was thus offered the opportunity to talk about Middle East history and reciprocate Waite's initial gesture. The Westerner Waite had to stifle his urge to talk directly about the situation at hand. They bided time, talking only indirectly around the present circumstance. This was, however, a necessary dance paying homage to Koranic traditions and building a measure of trust.

Question

8. What are some of the ways that a negotiator in the United States can create trust with a counterpart that he knows only by reputation or by Googling? Might your answer be different if the context is the negotiation of a transaction, rather than the settlement of a lawsuit?

Note: Rapport and Reciprocity

Considerable research has been done on ways to build rapport and influence attitudes for purposes of marketing and sales. Much of this research has applicability to negotiation and can be put to good use, provided it is implemented subtly enough that you appear sincere and don't come across as a salesman. One core finding of the research is that people tend to reciprocate small favors and concessions by giving more than they receive (see Cialdini 2001).

In our chart of negotiation stages at the beginning of this chapter, we listed first demands and offers as part of initial interactions under the competitive/adversarial approach, but omitted them in the interest-based approach. Interest-based negotiators seek to establish a positive relationship through reciprocal small concessions and exchange of information before discussing proposals. We return to demands and offers after the following discussion about gathering and managing information.

D. Exchanging and Refining Information

The task of finding out all that you can about the other side, their needs, their case, their BATNA, and other factors affecting their reservation point is a significant part of the preparation stage and pervades the entire negotiation process. Similarly, disclosing and managing information in your control that may shape the other side's perceptions or that they want to know is also a continual part of the process. Exchanging and refining information are listed as a separate step only to emphasize their importance in the process and to recognize that there are points in the negotiation where information is expected to be exchanged formally or informally. This "stage" could just as well have been listed before initial interactions and offers. Exchanging and refining information is a dynamic that continually shapes expectations and effects negotiation and decision making. Information may be bargained before negotiating over outcomes.

A hallmark of effective negotiators, whether competitive or cooperative, is their ability to listen, their propensity to ask questions, and their desire to continually gather information. (As will be presented later, information is power in negotiations.)

1. Listening and Questioning

Lawyers are often characterized as good talkers, who love to argue. In court, being a "silver-tongued" attorney may be valued. In negotiations, as in conversations, being a good listener and knowing how to obtain information through the use of questions is more important than talking. This is true in interacting with clients when preparing to negotiate for them, as well as in negotiating. The old wisdom that "we were born with one tongue and two ears so that we can hear from others twice as much as we speak," is good advice for negotiators.

If you can learn what is in the brain and heart of an opponent, you can make a personal connection, satisfy their needs, and get what you want at the lowest possible cost. If you actively allow others to openly express themselves, they usually will tell you what you want to know. The more you talk, the less they can say, and the less you can listen and learn. We seldom learn anything new by speaking. The key lesson here is easy: Talk less and listen more. When you do speak in a negotiation, do so in a way that elicits more information, directly or indirectly, or that helps shape the negotiation. Sometimes giving information is a way to get information, but know when and how to listen.

Research results confirm that effective negotiators are better at eliciting information and do more of it than less effective negotiators. Disclosing information, whether by arguing the merits of your case or asserting your position early on, generally results in worse outcomes than first asking questions and listening. Neil Rackham and John Carlisle studied the behavior of English labor and contract negotiators. The more successful negotiators asked twice the number of questions asked by less successful negotiators and spent twice as much time acquiring information. Effective negotiators tested their understanding of what was said and summarized what they heard (Rackman & Carlisle 1978).

Their research supports what psychologists and interviewers have known: The most effective listening is active listening. Active listening is the opposite of deadpan, silent, passive listening. During active listening you focus your energy on what the speaker is communicating and provide responses that encourage the speaker to open up and say more. In active listening you hear not only the content, but also identify the emotion or sentiment expressed. You then briefly restate in your own words the feeling and some of the content you heard communicated so the speaker can confirm, clarify, or amplify. Most important, your response lets speakers know you heard what they said and that you care about how they feel.

The following selection provides a guide for active listening and purposeful questioning when you are negotiating.

❖ **Lee E. Miller & Jessica Miller,** *A Woman's Guide to*
Successful Negotiating

66 (McGraw-Hill, 2002)

Active Listening

There are numerous ways to encourage others to talk so you can find out what their real concerns are. These techniques are referred to as active listening and include the following:

Reflect Back

Restate what the other person has said in your own words. This ensures that you correctly understand what has been said, and it also shows the other person that you are trying to see things from their perspective. For example, if someone says, "I can't understand how you could come up with such an unworkable solution to our problem," you might paraphrase that by stating, "I guess we don't understand what your real needs are here."

Clarify

When something is not clear or you want a better understanding of what has been said, you can ask for clarification. For example, in response to the previous statement, you might say, "I don't understand. What do you mean by unworkable?" Or you could ask them to explain: "Why do you think it's unworkable?" In addition to giving you additional information, clarifying signals that you care about their concerns.

Encourage

Nod and smile, lean forward when others are talking, look them in the eye, and occasionally interject phrases such as "I see," "Go on," or "Really." This will encourage those who are speaking to expand upon what they are saying. The more they speak, the more information you will get. Again, by engaging in this behavior, you signal your willingness to listen and your interest in what is being said.

Acknowledge Effort

Provide positive reinforcement when the speaker tries to work with you or says something you agree with. For example, you might respond by saying "I appreciate your efforts," or "That's a good point." This will encourage further efforts to find common ground with you.

Recognize Feelings

It often helps to address the feelings that people may be experiencing but not openly sharing. In response to the statement that "The proposal is unworkable," you could reply, "I see that you're frustrated with how the discussions are proceeding." Recognizing others' feelings often defuses anger and allows them to open up. This is frequently necessary before you can move on to problem solving.

Summarize

When you believe that you understand the other person's point of view, summarize your understanding of what has been said and ask whether your understanding is correct. Do the same when you reach an agreement on a particular issue. Summarizing helps to prevent misunderstandings, and you should use it continually throughout the course of negotiations. When done on an ongoing basis, it reinforces that the parties are making progress and encourages continued efforts toward reaching an agreement.

It doesn't do much good to listen, however, if you don't act on what you hear. Don't be afraid to stray from what you had planned to say if you get signals the other side is not receptive to the approach you are taking. Moreover, nothing works better than using what the other side says. You can achieve many of your objectives just by listening carefully to what is being said and agreeing to those points that are helpful. That is why it is always best to listen first.

Purposeful Questioning

Good negotiators ask different types of questions for different reasons, from open-ended, information-gathering questions to focused questions intended to lead someone to a specific conclusion. The two primary reasons for asking questions during negotiations are to get information or to support your argument. How you ask a question will depend on what you are trying to achieve.

Ask Open-Ended Questions

You should ask open-ended questions if your goal is to obtain information or to find out what the other person is thinking. Open-ended questions can't be answered with a yes or a no. They usually begin with "who," "what," "where," "when," "why," or "how," which allow for wide latitude as to responses. Their unstructured nature often enables you to find out what the real issues are and how you might satisfactorily resolve them. Open-ended questions such as "Tell me how you reached that conclusion" can also give you an insight into how someone else thinks.

Often, asking the right question at the right time can give you the information you need to completely turn around a negotiation. I recall one such situation. . . . I was practicing law, representing an executive who was taking a job with a new company and being asked to relocate from California to Connecticut. We had worked out the major issues — salary, bonus, stock options — to his satisfaction. The new company had a generous relocation policy, but it provided for only a 30-day temporary living allowance. My client's daughter was a senior in high school and he was not going to move his family until after she graduated. So he asked the company to pay his temporary living expenses for one year. The company representative insisted that they could not deviate from their relocation policy. My client was equally adamant and felt that if the company was taking such a bureaucratic approach to his request, it was probably not a place where he would want to work. Just when I thought the deal was about to fall through, I asked a question that allowed us to successfully conclude the negotiation. What was this brilliantly insightful question? It was simply "Why?" More specifically, I told the vice president of human resources that I couldn't understand why we were arguing about this issue. He explained that the relocation policy was written that way because the company had been burned by a senior executive who, after being paid temporary living expenses for well over a year, could not get his wife to move and rejoined his previous company. Having been embarrassed once, the vice president was not about to ask for another exception to the policy. Understanding his reasons for refusing our seemingly reasonable request enabled us to readily resolve the problem. We agreed that if my client did not move his family to Connecticut, he would repay the company for his temporary living expenses. This allowed the vice president to ask for and receive a modification to the relocation policy without the fear of looking foolish if things didn't work out. . . .

One purpose of asking open-ended questions is to keep the other side talking. The more someone talks, the more likely they are to provide valuable information. An added benefit is that it helps you develop a relationship with that person, which, in and of itself, is helpful. When you ask questions of others, people feel that you are working with them to find solutions, not negotiating against them.

Ask "Why?"

As mentioned above, often the most useful question you can ask is "Why?" Asking why works particularly well as a response to statements such as, "We can't agree to that" or "That would be contrary to policy." When you ask, "Why can't you agree to that?" or "Why do you have that policy?," you are calling for a reasoned response. After you are given a reason, you can make a case that the reason is not applicable in this instance. Alternatively, you have an opportunity to satisfy the other side's objections.

Repeat Back in Question Form

Another way to ask why is to use a variation on the reflecting back technique described above. Simply repeat what has just been said, but in question form . . . reflecting back the other side's own words when a proposal is not reasonable can be very effective. Similarly, when people make unqualified statements such as, "We never do that," a simple "Never?" will force them to either confirm that this is really the case, or, more likely, cause them to retreat to something like, "Except in very unusual circumstances." Once you get that kind of admission, you are well on your way to making your case because now you know what argument to make: that yours are unusual circumstances and require an exception to the normal practice. Once someone concedes that exceptions have been made in the past, it becomes much harder to claim that you don't deserve the same treatment.

Answer Questions with Questions

Sometimes you can answer a question with a question. If you don't want to respond to a particular question or you want to understand why someone is asking a particular question, you can respond by asking, "Well, what do you think?" If you do this too often you may appear evasive and argumentative, but using this approach sparingly can be effective.

Ask What They Would Do

Finally, if you find yourself at an impasse, you can always ask what they would do if they were in your position. This can sometimes completely change the dynamics of the negotiations by forcing the other side to come up with a solution to the problem, rather than trying to convince you that there is no problem. In doing so, a solution may emerge that would be acceptable to you or could be made so with slight modification.

Questions

9. The selection above on active listening and questioning is excerpted from a book written as a guide for women. Do you consider the advice given to be gender specific? Do you think men or women are generally better listeners? Why?

10. Are there times when active listening or responding to a question with a question should not be used? When would you find these techniques annoying or counterproductive?

11. The use of silence to elicit additional information after someone stops speaking can also be effective in situations other than negotiation. The silence should be accompanied by continued eye contact to convey an expectation or invitation for more information. Have you used this method with friends, a spouse, or children? Do you think you are susceptible to this technique when used by others?

2. Managing Information

Effective negotiators also know how to manage information and thoughtfully determine when and what information to provide. Generally, it is better to receive more information than you provide, but this is not an absolute. The distinction between managing information and purposely deceiving is a thin line and is examined in the section on negotiation ethics.

The following selection provides advice and discusses issues regarding obtaining and providing information. Professor Nelken first focuses on managing and bargaining for information in distributive situations and then on the benefits and concerns of sharing information in more integrative negotiations. The separation between distributive and integrative negotiation is not always clear, so her comments may apply to both.

❖ Melissa L. Nelken, *Negotiation: Theory and Practice*

41 (Anderson Publishing, 2007)

In the course of the negotiation, you will try to learn things about the other party's case, and about his perception of your case, that you don't know when the negotiation starts. He, of course, will do the same with you. Another important aspect of preparation, then, is deciding what you need to find out before you actually make a deal. Without considering what information you need to gather in the early stages of the negotiation, you will not be able to gauge how well the actual situation fits the assumptions you have made in preparing to negotiate. You may have overestimated how much the other party needs a deal with you, or underestimated the value he places on what you are selling. Only careful attention to gathering information will enable you to adjust your goals appropriately. In addition to what you want to learn, you also have to decide what information you are willing, or even eager, to divulge to the other party — for example, the large number of offers you have already received for the subject property — and what information you want to conceal — for example, the fact that none of those offers exceeds the price you paid for the property originally. Managing information is a central feature of distributive bargaining, and you have to plan to do it well.

A beginning negotiator often feels that she has to conceal as much as possible, that virtually anything she reveals will hurt her or be used against her. . . . [Y]ou are more likely to feel this way if you have not thought through your case and prepared how to present it in the best light that you realistically can. If you choose when and how you will reveal information, rather than anxiously concealing as much as possible, you gain a degree of control over the negotiation that you lack when you merely react to what your counterpart says or does. Increasing the amount of information you are prepared to reveal, and reducing the amount you feel you absolutely must conceal, will help you make a stronger case for your client. In addition, the more willing you are to share information that the other party considers useful, the more likely you are to learn what you need to know from your counterpart before you make a deal.

Using Outside Sources

As part of your preparation, you need to consult outside sources of information to help you understand the context of a given negotiation. You will need data about the subject of the negotiation — market prices, alternate sources of supply, industry standards, market factors affecting the company you are dealing with, and so on. In addition, information about the parties and their representatives from others who have negotiated with them in the past will be helpful in planning your strategy. You will also want to learn about any relevant negotiation conventions, for example, the convention in personal injury litigation that the plaintiff makes the first demand. . . .

Bargaining for Information

A central aspect of distributive bargaining is bargaining for information. In the course of planning, you have to make certain working assumptions about the motives and wishes of the other side, as well as about the factual context of the negotiation. In addition, we all have a tendency to "fill in" missing information in order to create a coherent picture of a situation. For a negotiator, it is imperative to separate out what you know to be true from what you merely believe to be true by testing your assumptions during the early stages of the negotiation. Otherwise, you risk making decisions based on inaccurate information and misunderstanding what the other side actually tells you. . . .

Many negotiators forget that they start with only a partial picture of the situation, and they push to "get down to numbers" before learning anything about the other side's point of view. Yet the relevant facts of a situation are not immutable; they are often dependent on your perspective. Knowing the other side's perspective is a valuable source of information about possibilities for settlement. The most obvious way to gather that information is by asking questions, especially about the reasons behind positions taken by the other party. Why does a deal have to be made today? How good are her alternatives to settlement with you? What is the basis for a particular offer? Asking questions allows you to test the assumptions that you bring to the negotiation about both parties' situations. Questions also permit you to gauge the firmness of stated positions by learning how well supported they are by facts. In addition, the information you gather can alert you to issues that are important (or unimportant) to your counterpart, opening up possibilities for an advantageous settlement if you value those issues differently.

In addition to asking questions, you have to learn to listen carefully to what the other party says, to look for verbal and nonverbal cues that either reinforce or contradict the surface message conveyed. If someone tells you that he wants $40,000-50,000 to settle, you can be sure that he will settle for $40,000, or less. If he starts a sentence by saying, "I'll be perfectly frank with you . . . ," take whatever follows with a large grain of salt and test it against other things you have heard. Asking questions is only one way to gather information, and not always the most informative one. You also have to listen for what someone omits from an answer, for answers that are not answers or that deflect the question, for hesitations and vagueness in the responses that you get. There is no simple formula for what such things mean, but the more alert you are for ways in which you are not getting information in a straightforward way, the better able you will be to sort through the information that you get. . . .

One of the most effective and underutilized methods of bargaining for information is silence. Many inexperienced negotiators, especially lawyer-negotiators, think that they are paid to talk and are not comfortable sitting quietly. If you can teach yourself to do so, you will find that you often learn things that would never be revealed in response to a direct question. When silences occur, people tend to fill them in; and because the silence is unstructured, what they say is often more spontaneous than any answer to a question would be. Since you are interested in gathering new information in the course of the negotiation, it is useful to keep in mind that if you are talking, you probably aren't hearing anything you do not already know. Therefore, silence is truly golden. . . .

Sharing Information

All that has been said so far about integrative bargaining suggests that lawyers will only be able to do a good job if they share substantive information about their clients' needs and preferences and look for ways to make their differences work for them in the negotiation. According to Follett (1942, p. 36), "the first rule . . . for obtaining integration is to put your cards on the table, face the real issue, uncover the conflict, bring the whole thing into the open." This is a far cry from the bargaining for information that characterizes distributive negotiations, where each side seeks to learn as much as possible about the other while revealing as little as it can. The more straightforward and clear the negotiators' communications are, the fewer obstacles there will be to recognizing and capitalizing on opportunities for mutual gain. This means, first, that they must be clear about their clients' goals, even if they are open as to the means of reaching those goals. In addition, there must be sufficient trust between them so that both are willing to reveal their clients' true motivations. Such trust may be based on past experience, but it may also be developed in the course of a negotiation, as the negotiators exchange information and evaluate the information they have received. It does not have to be based on an assumption that the other side has your best interest at heart, but only that he is as interested as you are in uncovering ways that you can both do better through negotiation. Self-interest can keep both sides honest in the process, even where there might be a short-term gain from misrepresentation. Of course, the need to share information in order to optimize results creates risks for the negotiators as well. . . .

Flexibility, rather than rigid positions, is key to integrative bargaining, since the outcome will depend on fitting together the parties' needs as much as possible. When the negotiators share adequate information, they may end up redefining the conflict they are trying to resolve. For example, what seemed a specific problem about failure to fulfill the terms of a contract may turn out to be a more fundamental difficulty with the structure of the contract itself. A better outcome for both sides may result if the contract is renegotiated. . . .

Strategic Use of Information

There is also anxiety because the amount of shared information needed for integrative bargaining to succeed may be more than a distributive bargainer wants to reveal. For example, a distributively-inclined buyer may prefer that his counterpart think that time of delivery, which he does not care much about, is very important to him, so that he can exact concessions on other aspects of the deal by "giving in" to a later delivery to accommodate the seller. Since it is hard to know in advance what issues will be most significant to the other side, it can be difficult to decide how much information to share and how to evaluate the quality of the information you receive about your counterpart's priorities. The fear of being taken advantage of often results in both sides' taking preemptive action focused on "winning" rather than on collaborating. Sometimes such strategies are effective; but they are also likely to impede or prevent what could be a fruitful search for joint gains.

E. Opening Demands and Offers

Problem

You are a new law graduate. A three-lawyer firm is interested in hiring you as its first associate. The firm's size, areas of practice and the personality of the partners is appealing to you. Your most viable alternative is as a staff lawyer with a government agency starting at $65,000. Large firms, which do not seem like a viable alternative, are starting associates at $165,000. You are scheduled to meet with the managing partner of the firm to discuss terms of employment, which have not previously been indicated.

1. In this situation, would you make the opening salary proposal or instead ask the partner to make a salary offer?
2. What are the advantages and disadvantages of making the first salary proposal versus allowing the managing partner to propose a salary?
3. What might it be helpful for you to know before making this negotiation decision?

As we noted earlier, the timing of offers and demands may vary between positional and interest-based approaches. Positional bargainers tend to make demands and offers early. Their initial interaction may commence with the presentation of a demand. The filing of a lawsuit without prior negotiation of the claim is one way to assert a demand and start negotiations. In contrast, interest-based negotiators seek information from their counterpart and prefer to establish a positive relationship before discussing proposals. One purpose of the information sought and perhaps exchanged is to discover interests that might lead to an acceptable solution that creates value, even if there might later be more competitive bargaining to allocate the added value.

Whether you prefer a competitive or cooperative approach, there will be negotiations in which you must decide if it is better to make the first offer or invite an offer from the other side. (Offers and demands are used here synonymously.) If choosing to make the first offer, should it be extreme, modestly favorable, exactly what you expect, or equitably calculated to be fair to all and maximize collective value? If the first offer is made by the other side, should you flinch, as recommended by Dawson, counteroffer immediately, or process the offer and come back with an exaggerated counteroffer or one closer to your reservation point? How does formulating the initial offer relate to what we have learned about perceptions, ripeness, anchoring, preparation, the role of expectations, and trust?

The negotiation guidebooks are full of advice on making offers, much of it contradictory. There appears to be consensus that in distributive negotiations more extreme or aggressive offers result in more favorable outcomes. (However, an exaggerated offer can come before or after learning the other side's opening position.) This consensus, focused on distributive negotiation, doesn't help you on how to start an integrative negotiation. The first selection below, which is based on Professor Williams's extensive empirical research of lawyer negotiators, weighs the advantages and disadvantages of three different opening strategies. Each strategy assumes that both sides seek to establish the illusion that they are inalterably committed to their opening positions. The second excerpt explores when to make the first offer and how to respond to an initial offer. It reviews the power of the first offer as an anchor, which you learned about in Chapter 2.

❖ Gerald R. Williams & Charles Craver, *LEGAL NEGOTIATION*

79 (West Publishing, 2007)

. . . The lawyers articulate their opening positions. At this early stage in the dispute, that exchange is not as simple as it appears. The facts are not all in, the legal questions are not fully researched, and unforeseen developments loom on the horizon. In the face of these uncertainties, the negotiators must leave themselves a certain amount of latitude, yet they must develop credible opening demands and offers. . . .

[T]here are essentially three strategies that can be used in framing an opening position. . . . Negotiators may adopt the *maximalist strategy* of asking for more than they expect to obtain, they may adopt the *equitable strategy* of taking positions that is fair to both sides, or they may adopt the *integrative strategy* of searching for alternative solutions that would generate the most attractive combination for all concerned. Each strategy has its own strengths and weaknesses.

Maximalist Positioning

Arguments for maximalist positioning begin with the assumption that the opening position is a bargaining position, and that no matter how long bargainers may deny it, they expect to come down from them to find agreements. Maximalist positioning has several advantages. These position statements effectively hide the bargainer's real or minimum expectations, they eliminate the danger of committing to an overly modest case evaluation, they provide covers for them while they seek to learn real opponent positions, and will very likely induce opponents to reduce their expectations. They also provide negotiators with something to give up, with concessions they can make, to come to terms with opponents. This last factor may be especially important when opponents also open high, and negotiators are required to trade concessions as they move toward mutually agreeable terms. These advantages may lead many to believe that negotiators who make high opening demands, have high expectations, make relatively small and infrequent concessions, and are perceptive and unyielding fare better in the long run than their opponents.

The potential benefits of the maximalist position need to be weighed against its potential demerits, which are those associated with competitive/adversarial strategies. . . . The most important weakness is the increased risk of bargaining stalemates. Competent opponents will prefer their non-settlement alternatives to the unreasonable demands and supporting tactics of the maximalist negotiators, unless the opponents themselves can devise effective strategies to counter such maximalist behaviors. We observe in the data that competitive attorneys at all levels of effectiveness are rated as making high opening demands. Yet, by definition, effective competitive/adversarials use the strategy proficiently, while ineffective competitive adversarials do not. We are forced to conclude that in the legal context the maximalist strategy does not consistently bring high returns for those who use it — only for those who employ it effectively. How high demands can be without losing their effectiveness depends on several considerations. One is the nature of the remedy being sought. By their nature, contract damages are less inflatable than personal injury damages, for example, and negotiators who multiply their contract damages as they do their personal injury claims will undermine their own credibility. Another consideration is local custom. Specialized groups within the bar develop norms and customs that provide measures against which the reasonableness or extremism of demands can be evaluated. Not all high demands are the same. Some demands lack credibility on their face by their inappropriateness and lack of congruity in the context in which they are made. But the level of demands is not the sole factor. The data suggest that effective competitive/adversarial negotiators are able to establish the credibility and plausibility of high demands by relying on convincing legal argumentation. Ineffective competitive/adversarials lack the skills to do this, and, in the absence of convincing support, their high demands lack credibility.

Finally, it should be noted that the effectiveness of high demands will depend upon the opponents against whom the high demands are made. In cases where opponents are unsure of the actual case values, high opening demands by maximizing negotiators have the desired effect. The opponents, unsure of case values, use the maximizer's high opening demands as standards against which to set their own goals. However, when the opponents have evaluated their cases and arrived at appropriate value judgments, the opponents interpreted maximizer high opening demands as evidence of unreasonableness. This causes maximizer credibility to be diminished, and the likelihood of bargaining breakdowns increases.

Equitable Positioning

Equitable positions are calculated to be fair to both sides. Their most notable proponent, O. Bartos, challenged the assumption of maximalist theorists that both sides to negotiations are trying to maximize their own payoffs or benefits. He argued that a competing value is also operative —that negotiators feel a cooperative desire to arrive at solutions fair to both sides. In support of this argument, he cited not only humanistic literature defending equality as an essential ingredient of justice, but also anthropological and sociological studies confirming the widespread existence and operation in society of an egalitarian norm of reciprocity. Bartos conducted numerous theoretical and experimental negotiation studies which lead him to believe that the human desire to deal fairly with others is preferable to a more competitive strategy.

This equitable approach is considered as the most economical and efficient method of conflict resolution. It minimizes the risk of deadlock and avoids the costs of delay occasioned by extreme bargaining positions. Bartos recommended that negotiators be scrupulously fair and that they avoid the temptation to take advantage of naive opponents. He cautioned that the equitable approach requires trust, which allows both sides to believe they are being treated fairly. Nonetheless, trust must be tempered with realism. It is out of trust that negotiators make concessions, but if their trust is not rewarded or returned in fair fashion, further concessions should be withheld until their opponents reciprocate. Equitable negotiators do not always open negotiations with statements specifying their desires to achieve mutually beneficial solutions. Rather, they open with positions that show they are serious about finding fair agreement, and they trustingly work toward mid-points between their reasonable opening position and the reasonable opening positions of their opponents. Unless both sides come forward with reasonable opening positions, it will be difficult for one side to compel the other to move toward an equitable resolution. Referring back to the data on cooperative/problem-solving and competitive/adversarial negotiators, we intuitively suspect that Bartos' equitable negotiators are cooperative/problem-solvers. This observation is borne out by the extremely high ratings received by cooperative/problem-solving attorneys on characteristics such as trustworthy, ethical, honest, and fair. Just as with our analysis of maximalist positioning by competitive/adversarial attorneys, it must be pointed out that the use of equitable positioning by cooperative/problem-solving attorneys does not always generate satisfactory results. It is obviously satisfactory as used by effective cooperative/problem-solvers, but it is likely to be deficient when used by ineffective cooperative/problem-solvers. We must conclude that the positioning strategy, whether maximalist or equitable, does not guarantee success. Whichever approach is used, it must be employed with care and acumen or it will not be effective.

Integrative Positioning

Integrative Positioning involves more than opening demands and offers. It describes an attitude or approach that carries through the other stages of the negotiation, and is an alternative to pure positional bargaining. The most effective advocates of this method have been Roger Fisher and William Ury who advise negotiators to avoid positioning completely. Among business people, the method is seen as the art of problem solving. Integrative negotiators view cases as presenting alternative solutions, and they believe that chances for reaching agreements are enhanced by discovering innovative alternatives reflecting the underlying interests of the parties, and seeking to arrange the alternatives in packages that yield maximum benefit to both parties. This strategy is often identified with exchange transactions involving many variables, and is generally seen as having limited utility in personal injury actions, for example, where the fundamental issue is how much money defendants are going to pay plaintiffs — a classic distributive problem. . . .

❖ **Deepax Malhotra & Max H. Bazerman,** *Negotiation Genius*

27 (Bantam Books, 2007)

Should You Make the First Offer?

The primary benefit of making a first offer in negotiation is that it establishes an *anchor.* An anchor is a number that focuses the other negotiator's attention and expectations. Especially when the other party is uncertain about the correct, fair, or appropriate outcome, they are likely to gravitate toward any number that helps them focus and resolve their uncertainty. As it turns out, first offers tend to serve this purpose well: they anchor the negotiation and strongly influence the final outcome. . . .

The power of anchors is substantial. Research has shown that anchors affect even those with negotiation experience and expertise. In one remarkable demonstration of the power of anchors, professors Greg Northcraft and Margaret Neale invited real estate agents to evaluate a house that was for sale. The agents were allowed to walk through the house and neighborhood, and were given the Multiple Listing Service (MLS) information sheet that provided details about the house, including its size and dimensions, the year it was built, the amenities included, etcetera. They were also given detailed information about other properties located in the same neighborhood. The information provided to each agent was identical with one exception: the "list price" on the MLS sheet that was given to the agent was randomly picked from one of the following: (a) $119,000, (b) $129,000, (c) $139,000, or (d) $149,000. In real estate, the list price is the "first offer" made by the seller. Thus, this study manipulated the first offer to see whether it would affect the perceptions of experienced real estate agents. After seeing the house and reading all of the information, agents were asked to evaluate the house on four dimensions:

1. What is an appropriate list price for this house? *(Appropriate List Price)*
2. What do you estimate is the appraisal value of this house? *(Appraisal Value)*
3. As a buyer, what is a reasonable amount to pay for the house? *(Willingness to Pay)*
4. What is the lowest offer you would accept as the seller? *(Lowest Acceptable Offer)*

[The chart] graphs the responses to these questions by agents who were provided each of the list prices. As you can see, agents were strongly influenced by whichever list price they were arbitrarily assigned! On every measure, those given a higher list price thought the house was worth more than did those given a lower list price. Furthermore, when the agents were asked whether their answers had been influenced *at all* by the list price given to them on the information sheet, more than 80 percent of them said no.

. . . [W]hether you should make the first offer or not depends upon how much information you have. If you believe you have sufficient information about the other side's reservation value, it pays to make a reasonable (i.e., *sufficiently* aggressive) opening offer that anchors the discussion in your favor. If you suspect that you may not have enough information about the ZOPA [zone of possible agreement], you'd be wise to defer an opening offer until you have collected more information. In this case, it may even be a good idea to let the other party make the first offer. You might forgo the opportunity to anchor the negotiation, but you also avoid the downside of not anchoring aggressively enough. Notice that a lack of information can also lead you to anchor *too* aggressively, demanding an amount that might offend the other side and drive them away. In other words, asking for too little diminishes the amount of value you can capture; asking for too much diminishes your chances of consummating the deal. . . .

How Should You Respond to Their Initial Offer?

When the other parry makes the first move, you become vulnerable to the effects of anchoring. Because anchoring effects can be very subtle, this is likely to be true even if you are aware of these effects. However, there are a number of ways you can protect yourself from being overly influenced by the other side's anchor:

Strategy 1: Ignore the Anchor

The best thing to do in the event that the other party makes an aggressive first offer — whether high or low — is to ignore it. This doesn't mean you should pretend you didn't hear it. Rather, respond to this effect: "Judging by your offer, I think we might be looking at this deal in very different ways. Let's try to bridge that gap by discussing. . . ." In this manner, you can shift the conversation to an entirely different topic, one that allows you to reassert control of the discussion.

Strategy 2: Separate Information from Influence

Every offer is a combination of *information* and *influence*. The other party's offer tells you something about what she believes and what she wants (information), but it also has the power to derail your strategy (influence). Your task is to separate the information contained in the particulars of the offer (and the way in which it was made) from the other side's attempt to influence your perceptions. The best way to stave off influence is to stick to your original game plan. If you walked in with a prepared first offer, don't allow the other side's anchor to soften it. This does not mean that you should ignore substantial information that changes your beliefs about the actual ZOPA. For example, if the other side has just provided credible evidence that she has an attractive offer from a competitor of yours, this might be reason to adjust your counteroffer. However, it is important to realize that anchors will affect perceptions and counteroffers even in the absence of any real information provided to you. For example, the negotiator's mind can sometimes fail to distinguish between these two statements:

- *Information and Influence*: "We have received a better offer from Company X. As a result, we think your initial offer is low. We would like you to increase it to $7 million."
- *Influence Only*: "As you know, there are other companies with whom we do business. We have spoken with them. As a result, we think your initial offer is low. We would like you to increase it to $7 million."

The first statement provides some (but not much) substantive information that should prompt you to think about whether to accept, challenge, or question the statement being made. The second statement simply reiterates what you already knew, but uses phraseology that helps the other side emphasize its anchor. Thus, you have every reason to ignore this statement.

Strategy 3: Avoid Dwelling on Their Anchor

Many negotiators believe that if someone anchors aggressively, you should push them to justify the anchor, thereby exposing the frivolous nature of their extreme demands. This is a dangerous strategy. Why? Because the more an anchor is discussed in a negotiation, the more powerful it becomes. If you ask the other party to justify their offer or discuss it further (e.g., "How did you come up with that number?"), you increase the power of that anchor to define the negotiation parameters. Almost always, your counterpart will find a way to frame the negotiation such that their offer makes at least a modicum of sense.

On the other hand, you do not want to miss out on the opportunity to learn something new about the deal or about your counterpart's perspective. To resolve this dilemma, try the following: if you are surprised by their offer, probe a little to find out if there is in fact any substantive new information that you can obtain. If no such information is forthcoming, quickly shift attention away from the anchor by sharing your own perspective and defining the negotiation in your terms.

Strategy 4: Make an Anchored Counteroffer, then Propose Moderation

Finally, if it is not possible to ignore or dismiss the other party's anchor, you should offset its influence by making an aggressive counteroffer. In doing so, you retain the ability to capture as much of the ZOPA as possible. However, countering aggression with aggression comes at a risk: the possibility that both parties will become entrenched and reach an impasse. To mitigate this risk, you should offset their anchor with an aggressive counteroffer, and then suggest that you need to work together to bridge the gap. In addition, you should offer to make the first move toward moderation by discussing your own perspective (i.e., by justifying your aggressive counteroffer). This allows you to deflate their anchor while shifting from an aggressive exchange to a quest for common ground. For example, in response to an aggressive anchor, you might say: Well, based on your offer, which was unexpected, it looks like we have a *lot* of work ahead of *us*. From our perspective, a fair price would be closer to $X [your counteroffer]. I will explain to you how *we* are valuing this deal, but it appears to me that if we are to reach any agreement, we will both have to work together to make it happen.

Strategy 5: Give Them Time to Moderate Their Offer Without Losing Face

If the other party's initial offer is *very* extreme — far outside the ZOPA — you may need to inform them that their offer is not even a basis for starting the discussion. This assertion should be followed by information regarding your own perspective and a candid invitation to reopen negotiation — from a very different starting point. . . .

To illustrate the point that your first offer or demand should not be so extreme that your opponent walks out of the room, consider the following scene from a popular book and movie. The non-fiction story chronicles the negotiation and trial of the claims of eight families in Woburn, Massachusetts, who sued the corporate owners of a tannery and chemical plants for cancer-related illnesses and deaths of their children. Even food and gifts could not prevent an impasse.

❖ **Jonathan Harr,** *A Civil Action*

277 (Vintage Books, 1996)

After a few minutes, the lawyers took their assigned seats at the table. Schlichtmann began talking about how he and his partners took only a few select cases and worked to the exclusion of all else on those. (This was Schlichtmann's way of saying there was no stopping them.) He said he wanted a settlement that would provide for the economic security of the families, and for their medical bills in the future. The families, he continued, weren't in this case just for money. They wanted an acknowledgment of the companies' wrongdoing, Schlichtmann said, a full disclosure of all the dumping activities.

"Are you suggesting there hasn't been a full disclosure?" Facher asked. "No," said Schlichtmann, who was suggesting exactly that, but now made an effort to avoid confrontation. "But as part of a settlement, we want a disclosure that the judge will bless." Another condition of settlement, he added, was an agreement that the companies clean their land of the toxic wastes, and pay the costs for cleaning the aquifer.

None of the defense lawyers had touched any of the food or drink. As Schlichtmann spoke, he saw Facher reach for a bowl of mints on the table and slowly unwrap the foil from one. Facher popped the mint into his mouth and sucked on it, watching Schlichtmann watch him.

Schlichtmann talked for fifteen minutes. Then Gordon laid out the financial terms of the settlement: an annual payment of $1.5 million to each of the eight families for the next thirty years; $25 million to establish a research foundation that would investigate the links between hazardous wastes and illness; and another $25 million in cash.

Cheeseman and his partners took notes on legal pads as Gordon spoke. Facher examined the pen provided courtesy of the Four Seasons, but he did not write anything on his pad. Facher studied the gilt inscription on the pen. It looked like a good-quality pen. These figures, he thought, were preposterous. They meant that Schlichtmann did not want to settle the case, or else he was crazy. Maybe Schlichtmann simply wanted to go to trial. This opulent setting, and Schlichtmann sitting at the table flanked by his disciples like a Last Supper scene, annoyed Facher. Where was Schlichtmann getting the money for all this?

When Gordon finished, silence descended.

Finally Facher stopped studying the pen. He looked up, and said, "If I wasn't being polite, I'd tell you what you could do with this demand."

Cheeseman had added up Gordon's figures. By Cheeseman's calculations, Schlichtmann was asking a total of four hundred ten million over thirty years. "How much is that at present value?" Cheeseman asked Gordon.

Gordon replied that he would rather not say. "Your own structured-settlement people can tell you that."

Facher took a croissant from the plate in front of him, wrapped it in a napkin, and put it into his pocket. That and the mint he had consumed were the only items the defense lawyers had taken from the sumptuous banquet that Gordon had ordered.

Cheeseman and his partners asked a few more perfunctory questions about the terms of disclosure, which Schlichtmann answered. Facher had gone back to studying the pen. "Can I have this?" he said abruptly, looking at Schlichtmann.

Schlichtmann, appearing surprised, nodded. Facher put the pen into his breast pocket. "Nice pen," he said. "Thank you."

Then Facher got up, put on his coat, and walked out the door. Frederico, who had not uttered a word, followed him.

Cheeseman and his partners stood, too, and in a moment, they followed Facher.

Schlichtmann and his colleagues sat alone on their side of the table. Gordon looked at his watch. The meeting had lasted exactly thirty-seven minutes, he announced. "I guess we're going to trial," Gordon added.

Schlichtmann was surprised, but only for a moment. He looked at his colleagues and shrugged. "We're going to get a jury in two weeks," he said. "The pressure's on them."

Conway got up and paced the room and smoked a cigarette. He didn't feel like talking. There was nothing to discuss. They'd gotten nothing out of this so-called settlement conference, not even information from the other side. He put on his coat and, along with Crowley, walked up Tremont Street back to the office.

Questions and Note

12. How did Schlichtmann go wrong? What advice offered by Shell and by Williams and Craver might have been helpful for Schlichtmann in making his demand?

13. Might local custom and the experience of opposing counsel, as well as the evaluation done by the other side, have been contributing factors to the defense walkout in the above scene? What would you have done differently than Schlichtmann in this situation?

In formulating your first proposal, whether it be a demand or offer, it is advised that you determine the most aggressive proposal for which you can state a credible justification. Never demand so much or offer so little that you can't explain the reason for it. Be able to phrase your first offer as "I propose this because. . . ." This will minimize the "Schlichtmann effect."

CHAPTER
6

Negotiation Step by Step—The Middle

A. Bargaining

Bargaining takes many forms and is not confined to a specific stage in the negotiation process. The term "bargaining" is more associated with the competitive/distributive approach. Phrases like "searching for solutions" and "problem solving" are frequently used to describe a more cooperative/integrative approach. However, at some point in any negotiation there must be movement from the differences that brought the parties to the table toward the agreement that will resolve the dispute or create a deal. Whether the movement results from arguments and persuasion or from proposed principles and criteria may be more a matter of semantics and tone than of real difference. For example, lawyers in negotiating a settlement of a lawsuit may agree, expressly or implicitly, that legal principles and precedent will be the criteria for settlement. Does this reduce the role of argument and attempts at persuasion regarding what case precedent is most analogous and applicable to the matter in dispute? A hallmark of integrative negotiation is trading off a lower priority to satisfy one more personally important. Is this not a form of bargaining concession?

1. Managing Concessions

Concessions are the compromises you make after your opening offer to move the negotiation forward, particularly in competitive bargaining. Usually the concessions you make are offered in return for those your negotiation opponent offers. Making concessions can be done strategically in recognition that the timing, amount, and nature of concessions are a form of communication by which each side sends signals about priorities and reservation points. The pattern of concessions forms a message. By carefully considering what you want to communicate you can manage concessions to shape the message, particularly about how close you are to your reservation point. (Diminishing concessions signal you are close.)

The timing of offering concessions can be telling and must also be considered carefully. Concessions given in rapid succession early on may signal risk aversion or desperation. Giving away too much in the initial stages of negotiation depletes the reserve of concessions that can be offered later, when they may be more appreciated.

By planning and using concessions strategically, you can influence the outcome of the negotiation. The flip side of anything that can be used strategically is that a similar or counterstrategy might be used to manipulate you. So be aware that the concession signals from a competitive bargainer can be deceptive and may mislead an adversary about how far the bargainer will go. The following reading is an exploration of concessions and their use, as explained by a leading negotiation trainer.

❖ **Theron O'Connor,** *Planning and Executing an Effective Concession Strategy*

(Bay Group International, 2003)

Concessions and the Negotiating Process

It is the concession piece of the negotiation process — the bargaining, the give-and-take, the "horse-trading," what the parties are willing to give up in order to reach an agreement — that will be discussed here. There are two principal sets of tasks to consider. The first is how to create the most advantageous negotiation context within which a concession strategy can be implemented. The techniques to establish a favorable negotiation context are discussed elsewhere in this volume. The second critical consideration is how to effectively handle the *execution* of the concession strategy or plan once the context has been established. This piece will focus upon the execution phase.

It should be noted that the many parts of the negotiation process are not strictly sequential. Rather, they occur and reoccur throughout the negotiation and must be attended to iteratively. That is particularly true of concession patterns. Often attention to concessions is mistakenly deferred until late in the game and concessions are used tactically, rather than strategically, as a closing tool.

Planning and Executing an Effective Concession Strategy

Once a desirable negotiating context has been established, the concession strategy can be executed. Whether to concede, when to concede, what to concede, how to concede are among a number of important considerations to keep in mind in dealing with concessions. Skilled negotiators develop plans for managing the process of making concessions, and thereby exert more control over the negotiation process. Conceding without a plan can doom you to failure in negotiation.

Concessions Should Be Made Only as Required

Notwithstanding that a sophisticated concession strategy has been developed — replete with creative and cost effective negotiables — no concessions should be made unless they are demanded by the other side. If the other side is willing to accept the initial proposal, then there has probably been a failure to accurately gauge the unexpectedly high value perception of the other side and a failure to take a sufficiently ambitious opening position. That error ought not to be compounded by then freely granting concessions from the largesse that has been built into the plan. While this should go without saying, there is often the temptation to "throw something in" simply because it is unexpectedly still there.

Concessions Should Be Made Slowly and Reluctantly

At the early stages of the negotiation, the focus should be on continuing to shape and influence the value perception of the other side and continuing to uncover and evaluate their wants and needs. With the range of reason advantageously set, it is imperative to hold the line and show resolve with respect to the value proposition and opening position. Reluctance to make concessions early on tends to increase their value in the mind of the other negotiator when they are in fact granted. Care should be taken, however, not to communicate too aggressive and inflexible a stance.

Try Not to Be the First to Make a Concession

If possible, get the other party to move first. Take the time to test the resolve of the other side by asking for concessions and suggesting ways that interests might be satisfied by them. First concessions can carry strong signals as to the flexibility of the other negotiator and can help calibrate the distance between the party's positions. Do not hesitate to make a concession, however, if it seems necessary to keep the negotiation going.

Get Something in Return for Any Concession

Concessions should be made in the context of trades or exchanges rather than given simply to see if the other side's point of satisfaction might be found. Demanding a concession in return both reinforces the value of what is being conceded and signals the resolve of the negotiator making the concession. It also helps to build the process of give and take and stimulate movement toward agreement.

First Concede Low Cost Negotiables That Represent High Value to the Other Side and Vice Versa

Having prioritized and ranked those things which might be offered to satisfy the wants and needs of the parties, it is important to evaluate each opportunity in terms of what might be offered that would be perceived to provide the highest possible value to the other side at the lowest cost. Likewise, in seeking concessions from the other side, it is important to seek concessions of high perceived value at comparatively low cost to them.

Use a Concession Pattern Designed to Leverage Fundamental Interests

Concession patterns communicate predictable messages to the other side. Holding firm and making one big concession at the end sends one message; making one large early concession and then holding firm sends another message. Making incremental but growing concessions sends one message; making incremental but diminishing concessions sends another message. Driving value early on and then executing a concession pattern of a large concession first and then progressively smaller ones often can be the most powerful pattern of all. It communicates resolve, then flexibility, and then diminishing returns moving toward closure.

Conclusion

It is critical to the ultimate success of the negotiation to deal with the concession process early on — even prior to initial contact — both to build the most advantageous context and to develop a strategy for execution of the concession plan. The context-building activities, anchoring, framing, positioning, setting high opening targets, discovering interests and negotiables, and managing emotions and behaviors, help to develop a robust value proposition and to stretch the range-of-reason within which an optimal outcome can be achieved.

Concession execution guidelines help to ensure that the negotiator will not give up too much too soon and that an appropriate balance will be maintained between self-interested competitiveness on the one hand and relational collaboration on the other. The concession execution guidelines are:

No Concession Unless Needed

Get the Other Party to Make First Concession

Concede Slowly and Reluctantly

Get Something in Return

Concede to High Value from Low Cost/Vice-Versa

Use Advantageous Pattern

Rigorous integration of both phases, building context and concession execution — from beginning to end — create the highest likelihood of successful negotiation.

Problem

Assume you are negotiating a personal injury claim on behalf of an injured pedestrian, and liability is not clear. You have spoken with the insurance claims adjuster five times. Each time you have conceded an additional $1,000 off your initial written demand of $80,000, while offering new information or arguments in support of your claim. What do you think the adjuster might be communicating to you with each of the following concession patterns (he would use only one of these four patterns), and how would each pattern influence your recommendation to your risk-averse client about accepting a $47,000 settlement after your fifth round of negotiation?

	A	B	C	D
1.	$ 0	$ 3,000	$40,000	$47,000
2.	$ 0	$ 6,000	$45,000	$47,000
3.	$ 0	$12,500	$46,500	$47,000
4.	$ 0	$25,000	$47,000	$47,000
5.	$47,000	$47,000	$47,000	$47,000

2. *Value-Creating Trades and Brainstorming*

A type of bargaining also occurs in cooperative, problem-solving negotiation. The focus is more on finding the best fit of interests rather than on gaining a one-sided advantage. The following reading proposes a way to generate value-creating options and trade-offs. The technique of brainstorming to generate more creative options based on different interests and values is described.

❖ **Robert H. Mnookin, Scott R. Peppet & Andrew S. Tulumello,**
Beyond Winning: Negotiating to Create Value in Deals and Disputes

37 (Harvard University Press, 2000)

Generate Value-Creating Options

Now . . . look for value-creating trades. But this is not as easy as it might appear. Many negotiators jump into a negotiation process that inhibits value creation. One side suggests a solution and the other negotiator shoots it down. The second negotiator proposes an option, only to be told by the first why it can't work. After a few minutes of this, neither side is willing to propose anything but the most conventional solutions. This method mistakenly conflates two processes that should be engaged in separately: generating options and evaluating them.

It often helps to engage in some sort of brainstorming. The most effective brainstorming requires real freedom — however momentary — from practical constraints. . . . [There are two ground rules for brainstorming.]

- No evaluation
- No evaluation

Premature evaluation inhibits creativity. We are all self-critical enough, and adding to our natural inhibitions only makes matters worse. When brainstorming, avoid the temptation to critique ideas as they are being generated. This includes avoiding even congratulatory comments about how great someone else's idea is, murmurs of approval, and backslapping. When you signal such approval, you send the implicit message that you're still judging each idea as it is generated — you're just keeping the *negative* comments to yourself. That does not encourage inventiveness. The goal is to liberate those at the table to suggest ideas. One person's idea may seem crazy, but it may prompt another person to suggest a solution that might otherwise have been overlooked. There will be time enough for evaluation. The idea behind brainstorming is that evaluation should be a separate activity, not mixed with the process of generating ideas.

The second ground rule of brainstorming is: *no ownership of ideas*. Those at the table should feel free to suggest anything they can think of, without fear that their ideas will be attributed to them or used against them. Avoid comments such as: "John, I'm surprised to hear you suggest that; I didn't think you believed that idea made much sense." John should be able to suggest an idea *without believing it*. Indeed, those at the table should feel free to suggest ideas that are not in their best interests, purely to stimulate discussion, without fear that others at the table will later take those ideas as offers.

In preparing for negotiations, brainstorming is often employed behind the table with colleagues in order to generate ideas. For many negotiators, however, it may feel very dangerous to engage in this activity with someone on the other side. Our own experience suggests, nevertheless, that by negotiating process clearly, brainstorming can also be productive across the table.

How do you convey these ground rules to the other side? You can get the point across without sounding dictatorial or rule-obsessed. Just explain what you're trying to achieve and then lead by example. . . . Generating these possible options may broaden the parties' thinking about the terms of their negotiated agreement.

Many of these options demonstrate that a negotiator's interests can often be met in a variety of ways. And often the simplest solution is to compensate one side by adjusting the price term . . . to accommodate the parties' needs and concerns. . . . In many deal-making situations, such "side-payments" can be an effective way to adjust the distributive consequences of value-creating moves. . . .

What happens to interest-based, collaborative problem-solving when you turn to distributive issues? Some negotiators act as if problem-solving has to be tossed overboard when the going gets tough. We could not disagree more. In our experience, it's when distributive issues are at the forefront that problem-solving skills are most desperately needed. . . .

Sometimes, of course, you won't be able to find a solution that satisfies both sides. No matter how hard you try, you will continue to disagree about salary, the amount to be paid in a bonus, or some aspect of a dispute settlement. Norms may have helped move you closer together, but there's still a big gap between the two sides. What should you do?

Think about process. How can you design a process that would fairly resolve this impasse? In a dispute settlement, you might be able to hire a mediator to address the distributive issues that are still open. Is there anyone both sides trust enough to decide the issue? Could you put five possible agreements into a hat and pick one at random?

Procedural solutions can often rescue a distributive negotiation that has reached an impasse. They need not involve complicated alternative dispute resolution procedures that cost money and time. Instead, you can often come up with simple process solutions that will resolve a distributive deadlock and allow you to move forward.

Changing the Game

Not everyone approaches negotiation from a problem-solving perspective. The basic approach described in this chapter — with its emphasis on the sources of value creation and the importance of a problem-solving process — obviously departs from the norm of adversarial haggling. To be a problem-solver, a negotiator must often lead the way and change the game. . . .

Conclusion

The tension between value creation and value distribution exists in almost all negotiations. But as our teaching and consulting have shown us, many people tend to see a negotiation as purely one or the other. Some people see the world in zero-sum terms — as solely distributive. We work hard to demonstrate to people that there are nearly always opportunities to create value. Others believe that, with cooperation, the pie can be made so large that distributive questions will disappear. For these negotiators, we emphasize that there are always distributive issues to address. . . .

The problem-solving approach we have suggested here will not make distributive issues go away or this first tension of negotiation disappear. But it does outline an approach that will help you find value-creating opportunities when they exist and resolve distributive issues efficiently and as a shared problem. . . .

Problem

Assume you represent the plaintiff family suing for wrongful death of a husband/father killed by a drunk driver. Bargaining has reached an impasse, with your last demand at $1 million and the defendant's last offer at $800,000 (combining a $500,000 insurance limit and defendant's personal funds). Would you consider brainstorming? If you knew that the affluent defendant was facing sentencing for vehicular manslaughter and a letter from your client could be beneficial to her, would this open the door to value creation? The following letter was written to the sentencing judge following brainstorming, which resulted in settlement of the case. (All names have been changed.) Is an ethical problem raised by the use of this letter to settle a wrongful death claim against a drunk driver?

> To whom it may concern:
> We are the mother and surviving widow of the deceased, David Baron, whose death has left us and his three young sons behind. We write this letter to request leniency for Ms. Dorian.
>> Mistakes were made by both Ms. Dorian and David, and we have all paid an enormous price. At this point, we do not believe that these consequences should be further multiplied by sending Ms. Dorian to jail.
>> We understand that this was an isolated incident of drinking and driving for Ms. Dorian and she seems truly sorry for what happened. She has taken steps to deal with the drinking problem and she has done her best to compensate us and the three boys for our loss. We believe it is time for everyone to put this tragedy behind them and to begin building new lives in its aftermath.
>> We want to ask that Ms. Dorian be placed on probation for a period of time. We would like to see her participate in programs and organizations for victims and substance abusers in the criminal justice system. We think David would agree.
>> Thank you for your time and consideration.
>
> Sincerely,
> Judith Baron and Martha Baron

---

3. Multiparty Bargaining — Coalitions and Holdouts

Legal disputes and transactions often involve multiple parties. The negotiation dynamic and trades then become more complex, and there may be sub-bargaining within the more comprehensive negotiation. In a multiparty lawsuit, a plaintiff must negotiate with the defendants and the defendants are likely to negotiate with each other. If there is also more than one plaintiff, negotiations occur on both sides of the table and across it. In multiparty transactions, there is a mix of complementary and competing interests that may require many negotiations within the larger negotiation context.

A key difference between two-party and multiparty bargaining is the formation of coalitions. A coalition forms when two or more parties discover that they have complementary interests or that they can form side deals. They can then leverage their combined bargaining strength against the others or reach a deal that leaves out another bargainer. It is the possibility of freezing someone out of participating in the deal or blocking a deal that gives a coalition leverage. The more parties, the more possible alliances or coalitions there are. The bargaining gets both more extracted and complex as each party weighs their bargaining options with each of the other parties and the possible combinations. Bargaining can become very strategic. Because there are different payoffs possible with each combination and these are not immediately known, coalitions may dissolve and change before a final agreement is reached.

An examplé of a classic coalition arises when an injured driver sues another driver, the dealer who sold the defendant her car, the automobile manufacturer, and the auto repair shop that last serviced the defendant's car. Although naturally allied in their defense against the injured plaintiff, because of joint and several liability each defendant has individual interests that may motivate him or her to bargain separately with the plaintiff and form a coalition against the remaining defendants. So if the auto dealership bargains with the plaintiff to pay a limited amount that caps the dealer's liability and reduces its actual payout if the plaintiff recovers full damages from the other defendants, then a coalition of interests is formed against the remaining defendants. The settling defendant may agree to stay in the case to testify favorably and also avoid creating the "empty chair" defense. (This is known as a "Mary Carter" agreement and is discussed in Chapter 11. See Abbot Ford, Inc. v. The Superior Court of Los Angeles County; Ford Motor Co., 43 Cal. 3d 858 (1987).) A similar coalition situation can occur in a breach of contract case or any other type of case involving multiple defendants or plaintiffs.

Another aspect of multiparty cases and transactions that can change the bargaining process is the prospect of one or more parties holding out from a settlement or deal knowing that the others want to close the deal and will pay proportionately more to bring in the holdout. A settlement requirement of unanimity among multiple parties in a negotiation increases the strategic motivation for one party to hold out for more and also increases the chance of a negotiation impasse. For example, one of four partners may hold out in negotiations to sell their business to a suitor unless the holdout is paid more than the other partners. One of several property owners may hold out until all other property owners have sold to a developer so he may demand more in order for the complete transaction to close. (For an analysis of the added complexities and obstacles to settlement created in multiparty situations, see Mnookin 2003.)

Multiparty disputes and transactions, which create the prospect of coalitions and holdouts, complicate the bargaining phase and require more detailed analysis of the potential payoffs and negotiation leverage. Correctly anticipating the behaviors and moves of others in multiparty bargaining situations can be particularly valuable. Game theory combines mathematical and economic concepts to calculate and quantify what others are likely to do in response to what you do. Game theory principles can be useful to systematically assess the probable actions of opponents in multiparty negotiations. (See Baird, Gertner & Picker 1994; Kaplow & Shavell 2004.)

Just as there may be a payoff for one seller in a multiple-seller situation or one plaintiff in a multiparty claim who holds out to be the last to agree, there are situations in which being the first defendant to settle is advantageous. Plaintiffs may, in effect, offer an attractive discount to the first to settle to obtain one defendant's cooperation and then leverage that agreement as pressure against the remaining defendants. The following excerpt illustrates such a situation in a class-action negotiation.

❖ **John M. Poswall, THE LAWYERS: CLASS OF '69**

248 (Jullundur Press, 2003)

On Monday morning, Leon and Bishop did what appeared to be poor strategy in negotiations. They went to the turf of their opponent to talk settlement — into the luxurious 28th floor conference room of the largest defense law firm in Northern California. There, overlooking the San Francisco Bay, they met with the firm's senior litigation partner, Martin Crosby, Jr., flanked by his committee of defense attorneys representing the various levels of defendants. A number of corporate senior vice presidents were also in evidence, each being given careful deference by his representative attorney. Jack Merchant was absent. . . .

"We're all realists here," Crosby went on. "All professionals. Litigation is costly, even when we win. I'll be candid with you. I think class actions are legal blackmail and should be resisted forcefully. But my clients, our clients," he corrected himself, gesturing with his hands to the assembled group, "are willing to resolve the matter now to save the costs of litigation. Of course, if the matter proceeds, this offer will be withdrawn, and I can give you my personal assurance, Mr. Goldman, that we are prepared to spend whatever it takes to win." . . .

"We're prepared to pay your class of clients $1 million" — Crosby said $1 million very slowly to let it sink in — "for any real or imagined slight they have endured and," he looked at Leon closely, "$1 million in fees and costs to your firm for its efforts in this matter." . . .

"Marty" — he knew no one called Martin Crosby, Jr., anything but Mr. Crosby — "you invite me over here, threaten me, and then insult me and my clients, and conclude with offering me what amounts to a bribe to sell out my clients. I think I should report you to the State Bar." . . .

Leon smiled. . . . He stood up, leaned on the table with both hands, and spent a few seconds on each corporate vice president, after passing his eyes over their attorneys.

"Here's how it's going to be, gentlemen. We will settle with each group separately. The first group will pay the least; the next a bit more; and so on. The last to settle will pay the most." . . .

"You should know that I met with Jack Merchant [a defense attorney not in the room] on Saturday and Sunday, and we have arrived at a settlement, signed last night, that includes all of the provisions I just outlined. The lenders group of defendants have agreed to pay $40 million in settlement with our guarantee that each remaining group will pay more."

He shifted his eyes around the room again. He sensed the shock bordering on panic.

"So gentlemen, I suggest each of you call me when you are ready."

He turned and walked to the door. . . .

B. Moving Toward Closure

1. The Role of Power and Commitment

Negotiation is often discussed in terms of power and how each side to a negotiation can use its power to move the negotiation in the direction it desires and get what it wants from the other side. Power comes from the mind of your negotiating opponents. If they believe that you can provide them what they want or deny it to them, then relative to them, you have power. Again, perception becomes reality for purposes of negotiation. What someone wants may be material or emotional. It may be a desire to gain something new or not to lose what they have. So, you have power if you control what your opponent wants, including peace of mind, looking good, or not being harmed — provided they think you will exercise your control.

Power is linked to commitment. If it is perceived that you are committed to do what another wants, or not do it, only if they give you what you want, then you have power to obtain what you want. For example, a hostage taker may have added power if one of several hostages is shot.

Power may be a factor from the beginning to the end of negotiation. However, the perception of power often changes as the process goes forward. Because power is in the mind of the perceiver, what is communicated verbally and nonverbally during the course of a negotiation determines how power is perceived at the time decisions must be made. Both parties will attempt to display or exercise the power they have over the other to move the negotiation to a successful closure. Each may communicate their power, or attempt to create a perception of power, by threats, displays of absolute commitment, or disclosure of better alternatives for themselves and worse alternatives for the opponent.

Getting to Yes did not place emphasis on negotiation power and was criticized for not addressing the topic more. In the article that follows, Roger Fisher, the lead author of *Getting to YES*, takes up the subject of negotiating power and ties it to commitment. He defines power and expands the traditional concepts of power in a way that makes using power consistent with being a principled negotiator.

❖ **Roger Fisher,** *Negotiating Power: Getting and Using Influence*

Negotiation Theory and Practice 127
(J. Z. Rubin & W. Breslin eds., 1991)

Getting to YES (Fisher and Ury, 1981) has been justly criticized as devoting insufficient attention to the issue of power. It is all very well, it is said, to tell people how they might jointly produce wise outcomes efficiently and amicably, but in the real world people don't behave that way; results are determined by power — by who is holding the cards, by who has more clout.

At the international level, negotiating power is typically equated with military power. The United States is urged to develop and deploy more nuclear missiles so that it can negotiate from a position of strength. Threats and warnings also play an important role in the popular concept of power, as do resolve and commitment. In the game of chicken, victory goes to the side that more successfully demonstrates that it will not yield.

There is obviously some merit in the notion that physical force, and an apparent willingness to use it, can affect the outcome of a negotiation. How does that square with the suggestion that negotiators ought to focus on the interests of the parties, on the generating of alternatives, and on objective standards to which both sides might defer? . . .

How Should We Define Negotiating Power?

If I have negotiating power, I have the ability to affect favorably someone else's decision. This being so, one can argue that my power depends upon someone else's perception of my strength, so it is what they *think* that matters, not what I actually have. The other side may be as much influenced by a row of cardboard tanks as by a battalion of real tanks. One can then say that negotiating power is all a matter of perception.

A general who commands a real tank battalion, however, is in a far stronger position than one in charge of a row of cardboard tanks. A false impression of power is extremely vulnerable, capable of being destroyed by a word. In order to avoid focusing our attention on how to deceive other people, it seems best at the outset to identify what constitutes "real" negotiating power — an ability to influence the decisions of others assuming they know the truth. We can then go on to recognize that, in addition, it will be possible at times to influence others through deception, through creating an illusion of power. Even for that purpose, we will need to know what illusion we wish to create. If we are bluffing, what are we bluffing about? . . .

Categories of Power

My ability to exert influence depends upon the combined total of a number of different factors. As a first approximation, the following six kinds of power appear to provide useful categories for generating prescriptive advice:

1. The power of skill and knowledge
2. The power of a good relationship
3. The power of a good alternative to negotiating
4. The power of an elegant solution

5. The power of legitimacy
6. The power of commitment. . . .

1. The Power of Skill and Knowledge

All things being equal, a skilled negotiator is better able to influence the decision of others than is an unskilled negotiator. Strong evidence suggests that negotiating skills can be both learned and taught. One way to become a more powerful negotiator is to become a more skillful one. Some of these skills are those of dealing with people: the ability to listen, to become aware of the emotions and psychological concerns of others, to empathize, to be sensitive to their feelings and one's own, to speak different languages, to communicate clearly and effectively, to become integrated so that one's words and nonverbal behavior are congruent and reinforce each other, and so forth. . . .

The more skill one acquires, the more power one will have as a negotiator. These skills can be acquired at any time, often far in advance of any particular negotiation.

Knowledge also is power. Some knowledge is general and of use in many negotiations, such as familiarity with a wide range of procedural options and awareness of national or negotiating styles and cultural differences. A repertoire of examples, precedents, and illustrations can also add to one's persuasive abilities.

Knowledge relevant to a particular negotiation in which one is about to engage is even more powerful. The more information one can gather about the parties and issues in an upcoming negotiation, the stronger one's entering posture. . . .

2. The Power of a Good Relationship

The better a working relationship I establish in advance with those with whom I will be negotiating, the more powerful I am. A good working relationship does not necessarily imply approval of each other's conduct, though mutual respect and even mutual affection — when it exists — may help, the two most critical elements of a working relationship are, first, trust, and second, the ability to communicate easily and effectively.

Trust. Although I am likely to focus my attention in a given negotiation on the question of whether or not I can trust those on the other side, my power depends upon whether they can trust me. If over time I have been able to establish a well-deserved reputation for candor, honesty, integrity, and commitment to any promise I make, my capacity to exert influence is significantly enhanced.

Communication. The negotiation process is one of communication. If I am trying to persuade some people to change their minds, I want to know where their minds are; otherwise, I am shooting in the dark. If my messages are going to have their intended impact, they need to be understood as I would have them understood. . . .

3. The Power of a Good Alternative to Negotiation

To a significant extent, my power in a negotiation depends upon how well I can do for myself if I walk away. In *Getting to YES*, we urge a negotiator to develop and improve his "BATNA" — his Best Alternative To a Negotiated

Agreement. One kind of preparation for negotiation that enhances one's negotiating power is to consider the alternatives to reaching agreement with this particular negotiating partner, to select the most promising, and to improve it to the extent possible. This alternative sets a floor. If I follow this practice, every negotiation will lead to a successful outcome in the sense that any result I accept is bound to be better than anything else I could do. . . . The better an alternative one can develop outside the negotiation, the greater one's power to affect favorably a negotiated outcome.

4. The Power of an Elegant Solution

In any negotiation, there is a mélange of shared and conflicting interests. The parties face a problem. One way to influence the other side in a negotiation is to invent a good solution to that problem. The more complex the problem, the more influential an elegant answer. Too often, negotiators battle like litigators in court. Each side advances arguments for a result that would take care of its interests but would do nothing for the other side. The power of a mediator often comes from working out an ingenious solution that reconciles reasonably well the legitimate interests of both sides. Either negotiator has similar power to effect an agreement that takes care of some or most of the interests on the other side.

5. The Power of Legitimacy

Each of us is subject to being persuaded by becoming convinced that a particular result ought to be accepted because it is fair; because the law requires it; because it is consistent with precedent, industry practice, or sound policy considerations; or because it is legitimate as measured by some other objective standard. I can substantially enhance my negotiating power by searching for and developing various objective criteria and potential standards of legitimacy, and by shaping proposed solutions so that they are legitimate in the eyes of the other side. . . .

To retain his power, a wise negotiator avoids advancing a proposition that is so extreme that it damages his credibility. He also avoids locking himself into the first principle he advances that he will lose face in disentangling himself from that principle and moving on to one that has a greater chance of persuading the other side. In advance of this process, a negotiator will want to have researched precedents, expert opinion, and other objective criteria, and to have worked on various theories of what ought to be done, so as to harness the power of legitimacy — a power to which each of us is vulnerable.

6. The Power of Commitment

There are two quite different kinds of commitments — affirmative and negative:

(a) Affirmative commitments
    (1) An offer of what I am willing to agree to.
    (2) An offer of what, failing agreement, I am willing to do under certain conditions.
(b) Negative commitments

(1) A commitment that I am unwilling to make certain agreements (even though they would be better for me than no agreement).

(2) A commitment or threat that, failing agreement, I will engage in certain negative conduct (even though to do so would be worse for me than a simple absence of agreement).

Every commitment involves a decision. Let's first look at affirmative commitments. An affirmative commitment is a decision about what one is willing to do. It is an offer. Every offer ties the negotiator's hands to some extent. It says, "This, I am willing to do." The offer may expire or later be withdrawn, but while open it carries some persuasive power. It is no longer just an idea or a possibility that the parties are discussing. Like a proposal of marriage or a job offer, it is operational. It says, "I am willing to do this. If you agree, we have a deal." . . .

A negative commitment is the most controversial and troublesome element of negotiating power. No doubt, by tying my own hands I may be able to influence you to accept something more favorable to me than you otherwise would. The theory is simple. For almost every potential agreement there is a range within which each of us is better off having an agreement than walking away. Suppose that you would be willing to pay $75,000 for my house if you had to; but for a price above that figure you would rather buy a different house. The best offer I have received from someone else is $62,000, and I will accept that offer unless you give me a better one. At any price between $62,000 and $75,000 we are both better off than if no agreement is reached. If you offer me $62,100, and so tie your hands by a negative commitment that you cannot raise your offer, presumably, I will accept it since it is better than $62,000. On the other hand, if I can commit myself not to drop the price below $75,000, you presumably will buy the house at that price. This logic may lead us to engage in a battle of negative commitments. Logic suggests that "victory" goes to the one who first and most convincingly ties his own hands at an appropriate figure. Other things being equal, an early and rigid negative commitment at the right point should prove persuasive.

Other things, however, are not likely to be equal.

The earlier I make a negative commitment — the earlier I announce a take-it-or-leave-it position — the less likely I am to have maximized the cumulative total of the various elements of my negotiating power.

The Power of Knowledge

I probably acted before knowing as much as I could have learned. The longer I postpone making a negative commitment, the more likely I am to know the best proposition to which to commit myself.

The Power of a Good Relationship

Being quick to advance a take-it-or-leave-it position is likely to prejudice a good working relationship and to damage the trust you might otherwise place in what I say. The more quickly I confront you with a rigid position on my part, the more likely I am to make you so angry that you will refuse an agreement you might otherwise accept.

The Power of a Good Alternative

There is a subtle but significant difference between communicating a warning of the course of action that I believe it will be in my interest to take should we fail to reach agreement (my BATNA), and locking myself in to precise terms that you must accept in order to avoid my taking that course of action. Extending a warning is not the same as making a negative commitment. . . .

The Power of an Elegant Solution

The early use of a negative commitment reduces the likelihood that the choice being considered by the other side is one that best meets its interests consistent with any given degree of meeting our interests. If we announce early in the negotiation process that we will accept no agreement other than Plan X, Plan X probably takes care of most of our interests. But it is quite likely that Plan X could be improved. With further study and time, it may be possible to modify Plan X so that it serves our interests even better at little or no cost to the interests of the other side.

Second, it may be possible to modify Plan X in ways that make it more attractive to the other side without in any way making it less attractive to us. To do so would not serve merely the other side but would serve us also by making it more likely that the other side will accept a plan that so well serves our interests.

The Power of Legitimacy

The most serious damage to negotiating power that results from an early negative commitment is likely to result from its damage to the influence that comes from legitimacy. Legitimacy depends upon both process and substance. As with an arbitrator, the legitimacy of a negotiator's decision depends upon having accorded the other side "due process." The persuasive power of my decision depends in part on my having fully heard your views, your suggestions, and your notions of what is fair before committing myself. And my decision will have increased persuasiveness for you to the extent that I am able to justify it by reference to objective standards of fairness that you have indicated you consider appropriate. That factor, again, urges me to withhold making any negative commitment until I fully understand your views on fairness. . . .

The Power of an Affirmative Commitment

Negative commitments are often made when no affirmative commitment is on the table. . . . To make a negative commitment either as to what we will not do or to impose harsh consequences unless the other side reaches agreement with us, without having previously made a firm and clear offer, substantially lessens our ability to exert influence. An offer may not be enough, but a threat is almost certainly not enough unless there is a "yesable" proposition on the table — a clear statement of the action desired and a commitment as to the favorable consequences which would follow.

Conclusion

This analysis of negotiating power suggests that in most cases it is a mistake to attempt to influence the other side by making a negative commitment of any kind . . . at the outset of the negotiations, and that it is a mistake to do so until one has first made the most of every other element of negotiating power.

This analysis also suggests that when as a last resort threats of other negative commitments are used, they should be so formulated as to complement and reinforce other elements of negotiating power, not undercut them. In particular, any statement to the effect that we have finally reached a take-it-or-leave-it position should be made in a way that is consistent with maintaining a good working relationship, and consistent with the concepts of legitimacy with which we are trying to persuade the other side. . . .

Questions

Getting to YES is one of the world's best-selling books and has been translated into every major language. Since its first publication in 1981, it has become the reference point for writing on negotiation. Other writers either agree and expand on its concepts or take issue with Fisher and Ury, as we have read in excerpts by James White and Roger Dawson. Roger Fisher has responded to some of the criticisms of cooperative/principled negotiation by either conceding that *Getting to YES* presents abbreviated concepts that need to be further expanded and specifically applied, or by elaborating on their principled theories and countering the criticisms.

1. Does the above essay by Professor Fisher on negotiating power depart from the principles of *Getting to YES*? How is it consistent or inconsistent?
2. Does an affirmative commitment always create more power than a negative commitment or threat? Are threats ever appropriate in negotiation? If so, when and under what circumstances?
3. Have you experienced or heard reports of threats that seemed irrational but succeeded in getting the threatening party what it wanted?

Note: Irrational Threats, Absolute Commitments, and Perception of Power

The selections you have read are all premised on rational behavior to get what your client wants through negotiation. Expressed and implied threats can also be conveyed very powerfully when viewed as irrational. Nikita Khrushchev gained immense power when, as premier of Russia, one of only two countries with a nuclear arsenal in the 1950s, he pounded his shoe on the table at the United Nations in an apparent fit of anger. An irrational, impulsive leader with his finger on the nuclear button had more power to get his way than a rational, restrained person, at least in the short run.

A threat does not become powerful unless the recipient believes the person making the threat has the capacity to carry it out. Khrushchev's behavior at the United Nations was powerful because it was known that the Soviet Union had nuclear capacity. Power can also come from creating the illusion that you have capacity to harm others. Iraq's Saddam Hussein was attributed with more power than he actually had because of our impression that he had weapons of mass destruction. This illustrates the statement that your power comes from the mind of your negotiating opponents.

A commercial negotiator can exert persuasive power by threatening to end a negotiation so that both sides will lose what they want, even if the result is irrational. The threat of going to trial over a small monetary dispute, for example, may seem irrational. However, if the commitment appears real and the means exist for the threat to proceed, the power of irrationality may prevail. The apparent irrationality may be explained by an absolute commitment to prevail, but it is no less effective. If in a game of "chicken" an opposing driver, headed toward you on a narrow road, removed her steering wheel and threw it out the window, would you get off the road? Would you be more persuaded to concede if you thought the oncoming driver was carrying a load of dynamite and you were on a road wide enough for only one vehicle?

The road-chicken example of the power of commitment and many others are discussed in an essay by Thomas Schelling, who shared the 2005 Nobel Prize in Economics for his writing on noncooperative bargaining and game theory. Schelling also provides this example of the power of irrational threats: "[I]f a man knocks at your door and says that he will stab himself on the porch unless given $10, he is more likely to get the $10 if his eyes are bloodshot." Schelling equates bargaining power with the firmness of one's commitment as communicated to an opponent. A sophisticated, rational negotiator has difficulty appearing obstinate and may have trouble bluffing. Threats and commitment to an outcome may be more believable from a madman or from someone irrevocably locked into a position by outside influences. Schelling cites examples of leverage derived from being locked into a position, including the added international bargaining power of a U.S. President negotiating under a congressional mandate on tariffs and a labor leader's leverage in negotiating with management following a union vote to strike if a set wage limit is not met.

Schelling notes that his examples have instructive characteristics in common:

> First, they clearly depend not only on incurring a commitment but on communicating it persuasively to the other party. Second, it is by no means easy to establish the commitment, nor is it entirely clear to either of the parties concerned just how strong the commitment is. Third, similar activity may be available to the parties on both sides. Fourth, the possibility of commitment, though perhaps available to both sides, is by no means equally available; the ability of a democratic government to get itself tied by public opinion may be different from the ability of a totalitarian government to incur such a commitment. Fifth, they all run the risk of establishing an immovable position that goes beyond the ability of the other to concede, and thereby provoke the likelihood of stalemate or breakdown. (1960, 22-28)

Power need not be based on the capacity to harm others. It can come from the positive ability to help others meet their needs. If they believe that you can provide them with what they want or deny it to them, then relative to them, you have power.

We know that perceptions can be manipulated to project power that otherwise would not exist. Perception becomes reality for purposes of negotiation. A classic example of perceived power resulting from illusion is portrayed in L. Frank Baum's popular tale the *Wizard of Oz*, which was made into the classic 1939 film featuring Judy Garland as Dorothy, and more recently the Broadway musical spin-off *Wicked*. The Wizard was created by the special effects of a meek, old man to be an image of power. The Wizard was able to create power and meet the needs of Dorothy and her rag-tag friends by manipulating their perceptions, and thus he also fulfilled his interest in banishing the Wicked Witch of the West. If only success in life and negotiation could be as easy as following the yellow brick road.

The next reading uses the *Wizard of Oz* to illustrate how power is in the mind of the beholder and that real power comes from being able to meet the needs of others. You will recognize many of the negotiation concepts covered in the previous readings, including packaging of "Trade Points," which the author defines as low-priority objectives that can be readily relinquished as concessions and exchanged for higher priority items that are more valued.

❖ **H. Lee Hetherington,** *The Wizard and Dorothy, Patton and Rommel: Negotiation Parables in Fiction and Fact*

28 Pepp. L. Rev. 289 (2001)

Perception is Reality — and Not Just in Oz

Proceeding on their arduous journey to The Emerald City, Dorothy and her new friends were totally unaware that they were on their way to a negotiation. They viewed themselves as supplicants seeking the grace of an all-powerful and benevolent Wizard possessed of magical powers. But as is so often the case in negotiations, appearances can be deceiving. . . . Though there was no way for Dorothy to know it, the Wizard's act was pure subterfuge. The would-be sorcerer was merely a carnival huckster whose hot air balloon was blown off course and ended up in Oz under circumstances similar to Dorothy's. But unlike the little girl with whom he was about to negotiate, the shrewd old man took advantage of his seemingly supernatural arrival by installing himself as the symbolic, yet inaccessible, ruler of Oz. The Wizard made the most of the old adage that perception is indeed reality. Ironically, it was the Wizard who assigned supernatural powers to the little girl with the black dog. After all, she was able to do what the Wizard never could — rid Oz of the Wicked Witch of the East. It occurred to the Wizard that everybody's life could be enhanced if he could find a way to get Dorothy to dispose of the Wicked Witch of the West, an impossible task which he had no idea how to accomplish. . . .

"I Am the Great and Powerful Wizard of Oz"

Who can forget the initial face to face encounter between Dorothy, her friends, and the all-powerful Wizard of Oz? When the four entered the Great Hall of Oz, they were greeted by a giant broiling fireball and a booming voice — all of which had a supernatural effect that transcended anything human. Of course, it was all an act, but an effective act nonetheless. Though the innocent quartet still did not know it, the parameters of a potentially deadly negotiation were set. The Wizard was prepared to trade a heart, a brain, courage, and a one-way ticket to Kansas for the broomstick of the Wicked Witch of the West. However, Dorothy had to first deliver her end of the bargain.

Once again, Dorothy and her friends were outflanked by the manipulative ruler of Oz. Because the old man was so successful in his efforts to cloak the Wizard's identity in myth and mystery, he was able to move freely about disguised as the crusty old gatekeeper of Emerald City. This allowed him a significant information advantage over the unsuspecting Dorothy and her friends. Upon their arrival in Emerald City, the gatekeeper was able to learn all he could about the unsuspecting visitors. As we know, the Wizard was able to transform this information into an effective negotiating agenda calculated to rid Oz of the menacing Wicked Witch of the West. . . .

The Wizard's Power — Superior Information and Credibility

The lesson for negotiators is clear — there is no substitute for good, solid information about one's bargaining counterpart. The more known about the opposite number's agenda, leverage, and deadlines, the more effective the negotiator will be in getting what the negotiator wants. Dorothy, the Scarecrow, Tin Man, and the Lion left Emerald City empty-handed, and because of the Wizard's high-tech packaging, he was able to maintain and project sufficient credibility necessary to convince the foursome to risk their lives in quest of the newly announced Deal Point: the Witch's broomstick.

The Wizard and Dorothy: The Second Round

Finally, after more adventure and close calls than most people experience in a lifetime, Dorothy and her friends made their triumphant return to Emerald City to redeem the promises made by the Wizard. Sensing his inability to uphold his end of the bargain, the ex-carnival-barker-turned- Wizard utilized delay tactics to keep the little girl and her brave friends from discovering his true identity and inability to keep his end of the bargain.

As the angry fireball boomed his displeasure, Toto nipped at a curtain off to the side of the Great Hall of Oz. To everyone's surprise, it revealed a man manipulating levers and speaking into a loudspeaker. "Pay no attention to that man behind the curtain . . . I am the great and powerful Wizard of Oz." Unfortunately for the Wizard, his secret was finally out. The great and terrible . . . ruler of Oz was in fact not a supernatural version of General Patton, but rather, a meek and kindly . . . imposter whose disguise was unveiled. In response to Dorothy's allegation that the Wizard was a "very bad man," he responded, "No, my dear. I'm a very good man, I'm just a very bad Wizard."

Defining the Quid Pro Quo

Now that Toto had uncovered the ruse, it was time for the Wizard to make good on his promise. Once again, the Wizard's ingenuity carried the day while providing all negotiators with an excellent lesson in packaging. To the Scarecrow, who so desperately wanted a brain, the Wizard gave a testimonial. Like so many of us, all the Scarecrow really wanted was validation. Likewise with the Lion, the intangible of courage, developed and tested through his adventures with Dorothy, was conclusively validated with a hero's medal. Finally, to the Tin Man, who clearly had the biggest heart of all, the Wizard gave a ticking heart-shaped clock. In all three instances, the benevolent old man found a way to satisfy the Deal Point needs of each of the three by making the effort to truly understand what they really wanted and responding with what was, in effect, three classic Trade Points. This demonstrates that all negotiators should look behind the positions of their counterparts to find the necessary common ground to seal the deal.

For all the Wizard's success with the others, Dorothy's Deal Point was admittedly a tougher wish to grant. There was no other alternative for the Wizard than to abdicate his Wizardry, dust off the hot air balloon that had transported him to Oz, and take Dorothy and her dog back to Kansas himself.

Dorothy's BATNA: The Ruby Slippers

On the appointed day amid great fanfare, just as the balloon carrying the Wizard and Dorothy was cut loose, Toto jumped from Dorothy's arms into the crowd. As Dorothy ran to follow, the balloon drifted away, and with it her last chance to return home. After all the trials and tribulations, circumstances, as they so often do, made it impossible to close the deal. For a negotiator who failed to develop a contingency plan, or as Fisher and Ury would call it, a BATNA position, all appeared lost. Dorothy was, however, wearing her BATNA in the form of the mysteriously powerful ruby slippers. With the help of Glenda, the Good Witch, Dorothy realized that the slippers represented her BATNA. By simply clicking the heels together and repeating the phrase, "There's no place like home" three times, she realized her objective even more surely, safely, and immediately than she would have with a balloon ride into the unknown. The lesson of the ruby slippers is ultimately that no matter how problematic a situation appears to be, the ultimate strength of every negotiator lies within. There is simply no substitute for perseverance, commitment, and resourcefulness when it comes to changing the status quo for the better. Throughout all of Dorothy's adventures, she never lost sight of her ultimate objective — to go home. Dorothy finally made her dream come true. Therefore, when the odds appear overwhelming and one feels outgunned in a negotiation, one should remember Dorothy and the Wizard of Oz and follow the Yellow Brick Road of planning, personality, and persistence.

Conclusion

Like so much of life, there is nothing particularly difficult about grasping the abstract principles of negotiation and personality assessment. However, consistent and effective application of this knowledge in a time-sensitive environment, characterized by competing needs, incomplete information, constantly changing circumstances, unrevealed deadlines, misleading signals, hidden agendas, and other ambiguous factors that combine to create the real world landscape of deal making and dispute resolution, is quite another matter. As with our fictional friend Dorothy Gale, necessity is the best and only true motivator we need. As lawyers, negotiation is a primary tool of the profession. For that reason alone, lawyers should strive to improve their negotiation skills in order to make the most of their potential. As any art student will claim, it never hurts to have another perspective on the use of light and color. So it is with the art of negotiation. . . .

---

2. Deadlines and Final Offers

The well-known maxim that work expands to fill the time available applies to negotiation. Negotiations often continue until time runs out. As available time to conclude an agreement decreases, slow-moving or stalled negotiations seem to move toward closure. Concessions are offered and compromises are sometimes reached near the forced end of negotiations even though they would not be considered at the earlier stages. As Dawson noted in *Secrets of Power Negotiating*, quoted in Chapter 3, "the rule in negotiating is that 80 percent of the concessions occur in the last 20 percent of time available." More competitive negotiators will attempt to take advantage of any perceived need of the other side to conclude a deal, while hiding their own need for quick closure. However, creative solutions also materialize for more cooperative negotiators as available time comes to an end. Experienced cooperative negotiators will discuss their time constraints and agree on a time frame for the negotiation.

The passage of time may be associated with costs or lost opportunities. Time is money in many situations. More often than not, both sides want to conclude an agreement as soon as practical. However, time and delay may be more costly for one side in a negotiation. An injured plaintiff may not have the financial resources to hold out during a protracted negotiation for payment of a claim, whereas the insurance company on the other side may benefit from delay if its claim reserves are earning interest. It is this type of asymmetrical time pressure that gives an advantage to one side and is subject to manipulation.

When it is to one party's favor to move to closure, particularly if it believes that it is advantageous to prevent the other side from exploring other alternatives or opportunities, that party will impose an accelerated deadline. The deadline may be linked to a concession or a desired sweetener in exchange for accelerating closure. ("Order now and receive a free set of 'Ginsu' knives.") The deadline may be imposed to accept the entire last offer or end the negotiation. ("Accept this settlement amount by 5 P.M. or we go to trial.") A take-it-or-leave-it deadline proposal is referred to as an "exploding offer."

Deadlines can also be used to test if the other side is serious about settlement. Of course, any test can fail, and the side imposing the deadline must be willing to live with the consequences. Consider the use of the bold and strategic deadline imposed by the plaintiff's attorney in a class-action civil rights lawsuit brought by African-American customers against the Denny's restaurant chain.

❖ **Guy T. Saperstein, *Civil Warrior: Memoirs of a Civil Rights Attorney***

384 (Berkeley Hills Books, 2003)

Tom Pfister showed up with the President of Denny's and began to present Denny's offer, as we sat and listened in our conference room. He explained what corrective action Denny's was willing to undertake, and, in some cases, had already undertaken. Much of that already was required under the agreement with the United States Department of Justice and we had no quarrel with the requirements of that agreement, except that it didn't go far enough. Then Tom addressed the damage issues, explaining that Denny's would donate $3 million to various civil rights groups. . . . I interrupted Tom before he finished, demanding, "Is that it? Is that all the money you're offering?" Tom said it was. So I said, "OK, I've heard enough" . . .

"You indicated Denny's is willing to donate $3 million to various civil rights groups. That is fine, but as far as I'm concerned, that is your client's charity. It has nothing to do with our lawsuit. We are not seeking charity, we are seeking damages for Denny's reprehensible behavior. You can give $3 million away to any group or groups you want, but you will get no credit from us for that. Frankly, I was astonished and angered at your money offer, as it bore no relation to the seriousness of our lawsuit. Your offer left me with the feeling that time spent in settlement negotiations with Denny's is time wasted. Therefore, I am going to tell you what Denny's has to do to maintain credibility with me. By 10 a.m. tomorrow morning, Denny's has to offer a *minimum* of $20 million to settle damage claims of the class. That $20 million offer which Denny's is going to make tomorrow morning will NOT settle this case. It is only Denny's down payment — a tangible expression of good faith that will allow Denny's to continue these discussions. In the end, Denny's will have to pay far more than $20 million to settle this case."

Tom and his cohort left the room. We went back to my office. The mood was heavy with gloom. No one said a word in support of what I had done; several attorneys quietly voiced negative opinions: "We overplayed our hand"; "They won't be back"; "It'll be a long time before we have settlement discussions again in this case." I responded, "We broke them today. Just watch."

I walked into the office the next morning around 9 a.m. Tom Pfister was sitting in our reception area, waiting for me. Tom, a former USC basketball player, and still trim and athletic, rose to his full height of about 6' 3'', shook my hand, and said, "You've got your $20 million."

Negotiations in the above case continued until a settlement was reached that included the payment by Denny's of $54.4 million, then the largest settlement in a public accommodations case in American history. This example also illustrates the power of commitment, the power of legitimacy, and the power of a good alternative, all explained by Roger Fisher in the previous selection. Guy Saperstein's power to successfully make this bold demand was enhanced by Denny's lawyers' awareness that Saperstein had tried and won a total of $250 million in a class-action gender discrimination case against State Farm Insurance companies.

Note: The Effect of Scarcity and Deadlines

Moving to closure by imposing deadlines or making an "exploding offer," which becomes unavailable if not accepted by a deadline imposed by the offerer, is a tactic in negotiation to take advantage of what is known as the "scarcity effect." The scarcity effect enhances the value of a desired item by making it appear less available or fleeting. We tend to pay more for something now if we believe it will not be available later. If something we want seems readily available, we tend to value it less and are less motivated to act decisively to obtain it. As examples, a New Yorker might never visit the Statue of Liberty until she discovers she must move to the Midwest, or the price of existing Volkswagen convertibles was bid up when it was announced that no more would be made.

Scarcity is enhanced if we discover that others want what we want, particularly if the item is limited in quantity or unique. A common ploy to close a negotiation is to suggest, directly or indirectly, that there is someone else interested in the deal if you do not accept it or that another offer is pending. (Lying about the existence of a competing offer is an ethical issue, as we will see in Chapter 10.)

Introducing deadlines into a negotiation is a way to create a vanishing opportunity or scarcity. Deadlines may be imposed by one side in the form of a threat, or created by external factors, like the end of a tax year. Time limits or deadlines can also be agreed to between the negotiating parties. Mutually imposed deadlines help structure negotiations and ensure a finite conclusion. So deadlines can be used cooperatively in negotiations, as well as in a unilateral, threatening way. Of course, agreed-upon deadlines can be extended by agreement and unilateral deadlines may also be subject to negotiation.

The following reading further explains the use of exploding offers and suggests a way to deal with them in select situations.

❖ **Robert J. Robinson,** *DEFUSING THE EXPLODING OFFER: THE*
FARPOINT GAMBIT

11 Negot. J. 277 (1995)

Why Are Exploding Offers Made?

It is not difficult to understand the thinking behind the use of exploding offers, in terms of the perceived advantage this affords the offeror. The ability to impose terms and back them up with a tight time limit may force the other side to capitulate or agree before it might otherwise have done so, increasing the value of the deal for the party making the offer. In many ways, the exploding offer is the ultimate hard bargaining tactic: Party A makes a final offer and then threateningly says, "And that's good until noon tomorrow. After that you can find another partner." In essence, the tactic defines an end to the negotiation process: An exploding offer is not only an offer in the traditional sense but is also the last offer. Rejection will automatically terminate the negotiation, and in some cases, the relationship as well. . . .

There is also another reason why the exploding offer is used. It can be a sign of offer weakness that might not be at all apparent to the recipient of the offer, but is almost always present. Negotiators who use exploding offers may perceive themselves to be at a disadvantage relative to their competitors. . . . Or they may have severe time or budget constraints. Once again, the function of the exploding offer can be either to force a quick acceptance by ending the negotiation (and thus avoiding the necessity of sweetening the deal to an unacceptably high level) or to restrict the ability of the recipient to comparison-shop, and therefore discover that the market was willing to pay at a significantly higher level.

Dealing with Exploding Offers: Try Being Reasonable First

In the tradition of *Getting to YES* (Fisher and Ury 1981), and *Getting Past No* (Ury 1991), there are a number of possibilities which exist for the individual faced with an exploding offer. Most of these involve getting away from positional stances, in order to explore underlying interests, and to look to create value via "principled negotiation" (Lax and Sebenius 1986). It is important to realize that exploding offers can be dealt with using these techniques, especially if there is some degree of goodwill in the interaction. An exploding offer is often made by a party who believes it stands to lose out in the negotiation, or is unsure of its power. Building trust and appealing to reason can go a long way toward addressing this underlying concern, resulting in the exploding aspect of the offer being withdrawn. . . .

The recipient of the exploding offer should also be prepared to make sensible counteroffers. He or she should be able to say when they *would* be in a position to accept, and to explain why this date makes sense (as opposed to choosing an equally arbitrary future time such as a week or ten days). . . . My first recommendation is, then, to engage in problem solving with respect to uncovering interests, generating and exploring options, moving to creative solutions, and emphasizing relationship issues. However, this can fail if the other party is unsympathetic, or locked into a positional or cynical stance. In such an instance, particularly if one feels that the other side is behaving in an ethically questionable fashion, I recommend the "Farpoint Gambit."

Fighting Fire with Fire: The Farpoint Gambit

While I always recommend first attempting a "principled" or integrative solution, I believe that when such tactics prove untenable, more assertive steps need to be taken. Doing this successfully depends on understanding where the power of the exploding offer resides. Exploding offers pivot on a credible, inviolable deadline. If the deadline is violated and the negotiation continues, the credibility of the explosion (the removal of the offer) is destroyed. And if the other side has depended on this threat as a central tactic, their entire position may collapse, putting the recipient of the initial offer in a very advantageous position. The technique I recommend, which I call the "Farpoint Gambit," is from the catalog of "hoist-them-by-their-own-petard" tools, which sometimes makes it particularly satisfying to employ.

The Farpoint Gambit derives from an episode of the science fiction television show, *Star Trek[: The] Next Generation*, in which the crew of the *Enterprise* (the spaceship from Earth) is put on trial by a powerful alien, "for the crimes of humanity." (The episode is called "Encounter at Farpoint," hence the name of the technique.) The alien creates a kangaroo court with himself as judge, and the captain of the *Enterprise* (Jean-Luc Picard) defends the human race. At a certain point, the alien judge becomes piqued by the captain's spirited defense, and says to the bailiff, "Bailiff, if the next word out of the defendant's mouth is anything but guilty, kill him!" He then turns to Picard and asks, "Defendant, how do you plead?" Picard thinks for a moment as the bailiff menacingly points a weapon at him, then firmly announces: "Guilty." As the courtroom gasps (and after an inevitable television commercial break), he adds, "Provisionally." This is essentially the Farpoint Gambit.

The alien has presented Picard with the ultimate coercive offer: Say you're guilty or I'll kill you. Obviously, Picard doesn't think he's guilty but he doesn't want to die. The power of the threat depends on getting Picard to admit that he's guilty — he does, but in such a way ("provisionally") that the alien judge is compelled to ask, "And what is the provision?" Picard then proceeds to talk his way out of the jam (as always happens with television heroes), and all is well. The point is that the alien is caught in his own trap: He's still arguing with Picard, who is still not guilty or dead. In the same way, an exploding offer can be defused by embracing it, using the Farpoint Gambit. . . .

The key is to make requests that are completely reasonable, but which will eventually result in the deadline being violated, due to the need for further clarification, or the lack of authority of the negotiator making the offer. Once the deadline passes, the credibility of the threat is destroyed, and successive attempts to set arbitrary deadlines can be dealt with in exactly the same way. The recipient of the offer can accept at his or her leisure, or reject the offer based on an unsatisfactory resolution of the provisions of the original acceptance.

The Farpoint Gambit also works by leveraging off fractures in the other side, or the imperfections in their informational strategies. . . . In such situations it is extremely easy to accept "pending satisfactory resolution of these issues," and then to continue to negotiate those and other issues.

The success of the Farpoint Gambit ultimately rests on the notion that the person receiving the exploding offer can eventually withdraw from the situation if no satisfactory resolution is forthcoming, without the offeror being able (or included) to sanction them for doing so. While this technique is about helping people get what they want from a coercive negotiating partner, it is not about helping people find a way to wriggle out of commitments given in good faith when they change their minds or get a better offer.

Inevitably, some negotiations, even those resuscitated by the Farpoint Gambit, are bound to fail. However, if conditions are attached to the acceptance — and these are not, by a reasonable assessment, met — then there really is not anything the company can do when the student withdraws, or the faculty candidate accepts an offer elsewhere, although possible reputational damage should still not be overlooked. It may be that each side has as much stake as the other, which will help to keep both reasonable — no organization wants to get the reputation for strong-arming prospective employees with techniques of dubious morality. In other cases, there may be actual legal provisions which allow the individual to withdraw within a specified time limit after accepting, such as in the case of signing an agreement to purchase a car.

The Farpoint Gambit has further advantage: It is nonescalative and non zero-sum in nature. Like the crew of the *Enterprise* in their endless quest for new frontiers, the Farpoint Gambit may force negotiators toward improved solutions at the "Pareto frontier" (see, e.g., Raiffa 1982). It moves the parties in the "right" direction, that is, toward one another rather than apart. In this sense, the Farpoint Gambit is not as dangerous as techniques that require one side to call the other's bluff, or see who can hold out the longest. In these latter cases, someone frequently wins, and someone loses. The Farpoint Gambit is about both sides being able to take care of underlying interests, and thus enable both to "win" and get what they want, with the offeror paying a fair price.

In Conclusion: When to Use — or Not Use — the Gambit

I would strongly caution against using the Farpoint Gambit as a routine technique to gain advantage. Nothing is more frustrating and unaccepting than someone who makes a habit of taking a deal, and who then continues to impose conditions or introduce new issues. Indeed, this is the flip side of the reprehensible lowballing technique employed by shady salespersons. In pondering this, I have come up with some guidelines for situations in which I believe it is legitimate to employ the Farpoint Gambit.

Ideally, I would make sure that all three of these conditions were present before I would feel completely comfortable in using this tactic:

* If the other side is perceived by the recipient of the exploding offer to be behaving unethically, and does not respond to appeals to reason;
* The recipient is truly interested in making a deal but needs more time to make a decision; and/or
* There genuinely are issues that need clarification, which would make the difference between accepting or rejecting the deal.

The Farpoint Gambit is a technique that should not be used lightly, in a spirit of deception, or with a lack of good faith. However, in situations where the individual is trapped by the hardball tactics of an offeror who relies on an exploding offer, the Farpoint Gambit offers a means whereby the pressure applied by the other side can be turned against them, much as a judo expert can use a foe's momentum to provide the energy which leads to the latter's own undoing. To be sure, this is itself a hardball tactic, and many might not feel comfortable using it. I offer the Farpoint Gambit as someone who has seen many friends, loved ones, and students put under enormous pressure, forced to make critical life decisions under unnecessarily difficult circumstances due to the callous use of power by people and institutions not operating in good faith.

---

3. Decision Tree Analysis

Moving toward closure by evaluating offers in light of probable BATNAs and making decisions about what is on the negotiation table may be aided by the use of decision tree analysis. Decision tree analysis provides a tool for making decisions in a rational, methodical, quantitative way, particularly in the face of uncertainty. Regularly taught in business schools to quantify strategic business choices, decision tree analysis has more recently been adopted within the legal community as an aid to decision making in complex litigation and in negotiations.

Decision tree analysis is a graphic version of the decision process we often engage in intuitively when we make common life decisions. Suppose, for example, that you are planning to go out, but it is threatening to rain. You listen to the weather report to learn the probability of rain to make a decision about taking an umbrella. After learning the percentage chance of rain, you then determine how far you have to walk to calculate the probable risk and degree of getting wet. Next, you calculate the discomfort and damage depending on how you are dressed. Each decision is discounted or multiplied by the next to make a rational final choice. The higher the likelihood of rain, the less far the walk need be before deciding to carry an umbrella. The more casually you are dressed, the lower the need to take an umbrella.

Making decisions in litigation and business settings can become more complicated because of the number of choices, the number of possible consequences and their probability, and the impact of decisions at each stage on later choices. More than intuition may be needed to make a rational series of decisions and keep track of the probabilities along the way. Decision tree analysis can help with this task.

The first step in decision tree analysis is to convert a set of possible decisions into a graphic format—a decision tree graph. The decision tree displays possible decision choices and the probable consequences of each choice. The decision tree graph then leads to the next set of decision choices on a new limb of the tree and all of those probable outcomes. The decision maker works through the tree graph in sequence, one limb at a time, and makes decisions based on the most favorable probable outcomes expressed in quantitative sums. The process is both logical and intuitive.

Decision tree analysis is also helpful because it requires that we and our clients write down all the explicit factors to be considered. This methodical process discourages us from taking mental shortcuts that leave out important points and considerations that should be factored into our clients' decisions. Going through a decision tree analysis with a client, in addition to promoting rationality, prevents misunderstandings and second guessing about strategic choices.

The following explanation will help you understand how to create and read decision trees as an aid to making decisions about settlement of pending litigation, even if you went to law school—because math is not on the LSAT.

❖ **Richard Birke,** DECISION TREES—MADE EASY
(2010)

Evaluating what a lawsuit is worth is difficult. The use of decision trees can make this difficult task somewhat easier. However, much of the literature on decision trees is too complicated for the average practitioner to use. This very short piece is an attempt to make this important tool more accessible.

Every negotiation or mediation of a legal dispute involves a comparison between the last offer made by the other side and the expected value of continuing on with litigation (or arbitration). On the one hand, there is a sure thing (the offer), and on the other is a risky alternative (litigation/adjudication).

In some cases, the client is unsure of how to compare the value of an offer to settle to the value of continuing litigation. In these cases, the client would do well to understand how to use a simple decision tree. The tree would help them determine the ballpark for an appropriate settlement.

There are seven simple steps that any person can take that will enable them to set up and use a decision tree to help them evaluate their claim. These are:

1. Use numbers when speaking about probability.
2. Pare the case down to no more than four major areas of uncertainty (fewer is better).

3. Learn to set up a simple tree in a logical order.
4. Assign probabilities based on the strengths and weaknesses in the case, working from left to right.
5. Add in the financial awards associated with the various ways the case might end.
6. Do the math to solve the tree.
7. Add in costs as appropriate.

Using Numbers

When lawyers talk about the value of trial with their clients, they tend to shy away from using numbers to express probabilities. This reluctance is understandable — law is not an exact science, and lawyers fear overpromising. So instead of saying "we have a 90% chance of winning," lawyers use phrases like "we have a good shot at winning" or "our case is strong." In workshops I have run in which I ask lawyers to assign a number to these phrases, they exhibit spreads of more than 50% between the intended probability and the understood probability. That is, the lawyer could say "we have a good shot," intending to express that the case is a winner 40% of the time, and the client could understand that the lawyer expressed an 80% likelihood. Words simply do not adequately express probabilistic estimates. Lawyers have to buckle under and start using numbers.

Determining the Significant Uncertainties

Lawsuits may be complicated, but disputes about the value of these lawsuits typically boil down to a small handful of disagreements between the parties. Ask what are the areas about which the parties are really far apart, and the answers are often differences like one side believes that a motion *in limine* will be granted and the other believes it will be denied. One side believes that their client will be believed by the jury and the other side believes that the client will be easily impeached. Each side is optimistic that the judge will use their jury instruction. The potential number of such disagreements is vast, but in any particular lawsuit, the number of really significant areas of disagreement is small. These disagreements represent the significant uncertainties in the case.

Setting up Trees

I like to think of decision trees as roadmaps with a few intersections, and each intersection has some discrete number of forks in the road. The intersections represent the areas of uncertainty and the number of forks represents the number of ways the issue could come out. For example, in a simple tort case in which the uncertainties are "will plaintiff prove duty," "will plaintiff prove breach," and "will plaintiff prove causation," there are three intersections, each with two forks — one for yes and one for no. Some intersections in some cases could have more than two forks. In a case in which one of the major areas of uncertainty is the credibility of a witness, there could be a fork representing "jury believes every bit of testimony," another for "jury believes nothing," and a third for "jury believes some but not all." Similarly, an intersection representing the various monetary awards that a jury might assign could have many forks.

An easy way to make sure that the tree is set up in a logical manner is to start at the left and move chronologically through the dispute. Our tort case might have duty as the first intersection, breach as the second, and causation as the third. A tree might be set up in a different manner (perhaps in order of most contested issue to least), but a chronological effort usually yields a competent result.

Each fork in the tree will end at a terminal point, and the package of terminal points represents all the different ways that a case could come out. In our tort liability case, there are four terminal points. One is where plaintiff fails to prove duty, in which case the lawsuit is over. The second is where plaintiff proves duty, but fails to prove breach, in which case the lawsuit is over. The third is where plaintiff proves duty and breach but not causation, and the fourth is where plaintiff proves all three elements.

Probabilities

First, look at each intersection and write down all the reasons why a case may travel each fork. In the tort case, the fork labeled "plaintiff proves duty" will have a yes fork and a no fork. The reasons why the case might go to the yes fork may be that plaintiff has good witnesses, a friendly judge, a good legal ruling or case, etc. The reasons why the case might go to the no fork might be related to uncertainty about witnesses, opposing legal case law, etc.

Analyze the factors that surround each intersection and then fill in the probabilities from left to right, and be careful not to double-count factors in your analysis. For example, imagine a case in which plaintiff was very concerned that a witness who would testify about duty and about breach might not show up for the trial. This might result in plaintiff assigning a lower probability to "prove duty," and it may appear again in the "prove breach" intersection. However, it would be incorrect to discount the case two times because of this witness. If the witness doesn't show up, plaintiff will not prove duty, and the case will not ever get to the "prove breach" intersection. Put another way, if plaintiff is at the "prove breach" intersection and is assigning a probability to that intersection, plaintiff has to take into account the fact that the witness has shown up. If you fill in from left to right and you take into account what has already happened in the intersections to the left, you will not run into dependent variable problems because you will have only counted each factor one time.

Add in the Awards

The awards attached to winning a lawsuit are sometimes clear — imagine our tort case involves an insurance policy with limits far below the value of the injuries, and that there is no possibility of an award in excess of the limits. So everyone in this case would know that if plaintiff prevailed, the award would be $1,000,000. In other cases, the awards might be highly variable, and that uncertainty would be another intersection in the tree with an appropriate number of forks.

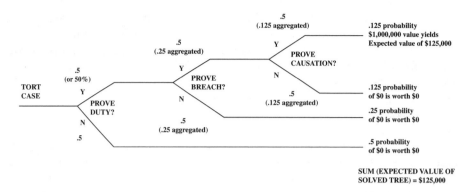

SUM (EXPECTED VALUE OF
SOLVED TREE) = $125,000

Solving the Tree

Now comes simple math. Each terminal point consists of a probability and a value. Assume for the moment that each element of our tort case has a 50/50 probability. That means that 50% of all cases result in a terminal point we can call "P didn't prove duty." The award is 0. The second terminal point "proved duty but not breach" will have a 25 percent probability (50% of 50%) and a value of 0. The third, "proved duty and breach but not causation" will have a 12.5% chance and a value of 0. The final terminal point shows a 12.5% chance of obtaining a $1,000,000 award value. A 50% chance of 0 is worth 0, a 25% chance of 0 is worth 0, a 12.5% chance of 0 is worth 0, and a 12.5% chance of a million dollars is worth $125,000. The sum is $125,000, and that is the solution of the tree.

Deduct Costs

If the trial would cost plaintiff $100,000—win or lose—we can deduct $100,000 from the solution of the tree, so that the net value of this lawsuit would be $25,000.

However, sometimes the costs vary depending on the nature of the uncertainties. For example, if the case has been tried already and is pending appeal, the uncertainties may be "will appellant win at the court of appeal" and "if they do, will they win at a new trial?" In this instance, if appellant loses at the court of appeal, they bear the costs of pursuing the appeal win or lose. If they win at the court of appeal and go to a new trial, they bear the cost of pursuing the appeal and the cost of the new trial. Thus the deductions of costs come not from the total expected value of the case, but at the end of each terminal point.

Still Not Simple Enough?

Here's a simple analogy that I like to use that helps me think of how these trees work. Imagine that there are 100 runners at the start of a race. The race course has a number of unmarked intersections. At each intersection, some number of runners will run in a way that brings them closer to the finish line, and some will turn in ways that will run them into a ditch, out of the race. Only runners who run the whole race will get a financial prize, and the rest will get nothing, and they may pay a fee for running.

Our 100 runners start, and 50 of them turn one way at the intersection of "prove duty" street and "don't prove duty" street. The 50 who run one way are still in the race with many intersections ahead, and the other 50 have run into a ditch and are out of the race. The remaining 50 split equally at the intersection of "prove breach" street and "don't prove breach" street, send 25 more into a ditch and 25 still in the race. At our third intersection, half run into a ditch and half run to the finish line where they each get a $1,000 prize. The average prize for each runner entering the race is $125, and if it cost each runner $100 to enter the race, the average take home reward is $25. If someone were to offer an individual runner $50 to buy her spot in the race, the runner would be well advised to take the money.

Of course, this assumes that the runner was in the race just for the money, and not to prove something to the defendant, or to herself, or to create a precedent. If the motivation for litigating has little to do with money, the decision tree is not a useful tool.

This is a very boiled-down discussion of a very well-studied topic. There are many wonderful, complex works on risk analysis, and the purpose of this short section is to whet your appetite. If this teaser was too much for you, then simply be aware that you can hire a consultant to help you in the appropriate case. If, on the other hand, this piece was not enough, then go to a search engine and find works by Marc Victor, Howard Raiffa, Bruce Beron, David Hofer, Marjorie Aaron, and others. They will help you get your fill.

Note: The Problem with Risk Analysis and Decision Trees

Decision trees create a mathematical model for risk analysis of the trial alternative to settlement. Although decision trees can be very helpful tools, they are based on what we know and, as Professor Birke points out, depend on "guesstimates." Even experienced trial attorneys and judges can only guess at a party's percentage chance of prevailing on a given set of facts, which are seldom clear. Some risk factors (uncertainty) come from factors that we may fail to build into our risk model or decision tree. For example, the decision tree might not factor in the possible bankruptcy of the defendant or his insurance carrier, or the death of a key witness. Nassim Taleb, in his book *The Black Swan* (2007), argues that in real-world situations there is always more that we don't know than we do, and that we tend to overvalue the known and undervalue the unknown and thereby expose ourselves to the most consequential risks when we least expect the outcome. Taleb reminds us that the "black swan" (his metaphor for highly consequential, improbable events) is produced in messy real-world circumstances where the gap between what we know and what we think we know can become dangerously wide. He postulates that our modern taste for data and "objective" decision-making models have increasingly undermined this part of the risk inquiry.

More questions about lawyer risk analysis are raised by a recent study of 4,532 civil litigation cases over a 44-year period. This study found that decisions to reject settlement offers and proceed to trial very often resulted in court outcomes no better than had the offer been accepted. Comparing the actual trial results with the rejected pretrial settlement offers, the study finds that 61 percent of plaintiffs and 24 percent of defendants obtained an award at trial that was the same as or worse than the result that could have been achieved by accepting the opponent's pretrial settlement proposal. Although plaintiffs experienced adverse trial outcomes more frequently than defendants, the financial costs incurred by defendants when they lost their litigation wagers were significantly higher than plaintiffs' error costs. The decision errors were worse in the most recent three years studied than in the previous 40 years, even with modern attention to jury verdict information and decision tree analysis. The average cost of "decision error," as the co-authors term these adverse trial outcomes, was $43,100 for plaintiffs and $1,140,000 for defendants during the 2002-2005 period (Kiser et al., 2008).

Questions

4. Is there any reason to think that the use of decision trees for case settlement would be favored more by plaintiffs or more by defendants? Why?
5. If you created a decision tree to assist you and your client in evaluating a case for settlement purposes, would you share it with the opposing side? Under what circumstances might you reveal it?
6. Are opposing sides likely to agree about the determinant events or decision points for constructing a decision tree? Are they likely to agree on the probability percentages assigned at each decision node, or the chance of the other side winning?
7. Would a decision tree be helpful in evaluating and settling a case on appeal? What would an appellate case decision tree look like, and how many branches would there be?

CHAPTER
7

Negotiation Step by Step—The End

A. Impasse or Agreement

Although a negotiation may appear to be moving toward closure, some gaps or differences can still exist. Both sides must assess if what is on the table is or is not better than no agreement. Adversarial negotiators may see this as the time to add new demands or conditions, and competitive bargainers may test an opponent's resolve by threatening to end the negotiation. More cooperative negotiators will see the need for joint problem solving and explore the possibility of improving the outcome for both sides. Several endgame moves or collaborative strategies are available to bring closure. Some of these focus on closing remaining economic gaps in the settlement or transaction, and some look for agreement by attending to matters beyond money. We now look at some approaches to breaking impasse.

1. Apologies

Some negotiations reach an impasse even though economic considerations do not seem to present an obstacle. Progress on substantive matters may stall because something gets in the way of a final agreement, but it is not always clear what that "something" is. As you now know, negotiated settlements depend on satisfaction of three sets of needs — economic, emotional, and extrinsic — that form the three sides of the settlement triangle, presented in Chapter 1. It may be difficult to quantify the emotional and extrinsic factors, but there are ways to satisfy emotional and social needs in a manner that creates value. Offering something other than money that fills a felt need can be worth more to the recipient than what is given up by the offering party. An apology and its acceptance illustrate this point.

The most readily identified words indicating an apology are "I'm sorry." This usually marks the beginning of an apology, but the most effective apologies contain several elements:

1. Expressing regret for the wrong suffered (I'm sorry);
2. Manifesting sympathy for the injury or hurt;
3. Admitting responsibility or blame;
4. Promising forbearance — not to do it again; and
5. Offering repair or compensation.

Saying you are sorry and showing sympathy without admitting fault is a partial apology that might help, but it can also make matters worse if perceived as insincere or a brush-off. A "full apology" would include at least the first three elements on the list. The third element, admitting fault, in many situations is the key component of an apology. However, admitting fault can be legally dangerous because the admission may be admissible evidence at trial to establish liability. The two elements of providing assurances that the wrong will not happen again and offering compensation create the perfect apology package.

The hoped-for counterpart or trade-off for an apology is forgiveness. Forgiveness may create value by filling needs for both the recipient and the forgiving party. An apology, even if not full or perfect, and expressions of forgiveness can unlock a stalled negotiation and facilitate closure. Although we have placed this material on apology at a late stage of the "negotiation dance," when impasse occurs, an apology that precedes negotiation or is offered in the earliest stages may be most effective. In resolving some disputes, the amount of compensation or other substantive considerations may be secondary to an apology and resulting forgiveness. In other cases, an apology might not matter or could be seen as manipulative.

The role of apologies in settling cases has become a subject of increased interest as states consider legislation providing evidentiary protection or "safe harbor" for apologies made by people who have done harm to those on the receiving end of a tort or wrong. Several significant law review articles have examined the appropriateness and effect of apologies on settlement, most drawing on psychological literature and anecdotal experience (see, e.g., O'Hara & Yarn 2002; Taft 2000; Cohen 1999). The following reading reports on new systematic studies using a large number of participants, presented with two personal injury factual scenarios, to gauge the effects of different types of apologies on settlement negotiations. Receipt of a full apology expressing responsibility increased the acceptability of a settlement offer. In contrast, a partial apology expressing regret and sympathy, but not responsibility, did not help, and in the case of more clear liability and greater injuries, it appears to increase the likelihood that a settlement offer will be rejected.

❖ **Jennifer K. Robbennolt,** *Apologies and Legal Settlement:*
An Empirical Examination

102 Mich. L. Rev. 460 (2003)

It is often said that U.S. legal culture discourages apologies. Defendants, defense counsel, and insurers worry that statements of apology will be admissible at trial and will be interpreted by jurors and judges as admissions of responsibility. In recent years, however, several legal commentators have suggested that disputants in civil lawsuits should be encouraged to apologize to opposing parties. They claim that apologies will avert lawsuits and promote settlement. . . .

Survey research suggests that claimants desire apologies and that some would not have filed suit had an apology been offered. In addition, there is anecdotal evidence of . . . settlement negotiations coming to a standstill over the issue of apology even after agreement on an appropriate damage amount has been reached, of plaintiffs who would have preferred an apology as part of a settlement, and of occasions on which a failure to apologize promoted litigation by adding insult to injury. . . . [The author explains her experimental simulation methods for studying the role of apologies in legal settlement negotiations.]

Effects of Apologies on Settlement Decisionmaking [First Study]

The first study examined recipients' interpretations of apologies and the effects of those apologies on willingness to accept a settlement offer in the dispute. The hypothetical scenario detailed a relatively simple personal-injury dispute: a pedestrian-bicycle accident. All participants reviewed this scenario and evaluated the same settlement offer.

Control participants evaluated a version of the scenario in which no apology was offered. Additional participants evaluated versions of the scenario in which two variables, the nature of the apology offered and the nature of the applicable evidentiary rule, were varied. First, the nature of the apology offered was varied to compare the effects of a partial apology, in which the other party merely expressed sympathy for the potential claimant's injuries, with the effects of a full apology, in which he or she also took responsibility for causing the injuries. Second, the evidentiary rule described to participants was varied to examine how different evidentiary rules influence the interpretation and effectiveness of an apology, comparing respondents' reactions to an apology where the evidentiary rules protected the apology, where the evidentiary rules did not protect the apology, and where no evidentiary rule was described. Thus, there were seven different variations of the basic scenario. One hundred forty-five people participated in the study and were randomly assigned to the experimental conditions.

Effects of Apology on Settlement

The first set of analyses compared the two different types of apology (partial and full) to the no-apology control where no evidentiary rule was specified. It was predicted that the nature of the apology would influence participants' settlement decisions. Moreover, based on the previous research on the psychological effects of apologies, it was predicted that an apology would influence settlement decisionmaking through its effects on participants' perceptions and attributions. That is, participants' interpretations of the apology, their affective reactions, and their evaluations of the situation and the offender were expected to mediate the effects of an apology on their settlement decisions: the nature of the apology would influence these perceptions and attributions, which would in turn influence settlement decisions.

Effect of Apology on Settlement Decisions

First, even though all participants were told that they had suffered the same injuries and received the same offer of settlement, the nature of the apology offered influenced recipients' willingness to accept the offer. . . . When no apology was offered 52% of respondents indicated that they would definitely or probably accept the offer, while 43% would definitely or probably reject the offer and 5% were unsure. When a partial apology was offered, only 35% of respondents were inclined to accept the offer, 25% were inclined to reject it, and 40% indicated that they were unsure. In contrast, when a full apology was offered, 73% of respondents were inclined to accept the offer, with only 13-14% each inclined to reject it or remaining unsure. . . .

Comparing each type of apology to the condition in which no apology was received, receiving a partial apology increased the likelihood that the respondent would be unsure about how to respond to the settlement offer, and receiving a full apology increased the likelihood that the respondent would choose to accept the offer and decreased the likelihood that the respondent would choose to reject the offer.

The Role of Perceptions and Attributions

Next, the study examined the effects of the nature of the apology on a number of constructs thought to underlie the effect of apology on settlement decisionmaking. Where there were differences in participants' responses across conditions, the differences follow a strikingly similar pattern: offering no apology or a partial apology elicited equivalent responses that were both different from the responses elicited when a full apology was offered. . . .

Thus, a full apology was viewed as more sufficient than either a partial apology or no apology. An offender who offered a full apology was seen as experiencing more regret, as more moral, and as more likely to be careful in the future than one offering a partial or no apology. While an offender offering a full apology was seen as believing that he or she was more responsible for the incident than one who offered a partial or no apology, the conduct of the full apologizer was judged more favorably than that of offenders who offered either a partial or no apology. Participants expressed greater sympathy and less anger at the offender who offered a full apology than they did at offenders who offered either a partial or no apology. Participants also indicated more willingness to forgive an offender who gave a full apology than they did for offenders offering a partial or no apology and expected that less damage to the parties' relationship would result following a full apology than they did following a partial or no apology. Finally, participants indicated that the settlement offer would better make up for their injuries when they had received a full apology than when they had received either a partial or no apology.

Therefore, apologies influenced the inclination to accept or reject a settlement offer. The effect of an apology on settlement decisions was complex, however, and depended on the type of apology offered. Only the full, responsibility-accepting apology increased the likelihood that the offer would be accepted. The partial, sympathy-expressing, apology, in contrast, increased participants' uncertainty about whether or not to accept the offer.

Moreover, apologies were found to influence ratings of numerous variables that are thought to underlie the settlement decision. The effects of apologies on these underlying constructs, however, were limited to the full apology in which the offender accepted responsibility. Offering a partial apology was no different from offering no apology at all. These underlying judgments are likely to favorably change the dynamics of the negotiation and also provided the mechanism by which apologies influenced settlement decisions. . . .

Factors Influencing the Effects of Apologies [Second Study]

A second study was conducted to explore the boundaries of these findings. This study, again, examined recipients' interpretations of apologies and the effect of those apologies on willingness to accept a settlement offer in the dispute. This time, however, in addition to the nature of the apology and the type of evidentiary rule, the strength of the evidence of the offender's fault and the severity of the resulting injury were manipulated. . . .

Consistent with the results of the first study, apologies influenced participants' attributions and perceptions of the situation and the offender. Overall, full apologies improved the participants' perceptions of the situation and the offender, while partial apologies did little to alter such perceptions. Exploration of the possible moderating influences of the severity of the injury and the evidence of the offender's responsibility revealed some interesting boundary conditions on these overall results. In particular, there were patterns in the data suggesting both that partial apologies may negatively impact perceptions where responsibility is relatively clear or where the injury is more severe and that partial apologies may positively impact perceptions where responsibility is relatively less clear or where the injury is relatively minor. . . .

Defendants

In the absence of statutory protection, defendants or potential defendants who desire to apologize are faced with balancing the effects of apologies on different types of judgments — settlement decisionmaking, liability decisions, and decisions about appropriate damage awards — as well as weighing the less strategic aspects of apologizing. The results of the instant studies inform one important component of these interrelated decisions — the impact of apology on settlement decisions. An important lesson for defendants to draw from these data is that apologies can have beneficial effects on settlement, altering the injured parties' perceptions of the situation and the offender so as to make them more amenable to settlement discussions and ultimately more likely to accept an offer.

As a general matter, the results of the present study provide evidence that a full apology that both expresses sympathy for the victim's injuries and accepts responsibility for those injuries influences a variety of perceptions and attributions about the situation and the other party that might lead to a settlement or allow the parties to begin discussions. Full apologies were seen as more sufficient apologies, as evidencing more regret and a greater likelihood of care in the future, and as offered by people of higher moral character. Full apologies favorably altered assessments of the conduct leading to the injuries and changed the emotions of the injured party so as to reduce anger and increase sympathy for the offender. Full apologies were seen as mitigating potential damage to the relationship, were more likely to lead to forgiveness, and inclined injured parties to look more favorably on the settlement offer. In addition, the results of the first study demonstrated that full apologies, through these effects on perceptions and attributions, increased the likelihood that the settlement offer would be accepted.

Accordingly, full apologies that include accepting responsibility for the incident may facilitate the settling of lawsuits. These "responsibility-accepting" apologies, however, are precisely the type of apologies that most clearly raise concerns about the effects of apologizing on liability decisionmaking and are not likely to be protected by evidentiary rules protecting apologies. Making a statement that admits fault and that might be admissible at trial, while improving the prospects for settling the case, is thought to increase the risk that the offender will be found liable.

For this reason, there is growing interest in ways in which offenders can apologize without exposing themselves to the same risks attendant to a full, responsibility-accepting apology. The present research suggests that the effects of such partial apologies are complex and identifies several aspects of the case that defendants ought to take into account when considering a partial apology. First, the effects of partial apologies on settlement decisionmaking appear to be much more complicated than the effects of full apologies. On the whole, partial apologies did not appear to facilitate settlement in the ways hoped by proponents. The most consistent finding was that partial apologies tended to be no better (or worse) than not offering an apology. Across both studies, regardless of the level of responsibility and the level of injury, there were no differences between those receiving partial apologies and no apology in their evaluations of the offender's conduct, the offender's regret, the offender's belief that he or she was responsible, damage to the relationship, anger, the degree to which the offer would make up for the injuries, or forgiveness. . . .

Overall, . . . it appears that a partial apology, while perhaps minimizing the risk that the apology will be considered an admission and result in an adverse liability decision, may not be terribly effective at improving the prospects for settlement. This may be because partial apologies do not communicate the same messages to recipients that full apologies do. In these studies, the partial apology, unlike the full apology, did not consistently convey to the recipient that the offender had accepted responsibility for his or her behavior, that he or she regretted the behavior, and, accordingly, that the offender would not repeat the conduct. . . .

Thus, a defendant or potential defendant who wants to fully apologize may face the uncertain effects of the apology on liability and damage-award decisions if settlement negotiations fail, but may benefit from an improved settlement climate and an improved chance of avoiding litigation altogether.
Defendants contemplating a partial, sympathy-expressing apology may not face the same liability risks. The beneficial effects of such apologies are not clear, however, and there is evidence of some risk that perceptions will be negatively impacted. Thus, defendants must be carefully attuned to the types of factors identified here, in particular the severity of the plaintiff's injury and the degree to which the offender appears to be responsible, in evaluating these rules.

Plaintiffs

In contrast to defendants, plaintiffs or potential plaintiffs must determine how to respond to an apology from someone they believe has wronged them. Many observers have expressed concern that plaintiffs may be induced by an apology to agree to a settlement that does not provide them with the monetary recovery to which they are entitled. Importantly, this concern is sometimes dismissed by assuming that plaintiffs are capable of evaluating an apology for its sincerity and strategic motivation and can assess apologies and settlement offers accordingly.

The results of the present studies suggest that plaintiffs may, in fact, be able to critically evaluate the content of an apology and to distinguish those that they find credible and that communicate the necessary information from those that do not. Participants in the studies evaluated partial apologies very differently from full apologies. Participants did not interpret partial apologies as conveying the same evidence of regret, acceptance of responsibility, or likelihood of greater care in the future as full apologies. . . . [H]owever, it is plausible that some plaintiffs would be willing to accept a smaller financial settlement if they receive an apology. If this is true, one explanation may be that they have been unfairly induced to forego their rightful compensation. An alternative explanation may be that they are more satisfied by a combination of financial compensation and the apology than they would have been with a larger monetary amount and no apology. Plaintiffs may value the apology more than or differently from financial compensation. Indeed, motivations other than legal entitlement and monetary recovery may be important to plaintiffs. While a monetary settlement may adequately restore financial losses resulting from an injury, an apology may be a better mechanism for restoring less tangible damage, expressing the proper relative moral positions of the parties, assuring the injured party that the offender will not reoffend, or achieving restorative justice. . . .

Note: Evidentiary Consequences of Apologies

Pursuant to the Federal Rules of Evidence and state evidence rules, admissions by party opponents are generally admissible at trial, as an exception to the hearsay rule. Apologies that include admissions of fault would be admissible under Federal Rule of Evidence 801(d)(2) and under state rules of evidence. However, most states now have confidentiality protections that preclude admission into evidence of what is said and done in mediation. Apologies offered as part of the mediation process are generally safe from evidentiary admission.

Several states have enacted laws intended to encourage apologies and "other benevolent gestures" on the scene of an accident and in negotiations afterwards. In 1986, Massachusetts became the first state to adopt a rule of evidence intended to preclude evidentiary admission of apologies for purposes of establishing liability. Following the lead of Massachusetts, Texas (1999), California (2000), Florida (2001), and Washington (2002) have amended their evidence codes to provide some protection for certain types of apologies. Although the language varies from state to state, California Evidence Code section 1160 is typical: "[S]tatements, writings, or benevolent gestures expressing sympathy or a general sense of benevolence relating to the pain, suffering, or death of a person involved in an accident . . . and made to that person or to the family of that person shall be inadmissible as evidence of an admission of liability in a civil action. The statement of fault, however, which is part of, or in addition to, any of the above shall not be inadmissible pursuant to this section." It is important to note that the California legislation, as well as that of other states, only encourages partial apologies that do not admit fault.

Colorado has gone further to encourage full apologies in medical malpractice situations. The Colorado "I'm Sorry" rule, effective in 2003, provides: "[I]n any civil action brought by an alleged victim of an unanticipated outcome of medical care, or in any arbitration proceeding related to such civil action, any and all statements, affirmations, gestures, or conduct expressing apology, fault, sympathy, commiseration, condolence, compassion, or a general sense of benevolence which are made by a health care provider or an employee of a health care provider to the alleged victim, a relative of the alleged victim, or a representative of the alleged victim and which relate to the discomfort, pain, suffering, injury, or death of the alleged victim as the result of the unanticipated outcome of medical care shall be inadmissible as evidence of an admission of liability or as evidence of an admission against interest" (Colo. Rev. Stat. Sec. 13-25-135). Since the passage of the Colorado statute in 2003, many states have enacted legislation providing some form of protection for apologies by health care providers, including Oregon, Oklahoma, Wyoming, Ohio, North Carolina, South Dakota, West Virginia, Maryland, Georgia, and Arizona.

Questions

1. The Colorado rule quoted above was part of a tort reform campaign. Do you feel that the protection provided to health-care providers by this exclusionary rule is likely to encourage meaningful apologies? Does the rule in any way favor health-care providers at the expense of malpractice victims? (See Dauer 2005, 47.)

2. Does the California "benevolent gesture" rule go far enough? Would you support legislation that protected from evidentiary admission full apologies that refer to a tortfeasor's blame or wrongdoing? Why or why not?

3. In what type of cases would an apology be most effective to bring closure? What needs might an apology fill in such a case? Are there cases in which an apology would not work or would not be appropriate?

4. During the 2004 Super Bowl halftime show, singer Janet Jackson experienced a notorious "wardrobe malfunction" in which her co-star, Justin Timberlake, pulled off part of her costume, exposing her breast. A week later at the Grammies show, Timberlake made this statement about the incident: "I know it has been a rough week on everyone and, umm, what occurred was unintentional, completely regrettable, and I apologize if you guys were offended." Evaluate the quality of Timberlake's statement. Do you think it accomplished its purpose? If you had been his advisor, what would you have advised about what, if anything, to say and how to say it?

5. A highly publicized apology from basketball star Kobe Bryant in 2004 played a role in the dropping of criminal rape charges by the recipient of the apology and the settlement of a related civil suit. Do you think the following apology by Mr. Bryant was a spontaneous, benevolent gesture, or the result of careful drafting and negotiation by attorneys? What policy issues are raised by this apology, the subsequent dropping of criminal charges, and the negotiated settlement in 2005 that resolved the civil suit? What considerations and motivations, from both sides, prompted the inclusion of the specific wording that was used? What purpose did this apology serve?

> *First, I want to apologize directly to the young woman involved in this incident. I want to apologize to her for my behavior that night and for the consequences she has suffered in the past year. Although this year has been incredibly difficult for me personally, I can only imagine the pain she has had to endure. I also want to apologize to her parents and family members, and to my family and friends and supporters, and to the citizens of Eagle, Colorado.*
>
> *I also want to make it clear that I do not question the motives of this young woman. No money has been paid to this woman. She has agreed that this statement will not be used against me in the civil case. Although I truly believe this encounter between us was consensual, I recognize now that she did not and does not view this incident the same way I did. After months of reviewing discovery, listening to her attorney, and even her testimony in person, I now understand how she feels that she did not consent to this encounter.*
>
> *I issue this statement today fully aware that while one part of this case ends today, another remains. I understand that the civil case against me will go forward. That part of this case will be decided by and between the parties directly involved in the incident and will no longer be a financial or emotional drain on the citizens of the state of Colorado.*

6. In testimony on June 17, 2010, before the U.S. House of Representatives Energy Committee, BP's then-CEO Tony Hayward offered this apology for the worst environmental catastrophe in U.S. history: "The explosion and fire aboard the deepwater Horizon and the resulting oil spill in the Gulf of Mexico never should have happened and I'm deeply sorry that it did." Hayward went on to detail what BP was doing to remedy the spill, and BP did pledge a fund of $20 billion to pay resulting claims. However, Hayward did not admit BP's fault. Does the Hayward "apology" help or hurt BP. Why?

2. Splitting the Difference and Dealing with Impasse

A deceptively simple concluding technique often used in both competitive and cooperative negotiations is "splitting the difference." The rationale for splitting the difference and a couple of caveats about agreeing to it are discussed in a popular book by Richard Shell. Professor Shell also offers advice on what to do when the remaining gap causes the negotiation to reach impasse.

❖ **G. Richard Shell, *Bargaining for Advantage: Negotiation Strategies for Reasonable People***

185 (Penguin, 2006)

Perhaps the most frequently used closing technique is splitting the difference. Bargaining research tells us that the most likely settlement point in any given transaction is the midpoint between the two opening offers. People who instinctively prefer a compromise style like to cut through the whole bargaining process by getting the two opening numbers on the table and then splitting them right down the middle.

Even in cases in which the parties have gone through several rounds of bargaining, there often comes a time when one side or the other suggests that the parties meet halfway between their last position. In situations in which the relationship between the parties is important, this is a perfectly appropriate, smooth way to close.

Why is splitting the difference so popular? First, it appeals to our sense of fairness and reciprocity, thus, setting a good precedent for future dealings between the parties. . . . Each side makes an equal concession simultaneously. What could be fairer than that?

Second, it is simple and easy to understand. It requires no elaborate justification or explanation. The other side sees exactly what you are doing.

Third, it is quick. For people who do not like to negotiate or are in a hurry, splitting the difference offers a way out of the potentially messy interpersonal conflict that looms whenever a negotiation occurs.

Splitting the difference is such a common closing tactic that it often seems rude and unreasonable to refuse, regardless of the situation. This is taking a good thing too far, however. There are at least two important situations in which I would hesitate to split the difference.

First, you should be careful that the midpoint being suggested is genuinely fair to your side. If you have opened at a reasonable price and the other party opened at an aggressive one, the midpoint is likely to favor the other party by a big margin. So don't split the difference at the end if there was a lack of balance at the beginning. Second, when a lot of money or an important principle is on the line and relationships matter, quickly resorting to a splitting may leave opportunities for additional, creative options on the table. . . .

When the gap between offers is too wide to split, another friendly way to close is to obtain a neutral valuation or appraisal. If the parties cannot agree on a single appraiser, they can each pick one and agree to split the difference between the two numbers given by the experts.

What Happens if Negotiations Break Down?

The concession-making stage of bargaining sometimes ends with no deal rather than an agreement. The parties reach an impasse. In fact, a no deal result is sometimes the right answer. No deal is better than a bad deal. . . .

In addition to escalation problems, the parties may start too far apart to close the gap. Many times there are miscommunications, misunderstanding, and simple bad chemistry that the parties fail to overcome. Now what?

Jump-Starting the Negotiation Process

Perhaps the easiest way to overcome impasse is to leave yourself a back door through which to return to the table when you get up to leave it. "In light of the position you have taken," you might say as you pack your bags, "we are unable to continue negotiations at this time." An attentive opponent will pick up on your use of the words "at this time" and tactfully ask you later if the time has come to reinitiate talks. This back door also allows you to contact the other side at a later date without losing face.

If the other negotiator leaves in a genuine fit of anger, he may not be very careful about leaving a back door open. If so, you should consider how you can let him back in without unnecessary loss of face. You must, in one expert's phrase, build him a "golden bridge" across which to return to the table. Such bridges include "forgetting" that he made his ultimatum in the first place or recalling his last statement in a way that gives him an excuse for returning.

When miscommunication is the problem, a simple apology may be enough to get the parties back on track. If the relationship has deteriorated beyond apologies, changing negotiators or getting rid of intermediaries altogether may be necessary.

In America, the sport of professional baseball lost nearly two full seasons in the 1990s because of an impasse in negotiations between the players' union and the club owners. The team owners from the big cities wanted to limit the size of team payrolls. The team owners from smaller cities wanted the team owners from big cities to subsidize their franchises. The players wanted more money. It was a three-ring circus. The breakthrough came when the owners hired a new negotiator — a lawyer named Randy Levine — to represent them at the table. Levine acted in the role of mediator as much as advocate and brought a high degree of both credibility and creativity to the process that, according to one participant, "broke the dam of mistrust" that had built up between the parties. Another move that helped move the talks beyond impasse was getting all parties to agree to stop talking to the press and taking public positions that made it hard for them to compromise at the table. . . . [P]ublic commitments can help you stick to your goals, but there comes a time when it is in everyone's interest to get unstuck from their positions. In a high stakes negotiation such as a labor strike, this often means getting the parties out of the spotlight so they can work in private.

The worst impasses are the products of emotional escalation that builds on itself: My anger makes you angry, and your response makes me even angrier. . . . The solution to this sort of collision, in business deals as well as wars, is what I call the "one small step" procedure. One side needs to make a very small, visible move in the other side's direction, then wait for reciprocation. If the other party responds, the two can repeat the cycle again, and so on. Commentator Charles Osgood, writing about the Cold War in the early 1960s, created an acronym for this process: GRIT (Graduated and Reciprocated Initiatives in Tension Reduction).

Egypt's late prime minister, Anwar Sadat, used the "one small step" technique to deescalate the Arab-Israeli conflict when he flew to Jerusalem on November 19, 1977 and later met with Prime Minister Menachem Begin. By simply getting off a plane in Israel — a very small step indeed — Sadat demonstrated his willingness to recognize Israel's existence. This move eventually led to the Camp David peace accords and Israel's return of the Sinai Peninsula to Egypt.

An executive once told me a bargaining story that nicely sums up how the "one small step" process can work in everyday life. Two parties were in a complex business negotiation. Both were convinced that they had leverage, and both thought that the best arguments favored their own view of the deal. After a few rounds, neither side would make a move.

Finally one of the women at the table reached in her purse and pulled out a bag of M&M's. She opened the bag and poured the M&M's into a pile in the middle of the table.

"What are those for?" asked her counterparts.

"They are to keep score," she said.

Then she announced a small concession on the deal — and pulled an M&M out of the pile and put it on her side of the table.

"Now it's your turn," she said to the men sitting opposite.

Not to be outdone, her opponents put their heads together, came up with a concession of their own — and pulled out two M&M's. "Our concession was bigger than yours," they said.

The instigator of the process wisely let the other side win this little argument and then made another concession of her own, taking another M&M for herself.

It wasn't long before the parties were working closely together to close the final terms of the deal. Call this the M&M version of the GRIT process. Any similar mechanism that restarts the norm of reciprocity within the bargaining relationship will have a similar, helpful effect.

Overall, when parties reach an impasse, it is usually because each sees the other's demands as leaving it below its legitimate expectations. Eventually, if the parties are to make any progress, they must change their frame of reference and begin seeing that they will be worse off with no deal than they would be accepting a deal that falls below their original expectations.

Sometimes this transition takes time. The impasse must be allowed to last long enough that one or both parties actually alter their expectations. A final agreement must be seen as a gain compared with available alternatives.

Questions

7. Have you ever "split the difference" to conclude a negotiation or sale? Looking back, was that the best way to close the deal? Are you now sure you were not manipulated into an outcome or price that was more favorable to the other side? Have you used this closing tactic to your advantage?

8. Do you agree with Shell that impasse can often be helpful? If so, when? Why would anyone plan an impasse as part of their negotiating strategy?

---

3. Logrolling and Packaging

You should now be familiar with the concept that value is created through negotiation when what is received in trade is worth more to the recipient than to the provider. Logrolling involves conceding on low-priority interests to satisfy high-priority interests. Legislators logroll when they trade their vote on a matter of little concern in their district for another legislator's vote on an important issue in their own district. For example, a congressman from Montana might agree to vote for a federal rapid transit subsidy bill in return for a New York City congressman's vote for federal animal grazing subsidies. Logrolling creates value, because both legislators are better off if both bills pass than if neither passes. The New York congressman strongly favors the rapid transit bill, while only moderately opposing the grazing bill, and the Montana legislator strongly favors the animal grazing bill and only moderately opposes the rapid transit bill.

You should also understand that the difference between overlapping reservation points, or "bottom lines," of negotiators creates a bargaining zone within which agreement is likely. Differences in the value that negotiators place on multiple items or promises allow for integrated solutions that expand the bargaining zone. Packaging multiple items, adding items to the mix, and taking advantage of an expanded zone of possible agreement can help close a deal. Packaging requires flexibility and creativity because the negotiators may have initially perceived the negotiation to be fixed on a single item or a more limited set of trade-offs. Selling a car by including a longer warranty or a reduced-price luxury package is a sales example of packaging. When negotiating for office space, the landlord may not budge on the rent but will include in the package the use of his building crew to make office improvements or the use of free conference rooms.

Packaging is also used in negotiating the settlement of lawsuits. An agreement may not be possible based on the claim in litigation, but a universal settlement that resolves other pending or potential claims between the same parties or those aligned in interest may expand the bargaining range, and allow more high-priority/low-priority trade-offs that allow an agreement to be reached. It was this type of packaging that led to the "universal" settlement of the *Microsoft v. Stac* litigation described in Chapter 3. Each side agreed to drop its claims in the lawsuit in exchange for cross-licensing all of their existing patents as well as future ones over five years, and Microsoft agreed to pay Stac license royalties totaling $43 million over 43 months, while also investing $39.9 million for a 15 percent equity stake in Stac. Although most often associated with problem-solving negotiation, packaging and logrolling are frequently utilized by competitive negotiators at the end of the day. Effective negotiators, regardless of their general approach, will do what it takes to reach a settlement or complete a deal if they end up getting more than they have to give up.

4. Agree to Disagree: Contingent Agreements

If impasse is reached because of different predictions of future events or disagreement over risks, an agreement might be structured based on these differences. In short, you can agree to disagree and write contingent outcomes into the deal.

Recognition of different views and probability assessments of uncertain events can help conclude a negotiation and result in an agreement that builds on differences by rewarding the side that most accurately predicts an unknown future event or outcome. An impasse over the amount of rent for a new restaurant can be resolved by the landlord agreeing to a lower base rent for the skeptical or risk-averse renter, with an additional amount to be determined by the restaurant's revenue. A personal injury settlement negotiation that is stalled because of different predictions about the ongoing need for medical treatment can be resolved by a lump sum amount, with a contingent amount based on the speed of recovery.

Agreeing to disagree and leaving economic questions open to uncertain results through the use of contingent agreements has a down side. The uncertainty and the temptation to manipulate the contingencies on which future rewards are based can create moral dilemmas and future disputes. The nature, potential, and dilemmas of contingent agreements are discussed in the next reading.

❖ **Michael Moffitt,** *Contingent Agreements:*
Agreeing to Disagree About the Future

87 Marq. L. Rev. 691 (2004)

"That won't happen." "Yes, it will." "No, it won't." "Will too." "Will not."

Negotiators generally find no shortage of things about which to disagree. For example, negotiators seeking to resolve a dispute often have sharply differing perceptions of the past. What happened? Whose decisions and actions caused the effects in question? How does their conduct compare with expectations or duties? In some circumstances, settlement is impossible without resolution of these backward-looking questions. A significant component of classical dispute resolution theory suggests that one might overcome impasse by shifting the focus of conversations toward the future. Sometimes, however, the shift to a forward-looking exploration merely provides fertile, new grounds for disagreement. Rather than arguing about what happened, the negotiators argue about what will happen. A wholesaler asserts that demand for the product will skyrocket in the future, and the retailer suspects otherwise. A defendant points to the relatively minor and temporary injuries caused in a car crash, but the victim fears that currently undetected injuries may manifest themselves down the road. Instinct may suggest that one negotiator will need to persuade the other about the likelihood of future uncertain events. Instead, genuinely held disagreements about the future present an important opportunity for negotiators to discover an attractive trade. The vehicle for capturing this potential is the contingent agreement.

Structurally, a contingent agreement is one in which the parties identify the universe of possible future conditions and agree to take on different obligations in each of those conditions. The simplest contingent deals are those in which the future has only two possible relevant conditions. X will happen, or it will not. If X happens, the terms of our deal are ABC; otherwise, we will do DEF. If I think X is unlikely to happen, I will be happy to give you terms you prefer for ABC, in exchange for terms I favor for DEF. Believing that she will get the work finished on time, an author signs a lucrative book contract with a very harsh penalty for late completion. Buyer loves Seller's house, but really wants a property with off-street parking. Seller firmly expects that the city council will approve a variance required for construction of a new garage, but Buyer is less confident about the likelihood of getting approval. Buyer agrees to purchase the property from Seller at a reduced price, with a substantial additional payment to Seller if the City Council grants a variance within the next twelve months. Negotiators can craft attractive trades by establishing obligations that are contingent on a future uncertain event that affects each side's valuation of the agreement.

Contingent agreements can also include variable terms, pegged to some benchmark to be measured in the future. I think interest rates will increase over the next few months, and you think they will go down. If I am loaning you money today, we will each be happy to agree to a deal with a floating interest rate. A school board is nervous about the future level of state funding to the districts, while the teachers' union is optimistic. The teachers' union agrees to a wage and benefit increase tied to a particular line in next year's state budget. The plaintiff believes that he may suffer long-term health effects of exposure to the defendant's product, while the defendant believes no significant health risks exist. The defendant agrees to pay specified medical monitoring expenses for the plaintiff and to assume any future medical costs associated with exposure. Parties to a joint venture agree to final, binding resolution of their intellectual property dispute by an appointed arbitrator. Without the possibility of contingent agreements, uncertainty regarding future conditions can make distributive decisions (for example, who gets how much money) difficult. By linking the allocation of resources to an externally measurable variable, negotiators can sometimes overcome otherwise paralyzing disagreements about the future.

Contingent agreements also present an opportunity to create favorable incentives. Some negotiated deals involve no future relationship between the negotiators and are self-executing. Buying a trinket in a marketplace involves a simple exchange of money for goods. In more complex circumstances, however, ongoing relationships exist and implementation of the agreement takes place over time. When the negotiated deal involves more than a simple, one-time exchange, parties' behavior after the agreement is relevant. Contingent agreements can help to create incentives for parties to behave well after the terms of the deal are fixed. A company may agree to tie a sales executive's compensation to sales performance, thus promoting sales-maximizing behavior out of the executive after the deal is signed. The health ministry of a developing country approaches a prospective donor, seeking support for particular health sector programs. Both the prospective donor and the developing country want to see multiple sources of funding. They agree to a matching program under which the donor will contribute an amount equal to the funds the ministry secures from other sources, giving the ministry officials added incentive to garner resources. In some contingent deals, one party can affect the likelihood of the contingent trigger — the salesman can make more sales calls, the ministry officials can approach more donors. Contingent agreements can affect parties' behavior after the agreement.

Precisely because contingent agreements can affect parties' behaviors, some contingent agreements risk creating conditions of moral hazard. Moral hazard is a condition in which one party, under the terms of an agreement, may undetectably or uncontrollably behave in a way that is adverse to the other party. How quickly do you take the speed bumps when you are driving a rental car? Moral hazard suggests that many drivers will drive more cautiously over the bumps if they are driving their own cars because they consider the long-term effects of their driving behavior. Athletes' contracts often contain contingent incentive clauses. If the athlete scores a certain number of points, for example, he or she receives additional money. Moral hazard arises when, toward the end of the season, a team notices that the athlete is only a few points away from the triggering contingent event. Will the team structure its play to enable the athlete to achieve the statistical goal? If an agent's contract provides for a thirty percent commission on sales this year, but only a ten percent commission in future years, the agent will have an incentive to push deals into the current year — even if the deal he or she could have struck next year would have been on terms more favorable to the company. Negotiators crafting a contingent agreement should foresee the possibility of moral hazard and, where appropriate, structure incentives and disclosures to minimize the incentive for subsequent adverse behavior. . . .

Contingent agreements may affect negotiators' perceptions of "winning" and "losing." Classical negotiation advice counsels negotiators to conceive of negotiations in terms other than win-lose, pointing to the risk that competitive behavior may cloud opportunities for joint gains. In one respect, contingent agreements may present an opportunity for negotiators to avoid the necessity of identifying a winner. Rather than forcing one side to concede on its forecast, contingent agreements permit (in fact, require) both sides to maintain their conflicting predictions about the future. At the time of the agreement, therefore, each side can declare "victory," to the extent such a declaration is important. On the other hand, contingent agreements have the nature of a wager or a bet. Unless one counts the sheer joy of gambling as a victory, both sides cannot win a wager. The contingent event either happens or it does not. Either way, one side may be disappointed. In some organizational cultures, failure is punished more harshly than success is rewarded. A negotiator fearful of identifiable failure (for example, a wager that visibly did not pay off) may forgo an elegant contingent agreement in favor of a less efficient non-contingent deal. Elegantly structured contingent deals may help to reduce the risk of visibly "losing." For example, if the plaintiff fears that a jury may award him nothing, and a defendant fears a runaway jury award of millions, the two could agree to a small guaranteed recovery in exchange for a cap on the maximum recovery. The losing party at trial will then be grateful to have made the contingent agreement, and the winner's regret will be dampened by having won a favorable verdict. . . .

A final, often overlooked, factor dissuading parties from crafting contingent deals is that parties place some value on certainty and finality. Particularly for negotiators embroiled in a dispute, achieving resolution may have an inherent value independent of the terms of the deal. Many disputants find it emotionally costly to carry around uncertainty. A contingent agreement does not represent complete finality, as at least some of the terms are yet to be determined. Uncertainty also can be costly for economic reasons. A company with an uncertain liability or benefit on its books faces considerable challenges in planning appropriate reserves of money, for example. If a company has a large collection of similar contingent agreements, it may be able to spread the risks and allocate money accurately in the aggregate. Similarly, some circumstances may permit parties to manage risks through the use of hedging instruments such as futures or options. Such allocations are not generally available to all individual negotiators, potentially making contingent agreements less attractive. For a contingent agreement to be appropriate in a given context, therefore, the perceived benefit it captures for each negotiator must exceed the transaction costs of discovering and implementing the agreement.

Negotiators arguing about the past sometimes "agree to disagree," preferring instead to focus on what they will do moving forward. Negotiators with differing perceptions of the future should similarly agree to disagree — using contingent agreements to capture the potential benefits of their differences.

Problem

Assume you are negotiating with a small law firm interested in hiring you as an associate. The firm is offering you a lower salary than larger firms are paying new associates. You do not want to accept a lower salary, but you prefer a smaller firm and believe that you will be able to generate some new business. What terms of agreement might you suggest that could benefit you and be attractive to the firm?

B. Finalizing and Writing the Agreement

After you reach decisions about how a case will be settled or a deal will be structured, your work as a lawyer is not complete. The relief you feel in reaching an agreement can induce you to neglect the important task of how the agreement will be worded and how the remaining details will be determined. Issues of implementation and execution may remain to be determined. The old maxim that "the devil is in the details" is an apt warning. Often a negotiated settlement about the amount to be paid or an agreement "in principle" triggers another set of negotiations, this time over the formal terms of the settlement agreement itself. Lack of clarity about the terms of the agreement can result in perceptual differences about what was decided and the unraveling of the agreement. Inattention to how the agreement is written can also put your client's interests at risk of intentional overreaching by the other side or unintentional differences of interpretation that do not favor your client. Not memorializing the agreement in writing as quickly as possible can lead to unnecessary expenses if more time is required to reconstruct exactly what was agreed or if uncertainty develops about the outcome. If you did well negotiating, the favorable result for your client can lead to buyer's remorse, causing the other side to look for ways to change the non-finalized terms or reject the not yet enforceable agreement.

A negotiated business transaction is usually memorialized in the form of a written contract that incorporates the terms of the deal and follows general contract principles. An agreement to settle a legal claim may have different characteristics and requirements. A release of claims, a dismissal or other disposition of the underlying lawsuit, enforceability by entry of judgment or liquidated damages, how and when money will be paid or performance of obligations will occur, costs, expenses, and tax aspects — all of these issues must be considered when writing an agreement to settle a lawsuit. Ambiguities must be avoided; a settlement document is written to resolve an existing dispute, not foster a future one.

It is also important to attend to the psychological and relationship aspects of closing the deal. Never celebrate a victory in the presence of an opponent. If you can leave the other side feeling they did well, there will be fewer questions regarding implementation of the agreement. The relationship is also strengthened if no one feels they were bested and if clients on both sides have reason to think they were well represented. (It is for this reason that a good negotiator on the other side will not give you an honest critique or tell you that you could have done better.) Even if the parties will not have an ongoing relationship, the attorneys may have future professional contact. There is value in the rapport that carries forward to future negotiations when each side is satisfied with the outcome and great cost if an opponent feels compelled to "get even" at the next opportunity because of regret over an outcome.

We present below the basics involving release of claims, structured settlements, ratification, and the use of single text agreements. Then relationship and practical issues involved in finalizing negotiated agreements, whether transactional or settlement based, are addressed. Tax considerations, which may affect some settlement terms and how the settlement agreement is written, are discussed in Chapter 11.

1. Release of Claims

If the settlement agreement resolves a legal dispute between parties, the agreement should contain a clause mutually releasing one another from future legal claims, either in general or relating specifically to the present controversy. The release-of-claims clause can be broad or narrow, depending on the case, but most settlement agreements should contain mutual releases. In tort cases, the release clause usually releases defendant from all future claims by the injured party. It may narrowly release defendant from claims arising out of the facts alleged, or more generally from all claims arising before the settlement date. If you represent the defendant, failing to obtain such a release in the settlement agreement could expose your client to future liability. You will want the broadest release possible. If you represent the plaintiff, especially in a personal injury case where the full extent of injury and complications may not be known, you will negotiate the narrowest release possible so that damages not now known may be sought later.

A tort defendant will usually seek a settlement provision that the settlement is not an admission of liability, which could be used in actions by other parties, particularly in product liability settlements. In many cases, the defendant, particularly in employment and sexual harassment claims, will want a confidentiality provision with liquidated damages. Such a provision may be the subject of added negotiation. In product liability and malpractice cases, confidentiality provisions may raise public protection and policy issues addressed in Chapter 10.

In settlement agreements between businesses, your client may not want to release the other parties from all claims arising before a certain date, since the business relationship may have ongoing conflicts, and some potential future claims may not be apparent. A blanket release may not take into account realities of the continuing relationship and latent claims, so it may be wise to propose and, if necessary, negotiate a limited release.

2. Structured Settlements

Structured settlements are commonly used where damages are substantial or otherwise difficult to meet in one lump-sum payment, and in cases of catastrophic injury or in significant settlements where the plaintiff is a minor. In a structured settlement, the amount recovered by the plaintiff is paid over time in installments. The defendant funds the payments by purchasing an annuity or bond, or by establishing a trust from which the plaintiff receives periodic payments. The structure can be tailored to meet a variety of circumstances. For example, an injured child whose future earning capacity is impaired by an accident may receive a sum now for medical expenses and escalating monthly payments beginning at age 18 for supplemental income. Experts and annuity representatives are readily available to help structure the future payments and offer annuities for a time-discounted payment.

3. Ratification

There are many situations where final authority to sign an agreement rests with someone not directly part of the negotiation. This can result in another opportunity to reopen negotiations to obtain approval of an absent authority and, in the process, for one side to "nibble" at what was thought to be an agreed deal. They might take advantage of asymmetrical timing needs or an opponent's investment in the anticipated outcome. Clarification of who has ultimate authority and whose signature is necessary to create an enforceable agreement should occur before the negotiation begins. (Issues of enforcement and defenses are covered in Chapter 11.)

The settlement of some disputes or transactions requires ratification by a constituent group. For example, the resolution of labor-management controversies may require ratification of union members. Some corporate issues may require a vote of stockholders. Disputes involving municipalities and other public bodies may rest upon final approval of elected councils or boards. Again, it is helpful to agree at the outset of negotiations on the approval/ratification process and on mechanisms to help ensure that those engaged in the negotiation have the confidence of the final decision makers. Good faith deposits or penalty provisions if approval is not forthcoming may help guard against last minute manipulations and disappointments.

The most effective way to ensure approval and ratification of "stakeholders" or interested parties not at the table is to involve those who hold final authority in the negotiation or to structure steps that require interim approval or endorsement along the way. If the stakeholder group becomes invested in the process and aware of the value being created, as well as the BATNAs involved and the concessions leading to the proposed agreement, its members are more inclined to concur with what they feel part of than if presented with an up-or-down vote on what appears to be a fait accompli. A gradual "buy-in" is more likely to result in endorsement than an after-the-fact request, even if a group process complicates the negotiation.

4. Single Text Agreements

One method used by mediators can also be of help in direct negotiation, particularly when ratification may be required. The single-text approach of building an agreement by writing the provisions or sections together at the table and then circulating that section for approval before the next section is written was made famous by President Jimmy Carter during the Camp David negotiations between Egypt and Israel (see Carter 1982). The resulting document grows section by section with the buy-in of all approving parties along the way. The completed agreement then reflects a joint effort that was grown to maturity by those who feel an ownership of what was built together. Of course, the pieces of an agreement are interrelated and final approval must await the completed document, so there is no guarantee that the end terms of a single text agreement will be accepted. However, using a single-text approach and getting buy-in along the way makes it more likely that there will be concurrence on the cumulative final document that represents the resulting agreement.

Questions

9. Can you identify additional situations that may require ratification, formal or informal, of a negotiated settlement or deal?
10. What are the potential advantages and disadvantages of a structured settlement?

❖ **Charles B. Craver,** *Effective Legal Negotiation and Settlement*

212 (Lexis, 2001)

Leave Opponent with Sense They Got Good Deal

As the overall terms are being finalized, negotiators should remember how important it is to leave their opponents with the feeling they got a good deal. If their adversaries are left with a good impression, they will be more likely to honor the accord and more likely to behave cooperatively when the parties interact in the future. Some advocates attempt to accomplish this objectively by making the final concession on a matter they do not highly value. Even a minimal position change at this point is likely to be appreciated by the other side. Others try to do it by congratulating their opponents on the mutually beneficial agreement achieved. Individuals must be careful, however, not to be too effusive. When negotiators lavish praise on their opponents at the conclusion of bargaining interactions, those individuals tend to become suspicious and think they got a poor deal.

Take Time to Review Agreement

When bargaining interactions are successfully concluded, many participants are anxious to terminate their sessions and return to other client matters. As a result, they fail to ensure a clear meeting of the minds. If both sides are not in complete agreement, subsequent misunderstandings may negate their bargaining efforts. To avoid later disagreements, the participants should take the time to review the specific terms agreed upon before they adjourn their discussions. In most instances they will encounter no difficulties and will merely reaffirm the provisions they have achieved.

Endeavor to Draft Final Agreement

Once the Competitive/Distributive, Closing, and Cooperative/Integrative Stages have been completed and a final accord has been achieved, many negotiators are readily willing to permit opposing counsel to prepare the settlement agreement. While this may save them time and effort, it is a risky practice. It is unlikely that they and the opponent would employ identical language to memorialize the specific terms agreed upon. Each would probably use slightly different terminology to represent his or her own perception of the matter. To ensure that their client's particular interests are optimally protected, bargainers should always try to be the one to draft the operative document.

No competent attorney would ever contemplate the omission of terms actually agreed upon or the inclusion of items not covered by the parties' oral understanding. Either practice would be wholly unethical and would constitute fraud. Such disreputable behavior could subject the responsible practitioner and his or her client to substantial liability and untoward legal problems. Why then should lawyers insist upon the right to prepare the final accord? It is to allow them to draft a document that unambiguously reflects their perception of the overall agreement achieved by the parties.

Each provision should be carefully prepared to state precisely what the drafting party thinks was mutually agreed upon. When the resulting contract is then presented to the other party for execution, it is quite likely that it would be reluctant to propose alternative language, unless serious questions regarding the content of particular clauses were raised. Doubts tend to be resolved in favor of the proffered document. This approach best ensures that the final contract will most effectively protect the interests of the party who drafted it.

Review Opponent's Draft Carefully

If negotiators are unable to prepare the ultimate agreement, they should be certain to review the terms of the document drafted by the other side before they permit their client to execute it. They should compare each provision with their notes and recollections of the interaction, to be positive that their understanding of the bargaining results is accurately represented. They should be certain that nothing agreed upon has been omitted and that nothing not agreed upon has been included. If drafters suggest that certain new terms are mere "boilerplate," reviewers should make sure those terms do not alter the fundamental substantive or procedural aspects of their agreement.

Unabashed Questioning of Drafts

Agreement reviewers should not hesitate to question seemingly equivocal language that may cause future interpretive difficulties or challenge phrases that do not appear to describe precisely what they think was intended by the contracting parties. Since practitioners now use word processors to draft contractual documents, it is easy to accommodate additions, deletions, or modification. Bargainers should never permit opponents to make them feel guilty about changes they think should be made in finally prepared agreements. It is always appropriate for non-drafting parties to be certain that the final language truly reflects what has been achieved through the negotiation process. If the other side repeatedly objects to proposed modifications because of the additional work involved, the participant suggesting the necessary alterations can quickly and effectively silence those protestations by offering to accept responsibility for the final stages of the drafting process. It is amazing how expeditiously these remonstrations cease when such an easy solution to the problem is suggested!

Tact in Questioning

When negotiators reviewing draft agreements discover apparent discrepancies, they should contact their opponents and politely question the pertinent language. They should not assume deliberate opponent deception. It is always possible that the persons challenging the prepared terminology are mistaken and that the proposed terms actually reflect what was agreed upon. The reviewers may have forgotten modifications quickly accepted near the conclusion of the negotiation process. It is also possible that the drafting parties made honest mistakes that they would be happy to correct once they have examined their notes of the bargaining interaction. Even when document reviewers suspect intentional deception by drafting parties, they should still provide their opponents with a face-saving way out of the predicament. The best way to accomplish the desired result is to assume honest mistakes and give the drafters the opportunity to "correct" the erroneous provisions. If reviewers directly challenged opponent integrity, the dispute would probably escalate and endanger the entire accord.

Vigilance Against Underhanded Tactics

In recent years, a few unscrupulous practitioners in the corporate area have decided to take advantage of the drafting stage of large documents to obtain benefits not attained during the negotiation process. They include provisions that were never agreed upon, or modify or omit terms that were jointly accepted. They attempt to accomplish their deceptive objective by providing their opponents with copies of the agreement at the eleventh hour, hoping that time pressure will induce their unsuspecting adversaries to review the final draft in a cursory manner. Lawyers who encounter this tactic should examine each clause of the draft agreement with care to be certain it represents the actual accord achieved. If necessary, they should completely redraft the improper provisions. If their proposed terms are rejected by opposing counsel, they should insist upon a session with the clients present to determine which draft represents the true intentions of the parties. When this type of meeting is proposed, deceitful drafters are likely to "correct" the "inadvertent misunderstandings" before the clients ever get together. If a client session were to occur and the other side enthusiastically supported the deceptive drafting practices of their attorneys, it would be appropriate for the deceived lawyers to recommend that their client do business with another party.

Addressing Unforeseen Ambiguities and Problems

On some occasions, ambiguities or actual disagreements may be discerned during this stage. Negotiators should not allow these difficulties to destroy their previous progress. When good faith misunderstandings are found, the advocates should strive to resolve them before they terminate their current interaction. At the conclusion of the Closing or the Cooperative/Integrative Stage, the parties tend to be in a particularly accommodating frame of mind. They feel good about their bargaining achievements and are psychologically committed to a final accord. It is thus a propitious time to address newly discovered problems. If they do not deal with these issues now, they are likely to encounter greater difficulties when these questions arise at a later date.

Writing and Signing Items as Safeguard

A few unscrupulous negotiators attempt to obtain a tactical advantage by deliberately creating "misunderstandings" as final agreements are being drafted. They hope to extract additional concessions from unsuspecting opponents as these seeming ambiguities are being resolved. Individuals who suspect that their adversaries may employ this tactic should insist on a careful review of the basic terms at the conclusion of the bargaining process. They should write out these items and have their opponents sign the draft to indicate their concurrence. This practice makes it difficult for adversaries to later create disingenuous "misunderstandings" that can be used to obtain unreciprocated benefits for their own side.

CHAPTER
8

Telephone and Cyber Negotiation

Effective negotiators use multiple forms of information gathering as the basis for formulating strategy and shaping responsive communication. Good negotiators employ all of their senses to obtain information from counterparts in order to comprehend their needs, feelings, resolve, strengths, and vulnerabilities. Skillful negotiators also send messages by nonverbal means, such as gestures and body language, to construct a desired context and build rapport. Therefore, face-to-face negotiation is the gold standard that allows for the fullest form of communication, using the senses of sight and hearing to create perceptions and put nonverbal cues in context. Meeting in person provides an opportunity to establish a relationship before jumping into negotiation details. Social psychologists and communication theorists refer to face-to-face discussions as a "rich medium" providing synchronous or "real-time" communication.

Our schedules, time restraints, distances, limited resources, and changing norms may require that we use telephone communications or e-mails to initiate, conduct, or conclude negotiations. These methods of communication limit nonverbal cues and other information. They are more "lean" forms of communicating than face-to-face negotiation. Thus, we must pay attention to a different skill set and approach to achieve effective negotiation results and avoid the potential traps of relying only on the spoken or printed word.

A. Negotiating by Telephone and Video Communication

Before the popular use of e-mail and texting, telephones were the efficient substitute for face-to-face negotiations. Like in-person communications, the telephone allows for real-time talk. The use of voice messaging adds to the efficiency factor by allowing sequential messages or "asynchronicity" when it is not practical for negotiating counterparts to be on the phone at the same time. Negotiation communication by telephone, rather than face-to-face meetings, may be a necessity when geographical distance or busy schedules prevent meeting in person. Teleconferencing in multiple-party negotiations offers exponential economies and convenience compared to getting several lawyers in the same room together.

Although negotiating by telephone strips us of visual cues, some audible cues beyond the words chosen can provide a richer medium of negotiation than the written word. Tone of voice, inflection, pitch, pace, volume, pauses, breathing, and sighs provide audible cues. These audible cues may be more pronounced with the elimination of visual distractions in face-to-face discussions. We also feel we can "read" meanings like friendliness, hostility, fear, and other emotions into what we hear from others over the telephone. Telephonic communication may be less personal than face-to-face negotiation, but the use of the telephone is generally more personal than the written word alone. It is more common to engage in "small talk" and other ice-breaking or rapport-building communication by telephone than in e-mail transmissions. We previously studied the role of trust in successful negotiations (see Chapter 5). Trust is fostered by getting to know a negotiating counterpart through conversation and identifying common interests before "getting down to business."

Telephone negotiations may be advantageous in some situations. It may be helpful to have your notes, concession points, and other reminders in front of you when negotiating by telephone. The use of outlines and prompts cannot so easily be relied upon in face-to-face talks. If your client is present with you when you are negotiating by telephone, you can visually communicate together in private in a way that cannot be done in face-to-face meetings with the other side. If you need to take time to gather your thoughts prior to making an offer or deciding what to do next, it is easier to interrupt the telephone conversation and offer to call back than excuse yourself from a face-to-face negotiation.

Telephoning a negotiation opponent offers the caller a degree of control beyond that provided by scheduling a negotiation meeting. Calling when you are prepared and ready may provide some advantage over the person who answers the call when she is not as focused as you are on the topic. (Courtesy and custom, however, may require scheduling the telephone conversation in advance.) In a significant negotiation, it may be easier to say no or be more insistent on favorable terms when negotiating by telephone than when facing a forceful opponent. It is also easier to strategically conclude a telephone negotiation that is not going well than to leave a negotiation meeting, particularly if it is in your office. Of course, an opposing lawyer might do the same or more easily use deceptive and strategic tactics on the telephone, including hanging up. Every advantage can be a double-edged sword.

Telephone follow-up to an in-person negotiation is common and presents fewer of the disadvantages and dangers noted above. If rapport and trust are established in face-to-face negotiations, communicating by telephone or videoconferencing to conclude the deal or settlement can be a cost-saving convenience.

Video technology is further transforming how we communicate and negotiate. Virtual meetings and teleconferencing through emersive telepresence and "halo" technology, maybe in 3-D, is becoming more of a reality to replace long-distance travel and scheduling of in-person negotiations. Tablet devices and smart phones with two-way cameras may become so ubiquitous that electronic video communication will be as ready an alternative to face-to-face negotiation as texting and e-mail now are to telephone conversation. Telephone negotiations, as well as newer technologies, present challenges that face-to-face negotiations behind closed doors do not.

Take the Deal!

Sports agents and others who negotiate for a living spend a lot of time on the telephone negotiating deals. One of the most successful lawyer agents is Leigh Steinberg, who, in his book *Winning with Integrity* (1998), discusses his use of telephone follow-up and other electronic aids to negotiation. Steinberg states that he can easily make a hundred telephone calls in a day. He cautions about the need to protect against invasions of privacy and eavesdropping. An interesting example provided is a contract he negotiated for Troy Aikman to become the star quarterback for the Dallas Cowboys. The negotiations began in a face-to-face meeting in Texas of Steinberg, Aikman, Cowboys owner Jerry Jones, the head coach, and others.

> This was a get to know you meeting. A lot of the conversation was about hunting and fishing. Everyone in that room, with the exception of me, was from Arkansas, Texas, or Oklahoma. I soon felt that I was the one with a heavy accent. . . . When I finally left Dallas that day and flew back home, we were far from finished. But the groundwork had been laid. . . . [W]e were on the phone constantly. . . . I had a particularly intense car phone conversation with Jerry Jones. I was stuck in the infamous Los Angeles rush-hour traffic on the San Diego Freeway, and Jerry was stuck at his offer of [$]10 million.
>
> "Jerry," I told him, "we've got to have eleven and a half."
> "Son," he said, "that dog won't hunt." "Jerry," I said, "this is fair."
> "Son," he answered, "we passed *fair* about eight million dollars ago." Back and forth it went, until suddenly a third voice came on the line, a stranger who had crossed cell phone signals with us.
> "Listen, buddy," the voice said, addressing me with a Texas drawl, "if you don't want the 10 million, I do. Take the deal."
> This deal was finally closed through a two-way telecommunications link-up between Los Angeles and Dallas as the parties sat in their offices watching one another on widescreen television.

B. E-Mail and Texting Negotiation

E-mail is now commonly used for purposes of conducting all types of negotiation or following up negotiations started through in-person or telephone discussions. In other words, e-mail has become a popular mode of communication in lieu of voice transmission, mail, or fax. We explore below some of the issues raised by e-mail negotiation.

This discussion of negotiation by e-mail should be placed in generational perspective. The communication norms and expectations of your generation of attorneys may be different than those who came before you. For many law students, e-mail and texting might serve as your primary mode of communication. You have probably grown up using computers and communicating with friends and family through the Internet. Laptops may have replaced your early desktop computers, and now you might use a handheld digital device, or smartphone, to send and receive messages. However, many older attorneys and clients may not be as comfortable or knowledgeable about cyber communication. The law relating to negotiation and the enforcement of negotiated agreements is, by nature, slow to catch up to technological advancement, as are some older lawyers.

As you know from your own experience, the ease and informality of e-mails and texting can be both a blessing and a curse. Experienced users of e-mail and texting develop shortcuts and abbreviations that among friends may be understood as acceptable conventions but can appear to others to be curt, abrupt, and sloppy. An informal choice of words may create misunderstandings and further disputes. Although e-mail and texting used in negotiation can and should be composed with care, it is easy to lapse into "cyber mode." As a "lean" form of communication, electronic words are not readily put in context by facial expressions, like a smile, and by posture or body language, like a shrug or a nod. The speed, convenience, and economy of electronic communication must be balanced against the risk of misinterpretation and the bareness of the medium. The following reading analyzes the pros and cons of e-mail negotiation and offers suggestions for overcoming practical and ethical concerns.

❖ **Lynn A. Epstein,** *Cyber E-Mail Negotiation vs.*
Traditional Negotiation: Will Cyber Technology Supplant
Traditional Means of Settling Litigation?

36 Tulsa L. J. 839 (2001)

Cyber e-mail negotiation offers numerous benefits and minimal detriments. These include:

Time and Distance

Cyber e-mail negotiation constitutes practice at leisure. When sitting down to a traditional face-to-face negotiation, time is often of the essence. Attorneys generally have allocated a specific amount of time to negotiate. When negotiating telephonically, talks often break down due to the ease with which often faceless parties can reject proposals. E-mail negotiation combines the luxury of negotiating as time permits in an attorney's schedule with the tools necessary to perform negotiation surgical strikes. Whether its 6:00 A.M. or 6:00 P.M., the attorney can make an offer or respond to an offer. The virtual time factor allows participants to reflect and review their positions before articulating them. They also have the luxury of taking a break without fanfare if emotions begin to run too high. Furthermore, e-mail negotiations avoid the frustrations inherent in telephone tag gamesmanship or the worry over violating the prescribed time limit set by the parties, the mediator, or the court.

Of course, one of the main benefits of online communications is that there are no distance barriers. You may negotiate by e-mail with an attorney one mile away or 1,000 miles away with the same force and effect. You may include or exclude as many parties as desirable. No more canceled flights, late arrivals, or car breakdowns. All parties are accessible and available. . . .

E-Mail Communication Is in Writing

The fact that cyber e-mail negotiation requires written as opposed to oral communication serves a positive and negative impact on the negotiation process. Typically, in face-to-face or telephone negotiations, there can often arise considerable disagreement by the parties as to what was actually said. This is often the case since there is no memorialization of the negotiation. With cyber e-mail, there is always a record and one that cannot easily be destroyed. Lawyers are less likely to lie in writing since they know the communication may last a lifetime. Even though the communication would be protected from admission in court, the fact that it is there may carry the imprimatur of a more genuine communication.

A written communication avoids the psychological games lawyers often engage in during face-to-face negotiations. For example, tactics such as feigned or real anger or boredom are difficult to accomplish by e-mail. While we've all been a witness to an attorney who storms out of the room and states, "You're wasting my time, I'll see you in court," it's difficult to have the same effect when leaving the virtual negotiating room. If you do not get a response from opposing counsel, it may be because opposing counsel is having a temper tantrum, attempting a stall tactic, or simply decided to go to the gym. Of course, it is possible to show anger by e-mail, often indicated by using all capital letters and exclamation marks, but such perversion in lawyer letter writing tends to not have the same effect as in person. Attorneys with an overly aggressive style may resort to excessive sarcasm in a face-to-face negotiation, but they may be unable to translate that approach through e-mail. Attorneys also frequently resort to branding their client as unreasonable and thus blaming them for being unable to effectuate a settlement in traditional negotiations. It is unlikely that an attorney would trash their client on e-mail since the client may very well be a part of the e-mail process, and even if not, the attorney would not risk the threat of the client reading that e-mail through later data recovery methodology. . . .

More Planned Negotiation

Since each e-mail communication is in itself a conversational demand letter, the successful e-mail negotiator must have a negotiation plan. The failure of many land-based negotiations is that attorneys go into them hoping to "wing" it. Often attorneys fail to do their homework. They do not adequately counsel their client to ascertain the client's needs, and they do not adequately seek information from the other side to determine the other side's needs. "Winging it" by e-mail is a transparent act. To effectively communicate the client's position, and to uncover the opposition's position through e-mail, requires advanced planning, deductive reasoning, and applied strategic effort. The more strategic planning the attorney applies to e-mail negotiation, the more likely a successful negotiation process will occur absent lengthy, wasteful and needlessly repetitive e-mail exchanges.

Likewise, if an attorney proceeds without a plan and attempts cyber e-mail negotiation, the result can very often be disastrous resulting in a squandering of both the client's financial resources and goodwill among the parties. A "seat-of-the-pants" cyber negotiation attempt will likely result in a tedious and fruitless exercise that will frustrate both parties and threaten to subvert the entire settlement negotiation process. Without adequate planning, it is likely that the negotiating would involve a multitude of miscued exchanges, where the attorneys chiefly react to the prior e-mail posting absent focus or direction. Just as in face-to-face negotiations, this effort will likely end in an exasperated exclamation of: "see you in court."

The Client Is Part of the Negotiation Process

Mediation has been successful, in part, due to the frequent requirement that the client attend the mediation session. While some attorneys balk at having to perform in front of the client, the logical interpretation of statistical results is that a case is more likely to settle when a client is available and actively participating. E-mail negotiation affords the opportunity for the client to monitor the ongoing negotiations without translation error and in virtual time. Since clients often complain their attorney fails to communicate and keep them informed about their case, the cyber e-mail negotiation affords clients the opportunity to be "present" and take an active part in the case. Knowing the client is present will likely decrease the gamesmanship and puffery that accompanies clientless negotiations and increase the pre-negotiation counseling process so that an attorney may adequately express the client's goals and objectives in the most effective manner to the opposing side.

E-Mail Negotiation Is Cost Effective

An efficient cyber e-mail negotiation should result in a reduction in cost exposure to the client. The time it takes to travel and conduct the negotiation is greatly reduced, or actually avoided, in cyber e-mail negotiation. When multiple parties are involved, cost avoidance or benefits are enhanced in an exponential degree. If the cyber e-mail negotiation process is effectively staged, the resultant billable time online should be effectively minimized. As client satisfaction is often equated with the economical management of legal expenses, client satisfaction is fostered by achieving this goal. . . .

Overcoming Ethical Problems

. . . [E]thical concerns may be overcome by consultation with the client and setting parameters with opposing counsel before the e-mail negotiation process commences. For example, an attorney should discuss with the client the process of e-mail negotiation and receive the client's approval for negotiation by e-mail before the process begins. In that discussion, the attorney should explain the procedure for conducting an e-mail negotiation, whether e-mail will be the sole means of negotiation or whether it will be utilized in a combination with face-to-face meetings. In order to address concerns with client confidentiality, the attorney should also explain the e-mail system being utilized and whether the transactions will be subject to encryption security measures. Additionally, the attorney should counsel with the client as to the information to be disclosed during the e-mail negotiations, and the potential for this information being discoverable. Finally, the attorney and client should agree upon the scope of client involvement in the e-mail negotiation process. For example, decisions as to whether the client will be copied on all e-mail negotiations, or simply provided a summary of the discussions, or a verbal assessment following the negotiation by the attorney.

After consultation with the client, an attorney involved in cyber e-mail negotiation should set parameters before the process begins. If there is a time frame in which the negotiations should conclude, that should be decided before the process starts. Additionally, the attorneys should discuss the interface between their respective e-mail systems including details of security guards such as encryption programs, in order to decide upon a mutually acceptable procedure for continuing the proceedings in the event of a technological breakdown. The attorneys should also discuss whether their clients will be part of the online process.

Attorneys can also protect themselves from e-mail disasters by taking a few cautionary steps. First, it is paramount that an attorney reviews an e-mail before it is sent. Not only should the recipient's name and address be verified, but also the content and tone should be reviewed. Unless the negotiations are restricted to one ISP (such as AOL), typically once an e-mail is sent, it is irretrievable. An attorney should also consider a disclaimer at the bottom of each e-mail, indicating the e-mail is confidential and is meant solely for the intended recipient. While case law and ethics opinions are not clear as to whether the use of a disclaimer shields a lawyer from liability a disclaimer undoubtedly alerts the recipient to the confidential nature of the transaction and shows the lawyer-sender's intent in keeping the message confidential.

Finally, the attorney must be diligent in retaining e-mail exchanges throughout the course of the negotiations. Separate filing systems, and the standby paper copies should be utilized. However, if the process becomes burdensome and tedious, the attorney should stop the madness. Many regrettable e-mails have been sent out of frustration and anger. If the process is not working, pick up the telephone or set up a face-to-face meeting to continue the negotiations.

Questions and Note

1. Are you persuaded that negotiating by e-mail or texting is significantly different in terms of necessary preparation, strategic considerations, or ethical issues than face-to-face or telephone negotiations?
2. Is checking with clients about system compatibility and encryption programs really necessary? Why is it necessary to get client approval of negotiating by e-mail before the process begins? How is this different than proceeding by telephone or face-to-face negotiation? Is permission required for any of these modes?
3. Is texting now so much a part of our daily communications that this article, written only a short time ago, is now passé or a statement of the obvious?

When lawyers know one another, either socially or from past dealings, the use of digital texting may have fewer disadvantages than when they do not have a relationship. Research indicates that the existence of a prior relationship between opposing counsel favorably affects the likelihood that they will settle a lawsuit. In a study of thousands of cases filed in federal courts, it was discovered that attorneys were less likely to go to trial and could settle cases more quickly when they had faced each other

> in the past than when they had not. (See Johnston & Waldfogel, 2002.)
> One explanation of this tendency is that those who know one another,
> even as opponents, are better able to communicate and know what to
> expect based on past interactions. They are able to put their commu-
> nications in context more easily based on past experience together.

How can lawyers who do not know one another tap the advantages of e-mail
for negotiation while minimizing the risks inherent in the "lean" nature of
digital communication and the absence of social cues? This question is answered by the empirical research described in the next reading. As explained by
Professor Nadler, law students were assigned to negotiate a commercial transaction with counterparts at a different law school using e-mail as the mode of
communication. Negotiators who spoke together in an introductory telephone
call established a relationship that tended to create rapport and trust, which
aided them in reaching agreement in the subsequent e-mail negotiation and
created positive feelings about one another. By contrast, those who began
e-mail negotiation without first engaging in telephone "small talk" were over
four times as likely to reach impasse and tended to end up feeling resentful and
angry about the negotiation. Professor Nadler concludes by discussing implications of this experiment for lawyers who use e-mail to negotiate.

❖ **Janice Nadler,** *Rapport in Legal Negotiation:*
How Small Talk Can Facilitate E-Mail Dealmaking

Harv. Negot. L. Rev. 223 (2004)

A. Procedure

The negotiation exercise used in the experiment involved the purchase of a
new car. Participants consisted of 146 law students, half of whom were students
at Northwestern University School of Law and half of whom were students at
Duke Law School. The students participated as part of a class assignment in a
Negotiation course. Thirty-five randomly selected Northwestern students were
paired with thirty-five randomly selected Duke students and were assigned to
the "Small Talk" condition. The remaining thirty-seven Northwestern students
were randomly paired with the remaining thirty-seven Duke students and were
assigned to the "No Small Talk" control condition.

Participants were given confidential role instructions which specified that
they were to conduct a two-party negotiation exclusively via electronic mail.
Each student received a packet of materials that contained a page of general
confidential instructions and guidelines, an e-mail address for their counterpart, and pre- and post-negotiation questionnaires. Participants were given one
week to complete the negotiation and questionnaires, and were specifically
instructed to not discuss the negotiation or procedures with their classmates.

Unbeknownst to participants in the "No Small Talk" control condition, the
participants in the "Small Talk" condition received an additional special
instruction: they were to have an initial "getting to know you" telephone

conversation lasting five to ten minutes with their partner before they began negotiating. Directions specified that participants should not talk about business (i.e., the negotiation) in this initial conversation, ensuring that it was a strictly social conversation. The goal was to have negotiators "break the ice." Regardless of group assignment, all negotiations took place exclusively via e-mail.

The negotiation itself involved the purchase of a new company car by a manager at a software company. The negotiation contained both distributive and integrative elements. Whereas both parties were motivated to claim as much value for themselves as possible, parties had different priorities; hence concessions by Party A on a given issue could be traded for gains on another issue which Party A values more but Party B values less. This type of logrolling increases the joint value of the agreement, creating more profit that can be allocated between the two parties. . . .

B. Results

"Small Talk" negotiators who had a brief "getting-to-know-you" telephone conversation prior to negotiating via e-mail reached superior economic outcomes and markedly better social outcomes than negotiators who did not talk on the phone. Differences between the "Small Talk" and "No Small Talk" conditions in economic and social outcomes are described below.

1. Economic Outcomes — Small Talk Led to More Negotiated Agreements

"Small Talk" negotiators were over four times as likely to reach an agreement as "No Small Talk" negotiators. Only three out of thirty-five "Small Talk" pairs (less than 9%) failed to reach an agreement, whereas fourteen out of thirty-seven "No Small Talk" pairs (nearly 40%) failed to reach agreement. The high percentage of "No Small Talk" pairs that were unable to reach agreement is especially noteworthy in light of the fact that a positive bargaining zone existed, making it economically desirable for each party to reach a negotiated agreement. Interestingly, the value of the outcome (measured both in terms of joint outcome and individual outcome) for the pairs that did reach agreement appears to be unaffected by small talk. . . .

An examination of precisely what occurred between negotiators who reached impasse is revealing. Because parties negotiated via e-mail, the transcripts of unsuccessful negotiations indicate the last offer on the table prior to the point at which impasse was declared. For all three "Small Talk" negotiators that failed to reach agreement, the last offer on the table had a value below the reservation price of one of the parties. In other words, none (0%) of the "Small Talk" pairs walked away from an offer that was more profitable than their outside option. For all three pairs, given the value of the last offer, it is understandable that one of the parties would refuse to agree to it. But the story for the "No Small Talk" pairs was quite different: the value of the last offer on the table exceeded both parties' reservation price for nine out of the fourteen pairs (64%). Thus, these eighteen negotiators (none of whom engaged in small talk) failed to reach agreement despite the fact that the last available offer would have made all of them better off than impasse.

The success of "Small Talk" negotiators cannot be explained by differences in motivation and ambition. Talking to the other negotiator on the telephone did not result in "Small Talk" negotiators setting higher reservation prices or more ambitious aspirations for themselves as measured prior to the negotiation, compared to negotiators who did not engage in small talk. The striking superiority of negotiation outcomes where negotiators chatted briefly about personal matters on the telephone prior to talking business via e-mail must be attributable to other mechanisms, which I explore in the next section.

2. Social Outcomes

What accounts for the huge differences between the "Small Talk" and "No Small Talk" negotiators in their propensity to reach a mutually beneficial agreement? Prior to negotiating (but after the phone call, if there was one) negotiators indicated on a scale from one to seven (1 ¼ Not at all; 7 ¼ Quite a bit) how "competitive" they were feeling toward their counterpart as they entered into the negotiation. They also indicated how "cooperative" they were feeling toward their counterpart. Negotiators who did not engage in small talk with their counterpart prior to negotiating reported feeling more competitive and less cooperative toward their counterpart than negotiators who did engage in small talk.

3. Negotiation Processes

Why would negotiators who adopt more cooperative, less competitive attitudes toward the negotiation achieve greater success economically than negotiators who adopt the opposite attitudes? After all, one might expect a negotiator who is too nice and unwilling to be tough to do poorly in a negotiation. By contrast, in this simulation, the cooperative attitude adopted by negotiators who engaged in small talk led them to come away from the negotiation in a position that was substantially more favorable economically than those who did not engage in small talk.

a) Small Talk Negotiators Shared More Information

One possible reason for why more cooperative, less competitive attitudes were associated with more successful negotiations is that negotiators who engaged in small talk were better able to exchange the kind of information necessary to reach a mutually beneficial agreement. Consistent with their cooperative mental model of the negotiation process, negotiators who engaged in telephone small talk prior to negotiating exchanged significantly more information relating to their relative priorities on multiple issues compared to negotiators who did not engage in small talk. Thus, negotiators who established initial rapport with a brief telephone chat felt more cooperative in the negotiation and trusted the other negotiator enough to share the kind of information necessary to reach an efficient solution.

b) Small Talk Negotiators Engaged in More Reciprocity

In addition to offering more freely their own information about relative priorities, information sharing was reciprocated more often for negotiators in the "Small Talk" condition than for negotiators in the "No Small Talk" condition. That is, compared to negotiators who did not engage in small talk, negotiators who chatted with their counterpart prior to negotiating were more likely to receive multiple issue priority information from their counterpart immediately following their own provision of such information. Negotiators who engaged in small talk expected more strongly to cooperate, did cooperate by sharing more relevant multiple-issue information, and received more cooperation in return from their counterpart. This pattern of multiple-issue information sharing is necessary for negotiators to avoid impasse by recognizing numerous, mutually beneficial solutions in the negotiation. In this mixed motive negotiation, failing to exchange information resulted in negotiators failing to integrate their interests, leaving little or no joint surplus to share.

c) Small Talk Negotiators Made Fewer Threats

The negotiation transcripts were also analyzed to examine whether negotiators provided information that related to one's own alternative, because such a reference can be akin to a threat to walk away from the table (e.g., "I can buy a similarly equipped car much more cheaply at another dealership"). Compared to negotiators whose initial contact was strictly business-like, negotiators who engaged in small talk before negotiating were less likely to reference their own alternative. Thus, in the absence of an initial getting-to-know-you telephone conversation, negotiators assumed a competitive mental model and behaved competitively during the negotiation by making subtle (or not so subtle) threats to walk away from the table. In sum, negotiators who did not engage in small talk both felt more competitive (as evidenced by their social perceptions prior to the negotiation described in Section 2a) and acted on these competitive inclinations by behaving more competitively in the negotiation.

Recall that threats to walk away from the negotiation table in fact materialized for nearly 40% of the pairs whose members did not have the opportunity to engage in small talk, compared to only 9% of pairs who did chat before negotiating. . . .

d) Small Talk Negotiators Developed More Respect and Trust

Negotiators who did not chat beforehand ended the negotiation with a substantially different attitude toward both the process and their counterpart than the negotiators who did chat initially. . . . Negotiators who did not chat found the process of e-mail communication more difficult. They ended up feeling significantly more angry, annoyed, and cold toward their opponent, as well as less friendly and pleasant, compared to negotiators who had the opportunity to chat with their opponent. These feelings are consistent with the competitive mindset and inferior economic outcomes of negotiators in the "No Small Talk" condition. The increased cooperation and trust that the telephone chat engendered led to smoother interactions and a friendlier attitude toward the opponent after the negotiation concluded. This attitude was also associated with respect — negotiators who engaged in small talk formed an impression of their counterpart as significantly more accomplished, skilled, effective, and perceptive than the impression formed by negotiators who did not engage in small talk. . . .

Finally, this experiment also measured the extent to which negotiators came away trusting their counterparts. One of the many ways to define trust is the expectation that the other person will cooperate with you when you are in a vulnerable position. In legal communities, lawyers who face each other in one negotiation often can expect to cross paths again in the future. If trust is eroded during negotiation in one matter, this is likely to affect the way the lawyers approach the negotiation in the next matter when they meet again. To explore the question of whether engaging in small talk prior to negotiating would increase trust, negotiators in this experiment answered two questions relating to trust. First, they were asked to suppose that they and their counterparts were in the position of working together on a future project and to rate how smoothly such a project would go. . . . Second, negotiators were asked to imagine that sometime in the future, they were in a vulnerable position in a dispute with their counterpart's firm. Would they prefer to negotiate with the same counterpart, or some other unknown attorney. . . . Negotiators who had an initial chat with their opponents left the negotiation with significantly more trust in their counterparts than did negotiators who did not chat initially.

C. Discussion

In the negotiation simulation involved in this experiment, a seemingly trivial intervention — a preliminary, brief, and informal chat on the telephone — increased the likelihood that the e-mail negotiations that followed would be characterized by cooperation, information exchange, reciprocity, liking, trust, and ultimately, agreement. These negotiators had the opportunity to establish common ground with the other negotiator through small talk, even if the basis for common ground was exceedingly trivial (e.g., "The weather is nice here in Chicago." "Yes, it is nice here, too."). Engaging in small talk enabled negotiators who were strangers to get to know one another and to connect in a fashion that did not spontaneously occur during the process of e-mail exchange. The seemingly inert act of small talk encouraged negotiators to adopt a cooperative mental model in the negotiation, leading to the sharing of crucial information with the other party. Negotiators who engaged in small talk were more willing to take the chance that the other negotiator would reciprocate and share their own private information, which is precisely what happened. This resulted in favorable impressions of the counterpart after the negotiation. Negotiators who engaged in small talk placed their trust in the ability of their counterpart to recognize the mutual benefit of information exchange. When the counterpart successfully recognized these benefits and shared crucial information, their abilities and skills were respected, and they were generally held in high regard.

By contrast, negotiators who did not have an opportunity to chat with their counterpart prior to e-mail negotiation approached the negotiation with a competitive mental model, and either failed to exchange the kind of information that would lead to identification of mutually beneficial solutions, or failed to recognize as beneficial the solutions which arose, leading to greater likelihood of impasse. In the absence of the phone call, the two negotiation counterparts were complete strangers, never having seen one another or heard one another's voice. Because the other person was, in this sense, an unknown quantity, negotiators could not be sure of the other person's motives. These circumstances were associated with negative impressions of the other person, as evidenced by negotiators' ratings of their opponents as less accomplished, skilled, effective, and perceptive than negotiators who engaged in small talk. In short, negotiators in the "No Small Talk" condition were less likely to reach agreement, which made them angry and annoyed and for which they blamed the other negotiator. By failing to reach agreement, pairs that reached an impasse achieved an outcome that was economically worse than any of the myriad of possible agreements that would have resulted in a profitable outcome for each party. The failure to reach an economically advantageous outcome is even more remarkable when one considers the circumstances under which this occurred — a substantial portion of the "No Small Talk" negotiators who reached an impasse did so despite an offer on the table that would have made both negotiators better off than impasse.

One reason that a cooperative mental model served negotiators well in this simulation (while an overly competitive mental model served negotiators poorly) is that cooperation helped participants solve the "negotiator's dilemma." This getting-to-know-you telephone call made e-mail interaction proceed more smoothly by creating rapport before the negotiation began. This rapport helped negotiators approach the negotiation with a more cooperative mental model, thereby trusting in each others' good intentions. This mental model, in turn, led to a successful negotiation that concluded with a contract and engendered positive feelings about one another. The negotiators who engaged in small talk solved the "negotiator's dilemma" by agreeing (albeit tacitly) to share enough information to determine what kind of agreement would satisfy their needs simultaneously.

Sharing information was crucial in the negotiation simulation used in this experiment because of the mixed motive nature of the exercise. While some issues were purely distributive, others could be profitably logrolled in a manner that inured to the benefit of both parties simultaneously. To successfully expand the pie of available resources (as opposed to simply compromising and "splitting the difference"), it was crucial for negotiators in this experiment to exchange enough information to allow them to determine, for example, that both parties preferred all airbags and yellow color, that financing was an especially important issue for the seller, but warranty was especially important for the buyer, etc. Without communicating this information in some form, negotiators were unable to maximize the joint value of the agreement. Adopting an attitude that was more cooperative than competitive allowed negotiators to trust the other party enough to share with them relevant private information, and to expect the other party to reciprocate by sharing their own relevant private information, which in turn resulted in identification of and agreement to efficient solutions. Because lawyers are repeat players within a legal community, and often expect to interact with each other again in the future, it is important to observe here that one deal that sours because of misunderstandings in the course of e-mail negotiations can affect the tenor of future negotiations — whether conducted via e-mail or more traditional means.

It is also interesting to note the similarity between the results of this study and a phenomenon identified by decision theorists and social psychologists called the "self-others discrepancy." In general, when we are asked to make predictions about the abilities or preferences of others, our predictions are strongly influenced by the extent to which we feel a personal connection with those others.

For example, if I am asked to judge how dependable, intelligent, considerate, etc. I am compared to others, my answer is likely to depend on the abstractness of the others. If the other is "the average person" then my comparison tends to be more favorable toward myself than if the other is an individual stranger sitting next to me. In other words, the less abstract the other person about whom I make a judgment, the more likely I am to judge that person as more similar to me. In addition to the abstractness of the other person, the degree of personal contact also encourages feelings of similarity: I judge myself more favorably in reference to a stranger on a videotape than I do in reference to a stranger who is in the same room. The "self-others discrepancy" extends to other judgments besides estimating personality traits. For example, people estimate that "an average person" making a decision will choose a riskier option than themselves, but the stranger sitting next to them will choose a similar option to the one chosen themselves. Finally, in Stanley Milgram's famous experiments in which the experimenter instructs a "teacher" to administer painful electric shocks to a "learner," the "teacher" is more likely to refuse to do so if the "learner" is visible and in the same room as the "teacher," compared to when the "learner" is not visible and in an adjoining room.

The "self-others discrepancy" has important implications for negotiating via e-mail. It suggests that conceptualizing one's negotiation counterpart as a concrete, identifiable individual person reduces the perceived difference between the counterpart and oneself. The anonymous character of e-mail leaves negotiators imagining a vague and abstract opponent whom they have never seen or met, making it more likely that negotiators will succumb to the self-others bias. Yet, the simple act of making personal telephone contact with the opponent prior to negotiating via e-mail enabled negotiators to substitute perceptions of an invisible, abstract opponent with a concrete human being who shares one's own characteristics. As a result, negotiators who engaged in small talk prior to negotiating via e-mail were more successful at exchanging the right kind of information necessary to reach agreement, and at recognizing a beneficial agreement when the opportunity for such an agreement presented itself. . . .

This study documents the importance for lawyers of establishing rapport when negotiating with another lawyer who is an "unknown quantity." When face-to-face contact between negotiators is not possible, it is important to find an alternative method of building rapport. This study demonstrates that a social, personalizing communication via telephone is one way to restore some rapport that may be missing from electronically mediated negotiations. . . .

Questions

4. Nadler's study appears to confirm the often repeated traveler's story of being invited to sit down for a cup of tea by a Turkish rug dealer before talking business or being asked by a Balinese beach peddler, how do you like Bali, and where are you from? What is the purpose of these benign gestures, and how do they relate to the previously described experiment?

5. If "schmoozing" is the social grease or foreplay that makes deals happen, are there ways other than a preliminary telephone conversation to schmooze or create rapport and promote cooperation before engaging in e-mail negotiations? In her article, Professor Nadler suggests the following:

> [A]n initial, non-business, getting-to-know-you chat over e-mail prior to beginning e-mail negotiations has been shown to increase the likelihood of reaching a mutually beneficial agreement. Moreover, outside of the negotiation context, social psychologists have shown that using flattery (even when people suspect the flatterer has ulterior motives) and humor, and mentioning points of similarity, can facilitate good feelings and relationship building, thereby engendering the kind of cooperation and trust that leads to discovery of mutually profitable negotiated solutions.

6. Professor Epstein makes reference to the tactic of starting with extreme demands as being comparably effective in e-mail negotiations as in face-to-face bargaining, and to other tactics, like splitting the difference and making successive concessions, which may be more effective by e-mail. What is the distinction that makes some tactics more and some less effective in e-mail negotiation mode? Are there other tactics that are likely to be more or less effective in e-mail negotiation, as compared to in-person negotiation?

7. How might the increasing affordability and use of digital video cameras and voice technology change the way we negotiate? Will the use of these technologies equate digital means of negotiation with in-person negotiation, or will differences remain? What might such differences be?

Note: Avoiding Costly E-Mail Mistakes

No doubt you have either experienced or heard e-mail horror stories. Knee-jerk reactions or damaging, unfiltered thoughts hastily entered via the computer keyboard and sent instantly through cyberspace without the benefit of delay or having to write them down longhand can cause long-lasting mischief. Hitting the "reply to all" button when sensitive information was intended only for the original sender can cause embarrassment and resentment. Misaddressing an e-mail that contains confidential or revealing information creates breaches of confidentiality, and the leaked information cannot be erased. Having an important message go unread because the subject line did not accurately indicate the content may result in a missed deal, or at least misunderstanding. The recipient taking offense because an abbreviated term was misinterpreted or an attempt at humor was misunderstood or coolly read out of context may be hard to turn around. These mistakes can be costly if committed in the course of e-mail negotiations. Why do people communicate differently in digital mode, and how can mistakes be avoided?

First, be aware of the false anonymity shield, or what has been referred to as "online disinhibition effect." We tend to believe that we are more anonymous in cyberspace and that we will not be held accountable in the same way as in face-to-face interchanges. Many people state in e-mails what they would not say face-to-face. When you are stuck in a room with a negotiation opponent, you see her reactions and the consequences of your comments. With e-mail you can, in effect, hit and run without staying around to see emotional reactions. Responses can only come later in digital form, so we tend to be bolder and less inhibited. However, if your name or e-mail address is on the message, you are not anonymous; you are accountable and can be held legally liable for what you send. E-mails also satisfy the writing requirement for a binding contract under the Statute of Frauds, because the Uniform Electronic Transactions Act provides that a "record or signature may not be denied legal effect or enforceability solely because it is in electronic form." See, e.g., International Casings Group, Inc. v. Premium Standard Farms, Inc., 358 F. Supp. 2d 863 (W.D. Mo. 2005); Donovan v. RRL Corp., 109 Cal. Rptr. 2d 807 (2001).

Second, e-mail communication can be highly "flammable." That is, without the schmoozing and face-to-face social lubrication that can soften spoken words, e-mail messages can be read with the most harsh and inflammatory interpretation. Devoid of eye contact, facial expressions, voice inflection, and body language, e-mail offers a "narrow bandwidth" or undressed mode to convey meaning. The flammable potential of naked e-mail, combined with the "hit-and-run" factor, is reason for caution and restraint in negotiating by e-mail.

Third, when representing clients, lawyers tend to write more formally and precisely because we understand the legal consequences of words and the downside of ambiguity. As agents of clients, we have a responsibility when negotiating not to be careless or sloppy in the words and phrases we use. If the medium is the message, as Marshall McLuhan said, then e-mails may not be an easy medium for lawyers to use in negotiating. The common style and "netiquette" of e-mail is informal and highly abbreviated. Although conventions of abbreviation and new definitions may be emerging, e-mail talk remains idiosyncratic and rapidly evolving, particularly when using handheld digital devices. Lawyers can use the speed and economy of the digital world to negotiate with composed and clear messages and more formally drafted attachments. Combining e-mail with other forms of communication, as we saw in the prenegotiation telephone schmoozing experiment described above, allows for the best use of different mediums. The use of e-mail to negotiate need not be all or nothing.

The following checklist[1] will help you avoid common e-mail and texting traps when negotiating, as well as when using digital communication generally.

✓ Use proper grammar, spelling, and punctuation.

Never send a message with an incomplete sentence, a misspelled word or referring to yourself as "i" because besides deleting them, people primarily do two things with e-mail: They forward them and they print them.

✓ Never send negative feedback or criticism through e-mail.

Criticism sent through an e-mail comes across like a slap in the face. It is always received more harshly than intended. At the very least, the recipient will

---

1. See Jay Sullivan, *Lawyers and Technology: A Crash course in Writing Effective E-Mails*, 229 N.Y. L.J. 5, Feb. 2003.

feel as if you should have picked up the phone to deliver your message, and you inevitably will appear to be "hiding behind your e-mail."

✓ **Refrain from humor and sarcasm.**

The nuances of face-to-face or spoken communication are lost with the written word. For instance, it is very hard to be funny in an e-mail. People who are humorous in person cannot necessarily write humor well. It requires a different discipline. Sarcasm, in particular, does not translate at all through e-mail, and it is often taken literally, with potentially disastrous consequences.

✓ **Think before sending an e-mail.**

This requires more than proofreading: It requires giving your brain a break between the drafting and the sending. Very few e-mails require an immediate response that you cannot build in a half-hour delay to improve the quality of your communication.

✓ **Put substance in the "subject" line.**

It is always easier to hit "reply" than to start a new message. Also, do not start your message in the subject line and continue it within the body. It is disconcerting to the reader and almost always requires that the recipient read the sentence twice.

✓ **Use a salutation.**

E-mail is generally an abrupt way of communicating, but by starting a message with the recipient's name, the tone is softened. It is especially important to use a salutation when copying someone on the message.

✓ **Get to the verb.**

Use short sentences and direct language in the body of the message. Avoid the passive voice. Many people check their messages on Blackberries, and they need to know right away what you want. Do not begin a professional e-mail with "How was your weekend?" or the recipient may think the message is more personal and never get to the meat of the message. This does not mean eliminate all niceties. Just keep it short.

✓ **Make it clear how you want the recipient to respond.**

People tend to respond to a particular communication in the same form they receive it. If we receive a formal letter, we reply in-kind. If we get a voicemail, we tend to reply by phone. When someone gets your e-mail, the instinct is to hit the "reply" button. However, if you are inaccessible for the next few hours or days, you need to indicate how you would like the reply delivered. For example, "Please respond by phone. I will not be able to check my e-mail for a few hours."

✓ **Review your "cc:" list.**

Who is on it and why? Is there a legitimate reason for including each individual? Do not include someone just to keep him or her "in the loop" unless you have first asked that person if they want to be included. The courtesy will be appreciated.

✓ **Be careful.**

Do not gossip (it will come back to haunt you), make off-color jokes or comments (they can, will and should get you fired).

✓ **Remember, e-mail does not get deleted, only subpoenaed.**

Deleting it from the hard drive does not "destroy" it. The document is still floating around somewhere in cyberspace.

✓ **Apply the Golden Rule.**

Only send e-mails you would like to receive.

Questions

8. Can you add any cautionary or advisory items to this checklist?
9. Are the potential mistakes noted previously and those in the checklist equally applicable to all forms of negotiation communications? What is truly unique about e-mail communications?
10. Have you negotiated via the Internet? Looking back on that experience, would you have done anything differently?
11. In Chapter 9 we consider the roles that gender, race, and ethnicity play in negotiation. Given the "lean" nature of e-mail communication and that the digitally transmitted word need not reveal the sender's gender, race, or ethnicity, does negotiation only via e-mail eliminate any influence of these factors? Why or why not?
12. Can you think of ways in which e-mail communication might exacerbate cultural differences and create obstacles to successful negotiation?
13. Can you think of any worse e-mail blunder than the one below, attributed to a Harvard summer associate at Skadden Arps by the *The New Yorker* on June 30, 2003? First, he made the mistake of sending it to all in the law firm rather than just to the friend he intended as the sole recipient, and then it was posted worldwide:

> "I'm busy doing jack shit. Went to a nice 2hr sushi lunch today at Sushi Zen. Nice place. Spent the rest of the day typing e-mails and bullshitting with people." He signed off, "So yeah, Corporate Love hasn't worn off yet. . . . But just give me time."

A helpful guide to business and legal use of e-mail is *Send: The Essential Guide to Email for Office and Home,* by David Shipley and Will Schwalbe (2007).

C. Online Dispute Resolution

Online dispute resolution (ODR) uses the ever-improving resources of cyberspace to offer programs for resolving disputes arising from online commerce, as well as off-line claims. The evolution of ODR reflects the expanding capacity and use of computers and the Internet. Initially used to organize and transmit information to assist traditional negotiation processes, ODR is increasingly used to replace precomputer ways of negotiating.

Sophisticated software and actively managed ODR sites use input information and variable formulas to present options that the parties can accept to resolve a damage claim or disputed transaction. Today's cyber-negotiation programs are not your father's keypunch electric calculator.

There are online and software programs to aid in planning and preparing for negotiations, which were described in Chapter 5 (see, e.g., *http://www.winx win.com*). There are secure platforms to facilitate communication between negotiators and train them to negotiate by identifying, quantifying, and maximizing interests (see, e.g., *http://www.smartsettle.com*). Cyber-negotiation sites also conduct monetary negotiations, primarily for insurance claims, using sophisticated algorithms to match demands and offers in a double-blind bidding process (see, e.g., *http://www.cybersettle.com*). Online commerce generates disputes that can be resolved online through affiliated negotiation and mediation services, such as *http://www.squaretrade.com*, offered through eBay. Many of these online negotiations involving online trading disputes are conducted without the assistance of lawyers. More advanced programs are being developed to offer cyber resolution in lieu of precomputer forms of negotiation.

The following reading is the story of how Cybersettle was created to resolve insurance claims by computer blind bidding and how it works. Next, Professor Katsh briefly explains the use of SquareTrade for negotiating settlements of eBay disputes and then contrasts two computer programs that resolve off-line disputes. He concludes with a look into the possible future of online negotiation and dispute resolution.

❖ **Douglas S. Malan,** *A NUMBERS GAME*

36 Conn. L. Trib. No. 4 (2010)

The idea started fairly simply about 15 years ago. Two New York City trial attorneys on opposite sides in an insurance claim dispute met in the courthouse in an attempt to settle their case.

They were tens of thousands of dollars apart, the story goes, but his veteran attorneys, they felt they knew roughly the amount for which the case would eventually settle. They just didn't want to show their hand to the other side.

The lawyers agreed to write down their bottom line numbers on a piece of paper and hand them to a clerk, who was instructed to indicate if the numbers were within $1000. If they weren't, the clerk would destroy the papers and neither side would know what had been written.

The numbers were in range, the lawyers split the difference and the case settled in minutes. That's the seminal moment that Cybersettle chief Executive Officer Robert Balou describes when asked about the origins of his Greenwich-based 19-person company, which offers online dispute resolution in insurance cases.

"No one ever wants to put the first offer on the table, and neither party wants to put their best offer on the table," said Bob Ballou, who was CEO of an e-discovery service provider to law firms before joining Cybersettle last June. "We eliminate the emotion behind the settlement negotiation process."

The paper process used by those New York attorneys is now automated, though the secrecy of the demands and offers remain intact. Cybersettle was launched 10 years ago and has become more visible as people turn to the Internet for assistance with legal problems. . . .

Price Negotiation

. . . [T]he company has become a go to resource for the Association of Trial lawyers of America, the New York State Trial Lawyers Association and the American Arbitration Association. Cybersettle counts among its clients

Wal-Mart, General Electric, and Zürich Insurance, along with the city of New York's Office of the Comptroller.

"We're very careful to frame what we do as simply the negotiation of a price," said Schwartz [Chief Operating Officer], who has spent 30 years as an executive and entrepreneur in the information technology field. "We accelerate the process of negotiating settlements. We don't get involved in the process of determining guilt or innocence or right or wrong."

Cybersettle's program is simple to understand. When a claim is filed against a client of Cybersettle's, the client receives a request to settle the matter on line. Both parties log-in to the system and submit three different amounts of money for their demands or offers.

Whenever the competing numbers come within a certain range, as determined by the Cybersettle client, both sides are alerted and a live person steps in to finalize the amount to be paid.

That payment is made online through the Cybersettle site.

The major benefit is a reduced amount of time spent going back and forth between attorneys, mainly because egos and emotions are removed from the process, Ballou noted.

If a settlement isn't reached, the parties can try the online process again, or they can opt for the more traditional routes of using live mediation or going to court. Neither side knows what dollar amounts were submitted during the online process.

Suzanne Beck, claims counsel for Acadia Insurance Co. in New Hampshire, said her company started using Cybersettle a few months ago as another tool that could lead to quicker settlements.

"We continue to press the use of it," Peck said. "It's amazing how our younger generation of claims adjusters is excited by the technology. There's been more skepticism among our older generation."

But the point, Beck said, isn't to replace traditional face-to-face negotiations, just to see if there is a way to speed up the process for certain cases. Already, the company has settled a six-figure claim through Cybersettle. "What we find when people engage online is that they want to settle," Ballou said.

New York City, which is Cybersettle's largest client, his reduced its claims backlog from 77,000 to 10,000 since hooking up with the company four years ago, Ballou said.

Many of the cases that are settled online, Ballou noted, are simple personal injury claims such as stepping in a hole and injuring a foot.

Squeeze On Business?

But not all defense lawyers have warmed up to the Cybersettle model. Charles F. Gfeller, a partner of West Hartford insurance defense firm Seiger Gfeller Laurie LLP, said removing the human element from settlement negotiations could actually hinder quicker settlements if the two sides are far apart.

"Often you need to hear the way the other lawyer delivers the message regarding a demand or offer to get a sense for how close the proposed number is to his or her bottom line," said Gfeller, . . . "If a client, for example, is stuck at a certain number or range, you need to provide some additional motivation to settle."

This could include a case involving an injury to a parent, Gfeller said, where a parent could be persuaded to settle because of the possibility that the parent's child may need to be deposed. "By letting a computer essentially serve as a mediator, you lose all of this," Gfeller said.

. . . But Ballou noted that Cybersettle was never designed to be a cure-all. "If we can help clients settle a large chunk of claims, it frees up clients' resources," he said.

And the online settlement tool is growing in popularity. Cybersettle has licensed its software to the American Arbitration Association so that parties who wish to settle disputes online can do so through the association's website as well as Cybersettle's site.

The key to growth, Ballou said, is to make the patented Cybersettle technology available through many different online outlets.

As Schwartz, Cybersettle COO said, "The adoption of the Web has accelerated in all businesses, just look at banking. Our general feeling is that human assisted processes will diminish as people become more comfortable using technology."

Problem

Assume you are consulted by a business client who purchased a computer server system from an out-of-state supplier in a private transaction for $80,000. The system is dysfunctional, and the client believes that the seller defrauded him by not revealing that the system would function only with customized software, which would require an additional $17,000 to create. Even with this software, the client says, the system will probably not handle the volume of data that he has to process, contrary to assurances given during the sales process. He wishes to revoke the transaction. He has heard about the Cybersettle system (see *www.cybersettle.com*) and wonders if it would make sense to use it. What would you advise your client and why?

❖ **Ethan Katsh,** *ONLINE DISPUTE RESOLUTION*

The Handbook of Dispute Resolution 425
(M. Moffitt & R. Bordone eds., 2005)

. . . Since March 2000, an Internet start-up, SquareTrade.com, has handled over two million disputes, mostly related to eBay transactions, wholly through online processes of negotiation and mediation. SquareTrade is probably the largest private dispute resolution provider in the world. . . .

eBay is an online auction site that makes it possible for sellers and buyers located anywhere to deal with one another. The service has over ninety-two million registered users and lists over fourteen million items for sale each day. eBay itself is not a party to any transaction and, in general, assumes no responsibly for problems that arise between buyers and sellers. In 1999, eBay decided that having a dispute resolution process might strengthen trust between buyers and sellers. After a pilot project conducted by the Center for Information Technology and Dispute Resolution mediated over two hundred disputes, eBay selected an Internet startup, SquareTrade, to be its dispute resolution provider. Before providing a human mediator, SquareTrade uses a technology-supported negotiation process in which parties try to resolve the dispute themselves before requesting a mediator. SquareTrade also uses the Web, rather than e-mail, as the means for communicating and working with disputants.

SquareTrade's use of the Web illustrates how relatively small changes in communication can have large consequences. Most who file complaints with SquareTrade have already tried to negotiate via e-mail and have reached an impasse. Not only do parties seem more willing to negotiate via the Web than through e-mail, but the negotiations are more frequently successful. Square-Trade's Website provides a more structured set of exchanges than does e-mail. SquareTrade recognized that almost all eBay disputes fall into eight to ten categories, allowing it to create forms that clarify and highlight both the parties' disagreements and their desired solutions. While parties have an opportunity to describe concerns in their own words, the forms and the form summaries they receive reduce the amount of free text complaining and demanding, and thus lower the amount of anger and hostility between them.

Negotiation, as classically defined, takes place between the disputants, without the presence of third parties. SquareTrade's use of the Web in negotiations adds a novel element to traditional negotiation, a kind of "virtual presence." The Website frames the parties' communication and provides some of the value traditionally provided by a mediator. Perhaps as parties increase their use of technology in negotiation, the distinction between negotiation and mediation will become less stark.

When Web-based negotiation fails, SquareTrade provides a human mediator for a modest fee. The conversation is facilitated by a third-party neutral using the Web interface. Because the parties are using the Web, they do not all need to participate at the same time. . . .

ODR for Offline Disputes: Enhancing ADR and Unbundling ODR

The SquareTrade . . . processes involve no face-to-face meetings. They are conducted wholly at a distance. The need for ODR with no physical meetings is most obvious in cases that arise online and when, because of distance, it is not feasible to meet face-to-face or go to court. It is not surprising that ODR was first directed at such disputes as well. ODR has grown in part because it is valuable for resolving traditional offline disputes. SquareTrade, for example, now resolves real estate disputes between home buyers and sellers. When the power of the computer to process information is added to the power of the network to transmit information the result is an array of dispute resolution processes that can be employed in any dispute, whether it arises, or is handled, online or offline.

A Simple Example: Automated Blind Bidding Processes

Blind bidding systems allow disputing parties to submit settlement offers to a computer and, if the offers are within a certain range, often thirty percent of each other, to split the difference. Blind bidding is attractive because if the parties do not reach settlement, the offers are never revealed. This practice encourages parties to be more truthful about their "bottom line."

Blind bidding is a negotiation tool, a technique that, if done offline and without a computer, would be cumbersome. The efficiency of blind bidding is that the computer transmits and receives information, processes it, and makes distinctions between what is private and public. If the offers are within the thirty percent range, for example, the parties are informed that there is a settlement. If not, no information about the offer is revealed to the parties. As Internet users come to understand how encryption and other techniques can protect confidentiality, trust in such systems and use of such systems will increase.

Thus far, blind bidding has been employed mainly in claims against insurance companies. These are claims that are generally settled at some point through negotiation. The traditional process of resolution in such cases, involving personal injury lawyers and insurance claim adjusters, is often lengthy and inefficient. There are problems with the parties and their representatives playing phone tag and posturing in ways that often take up time. A human third party could accept offers in a manner similar to the way a computer accepts offers in a blind bidding system, but could never do so as efficiently.

Blind bidding systems are both efficient and simple to use. They are also extremely limited, since they work only with disputes in which a single variable is contested. This variable must involve numbers so that the machine can make the necessary calculations. The insurance context is a fitting first arena for blind bidding because such differences often focus exclusively on money and the existing dispute resolution system is both expensive and inefficient.

The future of blind bidding will inevitably broaden beyond insurance company disputes. In many mediations or arbitrations, there are initially numerous differences, but ultimately only a monetary issue. Blind bidding technology could be helpful in such situations. In other situations, blind bidding might be an option before beginning a lengthier process. Blind bidding is a tool that can be added at any phase of a dispute resolution process.

Blind bidding also raises the question of what else a network-connected computer can do to assist parties involved in a dispute. Blind bidding is such a simple tool that it could easily be taken for granted if viewed only as a merging of a calculator with the network. Computers, however, are much more than calculators, and systems can be built to process and evaluate qualitative information.

A More Complex Example: SmartSettle

SmartSettle is much more sophisticated negotiation software than the blind bidding systems. It is intended for use in a range of disputes — simple or complex, single-issue or multi-issue, two-party or multiparty, comprising quantitative or qualitative issues, of short or long duration, or involving interdependent factors and issues. SmartSettle will never be as easy to use as blind bidding, and may not be needed for common and relatively simple disputes. However, experience with the software has demonstrated that network-connected computers can bring solutions that may not have been apparent to disputing parties.

SmartSettle moves disputants through several stages that clarify the issues in dispute, how strongly the parties feel about these issues, and the range of acceptable outcomes. In the early phases, SmartSettle provides a structure to clarify and assess issues that, by itself, can help parties reach consensus. What is most novel about SmartSettle, however, is that it can take a tentative agreement and suggest alternative approaches that may give each party a more favorable outcome.

While blind bidding involves only one quantifiable issue, SmartSettle may involve many issues. At the beginning of negotiations, parties are asked to place values on their different interests and demands. A family dispute, for example, may include issues of child support, the division of assets, care and custody schedules, and other relationship issues. A successful end result will involve trade-offs by each party. SmartSettle works to combine interests and issues into packages or groups so that the parties can see the impact of various decisions, enabling them to reach an end result that meets their needs. With SmartSettle, the computer not only stores the users' information and transmits it electronically, but also makes suggestions that will provide the parties with an attractive combination of settlement options. . . .

Conclusion

As of this writing, the World Wide Web is only fifteen years old and yet has already touched every important societal institution. Dispute resolution has felt the impact of the Web both in the generation of disputes and in the building of systems to respond to disputes. Yet, what has occurred is only a beginning. . . .

Cyberspace is, increasingly, a place where there are *processes* available to users as well as *information*. This should not be surprising since processes are sets of informational transactions and exchanges. What makes building processes out of informational transactions challenging is structuring and regulating the flow of information and the numerous informational exchanges among the parties. What makes building processes interesting, and what makes ODR a field with an exciting future, are innovations in software design and advances in the ability of software to manage complex interactions. ODR will grow in importance as offline activities migrate to the Web. The growth of ODR is partly a recognition that disputing is a kind of growth industry on the Internet. ODR is also, however, a sign or indicator that cyberspace is maturing. Many of the same tools that built such online venues as auctions, stores, and casinos can contribute to building online civic institutions such as courts and dispute resolution systems.

CHAPTER
9

Gender, Culture, and Race

A. Moving Beyond Gender Stereotypes

A generation ago, the issue of gender in negotiation was addressed as a question of how women should approach bargaining in a male-dominated profession. Although this issue has not totally disappeared, it is no longer the central question. More than half of law students are women, and quantitative gender balance among attorneys will soon approach equanimity. If there is a "male" model of practice, it is no longer necessary that women conform to it. Nor is it any longer necessary to ask whether women can succeed as negotiators. Experience and research have clearly shown that women can excel in all lawyering roles, including negotiation. We have seen that negotiation is increasingly approached as a process of problem solving and that effective negotiation draws upon a different set of qualities and skills than those associated with stereotyped male competitiveness. The game, as well as the players, has changed, and the old stereotypes of gender-based behavior are also changing, if not forgotten.

The fact that women have taken their place at the negotiation table does not necessarily mean that gender is irrelevant in negotiation. Questions remain about whether men tend to negotiate differently than women, whether negotiating with someone of the other gender is different than when a negotiating opponent is of the same gender, and whether any differences can be used to advantage or disadvantage. There is also a question of whether men and women tend to communicate differently — whether we speak the same language.

In considering matters of gender, as well as culture and race, it is important to note that there are no generic beings, no common man or woman. Every individual is unique, defined by genetic makeup, environment, and personal experience. Emphasizing gender differences detracts from considering women and men across culture, class, race, ethnicity, age, and gender orientation. However, culture and perhaps chromosomes foster some male- and female-associated behaviors that identify us with our gender and set us apart. The phenomenon of selective perceptions, and its children, stereotyping and self-fulfilling prophecies, along with attribution errors, magnify these differences and create cognitive traps that may shape and limit how we interact with those of the opposite gender when negotiating. The way to open these traps is to understand our individual uniqueness, as well as our gender differences, and work with them. Even if there are no actual differences, the belief by some that differences exist between male and female approaches to bargaining can be as important as reality in driving their behavior. Gender stereotyping may not be important to a new generation of enlightened lawyers who experience and assume more equality than previous generations, but gender may influence older lawyers and clients.

Carol Gilligan has written about a theory of moral development, which has been much cited and discussed in negotiation literature. Her theme is that men and women think and speak differently when confronted with ethical dilemmas. Gilligan distinguishes a feminine "ethic of care" with a masculine "ethic of justice" and believes that these gender differences in moral perspective are due to contrasting images of self:

> My research suggests that men and women may speak different languages that they assume are the same, using similar words to encode disparate experiences of self and social relationships. Because these languages share an overlapping moral vocabulary, they contain a propensity for systematic mistranslation, creating misunderstandings which impede communication and limit the potential for cooperation and care in relationships. (1982, 173)

Several more recent books provide guides for women on how to succeed at negotiating in what is assumed to be a male-dominated environment. Some, in effect, educate women to negotiate more like men. Some advise women on how to take advantage of what are described as feminine differences and qualities. Others rewrap traditional negotiation lessons in a package designed for the female market. The next reading describes the shadow negotiation — the often determinative negotiation within a negotiation — and provides a helpful guide for both men and women. The book from which this passage is taken draws on some of the principles previously developed, including hidden agendas, the role of trust and rapport, and reciprocity of listening to demands and making concessions. However, the authors caution that a seemingly even playing field may slope against women.

❖ Deborah M. Kolb & Judith Williams, *The Shadow Negotiation: How Women Can Master the Hidden Agendas That Determine Bargaining Success*

20 (Simon & Schuster, 2000)

The Shadow Negotiation

As we talked to women about what happens when they negotiate, we learned that a good idea alone rarely carries the day. Negotiations are not purely rational exercises in problem solving. They are more akin to conversations that are carried out simultaneously on two levels. First there is the discussion of substance — what the bargainers have to say about the problem itself. But then there is the interpersonal communication that takes place — what the talk encodes about their relationship. Yes, people bargain over issues, but they also negotiate how they are going to negotiate. All the time they are bargaining over issues, they are conducting a parallel negotiation in which they work out the terms of their relationship and their expectations. Even though they seldom address the subject directly, they decide between them whose interests and needs command attention, whose opinions matter, and how cooperative they are going to be in reaching an agreement. This interchange, often nonverbal and masked in the positions taken on issues, has a momentum all its own, quite apart from the substance of what is being discussed.

We call this parallel negotiation the *shadow negotiation*. This shadow negotiation takes place below the surface of any debate over problems. As bargainers try to turn the discussion of the problem to their advantage or persuade the other side to cooperate in resolving it, they make assumptions about each other, what the other person wants, his or her weaknesses, how he or she is likely to behave. They size each other up, poking here and there to find out where the give is. They test for flexibility, trying to gauge how strongly an individual feels about a certain point.

How you resolve the issues hinges on the actions you take in the shadow negotiation. If you don't move to direct the shadow negotiation, you can find the agreement tipping against you. The shadow negotiation is no place to be a passive observer. You can maneuver to put yourself in a good position or let others create a position for you. Your action — or inaction — here determines what takes place in the negotiation over problems.

Impressions count. Slight changes in positioning can cause a major shift in the dynamics within the shadow negotiation. You want to move into a position from which you can claim your place at the table. At the same time, you need to encourage your counterpart to collaborate with you in fashioning an agreement that works for both of you.

The Twin Demands of the Shadow Negotiation: Advocacy and Connection

To hold your own in the shadow negotiation, you don't have to be brash or aggressive. You do need to be an advocate for your interests. Through strategic moves you position yourself in the shadow negotiation so that the other party takes your demands seriously. You also turn any attempts to put you on the defensive. In effect, your advocacy defines your claim to a place at the table. It tells the other side not only that you are going to be an active player, but that you will not and do not need to settle for less than you deserve.

Active positioning is critical to how you negotiate the issues. The impressions you create in the shadow negotiation determine how much give and take there will be over the issues. If you are unsure of yourself or doubt whether your demands are justified or legitimate, you will have a tough time convincing others to give them much weight. Bargainers are quick to ferret out points of weaknesses, where you are tentative or vulnerable. You must be ready to move in the shadow negotiation not just to promote your interests but to block any attempt to undermine your credibility.

The messages you send in the shadow negotiation establish your advocacy. But you cannot pay attention only to gaining an advantage for your demands and to how you are positioned in the negotiation conversation. Any good solution requires compromise, concessions, and creativity on both sides. Concentrate only on your agenda, promote it at the other party's expense, and she has little incentive to cooperate. Regard her as an enemy and pretty soon she starts acting like one — blind to the interests you share.

To find common ground, you have to work together, not against each other. This is where the *skills of connection* come into play. It takes sensitivity and responsive action to draw out what other people have on their minds in a negotiation. Often these hidden agendas are their real agendas. Unless bargainers are explicitly encouraged to talk about them, they will hesitate, fearing that any candor will be used against them. They don't want to tip their hand.

There is a pragmatic reason behind this attentiveness to relationship building in the shadow negotiation. Show the others involved that you value them and their ideas, and there is a good chance they will reciprocate. You'd be surprised how quickly they become more open in voicing the reasons for their demands *and* more receptive to listening to yours. But establishing a connection with the other party does a good deal more than facilitate equal airtime. When you each feel free to engage in an open exchange that flows both ways, you can confront the real issues rather than their proxies. Different perspectives surface and point to other, more creative ways of resolving the issues than either of you can contemplate on your own.

Advocacy and connection go hand in hand in successful negotiation, and you establish the terms of both in the shadow negotiation. Using strategic moves and turns, you create your own space in the conversation. You cannot let a need for responsive and open exchange hold your own interests hostage. You must lay the groundwork for dialogue with a forceful advocacy. The other person has to have something and someone to connect with for the skills of connection to work. But those skills hold a larger promise. They enable you to build a relationship across differences so that you are both committed to working collaboratively on a mutual solution.

What Does Gender Have to Do with Negotiation?

Almost without exception, the women we interviewed could analyze a problem or a situation with great skill. Yet they stumbled in the shadow negotiation. The reason became clear the more we talked with them. Problems can be and often are gender neutral. But surprising things happen in negotiation. Unrecognized expectations and unwarranted assumptions come into play. And gender often sets them off.

Because we experience negotiation in such a personal way, we look for personal reasons why being a woman matters more at some times than at others. Something in the chemistry of this party negotiation, we figure, makes gender an issue. But even when we don't have a strong visceral reaction, gender colors our experience. Any negotiation is caught in a web of influence, social values, and informal codes of conduct. Social norms or standards that seem at first blush to have nothing to do with gender might generate troubling expectations about what we should and can do as women. Resources are often unevenly divided along gender lines. As a result, what appears to be a benign or even playing field might, in fact, slope against us.

Gender Frameworks

To a great extent, how we see gender determines how we deal with its effects in the shadow negotiation. We can consider being a woman a hindrance in negotiation and take seriously Professor Higgins's exhortation in *My Fair Lady*: "Why can't a woman be more like a man?" Alternatively, we can celebrate our differences and adopt the approach of Sally Field and Dolly Parton in the movie *Steel Magnolias*. When Steel Magnolias negotiate, they tap feminine strengths to temper confrontational impulses and encourage collaborative exchange. Or we can focus on the social dynamic set in motion when common yardsticks used to measure performance don't fit a woman's experience.

Professor Higgins' Advice

For the Professor Higginses of this world, the gender glass is half empty for women. They are not, by nature, bad negotiators. Socialized to be mothers and caretakers, they have never been schooled in the art of hard-nosed bargaining. They can, however, learn the "rules of the game." A woman need not fare badly in a salary negotiation or put in a double shift at home and at work. If she has not been able to argue her case for equal pay for equal work or prevent her colleagues from taking over her, she can study how to be more assertive, more strategic in her thinking, and less emotional.

The Professor Higgins approach is a remedial one. It assumes that individual deficiencies can be patched up with sufficient study and rigorous discipline: Passivity, for example, is a personal liability that can be corrected by training. The fault rests squarely on the particular woman's shoulders. She needs a "cure." Conveniently overlooked is the extent to which that cure will always be incomplete. No matter how hard a woman tries to learn the rules of the game, she will always play the game as a woman. Adopting aggressive behavior or a more "masculine" way of speaking in a negotiation can backfire. Instead of gaining her a voice and acceptance, it can provoke censure or backlash.

Remedial programs like these hold out a dubious promise: If you patch yourself up — fill in your obvious deficiencies and acquire the necessary skills — you can play the game as well as, or better than, many men. By recommending the wholesale assimilation of "good" masculine qualities, however foreign, advice like this encourages a woman to blame only herself when she is underpaid, overworked, or simply overlooked, invisible. The fault lies with her — in some inadequacy, in something she did or failed to do — not in the imbalances in the system itself.

The Steel Magnolias' Answer

Wait a minute, some critics say. Femininity is *not* an encumbrance. It gives a woman an edge, assets she can use to her advantage. Rather than lament the lack of assertive independence or competitive drive in women, why not celebrate an expressive, emotional, caring femininity? Women, through their capacity to mother and from their subordinate status at work, have developed not just coping mechanisms but real strengths. Empathy, an intuitive aptitude for collaboration, the ability to connect with others rather than to remain distanced as an independent actor, an instinctive feeling for "relationship" — these skills and inclinations carry an unrealized advantage in the new interconnected world of business. Women, it is suggested, build rapport and reach joint solutions more easily than men do precisely because they cooperate and empathize more naturally.

This thinking successfully challenges the notion that women are in some way deficient or inadequate. It runs into difficulty, however, when it assumes that a constellation of certain traits and qualities makes up the "female essence." This premise washes out differences among women. The problem is not that women do not have these special qualities. Many do. But others enjoy the challenge of competition; they are not by nature *only* concerned with others.

There is also some wishful thinking involved in declaring feminine attributes unqualified assets uniformly useful in negotiation. These "feminine" skills, far from being an advantage, can undermine a woman when she negotiates. If she is not careful, her attachment to relationship can be exploited and used against her. Of course, the helpful female colleague does not mind shouldering the lion's share of the work and ending up with none of the credit. Of course, a woman negotiating a severance package will sacrifice her financial interests to maintain cordial relations with her former employers. Taken to extremes, the feminine advantage does not gain a woman much credit when she negotiates.

While her empathetic male counterpart earns praise for his "people" skills, she is just acting like a woman. And if she is really successful, she is accused of being manipulative, of using feminine wiles to get her way. That is the flint behind the honey in Steel Magnolia's voice, the reason for the hint of the pejorative in the term's common usage.

There is a more damaging objection. Praise of the "feminine," when unqualified, makes it easy to discount or ignore the extent to which influence follows gender lines. As one commentator put it, an emphasis on women's special qualities of caring and nurturing amounts to a "setup to be shafted." In an unequal world, such critics argue, difference will always mean less and women will generally get less when they negotiate. In other words, the doubts women experience about their ability to do well often tell more about status, about bumping up against seemingly immovable walls and ceilings, about having less clout, than they reveal about underappreciated skills and abilities.

We are using the exaggerations of Professor Higgins and the Steel Magnolia for effect. They point to the extremes in the advice directed at women, but they also illustrate the extent to which we personalize the challenges gender creates in negotiation. On the one hand, it is our weakness and so we need to remedy it. On the other, it is *our* strength, but we must be wary in how we use it. But not all the challenges gender poses in negotiation are rooted in personal causes. However inclined we as individuals might be to view supposed differences as a handicap or a strength, a woman quite simply has to work harder than a man to get what she wants in a negotiation. . . .

The Yardstick Explanation

Gender is not a "woman's" problem — a question of whether women have deficiencies or special qualities. Although gender figures in most human relations, we deny its pervasiveness, preferring instead to see egalitarian gender neutrality in our relationships and in our organizations. Yet to a large extent, we still maintain implicit standards for behavior that can have a different impact on women than men. Standards generally reflect the experience of the people setting them. And, by and large, men do the setting in our society. As a result, their experience becomes the yardstick for measuring what is normal. And, in a masked exercise of power, that standard is then rather cavalierly assumed to be gender neutral. . . .

The authors of *The Shadow Negotiation* are esteemed and experienced in negotiation research and education. Their book has generally been well received and popular. However, some critics have questioned categorizing negotiators by gender and juxtaposing behaviors of women on a binary scale of male-female distinctions. The following reading raises some of these issues.

❖ **Amy Cohen,** *GENDER: AN (UN) USEFUL CATEGORY OF PRESCRIPTIVE NEGOTIATION ANALYSIS*

13 Tex. J. Women & L. 169 (2003)

. . . [R]epresentations of gender as either male-female difference or male-female similarity, as the basis for describing interpersonal skills and theoretical analysis, draw artificial parameters around the range of behavioral and communicative capabilities available to us each to imagine and perform. Naming negotiating skills and analysis as "masculine" versus "feminine" in the first instance is of little, if any, pedagogical advantage and potentially considerable pedagogical harm insofar as such binary coding works to narrow and normalize the emancipatory possibilities inherent in the process of learning and achieving. In arguing for a pedagogy of negotiation that decodes behaviors and skills as masculine and feminine, I begin with a detailed look at Deborah Kolb and Judith Williams' construction of gender and women bargainers in *The Shadow Negotiation: How Women Can Master the Hidden Agendas that Determine Bargaining Success.* I focus on *The Shadow Negotiation* because it presents a recent, widely acclaimed, and perhaps the most extensive attempt to link feminist theory and empirical research with prescriptive negotiation advice. . . . Much of their advice is written in second person—the "you" is presumably female throughout. Kolb and Williams begin by critiquing conventional "rational" (read: masculine) negotiation advice to "take the people out of the problem" and suggest that as individuals bargain over issues, they are simultaneously negotiating the terms of their relationships, albeit in the "shadow." Thus, Kolb and Williams propose we learn to focus on active interpersonal positioning—both assertive and collaborative—within the "shadow negotiation" in order to best resolve the issues that form the substance of the "real" negotiation.

Unsurprisingly, if not ironically, the "shadow" is also the location of gendered expectations and frustrations. In aiming to allow women a nonessentialized space to overcome stereotypical gender barriers, Kolb and Williams reject paradigmatic, if purposefully oversimplified, liberal feminist (Professor Higgins's advice) and cultural feminist (Steel Magnolias' answer) attempts to resolve the tension they assume exists between women and negotiation. Namely, they discount conventional wisdom suggesting that with equal access to personal and institutional resources, individual women will negotiate just like individual men. Instead, they remind us "she will always play the game as a woman." Alternatively, they admit there is a risk of unqualified praise of women as empathic and relational that may cloud differences among women. Nonetheless, they conclude that even though "many" women do have "these special qualities," such feminine skills become structural liabilities in real world negotiations where yardsticks of success are typically correlated with "masculine" experience and standards.

Ultimately, "the effective negotiator," they tell us, "turns out to look remarkably like a man": independent, self-confident, active, objective, and unruffled by pressure. Kolb and Williams are correct in their observation that this reified model hurts men and women alike — men when they show their "feminine" side and women when they fall short of the "masculine" ideal, for "no woman, however competent, can pull off what is essentially a male performance." Thus, their prescription is not a matter of choosing between masculine and feminine styles, but rather encouraging women to draw on "all our skills" as we learn to recognize and manage gendered behavioral patterns and expectations in the shadow negotiation.

However, in maintaining a binary distinction between what is feminine and what is masculine as the basis for prescriptive negotiating advice, as well as in creating a "shadow" as the locus of the interpersonal that can be analyzed separately from the substance of the problem, Kolb and Williams solidify the categories of analysis they in fact attempt to discredit. Perhaps even more importantly, by encouraging women to place "ourselves" in negotiations based on descriptive assumptions about the way we as women are, they draw unnecessary parameters around their own useful and seasoned interpersonal negotiating advice that limit our range of imagining the ways in which individuals and groups might communicate with each other. . . .

The challenge for women, then, is to "learn how to use their strengths and manage the dual impressions of femininity and strategic resolve." Thus, for women learning the art and science of negotiation, gender is the point of entry; it is the preexisting condition we bring to the table and then use to position ourselves as we interact with other parties. However, the conclusion that women do not fare as well as men, Kolb argues, follows not from our skills or abilities, but rather from the technical and rational prescriptions underlying conventional negotiation advice that excludes a "subjective and embedded feminine approach.". . .

Thus, "as women," Kolb and Williams tell us in *The Shadow Negotiation*, "we take our differences and our competence into every negotiation. These can be turned to our advantage, but they have to be recognized as valuable. . . . We need, in effect, to revise the standard." Using gender both as a descriptive indicator of women bargainers and as a method of feminist critique, Kolb, together with Williams, provides a series of behavioral and analytical skills to help women negotiate effectively in a feminine voice. . . .

Questions

1. Is the legal negotiation table still slanted against women? Are there situations in which it might be slanted against men? Can you give examples?

2. Are female law students a self-selected group that does not reflect the characteristics described by Kolb and Williams? For a general report on gender differences in negotiation, see Bebcock & Laschever, *Women Don't Ask: Negotiation and the Gender Divide* (2003). See also Korobkin & Doherty, *Who Wins in Settlement Negotiations?* (2009)

3. If relationships matter and effective negotiation results from making connections and problem-solving skills, could men benefit by signing up for seminars on how to negotiate like a woman?

4. The above selection and the literature on gender and negotiation focuses on male perceptions of females and, to a lesser extent, on female perceptions of males. Isn't the perception that women have of women, and that men have of men, just as important in explaining our negotiation approaches and behaviors? Do you believe from what you have read and experienced that patterns between women negotiating with one another would be significantly different than negotiations between men? If so, how?
5. Might gender orientation be a factor in negotiation style? What effect might it have, and why?
6. Do you agree with the statement by Kolb and Williams that "a woman quite simply has to work harder than a man to get what she wants at a negotiation"?

Problem — The Power of Underestimation

In a paper on the subject of gender in negotiation, a female law student argued that being underestimated as a woman negotiator was an advantage. Do you agree with what she states below? Is use of an opponent's underestimation of your negotiation savvy an acceptable manipulation?

Both men and women underestimate women in male-dominated settings, particularly if the female is young. People tend not to expect women to be highly competitive or manipulative. This works to the advantage of the female negotiator. She can not only perform beyond her employers' or colleagues' expectations, but more importantly, she can also outsmart her opponents without their even realizing it. For example, if a male negotiator feels less intimidated by the young female negotiator, he may not fully engage his competitive skills and simply give her his "bottom line." The young female negotiator may then use that figure as the starting point for her negotiations. Being underestimated can also be a great psychological motivator for women. Such offensive attitudes can act as a powerful catalyst to prove their opponents wrong. From this vantage point, women can see how being underestimated can be a highly underrated advantage.

B. Cultural Differences, or Why the World Is Not Boring

We tend to be most comfortable and trusting among people like ourselves and most fascinated with those who are different. Negotiating with people from other cultures can be challenging because trust and rapport affect negotiations, as do cultural values and traditions, which color what we perceive.

Cultural differences are difficult to discuss and apply to negotiation because the meaning of culture is elusive. Like gender, focusing on culture lends itself to stereotypes and creates a risk of substituting categorical norms for the uniqueness of individuals. Cultural considerations are so complex and ever-changing in our globalized world that defining a person by identity to a single culture and using that identity to predict values or behavior is prone to error.

However, because it is helpful to have clues about how our negotiating counterparts perceive the world and perhaps value things differently than us, cultural variations should be considered. Sensitivity to cultural differences can assist in preparing for negotiations, interpreting behavior, and providing ideas for how impasse can be avoided and value might be created in a negotiation. Cultural awareness can also help us avoid unintended consequences of what we say and do, as well as alert us to what others may anticipate from us because of our own cultural identity.

Cultural classifications are similar to many conveniences in life that we use but wish we did not need. Like automatic home appliances, disposable products, computers, and other of life's shortcuts, we may wish we did not need them, but we cannot seem to live without them. We use culture as a label or shortcut about categories of people with whom we do not confidently identify. We know that there are shortcomings to this convenience, but we use it anyway. We know that no culture or grouping of people is monolithic or truly homogenous. Although a group of people may have some common characteristics, those characteristics are not distributed or shared uniformly. Even if we could be sure of the nature of a group, few people are part of only one cultural identity. So we can never be sure of which of several cultural influences will be most applicable. Will the culture of a person's national origin, ethnicity, religion, schooling, professional identity, or economic class predominate in a particular contextual situation? Finally, can we ever know if the culture of the last generation, when cultural norms for that group may have been identified or popularized, is the behavioral or value norms of that group today? We know that cultural generalizations, although convenient, are inherently unreliable. In constitutional parlance, they are necessarily underinclusive and overinclusive.

With all of these caveats, cultural considerations are of great interest because we feel we need all the help we can get in better understanding others. Travel guides feature a section on the culture you will encounter in another country. One book claims to provide clear and concise information on how to negotiate in 50 different countries that account for 90 percent of the world economy (Llamazares 2009). Sociologists and political scientists, among others, study the impact of culture. People regularly talk about cultural behavior and analogize that culture is the software of the mind. Most books on negotiation include advice on how to utilize cultural awareness and knowledge to improve negotiation results. The next article explains both the value and shortcomings of using cultural categories. The perception errors referred to by Professor Sebenius, by now, should be familiar to you.

❖ **James K. Sebenius,** *Caveats for Cross-Border Negotiations*

18 Negot. J. 122 (2002)

While some of the work on culture and negotiation is at best superficial, much of the relevant academic literature is well grounded and accompanied by careful statements as to its limits and the conditions under which it should apply. While holding on to the truth that some characteristics do systematically vary across national borders, however, there is often a general uneasiness about unwarranted use of purported cross-cultural insight. . . . My objective is to make analysts and negotiators more sophisticated consumers of this advice by suggesting four classes of caveat, each with a slightly tongue-in-cheek name that will, I hope, be usefully evocative.

1. The John Wayne v. Charlie Chan Fallacy: Stereotyping National Cultures

Start with the obvious: All American negotiators are not like John Wayne and all Chinese negotiators are not like Charlie Chan. . . . In the face of such internal variation, we wisely caution ourselves against mindless stereotyping by nationality (as well as by gender, religion, race, profession, or age). Even so, in many situations it remains all-too-common to hear offhand remarks such as "all Chinese negotiators . . ." (as well as generalizations about "women" . . . or "engineers"). To combat this, a strong version of the anti-stereotyping prescription calls for ignoring nationality altogether in preparing for negotiation.

That advice is too strong. Nationality often does have a great deal to do with cultural characteristics, particularly in relatively homogeneous countries like Japan. The careful work of many researchers confirms significant associations between nationality and a range of traits and outcomes. . . . It would be foolish to throw away potentially valuable information. But what does information on a particular group's behavioral expectations or deeper cultural characteristics really convey? Typically, cultural descriptions are about central *tendencies* of populations that also exhibit considerable "within-group" variation. . . .

Inferences about individuals from central tendencies are often misleading or wrong. *You negotiate with individuals, not averages.*

But viewing the world without the aid of stereotypes is difficult. Forming stereotypes is a natural reflex that helps order the overflow of information that barrages people. Social psychologist Ellen Langer argues that a solution to the negative effects of stereotyping is "mindfulness," which she defines as a willingness to create new categories, an openness to new information, and an awareness that more than one perspective exists. Rather than straining against forming stereotypes, a more realistic strategy is to allow stereotypes room to change, multiply, and adapt to new information.

In sum, remember that "national traits" — as well as traits supposedly associated with gender, ethnicity, etc. — are *distributions* of characteristics across populations, not blanket descriptions applicable to each individual. Be very cautious about making inferences about characteristics of specific individuals from different groups — even where the groups are, on average, sharply different. Avoid stereotyping and the "prototypicality" error of assuming an individual will exhibit the most likely group characteristic. Even if U.S. negotiators are on average more impatient, deal-focused, and individually oriented than their Chinese counterparts, be careful not to help amplify that stereotype in the mind of the other side. . . .

2. The Rosetta Stone Fallacy: Overattribution to National Culture

National culture clearly matters. But there is a tendency to see it as the Rosetta Stone, the indispensable key to describe, explain, and predict the behavior of the other side. Of course there are many possible "cultures" operating within a given individual. . . . National culture can be highly visible but, obviously, it is only one of many possible influences. For example, Jeswald Salacuse surveyed executives from a dozen countries to determine national tendencies on ten important bargaining characteristics, such as negotiating goal (contract v. relationship), orientation (win-win v. win-lose), formality level, communication style, risk-taking, etc. While his results showed significant national differences, he also analyzed the data according to profession and occupations of the respondents such as law, engineering, marketing, the military, diplomacy, accounting, etc. These categories, too, showed systematic association with different bargaining styles. Finally, Salacuse could also differentiate many of these characteristics by gender. Other extensive studies extend and elaborate analogous findings. Nationality often matters when considering someone's bargaining characteristics but so too does gender, ethnicity, functional specialty, etc. . . . [N]ational culture is but one of many "cultures" that can influence bargaining behavior. . . .

B. Attribution Bias

Cultural differences, often evident in surface behavior, are easy to see; richer contextual factors frequently are not. In unfamiliar cross-border settings, factors like strategic incompatibility, politics, or even individual personality are less likely to be "blamed" for undesirable outcomes. The powerful but unconscious tendency to overattribute behavior to culture, all too often clouds negotiators' vision of the full range of factors that can affect a negotiation. Psychologists have extensively documented this dynamic, a systematic tendency to focus on supposed characteristics of the person on the other side of the table, rather than on the economic or other powerful contextual factors. . . . The antidotes? First, remember that "culture" doesn't just mean nationality; instead there are many potentially influential "cultures" at work. Second, beyond "culture" are many other factors that have potential to affect negotiation behavior. Nationality can carry important information, but with many other cultures and many other factors at work, you should be careful not to treat your counterpart's passport as the Rosetta Stone.

3. The "Visual Flying Rules" at Night Fallacy: Falling Prey to Potent Psychological Biases

Self-Serving Perceptions of Our Own Side

There is a powerful tendency, formally studied as "biased assimilation," for people to interpret information in negotiation self-servingly. For example, experiments give a number of people identical information about a pending court case but randomly assign them to the role of plaintiff or defendant. When each person is asked for his or her private assessment of the probability that the plaintiff will win, those assigned the role of plaintiff on average give much higher odds than those (randomly) assigned to the role of defendant (but, again, on the basis of identical information). People tend to "believe their own lines" or self-servingly interpret information. . . . And this tendency runs deep: Back in the 1950s, researchers conducted an experiment at a boy's camp, sponsoring a jelly bean hunt among the campers. After the hunt, the boys were shown an identical picture of a jar of jelly beans. Each boy evaluated the total number of beans in the jar according to whether he was told the jar belonged to his own team or to the other side. The same photograph was estimated to contain many more beans when it was presented as "your team's" and far fewer when it was alleged to be the "other side's."

Partisan Perceptions of the Other Side

If our capacity to process information critical of our own side is flawed, it is even more the case for our assessments of the other side in a conflict or negotiation. In part, this stems from the in-group/out-group phenomenon. Persons from different cultures, especially on the opposite side of the bargaining table, are more readily identified as belonging to an out-group, or the Other. Once that labeling is in place, powerful perceptual dynamics kick in (beyond the tendencies toward stereotyping and overattribution). Robert Robinson describes extensive research over the last 40 years, documenting an unconscious mechanism that enhances "one's own side, portraying it as more talented, honest, and morally upright" while simultaneously vilifying the Other. This leads to a systematic exaggeration of the other side's position and the overestimation of the extent of the actual conflict. As a result, negotiators are often unduly pessimistic about their ability to find common ground, and can be unwilling to pursue it.

Self-Fulfilling Prophesies

Such partisan perceptions hold the power to change reality by becoming self-fulfilling prophesies. The effects of labeling and stereotyping have been documented thoroughly to show that perceptions have the power to shape reality. . . . At the negotiating table, the same principle holds true: Clinging firmly to the idea that one's counterpart is stubborn, for example, is likely to yield intransigence on both sides, precluding the possibility of a compromise that might have occurred had the label of "obstinacy" not been so rigorously affixed.

In short, just as a pilot trying to navigate by visual flight rules[VFR] at night or in a storm is prone to dangerous misjudgments, the psychology of perception in cross-cultural situations is rife with biases. Not only do we stereotype and overattribute to nationality, we are also poor at interpreting information on our own situation, vulnerable to partisan perceptions of the other side, and likely to act in ways that become dangerously self-fulfilling.

4. St. Augustine's Fallacy: "When in Rome . . ."

Assume that you have undertaken a full analysis of the culture of the person you will meet on the other side of the bargaining table. St. Augustine gave the classic cross-cultural advice: When in Rome, do as the Romans do. While this admonition certainly has merit, it is not always good advice . . . much better options may be available. For example, learning that the Chinese, on average, are more hesitant than North Americans to take risks is only a first step. Clearly, a responsive strategy would not mimic this hesitancy, but effectively anticipate it.

Rather than learning to behave as the Romans do (while in Rome or elsewhere), strategies should accommodate the degree of cross-table understanding each side has of the other. For example, consider the best approach for a U.S. manager on his first visit to Japan dealing with a Yale-educated Japanese executive who has worked extensively in Europe and North America. Here it would be sensible to let the Japanese take the lead. If a negotiator is far more familiar with a counterpart's culture than vice versa, the best strategy might be to embrace the counterpart's negotiating "script." If both sides are equally "literate," an improvisational and mutually-accommodating approach might be most appropriate. A lower degree of familiarity dictates bringing in locally familiar expertise, perhaps on your side and perhaps even as a mediator.

A great deal depends on how familiar you are with "Roman" culture and how familiar your "Roman" counterpart is with your culture. And of course you want to avoid the previous fallacies as well. The nationalities across the table from each other may be Chinese and U.S., but both players may be regulars on the international business circuit, which has its own, increasingly global negotiating culture. Again, assess — etiquette, deeper traits, negotiation-specific expectations, and caveats; do not assume and project your assumption onto your counterpart.

In Conclusion

Cross-cultural negotiation analyses offer insight as to systematic differences in gestures and body language, etiquette and deportment, deeper behavioral traits, as well as organizational decision-making processes and forms of corporate and public governance. Accurately applying the very real insights from such studies can be challenging, but the difficulties perhaps lessened by thinking of four unlikely categories that themselves derive from cultures most dissimilar: John Wayne and Charlie Chan, the Rosetta Stone, VFR at night, and St. Augustine.

Note: Research on Culture and Negotiation

Professor Sebenius provides important caveats about the limits of cultural references. He also concludes that cultural analysis offers insight into systematic differences about how people from different cultures negotiate. With his caveats in mind, we now turn to some of the salient features that research indicates do distinguish the way people from different cultures negotiate.

The negotiation approaches and behaviors common within a culture are related to other aspects of that culture and are based on societal values, social structure, and modes of communication. The three distinguishing features most often mentioned in relation to negotiation norms within a culture are the value of individualism versus collectivism, egalitarianism versus hierarchy, and direct versus indirect modes of communication. Understanding these norms is helpful in forming working assumptions about different cultures and also in understanding our own values. The sharpest differences between societal values are often framed as differences between Eastern and Western cultures; however, this is too simple and can be misleading. The counter-posed sets of values can be summarized as follows:

- *Individualism versus collectivism*: Some societies appear to value individual needs over the collective needs of the group. Economic rewards, as well as social standing, are based on individual accomplishments. Individual autonomy is more important than societal interests. Individual rights tend to be most highly valued. In contrast, other societies place a higher priority on the interdependence of individuals and their social obligations to one another. Collective interests are valued more highly than individual rights.

- *Hierarchy versus egalitarianism*: This cultural juxtaposition distinguishes societies in which power and status are seen as vertical rather than horizontal. In hierarchical societies, social superiority is based on others being socially inferior and deference is given to those who are higher on the social and economic ladder. In egalitarian societies, there are no social castes and social status is undifferentiated.

- *Direct versus indirect communication*: In more direct communicating societies, information is explicit, with minimum nuance, and can be readily understood regardless of the context. Meaning is on the surface rather than embedded in other layers of pretext or context. People in societies with more indirect communication embed the meaning of their words in the context of the situation. Meaning must be inferred to be fully understood.

Interdisciplinary research is increasingly focusing on cultural variations in negotiation. Although very interesting, much of the research is highly theoretical and is written in research parlance. Practical application of the research findings is just starting to emerge and should be of considerable value to negotiators, subject to the caveats explained by Professor Sebenius. The following excerpt is from an extensive volume of research findings on negotiation and culture.

❖ **Wendy L. Adair & Jeanne M. Brett,** *CULTURE AND NEGOTIATION PROCESSES*

**The Handbook of Negotiation and Culture 158
(M. Gelfand & J. Brett eds., 2004)**

Culture is a distinctly group construct. Individuals have personalities; groups have cultures. Culture consists of group members' shared beliefs, attitudes, norms, and behaviors, and the group's social, political, economic, and religious institutional structures. . . . Social institutions carry culture in their ideology and reinforce it by rewarding and sanctioning social interaction within the group. . . . [We] use national boundaries to identify cultures, because national boundaries define institutional boundaries, and as a result provide an objective way to distinguish cultural groups. . . .

Culture and Beliefs about Negotiation

People from Western cultures tend to have independent, also called individualistic, self-construals. They understand themselves as independent or detached from the social groups to which they belong and view themselves as agents free to focus on personal goals to self-actualize rather than on social obligations. People from Eastern cultures tend to have interdependent, also called collectivist, self-construals. They tend to understand themselves within the context of the social groups to which they belong and view themselves as agents constrained by social obligations to maintain harmony and preserve "face" within their social groups.

An independent self-construal seems to be a worldview that is naturally associated with the perspective that negotiation is about distributing resources, not so much about relationships. An interdependent self-construal seems to be a worldview that is naturally associated with the perspective that negotiation is about relationships first, and then about distributing resources. This is the first distinction reflected in our model of culture and negotiation processes. . . .

This leads us to predict that a relationship frame will be more salient for negotiators in Eastern cultures, while a resource distribution frame will be more salient for negotiators in Western cultures. This implies that negotiators in Eastern cultures are more likely to think about negotiation in terms of relationships and that this frame should influence their negotiation goals. Negotiators in Western cultures are more likely to think about negotiation in terms of outcome, and this frame should influence their negotiation goals.

Culture and Negotiators' Goals

Because negotiation is a mixed-motive, cooperation and competition are both central elements of negotiation in the East and the West. Cooperative goals focus negotiators on integrative outcomes or joint value creation, while competitive goals direct the distributive or value-claiming aspects of negotiation. We propose that the normative behaviors that negotiators from different cultures use to enact cooperative and competitive goals are different and can be predicted from cultural differences in goals and how negotiation is framed in Eastern and Western cultures.

If people from Eastern cultures believe negotiation is more about relationships, the interplay between cooperative and competitive goals may represent an attempt to create a long-term relationship that is not too cooperative but has enough social distance to justify claiming value. For example, the primary cooperative goal may be to build trust, and the primary competitive goal may be to establish dominance. If people from Western cultures believe negotiation is more about the distribution of resources, the interplay between cooperative and competitive goals may represent an attempt to both create joint gains and claim the largest possible portion of that gain. . . . Thus, although negotiators from Eastern and Western cultures have both cooperative and competitive goals, the meaning of those goals may be different and may be one factor affecting normative negotiation behavior.

Culture and Negotiators' Norms

Norms are standards of appropriate behavior in social interaction. As with negotiation beliefs and goals, we argue that culture affects negotiation norms and therefore the behaviors that negotiators are more or less likely to use. In addition to cooperative and competitive goals, another major difference between Eastern and Western cultures that may affect negotiation behavior is low-versus high-context communication. In Eastern cultures that tend to be high context (e.g., Japan and China), meaning is communicated not just by a person's words or acts, but also by the context in which those words or acts are communicated. High-context communication is indirect and requires considerable familiarity with the cultural meaning conveyed by various contexts. In Western cultures that tend to be low context (e.g., the United States and Germany), meaning is embedded in words or acts. Low-context communication is direct, and although it requires familiarity with words and acts, it does not require familiarity with contexts.

Discussions of low- and high-context communication emphasize the differences between direct and indirect communications, but the dimensions on which high- and low-context communication cultures differ go beyond directness. For example, a negotiator from a low-context culture might suggest that his company is so financially weak that without a good price, his company will not be able to buy the product at all. In the same situation, a negotiator from a high-context culture might appeal to sympathy: "We've had a bad quarter, and our acquisitions budget is extremely limited." In the first example, the negotiator's message is explicit: "If you do not give us a good price, we will not be able to buy from you." In the second example, the negotiator's message is implicit; the other negotiator has to infer that a sale depends on an especially competitive price. The appeal is different in each case, too. In the first example, the appeal is to fact: "If you do not give us a good price, we will not be able to buy." In the second example, the appeal is to a more general principle: you are stronger, and you should take care of us. Logic in low-context communication therefore tends to be linear, developed in "if-then" terms. Logic in high-context communication tends be more amorphous and may require the listener to infer the focus of the argument.

Several research studies on negotiation processes support the low- and high-context communication distinction in the East and West. In low-context cultures, persuasion makes appeals to rationality; and in high-context cultures, persuasion makes appeals to emotions and affect. For example, in a content analysis of U.S.-Taiwanese cross-cultural negotiation transcripts . . . U.S. negotiators used more analytic statements, relying on logic and reasoning to persuade. In contrast, Taiwanese negotiators used more normative statements, relying on social roles and relationships to persuade. Other research has found U.S. negotiators using more commitments, a form of rational persuasion, than Chinese negotiators, and making more promises, a form of rational persuasion, than Soviet negotiators. In low-context cultures, information sharing is explicit and direct, whereas in high-context cultures, information sharing is implicit and indirect. For example . . . U.S. negotiators used more no's, a direct form of information exchange, than Chinese negotiators. Our own research also reveals that negotiators from low-context cultures engage in more direct information sharing, whereas negotiators from high-context cultures favor more indirect, implicit communication. . . .

In sum, our model implies an East-West distinction in negotiation with respect to beliefs, goals, and norms. Negotiators from the East tend to frame negotiation as a relationship. They have both cooperative trust goals that we propose are enacted through indirect information sharing behaviors, and competitive dominance goals that we propose are enacted through affective influence behaviors. Negotiators from the West tend to frame negotiation as a distribution of resources. They have both cooperative joint-gain goals that we propose are enacted through direct information sharing behaviors, and competitive claiming goals that we propose are enacted through rational influence behaviors. . . .

Of course, the East-West divide is not a dichotomy, but rather a continuum representing cultures that are more high-context on one side and more low-context on the other. Culturally normative behaviors occur in degrees of more or less, and contextual cues less subtle than culture may cause the frame to flip from what is culturally normative to what is not. For example, even high-context culture conflict avoiders may make a direct refusal in a competitive negotiation situation. . . .

Culture and Negotiation Process

In a study comparing negotiation behaviors and six cultures (the United States, Russia, France, Brazil, Japan, and Hong Kong), we looked at behavioral differences along a low-high context culture continuum (Adair, Brett, Lempereur, Okumura, Shikhirev, Kinsley, and Lytle, 2004). U.S. negotiators used relatively more direct information sharing than negotiators from the other five cultures. Russian, Japanese, and Hong Kong Chinese negotiators were more likely to use indirect information sharing than other negotiators, and, Russian and Japanese negotiators were more likely to use both rational and affective influence than negotiators from the other four cultures. These results confirm a relatively consistent low-high context continuum, with the U.S. negotiators more low context, Japanese and Russian negotiators more high context, and French, Brazilian, and Hong Kong Chinese negotiators somewhere in the middle of the continuum. . . .

Conclusion

Because researchers are just beginning to study culture and negotiation processes, the research . . . is not yet cumulative. Thus, our model of culture's effect on negotiation behaviors and sequences is tentative; our understanding of how negotiators in a cross-cultural setting can most effectively adapt their behaviors to maximize effective communication is limited; and, our evidence for what patterns of adaptation lead to joint satisfaction and joint gain is restricted. . . .

Much of the research and writing on culture as a factor in negotiation focuses on cultural norms as traits we should be aware of in those with whom we negotiate, particularly across borders. If the research on cultural norms is reliable, our own cultural identity can offer clues to others about our negotiating tendencies and can provide us personal insight into our negotiating behaviors and responses. Even though our own cultural or group identity may influence how we perceive ourselves and how others view us, these categorical attributes are subject to error and oversimplification to the point of being misleading and insulting. This limitation will not stop others with whom we negotiate from generalizing about us in a way that might affect their behavior toward us. Just as important, our self-identity helps shape our beliefs, emotions, and behaviors. This can have an impact on how we negotiate.

If you would like to test your own cultural, gender, or racial sensitivities and biases online, go to *https://implicit.harvard.edu/implicit/demo/selectatest.html*, where you will have the opportunity to participate in a Web-based research study. The results can be revealing and might be discussed in class.

Questions

7. What is the dominant culture with which you identify? Is this the same culture that those who do not know you well would assume you belong to? Are there other cultural subgroups that help define who you are? Are there stereotypes that opposing negotiators might have about you? Is there any way you can use those likely stereotypes to your advantage?

8. Does the downside of thinking about people as part of a cultural group outweigh the possible benefit of grouping people to help understand their values and anticipate their behavior?

9. Does the Adair and Brett writing contrasting Eastern and Western cultural differences to negotiating contradict Sebenius's warning about cultural stereotyping? Do you find Adair and Brett's report on cultural research helpful?

10. Do you agree that "culture is the lens through which we make sense of the world"? If so, is there any doubt that people of different cultures will see the world so differently that world conflict is inevitable? Is conflict and how to deal with it culturally defined? For a comprehensive and instructive collection of provocative readings on both culture and gender as they relate to conflict, see Chew (2001).

11. Based on selection, training, and shared values, do lawyers constitute a cultural subgroup that helps others understand them and predict their behavior? Is your answer the same for doctors, accountants, or clergy?

C. Is Race a Factor in Negotiations?

Earlier studies on race as a factor in negotiation outcomes found significant differences based on race (Ayers 1991, 1995). These studies compared prices arrived at for new cars in the Chicago area between white and black testers posing as otherwise similar buyers. Although cited in the negotiation literature as disturbing evidence that African-Americans "often get worse outcomes in negotiations," this evidence cannot be extrapolated to indicate that race is a predictor of negotiation skill. These studies documented discrimination in the offers that sales personnel made to African-American versus Caucasian testers, rather than differences in negotiating ability among the testers. Indeed, the studies were later introduced as evidence of discrimination in a class-action lawsuit against General Motors Acceptance Corporation (see Hawkins 2004).

We live in an age in which an African-American U.S. President has been elected, an increasing number of professionals are people of color, and many more people identify themselves as interracial or blended — or choose not to identify with any racial classification. Even though discrimination still exists and race may matter in important social justice issues, does it make a difference in negotiation among lawyers, who are a self-selected group of achievers with similar training?

We are not aware of empirical data about race as a factor in negotiation among attorneys, but Professor Charles Craver, who has taught negotiation for more than 25 years, has tracked simulated negotiation outcomes by gender and race among law students. In the next reading, Professor Craver presents the results and notes how race can influence negotiation encounters. He introduces his article by discussing one specialized practice of negotiation where client statistics can be accessed — sports agents, many of whom are lawyers. The disproportionately small percentage of African-American sports agents sets the stage for his report on negotiation outcomes between law students.

❖ **Charles B. Craver,** RACE AND NEGOTIATION PERFORMANCE: *DOES RACE PREDICT SUCCESS AS A NEGOTIATOR?*

8 ABA Disp. Resol. Mag. 22 (Fall 2001)

In major league baseball, nineteen percent of the players are black. As of 1992, 150 of the 200 agents registered with Major League Baseball Players Association had active clientele; black agents accounted for a mere three percent of this 150. In professional football, sixty-nine percent of the players are black, but black agents comprise only fourteen percent of the registered agents with active files. Worse yet, more than eighty percent of the NBA's players are black, but less than ten percent of them have black agents.

Why are many prominent black athletes reluctant to retain black agents to represent them? One factor undoubtedly concerns the high profile success of white agents such as David Falk in basketball and Leigh Steinberg in football, and the ability of these super-agents to attract draft-eligible black athletes. Another may involve the fact that "many black players have internalized racial stereotypes about blacks and thus, discriminate against their own people." These athletes may privately believe that white agents can negotiate better contracts than black agents. . . .

Real, Perceived Racial Differences

Negotiations involving participants from diverse ethnic backgrounds frequently develop differently than bargaining interactions involving persons from similar backgrounds. People tend to negotiate more cooperatively with opponents of the same race and culture than with adversaries of different races and cultures. Apparently, similarity induces trust and reduces the need for each interactor to maintain a particular "face" in the other's eyes. . . .

Students I have taught at various law schools over the past 25 years have often allowed their stereotypical beliefs to influence their bargaining encounters. Many of my students — regardless of their ethnicity — think that Caucasian males are the most Machiavellian and competitive negotiators. They expect these men to employ adversarial and manipulative tactics to obtain optimal results for themselves. On the other hand, numerous students expect African-American, Asian-American, and Latino-American negotiators to be more accommodating and less competitive. Even members of one race often stereotype other members of the same race. When opponents fail to behave in the anticipated manner, the bargaining process may be adversely affected.

Despite the unreliability of many stereotypical beliefs and the absence of more recent surveys, several empirical studies have found a few relevant differences between black and white interactants. Blacks tend to be high in terms of Interpersonal Orientation (IO). High IO individuals are more sensitive and responsive to the interpersonal aspects of their relationships with others. This tendency should make blacks more effective negotiators. Because bargaining outcomes are directly affected by the interpersonal skills of the participants, high IO individuals should be able to achieve better results than their low IO cohorts.

During verbal encounters, blacks tend to speak more forcefully and with greater verbal aggressiveness than whites. In competitive settings, this trait might enhance the bargaining effectiveness of individuals with these traits, while in cooperative situations it might undermine their ability to achieve mutual accords. When they interact with others, blacks tend to make less eye contact while listening to others than do whites, which may be perceived by speakers as an indication of indifference to what is being said or of disrespect toward the speaker. Such behavior might undermine the ability of the persons with minimal eye contact to establish the kind of rapport that can advance bargaining discussions.

Most negotiators tend to employ a cooperative/problem-solving or a competitive/adversarial style when they bargain with others. Cooperative/problem-solvers tend to be open with their information, prefer to use objective criteria to guide their discussions, and endeavor to maximize the joint return achieved by interactants, while competitive/adversarials tend to be less open with information, focus more on stated positions than objective factors, are manipulative, and attempt to maximize their own side's return. White negotiators usually employ relatively consistent bargaining styles, while black negotiators tend to adopt styles that are reflective of the race of their opponents. Blacks tend to perform more effectively when they compete with whites and when they cooperate with other blacks.

Statistical Findings

. . . This study evaluates the possible relationship between race and performance on negotiation exercises. The Null Hypothesis is that there is no correlation between race and the results students achieve on Legal Negotiation course exercises. The Alternative Hypothesis is that there is a relationship between race and the results students achieve on Legal Negotiation course exercises.

Although I have 16 years of Legal Negotiation course data at George Washington University, I decided to focus on the data covering the past nine years because the classes I taught from 1986 through the spring of 1992 contained insufficient numbers of black students to permit meaningful statistical comparisons. . . .

The statistical data . . . provide strong support for the Null Hypothesis . . . for three of the nine years, the mean negotiation scores for white students were slightly above the mean scores for black students, while for the other six years, the mean negotiation scores for black students were slightly above the mean scores for white students.

Implications

Individuals who commence negotiations with people of different races should appreciate the need to establish trusting and cooperative relationships before the serious substantive discussions begin. This approach should significantly enhance the likelihood of mutually beneficial transactions. The preliminary stage of their interaction may be used to generate a modicum of rapport. Negotiators should try to minimize the counterproductive stereotypes they may consciously or subconsciously harbor toward persons of their opponent's ethnicity. If negotiators anticipate difficult interactions as a result of such usually irrational preconceptions, they are likely to generate self-fulfilling prophecies. If negotiators conversely expect their opponents to behave more cooperatively and less manipulatively because of their ethnicity, they may carelessly lower their guard and give their opponents an inherent bargaining advantage. Negotiators must also try to understand any seemingly illogical reactions their opponents may initially exhibit toward them as a result of those individuals' stereotyping of them.

If the first contact negotiators have with opponents indicates that those persons are expecting highly competitive transactions, they should not hesitate to employ "attitudinal bargaining" to disabuse their opponents of this preconception. They should create cooperative physical and psychological environments. Warm handshakes and open postures can initially diminish combative atmospheres. Cooperative negotiators can sit adjacent to, instead of directly across from, opponents. In a few instances, it may be necessary to directly broach the subject of negative stereotyping, since this may be the most efficacious way to negate the influence of these feelings.

People who participate in bargaining transactions should recognize that the specific circumstances and unique personal traits of the individual negotiators — rather than generalized beliefs regarding ethnic characteristics — determine the way in which each interaction evolves. Each opponent has to be evaluated and dealt with differently. Is that individual a cooperative or a competitive bargainer? Does the other side possess greater, equal, or less bargaining power concerning the issues to be addressed? What bargaining techniques are likely to influence that person? What negotiating techniques has that individual decided to employ, and what are the most effective ways to counter those tactics? As the instant transaction unfolds, each negotiator will have to make strategic changes to respond to unanticipated disclosures or to changed circumstances.

When negotiators find themselves attributing certain characteristics to opponents, they must carefully determine whether those attributes are based on specific information pertaining to those particular opponents or to vague generalizations regarding people of their race. If people bargained only with individuals of the same race, they would quickly realize how different we all are. Some opponents would behave cooperatively, while others would act in a competitive manner. Some would exhibit win-lose tendencies, while others would evidence win-win attitudes. Techniques that would be effective against some opponents would be ineffective against others.

The nine years of Legal Negotiation course data evaluated by me indicates the absence of any statistically significant correlation between student race and the results achieved on negotiation exercises. These findings would suggest that even if cultural and behavioral differences between black and white students exist, those differences have no impact on students' ability to achieve beneficial negotiation exercise results.

Questions

12. Is race distinguishable from culture for purposes of negotiation? If so, what is the difference?
13. Are the "differences between black and white interactants," as cited by Professor Craver, valid? Are any generalizations about the speaking patterns, eye contact, or bargaining style of black people in comparison to white people reliable or of any value? In a multicultural, increasingly blended society, is race relevant?
14. Are there any possible factors or explanations for the disproportionate number of African-American sports agents other than the high profile of white agents and "internalized racial stereotypes," as noted by Professor Craver?
15. Is there any different explanation for the relatively few female sports agents?
16. If other bargainers assume that male Caucasian negotiators are "Machiavellian and competitive," how might this affect the bargaining process? Could a white male minimize such assumptions? How?

Note: Response of an African-American Law Professor[*]

As a law professor, and as a teacher of ADR, I was interested in what Professor Craver had learned in 16 years of teaching negotiations (9 years of which constituted the basis of his study). What I wonder, however, for your readers, is what his student negotiations in mock exercises in law school tells us about negotiations among lawyers and clients in the real world of sports negotiation. In my mind, the more interesting question concerning race has to do with the perception among many black athletes that they would do better with white lawyers (and some would say Jewish lawyers) serving as their agents. There are interesting questions about the impact of race and how that perception gets internalized in the individual coming into a world with which he or she did not have prior experience. What goes on in the world of high-level (i.e., a great deal of money involved) sports negotiations that leads to the perception in the NBA and NFL that a black athlete needs s white lawyer (agent) to be truly successful in the negotiations with the owners?

I appreciate the fact that Professor Craver has used his experience in teaching Legal Negotiation in law school to provide some empirical data about race and its impact on student results in law school negotiations. I think that Professor Craver may agree that his study tells only about law students in mock legal negotiations in law school. Does the study reliably tell us much about perceptions and actions among black and white negotiators serving as agents for athletes and representatives of owners in sports negotiations?

---

[*] The following comment is from a colleague who reviewed this chapter.

CHAPTER

10

Negotiation Ethics

A. Deception vs. Disclosure

As a lawyer, you will find yourself governed by rules that may seem both contradictory and personally uncomfortable. Ethics codes forbid you from lying in court but permit you to lie in negotiation, at least as most non-lawyers would define lying. Even if you would not deceive or lie on your own behalf, the obligation to be a zealous advocate for clients will confront you, as a lawyer, with the dilemma of deciding how far to go in gaining a negotiation advantage for your client by misstating or not revealing information.

This dilemma has contributed to an image problem for our profession. "Lawyer" is considered by many to be synonymous with "liar." The 1997 movie *Liar, Liar*, featuring actor Jim Carrey, was advertised by displaying the words "Lawyer, Lawyer," crossed out, with "Liar, Liar" written over them in red. This theme was repeated in the first scene of the film, where the lawyer's son is asked in his kindergarten class what his father does for a living. He innocently tells the class that his father is a "liar." The public image of lawyers is also reflected in unflattering and prolific jokes ("How do you know when a lawyer is lying? His lips are moving.").

Because negotiation occurs in private, usually without clients present, there is little check on what is said or not said in negotiation between lawyers. The ethics rules for negotiation are not precise and are sometimes contradictory, especially regarding what must be revealed to an opposing party. These elements result in constant and challenging choices facing attorneys in terms of ethics, morality, and negotiation effectiveness.

Ethics rules attempt to provide a guide for lawyers on how to balance our obligation to a client's interests and the integrity of the profession in a negotiation, but the specifics of applying the rules are elusive. Ethical limits can be found in each state's Rules of Professional Conduct or Code of Professional Responsibility and in its case and statutory law. The American Bar Association's (ABA's) Model Rules of Professional Conduct are the basis for most state ethics rules. The beginning point is Rule 4.1, which states that a lawyer shall not "knowingly (a) make a false statement of material fact or law to a third person; or (b) fail to disclose a material fact to a third person when disclosure is necessary to avoid assisting a criminal or fraudulent act by a client, unless disclosure is prohibited by Rule 1.6."

A serious limitation of knowing what should or should not be revealed is the qualification that only "material" facts must be revealed. The official comment to Rule 4.1 states that "under generally accepted conventions in negotiation, . . . estimates of price or value placed on the subject of the transaction" are not considered material, nor are "a party's intentions as to an acceptable settlement of a claim" covered by Rule 4.1's prohibitions against making false statements. (See Comment 2.)

Also, as you may recall, Rule 1.6 protects client confidences. So an attorney whose client reveals a bottom line, or any other information that the client regards as confidential, cannot disclose that information, unless the client authorizes the disclosure. In effect, the requirement that a lawyer may not reveal client confidences swallows the rule requiring disclosure, even of most criminal conduct.

The net result of the ethical rules is that lawyers in negotiation can lie about some things, but not others. You can puff and bluff because that's the expected convention. So, as a lawyer you can tell the other side that "this is a seven-figure case if it gets to a jury," even though you believe a verdict would not exceed $500,000, or that your client's bottom line is $100,000 when it is really $80,000. However, you cannot say your client sustained a broken neck, knowing that she did not. In other words, deception is still considered an acceptable aspect of negotiation, but only to a point. (See the next chapter for the limits imposed by contract law.) This creates a dilemma for the ethical negotiator and lends itself to a lot of debate and literature on the subject.

Richard Zitrin and Carol Langford, in their book *The Moral Compass of the American Lawyer* (1999), explain that lawyers are perennially rated among the least beloved people in America because almost everyone thinks lawyers lie when we engage in "strategic speaking," or "shading the truth" when negotiating. According to them, negotiation necessarily "involves some measure of misleading the opponent [and] concealing one's true position. . . . Negotiation is not, and never will be, a matter of 'putting all our cards on the table'" (165). Zitrin and Langford summarize lawyers' excuses for lying in negotiation:

- "I didn't lie," which includes "My statement was literally true" (although misleading), "I was speaking on a subject about which there is no absolute truth," and "I was merely putting matters in the best light."
- "I lied, if you insist on calling it that, but it was . . .": "ethically permissible" (and thus okay); "legal" (and thus okay); "just an omission"; or "ineffectual," because it was just a white lie or because it was simply not believed.
- "I lied, but it was justified by the very nature of things." This includes situations where lying is considered part of the rules of the game, such as negotiations, where most lawyers feel that candor defeats the very purpose of the exercise.
- "I lied, but it was justified by the special ethics of lawyering," especially the duties owed clients: loyalty, confidentiality, and, of course, zealous representation.
- "The lie belongs to someone else," usually the client, so that the lawyer is "just the messenger."

- "I lied because my opponent acted badly." This includes "self-defense," or "having to lie" before the opponent does, and lying to teach the opponent a lesson, or because bad behavior means the opponent has forfeited any right to candor.
- "I lied, but it was justified by good consequences," that is, justice triumphed. . . .

Professor Longan, in the next reading, provides hypotheticals that highlight some of the ethical issues in negotiation. In considering these hypotheticals, he analyzes the ABA Model Rules and opinions on point, but goes beyond these in urging consideration of both what is wise and most effective in the long run.

❖ **Patrick E. Longan,** *ETHICS IN SETTLEMENT NEGOTIATIONS: FOREWORD*

52 Mercer L. Rev. 810 (2001)

There are two issues lurking within and behind . . . [Rule 4.1]. First, as to misrepresentations, comment two to Rule 4.1 contains a special qualification for statements in the context of settlement negotiations. It exempts from the requirements of Rule 4.1(a) certain statements that "under generally accepted conventions in negotiation" are not taken as statements of fact, such as the acceptability of a particular amount in settlement. In other words, there is room in negotiations for puffing and bluffing because those practices are what everyone involved expects. Second, the last phrase of Rule 4.1(b) appears to prohibit disclosure, even to prevent fraud, if Rule 1.6 would prohibit the disclosure. Rule 1.6 forbids disclosure of "information related to the representation of a client," absent client consent and with some very limited exceptions. The exception, therefore, threatens to swallow the rule about disclosure. . . .

A.   The Limits of Representations

. . . You represent the plaintiff in a breach of contract action. You are seeking lost profits. What can you say in negotiations about the lost profits if:

1. Your expert has come to no conclusion about their cause.
2. Your expert has told you the breach did not cause the lost profits.
3. Your expert has given you a range between $2,000,000 and $5,000,000 for the lost profits.
4. Your expert says the maximum lost profit is $2,000,000.
5. You do not have an expert; your client says the loss was $5,000,000.

It is common in negotiation for each side to emphasize the strength and persuasiveness of its evidence. On the other hand, each side in discovery has the opportunity to explore the other side's evidence. In this scenario, each side would be entitled to a report and a deposition of the other's testifying expert. Any statement about the expert would be a statement of fact. Because of the importance of expert testimony to this case, any statement of this sort would be material. The lawyer must be careful to tell only the truth to avoid violating Rule 4.1. Good lawyers, however, will test the assertions in discovery, consistent with the now-famous Russian proverb, "Trust, but verify."

Beyond the rules of ethics, however, it is proper to ask what the best strategy is for a lawyer in this negotiation. Here, any statement about the expert's conclusions probably will be the subject of discovery. If the statement is found to be false, the lawyer who made it will lose some credibility. That loss, which will likely survive the conclusion of this particular case and affect negotiations with the other lawyer in future cases, will cause these future negotiations to be more strained, more lengthy, and probably less fruitful. To the extent that the lawyer gains a reputation for untruthfulness as a result of statements about the expert, the lawyer may be impeding all his or her future negotiations. In other words, this hypothetical involves a happy situation in which it is both the right strategy and the smart strategy to tell the truth. . . .

In this breach of contract action, can you:

1. tell opposing counsel that you will not settle for less than $3.5 million when you have authority to settle for $2 million?
2. tell opposing counsel that five major buyers stopped buying from your client after the breach, knowing that they stopped buying for other reasons?

As discussed, comment 2 to Model Rule [4.1] defines statements about settlement authority not to be material. Technically, therefore, the lawyer should feel free to lie about his or her authority. Another strategy, however, and one that may be more effective in the long run, is simply to deflect any questions of authority with statements such as, "You know neither one of us can discuss our authority — let's talk about a fair settlement of this case." The reason a deflection may be more effective in the long run is the same reason exaggerations about the expert's conclusions may cause long term harm. You may be ethically permitted to lie about your authority, but if you do it, and the other lawyer catches you at it, he or she will not trust you again.

The misleading statement about the lost customers raises a persistent and subtle issue for lawyers about the use of language. The statement is literally true. These customers have left, and they did so at a time after the defendant's breach. The only reason the statement is made, however, is in the hope that the defendant will make the leap and conclude that the customers left because of the breach or, at least, that the plaintiff will attempt to prove that they did. The statement is, therefore, an intentionally misleading, sly use of language. It is reminiscent of former President Clinton's response to a question before the grand jury about his deposition testimony: "It depends on what the meaning of is is." The lawyer who engages in this type of deception is more clever, perhaps, than a straightforward liar, but the lawyer is no less worthy of condemnation. Once again, however, we can rely on the power of reputation to deter lawyers (at least those who care about their reputations) from engaging in these tactics. Word gets around.

B. Disclosure of Factual Errors

The second hypothetical concerned a duty to disclose facts when the other lawyer has made a settlement offer containing obvious mistakes:

You represent the husband in a divorce action. You receive from opposing counsel a proposed property settlement with the following errors: (1) a transcription error that undervalues an asset; (2) an arithmetical error that undervalues an asset; (3) a valuation by purchase price of an asset when market value is much higher. All the errors work to your client's advantage. What, if anything, should you do about them?

To the extent that the first two errors are "scrivener's errors" (the other lawyer missed a typographical error or failed to add the numbers correctly), the lawyer has the duty to correct the mistakes. The third problem may raise more difficult issues because the error may come from opposing counsel's conscious but erroneous judgment about what valuation is best for his or her client. Can the lawyer in the hypothetical take advantage of his or her adversary's error in judgment?

The question is a species of a fundamental, recurring question in an adversarial system. The lawyer owes a primary duty of loyalty to the client. In most respects, the lawyer is not expected to be his or her brother's keeper. One answer to the particular ethical question presented is to say that it is not the interesting or important question. The client is not perpetrating a fraud or a crime by taking advantage of a bad lawyer on the other side. There is no duty to disclose under Rule 4.1.

Abiding by the rules of ethics, however, is necessary but not always sufficient for good lawyering. Ethically, the lawyer need not correct every misstep of opposing counsel. But sometimes correcting the mistake would be the wise thing to do. For example, if the mistakes involved in the proposal were fundamental mistakes, ones that under the law of contract the opposing party would provide grounds later to void the transaction, then the lawyer may best serve his or her client by alerting opposing counsel to the mistakes now. If the parties to the transaction will have a continuing relationship, such as shared responsibility for minor children, the best strategy might be to correct the mistakes and buy some trust, which may be sorely needed later. Here, as in many situations, ethics tells you the options available, but the lawyer must still exercise good judgment among the options.

C. Disclosure of Legal Errors

The final hypothetical . . . highlighted the fact that Model Rule 4.1 forbids a lawyer from making a material misrepresentation about the law. The hypothetical does so in the context of an interaction with a young lawyer who is operating under a mistake about the state of the law:

> You represent the defendant in a personal injury case. In negotiation with plaintiff's counsel (a young, relatively inexperienced lawyer), it becomes clear to you that this lawyer believes his or her client's potential recovery is limited by a tort reform statute. You know that this statute has been found unconstitutional by the state supreme court. May you, and should you, correct opposing counsel's mistake about the law?

Most practicing lawyers would not think twice about taking advantage of this younger lawyer. Again, the client is not perpetrating a fraud or a crime, and the client might be very happy to save some money because his or her adversary's lawyer is clueless. No rule of legal ethics requires the lawyer to be the opposing party's lawyer also. No rule requires that lawyers settle cases only on "fair" terms.

Again, however, the strictly ethical inquiry cannot end the discussion. For example, lawyers might find that taking advantage of the mistake in particular circumstances, such as a horrific injury to a young child, would be morally wrong although ethically permissible. The lawyer is free to counsel the client about nonlegal matters, such as the morality of leaving the injured child unable to obtain the life-long care the child needs. The lawyer is even free to seek to withdraw if assisting in a settlement under these circumstances would be repugnant to the lawyer. Here, as in the prior examples, the best lawyers consider all the circumstances and determine first whether the rules of ethics require a particular course of action and, if they do not, what under all the circumstances is the wisest choice. . . .

Questions

1. Assuming that a lawyer can lie about a client's bottom line and matters of value in negotiation without violating ethical rules, when might doing so be a good tactic, and when not? What is the tactical advantage of candor? If there is reason to be candid when not ethically required, should it be selective candor depending on the situation or is a uniform policy of candor more advantageous? Why?

2. Should the client have a say in what is revealed in the above hypotheticals? If you disagree with your client, must the client's wishes govern? (See the next section, Client Control vs. Lawyer Integrity, for discussion of these issues.)

3. Zitrin and Langford suggest that "instead of putting lawyers in the position of having to lie, as the rule does now, it could simply forbid lawyers from asking their opponents their ultimate positions on value" (168). Would this be an effective, or at least preferable, solution to the dilemma between zealous representation and candor? Why or why not?

4. Is there any reason to behave differently toward people in negotiation than you would in other interactions? In other words, what distinguishes negotiation from interpersonal interactions generally? (For an interesting analysis of this question, see Cohen 2001.)

5. There is much debate and also some case law on what is "a material fact" that must be revealed in a negotiation pursuant to Model Rule 4.1(a). For example, if you are representing a client injured in an automobile accident, need you reveal the client's death prior to finalizing settlement of a claim for his injuries? Why or why not? (See Kentucky Bar Assn. v. Geisler, 938 S.W. 2d 578 (1997).)

6. Assuming that your client in the above question was alive at the initiation of the claim and the beginning of negotiation, the question raises an issue of what must be revealed when facts change or when what was revealed earlier is no longer true. This occurs frequently in the context of formal discovery. If a response to a question asked in formal discovery is no longer true, rules of civil procedure generally require an attorney to inform the opposing side of the change. (See FRCP Section 26(e).) If a fact material to a negotiation changes, is silence on the part

of the knowing attorney a violation of Model Rule 4.1? Should the ethics rules governing attorneys permit silence when rules of procedure would require correction? Can you articulate a meaningful distinction? (See White 1980.)

7. How does what Rule 4.1 requires of lawyers compare with your personal moral values? If your personal ethics are more restrictive than the rules, is there a risk that your interests might conflict with those of your client? This topic is covered in the following section.

Problem

You are defending an insured driver in a serious auto accident that injured the plaintiff, a young man in his late teens. You properly insisted that the plaintiff be examined by a doctor of your choosing paid by your client, the insurance company. Your doctor discovered something that the youth's own physician had missed: a life-threatening aortic aneurysm that could burst at any time, and had likely been caused by the accident. Revealing the results of a physical exam obtained by the defense is not generally required in your jurisdiction. If the plaintiff learns about the aneurysm it will result in a much higher settlement to be paid by your client. Your client instructs you not to reveal the aneurysm.

Do you have an ethical obligation to reveal the aneurysm? (See Spaulding v. Zimmerman, 263 Minn. 346, 116 N.W.2d 704 (1961).)

B. Client Control vs. Lawyer Integrity (Conflicts of Interest)

Ethical issues in negotiation are often compounded for lawyers because their interests are seldom in complete congruity with those of their client's. When lawyers are employed to negotiate for principals, the interests in the timing, costs, trade-offs, goals, and relationships involved in a settlement may be different for the lawyer than for the client. However, lawyers work for clients and, at least to some extent, clients get to call the shots. ABA Model Rule 1.2(a) states that "A lawyer shall abide by a client's decisions concerning the objectives of representation . . . and shall consult with the client as to the means by which they are to be pursued. A lawyer shall abide by a client's decision whether to accept an offer of settlement of a matter." This rule distinguishes the end goal, decided by the client, from the means of achieving it, decided by the lawyer in consultation with the client. The rule is clear that the decision whether to settle and under what terms is the client's choice. The application of the rule to how lawyers should negotiate is less clear.

We suggested earlier, in discussing cultural identities, that being a lawyer identifies you with what may be considered a cultural subgroup. Another way to view the relationship between lawyers is to analogize the relationship among lawyers to a "community." Whether viewed as a community or subculture, lawyers have long-term relationships with one another and repeatedly interact in ways that have their own norms of behavior and shared expectations. This may be in contrast to the relationship of clients to the legal/judicial system, which is likely to be a one-time occasion. A potential conflict exists between the client's interest in maximizing gain from a one-time transaction or settlement and a lawyer's longer term interest in maintaining credible and amicable relations with other lawyers. The gain from deceit and lying may benefit a client at the expense of the lawyer's reputation and relationships within the community.

Both economic and ethical considerations may conflict with your ideals and commitment to self-defined professional integrity and honesty. Preserving your client's confidences may prevent you from candidly discussing with an opposing lawyer how your client has asked you to negotiate or giving your counterpart warning that she should be cautious.

> ### Questions
>
> 8. If a client you represent in the sale of a business instructs you to make a first offer of $1 million to eventually sell for his target of $500,000, can you refuse because you feel the bloated offer compromises your integrity? If you do refuse, over the client's objection, is the representation necessarily ended? Can you make the first offer to opposing counsel with a wink and not be breaching a client confidence?
> 9. Does Model Rule 1.2(a), which divides bargaining decision responsibilities along an end-means line (client decides the end goal, lawyer decides the means of obtaining client's goal), provide a helpful distinction for you?
> 10. Is there a cleaner end-means line when representing an injured tort claimant than when representing a businessperson in a commercial transaction? Is an insurance company that retains a lawyer to defend a personal injury claim more likely to control the means of lawyer negotiating than is an injured plaintiff? Do different ethics rules apply to lawyers depending on who employs them?

A conflict may also exist between a client's personal economic needs, which drive her to value an attractive settlement offer more than societal interests, and a lawyer's ideals, which may focus more on broader policy concerns. This conflict can cut the other way if an idealistic client wants to reject a settlement on principle when the lawyer is coveting the immediate fee payoff.

Consider the settlement situation described in the following example and the conflicts it raises.

❖ **Richard Zitrin & Carol M. Langford,** THE MORAL COMPASS OF THE AMERICAN LAWYER

183 (Ballantine Books, 1999)

E.J. Boyette was a forty-eight-year-old computer programmer when he died, leaving a wife and five kids. Always active, Boyette had worked out three times a week, and on the weekends he rowed with a group of guys he knew from college. Shortly after his forty-seventh birthday he noticed that he was getting tired easily and was often short of breath. He made an appointment with his doctor, who referred him to a cardiologist. After extensive tests, the cardiologist recommended surgical placement of a new kind of heart valve from the Jones/Henning/Wharton Company that had been highly praised in all the medical journals.

At first everything seemed fine. Boyette was released from the hospital, started mild workouts, and had even begun dreaming of joining his rowing mates on the water again. But after three months Boyette's physical condition began deteriorating quickly. In another month he was dead. His widow consulted attorney Andrea Hardy, partner in a small firm that represents plaintiffs in injury cases. . . .

Now eighteen months later, after extensive discovery and a review of thousands of documents, Andrea and her paralegal have just found a memo that seems to show that the company knew its first-generation heart valves had design flaws that could cause some patients to get worse and even die. She and her paralegal can barely contain their excitement. They quickly draft a new and very specific demand for the other side to produce more documents, which Andrea believes will include the smoking gun she can use to prove that the manufacturer knew the heart valves were defective. . . .

On the appointed day for delivery, Andrea is surprised to find Burger himself [chief defense counsel] at her office. He asks if they can talk.

"Look," he says, "I'll hand over these documents in a minute. I think you know what's in them. But there's something I'd like you to consider. We'll offer you five million dollars right now to settle the case. There are just two conditions: the amount we pay must be secret, and the documents you've gotten from us must be returned. All of them, including copies." Andrea is dumb-struck. Until this moment Burger had maintained his client's innocence and never breathed a word about settlement. She knows $5 million is a lot more than she's likely to get for a case at trial, even with punishment damages. And the fee would easily be the largest her firm has ever received. She's sure the documents in George Burger's briefcase include the smoking gun she'd been looking for.

Andrea tells Burger that she'll have to review the documents and discuss things with her client before making a decision. "Fine," says Burger, "I'll give you a week." Later that day, with her paralegal and her law partners gathered around her, Andrea reads three memos from senior Jones/Henning/Wharton officials that conclusively prove that the manufacturer knew that the heart valve's design was defective before Mr. Boyette's valve was implanted. One memo summarizes 107 incidents in which the valve was considered a contributing cause in a patient's death. The other two discuss how the company should deal with the design flaw, eventually concluding that nothing should be done to take it off the market until a new product could be developed to replace it.

Andrea knows she must talk to Mr. Boyette's widow. But she ponders what to advise her about accepting Burger's offer. She loves her practice because she gets to expose dangerous products, not conceal them. She knows that if she agrees to keep the documents secret, other people with heart valves like Mr. Boyette's could be in danger, even die. But she also knows the guiding principle that her first duty is to her client, not the public at large. And the amount her client has been offered is enormous. . . .

She was not surprised when John Boyette called the next day to say that the family had met, discussed the offer, and decided to accept it.

Questions

11. After describing the $5 million Boyette secret settlement, Zitrin and Langford discuss some state laws that ban secret settlements to prevent protection of public health and safety. What are the arguments for and against statutory restrictions on secret settlements involving claims of defective products, fraud, and malpractice? Should lawyers be required to report such settlements? Why or why not? (See Doré, 1999; Zitrin, 1999.)
12. How can you as a lawyer deal with this type of conflict or the more common one of the client's desire to have her lawyer shade the truth or conceal adverse bargaining information?

Both economic and ethical considerations may require lawyers to compromise their ideals and commitment to self-defined professional integrity. Preserving clients' confidences may prevent opposing lawyers from candidly discussing how their clients have instructed them to negotiate or giving warning that the other side should be cautious. In the next reading, Robert Condlin discusses how the ethical conflict created by trying to get the most for your client can lead to unproductive behavior and ritualized aggression in negotiation that feeds the public's negative view of lawyers.

❖ **Robert J. Condlin,** *BARGAINING IN THE DARK:*
THE NORMATIVE INCOHERENCE OF LAWYER DISPUTE BARGAINING ROLE

51 Md. L. Rev. 1 (1992)

There is a contradiction in the prevailing understanding of [a lawyer's] dispute bargaining role, between what might be thought of as bargaining's practical norms and its ethical norms. The practical norms provide rules for maximizing long range client and lawyer returns. They tell lawyer bargainers to distribute resources efficiently, preserve bargaining relationships, and satisfy party interests in the aggregate. The ethical norms provide rules for representing clients competently and diligently. They tell lawyers to get the most they can for present clients, when so instructed, irrespective of the effects on resource distribution and future bargaining. Trying scrupulously to comply with both sets of norms, each for different reasons, lawyers frequently find themselves under contradictory commands, without meta norms to sort out the contradictions or rank order the commands, and thus, "in the dark" with respect to the central question of how they should act. This contradictory set of role commands has several effects, but one of the least salutary is that it seems to encourage the stylized adversarial maneuvering commonly associated with lawyers and dispute bargaining (e.g., exaggerated argument, insulting tone, routinized trading, circumspect and deceptive disclosure), which is now widely thought to make such bargaining inefficient, unpleasant, and unfair. If these effects are to be avoided, and bargaining roles to be made more coherent, it is necessary that bargaining's ethical and practical norms be reconciled, or if that is too ambitious, at least their contradictions described in sufficient detail so that others may work on the problem. . . .

While lawyers may not take action that is frivolous (i.e., primarily to harass or maliciously to injure) or prohibited by law, they must use any legally available move or procedure helpful to a client's bargaining position. Among other things, this means that all forms of leverage must be exploited, inflated demands made, and private information obtained and used whenever any of these actions would advance the client's stated objectives, even if such action would jeopardize a lawyer's long-term, working relationship with her bargaining counterpart.

Lawyers also must show enthusiasm for the bargaining task. Once described as the obligation of zealous representation, and now expressed as the duty of diligence, this duty requires lawyers to act with "commitment and dedication to the interests of the client," and to "carry to a conclusion all matters undertaken" on the client's behalf. Lawyer bargainers, in other words, must develop and play out client-bargaining hands with energy and believability, and not undercut those efforts with a tone or attitude which indicates that their hearts are not in it, or that they do not believe what they say. Plausibility and sincerity are the most important attributes of effective bargaining maneuvers; the duty of competence requires the first, and the duty of diligence the second.

The duty of deference is concerned with which objectives are pursued, not how they are pursued. It makes client judgments supreme in disagreements with lawyers about which objectives to seek and, absent criminality or fraud, obligates lawyers to pursue all goals clients set. Deference is the centerpiece of lawyer-client relations and the feature of [a lawyer's] role that makes law practice a fiduciary enterprise. In bargaining, the main function of deference is to require that clients alone decide whether to accept or reject offers of settlement. . . .

When these duties are combined, as they must be, it may appear that lawyers are ethically obligated to be skillful, energetic, uncritical, and obedient instruments of selfish client ends, but the reality of [a lawyer's] dispute bargaining role is slightly less harsh. Lawyers are persons in their own right, with moral and political rights and obligations of their own, and even though they must take direction from their clients, they need not do everything asked. For example, the duty of deference distinguishes between questions of ends and questions of means, and reserves to lawyers the tactical and technical decisions of how best to advance client objectives. If a client asks a lawyer to use tactics that are repugnant, lawyers may refuse. Lawyers owe clients only substantive competitiveness; they may choose their own style. While clients should decide mixed questions such as how much expense to incur or how much harm to inflict, for the most part lawyers and clients divide bargaining decision responsibility along an ends-means line.

Similarly, as officers of the court and citizens of the community, lawyers have public responsibilities, to third parties and to the law, that clients may not trump. Lawyers may not lie for clients (though they may tell half truths and puff), either to adversaries or courts, or mislead opponents, either by act or omission, when to do so would be civilly actionable. In limited circumstances,

occasionally present in bargaining, lawyers must correct adversary misappre-
hensions and remedy ignorance. They must bargain in good faith, not seek or
agree to unconscionable settlements, and deal fairly with opponents by avoiding the use of force and fraud. These are limited obligations, imposed by law as
much as by ethical rules, and while they prohibit few competitive maneuvers —
there is still no obligation to make an adversary's factual case, correct analytical
errors, or refuse any deal a court would enforce — they are supreme in their own
realm. . . .

The Bargainer's Dilemma

Practical bargaining is cooperative bargaining. Clients do better, at least
clients in the aggregate, when represented by lawyers who bargain cooperatively and are known to do so. Nevertheless, a particular client, valuing her own
immediate return in an individual case more highly than the interests of clients
in the aggregate (which may include the particular client's own future interests),
may seek to trade on rather than contribute to her lawyer's history of cooperating. She may instruct the lawyer to defect when the adversary cooperates, and
may ground this instruction on the lawyer's ethical obligations to be deferential
and competent. This places the lawyer in a bind. Does she bargain ethically or
practically? Does she reject the instruction and preserve her reputation for
cooperating, so that she can secure better settlements, on average, for all of her
clients, including those in the future? Or does she follow her client's instruction,
exploit the adversary's reasonable but, as it will turn out, unwarranted cooperation, and plant the seeds of future retaliation?

The dilemma is serious, not necessarily because it is widespread — it may or
may not be — but because lawyers seem to assume that it is the paradigm case.
They see the defecting client as every client, and feel the pressure to bargain
competitively across the board. Clients do not correct the assumption, some
perhaps because they agree with it, others perhaps because they do not know
that it has been made, and still others perhaps because they see legal representation as a technical process in which following the lawyer's lead is the proper
(and safest) course. Whatever the reasons, the view that clients invariably want
to compete has developed a life of its own, and is now treated as received
wisdom in large parts of the profession. . . .

When a client asks a lawyer with a reputation for cooperating to defect on an
adversary who also expected to cooperate, the lawyer's reputation for cooperating is likely to be jeopardized. She understandably will be reluctant to
undercut this reputation because it allows her to coordinate activities and
produce the largest aggregate returns over a bargaining career. This reluctance
will make it difficult for the lawyer to make and carry out the decision to defect.
Because lawyers may not represent clients when the lawyers' interests prevent
them from considering and carrying out courses of action desired by clients, it
may seem, at first glance, that a lawyer must either defect or refuse representation. Yet, a closer look at the Model Rules will show that they are more
concerned with lawyer "income" and "business interests" specific to the particular representation than to the undifferentiated interest of doing well generally
over time. The Rules try to make sure that lawyers do not exploit the influence
provided by their clients' dependent circumstances to advance their own (the
lawyers') interests by making favorable book deals, buying property at bargain

prices, receiving gifts, unfairly appropriating resources held by clients, and the like. The Rules are less concerned with preventing lawyers from representing clients in ways that also maximize lawyer long range monetary return. In fact, if the latter was prohibited, representation would be denied to all but the most compliant clients. . . .

Seemingly trapped in a no-win situation, lawyers have made an interesting and clever, albeit probably unselfconscious, adaptation. Lawyer bargaining is not just adversarial; it is also stylized. It is adversarial because it is made up, in the main, of aggressive communication maneuvers such as argument, challenge, and demand. It is stylized because this aggressive maneuvering is carried out in a slightly exaggerated, somewhat predictable, and essentially impersonal fashion. Both dimensions are important to wriggling out of the dilemma of lawyer bargaining role. The adversarial part allows lawyers to believe that they have fought hard for their clients, and in the process that they have been deferential to client wishes and diligent in their pursuit. The stylized part allows them to preserve bargaining relationships with other lawyers by signaling, through a set of rhetorical conventions, that the aggressiveness is not personal, but is just part of the lawyer act. Behavior that is both adversarial and stylized is a lawyer's way of being (or believing she has been) both ethical and practical, of protecting her reputation for cooperating, while at the same time arguing zealously for the interests of her clients. It is an effort to walk a line between the important but conflicting normative pulls of bargaining's ethical and practical sides, complying minimally with each and not openly violating either. . . .

Question

13. Professor Condlin states that, "If a client asks a lawyer to use tactics that are repugnant, lawyers may refuse." He divides "bargaining decision responsibilities along an end-means line." Is this a helpful distinction for you?

Problem

Assume that you are a third-year law student who has landed a plum job as an associate with a boutique intellectual property law firm to commence after graduation. You were to be paid $160,000 a year. Although a very good law firm, the written offer, which it prepared and you accepted, was an absolute commitment on the part of the firm with no conditions. Since your acceptance, economic conditions have worsened and the type of litigation in which the firm primarily engages has declined. A couple of weeks ago you met with the managing partner, Jerome Higgins, who cordially explained the circumstances and indicated that the firm needed to cancel the employment arrangement but wanted to be fair with you. You indicated that you relied on the early offer and turned down other employment offers during the law school interview season, which is now concluded. You also truthfully revealed that you had rented a new apartment and purchased a car in reliance on the employment agreement. You acknowledged that economic conditions have tightened since you accepted the offer, but pointed out that the offer was unconditional and that the bad economic times would make it difficult for you to find a comparable position.

You agreed that you would meet again with Mr. Higgins in a few weeks to discuss severance terms. While discussing your situation with your IP law professor, he told you of an alum who recently was appointed General Counsel for a tech startup and had asked him for a recommendation of a graduating student who might be interested in working with him. He passed on your name, and you have been offered the position at a starting salary of $120,000 to commence immediately following the Bar exam. Although the position pays less than the law firm job, you are thrilled because of the excitement of the startup and the unique opportunity it presents, as well as the fact that the other job offer was withdrawn. You plan to accept the Associate General Counsel position. However, you first want to talk with Mr. Higgins to see what you can work out with him regarding the breach of your employment contract by his law firm. You are truly concerned about your immediate economic needs and your heavy student loan debt. Although Higgins's law firm may not be expanding, you are aware of its high per-partner income and the firm's solid economic base. You would like to get as much from them as you can. You know that if you personally negotiate with Mr. Higgins, you will feel compelled to tell him about your new job offer, even if he doesn't ask. If you do that, your severance package won't be worth much.

Can you hire a lawyer to negotiate for you and not tell the lawyer about your pending job offer? If you do tell the lawyer about the other job offer, would she be acting unethically not to disclose it if Higgins does not ask if you have other offers? If Higgins does ask about what you have done to mitigate damages, then must your attorney reveal the other offer? Can your lawyer insist on revealing the terms of the other job offer even if you instruct her not to do so? If you were to switch roles, would you agree to negotiate on behalf of someone in these circumstances? What would you advise your client to do and why?

❖ **Robert H. Mnookin, Scott R. Peppet & Andrew S. Tulumello,**
Beyond Winning: Negotiating to Create Value in Deals and Disputes

282 (Harvard University Press, 2000)

What If My Client Wants Me to Mislead the Other Side?

Seek to Understand the Client's Choice

If a client is asking you to mislead the other side, the first step, as always, is to try to understand why. In what ways does this request make sense for the client? Put yourself in her shoes. If you were the client, would you propose the same thing that she's proposing?

By identifying the incentives that motivate your client to ask you to mislead the other side, you may be able to relate better to the client as you talk about his request. The key is to learn why the client thinks you should manipulate the truth. What does he see as the advantages? What does he see as the risks? What are the client's concerns? By listening and demonstrating understanding, you can often draw out the client to talk about the underlying choice of strategy.

Raise Your Concerns Explicitly

Lawyers also must learn to discuss ethical dilemmas explicitly. You can find yourself in a very uncomfortable situation if neither you nor your client is willing to discuss ethical conflicts. Learning to have such conversations productively is a critical skill.

If your client asks you to mislead the other side, you should negotiate with her and try to help her understand your views. You must explain that you don't want to violate established rules of professional responsibility, and that you don't want to do something that isn't in your client's best interests. You don't want to go against your personal beliefs, and you don't want to do something that hurts your reputation. By explaining your interests and perspective — while continuing to demonstrate understanding for the client's views — you can begin a conversation about the dilemma you face.

Ed's lawyer, for example, would want to explain that in the face of questioning by Mr. Jenks he would either have to tell the truth about a competing offer or refuse to answer a direct question. "That would probably give away the issue right there," Ed might say. "Couldn't you just say 'No, he has no other offers'?" "No," his lawyer might explain. "I can't lie about a material piece of information like that. And I've got to tell you, it would probably amount to fraud. Given that sooner or later he's going to find out whether you're working again, lying about it could cause serious problems later."

Remember That Your Reputation Is a Valuable Asset

Clients sometimes want to use a lawyer's reputation for honesty as a cover for their own unethical behavior. If a lawyer is known for telling the truth, this reputation can be a perfect smokescreen for throwing the other side off track. If your client persuades you to lie, however he may take advantage of your reputation for his own short-term gain, disregarding the long-term effect on your career and well-being.

We learned of a recent example in a divorce case. After discovering that his wife had hired an attorney, the husband hired an outstanding family lawyer — known in his community as an honorable problem-solver. The two lawyers had done many divorce cases together in the past and had built up a great deal of trust. Ordinarily they did not rely on formal discovery procedures, choosing instead to exchange information informally. This saved their clients a great deal of time and money.

The husband in this case insisted that his lawyer not disclose certain financial information to the other side unless forced to do so through formal discovery. The husband's lawyer faced a real ethical dilemma. When his colleague proposed that they informally exchange information as they had in the past, what was he to do? He knew that if he disclosed partially but withheld the information in question, it would go against his counterpart's clear expectation and would ultimately hurt his own reputation as an honest negotiator. At the same time, he was obligated to obey his client's wishes not to disclose the financial information.

Ultimately, he chose to refuse to engage in the informal information exchange process with the other attorney. This implicitly signaled, of course, that this divorce was unlike the others they had negotiated together before. Many lawyers had told us that in such situations they are likely to signal to the other side that the normal rules of play are suspended and that the baseline professional ethics rules are all that should be expected. One lawyer told of a case in which he entered the room where the negotiation was to occur, sat down across the table from a long-time colleague, and simply said "On guard." Both knew immediately that their normal collaborative rules of engagement were temporarily suspended.

Such signaling raises difficult ethical issues, of course. On the one hand, why should a client be able to gain distributive advantage by hiding behind his lawyer's reputation? Doesn't that disserve the attorney's other clients who rely on his problem-solving abilities? By refusing to engage in the informal discovery process that was based on trust, doesn't the lawyer merely give his client what the client would get from any other attorney that *didn't* have a reputation for honesty? On the other hand, is it ever legitimate for an attorney *not* to do something that would maximize the distributive benefit for a given client? If a lawyer's approach conflicts with his client's, would the best approach be simply to withdraw?

In our view, withdrawal is one possible solution. In practice, as we've discussed, however, lawyers *and clients* face real financial and logistical constraints that may make withdrawal unattractive. Once an attorney has worked with a client over time, the lawyer has built up a store of knowledge and experience relevant only to that client, and the client has invested time and money in educating his lawyer about the particulars of the case. Under such circumstances, rather than withdraw, it seems reasonable for an attorney to signal to the other side that for this negotiation they should not expect anything beyond what the formal discovery rules require.

The lesson we draw, however, is that lawyer-client preparation is essential. As a lawyer-client relationship begins, an attorney must be clear with his client about his problem-solving orientation and what that requires. If a lawyer is unambiguous about what he will and won't do, the client can make an informed choice about which lawyer to retain. Such ethical conflicts are thus much less likely to arise.

Lawyers' fees and how they are determined may influence how lawyers negotiate on behalf of both plaintiffs and defendants. In the next article, Herbert Kritzer discusses this factor and particularly how a contingent fee arrangement may influence negotiation decisions.

❖ **Herbert M. Kritzer,** *Fee Arrangements and Negotiation*

21 Law & Soc'y Rev. 341 (1987)

My central argument is that discussions of the settlement process, and particularly of manipulations of that process, must consider the interests of *all* involved in litigation. Regular participants in litigation are well aware of this point. In my series of interviews with corporate lawyers and their clients in Toronto regarding the impact of fees and fee shifting a number of respondents mentioned the importance of taking into account the interest of the opposing lawyer. For example, a litigation partner in a firm with one hundred lawyers said, "If you can satisfy the lawyer [with regard to his fee], you'll be a lot closer to settlement." A lawyer for a large retailer similarly stated that to achieve settlement, "you need to provide an incentive for the [opposing] lawyer." Yet despite the evidence that litigation lawyers do not selflessly ignore their own interests, little attention has been paid to how these interests affect settlement and negotiation.

I am not suggesting that lawyers engage in questionable actions for financial gain. The argument is more subtle: Lawyers, like all of us, when forced to make a choice for which there is no definitive answer, will tend to select the option that is in their own interest. In other words, the financial incentives of their work will often influence the decisions, and it is not coincidental that they will personally benefit from these choices. Thus, although the plaintiffs' bar may truly believe that the contingent fee is the poor man's key to the courthouse door, this belief is shaped by the fact that the key to the courthouse also brings clients — and therefore a livelihood — to the plaintiffs' lawyers. Elsewhere I have pointed out that the relationship between lawyers and clients is shaped by professional, personal, and business considerations, the last, at their most basic, meaning income (and income streams.) But what is the significance of this type of analysis for settlement and negotiation? . . .

Contingent fee lawyers in cases with modest amounts at stake have an incentive to arrive quickly at a settlement, even if that settlement is not the best for the client. Whether this means that the fee arrangement directly affects the amount of time the lawyer spends on settlement negotiations (although I could in fact find no systematic difference in time spent on such activities between hourly and contingent fee lawyers), the same theoretical considerations apply to the content of the actual negotiation. Specifically, since the contingent fee lawyer is to receive a share of the ultimate recovery, she has an incentive to see to it that the recovery can in fact be shared.

A contingent fee lawyer who sought nonmonetary resolutions of her clients' cases, even if those resolutions were better from the clients' perspectives, would soon go out of business unless some alternate payment method were available for such settlements (e.g., fee shifting, whereby the defendant pays the plaintiff's attorney for his time, or a central fund, created by taxing contingent fees, from which the lawyer could receive compensation).

. . . Although lawyers are professionals who are concerned with the needs and interests of their clients, their behavior is nonetheless influenced (note the use of *influenced* rather than *determined*) by the forces of economic rationality or necessity or both, and this influence is felt as well in the lawyers' means of negotiating. If we want lawyers to consider actively what Menkel-Meadow calls the problem-solving approaches to negotiation, we must insure that their livelihood is not dependent upon adversary approaches to negotiation.

Questions

16. Might there be some settlements that are better from the client's perspective, but not necessarily in the economic interests of the plaintiff's lawyer? What is the meaning of the saying that "all contingent fee settlements need to be divisible by 3"?

17. Do contingent fee arrangements create an attorney-client conflict of interest? Should they be considered unethical? Why or why not?

18. Would Kritzer's suggestion, that contingent fees be replaced by a fee shifting method where the defendant pays the plaintiff's attorney for time spent or a tax on contingent fees to create a central lawyers' fee fund, eliminate attorney-client conflicts of interest in settlement or create new ones? Would you support these "reforms"?

C. Good Faith vs. Threats, Exposure, and Coercion

Although it can be hoped that lawyers will be retained to negotiate only when the client desires to reach an agreement and bargain in good faith, there may be occasions when settlement is not the goal or when compromise for purposes of agreement is not an option. On occasion a client may pursue negotiation for purposes of delay or distraction, to obtain information from a competitor, or to harass. As previously discussed, clients have the right to decide the purpose and objectives of negotiation, but lawyers can usually decline to represent a party or withdraw. Indeed, ethical rules may require the lawyer to withdraw if continued representation will result in violation of ethical rules. (See ABA Model Rule 1.16(a)(1).)

There is no general ethical duty to bargain in good faith, but if the parties have agreed by contract to negotiate in good faith, for example, before ending a business relationship or going to court, they may be held to their bargain. In some labor management disputes under the National Labor Relations Act, 29 U.S.C.A. 158(d), there may be a good faith negotiation requirement. Rules of court and court orders may also require "good faith" negotiation or mediation before a dispute will be heard.

Even if good faith in negotiation is not required, ethical rules and contract law limit certain types of "bad faith" bargaining. A prohibition against bad faith negotiation is indicated by ABA Model Rule 4.4, which states:

> "*Respect for Rights of Third Persons*: In representing a client, a lawyer shall not use means that have no substantial purpose other than to embarrass, delay, or burden a third person, or use methods of obtaining evidence that violate the legal rights of such a person."

Tort law, contract law, and criminal law may also restrict the use of threats, extortion, and some forms of coercion. However, threatening to file a civil lawsuit to resolve the matter in dispute when the lawyer has a good faith basis for the claim is not prohibited. (See *Restatement, Second of Contracts*, Sec. 175, Comment (b) (1981).) Indeed, every legal negotiation carries, at least, an implicit threat that if agreement is not reached, further action will be taken or alternatives will be pursued. Adversarial negotiations and pressure from clients may tempt lawyers to go further and use threats of unrelated legal action or exposure of wrongdoing if negotiation demands are not met. The law, rather than ethical rules, may be used to decide when threatening exposure of wrongdoing or a ruinous lawsuit becomes criminal extortion, and also when lying becomes fraud.

A threat by a lawyer to punch an opponent in the nose if a demand is not met is clearly unethical and criminal. A threat to do something adverse to your opponent, even if not unlawful, only for the purpose of gaining an advantage in a negotiation, presents more challenging issues. For example, deciding to expose or not expose an opposing lawyer's unethical behavior in conjunction with a negotiation may place you between the proverbial "rock and a hard place." Power imbalances may also create questions of intimidation in the negotiation process, as might the otherwise legitimate threat of filing a class action against a modest-sized company if monetary demands are not met. In addition to being ethically risky, threats may jeopardize the enforceability of a settlement because of duress or other contract grounds for voiding or rescinding agreements.

The article that follows addresses some of these issues and is included to help you understand that even though the limits of what lawyers can do in negotiations are murky, tort, contract, and criminal law do impose outer limits on negotiation conduct and communications. It explains negotiation constraints, particularly where there is unequal power.

❖ Robert S. Adler & Elliot M. Silverstein, *WHEN DAVID MEETS GOLIATH: DEALING WITH POWER DIFFERENTIALS IN NEGOTIATIONS*

5 Harv. Negot. L. Rev. 1 (2000)

. . . Although the superior bargaining power of one party, standing alone, does not generally provide the basis for invalidating an agreement, the law does set limits within which bargainers must operate. These limits apply both with respect to the terms that can be negotiated and to the methods one can use to influence an opponent to agree to the terms. They are premised on the assumption that at some point in the bargaining process, power advantages can produce inequities so pronounced that the law must step in to protect the weak. In negotiations involving power imbalances, most abuses arise when the stronger party, either through threats or other overt displays of power, intimidates the other into entering an agreement so one-sided that it offends reasonable sensibilities. Of course, not all bargaining abuses result from overt power displays. Some arise from shifting the balance of power by exploiting trust or employing deceit.

Depending on the nature of the abuse, the law may take different approaches — regulating modestly where "arm's length" conditions exist or expansively where a "special relationship" requires protection for particularly vulnerable individuals. Where special relationships exist, special protections apply.

A. Undue Influence

When a relationship of trust and dependency between two or more parties exists, the law typically polices the relationship closely and imposes especially stringent duties on the dominant parties. For example, although tort law generally imposes no obligations on citizens to assist those in danger, the courts take the opposite position when they determine that a special relationship exists. In those cases, the courts unhesitatingly find an affirmative duty to rescue.

Contract law imposes similar duties in the case of agreements involving undue influence in special relationships. Where one party — because of family position, business connection, legal authority or other circumstances — gains extraordinary trust from another party the courts will scrutinize any agreements between them with great care to ensure fairness. Common examples of special relationships include guardian-ward, trustee-beneficiary, agent-principal, spouses, parent-child, attorney-client, physician-patient, and clergy-parishioner. To treat negotiations in these settings as arm's length interactions would invite "unfair persuasion" by the dominant parties either through threats, deception, or misplaced trust. Accordingly, the law imposes special obligations on those who play the dominant role in such relationships, requiring them to exercise good faith and to make full disclosure of all critical facts when negotiating agreements with dependent parties. In determining whether a dominant party in a special relationship exerted undue influence, the courts generally look to the fairness of the contract, the availability of independent advice, and the vulnerability of the dependent party. An agreement entered into as a result of undue influence is voidable by the victim.

B. Protections in Arm's Length Transactions

Under the "bargain theory" of contracts, parties negotiate at arm's length to exchange consideration. An arm's length transaction is one in which the parties stand in no special relationship with each other, owe each other no special duties, and each acts in his or her own interest. The vast majority of contracts fall within the arm's length category, which means that no special obligations of disclosure, fair dealing or good faith are generally required. This is not to suggest that parties are free to operate without rules, but it does mean that they are accorded substantial leeway in negotiating contracts. They certainly maintain the freedom to assume even foolish and shortsighted contractual obligations, so long as they do so knowingly and voluntarily. Once one of the parties acts in a patently abusive manner, however, the law does provide protection, as, for example, with fraud, duress, and unconscionability.

1. Fraud

Negotiated agreements, to be binding, must be entered into by the parties in a knowing and voluntary manner. Lies undermine agreements by removing the

"knowing" element from the bargain. That is, one induced by misrepresentations to purchase a relatively worthless item of personal property typically buys
the product "voluntarily" — in fact, eagerly — with enthusiasm generated by
the false promise of the product's value. The catch is that because of the
defrauder's lies, the victim has unfairly lost the opportunity to "know" the
precise nature of what he or she has bought. Lies of this nature clearly alter
the normal contractual dynamic, unfairly shifting power from the victim to the
defrauder. Because of the dramatic impact that fraud has on the power balance
in negotiations, we necessarily review this doctrine.

In its classic formulation, common law fraud requires five elements: (1) a false
representation of a material fact made by the defendant, (2) with knowledge or
belief as to its falsity, (3) with an intent to induce the plaintiff to rely on the
representations, (4) justifiable reliance on the misrepresentation by the plaintiff, and (5) damage or injury to the plaintiff by the reliance. Fraud entitles the
victim to void the transaction and permits him or her to pursue restitution or
tort damages. A false representation may be made in several ways — through a
positive statement, through misleading conduct, or by concealing a fact that the
defrauder has a duty to disclose. . . .

2. Duress

Coercion, whether express or implied, takes many forms. One party, for
example, might threaten to take its business elsewhere if its terms are not met.
Another might threaten to file suit if its financial claims are not resolved. Still
another might insist that it will no longer provide a discount or expedited
delivery if a deal cannot be struck. These threats, designed to exert pressure on
an opponent to secure his or her cooperation, generally fall into a category that
the law would consider to be hard bargaining, but not illegal. At some point,
however, coercion becomes objectionable. How does one distinguish between
proper and improper behavior? Unfortunately, there is no clear dividing line.
As various commentators and courts have stated, threats per se are acceptable;
only wrongful threats are forbidden. What makes one threat "wrongful" and
another not depends on the circumstances of each case. To constitute duress,
threats must be of a particularly virulent nature. . . .

Threatened action need not be illegal — even acts otherwise legal may
constitute duress if directed towards an improper goal. For example, a threat to
bring a lawsuit — normally a legitimate form of coercion — becomes abusive if
"made with the corrupt intent to coerce a transaction grossly unfair to the victim
and not related to the subject of such proceedings." Similarly, a threat to release
embarrassing, but true, information about another person, although abhor-
rent, would not constitute duress (in the form of blackmail) unless accompanied
by an improper demand for financial or other favors.

Should negotiators with a decided power advantage feel inhibited from
pushing for as hard a bargain as they can in light of the law of duress? Generally,
no. Judging from the language in the courts' opinions, hard bargainers should
have little to fear from the doctrine of duress. Nothing in the law of duress
prevents negotiators from pushing to the limits of their bargaining power or
from taking advantage of the economic vulnerabilities or bad luck of their
opponents. Trouble arises only when a party makes threats that lapse into the

illegal, immoral and unconscionable. Of greater impact on negotiators concerned about legal protections is the law of unconscionability, to which we now turn.

3. Unconscionability

The doctrine of unconscionability functions to protect bargainers of lesser power from overreaching by dominant parties. Invoked in a variety of cases under the Uniform Commercial Code and elsewhere, the term has never been precisely defined, no doubt to provide greater flexibility in its use. . . .

What is an unconscionable contract? Given that the UCC drafters deliberately avoided an explicit definition, one cannot simply and easily capture the concept. At a minimum, an unconscionable contract is one "such as no man in his senses and not under delusion would make on the one hand and no honest and fair man would accept on the other." Unconscionability seeks to prevent two evils: (1) oppression and (2) unfair surprise. In a seminal analysis, Professor Arthur Allen Leff labeled these two concepts "substantive" and "procedural" unconscionability, respectively. Substantive unconscionability includes the actual terms of the agreement; procedural unconscionability refers to the bargaining process between the parties. . . .

Virtually all cases in which unconscionability arises as an issue involve significant disparities in bargaining power, but that, standing alone, rarely justifies a finding of unconscionability according to most courts and commentators. What draws judicial fire is when the party endowed with superior bargaining power imposes an extremely unfair and one-sided agreement on the weaker. In effect, the stronger party oppresses the weaker party through the application of brute power, thereby removing any real "choice" from the victim. Accordingly, inequality of bargaining power seems a generally necessary, but not sufficient, condition of unconscionability. . . .

How concerned should a negotiator be — especially one with superior bargaining power — that pursuing an advantage in a contract will result in a court ruling that the agreement is unconscionable? Our best answer: some, but not much. For the most part, the courts have taken a cautious approach to finding unconscionability in negotiated agreements. The vast majority of successful unconscionability claims involve poor, often unsophisticated, consumers challenging oppressive adhesion contracts foisted on them by retail merchants or credit sellers. . . . No doubt this reflects the general view that persons of greater sophistication suffer less contractual abuse and need less protection. . . .

Questions

19. If you become aware that an opposing lawyer is lying about a material fact, like the amount of medical damages incurred by a client, what should you do? Must you report the lie to the Bar? Should you first confront the lawyer or state your intent to report? Might this be considered a threat? Must you wait until after the negotiation is completed to report the ethical breach?

20. Suppose during a lawsuit you receive a copy of a letter from your opponent instructing one of their witnesses to lie under oath. May you use this letter in settlement negotiations? May you use the threat of a Bar disciplinary proceeding or a criminal prosecution for obstruction of justice? In exchange for a favorable settlement, may you agree not to report the opponent's instructions? (See ABA Comm. on Ethics and Professional Responsibility, 1992.)

21. There is a generally recognized privilege for statements made in the course of judicial proceedings. (See Silberg v. Anderson, 50 Cal. 3d 205 (1990), holding that a letter with threats of criminal prosecution sent in the course of judicial proceedings is privileged.) Should a threat of physical violence be covered by this privilege?

22. Assume a client asks you to represent her against a prominent, wealthy man she claims had forced sex with her. She wants you to inform him that if he reasonably compensates her, she will not "go public." Would you accept this assignment, and, if so, how might you proceed? Do you risk criminal prosecution or a civil action against you for extortion? (See Flatley v. Mauro, 18 Cal. Rptr. 3d 472 (2004).)

23. The greatest power differentials in negotiation are associated with consumer cases and bargaining where one side is not represented by an attorney. Can undue influence and unconscionability in negotiations occur when all parties are represented by competent lawyers? By definition, if undue influence or unconscionability is found to void a settlement or transaction negotiated by lawyers, do incompetence and malpractice exist?

Problem

Your client is a small business tenant who is involved in a civil dispute with his landlord regarding whether the lease entitles him to use certain space in the basement of the building for the storage of inventory items. You have requested that the landlord give your client access to the space, but the landlord will not agree unless your client pays significantly more rent. During the course of negotiations you discover that the landlord has failed to maintain the property in accordance with local building codes, and this may subject him to criminal prosecution. Can you inform the landlord that you intend to report him to the appropriate authorities if he fails to agree to your settlement terms? (See Peter H. Geraghty, *Making Threats*, ABA 2008, *www.abanet.org/media/youraba/200810/article11*.)

D. Ethics Reform and New Forms of Practice

1. Reform Proposals and Guidelines

The absence of a rule explicitly prohibiting deception by lawyers during negotiation has disturbed many who feel that a change in lawyer ethics is necessary to promote honesty and correct the lawyer-liar image. For decades there has been a debate within the Bar about prohibiting false statements of fact in negotiation, whether material or not. The ABA, when drafting the Model Rules in the early 1980s, considered requiring that lawyers be "fair" in negotiations and not permit "unconscionable" agreements, but these requirements, following much debate, were rejected as untenable. Some believe the ethics requirements should be enhanced to promote honesty and professional integrity. For others, requiring truthfulness in all matters relating to negotiation would be naive and undermine the enforceability of negotiated agreements, particularly when truthfulness regarding nonmaterial facts is not required of those who are not lawyers. An array of proposals has been urged to formally change Model Rule of Professional Conduct 4.1, which prohibits only lying about material facts, and Comment 2, which acknowledges and does not disapprove the use of deception about bottom lines and puffery about value. The rule would be easy to rewrite, but the revisions could be difficult to sell and enforce. (For a specific proposal, see Alfini 1999.)

The Litigation Section of the ABA in 2002 approved Ethical Guidelines for Settlement Negotiations. Although the Guidelines do not change the ABA Model Rules, they do suggest best practices and aspirational goals that go beyond the rules regarding honesty in negotiation. (See *www.abanet.org/ litigation/ethics/settlementnegotiations*.)

The work of the ABA's Commission on Evaluation of the Rules of Professional Conduct, known as the "Ethics 2000 Commission," resulted in a slight change to Comment 2 of Rule 4.1. The official comment now states that "a party's intentions as to an acceptable settlement of a claim are *ordinarily* not in the category of facts" where candor can be expected (see Mahoney 2002).

The prevailing view is opposed to requiring fairness as a matter of lawyer ethics and against prohibiting lawyers from making false statements regarding "nonmaterial" facts. This practical, minimalist view of regulating lawyer negotiation is rooted in our adversary legal system and a lawyer's duties to his client of loyalty and confidentiality.

2. Collaborative Law, Cooperative Practice, and Mindfulness

A movement by some lawyers to commit to a nonadversarial, interest-based approach and more openness in how they represent clients may have a more profound impact on lawyering ethics and the negotiation of disputes than changes in ethics rules alone. The discontent with the practice of adversarial law, fueled in part by the tension created between the expectation of zealous representation and the desire for personal integrity, has caused some lawyers to explore other models of practice. These efforts have been thoughtful and courageous, as well as controversial. Individual lawyers have reshaped their practices by emphasizing aspects of representation that they find more comfortable and rewarding. We have previously covered the problem-solving approach in contrast to adversarial negotiations. This approach changes the practice paradigm and has implications for personal standards of professional integrity.

Some lawyers have gone further, forming regional groups of practitioners who pledge between them to abstain from litigation and adhere to enhanced standards in their interactions. The most notable example is the collaborative law (CL) movement in domestic relations, where subscribing lawyers contract with clients about standards and limits of representation. A collaborative lawyer will not represent the client if the case goes to court and will not mislead another lawyer during negotiations. (For an explanation of the collaborative practice model, see Lawrence 2003; Tesler 2001.)

The basic elements of CL, as explained by Pauline Tesler (2003), one of its founders, are:

- Each party is represented by separate counsel specially trained to provide effective collaborative representation.
- All parties and attorneys sign a binding participation agreement providing that the attorneys are retained solely to facilitate reasonable, efficient settlement of all issues (a "limited purpose" retention).
- The agreement commits all participants to good-faith negotiations, without the threat of or resort to litigation during the pendency of the collaborative process. All parties agree to provide early, voluntary, continuing disclosure of all information that a reasonable decision maker would need to make an informed decision about each issue in the dispute. If a party refuses to disclose information that counsel considers relevant and material to the dispute, collaborative counsel commit to withdraw and/or terminate the process. In other words, although collaborative lawyers remain bound by attorney-client privilege, they will not assist a client to participate in bad faith in the collaborative process or to misuse the process for undue advantage.
- Clients are free to terminate the process at any time and seek third-party dispute resolution, including litigation, but if any party does so, all attorneys are disqualified from participating in any way in nonconsensual third-party proceedings brought by any party to the dispute against any other party or parties.
- If the process is terminated and litigation follows, the collaborative agreement may give the court jurisdiction to make awards of attorneys' fees and costs against any party who has misused the collaborative process for delay, deception, or other bad-faith purposes. The collaborative lawyers, however, could not be witnesses in such proceedings.

CL practice is designed to encourage parties to stay in the negotiation process, but this may cause some clients to feel stuck, having invested time and money and then being at risk of losing their lawyer if the collaborative process terminates and the conflict continues. Ethical issues have been raised about attorneys limiting their practice to provide clients with representation only if the other side collaborates. Several states, including Kentucky, Pennsylvania, and New Jersey, have examined CL practice in light of Model Rule of Professional Conduct 1.2(c), which requires informed client consent before lawyers can limit the scope of their practice, and Rule 1.7, which prohibits representation if there is a conflict of interest with the lawyer's responsibilities to others. The CL lawyer's commitment to other CL attorneys, as well as her own interest in a limited practice, raises conflict of interest questions. Several ethics opinions have found that these two provisions create a duty for a CL lawyer to assess whether the limitation and commitment are in the client's best interest and screen cases for CL appropriateness. Clients must be clearly informed about the risks of the process. Although considerable effort has been made by proponents of CL to expand the practice to non-family civil matters, the effort has not met with much success (see Lande & Mosten 2010; Peppet 2008). The Colorado Bar Association's Ethics Committee ruled in 2004 that the disqualification provision, a hallmark of CL, violates the lawyer's duty of client loyalty and creates a non-waivable conflict of interest:

> It is the opinion of this Committee that the practice of Collaborative Law violates Rule 1.7(b) of Colorado Rules of Professional Conduct insofar as a lawyer participating in the process enters into a contractual agreement with the opposing party requiring the lawyer to withdraw in the event that the process is unsuccessful. The Committee further concludes that pursuant to Colo. RPC 1.7(c) the client's consent to waive this conflict cannot be validly obtained.

The comment to Rule 1.7 explains:

> Loyalty to a client is also impaired when a lawyer cannot consider, recommend or carry out an appropriate course of action for the client because of the lawyer's other responsibilities or interests. The conflict in effect forecloses alternatives that would otherwise be available to the client.

Despite the controversy over the withdrawal aspect, or perhaps because of it, the Uniform Law Commission in 2009 voted to adopt the Uniform Collaborative Law Act. The Act recognizes CL as an ADR process. It also articulates requirements for informed client consent to participate and a duty upon lawyers to protect the safety of clients from domestic violence during the collaborative process. The Act was sent to the ABA House of Delegates in 2010 for its consideration and, if approved, was to be sent to states for adoption (see Schepard 2009, *http://lawprofessors.typepad.com/family_law/2009/week30/index .html*).

A variant on CL is known as "cooperative law." Interestingly, the Colorado ethics opinion distinguished cooperative law from CL. It found that cooperative law is not per se unethical because it "lacks the disqualification agreement found in Collaborative Law." As explained by Professor John Lande, its principal advocate, cooperative practice also involves a "participation agreement" between lawyers and parties setting out a negotiation process with a goal of reaching a resolution that is fair for all parties. These agreements vary and may include terms committing to negotiate in good faith, act respectfully toward each other, disclose all relevant information, use jointly retained experts, protect confidentiality of communications, and refrain from formal discovery and contested litigation during negotiation. The participation agreement may provide for use of a mediator or a "cooling off" period before engaging in contested litigation. It may also state that if the parties do litigate, the lawyers would focus solely on the merits of the issues. The process generally begins before the parties file a lawsuit or soon afterward. The process typically involves "four-way meetings" with the parties and lawyers, although some negotiation may be directly between the lawyers or parties when appropriate.

The main difference between cooperative practice and CL, as noted in the Colorado ethics opinion, is that the participation agreement in cooperative practice does not include a "disqualification agreement" or "withdrawal agreement," so that if any party chooses to litigate (or threatens litigation), the lawyers are not disqualified from representing the parties, and there is no need to hire new lawyers. In addition to this distinction, there may be other differences in tailoring the procedure to the particular circumstances. For example, cooperative practitioners may not use four-way meetings as much or involve as many other professionals in the meetings as in collaborative practice. (See Lande 2009.)

Another developing concept and practice that may influence how some lawyers negotiate is "mindfulness" in lawyering. Although difficult to simply describe and pigeonhole, mindfulness derives from meditative qualities that put immediate demands in a larger perspective. Mindfulness builds individual capacity for non-judgmental awareness of ourselves and all around us. It amounts to paying attention, being present, and developing insight through concentration. It is a way of being that focuses the practitioner on the big picture and not only on the discrete transaction of the moment. Mindfulness redirects the context of practice to the integrity of the person and the system, rather than the immediate needs of the situation. Mindfulness focused on ethical decision making and compassion is not necessarily the opposite of adversarialness, but they may be difficult to reconcile. (See generally Riskin 2006.)

Mindfulness is finding its way into law school curriculums, law firm programs, and legal publications. An issue of the *Harvard Negotiation Law Review* was dedicated to meditation and mindfulness in the practice of ADR. One commentator in that *Review*, Professor Scott Peppet, takes on the logical extension of mindfulness, perhaps tongue-in-cheek, to reach an analogy between the mindful lawyer and a saint or holy man and then questions whether two saints could negotiate. His article helps put our earlier consideration of Model Rule 4.1 in perspective and recasts the question of whether a lawyer can reconcile personal integrity with the conduct allowed, if not required, by Model Rule 4.1.

❖ **Scott R. Peppet,** *Mindfulness in the Law and ADR:*
Can Saints Negotiate?

7 Harv. Negot. L. Rev. 83 (2002)

. . . [I]magine that, at the extreme, a diligent mindfulness practitioner might eventually reach a state of complete dedication to an ethical life. I will call this person a "saint" because she adopts a more conscientious stance toward her relations with the world and others than most of us will ever achieve. Our saint would also have to be sufficiently strong-willed to live up to her moral commitments. She must have developed herself to the point that the contingencies of her life — her history, attachments, psychology, and emotions — no longer lead her to act against these deeply-held beliefs. She is so mindful as to be somewhat frightening.

What sort of ethical commitments would our saint adopt? For the sake of argument, I will assert that at the very least such a person would commit to both honesty and fairness, resolving neither to deceive nor to take advantage of other human beings for her own ends and to respect and take others' interests into account. There is good reason to believe that a very mindful person would adopt such a saintly view of life. Even without turning extensively to religious doctrine, one can imagine that our saint would be consistently non-partisan when it came to her own and others' interests. . . .

Consider the negotiating standards of two holy men, one a willing buyer and the other a willing seller. If their personal commitments to holiness prevented them from making the slightest misrepresentation or from engaging in any abuse of their bargaining positions, how would the ultimate outcome of their negotiations differ from the outcome achieved by two lawyer negotiators? If deceit truly is inherent to negotiation, the outcome achieved by the holy men could not be defined as the product of a negotiation. . . .

Not everyone agrees with this characterization, but it is certainly common. Perhaps the best example of this sort of thinking is, again, Model Rule 4.1's permission of misrepresentations about reservation price. According to the Rule's Comments, misleading statements of this sort are permitted because "under generally accepted conventions in negotiation, certain types of statements ordinarily are not taken as statements of material fact." Although the Rules do not say so explicitly, this Comment seems to imply that barring all types of misrepresentation would demand too much — it would make negotiation as we normally understand it impossible.

I disagree with this view. . . . Although many negotiators may deceive and manipulate, I see nothing that requires one to do so, nor do I think that one can be effective only by doing so. Negotiation requires parties to manage different and sometimes conflicting interests to determine whether a jointly-created outcome can be found that is more satisfying than any self-help alternative. Two saints could honestly disclose their alternatives and reservation values, their interests and priorities, and still face a variety of challenging decisions regarding how best to maximize achievable joint gain and divide the pie. Even for the enlightened there would likely be no easy answer as to whether to give more of the economic surplus in a transaction to the person who needed it more, wanted it more, or deserved it more. Two saints might disagree about how to classify a used car in the "blue book" scheme, or about when an employment agreement should vest an executive's stock options. I see no reason to redescribe their interaction over these matters as something other than negotiation merely because they chose to avoid dishonesty or manipulation.

I must make one caveat, however. One can imagine a person who becomes so universal in her views — so detached from the particulars of her individual position — that she no longer values her own interests at all. Her only interest becomes to serve others' interests. Although it is difficult to imagine how two such people could interact (wouldn't they merely circle each other endlessly, each trying to help the other?), I think the introduction of even one such person into what would otherwise be a negotiation does require redescription of the interaction as something other than bargaining. In this extreme circumstance there would not be two people with differing or conflicting interests; only one with interests and another with a desire to serve. There would be nothing to negotiate about — person A would express needs and person B would satisfy them to the best of B's ability.

Finally, one might object that lawyers have a duty to compete. If a lawyer refuses to do so because of ethical commitments that include consideration of an opponent's interests, then even if we cannot redescribe that lawyer's inter-actions as something other than negotiation, perhaps we should simply decide that the person can no longer be a lawyer. Robert Condlin, for example, has written that lawyers "must use any legally available move or procedure helpful to a client's bargaining position. Among other things, this means that all forms of leverage must be exploited, inflated demands made, and private information obtained and used whenever any of these actions would advance the client's stated objectives. . . . " If negotiating lawyers will not play the game, they should be disqualified as players.

Although it opens yet another difficult line of argument, I think it unlikely that a saint, or even just a very reflective person, would decide, like Condlin, to prioritize client loyalty over the saint's already-discussed ethical commitments. As Riskin explains, mindfulness loosens one's attachments — one's loyalties. This is, again, what suggests that these practices might aid in adopting a more universal perspective on moral questions. It also suggests, however, that a loyalty-driven ethic, peculiar to one's particular duties to a particular client, will be relatively unpersuasive to our saint as compared to the basic obligations to honesty and fairness. . . .

Questions

24. How might a "disqualification agreement," as used in collaborative practice, benefit a client?
25. What might be the barriers to the acceptance of collaborative law in general civil cases?
26. If cooperative practice does not involve a disqualification agreement, how does it differ from more traditional practice by competent attor-neys, who attempt to negotiate settlements before initiating litigation?
27. Would a "saint," as described by Professor Peppet, who negotiates on behalf of a client, be subject to discipline by the Bar for failing to make the client's interests a priority and for not being a zealous advocate? Would you retain such a saint as your lawyer for purposes of negotia-tion?
28. Would you change Rule 4.1 and the comments to it? If so, what would you change and why?

29. A corporate defendant may desire to restrict a plaintiff's lawyer from representing other plaintiffs with similar claims or may feel vulnerable to future lawsuits based on information the plaintiff's lawyer obtained through discovery. As part of a negotiated settlement, the defendant in this situation may request that the plaintiff's attorney agree not to represent other plaintiffs with similar claims. Such a provision would contravene Model Rule 5.6, which provides, "A lawyer shall not participate in offering or making . . . an agreement in which a restriction on the lawyer's right to practice is part of the settlement. . . ." What do you think is the rationale and justification for this prohibition?

30. Is the "mirror test" the ultimate guide for negotiation ethics? That test takes into account your own values following a completed negotiation by asking, "Can you look at yourself in the mirror and feel okay?"

CHAPTER
11

The Law of Negotiation

A. How Law Impacts Negotiation

The purpose of most negotiation by lawyers is to reach an agreement to settle a claim or transact a business deal. The resulting agreement is a contract intended to be enforceable. Therefore, contract law is in play during negotiations and becomes the focus when enforcing or challenging a negotiated agreement. The basic contract principles of offer, acceptance, and consideration are the foundation of understanding the law of negotiated agreements. When a negotiated agreement is challenged, it is most often for contract-based failure of consideration, fraud, misrepresentation, or duress.

A related legal issue in negotiations conducted by lawyers is what authority the lawyer as agent has to commit the client as principal to an agreement. Questions about a lawyer's authority to represent a party's interests in settlement negotiations and bind the client can surface when a settlement or transaction is challenged. Case law and statutory limits on remedies and lawyer's fees can also result in collateral litigation, particularly in class actions where negotiations may create a conflict between the interests of the plaintiff class and its attorneys. (See, e.g., Evans v. Jeff D., 475 U.S. 717, 106 S. Ct. 1531 (1986).) The imprecise drafting of settlement agreements may create subsequent litigation about what was negotiated and what was mutually intended as a settlement. The law relating to releases, confidentiality provisions, and promises to do or not do something in the future can be critical in fashioning a lasting negotiated settlement.

As explored more in Chapter 14, most settlement negotiation occurs in the "shadow of the law," insofar as the prospect of the law of the case and what would happen in court if the claim is litigated influence bargaining. (See Mnookin & Kornhauser 1979.) The substantive law of the matter being negotiated affects lawyer negotiations and forms the backdrop for bargained outcomes. So, the entire law school curriculum bears in some way on the process, substance, and outcomes of negotiations by lawyers.

We focus on five areas in which the law may shape negotiation conduct. First, negotiated settlements can be encouraged by allocating attorneys' fees and litigation costs based on the reasonableness of rejected settlement offers. The statutory and case law regarding offers of settlement and fee shifting is covered.

Second, strategic moves by lawyers to settle with only some of several defendants have spawned appellate decisions about the consequences when some defendants settle and others do not. We look at "Mary Carter" agreements, as these secret, selective settlements have become known. Third, because a settlement agreement is a contract, this chapter examines how the law may limit the extent to which the settlement can be enforced if it is the result of fraud, misrepresentation, or duress. Fourth, the tax aspects of settlements can influence negotiation tactics and results, so we provide a primer on tax considerations in negotiating settlements. Finally, lawyers must be aware that what they do or fail to do as negotiators for clients can lead to charges of professional malpractice. We include material on potential claims by disappointed clients against their lawyers after the negotiation is concluded.

Other areas of law that significantly impact negotiations are not covered here, but should be noted. Insurance coverage issues and the role of insurance in paying settlement agreements loom in the background of tort and other lawsuit settlement negotiations. However, this topic cannot adequately be presented in a general negotiation course. There are distinct legal issues and possible reporting requirements regarding settlements when bankruptcy lurks in the shadows or when the negotiation may impact publicly traded securities of a company. Unique factors of which negotiators must be aware may also exist in domestic relations, environmental, and civil rights cases, particularly when courts must approve the settlement. Class actions create unique issues about the fairness of settlements and the need for court approval. Finally, settlement discussions may postpone filing an action and a question may arise about whether negotiation can stop a statute of limits from running and barring the claim. Although negotiation does not generally stop the statute from running, there are exceptions. What follows is intended to help familiarize you with a few critical areas in which the law does matter in lawyer negotiations and to help you spot red flags.

B. Offers of Settlement and Fee Shifting

The attorneys' fees and costs of bringing or defending a lawsuit are a major factor in negotiating settlement of a dispute. Whether legal action is threatened or pending, each side must consider in its risk analysis the potential costs of court proceedings. Favorable verdicts must be discounted by the amount required to obtain them; a defendant's exposure to loss is enhanced by the amount required to defend. Modest victories in court can be dwarfed and losses magnified by the costs expended, particularly for attorneys' fees. Anticipation of litigation costs affects reservation price calculations and can have a profound influence on negotiations.

In the United States the general rule is that each party pays its own legal expenses. This rule is modified by statute for some causes of action, like civil rights cases, or by predispute contractual agreements. In contrast to the "American rule," England and most of Europe impose costs on the losing party by awarding costs to the prevailing party. The "English rule," as this approach is known, tends to discourage litigation, particularly for those of limited means, by increasing the costs of losing. The leverage of increased costs on the loser increases the incentive for settlement. "Loser pays" legislative proposals in the United States have been favored by business defendants as part of "tort reform" to discourage frivolous lawsuits.

One problem with "loser pays" is defining who is the "loser." Is the person who obtains a verdict of $10,000, after bringing a lawsuit claiming damages of a million dollars and rejecting an offer of $100,000, the winner or loser? To more clearly define a court "win" for purposes of determining who pays the costs of a suit, a modified loser-pays approach is to allow a defendant to offer a judgment against itself for a designated amount. This offer, if not accepted, then becomes the benchmark to decide who the winner is relative to the money put on the table before the trial begins. This approach, known as an "offer of judgment," is embodied in Federal Rule of Civil Procedure 68, which has many state counterparts and variants. Pursuant to this rule, a plaintiff who rejects the defendant's formal, unconditional settlement offer, made within a specified time prior to trial, and is then awarded less than the offered amount, is responsible for the defendant's court costs and fees incurred after the date of the offer. It is important to note that court costs and fees, as used in the rule, do not include actual attorneys' fees, but may include certain discovery expenses incurred after the offer is made, as well as filing fees and other statutory costs. Although the cost-shifting mechanism of Rule 68 is only available for defendants, it is thought to provide an incentive for both sides to make more reasonable offers of settlement. See Robert G. Bone, *To Encourage Settlement: Rule 68, Offers of Judgment, and the History of the Federal Rules of Civil Procedure*, 102 Nw. U. L. Rev. 1551 (2008).

Note: Rule 68 Requirements

There are explicit and implicit requirements for making a Rule 68 offer of judgment. Failure to follow the requirements can defeat the recovery of costs and have other adverse consequences. The principal requirements to invoke Federal Rule 68 and most of its state counterparts include the following:

- The offer must be in writing.
- The offer must be served more than ten days before the trial begins (the date the actual hearing commences), although the time requirement varies state by state.
- The terms and amount of the offer must be clear.
- The offering defendant must agree to have a formal judgement entered on the record.
- The acceptance must be in writing and unconditional.

Once an offer of judgment is made, it is irrevocable until the trial begins, and it is then considered withdrawn and inadmissible as evidence at trial. Because the offer is treated as unconditional, there is no relief to a defendant for a unilateral mistake or misstated offer. On occasion this can result in a windfall for an accepting plaintiff, as in the following case of the free BMW.

❖ BMW OF NORTH AMERICA, INC. v. KRATHEN

471 So. 2d 585 (1985)

HURLEY, Judge.

BMW appeals from an order of the circuit court denying its motion to vacate judgment and, alternatively, its motion for relief from judgment. We affirm.

The Krathens filed suit against BMW, seeking money damages for breach of express and implied warranties under the Uniform Commercial Code, and for alleged violations of the Magnuson-Moss Warranty Act, 15 U.S.C.A. §§ 2301-2312 (1982). The gravamen of the complaint was that BMW sold the Krathens an automobile, at a purchase price of $26,534.13, (with a deferred payment price of $32,501.88), which had a shimmy in the front end that could not be corrected.

BMW responded by mailing an offer of judgment to the Krathens which reads, in its entirety: Pursuant to Fla. R. Civ. P. 1.442, Defendants hereby offer to allow the Plaintiffs to take judgment against them in the amount of Twenty Thousand Five Hundred ($20, 500) Dollars, plus reasonable attorneys fees and costs heretofore accrued.

The Krathens promptly mailed their acceptance of the offer "as written" pursuant to rule 1.442, Fla. R. Civ. P. After the offer of judgment was filed, the clerk of the court entered judgment against BMW for "the total sum of twenty thousand five hundred ($20, 500) dollars, plus reasonable attorneys fees and costs."

BMW thereafter filed a motion to clarify offer of judgment and to vacate judgment by the clerk of the court and, alternatively, a motion for relief from judgment pursuant to rule 1.540, Fla. R. Civ. P. Essentially, BMW argued that "return of the vehicle was always a condition precedent to all settlement negotiations with the plaintiffs," and that the offer of judgment should therefore be clarified to reflect that understanding. In its motion for relief from judgment, BMW further argued that even if return of the vehicle were not a condition precedent to the offer, it should be granted relief under rule 1.540, Fla. R. Civ. P., because the offer "was made as a result of mistake, inadvertence, or excusable neglect on the part of [BMW's] counsel." Both motions were denied and this appeal ensued.

As to the denial of the motion to vacate and clarify, the trial court properly refused to look at the pleadings in this case for purposes of interpreting the offer of judgment which unambiguously states that $20,500 is offered "to allow the Plaintiffs [the Krathens] to take judgment against them." The Krathens accepted the offer "as written"; BMW therefore cannot now be heard to complain that a condition precedent should be read into the offer merely because the attorney who drafted the offer "assumed" that both parties contemplated return of the vehicle in exchange for the $20,500.

A judgment entered pursuant to rule 1.442, Fla. R. P., may properly be analogized to a consent judgment, which is in the nature of a contract. As such, the construction of a rule 1.442 judgment should be governed solely by the language employed by the parties if it is without ambiguity. When contractual language is clear and unambiguous, courts cannot indulge in construction or interpretation of its plain meaning. Further, where a contract is silent as to a particular matter, courts should not, under the guise of construction, impose on parties contractual rights and duties which they themselves omitted.

Thus, in construing the rule 1.442 judgment at issue in this case, the trial court properly refused to look to the pleadings for evidence of the parties' intent because the offer and acceptance were unambiguous on their face.

Next, we turn to BMW's assertion that the judgment should have been vacated because it was the result of a mistake. Under the rule in most states, a contract cannot be opened, changed or set aside without the assent of the parties in the absence of fraud, *mutual mistake*, or actual absence of consent. Florida, however, follows the minority rule which permits a contract to be set aside on the basis of *unilateral mistake* unless (a) the mistake is the result of an inexcusable lack of due care or (b) the other party has so changed its position in reliance on the contract that rescission would be unconscionable.

The facts in the case at bar provide ample support for the trial court's implied finding of inexcusable lack of due care on the part of BMW's counsel. The offer of judgment did not involve a complex transaction. The terms were few and easily understood. Thus, the omission of what is now claimed to be an essential term, cannot be characterized as a minor, inadvertent error. On the contrary, it evidences a total lack of forethought and such poor draftsmanship as to be well below accepted professional standards. Accordingly, the trial court was justified in refusing to grant relief from a unilateral mistake which resulted from an inexcusable lack of due care.

With respect to the trial court's denial of the defendant's motion for relief from judgment under rule 1.540(b), Fla. R. Civ. P., this court may reverse only if the denial amounted to an abuse of discretion.

Under rule 1.540(b), the trial court is authorized to relieve a party from a final judgment or decree on grounds of "mistake, inadvertence, surprise or excusable neglect." A party to a consent judgment who files a rule 1.540(b) motion is not entitled to relief because he misunderstood the legal effect of his consent, nor is a party to a stipulation for dismissal entered after a negotiated settlement entitled to relief on grounds of inadvertence or excusable neglect where a belated discovery of a more serious injury sustained by one plaintiff is discovered, even though the defendants were in possession of a physician report describing said injury, where plaintiffs failed to avail themselves of available methods for obtaining the report. Neglect of counsel amounts to excusable neglect sufficient to warrant relief from judgment only where it is the result of generally accepted practices and amenities among the local bar. In this case, the omission of a key contractual provision simply cannot be classified as a generally accepted practice among the local bar.

Therefore, we find that the trial court acted well within its discretion by denying BMW's motion for post-judgment relief.

In *Randle-Eastern Ambulance Service, Inc. v. Vasta*, 360 So. 2d 68 (Fla.1978), the supreme court observed:

> It has never been the role of the trial courts of this state to relieve attorneys of their tactical mistakes. The rules of civil procedure were never designed for that purpose, and nothing in Rule 1.540(b) suggests otherwise. . . .

Similarly, we hold that the court below correctly concluded that it was without authority to grant relief under rule 1.540(b) in order to relieve BMW's counsel

of his mistaken assumptions and neglect in failing to specifically provide for return of the vehicle as a condition precedent to its offer of judgment. The trial court's denial of BMW's motion is
AFFIRMED.

Questions

1. Who is likely to pay for the BMW car the plaintiffs are allowed to keep, along with return of $20,500, attorneys' fees, and costs? (Negotiation malpractice is presented in more detail later in this subsection.)
2. Why did the trial court refuse to look at the pleadings for purposes of interpreting the offer of judgment? Does the appellate court's decision not to discern the intent of the parties based on the pleadings seem correct? Why?
3. If the negotiations preceding the offer of judgment in *BMW of North America v. Krathen* were clearly premised on Krathen returning the BMW in exchange for repayment of the purchase price, would you as Krathen's attorney have any ethical obligation to have corrected the wording of the plaintiff's offer of judgment or advised your client to return the car?

When the plaintiff brings a cause of action pursuant to a statute that provides attorneys' fees if the plaintiff "prevails," is the right to statutory attorneys' fees lost when the judgment obtained is less than the rejected Rule 68 offer? This important question, and the settlement-promoting rationale for Rule 68, are considered by the Supreme Court in the opinion that follows.

❖ *MAREK v. CHESNY*

473 U.S. 1, 105 S. Ct. 3012 (1985)

Justice BURGER delivered the opinion of the Court.

We granted certiorari to decide whether attorney's fees incurred by a plaintiff subsequent to an offer of settlement under Federal Rule of Civil Procedure 68 must be paid by the defendant under 42 U.S.C. §1988, when the plaintiff recovers a judgment less than the offer.

Petitioners, three police officers, in answering a call on a domestic disturbance, shot and killed respondent's adult son. Respondent, in his own behalf and as administrator of his son's estate, filed suit against the officers in the United States District Court under 42 U.S.C. §1983 and state tort law.

Prior to trial, petitioners made a timely offer of settlement "for a sum, including costs now accrued and attorney's fees, ONE HUNDRED THOUSAND ($100,000) DOLLARS." Respondent did not accept the offer. The case went to trial and respondent was awarded $5,000 on the state-law "wrongful death" claim, $52,000 for the §1983 violation, and $3,000 in punitive damages.

Respondent filed a request for $171,692.47 in costs, including attorney's fees. This amount included costs incurred after the settlement offer. Petitioners opposed the claim for postoffer costs, relying on Federal Rule of Civil Procedure 68, which shifts to the plaintiff all "costs" incurred subsequent to an offer of judgment not exceeded by the ultimate recovery at trial. Petitioners argued that attorney's fees are part of the "costs" covered by Rule 68. The District Court agreed with petitioners and declined to award respondent "costs, including attorney's fees, incurred after the offer of judgment." The parties subsequently agreed that $32,000 fairly represented the allowable costs, including attorney's fees, accrued prior to petitioners' offer of settlement. . . . [The first question addressed was whether the rejected lump sum offer, which included attorney fees to that point, was "more than" the judgment obtained for damages alone. The Court held the Rule 68 lump sum offer was more than the judgment.]

The second question we address is whether the term "costs" in Rule 68 includes attorney's fees awardable under 42 U.S.C. §1988. By the time the Federal Rules of Civil Procedure were adopted in 1938, federal statutes had authorized and defined awards of costs to prevailing parties for more than 85 years. Unlike in England, such "costs" generally had not included attorney's fees; under the "American Rule," each party had been required to bear its own attorney's fees. The "American Rule" as applied in federal courts, however, had become subject to certain exceptions by the late 1930's. Some of these exceptions had evolved as a product of the "inherent power in the courts to allow attorney's fees in particular situations." But most of the exceptions were found in federal statutes that directed courts to award attorney's fees as part of costs in particular cases. . . .

The authors of Federal Rule of Civil Procedure 68 were fully aware of these exceptions to the American Rule. The Advisory Committee's Note to Rule 54(d), 28 U.S.C. App., p. 621, contains an extensive list of the federal statutes which allowed for costs in particular cases; of the 35 "statutes as to costs" set forth in the final paragraph of the Note, no fewer than 11 allowed for attorney's fees as part of costs. Against this background of varying definitions of "costs," the drafters of Rule 68 did not define the term; nor is there any explanation whatever as to its intended meaning in the history of the Rule.

In this setting, given the importance of "costs" to the Rule, it is very unlikely that this omission was mere oversight; on the contrary, the most reasonable inference is that the term "costs" in Rule 68 was intended to refer to all costs properly awardable under the relevant substantive statute or other authority. In other words, all costs properly awardable in an action are to be considered within the scope of Rule 68 "costs." Thus, absent congressional expressions to the contrary, where the underlying statute defines "costs" to include attorney's fees, we are satisfied such fees are to be included as costs for purposes of Rule 68.

Here, respondent sued under 42 U.S.C. §1983. Pursuant to the Civil Rights Attorney's Fees Awards Act of 1976, 90 Stat. 2641, as amended, 42 U.S.C. §1988, a prevailing party in a §1983 action may be awarded attorney's fees "as part of the costs." Since Congress expressly included attorney's fees as "costs" available to a plaintiff in a §1983 suit, such fees are subject to the cost-shifting provision of Rule 68. This "plain meaning" interpretation of the interplay between Rule 68 and §1988 is the only construction that gives meaning to each word in both Rule 68 and §1988.

Unlike the Court of Appeals, we do not believe that this "plain meaning" construction of the statute and the Rule will frustrate Congress' objective in

§1988 of ensuring that civil rights plaintiffs obtain "'effective access to the judicial process.'" Merely subjecting civil rights plaintiffs to the settlement provision of Rule 68 does not curtail their access to the courts, or significantly deter them from bringing suit. Application of Rule 68 will serve as a disincentive for the plaintiff's attorney to continue litigation after the defendant makes a settlement offer. There is no evidence, however, that Congress, in considering §1988, had any thought that civil rights claims were to be on any different footing from other civil claims insofar as settlement is concerned. Indeed, Congress made clear its concern that civil rights plaintiffs not be penalized for "helping to lessen docket congestion" by settling their cases out of court.

Moreover, Rule 68's policy of encouraging settlements is neutral, favoring neither plaintiffs nor defendants; it expresses a clear policy of favoring settlement of all lawsuits. Civil rights plaintiffs — along with other plaintiffs — who reject an offer more favorable than what is thereafter recovered at trial will not recover attorney's fees for services performed after the offer is rejected. But, since the Rule is neutral, many civil rights plaintiffs will benefit from the offers of settlement encouraged by Rule 68. Some plaintiffs will receive compensation in settlement where, on trial, they might not have recovered, or would have recovered less than what was offered. And, even for those who would prevail at trial, settlement will provide them with compensation at an earlier date without the burdens, stress, and time of litigation. In short, settlements rather than litigation will serve the interests of plaintiffs as well as defendants.

To be sure, application of Rule 68 will require plaintiffs to "think very hard" about whether continued litigation is worthwhile; that is precisely what Rule 68 contemplates. This effect of Rule 68, however, is in no sense inconsistent with the congressional policies underlying §1983 and §1988. Section 1988 authorizes courts to award only "reasonable" attorney's fees to prevailing parties. In *Hensley v. Eckerhart*, [*supra*], we held that "the most critical factor" in determining a reasonable fee "is the degree of success obtained." We specifically noted that prevailing at trial "may say little about whether the expenditure of counsel's time was reasonable in relation to the success achieved." In a case where a rejected settlement offer exceeds the ultimate recovery, the plaintiff — although technically the prevailing party — has not received any monetary benefits from the postoffer services of his attorney. This case presents a good example: the $139,692 in postoffer legal services resulted in a recovery $8,000 less than petitioners' settlement offer. Given Congress' focus on the success achieved, we are not persuaded that shifting the postoffer costs to respondent in these circumstances would in any sense thwart its intent under §1988. . . .

Justice POWELL, concurring.

Justice REHNQUIST, concurring.

Justice BRENNAN, with whom Justice MARSHALL and Justice BLACKMUN join, dissenting.

. . . I dissent. The Court's reasoning is wholly inconsistent with the history and structure of the Federal Rules, and its application to the over 100 attorney's fees statutes enacted by Congress will produce absurd variations in Rule 68's operation based on nothing more than picayune differences in statutory phraseology. Neither Congress nor the drafters of the Rules could possibly have intended such inexplicable variations in settlement incentives. . . . Finally, both Congress and the Judicial Conference of the United States have been engaged for years in considering possible amendments to Rule 68 that would bring attorney's fees within the operation of the Rule. That process strongly suggests that Rule 68 has not previously been viewed as governing fee awards, and it illustrates the wisdom of deferring to other avenues of amending Rule 68 rather than ourselves engaging in "standardless judicial lawmaking."

. . . The Court argues, however, that its interpretation of Rule 68 "is neutral, favoring neither plaintiffs nor defendants." This contention is also plainly wrong. As the Judicial Conference Advisory Committee on the Federal Rules of Civil Procedure has noted twice in recent years, Rule 68 "is a 'one-way street,' " available only to those defending against claims and not to claimants. Interpreting Rule 68 in its current version to include attorney's fees will lead to a number of skewed settlement incentives that squarely conflict with Congress' intent. To discuss but one example, Rule 68 allows an offer to be made any time after the complaint is filed and gives the plaintiff only 10 days to accept or reject. The Court's decision inevitably will encourage defendants who know they have violated the law to make "low-ball" offers immediately after suit is filed and before plaintiffs have been able to obtain the information they are entitled to by way of discovery to assess the strength of their claims and the reasonableness of the offers. The result will put severe pressure on plaintiffs to settle on the basis of inadequate information in order to avoid the risk of bearing all of their fees even if reasonable discovery might reveal that the defendants were subject to far greater liability. Indeed, because Rule 68 offers may be made recurrently without limitation, defendants will be well advised to make ever-slightly larger offers throughout the discovery process and before plaintiffs have conducted all reasonably necessary discovery.

This sort of so-called "incentive" is fundamentally incompatible with Congress' goals. Congress intended for "private citizens . . . to be able to assert their civil rights" and for "those who violate the Nation's fundamental laws" not to be able "to proceed with impunity." Accordingly, civil rights plaintiffs " 'appear before the court cloaked in a mantle of public interest' "; to promote the "*vigorous* enforcement of modern civil rights legislation," Congress has directed that such "private attorneys general" shall not "be deterred from bringing good faith actions to vindicate the fundamental rights here involved." Yet requiring plaintiffs to make wholly uninformed decisions on settlement offers, at the risk of *automatically* losing all of their postoffer fees no matter what the circumstances and notwithstanding the "excellent" results they might achieve after the full picture emerges, will work just such a deterrent effect. . . .

Questions

4. Does the Court's holding in *Marek* seriously impair the incentive to bring civil rights cases, as intended by Congress when it provided for recovery of plaintiffs' attorneys' fees?

5. In Chapter 2 you read about risk averseness and the role of this concept in negotiation. Professor Ed Sherman suggests, "that a well-heeled defendant is less likely to be deterred from defending a weak suit by the threat of having to pay its opponent's attorneys' fees than a plaintiff from prosecuting a possibly meritorious suit. Since plaintiffs are generally more risk averse than defendants, a 'loser pays' rule impacts disproportionately on plaintiffs' access to the courts" (Sherman 1998, 1863). Is it convincing to you that well-heeled defendants are less risk averse than less financially well-off plaintiffs? Why might or might not this be correct?

6. You also read previously about the tendency of parties and lawyers to be overly optimistic about the strength of their cases and their chances of winning. If both sides in a case are confident about their chance of prevailing, does a "loser pays" rule promote or impede settlement? Are both sides likely to insist on more in their negotiations because each believes the other will have to pay all costs and fees following trial?

7. Often, attorneys negotiate the amount of statutorily allowed fees at the same time that they seek substantive payments for their clients. The defendant may seek trade-offs of lower attorneys' fees, or waiver of fees, in exchange for a higher payment to the client. This principal-agent conflict can pit client interests against those of the lawyer. The Supreme Court addressed this issue in Evans v. Jeff D., 475 U.S. 717 (1986), and held that the plaintiff's waiver of statutory attorneys' fees to obtain a better settlement for his client would not be set aside and that the trial court could consider the propriety of such a trade-off on a case-by-case basis. Is the ethical dilemma greater for the plaintiff's attorney confronted with a coercive offer to waive or reduce fees to obtain a better settlement for his client, or for the defendant's attorney whose client insists that the trade-off be proposed? Do you feel that such proposals for a fee waiver or reduction should be ethically prohibited?

Justice Brennan in his dissent in *Marek* notes that the Judicial Conference, which proposes the wording of the Federal Rules, and Congress have on multiple occasions considered amending Rule 68 to include attorneys' fees and to make the Rules mechanism available to plaintiffs as well as defendants. Congressional bills continue to propose expansion of Rule 68 to increase its impact on promoting settlement. This ongoing interest in amending Rule 68 is prompted, in part, by a sense that in its current form Rule 68 is not enough of an incentive in the negotiating process to make a meaningful difference in settlement rates and fails to shift enough expense risk to plaintiffs if they reject an offer. Although the frequency with which Rule 68 is invoked in negotiating lawsuit settlements is not regularly tracked, its incidence of use is thought to be relatively low.

On the other hand, increasing the economic incentive or coercion for plaintiffs to settle may diminish access to courts by less wealthy plaintiffs attempting to right wrongs or pursue public interest causes. This concern, along with the complexities of expanding Rule 68, has defeated attempts to broaden the Federal Rule. However, the beat goes on to promote more negotiated settlements by increasing settlement incentives and litigation disincentives. The issue is sometimes framed in terms of putting more "teeth" in Rule 68.

Problem

You are serving as a representative of the Law Student Section on an ABA task force to suggest revisions to FRCP 68, which has not been substantively changed since 1946. The task force is composed of attorneys representing plaintiffs and defendants, as well as several judges. The judges report that the use of FRCP 68 appears to be declining. Several amendments to the Rule have been proposed, including adding attorneys' fees to costs when the Rule is invoked, creating mutuality by allowing plaintiffs to propose an FRCP 68-triggering settlement, and requiring a 10 percent differential between the judgment and the settlement offer before triggering a cost shift. What, if any, changes would you support and why? What additional information would you find helpful? Are there any other amendments to FRCP 68 that you might suggest?

The next reading discusses the impact of "loser pays" rules on negotiation incentives and some state modifications to Rule 68 offers of settlement mechanisms that may pave the way for change to Federal Rule 68.

❖ Anna Aven Sumner, *IS THE GUMMY RULE OF TODAY TRULY BETTER THAN THE TOOTHY RULE OF TOMORROW? HOW FEDERAL RULE 68 SHOULD BE MODIFIED*

852 Duke L.J. 1055 (2003)

Introduction

Federal Rule of Civil Procedure 68, the offer-of-judgment rule, has a portentous past and purpose, but it has never lived up to the hype surrounding its creation. Touted as a tool of settlement, the rule lacks the "teeth" necessary to effect settlements. The absence of any such teeth also means that the rule lacks the power to create disincentives for bringing frivolous suits — a second, complementary goal of the rule.

Despite these shortcomings, federal rulemakers have not amended the substance of Rule 68 since 1946. In contrast, state lawmakers have been more responsive to criticisms of the rule. Many states have either amended their respective versions of Federal Rule 68 or have completely rewritten the rule. Such state rules concerning attorney's fees may serve as useful models for amending Federal Rule 68 to better serve the rule's twin goals — those of encouraging settlement and deterring frivolous litigation. . . .

I.   Attorney's Fees and Federal Rule 68

A. An Explanation of Attorney's Fees Under Offer-of-Judgment Rules

The most controversial of potential amendments to Rule 68, and perhaps the most necessary, would be the inclusion of attorney's fees, also referred to as "fee shifting," in the language of the rule, or the inclusion of attorney's fees in post-offer costs. In their most basic incarnations, statutes or procedural rules aimed at fee shifting require, under specified circumstances, the "loser" in a suit to pay the "winner's" attorney's fees. It is difficult to speak of fee-shifting rules in very specific terms without recourse to actual state statutes because the statutes vary in several respects, including the definition of "success," the inclusion of interest, and the "specified circumstances" under which fee shifting would occur.

Nonetheless, as a general example, suppose that, under a fee-shifting rule, A makes an offer of judgment to B for $10,000. B rejects this offer and recovers some amount less than $10,000, or fails to recover anything at trial. A would be considered the "winner." As the "winner," A would be entitled to recover from B all attorney's fees and costs A incurred in defending against the suit after its offer of judgment was made and rejected. If B does not pay immediately, A may be entitled to interest on the amount. The precise amount B must recover to avoid paying A's attorney fees depends upon the relevant statutory language.

If, on the other hand, after B's rejection, B recovers $10,000 or more at trial, two options are possible. First, each party might be responsible for its own attorney's fees. Alternatively, as a statutorily defined "loser," A might have to pay whatever attorney's fees and costs B incurred after A made the offer of judgment. Again, B may be entitled to interest on the costs and fees.

B. Why Is Including Attorney's Fees a Necessary Change to the Rule?

The two most logically appealing reasons to include attorney's fees in an offer-of-judgment rule are (1) to encourage parties to consider settlement carefully, and (2) to discourage frivolous litigation. Although encouraging settlement has long been an enunciated goal of offer-of-judgment rules, discouragement of frivolous litigation is less vocally supported. Perhaps if fears about this "penalty enhancement" justification for the addition of attorney's fees can be assuaged, an amendment including attorney's fees to Federal Rule 68 may be successful. . . .

II.   State Modifications Permitting Inclusion of Attorney's Fees

. . . Various states have adopted modified versions of Federal Rule 68 to include attorney's fees. These state rules provide models for improving Federal Rule 68. This Note now turns to a discussion of the mechanics of the approaches that these states have taken.

A. The Expansive Extreme: Alaska

Alaska has adopted an offer-of-judgment rule that supports the award of attorney's fees in virtually all circumstances. In Alaska's version of Federal Rule 68, if the judgment of the court is either 5 or 10 percent less favorable than the refused offer, the offeror is entitled to costs and "reasonable actual" post-offer attorney's fees. Attorney's fees, under the statute, are awarded according to when the offer was made. If the offer was made within sixty days of discovery, the offeror is entitled to have 75 percent of its attorney's fees paid. If the offer was made between sixty and ninety days after discovery, the offeror is entitled to have 50 percent of its attorney's fees paid. If the offer was made more than ninety days after discovery but at least ten days before the commencement of trial, the offeror is only entitled to have 30 percent of its attorney's fees paid. . . .

B. The Middle of the Road: California and Nevada

Other states have embraced the middle road, permitting an award of attorney's fees only in cases of bad-faith actions of parties during litigation. California has adopted its rule explicitly in a state rule of civil procedure, while Nevada has generated similar results through case law interpreting a similar rule of civil procedure.

1. The California Framework

California's offer-of-judgment rule is section 998 of the Civil Procedure Code. Although the text of this rule differs greatly from that of Federal Rule 68, the relevant fee-shifting provision differs from the federal rule only in that it permits plaintiffs to make offers of judgment, and in that it applies equally to arbitration proceedings. To supplement section 998, California, in 1987, enacted as a pilot project Civil Procedure Code section 1021.1, a provision for discretionary awards of attorney's fees in conjunction with offers of judgment. . . . Together, these two sections create a possible model for amending Federal Rule 68. . . .

California courts have determined that inherent in any offer-of-judgment rule is the requirement that the offer not be token or in bad faith. A one-dollar offer of judgment, for instance, was found to have been made in bad faith, and, as such, no expert witness fees were awarded to the offering party, even though the offering party prevailed. This requirement of a good-faith offer of settlement has been applied when a nominal offer was as high as $15,001, in a case in which the ultimate judgment was for more than $1 million. Although the good-faith standard cannot be applied across the board, it appears that, at least in California, judicial discretion comfortably steps in and applies the standard as needed.

2. The Nevada Framework

Unlike California, Nevada's offer-of-judgment rule does not explicitly address the same concerns. On the face of the rule, when a party rejects an offer and fails to obtain a more favorable judgment, several penalties follow. The first is that a party cannot recover "any costs or attorney's fees and shall not recover interest for the period after the service of the offer and before the judgment." Additionally, the offeree is bound to pay the offeror's post-offer costs from the time of the offer, and reasonable attorney's fees actually incurred by the offeror since the time of the offer. What the rule does not facially address is in what circumstances attorney's fees should be awarded under Nevada's Rule 68. Thus courts were left with the job of interpreting the rule to determine when attorney's fees were to be shifted.

The first case to address the appropriateness of an assessment of attorney's fees was *Beattie v. Thomas*, in which the Nevada Supreme Court enunciated four factors to guide the exercise of discretion for awarding attorney's fees: (1) whether the plaintiff's claim was brought in good faith; (2) whether the defendants' offer of judgment was reasonable and in good faith in both its timing and amount; (3) whether the plaintiff's decision to reject the offer and proceed to trial was grossly unreasonable or in bad faith; and (4) whether the fees sought by the offeror are reasonable and justified in amount. After weighing the foregoing factors, the district judge may, where warranted, award up to the full amount of fees requested. . . .

C. The Restrictive Extreme: Arizona

Arizona exemplifies the most restrictive approach to the modification of Federal Rule 68 by the imposition of attorney's fees, permitting an award of fees only if the parties agree to such fee shifting at the outset. First, attorney's fees, if contemplated by the parties, must be identified separately as a part of the offer. After an offer has been made, the offeree essentially has three different options. The first option, naturally, is to accept the offer in full. The second option is to permit the offer to lapse. If the offer is permitted to lapse, then and only then may an award of expert witness fees and double costs be permitted as sanctions, if the rejecting party recovers less than the offer. If the offer lapses, however, attorney's fees cannot be imposed. The third option is for the offeree to accept the offer in part. Partial acceptance of the offer occurs when the parties agree as to the monetary award for the causes of action asserted, but disagree as to whether attorney's fees should be awarded, and if awarded, disagree as to the specific amount. In such an instance, the parties may file the offer and acceptance thereof with the court, and apply to the court for a determination of whether or not an award of fees is appropriate, and if so, in what amount. . . .

Note: Does FRCP 68 Create More Risk Taking Rather Than Less?

The study referred to in Chapter 6 of 4,532 civil litigation cases over a 44-year period was based on California Code of Civil Procedure Section 998, the California equivalent of FRCP 68, intended to encourage settlement by financially penalizing parties whose trial result is worse than the settlement offer made by an adversary. That study shows that Section 998-inspired offers, available to both plaintiffs and defendants, could be counterproductive. Parties who received settlement offers under Section 998 were more likely to take aggressive settlement positions, resulting in financially adverse outcomes, than were those in the study who didn't receive such offers. The decision error rate (defined as getting less at trial than the pretrial offer) for plaintiffs who risked the imposition of statutory financial penalties for not accepting written settlement offers was 83 percent, compared with 61 percent for plaintiffs who did not receive such offers. Similarly, defendants faced with statutory penalties for unreasonable settlement positions exhibited a decision error rate of 46 percent, compared to an error rate of 22 percent for defendants who did not negotiate under the threat of statutory penalties. These findings complement other empirical and experimental studies indicating that legislation intended to increase settlement rates or curb risk-taking settlement negotiation behavior may be ineffective. Whether this particular California statutory procedure provokes risk-taking behavior, the co-authors caution, is unclear, as other factors may cause the high decision error rates associated with the procedure (see Kiser et al. 2008).

C. Mary Carter Agreements

Negotiation between a plaintiff and multiple defendants can be legally and ethically complex. When one or more of multiple defendants with joint and several liability settles with a plaintiff and the others do not, it is commonly referred to as a "Mary Carter" or sliding scale agreement. The settling defendant typically makes a deal with the plaintiff about the maximum amount that the defendant will pay, regardless of the trial outcome or later settlement by the plaintiffs with other defendants. The agreement also allows a decrease in the settling defendant's payment if the plaintiff obtains more from all the defendants combined than the total amount of damages (sliding scale). In other words, the settling defendant caps his liability and potentially benefits from the plaintiff's success against the remaining defendants. It is possible that the settling defendant will pay nothing if the plaintiff collects the full amount of damages from the other defendants (a "zero bottom" settlement.)

Mary Carter agreements are named after the Florida case Booth v. Mary Carter Paint Company, 202 So. 2d 8 (Fla. App. 1967), in which the plaintiff, Booth, brought a negligence action against multiple defendants for the motor vehicle death of his wife. During settlement negotiations, the defense counsel for two of the defendants made a deal with the plaintiff, separately from Mary Carter Paint Company, also a defendant in the case, about the maximum amount that they would pay. The signing defendants were not released from liability and remained in the case tried to a jury, which was unaware of the settlement agreement. In essence, the settling defendants switched to the plaintiff's side while seeming to the jury to still be defendants. The Carter Paint Company lost its post-trial objections to the secret settlement deal, which could have resulted in it paying the entire settlement (but did not). The Florida Court of Appeal confirmed the ruling and upheld the partial settlement agreement.

Mary Carter agreements classically involve four major features:

1. The plaintiff is guaranteed a certain amount of recovery from the settling defendants.
2. The dollar liability of the settling defendants is limited to the guaranteed amount and may be reduced by the plaintiff's recovery from other defendants.
3. The agreement between the settling defendant and the plaintiff is kept secret from the jury and often from the nonsettling defendants.
4. The settling defendant remains in the lawsuit.

Although a few states have banned Mary Carter agreements as collusive and against public policy, most allow some form of this negotiated partial settlement, even if only on a case-by-case basis or referred to by another name. In Arizona, this type of selective settlement is known as a "Gallagher covenant," from the case City of Tucson v. Gallagher, 14 Ariz. App. 385, 483 P.2d 798 (1971). A majority of states now require Mary Carter agreements to be disclosed to co-defendants and the jury. (See Hodesh v. Korelitz, 123 Ohio St. 3d 72, 2009.)

California relies on the wording of a state statute (Cal. Civ. Proc. Code 877 and 877.6) to allow "sliding scale recovery agreements," provided the value of the settlement indicates it was entered into in "good faith." As the California Supreme Court explained in the case that follows, the negotiated cap amount and other financial obligations must be within a reasonable range of the settling defendant's proportional share of comparative liability among the tortfeasors.

❖ *ABBOT FORD, INC. v. THE SUPERIOR COURT OF LOS ANGELES COUNTY;*
FORD MOTOR CO.

43 Cal. 3d 858 (1987)

PANELLI, J.

The issue presented here is whether a "sliding scale recovery agreement," entered into by plaintiffs and one of several defendants in a personal injury action, represents a "good faith" settlement within the meaning of sections 877 and 877.6 of the Code of Civil Procedure, so as to relieve the settling defendant of any liability for contribution or equitable comparative indemnity to other defendants in the action. The trial court concluded that the agreement in question was not a good faith settlement and denied the settling defendant's motion to bar cross-complaints by the remaining defendants. The settling defendant then sought review by writ of mandate, and ultimately the Court of Appeal — after remand by this court — concluded that while the "good faith" of such a sliding scale agreement must properly be measured by the standard set forth in our recent decision in *Tech-Bilt, Inc. v. Woodward-Clyde & Associates* (1985) 38 Cal. 3d 488, the agreement at issue here satisfied that standard as a matter of law. We granted review to consider the question of the appropriate application of the statutory "good faith" requirement in the context of sliding scale agreements.

To place the issue in perspective, we review the facts and the litigation background as revealed by the declarations and other materials that were presented to the trial court in connection with its hearing on the good faith settlement question.

The underlying personal injury action in this case arose out of a somewhat unusual automobile accident that occurred on September 10, 1981. At the time of the accident, Ramsey Sneed was driving a used 1979 Ford Econoline van that he had purchased from Abbott Ford, Inc. (Abbott). As Sneed was driving, the left rear wheel came off the van and crashed into the windshield of an oncoming car, a 1965 Mercury station wagon driven by Phyllis Smith. The windshield shattered and Smith suffered serious injuries, including the loss of sight in both eyes and the loss of her sense of smell.

Thereafter, Smith and her husband (hereafter plaintiffs) filed the underlying lawsuit against four defendants — (1) Sneed, (2) Abbott, (3) Ford Motor Company (Ford) and (4) Sears, Roebuck & Co. (Sears) — seeking recovery on a variety of theories. . . .

With the case in this posture, a mandatory settlement conference was set for March 26, 1984. In anticipation of that conference, representatives of Abbott, Ford and Sears met on March 14, 1984. At that meeting, Abbott's counsel stated that he believed a reasonable settlement value for the case was $2.5 million and that Abbott was willing to contribute 70 percent of that sum. Counsel for Ford and Sears, however, maintained that their clients had only minimal, if any, responsibility for the accident and were unwilling to bear 30 percent — $750,000 — of such a settlement.

At about the same time, plaintiffs offered to settle with Ford or Sears if they would enter into a sliding scale agreement guaranteeing plaintiffs $1.5 million. Both Ford and Sears declined the offer.

On March 23, 1984, three days before the settlement conference, plaintiffs filed their "mandatory settlement conference statement" setting forth the facts of the case, their theories of liability against all parties, and their expected recovery. With respect to liability, the statement concluded: "The liability of Abbott Ford in this case is clear on either a products liability theory or on a negligence theory because Abbott Ford modified the van with unsafe, defective after-market wheels and tires notwithstanding Ford's warning to the contrary. Ford's and Sears' liability is not as clear as Abbott Ford's, but it is for the jury to decide whether they should be held accountable for this accident. The liability of Sneed is also clear because he had the last opportunity to avoid the accident." With respect to damages, the statement declared that — on the basis of a detailed review of damage awards in numerous cases involving similar injuries — "[p]laintiffs expect a favorable verdict in this case in an amount not less than $3,000,000."

Three days later, at the mandatory settlement conference, Abbott's insurer announced that it had agreed in principle to enter into a sliding scale agreement with plaintiffs, guaranteeing plaintiffs a recovery of $3 million. Several months later, plaintiffs and Abbott's insurer formally entered into the sliding scale agreement that is the focus of the present proceeding.

The agreement — which took the form of two separate contracts, one with each plaintiff, twenty-two and twenty pages in length respectively — contained three key and interrelated elements: (1) Abbott's insurer guaranteed Phyllis Smith an ultimate recovery of $2.9 million, and her husband an ultimate recovery of $100,000; if, at the conclusion of the lawsuit, plaintiffs had not collected the guaranteed amounts from the remaining defendants, Abbott's insurer would pay the balance up to the guaranteed sum. Thus, if plaintiffs recovered $3 million or more from Ford and Sears, Abbott would not bear any ultimate liability to plaintiffs; if plaintiffs recovered less than $3 million from Ford and Sears, Abbott would be obligated to pay plaintiffs the difference. In return for these guaranties, plaintiffs agreed (a) to dismiss all of their actions against Abbott and (b) to continue to prosecute their action against Ford and Sears in the same way that they would have in the absence of the agreement — through appeal, if necessary — "except that [plaintiffs] shall not settle all or any portion of this litigation with defendants Ford and Sears

Roebuck for less than the amount of [their] guaranty, without the express written consent of " Abbott's insurer.

In addition to providing the guaranties, Abbott's insurer agreed to make substantial, periodic no-interest loans to plaintiffs and their attorneys during the course of the litigation. Under the agreement, a total of $390,000 in interest-free loans had been made to plaintiffs and their attorneys by January 1986, and Abbott's insurer was obligated to pay plaintiffs and attorneys the full $3 million — in the form of a loan — by July 1, 1987, if plaintiffs' action had not been terminated by then. The agreement provided that the loan payments would serve as credits for the insurer's obligations under the guaranty provision; if plaintiffs collected $3 million or more from Ford and Sears, plaintiffs were obligated to repay the loans in full — but without interest — to Abbott's insurer.

Finally, the agreement contained an additional provision under which the insurer agreed to pay plaintiffs the full $3 million outright if the agreements were found to be invalid or not in good faith. . . . As Ford and Sears point out, sliding scale — or, as they are more commonly known throughout the country, "Mary Carter" — agreements have engendered a considerable body of academic commentary, much quite critical of this genre of settlement agreements. Relying on this literature, and a few out-of-state cases, Ford and Sears urge us to hold all such agreements contrary to public policy and invalid as a matter of law.

The majority of out-of-state decisions have, however, declined either to condemn or condone such agreements categorically and, for a number of reasons, we believe such a cautious approach to the problems posed by sliding scale agreements is appropriate. First, an enormous variety of contractual arrangements fall within the general rubric of sliding scale or Mary Carter agreements. Although in all such agreements the settling defendant's ultimate liability to the plaintiff is dependent, at least in part, on the amount of money which the plaintiff recovers from the nonsettling defendants, there are a virtually unlimited number of additional provisions that may be included in such agreements — for example, provisions which mandate secrecy, restrict settlement with the remaining defendants, or provide various forms of financing for the plaintiff's action — that will often substantially affect the operation and validity of the agreements. These differences caution against hasty overgeneralization of the merits or demerits of sliding scale agreements as a class.

Second, in addition to the variety of provisions that may supplement the sliding scale or "guaranty" clause of such agreements, the content and effect of the sliding scale provision itself and the factual background against which the agreement is negotiated frequently vary significantly from case to case. In some cases, like this one, the sliding scale clause may be structured so that the settling party may ultimately bear no liability to the plaintiff; in other cases, the settling party may make a substantial noncontingent payment to the plaintiff, and the sliding scale element may simply provide a supplemental guaranty of some additional recovery. In some cases, again like this one, the guaranty figure may be for an amount equal or close to the plaintiff's total damages; in others, the guaranty figure may represent only a relatively small share of the plaintiff's damages. In some cases, the settling defendant who may potentially be relieved of all liability by virtue of the agreement may be clearly the most culpable of all of the defendants, while in other cases a sliding scale agreement may be entered into by only peripherally involved defendants in order to obtain an escape from a potentially lengthy and costly suit. Finally, in some cases a sliding scale agreement may be obtained by one defendant in the early stages of negotiation without regard to the willingness of other defendants to engage in settlement negotiations in good faith, while in others such an agreement may be resorted to only as a last resort, after one or more defendants unreasonably refuse to make any settlement offer that may be commensurate with their fair share of responsibility for the plaintiff's damages, thwarting a fair and complete settlement of the litigation. These differences too may have a significant bearing on the fairness and propriety of a particular agreement.

Third, and finally, a broad ruling on the inherent validity or invalidity of sliding scale agreements "in general" is inappropriate because such agreements may have a variety of effects at different stages of the litigation process — discovery, settlement, trial or appeal. The potential problems posed by a particular provision in such an agreement may call for one remedy — e.g., disclosure of the agreement to the nonagreeing parties or to the jury — in one context, and another remedy — e.g., invalidation of a specific provision, or the agreement as a whole — in a different context. Thus, analysis requires close attention to the specific provisions of the agreement itself, the factual setting in which the agreement is entered into, and the agreement's effect on the particular aspect of the judicial process at issue.

In the present case, the question before us is not the broad one of the validity of sliding scale agreements in general, but the more limited question of whether the sliding scale agreement at issue here should properly be considered a "good faith" settlement under the relevant statutory provisions so as to absolve Abbott from any liability for contribution or indemnity to the remaining codefendants, Ford and Sears. As we shall see, that issue in itself raises a number of complex questions. . . .

[The court next enunciates the statutory requirements and reasons for "good faith" and proportionality based on Cal. Civ. Proc. Code 877, which reduces the plaintiff's claim against other defendants by the amount actually paid by the settling defendants.]

As Abbott suggests, in some instances sliding scale agreements have been entered into only as a matter of last resort, when one defendant in a multidefendant action refuses to participate in settlement negotiations or to make a good faith offer commensurate with its fair share of responsibility for plaintiff's damages. In such a setting, the recalcitrant defendant's unyielding position may threaten to make it impossible for any of the defendants to settle the litigation with the plaintiff, because the plaintiff may be unwilling to release any of the joint-and-severally liable defendants without an assurance that he will at least recover a minimum sum which he feels is necessary to compensate him for his injuries. While a defendant is, of course, ordinarily under no "legal obligation" to enter into a settlement with the plaintiff and has the "right" to insist that the plaintiff prove its case at trial, when a defendant acts unreasonably in settlement negotiations and its action or refusal to act threatens to frustrate the good-faith settlement efforts of other defendants and the plaintiff, such a defendant may be on shaky equitable grounds when it thereafter seeks to attack the "good faith" of a sliding scale agreement that has been occasioned by its own recalcitrance. We agree with Abbott that in such a setting it is appropriate for a trial court to take into consideration the conduct of the nonsettling defendant in determining whether a sliding scale agreement is a good faith settlement for purposes of sections 877 and 877.6. . . .

In sum, we conclude: (1) that *Tech-Bilt's* good faith standard applies to sliding scale agreements, (2) that to satisfy the statutory objective of a fair apportionment of loss (i) the "consideration" paid by a defendant who enters into a sliding scale agreement must fall within the *Tech-Bilt* "ballpark" and (ii) the plaintiffs' claims against the remaining defendants must be reduced by the amount of the "consideration paid" by the settling defendant, (3) that any unreasonable or bad faith conduct of the nonsettling defendants which impeded the settlement process and led to the sliding scale agreement may be taken into account in determining whether the agreement satisfies the "ballpark" standard, and (4) that any provision which purports to give a settling defendant a "veto" over subsequent settlements is valid only if it is limited to settlements which would leave the earlier settling defendant to bear more than its fair share of liability for the plaintiff's damages.

Questions

8. One reason for the California requirement of "good faith" or proportionality of the settling defendant's obligation is that a Mary Carter agreement between a plaintiff and one of multiple defendants stops a co-defendant/tortfeasor with joint and several liability from cross-complaining or suing the settling defendant for contribution. Why is this protection of the settling defendant necessary?

9. What are the policy reasons that justify the approval of Mary Carter agreements by most courts that have considered challenges to them?

10. Do Mary Carter agreements promote settlement or promote trials? Is a trial more or less likely to continue to conclusion if one of several defendants has negotiated a Mary Carter type settlement? Why?

11. Does the California requirement of "good faith," linked to proportionality of the settling defendant's comparative fault, improve or unduly complicate assessment of Mary Carter or sliding scale settlement agreements? Does the California "case-by-case" determination of good faith promote negotiated settlements?

12. Why would the plaintiff want to keep secret from the jury that one of multiple defendants has settled or capped his payment to the defendant? Is the settling defendant then adverse to the plaintiff, or are their interests aligned? Should the jury know this? (See Alcala Co., Inc. v. Sup. Ct., 49 Cal. 4th 1308, 1317, 57 Cal. 2d 349, 354, (1996).) What difference might this information make to the jury?

13. Does proposing, negotiating, or fulfilling a Mary Carter agreement kept secret from the judge, jury, or other defendants raise any ethical questions for lawyers? If so, what are they? Should other defendants be informed of Mary Carter agreements? (See Cal. Civ. Proc. Code 877.5(c) for one statutory solution to this question.)

D. Common-Law Limits — Fraud, Misrepresentation, and Duress

A settlement agreement is usually drafted to bind the parties to each do something, like paying money to dismiss a lawsuit or appeal, or refraining from actions, most often from pursuing a lawsuit. If there is not compliance with the settlement terms, the agreement can be enforced as a contract. Courts are called on to enforce settlement agreements and, on occasion, to rescind them or declare their meaning. Defenses of fraud, misrepresentation, or duress may be invoked.

Problem

Your client successfully sued Goodyear for damages resulting from a defective hose and valve that they manufactured. The verdict was for $1.3 million, but you appealed because the award did not grant prejudgment interest. The Court of Appeals remanded to the trial court for determination of interest. The parties agreed as to the dates from which interest should be calculated, but their calculations about the amount of interest owed were apart by several hundred thousand dollars. Goodyear sent an e-mail offering to negotiate a settlement, in which it accidentally overstated the damages it owed by $550,000. You accepted immediately. While Goodyear was drafting the satisfaction of judgment, it noticed its mistake and sent a revised document, with $550,000 deducted. You refused to sign and instead moved the district court to enforce the "settlement agreement." The district court did so, and Goodyear appealed.

What argument might Goodyear make to overturn the district court decision? What would you argue in support of the favorable ruling? Are some things too good to be true? (See Sumerel v. Goodyear Tire & Rubber Co., Colo. App., May 27, 2009.)

Courts, in applying the common law when enforcing or declining to enforce settlement agreements, set limits on bargaining behavior. Those limits are discussed in the following reading.

❖ **Russell Korobkin, Michael Moffett & Nancy Welsh,**
     THE LAW OF BARGAINING

------

87 Marq. L. Rev. 839 (2004)

When a negotiated agreement results from false statements made during the bargaining process, the common law of tort and contract sometimes holds negotiators liable for damages or makes their resulting agreements subject to rescission.[1] The common law does not, however, amount to a blanket prohibition

---

1. *See generally* Restatement (Second) of Torts §525 (1986), Restatement (Second) of Contracts §164 (1982).

of all lying. Instead, the common law principles are subject to the caveats that false statements must be material, the opposing negotiator must rely on the false statements, and such reliance must be justified. Whether reliance is justified depends on the type of statement at issue and the statement's specificity. A seller's specific false claim ("this car gets 80 miles per gallon gas mileage") is actionable, but his more general claim ("this car gets good gas mileage") is probably not, because the latter statement is acknowledged as the type of "puffing" or "sales talk" on which no reasonable buyer would rely.

While it is often said that misrepresentations of fact are actionable but misrepresentations of opinion are not, this statement is not strictly accurate. Statements of opinions can be false, either because the speaker does not actually have the claimed opinion ("I think this Hyundai is the best car built in the world today") or because the statement implies facts that are untrue ("I think this Hyundai gets the best gas mileage of any car"). But statements of opinion are less likely to induce justified reliance than are statements of specific facts, especially when they are very general, such as a claim that an item is one of "good quality."[2]

Whether reliance on a statement of fact or opinion is justified depends significantly on the context of the negotiation and whether the speaker has access to information that the recipient does not. A seller "aggressively" promoting his product whose stated opinions imply facts that are not true is less likely to find himself in legal difficulty if the veracity of his claims are easily investigated by an equally-knowledgeable buyer than if his customer is a consumer unable to evaluate the factual basis of the claims.[3] The case for liability is stronger still when the negotiator holds himself out as being particularly knowledgeable about the subject matter that the expressed opinion concerns.[4] Whether a false statement can be insulated from liability by a subsequent disclaimer depends on the strength and clarity of the disclaimer, as well as on the nature of the false statement. Again, the standard is whether the reasonable recipient of the information in total would rely on the statement at issue when deciding whether to enter into an agreement.[5]

It is universally recognized that a negotiator's false statements concerning how valuable an agreement is to her or the maximum she is willing to give up or exchange in order to seal an agreement (the negotiator's "reservation point," or "bottom line") are not actionable, again on the ground that such false statements are common and no reasonable negotiator would rely upon them. So an insurance adjuster who claimed that $900 was "all he could pay" to settle a claim is not liable for fraud, even if the statement was false.[6] The law is less settled regarding the status of false statements concerning the existence of outside alternatives for a negotiator. A false claim of an offer from a third-party is relevant because it implies a strong reservation point, so a negotiator might

---

2. *See* Royal Bus. Machs., Inc. v. Lorraine Corp., 633 F.2d 34, 42 (7th Cir. 1980) (calling such statements "'puffing' to be expected in any sales transaction").

3. *See, e.g.,* Vulcan Metals Co. v. Simmons Mfg. Co., 248 F. 853 (2d Cir. 1918).

4. *See* Pacesetter Homes v. Brodkin, 85 Cal. Rptr. 39, 43 (Cal. Ct. App. 1970).

5. *See, e.g.,* In re Trump, 7 F.3d 357, 369 (3d Cir. 1993) (finding that repeated warnings of risk meant that "no reasonable investor could believe anything but that the . . . bonds represented a rather risky, speculative investment," despite other optimistic claims about the financial stability of the issuer).

6. Morta v. Korea Ins. Corp. 840 F.2d 1452, 1456 (9th Cir. 1988).

logically argue that such a claim is no more actionable than a claim as to the reservation point itself. But courts have occasionally ruled that false claims of a specific outside offer are actionable, on the ground that they are material to the negotiation and that the speaker has access to information that cannot be easily verified by the listener's independent investigation.[7]

The most inscrutable area of the law of deception concerns when a negotiator may be held legally liable for failing to disclose information that might weaken his bargaining position (rather than affirmatively asserting a false claim). The traditional laissez-faire rule of caveat emptor eroded in the twentieth century, with courts placing greater disclosure responsibility on negotiators. It is clear that any affirmative action taken to conceal a fact, including the statement of a "half-truth" that implies a false fact, will be treated as if it were an affirmative false statement. Beyond this point, however, the law becomes murky. Although the general rule is probably still that negotiators have no general disclosure obligation, some courts require bargainers (especially sellers) to disclose known material facts not easily discovered by the other party.[8]

Just as the law places some limits on the use of deceptive behavior to seal a bargain, so too does it place some limits upon negotiators' ability to use superior bargaining power to coerce acquiescence with their demands. In general, negotiators may threaten to withhold their goods and services from those who will not agree to their terms. Courts can invoke the doctrine of duress, however, to protect parties who are the victims of a threat that is "improper" and have "no reasonable alternative" but to acquiesce to the other party's demand,[9] such as when one party procures an agreement through the threat of violence,[10] or through the threat to breach a prior agreement after using the relationship created by that agreement to place the victim in a position in which breach would cause noncompensable damage.[11] Judicial intervention is most likely when the bargaining parties' relationship was not arms-length. For example, the common law provides the defense of undue influence to negotiators who can show that they were dependent upon and thus vulnerable to the other, dominant negotiator.[12] . . .

E. Tax Considerations

Knowing the rudiments of how taxes impact settlement outcomes can help you create value and enhance what your client ends up keeping. Early identification

---

7. *See, e.g.,* Kabatchnick v. Hanover-Elm Bldg. Corp., 103 N.E.2d 692 (Mass. 1952) (falsely claiming a "bona fide offer from one Melvin Levine . . . of $10,000 per year"); Beavers v. Lamplighters Realty, 556 P.2d 1328 (Okla. 1976) (falsely claiming a prospective buyer was willing to pay the asking price for a house and would be delivering a check that same day).

8. *See, e.g.,* Weintraub v. Krobatsch, 317 A.2d 68 (N.J. 1974) (sellers must disclose known insect infestation of house).

9. *See* Restatement (Second) of Contracts, §175(1) (1982).

10. *See, e.g.,* Rubenstein v. Rubenstein, 120 A.2d 11 (N.J. 1956); Restatement (Second) of Contracts §176(1)(a) (1981).

11. *See, e.g.,* Austin Instruments, Inc. v. Loral Corp., 272 N.E.2d 533 (N.Y. 1971).

12. *See* Restatement (Second) of Contracts §177 (1979).

of tax liabilities and likely tax treatment of what is paid and received in settlement allows you to favorably shape negotiation strategy and better frame issues for negotiation. The next article presents a basic primer on what you need to know about the tax consequences of settlements.

❖ **Robert W. Wood,** *Taxing Matters in Settling Cases*

27 California. Lawyer 41 (June 2007)

Even practitioners who have assiduously avoided concentrating on the intricacies of tax law still need to be aware of the possible tax ramifications in case settlements before finalizing them. Luckily, if you keep in mind a few basic principles, you should be in a position at least to help assess the risks, and to know when to get or recommend outside tax advice.

First, consider whether your client is receiving money or paying money. Receiving income is usually more important from a tax perspective, so most plaintiffs are more worried about tax issues than most defendants.

Tax Concerns for Plaintiffs

The overarching rule is that the origin of your client's claim will determine the tax consequences of a settlement The U.S. Supreme Court laid down that rule more than a half century ago in *Arrowsmith v. Commissioner* (344 U.S. 6 (1952)). For example, if your client's claims are for wages, a settlement will generally be treated as wages for both income tax and employment tax purposes. *(See* Rev. Ruling 78-336, 1978-2 C. B. 225.) And if a business sues for harm to its goodwill, the resulting settlement should be treated as a recovery of goodwill, which usually means a capital gain.

Another fundamental tax rule is that all income is taxable unless there is a special rule to the contrary. In other words, you and your client should assume everything is taxable as a starting point. The biggest statutory exception to this rule is section 104 of the Internal Revenue Code, which states that damages for "personal physical injuries or sickness" are tax-free. . . .

Unfortunately, it is not clear what constitutes physical injury or sickness under the codes. The IRS view of physical injury is that there must be serious physical contact involved, such as an auto accident or battery. And the resulting injury needs to be serious enough to see—broken bones or bruises, for example. Prior to 1996, emotional-distress damages were tax-free, but the Internal Revenue Code was amended that year to add the "physical" requirement, dramatically tightening the scope of this exclusion. (I.R.C. §104(a)(2), as amended by the Small Business Job Protection Act of 1996.) The primary target of the 1996 amendment was employment litigation, in which plaintiffs generally excluded from income emotional-distress and discrimination recoveries.

Figuring out what is excludable is tough. The legislative history of the 1996 Act indicates that mere symptoms of emotional distress, such as headaches, insomnia, and stomach aches, do not qualify as physical injuries or sicknesses, so recoveries for such items are not excludable. (H. Conf. Rept. 104-737 at 301 (1996), 1996-3 C.B. 741, 1041.) However, it is not clear whether an ulcer would be treated as a mere symptom of emotional distress and taxable, or as a bona fide physical injury or sickness, and therefore tax-free.

Not surprisingly, much of the relevant case law comes from employment claims, in which employees often allege that some portion of their recovery relates to physical injuries or sickness. The IRS is strict in imposing limits. However, when there is actual physical contact, such as sexual assault in a sexual-harassment case, it may be appropriate to claim some exclusion. In such cases, it is usually wise to get a tax professional involved for specific guidance.

The language of the settlement agreement is also important. Ideally, the plaintiff and the defendant should agree on what a settlement payment represents. The IRS and the California Franchise Tax Board will usually ask for a copy of the complaint in an audit to see the genesis of the claims and will also request a copy of the settlement agreement. And though government auditors are not bound by the agreement, they do consider it. A plaintiff who fails to include tax allocation and characterization language in a settlement agreement misses an opportunity to help mold the tax treatment of the recovery.

Another matter of critical importance is how the payments to the plaintiff are reported. IRS Form W-2 is used to report the wages paid to an employee each year; Form 1099 is used for most other payments.

If a payment is excludable from income, it should not be reported on a 1099. Virtually every business issues 1099s for payments made in the course of business. The 1099 forms reporting all payments made in the prior year are due to the taxpayer who receives the payment by January 31 of the following year. Then, the business must send copies of all of its 1099s, along with transmittal Form 1096, to the IRS before the end of February, leaving a one-month delay between the time Forms 1099 are due to the taxpayer and the time they must be sent to the IRS. That delay may provide a tactical advantage for your clients. If a client receives a Form 1099 that is incorrect, and immediately notifies the payer, there may be enough time to change it before the IRS receives it.

Returning to the primary precept that all settlements are taxable unless you can prove otherwise, it is also important to recognize that section 104 does not shield all damages from taxation, even in a case indisputably involving physical injury. For example, if a plaintiff is injured and rendered a quadriplegic, punitive damages awarded for the injury are still taxable. (*O'Gilvie v. United States*, 519 U.S. 79 (1996).) The same is true for prejudgment and postjudgment interest. (*Kovacs v. Commissioner*, 100 T.C. 124 (1993).) So if your client recovers money in a personal injury case, you still need to differentiate between damages for physical injuries and any amount awarded for interest or punitive damages in determining whether the money is excludable.

The toughest calls in determining the treatment of punitive damages or interest are in cases that settle on appeal. For example, suppose that an auto accident case in which your client was awarded $500,000 in compensating damages and $2 million in punitives settles for $1 million pending appeal. Some portion of that settlement might be allotted to interest or punitive damages at trial. (*Rozpad v. Commissioner*, 154 F.3d 1 (1998).) It may be appropriate to seek the advice of competent tax counsel if you have a case involving such issues, preferably before the case settles.

Tax reporting rules are one reason to expressly address tax issues in a settlement agreement. For example, if your client's settlement agreement says nothing about IRS Form W-2 or 1099, and those forms are incorrect when issued, you may have little recourse. You can contact the defendant and plead your case, but very few defendants take such requests seriously.

In contrast, if the settlement agreement is specific—for example, there will be a W-2 for $500, a Form 1099 for $20,000, and a Form 1099 to the attorney for $10,000 you have something specific to address. If the forms come in any other manner, you can contact the defendant and assert that the settlement agreement was breached. Such discussions generally lead to corrections.

Other plaintiff recoveries.   In addition to the tricky personal injury area, tax considerations play a part in virtually all other kinds of recoveries too. Again, assume everything is taxable.

You may also face the question of whether a recovery is ordinary income or a capital gain. The top tax rate for ordinary income is 35 percent while the top capital gain rate is 15 percent, so clients have big incentives to try to characterize their recovery as capital gains. In general, a recovery for a capital asset such as a business, a personal residence, or shares of stock follow a particular pattern. If the case you are handling relates to damages to assets, you must be mindful of the distinction between ordinary income and capital gains.

Intellectual property is another area ripe for tax planning. An intellectual property recovery may be treated as lost profits, such as lost royalty income on a patent license. It may also be treated as harm to the patent itself, in which case the recovery may be viewed as a capital gain, or even as a recovery of the patent holder's basis in the patent, and not taxable at all. Plainly, there can be huge tax savings depending on the characterization. It may also be wise to get tax counsel involved when you are handling an intellectual property case—again, preferably before the case is settled.

As added complications, there are special tax rules that apply when property is damaged, and unique provisions for gain on the sale of a personal residence, as well as tax provisions applying when property is involuntarily converted, for example, by fire or condemnation.

Attorneys fees.   Finally, when considering awards to plaintiffs, be wary of the tax treatment of attorneys fees. In 2004, the tax law was amended to expressly allow an "above-the-line" deduction for attorneys fees in employment cases. (I.R.C. §62, as amended by the American Jobs Creation Act of 2004.) The tax issue here is a fundamental one. Suppose you handle contingent-fee litigation for a client and recover $100,000, and your fee is 40 percent. Does the client have gross income of $60,000, or gross income of $100,000, followed by a $40,000 deduction? Economically, this may sound like a distinction without a difference, yet these two alternatives generally do not mean the same thing from a tax standpoint,

Resolving a vehement split in the circuit courts, the U.S. Supreme Court ruled in 2005 that a plaintiff in contingent-fee litigation generally must be treated as receiving 100 percent of the recovery for tax purposes, regardless of how the checks are cut or whether the plaintiff's lawyer is paid his or her share directly. (*Commissioner v. Banks*, 543 U.S. 426 (2005).) The statutory change, made a few months before the Supreme Court's holding, allows employment plaintiffs an above-the-line deduction so that, in effect, they are not taxed on the money paid to their lawyers.

However, excluding employment litigation, the client in the example above generally will have gross income of $100,000 and will have to find a way to deduct the $40,000 in legal fees. Usually those fees can be deducted only as a "miscellaneous itemized deduction," which means there are limitations and restrictions. In particular, the client will often be stung by the dreaded alternative minimum tax, or AMT.

Deductibility for Defendants

If you are representing a defendant, tax worries are less obvious than those of plaintiffs. But there are a few key rules to keep in mind. First, nearly all defendants want to make sure they can deduct a payment as a business expense. In business litigation, this is usually not a problem, but it still merits close consideration. Some defendants get stung by capitalization rules, having to add the cost of a settlement to their tax basis, so they get no current deduction. That can occur in litigating environmental matters and in settling title to assets.

For example, if your client pays a settlement to resolve a dispute over who owns the land under an office building, that settlement payment will probably be viewed for tax purposes as a payment to quiet title. As such, the client probably cannot deduct it as an ordinary business expense, but instead would have to add it to his or her basis for tax purposes. Although the client would eventually receive a tax benefit for this payment when he or she sold the building, that may be a long wait. A current tax deduction is always better than a delayed tax benefit.

The tax treatment of attorneys fees generally follows the tax treatment of the underlying settlement or judgment. So, if your defendant client must capitalize, rather than deduct, a settlement payment, the attorneys fees the defendant pays will likely face the same unfavorable treatment.

Sometimes, tax planning at settlement time can help ameliorate these harsh tax consequences. Still, most settlement payments in a business context are tax-deductible, even punitive damages. Generally, a defendant wants to make sure to get a current deduction, even where there is some delay in getting the money to the plaintiff.

A larger topic relates to tax reporting and withholding. Business clients are subject to strict rules. If you are a defense lawyer, when the plaintiff's lawyer asks for certain tax language to be included in the agreement, review it carefully before incorporating it. If the plaintiff asks your client to characterize a patent royalty payment in a settlement agreement as "personal physical injury damages," don't do it. It may be tax fraud, and it is certainly inappropriate. However, if the plaintiff asks your defendant client not to issue a Form 1099 for one-third of a sexual harassment settlement, this may be perfectly fine, depending on the facts. Consider whether that third of the settlement payment represents a fair allocation.

Probably the biggest exposure defendants face is for failure to withhold on taxes. If it is an employment case and the amounts paid to settle the case are wages, the defendant's liability for failing to withhold can be serious. For example, if your client is an employer and the case involves a claim for back wages, what if the plaintiff asks that there be no withholding on the settlement payment? If the case is 100 percent about wages, then under the origin-of-the-claim doctrine, the settlement payment should likewise be 100 percent wages. Wages are subject to withholding—and an employer that fails to withhold is liable for the taxes the employee does not pay, as well as for penalties and interest.

Thus, a plaintiff's seemingly simple request not to withhold taxes can result in major liability if the defendant agrees and the characterization is later determined to be improper. Often, a plaintiff will offer to indemnify the defendant for any tax problems as a way to get the tax language the plaintiff wants into the settlement agreement. But don't simply rely on the plaintiff's indemnification obligation, because those are rarely enforced. If your client is making a wage payment, but the plaintiff insists that it not be reported as wages, beware.

A defendant in a case that involves damages for personal injury or sickness can legitimately agree not to issue a Form 1099 for a portion of the settlement that is fairly allocated to such claims.

The attorneys fees tax-reporting rules are also highly complex. In general, in contingent-fee litigation, the defendant must issue a Form 1099 to both the plaintiff and to the plaintiff's lawyer.

F. Negotiation Malpractice

Client dissatisfaction, after the fact, with claim settlement and transactional agreements negotiated by their attorneys, is not uncommon. An agreement that seemed appealing at the time it was obtained, when uncertainty, fear of the worse alternatives, and time pressure drove acceptance may, in hindsight, be unsatisfactory. A good negotiated result is attributed to a strong case and a resolute client; a marginal result, after the dynamics and trade-offs of the negotiation are forgotten, is attributed to poor representation.

The frequency of complaints filed against attorneys for malpractice in negotiations is not precisely known but is thought to be high, as noted by Professor Epstein in a reading that follows. Even though there is a general requirement that clients must agree to a negotiated settlement or transaction before it becomes final, consent to the result is not a total barrier to a claim of malpractice. Clients have reason to rely on the professional expertise, skill, and integrity of the attorney negotiating on their behalf and may sue when that reliance is misplaced.

Malpractice is grounded in tort and requires proof of the classic tort elements:

- Duty to the plaintiff;
- Breach of that duty;
- Causation; and
- Damages.

Proving causation and damages is difficult in claims of negotiation malpractice because, as we have presented throughout this text, there is no one right or sure way to negotiate. Damages cannot be easily established by comparing a negotiated outcome to a trial result that did not occur or to another negotiation with all the same variables. Richard Posner, Chief Judge of the Seventh Circuit, stated the issue and the challenge succinctly:

Proof of causation is often difficult in legal malpractice cases involving representation in litigation — the vast majority of such cases — because it is so difficult, yet vital, to estimate what difference a lawyer's negligence made in the actual outcome of a trial or other adversary proceeding. How many criminal defendants, required as they are to prove that their lawyer's ineffective assistance prejudiced them, succeed in overturning their convictions on this ground? Proof of causation is even more difficult in a negotiating situation, because while there is (at least we judges like to think there is) a correct outcome to most lawsuits, there is no correct outcome to a negotiation. Not only does much depend on the relative bargaining skills of the negotiators, on the likely consequences to each party if the negotiations fall through, and on luck, so that the element of the intangible and the unpredictable looms large; but there is no single right outcome in a bargaining situation even in principle. Every point within the range bounded by the lowest offer that one party will accept and the highest offer that the other party will make is a possible transaction or settlement point, and none of these points is "correct" or "incorrect". (Nicolet Instrument Corp. v. Lindquest & Vennum, 34 F.3d 453 (7th Cir. 1994)).

The following opinion reflects and articulates these difficulties of proof. However, this appellate court reverses summary judgment and requires the alleged negligent law firm to defend itself at trial and argue the question of damages there.

❖ NICOLET INSTRUMENT CORP. v. LINDQUEST & VENNUM

34 F.3d 453 (7th Cir. 1994)

POSNER, Chief Judge.

Nicolet Instrument Corporation brought a diversity suit for legal malpractice against its former counsel, Lindquist & Vennum. The district judge granted summary judgment for the law firm on the ground that Nicolet had failed to establish a causal connection between its loss and the law firm's alleged negligence. Wisconsin law governs the substantive issues.

Nicolet had a wholly owned subsidiary named "Nicolet Zeta Corp." that made computer graphics equipment, and in 1982 Nicolet leased a building in California for Zeta to occupy. The lease was for 10 years from the date of occupancy (which turned out to be 1984), and the landlord insisted that Nicolet rather than the subsidiary be the lessee. In 1986 Nicolet sold all the stock of Zeta to AM International for $22 million, and Zeta became a wholly owned subsidiary of that firm. Nicolet assigned its rights under the lease to Zeta, which agreed to pay the rental due under the lease, but AM International assumed no obligations under it and Zeta's landlord refused to substitute Zeta for Nicolet as the lessee. The remaining rental due under the lease until its expiration in 1994 was $5.4 million. In 1990 AM International sold Zeta, and the following year Zeta collapsed and ceased paying rent. The landlord insisted that Nicolet pay. Nicolet complied, and by the time the lease expired had paid $2.6 million in rental, taxes, and maintenance fees. . . .

Nicolet charges Lindquist & Vennum, which negotiated the sale of Zeta to AM International on Nicolet's behalf, with negligence in having failed to make any effort to eliminate Nicolet's contingent liability under the lease. Nicolet was getting rid of Zeta lock, stock, and barrel and wanted nothing more to do with it, and certainly did not want to retain a large contingent liability for the rent of a building used in a business with which it hoped to have nothing further to do. Nicolet claims that it made all this clear to the law firm, which for the purposes of this appeal we may assume was negligent in making no effort to shift or at least reduce the contingent liability. The law firm could have tried to persuade AM International, and the landlord of Zeta's building, to consent to substitute AM International for Nicolet on the lease or, if the landlord would not go along, it could have tried to persuade AM International to agree to indemnify Nicolet should the latter ever be called on to make payments under the lease. . . .

The district judge dismissed the suit because he was convinced that Nicolet had failed to prove that obedience by the law firm to Nicolet's instructions would have made any difference. The judge thought it sheer conjecture that if Nicolet had insisted on AM International's agreeing to indemnify it for any liability arising out of the lease of Zeta's building, AM would have acceded, rather than walk away from the deal. And in the latter case Nicolet would be worse off than it is today, for in light of Zeta's subsequent collapse it appears that $22 million was a very good price for Nicolet to get for the subsidiary.

Proof of causation is often difficult in legal malpractice cases involving representation in litigation — the vast majority of such cases — because it is so difficult, yet vital, to estimate what difference a lawyer's negligence made in the actual outcome of a trial or other adversary proceeding. How many criminal defendants, required as they are to prove that their lawyer's ineffective assistance prejudiced them, succeed in overturning their convictions on this ground? Proof of causation is even more difficult in a negotiating situation, because while there is (at least we judges like to think there is) a correct outcome to most lawsuits, there is no "correct" outcome to a negotiation. Not only does much depend on the relative bargaining skills of the negotiators, on the likely consequences to each party if the negotiations fall through, and on luck, so that the element of the intangible and the unpredictable looms large; but there is no single "right" outcome in a bargaining situation even in principle. Every point within the range bounded by the lowest offer that one party will accept and the highest offer that the other party will make is a possible transaction or settlement point, and none of these points is "correct" or "incorrect."

But to withstand summary judgment Nicolet was not required to prove that but for the law firm's negligence it would have avoided the $2.6 million rental expense that it incurred as a result of its remaining on the Zeta lease with no promise of indemnity by AM. All it had to show was that a rational trier of fact, confronted with the evidence produced in the summary judgment phase of the litigation, could conclude that, yes, Nicolet had suffered some harm as a consequence of the law firm's negligence and could quantify that harm to a reasonable, which is not to say a high, degree of precision. This not very demanding standard was satisfied, when, as is required given the posture of the case, Masson v. New Yorker Magazine, Inc., 501 U.S. 496, 520, (1991), the evidence is construed as favorably to Nicolet as the record will permit.

. . . [W]e do not know how much AM International was willing to pay for Zeta. All we know is that it paid $22 million, which happens to have been exactly midway between the ranges from which the negotiations started. (AM International hoped to pay between $15 and $18 million, which averages to $16.5 million; Nicolet hoped to get between $25 and $30 million, which averages to $27.5 million; $22 million is the midpoint between $16.5 million and $27.5

million.) Had Nicolet through the law firm made clear at the outset that it didn't want to remain stuck with potential liability on the lease, AM International might have raised its estimate of Nicolet's reservation price and have decided to accept the contingent liability on top of paying $22 million. For all we know, it thought $22 million a good price and was willing to pay more, whether in cash or in the assumption of a contingent liability. . . .

The negotiator for AM International testified that he might have asked Nicolet for a $2 million price reduction in exchange for a promise to guarantee the lease. Indeed he might have; but a lot of demands are made in negotiations that do not represent a party's final, unbudgeable position. It would have been irrational for AM International to insist on such a reduction unless it was buying Zeta in the expectation that Zeta would fail. To price the contingent liability represented by such a promise of indemnity at $2 million would be to assume that there was about a 75 percent chance that Zeta would fail by the end of the fifth year, putting AM International $2.6 million in the hole. There is as yet no evidence to support such an assumption.

The law firm points out that $22 million even with the retention of the contingent liability was a good deal for Nicolet, given Zeta's dismal, though hidden, future. That is true but it would have been an even better deal if Nicolet could have shifted the liability or at least most of it to AM International with little or no reduction in the purchase price. The baseline for measuring damages is the world as it would have been had it not been for the defendant's wrong. It is also true that Nicolet's then chief executive testified that if AM International had been adamant against taking on the liability, he would not have insisted; for, ex ante as well as ex post, he considered $22 million a good price even with the contingent liability under the lease retained. But as already explained we cannot assume that AM International would have credibly threatened that it would break off negotiations unless Nicolet agreed to pay it a huge premium to assume Nicolet's contingent liability.

One might think that even though the issue of causation—is it more likely than not that, but for the law firm's alleged negligence, Nicolet would not have sustained a loss of $2.6 million?—is susceptible of rational determination, the issue of damages—how much better off would Nicolet have been if the law firm had not dropped the ball?—is hopelessly speculative. But the law firm does not make the argument, which in any event is premature. Should Nicolet be unable to present at trial evidence upon which a rational jury can base a reasonable estimate of damages—a requirement that we take seriously, . . . —Nicolet will lose.

REVERSED AND REMANDED.

Note: Gravamen of Malpractice

Lawyers have both procedural and substantive duties when advising and representing clients in negotiations. Breach of the procedural duties, as well as the substantive ones, result in malpractice. The procedural duties reflect ethical responsibilities that lawyers have toward clients. These responsibilities are discussed in Chapter 10. Procedural requirements that are often the gravamen of malpractice claims against attorney negotiators include the following:

- Duty to communicate settlement offers to client (see ABA Model Rule 1.4(a)).
- Duty to not exceed authority given by client in making or accepting offers (see ABA Model Rule 1.2(a)).
- Duty to be diligent (see ABA Model Rule 1.3).
- Duty to reveal conflicts of interest (see ABA Model Rule 1.7) and not trade off clients' interests to cover up attorney error (see ABA Model Rule 1.7(2)).

Substantively, lawyers owe their clients the duty to know the law and properly advise clients about how law and practice affect their situation. Accurate information is necessary for clients to make informed decisions about settlement. The test for purposes of malpractice is commonly stated as whether the attorney exercised that degree of skill, prudence, and diligence in investigating facts, in legal research, and in giving legal advice that lawyers of ordinary skill and capacity would do in similar situations.

Only disappointed clients sue their lawyers. Domestic relations is an area of legal practice in which client expectations are often unrealistically high, as are emotions. It is not unusual for clients to have second thoughts and be disappointed with a negotiated settlement. "Buyer's remorse" can lead to claims against lawyers following an accepted settlement, particularly in divorce. Consider the following malpractice case and the lessons you can learn from it.

❖ ZIEGELHEIM v. APOLLO

128 N.J. 250, 607 A.2d 1298 (1992)

HANDLER, J.

. . . In September 1979, Mrs. Ziegelheim retained defendant, attorney Stephen Apollo, to represent her in her anticipated divorce action. Because this appeal relates to the trial court's granting of summary judgment against plaintiff, we assume for the purposes of our decision that all of the facts she alleges relating to Apollo's handling of her divorce are true. According to Mrs. Ziegelheim, she and Apollo met on several occasions to plan various aspects of her case. She told him about all of the marital and separate assets of which she was aware, and they discussed her suspicion the Mr. Ziegelheim was either concealing or dissipating certain other assets as well. In particular, Mrs. Ziegelheim told Apollo that she thought her husband had $500,000 hidden in the form of cash savings and bonds. Accordingly, she asked Apollo to make a thorough inquiry into her husband's assets, including cash, bonds, patents, stocks, pensions, life insurance, profit-sharing plans, and real estate. . . .

According to Mrs. Ziegelheim, Apollo failed to discover important information about her husband's assets before entering into settlement negotiations with Mr. Ziegelheim's attorney, Sheldon Liebowitz. Apollo hired an accountant who valued the marital estate at approximately $2,413,000. Mrs. Ziegelheim claims that the accountant substantially underestimated the estate because of several oversights by Apollo, including his failure to locate a bank vault owned by Mr. Ziegelheim; to locate or determine the value of his tax-free municipal bonds; to verify the value of his profit-sharing plan at Pilot Woodworking, a company in which he was the primary shareholder; to search for an estimated $500,000 in savings; to contact the United States Patent Office to verify the existence of certain patents he held; to inquire into a $1,000,000 life insurance policy naming an associate of his as the beneficiary; to verify the value of certain lakefront property; and to verify the value of his stock holdings. She alleges that had Apollo made a proper inquiry, it would have been apparent that the marital estate was worth approximately $2,562,000, or about $149,000 more than the accountant found. . . .

In sum, Mrs. Ziegelheim was to receive approximately $333,000 in alimony, $6,000 in contributions to insurance costs, and $324,000 in property, the last figure representing approximately fourteen percent of the value of the estate (as appraised by Apollo and the accountant). Mr. Ziegelheim was to receive approximately $2,088,000 in property, approximately eighty-six percent of the value of the estate.

When testifying before the court immediately after the settlement was read into the record, both Mrs. Ziegelheim and Mr. Ziegelheim stated that they understood the agreement, that they thought it was fair, and that they entered into it voluntarily. Mrs. Ziegelheim now asserts, however, that she accepted the agreement only after Apollo advised her that wives could expect to receive no more than ten to twenty percent of the marital estate if they went to trial. She claims that Apollo's estimate was unduly pessimistic and did not comport with the advice that a reasonably competent attorney would have given under the circumstances. Had she been advised competently, she says, she would not have accepted the settlement. . . .

The trial court ruled in favor of defendant on all counts. It noted that Mrs. Ziegelheim had stated on the record that she understood the settlement and its terms, that she thought the terms were fair, and that she had not been coerced into settling. . . .

In accepting a case, the lawyer agrees to pursue the goals of the client to the extent the law permits, even when the lawyer believes that the client's desires are unwise or ill-considered. At the same time, because the client's desires may be influenced in large measure by the advice the lawyer provides, the lawyer is obligated to give the client reasonable advice. As a legal matter progresses and circumstances change, the wishes of the client may change as well. Accordingly, the lawyer is obligated to keep the client informed of the status of the matter for which the lawyer has been retained, and is required to advise the client on the various legal and strategic issues that arise.

In this case, Mrs. Ziegelheim made several claims impugning Apollo's handling of her divorce, and the trial court dismissed all of them on Apollo's motion for summary judgment. As we explain, we believe that the trial court's rulings on several of her claims were erroneous. . . .

On Mrs. Ziegelheim's claim that Apollo negligently advised her with respect to her chances of winning a greater proportion of the marital estate if she proceeded to trial, we conclude, as did the Appellate Division, that there was a genuine dispute regarding the appropriate advice that an attorney should give in cases like hers. According to the expert retained by Mrs. Ziegelheim, women in her position — who are in relatively poor health, have little earning capacity, and have been wholly dependent on their husbands — often receive upwards of fifty percent of the marital estate. The expert said that Mrs. Ziegelheim's chances of winning such a large fraction of the estate had she gone to trial would have been especially good because the couple had enjoyed a high standard of living while they were together and because her husband's earning capacity was "tremendous" and would remain so for some time. Her expert's opinion was brought to the trial court's attention, as was the expert report of Mr. Ziegelheim. If plaintiff's expert's opinion were credited, as it should have been for purposes of summary judgment, then Apollo very well could have been found negligent in advising her that she could expect to win only ten to twenty percent of the marital estate.

Apollo urges us to adopt the rule enunciated by the Pennsylvania Supreme Court in *Muhammad v. Strassburger, McKenna, Messer, Shilobod and Gutnick,* 526 Pa. 541, 587 A.2d 1346 (1991), that a dissatisfied litigant may not recover from his or her attorney for malpractice in negotiating a settlement that the litigant has accepted unless the litigant can prove actual fraud on the part of the attorney. Under that rule, no cause of action can be made based on negligence or contract principles against an attorney for malpractice in negotiating a settlement. The Pennsylvania Supreme Court rationalized its severe rule by explaining that it had a "longstanding public policy which encourages settlements."

New Jersey, too, has a longstanding policy that encourages settlements, but we reject the rule espoused by the Pennsylvania Supreme Court. Although we encourage settlements, we recognize that litigants rely heavily on the professional advice of counsel when they decide whether to accept or reject offers of settlement, and we insist that the lawyers of our state advise clients with respect to settlements with the same skill, knowledge, and diligence with which they pursue all other legal tasks. Attorneys are supposed to know the likelihood of success for the types of cases they handle and they are supposed to know the range of possible awards in those cases.

As we noted in *Levine v. Wiss & Co,* 97 N.J. 242, 246, 478 A.2d 397 (1984), "One who undertakes to render services in the practice of a profession or trade is required to exercise the skill and knowledge normally possessed by members of that profession in good standing in similar communities." We have found in cases involving a great variety of professionals that deviation from accepted standards of professional care will result in liability for negligence. . . . Like most courts, we see no reason to apply a more lenient rule to lawyers who negotiate settlements. *After all, the negotiation of settlements is one of the most basic and most frequently undertaken tasks that lawyers perform* [emphasis is court's]. . . .

The fact that a party received a settlement that was "fair and equitable" does not mean necessarily that the party's attorney was competent or that the party would not have received a more favorable settlement had the party's incompetent attorney been competent. Thus, in this case, notwithstanding the family court's decision, Mrs. Ziegelheim still may proceed against Apollo in her negligence action.

Moreover, another aspect of the alleged professional incompetence that led to the improvident acceptance of the settlement was the attorney's own failure to discover hidden marital assets. When Mrs. Ziegelheim sought to reopen her divorce settlement, the family court denied her motion with the observation that "[a]mple opportunity existed for full discovery," and that "the parties had their own accountants as well as counsel." The court did not determine definitively that Mr. Ziegelheim had hidden no assets, but stated instead that it "suspected that everything to be known was known to the parties." The earlier ruling did not implicate the competence of counsel and, indeed, was premised on the presumptive competence of counsel. Hence, defendant cannot invoke that ruling now to bar a challenge to his competence. Mrs. Ziegelheim should have been allowed to prove that Apollo negligently failed to discover certain assets concealed by her former husband. . . .

In holding as we do today, we do not open the door to malpractice suits by any and every dissatisfied party to a settlement. Many such claims could be averted if settlements were explained as a matter of record in open court in proceedings reflecting the understanding and assent of the parties. Further, plaintiffs must allege particular facts in support of their claims of attorney incompetence and may not litigate complaints containing mere generalized assertions of malpractice. We are mindful that attorneys cannot be held liable simply because they are not successful in persuading an opposing party to accept certain terms. Similarly, we acknowledge that attorneys who pursue reasonable strategies in handling their cases and who render reasonable advice to their clients cannot be held liable for the failure of their strategies or for any unprofitable outcomes that result because their clients took their advice. The law demands that attorneys handle their cases with knowledge, skill, and diligence, but it does not demand that they be perfect or infallible, and it does not demand that they always secure optimum outcomes for their clients. . . .

Questions

14. The Supreme Court of New Jersey's opinion in *Ziegelheim v. Apollo* states that, "In holding as we do today we do not open the door to malpractice suits by any and every dissatisfied party to a settlement." Does the New Jersey court, in reviewing the summary judgment for the defendant and allowing the negligence action against the attorney to proceed, shut the door or, rather, leave it open?

15. The court advises that, "Many such claims could be averted if settlements were explained as a matter of record in open court in proceedings reflecting the understanding and assent of the parties." This advice may be practical in divorce cases, where the court is asked to approve and incorporate the marital settlement agreement into a court judgment, but is this cautionary step of making a court record practical as a conclusion to other lawsuit settlements? Does this help explain why settlement agreements prepared by attorneys often recite the facts, premises, and underlying reasons for the settlement?

16. Is *Ziegelheim v. Apollo* likely to be tried following this remand? If you represented defendant Apollo, how would you negotiate a final settlement of the Ziegelheim claim, and what amount would you anticipate it would take to conclude this matter?

17. If prior to finalizing the divorce settlement agreement that lawyer Apollo obtained for Ms. Ziegelheim, she fired him and retained another lawyer who negotiated a substantially similar settlement that was approved and adopted by the court following Ms. Ziegelheim's testimony that it was fair, would she be estopped from suing Apollo? (See Puder v. Buechel, 183 N.J. 428, 2005.)

The New Jersey Supreme Court in the *Apollo* case expressly rejects the reasoning of the Pennsylvania Supreme Court in *Muhammad v. Strassburger et al.*, which barred a client who accepted a negotiated settlement from suing his attorney in the absence of fraud. The *Muhammad* decision has been rejected by other courts, as illustrated by *Apollo*. In the following article, Professor Epstein explains why courts have rejected the *Muhammad* opinion reasoning and then contrasts malpractice actions arising from the negotiation process with other types of malpractice cases. She also offers advice on how to defend and avoid malpractice claims when clients initially accept the negotiated settlement.

❖ **Lynn A. Epstein,** *Post-Settlement Malpractice:*
Undoing the Done Deal

46 Cath. U. L. Rev. 453 (1997)

Clients voice their approval to mediators and judges as a settlement agreement is reached. A release is signed, the file is closed, and from the lawyer's perspective, another case ends. The settled case joins an overwhelming majority of civil cases that are resolved in pretrial settlement. Buried within this figure, however, is a more troubling statistic: Over twenty percent of civil cases will be resurrected in the form of malpractice actions initiated by dissatisfied clients. In those instances, and for various reasons substantiated by expert opinions, the client will charge that they could have received a better result in the settlement even though the client knowingly and willingly agreed to end the case.

In every state except Pennsylvania, a client is permitted to proceed with the theory that his attorney negligently negotiated an agreement despite the fact that the client consented to settlement. In *Muhammad v. Strassburger, McKenna, Messer, Shilobod & Gutnick,* the Pennsylvania Supreme Court determined that an attorney is immune from malpractice based on negligence where the client consented to settle. Court decisions after *Muhammad,* however, have uniformly rejected immunity for the attorney, permitting post-settlement malpractice actions to proceed in the same manner as the prototypical malpractice case.

This Article analyzes the Pennsylvania Supreme Court's decision to bar malpractice lawsuits based on settled cases. This Article then contrasts the opinion with the contradictory majority rule in other states. Next, this Article addresses the difference between mainstream malpractice actions and those malpractice actions arising from the negotiation of settled cases. . . .

Muhammad **and its Successors**

Conventional wisdom dictates that attorneys settle cases effectively, as an estimated ninety-five percent of civil cases are resolved by settlement. Yet, an emerging trend of post-settlement malpractice claims threatens the integrity of the settlement negotiation process. While malpractice actions are on the rise, most attorneys reasonably believed they were insulated from liability because the client had consented to settlement, and because there was no affirmative wrongdoing by the attorney. Because so many factors influence a client's decision to settle, and because so many individuals, such as judges and mediators, are a part of the process, it would appear fundamentally unfair to hold the attorneys solely responsible for such malpractice claims. This is buttressed by a majority viewpoint which looks unfavorably upon malpractice claims that require the judiciary to infiltrate the negotiation process, a process traditionally viewed as immune from judicial scrutiny.

Balancing these competing interests, the Pennsylvania Supreme Court barred such malpractice actions to foster the negotiation and settlement process. In *Muhammad*, the Pennsylvania Supreme Court held that, absent fraud, an attorney is immune from suit by a former client dissatisfied with a settlement that the former client agreed to enter.

Pamela and Abdullah Muhammad sued the firm of Strassburger, McKenna, Messer, Shilobod, and Gutnick for malpractice arising from the settlement of an underlying medical malpractice suit. In the underlying action, the Muhammads sued the physicians and hospital that performed a circumcision on their son who died as a consequence of general anesthesia used during the procedure.

The Muhammads retained the Strassburger law firm. The physicians and hospital offered to settle the malpractice claim for $23,000, which was subsequently increased to $26,500 at the suggestion of the trial court. The Muhammads accepted the settlement offer. The Muhammads later grew dissatisfied with the amount received in settlement and instructed the Strassburger law firm to communicate this discontent to defense counsel. An evidentiary hearing ensued where the court upheld the settlement agreement, reasoning that the Muhammads agreed to the settlement amount and, thus, there existed a binding and enforceable contract.

Unable to reopen the medical malpractice proceeding, the Muhammads initiated a claim against the Strassburger law firm alleging legal malpractice, fraudulent misrepresentation, fraudulent concealment, nondisclosure, breach of contract, negligence, emotional distress, and breach of fiduciary duty. The court dismissed the fraud counts because the Muhammads had not pled fraud with specificity. Surprisingly, the court then barred the Muhammads from proceeding with their remaining negligence claim against the Strassburger firm, based on articulated public policy encouraging civil litigation settlement. In granting immunity, the court wrote:

> [W]e foreclose the ability of dissatisfied litigants to agree to a settlement and then file suit against their attorneys in the hope that they will recover additional monies. To permit otherwise results in unfairness to the attorneys who relied on their client's assent and unfairness to the litigants whose cases have not yet been tried. Additionally, it places an unnecessarily arduous burden on an overly taxed court system.

The court emphasized that this immunity extends to specific cases where a plaintiff agreed to settlement in the absence of fraud by the attorney. This is distinguished from the instance when a lawyer knowingly commits malpractice, conceals the wrongdoing, and convinces the client to settle in order to cover up the malpractice. According to the court, in this instance, the attorney's conduct is fraudulent and actionable. . . .

Muhammad has suffered widespread criticism and is uniformly rejected in every reported opinion reviewing post-settlement legal malpractice litigation. . . . While most courts are expeditious in determining that an attorney is not absolutely immune from legal malpractice actions when the client consents to settlement, they are also uniform in expressing a desire to foster protection over the negotiation process.

Courses of Action for Attorneys Confronting Post-Settlement Malpractice Claims

A. The Contributory/Comparative Negligence Defense

In a post-settlement malpractice action, an attorney should defend the action by claiming client contributory/comparative negligence. The defense should be presented by introducing evidence of the client's subjective reasons for settling the case.

The client contributory/comparative negligence defense is generally recognized in legal malpractice actions; however, some courts do not permit the issue to reach a jury. This reluctance is supported by the Restatement (Third) of Law Governing Lawyers, which asserts that the client contributory negligence defense is available in jurisdictions that recognize the same defense to general negligence actions. The Restatement cautions, however, that the lawyer/client relationship imposes fiduciary duties by which "clients are entitled to rely on their lawyers to act with competence, diligence, honesty, and loyalty." The lawyer/client relationship imposes numerous duties on the lawyer, while imposing few on the client. Yet, this cannot relieve clients from accepting responsibility for their own acts or omissions which result in unfavorable settlements.

Courts that permit the client comparative negligence defense, however, proceed with caution, premised on the view that attorneys should not be permitted to circumvent responsibility to former clients under the guise that the client should have known how to respond or act. Thus, even when a legal document contains simple English that needs no interpretation by a lawyer, the defense of client contributory negligence has been barred in certain jurisdictions. . . .

Courts should, however, permit the comparative negligence defense to proceed to the fact finder where the client settled a claim and now seeks to hold an attorney liable for malpractice committed in the negotiation of that settlement. In a majority of post-settlement malpractice claims, the former clients do not claim they did not understand the settlement agreement. Instead, this majority group freely admits they voluntarily entered into settlement, conceding they understood the agreement and abandoned their right to a trial. Only after settlement did these former clients contend there was "something else" their former lawyer should have done to secure a better result.

Although there will be cases where the client is genuinely aggrieved by a negligent attorney, the majority of post-settlement malpractice litigation arises from the client's own conduct. In those cases, the comparative fault defense should be considered by the fact finder.

While the comparative fault defense is available in the typical legal malpractice action, its use has been limited in post-settlement malpractice litigation. . . . [Courts] provide minimum guidelines to which an attorney should adhere in advising a client regarding settlement. . . . [T]he lawyer should hold an appreciation of (1) the relevant facts; (2) the present and future potential strengths and weaknesses of his case; (3) the likely costs, both objectively (monetarily) and subjectively (psychological disruption of business and family life) associated with proceeding further in the litigation; and (4) the likely outcome if the case were to proceed further.

Many cases of legal malpractice occur from "perceived" negligence by attorneys who fail to adhere to the [above] criteria. Common practice dictates that attorneys review the four factors in detail with their client prior to settlement. In post-settlement malpractice litigation analysis, courts tend to focus only on the result obtained (the settlement sum) to gauge the lawyer's liability exposure, ignoring the traditional factors preceding settlement. Hence, an attorney wishing to marshal an effective defense must take pre-settlement steps aimed to protect his client's interest. This will safeguard against subsequent malpractice claims within the framework developed by the courts.

B. The "Release and Settlement Agreement": Solidifying the Deal

The "release and settlement agreement" is the final written document ending the litigation and, in many instances, the lawyer-client relationship. An historical review of related lawyer-client concern over apparent complications arising from contingency fee arrangements creates an additional post-settlement malpractice defense. To assure a client's comprehension of contingency fee contracts, many state bar associations require clients and attorneys to review and execute a "statement of client rights" which thoroughly explains the contingency fee agreement. This statement obligates the attorney to adhere to specific reporting and accounting requirements concerning fees throughout the client's case. It also provides the client with a remedy against unscrupulous attorneys.

Similar to the "statement of client rights," an attorney should be required to provide a client with a statement of the case before settlement. This statement would precisely articulate the ramifications of settlement and act as written confirmation of the attorney's work on the case. . . .

Conclusion

Post-settlement malpractice actions are quite unique. While the Pennsylvania Supreme Court effectively banned these lawsuits, providing former counsel immunity rather than engaging in the arduous analysis inherent to malpractice litigation, the better course of action is to permit attorneys to present the client comparative fault defense. This will allow an attorney to present evidence of the client's subjective reasons for settling the litigation. Additionally, through the use of a pre-settlement statement of the case form, attorneys will provide their clients sufficient information to adequately prepare for a successful negotiation and settlement process.

Note — Preventing Negotiation Malpractice

In the *Muhammad* case, Justice Larsen wrote a stinging dissent accusing the majority of creating a "LAWYER'S HOLIDAY" by barring malpractice against lawyers for negligence committed in the negotiation of civil settlements. He reasoned by comparison, "If a doctor is negligent in saving a human life, the doctor pays. If a priest is negligent in saving the spirit of a human, the priest pays. But if a lawyer is negligent in advising his client as to settlement, the client pays." Justice Larsen's dissent reflects the general view that most courts have taken in rejecting the Pennsylvania Supreme Court's protection of the negotiation process from claims of malpractice.

When negotiation malpractice cases do proceed to a jury trial, the jury is required to assess the negotiated outcome. The dilemma of evaluation confronted in these cases is "compared to what?" Most often the comparison is to the likely result if the negotiated claim had proceeded to trial. This requires, in effect, a "trial within a trial." Although this approach is thought to apply an objective standard, it does not take into account the give and take of the negotiation process and the subjective, or nonmonetary, interests that may in reality have driven the negotiation. The "trial within a trial" approach reverts to a distributive negotiation model that launders out integrative aspects that favorably distinguish negotiation from trial.

Judging a negotiated outcome by an objective, monetary gauge fails to factor in the interest-based approach to which most of the new negotiation literature is directed. It raises the same concerns as does grading law students at the end of a negotiation course only on the quantitative, money results of a final negotiation role-play. As expressed by Epstein, "[E]very aspect of a negotiated settlement, particularly its conclusion, is a subjective evaluation premised on the client's needs and desires, coupled with the various influences that affect that client's ultimate desire to settle".... Gauging a lawyer's liability exposure only on the monetary result obtained can have a chilling effect on good integrative bargaining by attorneys.

Professor Epstein proposes that attorneys protect themselves from malpractice claims by regularly using a form entitled, "Pre-Settlement Statement of Client's Case," which the client is to sign before settlement. This form memorializes all the facts, assessments, and advice that were considered to decide upon settlement. The concluding sentence of the form states "[Y]our attorney may use this document as a defense in a malpractice action if permitted by law." Although not a release per se, it is clearly intended to relieve the attorney of malpractice liability.

This "CYA" approach may or may not be effective protection, but is it the way you want to practice law? Each of us must ask how a precautionary approach with an eye ahead to defending malpractice claims will influence our relations with clients and affect our interaction with other attorneys. Will fear of malpractice hinder our nimbleness and creativity as negotiators? Was the *Muhammad* decision correct in its premise that opening up negotiation to after-the-fact legal scrutiny may impede negotiation and discourage settlement? If so, will judicial resources and client interests be adversely impacted?

As you consider these questions, please be aware that malpractice verdicts against lawyers for their good-faith efforts in negotiating on behalf of clients appear to be rare. Keeping clients informed is the best prevention. Reading this book and studying the negotiation process will prepare you to be an effective negotiator, with appreciative clients. Satisfied clients whose needs are met, including the need to know you have faithfully attended to their interests, do not sue their lawyers.

Obstacles to Agreement and Negotiation Assistance

A. Obstacles

Negotiation does not always result in agreement. Negotiations may stall due to a variety of obstacles. Indeed, some negotiations never get started because talking together is prevented by the history of the relationship or other barriers.

The psychological traps and different perceptions that create conflicts can persist or reappear to serve as obstacles that prevent a negotiated resolution of the conflict. Drawing from your own experience, as well as from the previous readings in this book, you are familiar with some of the obstacles that can get in the way of a negotiated settlement. Many of these arise from the cognitive and emotional factors, as well as interpersonal dynamics, discussed in Chapter 2. Other barriers are structural or strategic. Common obstacles to negotiated settlements, as well as some negotiated transactions, include the following:

- Being over-competitive
- Complexity of issues
- Concern about setting precedent
- Demonizing opposition
- Different perceptions
- Different case evaluations
- Egos/reputations
- Fear of looking weak
- Fixation on single position/solution
- Greed
- Hidden agendas

- Lawyer incentives not to settle
- Linear thinking
- Optimistic overconfidence
- Over-investment in case
- Past baggage
- Personality clashes
- Poor communication
- Reactive devaluation
- Self-fulfilling prophecies
- Stereotypes
- Strong feelings

When any of these barriers make negotiations difficult, cumbersome, or unlikely to succeed, assistance is available. Using a third-party neutral to facilitate or manage the negotiation, and perhaps to make suggestions, can be helpful in promoting settlement. The third party may be a judge with power to order the parties to participate, a special master or evaluator appointed by the court to provide settlement assistance, or a mediator connected to the court or in private practice.

We examine here procedures available through the courts and from private mediators to help reach settlements. First we learn more about barriers and how neutral third parties can overcome some of the most persistent barriers to negotiated resolution.

❖ Robert H. Mnookin, *Why Negotiations Fail: An Exploration of Barriers to the Resolution of Conflict*

8 Ohio St. J. Disp. Resol. 235 (1993)

Conflict is inevitable, but efficient and fair resolution is not. Conflicts can persist even though there may be any number of possible resolutions that would better serve the interests of the parties. . . . In our everyday personal and professional lives, we have all witnessed disputes where the absence of a resolution imposes substantial and avoidable costs on all parties. . . .

My first example involves a divorcing family in California who were part of a longitudinal study carried out by Stanford psychologist Eleanor Maccoby and me. Mary and Paul Templeton spent three years fighting over the custody of their seven-year-old daughter Tracy after Mary filed for divorce in 1985. Mary wanted sole custody; Paul wanted joint physical custody. This middle-income family spent over $37,000 on lawyers and experts. In the process, they traumatized Tracy and inflicted great emotional pain on each other. More to the point, the conflict over who would best care for their daughter damaged each parent's relationship with Tracy, who has suffered terribly by being caught in the middle of her parents' conflict. Ultimately the divorce decree provided that Mary would have primary physical custody of Tracy, and Paul would be entitled to reasonable weekend visitation. The parents' inability to negotiate with one another led to a result in which mother, father, and daughter were all losers. . . .

My last example is an Art Buchwald story — but it isn't a laughing matter, at least, not for Buchwald. He and his partner, Alain Bernheim, submitted Buchwald's two and a half page "treatment" for a story called "King for a Day" to Paramount Pictures pursuant to contracts providing that Bernheim would produce any film based on the story idea and that Buchwald and Bernheim would each share in the profits. In 1989, Buchwald and Bernheim sued Paramount for breach of contract. They claimed that the studio had based Eddie Murphy's film, "Coming to America." on their treatment but had failed to give them their due. After three years of bitter litigation, a trial judge awarded Buchwald $150,000 and Bernheim $750,000. In the initial newspaper accounts, both sides claimed victory, but this is hardly an example of "win-win." Paramount claimed to be the winner because the legal fees of the plaintiffs' lawyers exceeded $2.5 million and the total recovery of only $900,000 was a small fraction of the $6.2 million Buchwald and Bernheim had requested in their final arguments. As it turns out, Buchwald and Bernheim will not have to pay the full legal fees because of a contingency arrangement with their law firm, but Buchwald has acknowledged that his share of out-of-pocket expenses alone exceeds $200,000 and that as a consequence, he will have no net recovery. On the other hand, Buchwald ridiculed Paramount's claim of victory. How, he asked, could it be a victory for a defendant to pay out nearly $1 million in damages, and, in addition, have legal fees of its own in excess of $3 million? Seems like lose-lose to me.

On her death bed, Gertrude Stein was asked by Alice B. Toklas, "What is the answer? What is the answer?" After a long silence, Stein responded: "No, what is the question?" Examples like these, and I am sure you could add many more of your own, suggest a central question for those of us concerned with dispute resolution: Why is it that under circumstances where there are resolutions that better serve disputants, negotiations often fail to achieve efficient resolutions? In other words, what are the barriers to the negotiated resolution of conflict?

Barriers to the Negotiated Resolution of Conflict

. . . I am not attempting [here] to provide a comprehensive list of barriers or an all-encompassing classification scheme. Instead, my purpose is to show that the concept of barriers provides a useful and necessarily interdisciplinary vantage point for exploring why negotiations sometimes fail. After describing these barriers and their relevance to the study of negotiation, I will briefly suggest a variety of ways that neutral third parties might help overcome each of these barriers.

Strategic Barriers

The first barrier to the negotiated resolution of conflict is inherent in a central characteristic of negotiation. Negotiation can be metaphorically compared to making a pie and then dividing it up. The process of conflict resolution affects both the size of the pie, and who gets what size slice.

The disputants' behavior may affect the size of the pie in a variety of ways. On the one hand, spending on avoidable legal fees and other process costs shrinks the pie. On the other hand, negotiators can together "create value" and make the pie bigger by discovering resolutions in which each party contributes special complementary skills that can be combined in a synergistic way, or by exploiting differences in relative preferences that permit trades that make both parties better off. Books like "Getting to Yes" and proponents of "win-win negotiation" emphasize the potential benefits of collaborative problem-solving approaches to negotiation which allow parties to maximize the size of the pie.

Negotiation also involves issues concerning the distribution of benefits, and, with respect to pure distribution, both parties cannot be made better off at the same time. Given a pie of fixed size, a larger slice for you means a smaller one for me. Because bargaining typically entails both efficiency issues (that is, how big the pie can be made) and distributive issues (that is, who gets what size slice), negotiation involves an inherent tension — one that [has been] dubbed the "negotiator's dilemma." In order to create value, it is critically important that options be created in light of both parties' underlying interests and preferences. This suggests the importance of openness and disclosure, so that a variety of options can be analyzed and compared from the perspectives of all concerned. However, when it comes to the distributive aspects of bargaining, full disclosure — particularly if unreciprocated by the other side — can often lead to outcomes in which the more open party receives a comparatively smaller slice.

To put it another way, unreciprocated approaches to creating value leave their maker vulnerable to claiming tactics. On the other hand, focusing on the distributive aspects of bargaining can often lead to unnecessary deadlocks and, more fundamentally, a failure to discover options or alternatives that make both sides better off. A simple example can expose the dilemma. The first involves what game theorists call "information asymmetry." This simply means each side to a negotiation characteristically knows some relevant facts that the other side does not know.

Suppose I have ten apples and no oranges, and Nancy Rogers has ten oranges and no apples. (Assume apples and oranges are otherwise unavailable to either of us.) I love oranges and hate apples. Nancy likes them both equally well. I suggest to Nancy that we might both be made better off through a trade. If I disclose to Nancy that I love oranges and don't eat apples, and Nancy wishes to engage in strategic bargaining, she might simply suggest that her preferences are the same as mine, although, in truth, she likes both. She might propose that I give her nine apples (which she says have little value to her) in exchange for one of her very valuable oranges. Because it is often very difficult for one party to know the underlying preferences of the other party, parties in a negotiation may puff, bluff, or lie about their underlying interests and preferences. Indeed, in many negotiations, it may never be possible to know whether the other side has honestly disclosed its interests and preferences. I have to be open to create value, but my openness may work to my disadvantage with respect to the distributive aspect of the negotiation.

Even when both parties know all the relevant information, and that potential gains may result from a negotiated deal, strategic bargaining over how to divide the pie can still lead to deadlock (with no deal at all) or protracted and expensive bargaining, thus shrinking the pie. For example, suppose Nancy has a house for sale for which she has a reservation price of $245,000. I am willing to pay up to $295,000 for the house. Any deal within a bargaining range from $245,000 to $295,000 would make both of us better off than no sale at all. Suppose we each know the other's reservation price. Will there be a deal? Not necessarily. If we disagree about how the $50,000 "surplus" should be divided (each wanting all or most of it), our negotiation may end in a deadlock. We might engage in hardball negotiation tactics in which each tried to persuade the other that he or she was committed to walking away from a beneficial deal, rather than accept less than $40,000 of the surplus. Nancy might claim that she won't take a nickel less than $285,000, or even $294,999 for that matter. Indeed, she might go so far as to give a power of attorney to an agent to sell only at that price, and then leave town in order to make her commitment credible. Of course, I could play the same type of game and the result would then be that no deal is made and that we are both worse off. In this case, the obvious tension between the distribution of the $50,000 and the value creating possibilities inherent in any sale within the bargaining range may result in no deal.

Strategic behavior — which may be rational for a self-interested party concerned with maximizing the size of his or her own slice — can often lead to inefficient outcomes. Those subjected to claiming tactics often respond in kind, and the net result typically is to push up the cost of the dispute resolution process. (*Buchwald v. Paramount Pictures Corp.* is a good example of a case in which the economic costs of hardball litigation obviously and substantially shrunk the pie.) Parties may be tempted to engage in strategic behavior, hoping to get more. Often all they do is shrink the size of the pie. Those experienced in the civil litigation process see this all the time. One or both sides often attempt to use pre-trial discovery as leverage to force the other side into agreeing to a more favorable settlement. Often the net result, however, is simply that both sides spend unnecessary money on the dispute resolution process.

The Principal-Agent Problem

The second barrier is suggested by recent work relating to transaction cost economics, and is sometimes called the "principal/agent" problem. . . . The basic problem is that the incentives for an agent (whether it be a lawyer, employee, or officer) negotiating on behalf of a party to a dispute may induce behavior that fails to serve the interests of the principal itself. The relevant research suggests that it is no simple matter — whether by contract or custom — to align perfectly the incentives for an agent with the interests of the principal. This divergence may act as a barrier to efficient resolution of conflict.

Litigation is fraught with principal/agent problems. In civil litigation, for example — particularly where the lawyers on both sides are being paid by the hour — there is very little incentive for the opposing lawyers to cooperate, particularly if the clients have the capacity to pay for trench warfare and are angry to boot. Commentators have suggested that this is one reason many cases settle on the courthouse steps, and not before: for the lawyers, a late settlement may avoid the possible embarrassment of an extreme outcome, while at the same time providing substantial fees. . . .

Overcoming . . . Barriers: The Role of Negotiators and Mediators

The study of barriers can do more than simply help us understand why negotiations sometimes fail when they should not. It can also contribute to our understanding of how to overcome these barriers. . . .

First, let us consider the strategic barrier. To the extent that a neutral third party is trusted by both sides, the neutral may be able to induce the parties to reveal information about their underlying interests, needs, priorities, and aspirations that they would not disclose to their adversary. This information may permit a trusted mediator to help the parties enlarge the pie in circumstances where the parties acting alone could not. Moreover, a mediator can foster a problem-solving atmosphere and lessen the temptation on the part of each side to engage in strategic behavior. A skilled mediator can often get parties to move beyond political posturing and recriminations about past wrongs and to instead consider possible gains from a fair resolution of the dispute.

A mediator also can help overcome barriers posed by principal/agent problems. A mediator may bring clients themselves to the table, and help them understand their shared interest in minimizing legal fees and costs in circumstances where the lawyers themselves might not be doing so. In circumstances where a middle manager is acting to prevent a settlement that might benefit the company, but might be harmful to the manager's own career, an astute mediator can sometimes bring another company representative to the table who does not have a personal stake in the outcome.

A mediator can also promote dispute resolution by helping overcome cognitive barriers. Through a variety of processes, a mediator can often help each side understand the power of the case from the other side's perspective. Moreover, by reframing the dispute and suggesting a resolution that avoids blame and stresses the positive aspects of a resolution, a mediator may be able to lessen the effects of loss aversion. My colleague for Tversky thinks that cognitive barriers are like optical illusions — knowing that an illusion exists does not necessarily enable us to see things differently. Nevertheless, I believe that astute mediators can dampen loss aversion through reframing, by helping a disputant reconceptualize the resolution. By emphasizing the potential gains to both sides of the resolution and de-emphasizing the losses that the resolution is going to entail, mediators (and lawyers) often facilitate resolution.

With respect to . . . reactive devaluation, mediators can play an important and quite obvious role. Reactive devaluation can often be sidestepped if the source of a proposal is a neutral — not one of the parties. Indeed, one of the trade secrets of mediators is that after talking separately to each side about what might or might not be acceptable, the mediator takes responsibility for making a proposal. This helps both parties avoid reactive devaluation by allowing them to accept as sensible a proposal that they might have rejected if it had come directly from their adversary. . . .

B. Negotiation Assistance

There are a variety of options available to resolve your clients' disputes. Direct negotiation anchors one end of a spectrum of dispute resolution procedures. At the other end is a trial in court. Negotiation and trial are polar opposites. Parties who opt for trial have relatively little control over either the process or the outcome. Trials are formal and public, conducted under detailed procedural and evidentiary rules, with a judge in control. A judge or jury decides the outcome, and in doing so is bound to follow established legal principles. By contrast, negotiation gives parties maximum control over both the process and its outcome.

In between direct negotiation and trial is a continuum of alternative dispute resolution (ADR) processes. The continuum moves from processes that have characteristics very similar to negotiation to ones that closely resemble a trial. The key characteristic that distinguishes negotiation-like processes from trial-like methods is whether a neutral party has the ability to impose a binding outcome on the participants. Proceedings in which the neutral can decide the result are all forms of adjudication. Processes that authorize the neutral to facilitate, persuade, even pressure parties to reach agreement — but not to impose a result on them — are all forms of assisted negotiation.

Mediators, for example, assist negotiators in reaching a settlement, but do not have the power to require disputants to reach agreement or impose a decision. For that reason, mediation and all of its variants are on the nonbinding, assisted-negotiation side of the spectrum. By contrast, in traditional arbitration the neutral does have the power to decide the outcome, so arbitration falls on the binding, adjudicative side of the spectrum. However, the terminology can be misleading. One example is a process known as advisory or judicial arbitration, which does not necessarily result in a binding decision and can promote a negotiated settlement. We present below dispute resolution processes as a spectrum of procedural shadings, with the central dividing characteristic or line being whether a neutral has authority to impose a binding outcome on the parties. All the procedures to the left of the dividing line are available as a form of third-party assisted negotiation.

Dispute Resolution Spectrum

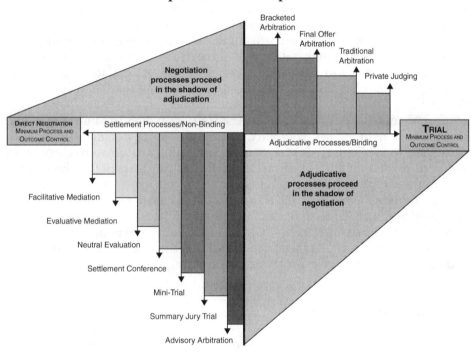

Whenever a dispute involves a legal claim, the plaintiff can, at least in theory, obtain a binding decision from a court. The elephant in the closet of nonbinding settlement efforts is the likely outcome if the dispute proceeds to trial. For this reason a "shadow of adjudication" extends across the nonbinding, negotiation side of the spectrum. Similarly, disputants can halt even a binding procedure by reaching agreement. Settlement negotiations, in effect, lurk in the closet of adjudication: We refer to this on our chart as the "shadow of negotiation."

The process possibilities on the nonbinding, negotiation side of the spectrum are infinite, limited only by what the parties can create, agree upon, and afford. The spectrum displays the settlement processes and methods that are most often discussed in the literature and commonly used, now or in the recent past. The most widely used nonbinding form of assisted dispute resolution is mediation. Mediation is available privately as a service for a fee and through court-connected or -mandated programs, where there may or may not be a fee. We look first at the process of mediation as an aid to reaching negotiated agreements and then explore the use of other nonbinding forms of assistance to lawyers in settling disputes. In the next chapter you will read about how to best represent clients in mediation and how to use mediation to their advantage for purposes of favorably negotiating agreements.

C. Mediation

1. What Is Mediation?

Mediation is a process of assisted negotiation in which a neutral person helps parties reach agreement. The process varies depending on the style of the mediator and the wishes of the participants. As noted above, mediation differs from direct negotiation in that it involves the participation of an impartial third party. The process also differs from adjudication in that it is consensual, informal, and usually private. The participants need not reach agreement, and the mediator has no power to impose an outcome.

In some contexts you may find that this definition does not fully apply. The process is sometimes not voluntary, as when a judge requires litigants to participate in mediation as a precondition to gaining access to a courtroom. In addition, mediators are not always entirely neutral; a corporate lawyer, for instance, can apply mediative techniques to help colleagues resolve an internal dispute, despite the fact that she is in favor of a particular outcome. Occasionally mediation is required to be open to the public, as when a dispute involves governmental entities subject to "open meeting" laws. And finally, a mediator's goal is not always to settle a specific legal dispute; the neutral may focus instead on helping disputants to improve their relationship.

2. What Do Mediators Do?

Mediators apply a wide variety of techniques. Depending on the situation, a settlement-oriented mediator may use the following approaches, among others:

- Help litigants, including attorneys, design a process that ensures the presence of key participants and focuses their attention on finding a constructive solution to a dispute.
- Allow the principals and their attorneys to present legal arguments, raise underlying concerns, and express their feelings directly to their opponents, as well as hear the other side's perspectives firsthand.
- Help participants to focus on their interests and identify imaginative settlement options.
- Moderate negotiations, coaching bargainers in effective techniques, translating communications, and reframing the disputants' positions and perceptions in constructive ways.
- Assist each side to assess the likely outcome if the case is litigated and to consider the full costs of continuing the conflict.
- Work with the disputants to draft a durable agreement and, if necessary, to implement it.

3. What Is the Structure of Mediation?

Because mediation is informal, lawyers and clients have a great deal of freedom to modify the process to meet their needs. In practice, good neutrals and advocates vary their approach significantly to respond to the circumstances of particular cases. That said, a typical mediation of a legal dispute is likely to proceed through a series of stages.

a. Pre-Mediation

Before the disputants meet to mediate, the neutral, or a case manager, often has conversations with the lawyers, and sometimes also with the parties, to deal with issues such as who will attend the mediation and what information the mediator will receive beforehand. Lawyers can use these contacts to start to build a working relationship with the mediator and educate her about their clients' perspectives on the dispute and obstacles that have made direct negotiations difficult.

b. The Opening Session

Many mediations begin with a session at which the parties, counsel, and the mediator meet together. The content and structure of a joint session can vary considerably, depending on the goals of the process and the wishes of the parties. When mediation is focused on reaching a monetary settlement, the opening session is likely to be dominated by arguments of lawyers, perhaps followed by questions from the neutral. If, by contrast, the goal of the process is to find an interest-based solution or to repair a ruptured relationship, then the mediator is much more likely to encourage the parties themselves to speak and to attempt to draw out underlying issues and emotions. The practice of holding a joint opening session in mediations of cases in litigation is declining. Some mediators, acting at the request of litigators, often begin the process with only a cursory "housekeeping" joint session or none at all, and spend virtually all their time in private caucusing. Others meet with each side separately before an opening joint session.

c. Private Caucusing

If there is a joint session, after disputants have exchanged perspectives, arguments, and questions, most civil mediators adjourn the joint session in order to meet with each side individually in private "caucuses." The purpose of caucusing is to permit disputants and counsel to talk candidly with the neutral. Keeping the parties separated, with communications channeled through the mediator, also allows the neutral to shape the disputants' dialogue in productive ways.

When the mediation process is focused on monetary bargaining, the participants usually spend most of their time separated, with the mediator shuttling back and forth between them. In very contentious cases, particularly sexual harassment and termination matters, parties may not meet together at all. If, however, parties are interested in exploring an interest-based resolution or repairing a broken relationship, then the mediator is much more likely to encourage them to meet and, perhaps, remain together so that they can work through difficult emotions, explore options, and learn to relate productively with each other.

d. Moderated Discussions

Even when a mediation is conducted primarily through private caucusing, neutrals sometimes ask the disputants to meet with each other for specific informational or negotiation purposes. This might be to examine the tax issues in a business breakup, explore a licensing agreement to resolve a patent claim, or to deal with a difficult emotional issue in a tort case. And in most mediations, whether or not conducted through caucusing, the lawyers and parties all meet at the end of the process to sign a memorandum of agreement or to decide on future steps in the case.

e. Follow-Up Contacts

Increasingly the mediation process is not limited to the specific occasions on which the mediator and disputants meet together. If a dispute is not resolved at a mediation session, then the neutral is likely to follow up with the lawyers or parties. Depending on the situation, the mediator may pursue continued telephone or e-mail negotiations, or convene additional face-to-face sessions if the parties wish.

f. Variations in Format

The above structural elements represent "default" models for mediation of legal claims, but you will encounter significant variations in the field. Mediators who handle family disputes, for example, often remain in joint session during the entire process, and some mediators are experimenting with no-caucus formats in other kinds of civil cases. Mediation of multiparty, mass torts, securities claims, other class actions and very complex cases may require joint pre-mediation planning sessions or separate pre-mediation meetings with the mediator to tailor the process to the particular demands of the dispute in order to increase the likelihood of a negotiated resolution.

Problem — Death of a Student

In late August, Scott Krueger arrived for his freshman year at the Massachusetts Institute of Technology. Five weeks later, he was dead. In an incident that made national headlines, Krueger died of alcohol poisoning following an initiation event at a fraternity. Nearly two years later, Krueger's parents sent MIT a demand letter stating their intent to sue. The letter alleged that MIT had caused their son's death by failing to address what they claimed were two long-standing campus problems: a housing arrangement that they said steered new students to seek rooms in fraternities, and what their lawyer called a culture of alcohol abuse at fraternities.

MIT's lawyers saw the case as one that could be won. An appellate court, they believed, would rule that a college is not legally responsible for an adult student's voluntary drinking. Moreover, under state law the university could not be required to pay more than $20,000 to the Kruegers (although that limit did not apply to claims against individual university administrators). MIT officials felt, however, that a narrowly drawn legal response would not be in keeping with its values. They also recognized that there were aspects of the institution's policies and practices — including those covering student use of alcohol — that could have been better. MIT's president, Charles M. Vest, was prepared to accept responsibility for these shortcomings on behalf of the university, and felt a deep personal desire for his institution to reach a resolution with the Krueger family. MIT also recognized that defending the case in court would exact a tremendous emotional toll on all concerned. The Kruegers would be subjected to a hard-hitting assessment of their son's behavior leading up to his death, whereas MIT would be exposed to equally severe scrutiny of the Institute's culture and the actions of individual administrators. Full-blown litigation in a case of this magnitude was also sure to be expensive, with estimated defense costs well in excess of $1 million.

How might mediation be initiated and used to satisfactorily resolve the Kruegers' claim?

Note: An Example of Mediation in Aid of Negotiation[*]

The question, as MIT saw the above situation, was not whether to seek to engage the Kruegers in settlement negotiations, but how. The university decided to forego a traditional legal response to initiate negotiations and reply instead with a personal letter from President Vest to the Kruegers, which noted the university's belief that it had strong legal defenses to their claims, but offered to mediate.

---

* [Confidentiality is one of the most important attributes of mediation. The facts in the following account that have not previously been published have been approved by attorneys for both parties. — EDS.]

The Kruegers responded with intense distrust. Tortuous negotiations ensued. The parents eventually agreed to mediate, but only subject to certain conditions: At least one session would have to occur in Buffalo, where the Kruegers lived. MIT would have to offer a sincere apology for its conduct; without that, no sum of money would settle the case. There would be no confidentiality agreement to prevent the parents from talking publicly about the matter, while at the same time any settlement could not be exploited by MIT for public relations purposes. The Kruegers would have the right to select the mediator. And President Vest would have to appear personally at all the mediation sessions. The university agreed to most of the conditions, and the mediation went forward.

MIT's lawyers believed that it was important that the Kruegers' lawyers and the mediator understand the strength of the university's defenses, but plaintiff counsel knew that subjecting the Kruegers to such a presentation would make settlement impossible. To resolve the dilemma, the lawyers bifurcated the process. The first day of the mediation, which the Kruegers would not attend, would focus on presentations by lawyers and would be held in Boston. One week later, the mediation would resume at a conference center located a 40-minute drive outside Buffalo, this time with the Kruegers present. Their counsel selected that location so that "no one could leave easily." On the second day the Kruegers would personally meet President Vest, and the parties would begin to exchange settlement proposals.

Counsel had agreed that the mediator, Jeffrey Stern, should begin the day by having a private breakfast with Mr. and Mrs. Krueger and their lawyers. The Kruegers vented their anger, first to Stern and later to President Vest. "How could you do this?" they shouted at Vest, "You people killed our son!" They also challenged Vest on a point that bothered them terribly: Why, they asked him, had he come to their son's funeral but not sought them out personally to extend his condolences? Vest responded that he had consulted with people about whether or not to approach the Kruegers and was advised that, in light of their anger at the institution, it would be better not to do so. That advice was wrong, he said, and he regretted following it.

Vest went on to apologize for the university's role in what he described as a "terrible, terrible tragedy." "We failed you," he said, and then asked, "What can we do to make it right?" Mrs. Krueger cried out again at Vest, but at that point her husband turned to her and said, "The man apologized. What more is there to say?" Their counsel, Leo Boyle, later said that he felt that, "There's a moment . . . where the back of the case is broken. You can feel it. . . . And that was the moment this day." The mediator gradually channeled the discussion toward what the Kruegers wanted and what the university could do.

Hard bargaining followed, much of it conducted though shuttle diplomacy by the mediator. In the end the parties reached agreement: MIT paid the Kruegers $4.75 million to settle their claims and contributed an additional $1.25 million to a scholarship fund that the family would administer. Perhaps equally important, President Vest offered the Kruegers a personal, unconditional apology on behalf of MIT that no court could have compelled and that would not have been believed if it were. At the conclusion of the process Vest and Mrs. Krueger hugged each other. For MIT the settlement, although expensive, made sense: It minimized the harm that contested litigation would have caused to the institution. And, most important, the university felt that it was the right thing to do.

What did the mediator contribute to overcoming obstacles in the negotiation process? During the first day, Stern questioned both lawyers closely about the legal and factual issues, creating a foundation for realistic assessments of case value later in the process. The initial money offers put forth by each party were far apart, but the mediator put them into context so that neither side gave up in frustration. According to plaintiff counsel Brad Henry, Stern's greatest contribution was probably the way he responded to the Kruegers' feelings: "What he did most masterfully was to allow a lot of the emotion to be directed at him. He allowed it almost to boil over when it was just him with the Kruegers, but later he very deftly let it be redirected at President Vest and the university. . . . He also prepared Charles Vest for the onslaught. . . . Mediation can be like a funeral — especially with the death of a child. He mediated the emotional part of the case, and then let the rest unfold on its own."

Questions

1. What barriers made it difficult for the parties in the Krueger case to negotiate with each other directly? In what ways was mediation likely to be more effective than direct negotiation at overcoming them?
2. What goals did the university have in proposing mediation? What did the student's family appear to be seeking from the process?
3. What did the Kruegers obtain in mediation that they could not likely have obtained in direct negotiation or have won at trial?

---

4. Goals for the Process

When you participate in mediation as an advocate, what will be your goals for the process? The answer may seem simple — to settle a legal dispute. But the question is often more complex. Many disputes involve issues, interests, and potential solutions that go beyond the legal issues that lawyers typically consider or the remedies that courts can grant. When a dispute arises from an important relationship, for example, repairing the rupture could be more significant to a client than how the current controversy is resolved. The goals that you pursue in mediation thus may change greatly from one situation to another, and these differences will in turn influence your choice of a neutral and structure for the process. As a lawyer representing clients, you may have one or more of the following purposes in deciding to mediate.

a. Resolve a Claim in Litigation on the Best Possible Monetary Terms

When litigators enter mediation, their goal is usually to settle a legal dispute. Most trial lawyers take a narrow approach to the process: They discuss only the legally relevant facts and issues and set as their goal to obtain the highest (for the plaintiff) or lowest (for the defendant) possible monetary payment in return for ending the case. When litigators talk about mediation, they often reflect this perspective. One lawyer, for example, has said that, "The effective advocate approaches mediation as if it were a trial . . . the overwhelming benefit of mediation is that it can reduce the cost of litigation" (Weinstein 1996). Perhaps in response, commercial mediators often see their primary role as to facilitate distributive bargaining. One successful New England neutral, for example, has written that, "In the typical civil mediation, money is the primary (if not the only) issue" (Contuzzi 2000), while a leading Southern mediator has said that, "The goal of resolution is always the same: allowing the parties to negotiate to a 'reasonable ballpark,' in which they, with the help of the mediator, identify 'home plate' based on what a jury will consider 'a reasonable verdict range'" (Max 1999).

In the typical commercial dispute, then, litigants and their counsel are likely to enter the process assuming that it will focus primarily on legal arguments and principled/positional bargaining over money. Although this kind of negotiation often produces less-than-optimal results, a mediator can do a great deal to assist parties even when money is the only issue about which the disputants are willing to bargain.

b. Develop a Broad, Interest-Based Resolution

As we have seen, parties to legal disputes often have interests that go far beyond money, and settlements that respond to these concerns can provide greater value to disputants than a purely monetary outcome. Some lawyers employ mediation to facilitate interest-based bargaining and obtain creative resolutions. One text for corporate attorneys, for example, emphasizes that, "The process creates an opportunity to explore underlying business interests [and] offers the potential for a 'win-win' solution . . ." (Picker 2003), while another describes the process as providing "a framework for parties to . . . privately reveal to the mediator in caucus sensitive interests that may assist the mediator to facilitate broad solutions" (CPR Institute, Scanlon ed. 1999).

c. Repair the Parties' Ruptured Relationship

Attorneys sometimes enter mediation not so much to obtain specific terms of settlement as to repair the parties' relationship. When parties enter litigation they typically sever any prior connection between them, but many supporters of mediation believe, in the words of Professor Lon Fuller, that "mediation has as its primary goal the repair of the troubled relationship" (Fuller 1971).

d. Change the Parties' Perspectives

In a still-broader view, the purpose of the mediation process is not to obtain any specific outcome. Instead its focus is to assist parties in transforming their perspectives on the dispute and each other, a change that may or may not lead to an improvement in their relationship. Advocates of this perspective, known as "transformative" mediation, argue that the disputants should be allowed to take charge of the mediation process, with the mediator serving as a resource to facilitate their conversations. Professor Baruch Bush and Joseph Folger, for example, contrast transformative mediation with processes oriented toward problem solving, stating that

> a *transformative approach* to mediation, emphasizes mediation's capacity for fostering empowerment and recognition. . . . Transformative mediators concentrate on empowering parties to define issues and decide settlement terms for themselves and on helping parties to better understand one another's perspectives. The effect of this approach is to avoid the directiveness associated with problem-solving mediation. Equally important, transformative mediation helps parties recognize and exploit the opportunities for moral growth inherently presented by conflict. It aims at changing the parties themselves for the better, as human beings. (Bush & Folger 2004)

e. Choices Among Potential Goals

Although a particular mediation can have more than a single purpose, one can think of possible goals for the process as falling along a continuum.

How likely is it in practice that if an attorney seeks one of these goals, he will be able to achieve it — how often, in other words, can parties in a civil mediation expect to leave the process with a purely monetary settlement, an interest-based solution, or a relationship repair?

The answer will be heavily influenced by the nature of the case, the attitudes of clients and counsel, and the skills and goals of the mediator. Relationship repair in mediation is often not feasible: In most auto tort cases, for example, there is no prior relationship to revive. Even when a dispute does arise from a relationship, the parties often litigate bitterly before mediating, and in such situations repairing the relationship is very difficult. Sometimes, however, both sides recognize that it is in their interest to heal their rupture. This is most common in settings where the parties' past connection has been strong and their alternatives to relating are not attractive. One example of such a situation is a quarrel between a divorcing couple over how they will parent their children. Relationships can be important in commercial settings as well; partners in small businesses may have a strong interest in seeking a repair of a troubled relationship because neither is able to buy out the other, and continued conflict will destroy the enterprise. A study of mediations of larger civil disputes arising from relationships (excluding unionized labor and divorce cases) found the following:

Outcomes of Legal Mediation in "Relationship" Cases			
Repair of relationship	Integrative term & money, but no repair	Money terms only	Impasse
17%	30%	27%	27%

In other words, when parties mediate a legal dispute arising from a significant prior relationship with a mediator open to imaginative solutions, there appears to be approximately a 15-20 percent chance that the process will culminate in a repair of the parties' relationship, a 30 percent chance of a settlement that has at least one significant integrative term in addition to money, a 25-30 percent probability of a settlement consisting solely of a monetary payment, and a 25-30 percent likelihood of impasse. Interestingly, focusing only on those cases that settled, agreements with at least one significant integrative term (either a relationship repair or another nonmoney term) totaled 47 percent, a much higher percentage than settlements consisting only of a monetary payment (27%) (Golann 2002).

As a lawyer you are likely to encounter many situations in which your client's only stated goal is to end her relationship with an adversary on the best possible terms. The data suggest, however, that in cases that arise from a prior relationship, more often than not it is feasible to obtain an agreement that includes some term of significant value to the parties in addition to money, and that in a small but appreciable portion of cases it is possible to repair the parties' relationship.

Questions

4. In what kinds of legal cases would you expect the parties to have a weak or nonexistent prior relationship?
5. In what types of disputes are the parties likely to find it very difficult or costly to sever their connection?

---

5. Mediator Styles

a. Classifying Styles

As a lawyer, it will be largely up to you to choose a mediator to assist with negotiation of your client's case. Matching the mediator to your goals for the mediation is important. Mediators are often classified according to the methods that they use and their mediation style. Professor Leonard Riskin created an often cited grid to classify mediators.

❖ **Leonard L. Riskin,** *MEDIATOR ORIENTATIONS,*
STRATEGIES AND TECHNIQUES

12 Alternatives 111 (Summer 1994)

. . . The classification system starts with two principal questions: 1. Does the mediator tend to define problems narrowly or broadly? 2. Does the mediator think she should evaluate — make assessments or predictions or proposals for agreements — or facilitate the parties' negotiation without evaluating? The answers reflect the mediator's beliefs about the nature and scope of mediation and her assumptions about the parties' expectations.

Problem Definition

Mediators with a *narrow* focus assume that the parties have come to them for help in solving a technical problem. The parties have defined this problem in advance through the *positions* they have asserted in negotiations or pleadings. Often it involves a question such as, "Who pays how much to whom?" or "Who can use such-and-such property?" As framed, these questions rest on "win-lose" (or "distributive") assumptions. In other words, the participants must divide a limited resource; whatever one gains, the other must lose.

The likely court outcome — along with uncertainty, delay and expense — drives much of the mediation process. Parties, seeking a compromise, will bargain adversarially, emphasizing positions over interests.

A mediator who starts with a *broad* orientation, on the other hand, assumes that the parties can benefit if the mediation goes beyond the narrow issues that normally define legal disputes. Important interests often lie beneath the positions that the participants assert. Accordingly, the mediator should help the participants understand and fulfill those interests — at least if they wish to do so.

The Mediator's Role

The *evaluative* mediator assumes that the participants want and need the mediator to provide some directions as to the approximate grounds for settlement — based on law, industry practice, or technology. She also assumes that the mediator is qualified to give such direction by virtue of her experience, training, and objectivity.

The *facilitative* mediator assumes the parties are intelligent, able to work with their counterparts, and capable of understanding their situation better than either their lawyers or the mediator. So the parties may develop better solutions than any that the mediator might create. For these reasons, the facilitative mediator assumes that his principal mission is to enhance and clarify communications between the parties in order to help them decide what to do.

The facilitative mediator believes it is inappropriate for the mediator to give his opinion, for at least two reasons. First, such opinions might impair the appearance of impartiality and thereby interfere with the mediator's ability to function. Second, the mediator might not know enough — about the details of the case or the relevant law, practices, or technology — to give an informed opinion.

Each of the two principal questions — Does the mediator tend toward a narrow or broad focus? and Does the mediator favor an evaluative or facilitative role? — yield responses that fall along a continuum. Thus, a mediator's orientation will be more or less broad and more or less evaluative.

Mediators usually have a predominant orientation, whether they know it or not, based on a combination of their personalities, experiences, education, and training. Thus, many retired judges, when they mediate, tend toward an evaluative-narrow orientation.

Yet mediators do not always behave consistently with the predominant orientations they express. . . . In addition, many mediators will depart from their orientations to respond to the dynamics of the situation. . . . [As an] example: an evaluative-narrow mediator may explore underlying interests (a technique normally associated with the broad orientation) after her accustomed

```
┌─────────────────────────────────────────────────────────────┐
│              Role of Mediator: Evaluative                    │
│         ┌────────────────────────┬────────────────────────┐  │
│         │                        │                        │  │
│         │     EVALUATIVE         │     EVALUATIVE         │  │
│         │     NARROW             │     BROAD              │  │
│         │                        │                        │  │
│ Problem │                        │                        │ Problem │
│ Definition: ├────────────────────┼────────────────────────┤ Definition: │
│ Narrow  │                        │                        │ Broad │
│         │     FACILITATIVE       │     FACILITATIVE       │  │
│         │     NARROW             │     BROAD              │  │
│         │                        │                        │  │
│         └────────────────────────┴────────────────────────┘  │
│              Role of Mediator: Facilitative                  │
└─────────────────────────────────────────────────────────────┘
```

narrow focus results in a deadlock. And a facilitative-broad mediator might use a mildly evaluative tactic as a last resort. For instance, he might toss out a figure that he thinks the parties might be willing to agree upon, while stating that the figure does not represent his prediction of what would happen in court. . . . Many effective mediators are versatile and can move from quadrant to quadrant (and within a quadrant), as the dynamics of the situation dictate, to help parties settle disputes. . . .

Professor Riskin has since modified his grid by replacing the word "evaluative" with "directive" and "facilitative" with "elicitive" (the "broad" versus "narrow" continuum remains the same). Most writing on mediator styles continues to employ Riskin's original evaluative-facilitative terminology. To avoid confusing you with inconsistent terms, we use evaluative and facilitive in this book. Students interested in exploring the issue of mediator style more deeply should read Professor Riskin's 2003 article, *Decisionmaking in Mediation: The New Old Grid and the New New Grid System*, 79 Notre Dame L. Rev. 1 (2003).

b. Do Mediators Have a Single Style?

To investigate if mediators maintain a consistant style, one of the authors asked several respected lawyer mediators to mediate a case in a role-play format while being filmed. The experiment found, as Professor Riskin suggests, that good neutrals do not maintain a single orientation, but instead adapt their approach to fit the evolving circumstances of a dispute. Indeed, neutrals typically changed their approach repeatedly during a single caucus meeting with a party. All of the mediators began in a broadly facilitative mode, asking about the parties' business and personal interests, but they were usually met with narrowly evaluative comments from the lawyers. In response, the mediators remained facilitative, but acceded to counsel's narrow subject-matter orientation. Periodically during the process, however, mediators would return to a "broad" orientation, asking about the client's interests and suggesting nonmonetary solutions.

This experiment confirms Riskin's observation that successful legal mediators are not consistently either facilitative or evaluative. The neutrals in the study did become increasingly evaluative over the course of each mediation, but their advice usually focused on the bargaining situation: They offered opinions, for instance, about how the other side was probably seeing the situation and what negotiating approach was most likely to be effective ("If you make that offer, I'm concerned that they will react by . . ."). As each of the filmed roleplays continued, the mediator became more willing to ask questions or make comments that suggested a view, or at least skepticism, about the disputants' legal arguments. However, when a neutral did make an evaluative comment about a legal issue, she almost always framed it in general terms ("The evidence on causation seems thin. . . . I'm concerned that a court might . . ."). Overall, changes in the style of each mediator appeared to be determined much more by the personalities and tactics of the parties and lawyers than by tendencies of the neutral. Lawyer advocacy and client attitudes, in other words, counted for more than a mediator's preferred technique in determining what occurred during each mediation.

6. Mediation Techniques to Overcome Negotiation Obstacles

Most mediation involving lawyers is focused on civil cases — that is, disputes involving the kinds of tort, contract, property, employment, and statutory claims that you have studied in law school, compared to marital or collective bargaining disputes. These are commonly referred to as "commercial" mediation cases. Commercial mediators almost all use a caucus-based format, and discussions in such cases tend to focus on what courts would consider legally relevant and on exchanges of money offers.

Mediators who specialize in divorce and other disputes between family members, by contrast, usually avoid caucusing and place more emphasis on the parties' nonmonetary interests. The setting in which mediation occurs — for example, whether it is an all-day private affair or a two-hour court-connected process — also affects how the mediation develops.

If mediation is invoked in litigated cases it is usually because parties are unable to negotiate effectively on their own, due to one or more of the barriers discussed above, or the court has a program encouraging mediation. The goal in using mediation is to stimulate constructive negotiations. A commercial mediator might begin by seeking information that answers two questions:

- What obstacles are preventing the parties from settling this dispute themselves?
- What strategy is most likely to overcome these barriers?

A mediator's understanding of what is keeping the parties apart will deepen over the course of a mediation, and the obstacles themselves may change as the process goes forward. Ideally a mediator's strategy will be attuned to each case. In practice, however, many commercial mediators use a standard sequence of techniques to deal with the barriers most likely to be present, customizing their approach as they go along. This section describes a six-step strategy suggested by the authors when training commercial mediators. By knowing what mediators are trained to do, you will have a better understanding of the process so you can prepare for it and shape the mediation to best meet the needs of your client.

a. Build a Foundation for Settlement

The Challenge: Missing Elements — People, Data, Interactions.   Negotiations often fail because some essential element is missing. One side may have the wrong people — a key decision maker may be missing, or one of the bargainers may be so emotional he cannot make good decisions. At other times, parties do not have the data they need to settle: Defense counsel may not, for instance, know how the claimed damages were computed and without this information cannot get authority to settle. Such problems are difficult to fix once mediation begins.

Response: Identify Issues and Address Them in Advance.   To identify and resolve such problems, it is best to start before the parties meet to mediate. The first step is to ask the lawyers for mediation statements and set up telephone conversations with each of them. Ask each attorney who he plans to bring and who needs to attend from the other party. If a decision maker is absent, work to bring her to the table. If key information is missing, suggest that a party provide it. Mediators can elicit information and persuade people to attend in circumstances in which the same request would be rejected if made by a party.

b. Allow Participants to Argue and Express Feelings

The Challenge: Unresolved Process and Emotional Needs.   If parties don't settle, it's often because someone wants something more than just particular settlement terms. A litigant might be looking instead for an empathetic hearing: the opportunity to appear before a neutral person, state his grievances or defense, and know he has been heard. Or a party may have a need to express strong feelings directly to an adversary. Until they feel heard, parties are often not ready to settle. The need to express strong feelings to one's adversary is a very human one, felt by executives and mailroom clerks alike

Response: Provide an Opportunity to Speak and Feel Heard.   Mediation is not a court session and mediators are not judges, but the process can give parties the satisfaction of receiving a hearing not bound by narrow rules of evidence. They can see their lawyer argue their case, or present it themselves, and listen to an opponent's arguments. The mediator will not decide the dispute and might never express an opinion about the merits, but she can demonstrate she has heard the disputants. The experience of telling one's story and feeling heard by a neutral person can have a surprising impact on a person's willingness to settle. Arguing the merits also focuses participants on the facts and legal principles relevant to the controversy, and knowing that a neutral person will be listening encourages them to think through their arguments and avoid extremes. Beyond the merits, parties can express some of their feelings about the dispute and each other.

c. Moderate the Bargaining and Offer Coaching

The Challenge: Positional Tactics Leading to Impasse. Negotiators often have trouble reaching settlement because they use a positional approach to bargaining, trading monetary concessions until they reach agreement. We have seen that positional bargaining can be successful but that it often makes negotiators frustrated and angry, for example, when one side makes an offer that the other perceives as "insulting."

Response: Become the Moderator of the Process and Coach. Earlier mediation training encouraged mediators to prevent adversarial bargaining over money alone by convincing parties to focus on principles and interests. In commercial mediation, however, parties usually arrive suspicious of each other, focused on legal issues, and determined to engage solely in money bargaining. A mediator's only practical option in such cases is often to facilitate the process the parties want while looking for an opportunity to move them toward a more effective approach.

One way to facilitate money negotiations is to act as a coach. You can, for example, in caucus ask a bargainer to support its number with an explanation ("I'll communicate it, but if they ask how you got there what should I tell them?"), or help a disputant assess how a planned tactic will work ("What do you think their response will be if you start at $10,000?"). A mediator can give bargainers advice about how to keep the process moving ("If you want them to get to $100,000 with the next round, I think your offer to them needs to be in the range of $700,000 to $800,000. . . . "). By using these steps in combination with a continuing discussion of the case, a mediator can often orchestrate a "dance" of concessions to move the parties toward settlement.

d. Seek Out and Address Hidden Issues

The Challenge: Disregard of Hidden Issues and Missed Opportunities. Negotiations in legal cases are often blocked by hidden psychological obstacles. Participants in commercial mediation typically arrive with "game faces on," presenting a businesslike demeanor even as feelings boil beneath the surface. When this occurs, simply giving a disputant the chance to express emotions, as discussed earlier, is often not enough.

Response: Probe for and Deal with Hidden Issues. Even as you are carrying out other tasks, look for clues to hidden emotions and overly narrow approaches to settlement. Try to broaden the negotiation by identifying unexploited opportunities for gain that may include nonmonetary terms.

e. Test the Parties' Alternatives; If Necessary, Evaluate the Adjudication Option

The Challenge: Lack of Realism About the Outcome in Adjudication.   Participants in legal disputes often justify hard-bargaining positions in terms of the merits of the dispute. They are asking for a great deal or offering little, they say, because they have a strong legal case. Both parties usually claim that they will easily win in court. To some degree parties bluff about litigation options to justify their bargaining positions and do not expect to be taken literally. To a surprising degree, however, disputants actually believe their clashing predictions. There are two basic causes for disputants' distorted thinking about legal alternatives. One is lack of information; the other, an inability to accurately interpret available data because of psychological traps and lack of objectivity (outlined in Chapter 2).

Response: Foster an Information Exchange.   Even though discovery rules are meant to require each side to disclose key evidence, discovery may not be completed and it is often surprising how little one party knows about the other's case even after years of litigation. As a mediator, you can be an effective facilitator of information exchange. If, for example, a plaintiff has explained its theory of liability in detail but has given no explanation for its damage claim, you can suggest it flesh out damages to help the defendant get authority to settle. Parties will often respond cooperatively to a mediator's request, although they would have refused the same inquiry coming from their opponent.

Response: Reality Test.   Even when parties have the relevant information, we have seen that they often do not interpret it accurately. The least intrusive way to solve merits-based problems is through questions that help parties focus on evidence and issues they have glossed over. It is important both to ask questions pointed enough to prompt someone to confront a problem and to avoid comments so tough the disputant concludes the mediator has taken sides against her. Begin with open-ended questions asked in a spirit of curiosity; in this mode, you are simply trying to understand the dispute and the parties' arguments. ("Tell me what you think are the key facts here," or "Can you give me your take on the defendant's contract argument?") Your questions can progress gradually from open-ended queries ("Have you thought about . . . ?") to more pointed requests ("They are resisting making a higher offer because they believe you won't be able to prove causation . . . . What should I tell them?"). You might also want to take a party through an analysis of each element in the case, using systematic questions to prevent disputants from skipping over weaknesses. This can help counteract disputants' tendency to be overoptimistic. It also assists lawyers who are dealing with an unrealistic client, and can give a disputant a face-saving excuse for a compromise it secretly knows is necessary.

Response: Evaluative Feedback.   In some cases questions and analysis are not enough; a disputant might be wedded to an unrealistic viewpoint or require support to justify a settlement to a supervisor. In such situations, a commercial mediator may go further and offer an opinion about how a court is likely to decide a key issue or even the entire case. Evaluations can be structured in a wide variety of ways; for example, "My experience with state court judges is that they usually deny summary judgment in this kind of situation," or "If the plaintiff prevails on liability, what I know of San Francisco juries suggests they would value damages at somewhere between $125,000 and $150,000." You should never say how you *personally* would decide the case, but rather you should frame your opinion as a *prediction* of the attitude of an *outside decision maker*. Expressing one's personal opinion about what is "right" or "fair" in a dispute is almost always a bad idea, because it is likely to leave a listener feeling that the mediator has taken sides against him. Properly performed, a neutral evaluation can be helpful in producing an agreement, but a poorly done or badly timed opinion can be harmful to the process.

f. Break Bargaining Impasses

The Challenge: Closing the Final Gap.   Often barriers to agreement are too high, causing bargaining to stall and provoking an impasse.

Response: Persevere and Project Optimism.   When in doubt, persevere. Parties get stuck at some point during a mediation, often during the late afternoon or early evening, when energy levels decline and each side has made all the compromises it feels it ought to and more. The key thing to remember at this point is that the mediation probably *will* succeed; if you can keep the parties talking, they will find a solution. The disputants will be looking for signals about whether it is worth continuing, and it is important to send positive ones if possible within the bounds of reality.

Response: Invite Disputants to Take the Initiative.   Another simple tactic is to ask the disputants to take the initiative. You could say, "What do you think we should do?" and then wait quietly. If disputants realize they cannot simply "hang tough" and demand that the mediator produce results, they sometimes offer surprising ideas.

Response: Test Flexibility or Make a Mediator's Proposal.   Another option is to privately test the disputants' flexibility. Parties may refuse to offer anything more to an opponent but be willing to give private hints to you. You could, for example, ask "What if?" questions ("What if I could get them down to $150,000; would that keep the process going?") or propose bracketed bargaining ("If I can get the plaintiffs to come down on their demand to $300,000, would you up your offer to $100,000"). A mediator's proposal will often break an apparent impasse and produce agreement. Even if it doesn't, the proposal may prompt parties to rethink their positions and restart direct bargaining. (These techniques are explained more in the next chapter.)

Response: Adjourn and Follow-up.   If the disputants are psychologically spent or have run out of authority, the best response may be to adjourn temporarily. You can follow-up with shuttle diplomacy by telephone, propose a second, shorter mediation session, or set a deadline to prompt parties to make difficult decisions. This is true even if a mediator's proposal has been offered and rejected.

7. *"Deal Mediation"*

You now understand, as many practicing lawyers do, the potentially significant role that a mediator can play in facilitating negotiation, enhancing communication, and even transforming relationships. It should therefore come as no surprise that some have theorized about — and in some cases implemented — intervention strategies that apply these same principles at points "upstream" from active disputes.

In the following reading, one scholar asks a simple question: Could third-party mediators be helpful in negotiating deals, just as they are in disputes? He posits a potential role for mediators in helping the parties to overcome psychological, emotional, and relational barriers to reaching an agreement in commercial transactions.

❖ Scott R. Peppet, *Contract Formation in Imperfect Markets: Should We Use Mediators in Deals?*

38 Ohio St. J. on Disp. Resol. 283 (2004)

[M]any of the same barriers to negotiation that plague litigation settlement exist in commercial transactions, particularly during the closing stage of a deal when lawyers attempt to negotiate terms and conditions. [A] transactional mediator could help lawyers and clients to overcome such barriers. By a "transactional mediator," the author means an impartial person or entity that intervenes in a transactional negotiation pre-closing to facilitate the creation of a durable and efficient contract.

In one experiment, for example, small teams of experienced executives were given detailed information about two simulated companies. They were then assigned to represent one company or the other and asked to evaluate the companies and negotiate a merger. Although agreement was possible, only nine of the twenty-one pairings reached agreement. In addition, the executives disagreed wildly about the relevant valuations — selling prices ranged from $3.3 million to $16.5 million. This suggests that occasionally transacting parties fail to "close the deal" because of strategic posturing. [Moreover], as in litigation, transacting parties may fail to find Pareto-efficient agreements. . . . Information asymmetries and strategic posturing may lead to inefficiencies. . . . Interestingly, the researcher in this corporate acquisitions experiment re-ran the simulation offering each negotiating pair the service of a trained mediator, but not requiring that they use the mediator. Those executives that made use of the mediator reached more efficient contracts than those that did not. . . . [M]ediators should theoretically be able to help merging companies resolve disagreements over "social issues," such as how to name the post-merger corporation, how to resolve status and position questions (e.g., who will be CEO), and where to locate the new company's headquarters.

Howard Raiffa also suggests that a mediator might serve as a "contract embellisher" in transactions. [A]t the start of bargaining a mediator could privately interview each party about its needs, priorities, and perceptions. The mediator would lock away that information and the parties would be left alone to negotiate a deal. At the conclusion of their negotiation, but prior to closing the deal, the intervenor would return [. . .] try to use his private information about the parties' interests to craft a superior deal. He would then show his substitute agreement to each party privately. If both sides agreed that the mediator's suggestion was superior to their own contract, the substitution would be made. There would be no haggling about the terms of the mediator's proposal — it would be a take-it-or-leave-it situation. . . .

In complex transactions, lawyers, accountants, bankers, and other agents are generally brought in to assist in the closing stage. Lawyers in particular are needed to draft legal language for an acquisition agreement or other contract. As the closing stage progresses, due diligence may not eliminate all uncertainties about the company or assets in question [and] [l]awyers will therefore bargain over contract language to shift the risks associated with these remaining uncertainties.

A lawyer-mediator might prevent the parties' lawyers from blowing up the deal unnecessarily, and, perhaps more importantly, from reaching an inefficient set of contract terms. Although the bargaining about a single contract term may be largely distributive contracting attorneys can generally create value by trading between terms. For example, if a contract contains ten legal provisions (A, B, . . . J), parties X and Y will value those terms differently. If X finds term A extremely important and Y term B, they can create joint gains by allocating the risk in term A as X prefers and the risk in term B as Y prefers. And so on.

Empirical analysis of contracts shows that parties often do not trade risk in complex — yet value-creating — ways. Instead, in many domains contracts are simpler than one might expect. Various explanations have been offered for this simplicity, including behavioral explanations and the network effects theory. Another, less-explored, explanation is that the threat of strategic behavior prevents parties from complex contracting. To create a tailored term requires disclosing information about one's interests and preferences. This, again, permits exploitation. In the absence of trust, parties may resort to a standard term to minimize this risk.

A mediator might help the parties to overcome these strategic difficulties, thereby permitting more complex contracting. Again, a mediator can solicit and compare information from each side, potentially finding value-creating trades. The mediator might test the viability of various packages of trades of legal terms, asking each side in confidence which of several sets of terms the party would accept, but not revealing the origin of the various packages. In this way, the mediator can surmount the adverse selection problems that might otherwise prevent tailoring contract language during the deal's closing stage. . . .

[Besides helping the parties to overcome strategic barriers to transactions, mediators can also help them to overcome psychological barriers.] A neutral is in an ideal position to identify self-serving assessments by one or both parties. At a substantive level, if the neutral has sufficient expertise she can check each side's assumptions about "what's fair" and keep the parties from locking in to diverging stories about how a transaction should be priced or closed. Moreover, the mediator may be able to offer a neutral assessment or fair proposal that the parties will adopt. At a procedural or process level, a neutral can also help the parties avoid spinning very biased interpretations of how their bargaining is unfolding.

Negotiating parties must constantly assess information received from the other side. Research has shown, however, that negotiators . . . sometimes overly devalue an opponent's proposal or concession merely because their opponent made it. This phenomenon is known as "reactive devaluation." [A] neutral can help parties to overcome reactive devaluation in transactional bargaining by either adding noise to the parties' communication or proposing solutions of her own. Adding noise may be as simple as raising Party A's proposed solution privately with Party B without telling B that the idea came from Party A. If B assumes that the idea originated with the neutral, B may be more willing to consider it on the merits.

A neutral may be less susceptible to the endowment effect than a partisan agent, and therefore able to help parties to overcome it. For example, a neutral may be able to provide both sides with market information against which they can test their (biased) evaluations. This is particularly plausible vis-à-vis the legal terms and conditions in a contract. A lawyer-neutral might be familiar with the legal norms in a given context and be able to point the parties towards compromise legal language. Rather than start with a standard form or with a first draft, which would typically become the original endowment against which the parties compared, the neutral could manage the negotiation process so that the parties instead would work collaboratively to build a contract draft from framework through to completion.

In addition to managing information exchange and helping parties to overcome these cognitive and social psychological biases, a neutral can help parties to manage emotional and relational difficulties in their negotiations. This may facilitate trust and permit more efficient outcomes.

. . . [N]egotiation breakdowns occur in transactional bargaining, sometimes to the detriment of both parties. To some extent, agents such as investment bankers and lawyers already serve to mediate emotional conflicts during mergers, acquisitions, and other transactions. A neutral sometimes has an advantage over an agent in this regard, however. An agent may naturally take his client's perspective as given and discount the likelihood that the other side has a valid interpretation of events or more benign intentions than the client understands. A neutral positioned between two parties can often help them to gain such perspective. In strategic situations it is easy to assume that when the other bargainer "starts high" or "holds out," they do so because they intend to harm you or to treat you unfairly. Bargainers are less likely to attribute such actions to the exigencies of circumstance. By screening some overly opportunistic offers and at times sending fuzzy rather than clear information between the parties, a mediator can blunt such emotions and thereby keep the negotiations on track. Over time, avoiding emotional disagreements may help the parties to establish trust. This not only leads to more amiable negotiations, but also has serious substantive benefits. If the parties trust each other they may be better positioned to find value-creating solutions to their substantive differences. They may be able to rely more on informal agreements rather than contractual obligations and may be more flexible in the face of unexpected bumps in the road. Perhaps most importantly, they may avoid the destructive cycle of misattributions that can lead parties to "blow up" a deal or reach a Pareto-inefficient agreement.

D. Judicial Settlement Conferences and Court ADR Programs

1. Judge-Led Settlement Conferences

Judges have an interest in encouraging settlement and have always been available to informally provide assistance to lawyers and their clients. Our court system currently depends on having over 95 percent of all cases filed settled prior to trial. Judges often used Rule 16 of the Federal Rules of Civil Procedure and its state equivalents to discuss settlement possibilities with attorneys in pretrial conferences. In 1983, Rule 16 was amended to specify that judicially hosted pretrial conferences with lawyers included the purpose of facilitating settlement of the case. Fed. R. Civ. P. 16(a)(5). The rule now specifies that judges may "take appropriate action with respect to . . . settlement and the use of special procedures to assist in resolving the dispute when authorized by statute or local rules." Fed. R. Civ. P. 16(c)(9). In addition, judges may "require that a party or its representative be present or reasonably available by telephone in order to consider possible settlement of the dispute." Fed. R. Civ. P. 16(c).

A judge-led settlement conference is similar to an evaluative mediation, usually conducted in an abbreviated fashion. However, when the mediator wears a judicial robe, the evaluation tends to carry more weight, particularly if the judge will be making rulings in the case or is assigned to conduct the trial. Judicial settlement conferences can be thought of as "muscle mediations." Some mediators bristle at equating judicial settlement conferences with mediation because of the muscle factor, which they see as coercive. In fact, judicial settlement conferences can be as varied as the judges who conduct them and the time available. Some judges take their settlement role very seriously and perfect a mediation style that incorporates their judicial power, which may be welcomed by attorneys for some cases.

So what is it that judges provide to help overcome obstacles and assist in negotiation? Federal Judge Magistrate Wayne Brazil, drawing on his extensive experience and a survey of attorneys, summarized judicial assistance as follows:

> What judges have to contribute to settlement that lawyers value most is . . . penetrating, analytical exposition and thoughtful, objective, knowledgeable assessment. They want the perspective of the experienced neutral. Data . . . shows that a judge's opinion that a settlement offer is reasonable is likely to have a great affect on a recalcitrant client, especially if that client is not often involved in litigation.
>
> There also are many ways judges can contribute to the quality of the settlement dialogue itself: they can defuse emotions, set a constructive and analytical tone, help parties focus on the pertinent matters, and ask questions that expose underdeveloped areas. Judges can help keep litigants talking when they otherwise might retreat into noncommunication. In these and other ways, a judicial officer

can improve visibility, efficiency, and efficacy of the negotiation process." (*Settling Civil Cases*, 1984, 45-46)

2. Court ADR Programs

Some judges are better than others in moving parties toward settlement, and many judges question the appropriateness of direct judicial intervention in the settlement process. Recognizing the importance of promoting settlement to relieve civil caseloads and reduce delay and the limits of settlement conferences, judges convened bench-bar committees in the 1980s to recommend alternative methods to resolve cases. Local experimentation led to successes, which were replicated and refined in other jurisdictions. Traditional settlement conferences conducted by judges were augmented and sometimes replaced by more innovative dispute resolution options to assist negotiation. A rich array of court-connected ADR processes developed. Informal "settlement weeks" and case evaluation panels, both utilizing volunteer lawyers, led to statutes and court rules that required litigants to engage in ADR.

Mediation of different types, often conducted for the court by lawyers in their own offices, became the most popular form of court-directed ADR. Some courts hired full-time staff to direct and manage cases in ADR programs. The Alternative Dispute Resolution Act of 1998 requires all federal district courts to establish an ADR program by local rule. Participation in some settlement processes, including early neutral evaluation and mediation, can be compelled in federal courts, as in many state courts. (We consider the policy arguments about mandatory participation in Chapter 14.)

Although court ADR processes vary greatly, they share some common elements. Court ADR is intended to:

- Relieve each attorney from being the one to initiate settlement discussions.
- Provide a stimulus or requirement for attorneys to explore settlement early.
- Promote or require involvement of key decision makers.
- Use attorneys as neutrals to augment judicial resources.
- Provide more flexibility than formal adjudication.
- Avoid involving the judge who will preside at trial.

One perhaps unintended consequence of court-connected ADR programs, particularly mediation, has been to educate attorneys and business executives about the positive potential of nonbinding forms of ADR. Even though most cases entered the early court programs involuntarily, satisfaction rates were high. Occasional complaints about the quality of volunteer neutrals or bureaucratic restrictions could be remedied by having mutually respected neutrals serve for a fee privately, outside the court. Corporate and insurance clients faced with long waits in court and increased litigation expenses pushed for more use of private ADR. Plaintiffs' lawyers, reluctant at first, became more supportive of nonbinding, voluntary forms of ADR when they realized that these could speed settlement and collection of damages for clients in need and payment of their contingent fees. Greater efficiency, lower costs, more control, less risk, and improved outcomes were the driving forces for increased use of both court-based and private ADR. The seeds were planted for what would later become a change in the legal culture regarding how disputes are negotiated and resolved.

Mediation, with which you are now familiar, is the most widely used of ADR processes in court-connected programs. Other nonbinding settlement processes are available to help overcome the most common obstacle to negotiated agreement—different assessments of what will happen if the dispute goes to trial. If all parties had the same estimate of the court outcome in a contested case and how much a trial would cost, each side's BATNA would be similar. Settlement would be much easier. Several ADR mechanisms provide all parties with the same proxy or forecast of what will happen in court if negotiations fail. The principal distinctions between these ADR procedures is the nature of the assessment, at what point in the litigation process it is provided, and based on what degree of case presentation.

Trailing mediation, *nonbinding arbitration* and *early neutral evaluation* are the next two most frequently used court-connected ADR programs. Nonbinding arbitration occurs after substantial trial preparation is completed. An experienced trial attorney drawn from a court list hears adversarial presentations, in summary form, presented by the parties' attorneys. Witnesses are sometimes called and exhibits may be submitted. The arbitrator issues a monetary award or decision on the merits. If neither party objects, the award is entered as a court judgment to conclude the litigation. Any party may object to the award and request a trial de novo, usually at the risk of paying the other side's court costs if it does not do better at trial than it fared under the arbitration award. The parties, informed by the arbitration result, may, of course, negotiate a settlement.

Early neutral evaluation (ENE) is a process designed to improve settlement prospects by giving litigants an advisory evaluation of the case well before preparation for litigation is completed. The next reading describes the background, design, and results of a mandatory federal court ENE program. Although public funds are used to support court-connected settlement assistance programs and parties may be mandated to use them, little empirical research had been done to measure their benefit in federal courts prior to the Civil Justice Reform Act of 1990. The study reported below was one of the first to use a control group and combine quantitative data with qualitative surveys and interviews to determine if ENE promoted negotiated settlements.

❖ **Joshua Rosenberg & Jay Folberg,** ALTERNATIVE DISPUTE
RESOLUTION: AN EMPIRICAL ANALYSIS

46 Stan. L. Rev. 1487 (1994)

During the past decade, courts at every level have begun to use alternative dispute resolution (ADR) processes. What began as an experiment in the methods used to resolve family disputes is evolving into what may become the most significant changes in civil practice since the adoption of the Federal Rules in 1938. Indeed, some commentators have cautioned that ADR is becoming not merely a supplement to adjudication, but a replacement for it: Litigants are seeking ADR on their own initiative, courts are making ADR available to litigants who request it, and many state and federal courts have implemented mandatory ADR programs. Despite the growing reliance on ADR, there is scant empirical research about its effectiveness outside of family cases. . . .

This article adds to the empirical research by reporting on a quantitative and qualitative study of the ADR program of the United States District Court for the Northern District of California. The Northern District is one of six courts designated as demonstration districts in the Civil Justice Reform Act of 1990 (CJRA). Prior to the enactment of the CJRA, the Northern District had generated significant national interest in its design and use of an ADR procedure known as early neutral evaluation (ENE). Pursuant to the CJRA, the court retained the authors to evaluate its mandatory ENE program and suggest improvements.

Our most important findings include the following: (1) Approximately two-thirds of those who participated in the mandatory ADR program felt satisfied with the process and believed it worthy of the resources devoted to it (dissatisfaction with the program resulted primarily from dissatisfaction with the particular neutral assigned to the case); (2) while the percentage of parties who reported saving money approximately equaled the percentage who reported that the process resulted in a net financial cost, the net savings were, on average, more than ten times larger than the cost of an ENE session; (3) approximately half the participants in the program reported that participation decreased the pendency time of their cases; (4) the majority of parties and attorneys reported learning information in the ENE session that led to a fairer resolution of their case; and (5) the ENE process varied significantly from case to case and from neutral to neutral, and the most important factor in determining the success of the process in any one case was the individual neutral involved. . . .

The ENE process was intended to lie somewhere between mediation, in which a third party with substantial procedural expertise facilitates communication among the parties in the interest of settling some or all of the issues in dispute, and nonbinding arbitration, in which a third party with substantial subject matter expertise reviews the case presented by the litigants and determines an appropriate outcome. . . .

Specific Outcomes

After determining that ENE participants on average saved money and time and were satisfied with the process, we next sought to identify the specific outcomes that produced these results. We found that to a great extent ENE was accomplishing just what its originators had intended: The ENE program organized, streamlined, and generally increased the efficiency of discovery and trial preparation; in many cases, it increased prospects for early settlement; and almost all participants who were satisfied with the ENE process reported gaining a better understanding of both the law and the facts of the case. Moreover, these participants noted that subsequent settlement discussions were informed by, and furthered as a result of, this increased understanding.

Thirty-five percent of the parties and 23 percent of the attorneys reported that their cases settled either in ENE or as a direct result of it. Fifty-four percent of the attorneys and 52 percent of the parties reported that ENE increased the prospects for early settlement of their cases. . . .

In addition to requiring participants to focus on their case earlier, ENE also eliminated another significant obstacle to serious settlement discussions — the fear that initiating settlement discussion would give the other side a strategic negotiating advantage. In cases that did not go through ENE, 27 percent of the attorneys reported that earlier settlement discussions were impeded because neither side wanted to initiate such discussions out of fear of being perceived as weak. By forcing the parties to discuss their case and possible settlement at an early stage, ENE facilitated useful discussions that might never have commenced otherwise.

For many participants, the primary factor improving both settlement prospects and discovery planning was their increased understanding of the case. Thirty-five percent of the attorneys and 51 percent of the parties reported developing a better understanding of the legal issues involved in the case as a result of ENE, 46 percent of the attorneys and 40 percent of the parties reported developing a better understanding of the factual issues, 42 percent of the parties reported developing a better understanding of the litigation process, and 70 percent of the parties reported gaining a better understanding of the other side's perception of the case.

The greater understanding that attorneys and parties developed in ENE also helped them more realistically evaluate their case. Sixty-seven percent of the parties and 52 percent of the attorneys stated that, as a result of the ENE process, they developed a more realistic assessment of the likely outcome of their cases, and that their changed assessment made at least a moderate contribution to improving the prospects for earlier settlement. Of those who did not go through ENE, 41 percent of attorneys reported that their own failure to fully understand the case impeded serious settlement discussions, and 53 percent reported that the other side's failure to understand the case impeded the successful conclusion of settlement discussions. A total of 57 percent of the non-ENE attorneys reported increased costs and fees because one or more sides did not have an adequate understanding of the case early on.

In addition to learning about the law and facts of their cases, ENE participants also gained valuable insights into procedural aspects of the litigation. Fifty-two percent of the parties and 31 percent of the attorneys stated that their development of a more realistic assessment of the costs of continuing litigation through trial improved settlement prospects.

Because ENE so effectively increased participants' understanding of their cases, many participants believed that when issues were resolved in or as a result of ENE the outcome was not only quicker but also fairer than it otherwise would have been. . . .

Notes and Questions

A subsequent, controversial study of six federal court ADR programs, four involving mediation and two using ENE, was less favorable. Known as the "RAND Study," it concluded that "we have no strong statistical evidence that lawyer work hours [or time to disposition] are significantly affected by mediation or neutral evaluation in any of the six programs studied . . ."

(Kakalik et al., 1996). However, another study by the Federal Judicial Center of five different federal courts was more encouraging (see Stienstra et al., 1997).

7. Based on what you know about early neutral evaluations and nonbinding arbitration, what cases are most appropriate, or inappropriate, for each process?

8. If you represented a small manufacturer with limited resources, sued for unlicensed use of another's patented manufacturing process, and settlement negotiations have failed, should your client be compelled to participate in a judicial settlement conference? See G. Heileman Brewing Co. v. Joseph Oat Corp., 871 F.2d 648 (7th Cir. 1989). See also FRCP 16 (b). Summary jury trial? See Strandell v. Jackson County, Illinois, 838 F.2d 884 (7th Cir. 1988). An early neutral evaluation? Are your arguments for one or the other of these processes different?

9. May the court compel the defendant's nonparty insurance company to attend a settlement conference if it appears there is coverage? See In re Novak, 932 F.2d 1397 (11th Cir. 1991).

10. If a court compels participation in a settlement program, what level of participation is required? Can anyone be compelled to settle? To speak? Can "good faith" participation be required? If so, how might "good faith" be defined? See John Lande, *Using Dispute System Design Models to Promote Good-Faith Participation in Court-Mandated Mediation Programs*, 50 UCLA L. Rev. 69 (2002); Edward F. Sherman, *Court-Mandated Alternative Dispute Resolution: What Form of Participation Should be Required?*, 46 SMU L. Rev. 2079 (1993).

11. In the above situation for the same client, if your client did agree to participate in one of the court's ADR programs, could you insist that it be conducted confidentially, without public or press access? See Cincinnati Gas & Electric Co. v. General Elec. Co., 854 F.2d 900 (6th Cir.1988).

12. Assuming it is appropriate for courts to compel participation in their ADR programs, may or should the courts require the parties to pay administrative costs? Should the lawyer neutrals in court ADR programs be compensated for their time? If so, who should pay them?

The *mini-trial*, which has more accurately been called "maxi-negotiation," evolved primarily as a private process outside the courts. In the 1980s, the CPR Institute for Dispute Resolution and other organizations promoting ADR in the business arena touted the benefits of mini-trials. The process is unique in that it brings together key decision makers from each party as members of a panel hearing "best shot" presentations of evidence and arguments by advocates for each side for each party to the controversy — thus potentially laying a foundation for focused negotiations aimed at settlement, which follow immediately upon the conclusion of the "hearing." In the typical mini-trial proceeding, principals of each party sit on either side of a neutral third-party referee or mini-trial "judge," who supervises the process. As lawyers for the parties present rigorously abbreviated cases, with summaries of best evidence (including, perhaps, videos of key witnesses) and arguments, the principals and the referee act as inquisitors, probing the main elements of each party's case. At the conclusion of the presentations, the principals have the opportunity to negotiate face-to-face, perhaps with the assistance of the neutral. The latter may at some point be called upon to offer a nonbinding advisory opinion regarding a resolution of the controversy. See ABA, Sub-committee on Alternative Means of Dispute Resolution, *The Effectiveness of the Mini-Trial in Resolving Complex Commercial Disputes: A Survey* (1986). Mini-trials are not widely used today, largely because of their expense and the significant lawyer and executive time they require. Moreover, when a mini-trial is not used until the conclusion of discovery, the possibility of deriving significant cost savings is substantially diminished. Today, whether or not they are so described, abbreviated mini-trial formats are sometimes employed in the context of mediation. Can you think of any types of cases in which a mini-trial might be cost effective and worth the effort?

3. A Perspective on ADR Principles

As a U.S. Magistrate Judge in California's Northern District, Wayne Brazil directed one of the nation's most innovative, multifaceted court-connected ADR programs and has written extensively on settlement. Here he examines the toxic tort litigation of families in Woburn, Massachusetts, depicted in the book *A Civil Action*, from which you read in Chapter 5 about a failed negotiation involving plaintiffs' lawyer Schlichtmann. Judge Brazil discusses another aspect of the obstacles to negotiation in that case and what the defendants might have done to promote an earlier settlement.

❖ Wayne Brazil, *A Judge's Perspective on Lawyering and ADR*

19 Alternatives 44 (Jan. 2001)

I choose . . . to examine a specific case — to search in the social wreckage it represents for lessons about lawyering and ADR — lessons that may apply broadly, from lawyering for the little guy(s) to lawyering in self-perceived cynicism for the largest of economic stakes.

The case is *Anderson v. Cryovac Inc.*, also known as *Anderson v. W.R. Grace, Co. and Beatrice Foods*, but best known, simply, as "A Civil Action." Made famous by a book and movie, this litigation pitted 33 individual plaintiffs against large corporations. The plaintiffs alleged that the defendants had contaminated the local public water supply — and that contamination was responsible for the deaths of five children and for serious injuries and illnesses suffered by other children and by adults.

My interest here is not in how the case was litigated, but on how it wasn't lawyered. With the benefit of hindsight, disengagement, and the considerable developments in ADR since the mid-1980s (when the case was tried), I would like to use this case to make an argument about what really good, really professionally responsible lawyering should be all about — and to show how essential a problem solving spirit, aided by ADR processes, is to lawyering that aspires to deem itself "the highest quality."

Many of the plaintiffs in "A Civil Action" had suffered in the most severe of ways — physically and emotionally. They felt confused, alone, and betrayed — even though they weren't sure by whom. Some probably felt, at some level, guilty and responsible for the terrible things that their children and they had suffered. They remained both afraid and angry. They wanted answers. Why did this happen? Who was really responsible? Can anything be done about the present and the future? They wanted help dealing with the consequences of their tragedies. They wanted restoration of and to their community.

Lawyers with insufficient vision might say that the plaintiffs were naive to think that they could achieve these kinds of ends through the legal system. Certainly the system as it was actually used by the lawyers who handled the case, traditionally and narrowly over a period of eight years, delivered precious little toward these ends. The transaction costs (not counting a dime of settlement money) were well above $15 million. But the huge investment of money and time yielded a judgment and a settlement that brought no answers to the biggest questions, no emotional healing, no restoration of community, no repair of severely damaged good will, and addressed only modestly the plaintiffs' need to respond financially to the consequences of their injuries (each plaintiff received through settlement about $100,000).

Really good lawyers, however, would have understood that in the aftermath of the tragedy there was an opportunity to build — to use ADR to create new, long-range value of great significance. What could have been?

Let's look at the situation primarily through the eyes of the defendant corporations. Even if the only value that really mattered to the defendants was profit, a good lawyer would have counseled them to move in a very different direction — and to use ADR to do so.

The defendants knew that the U.S. Environmental Protection Agency[EPA] had designated the accused area as a Superfund site and had been investigating the extent and sources of the obvious contamination for some time before the lawsuit was filed. The defendants knew that they were required by law to cooperate fully with the EPA investigation. The defendants knew that there was a substantial possibility that the EPA would order them to contribute toward the cost of clean up. The defendants knew that the U.S. Geological Survey also was studying contamination in the area. And the defendants should have known that if they were not truthful with federal authorities, the U.S. Department of Justice might well intervene. In fact, the Justice Department ultimately indicted one of the corporate defendants for just such untruthfulness — and that defendant ultimately pled guilty.

The defendants also could foresee that a case like this would generate a great deal of press coverage (as it did), and that the defendants would not be favored in the sympathy slant (77% of people polled in surveys taken as the trial date approached believed that the corporate defendants were responsible for the deaths of the children). Moreover, two of the three companies that ended up being pulled into the case knew they would remain in the community — that they would employ local workers, work with local politicians, and need local services.

Given these circumstances, a good lawyer would have counseled his or her client to use an ADR process early in the pretrial period — well before most of the litigation transaction costs were incurred and before the litigation process further alienated the plaintiffs and rigidified their positions. The goal would be to use ADR to explore what was most important to the plaintiffs themselves (as opposed to their lawyers), to de-demonize the defendants, and to reach out to the plaintiffs in a constructive and civic spirit that might make it possible to work out a settlement that would simultaneously save the defendants money and yield potentially huge public relations benefits.

A good lawyer would have urged each corporate defendant to send its chairman or its CEO to the ADR session — to demonstrate graphically that the company understood the gravity of the losses that plaintiffs had suffered. This was a big case — economically, "politically," and emotionally. Direct participation by the highest level corporate officers was fully justified (by financial considerations alone) and would have improved the odds, considerably, that the companies' presentations would elicit favorable responses from the plaintiffs.

A good lawyer would have advised the representative of the company to begin the neutraled ADR session by listening to the plaintiffs — actively, openly, and sympathetically. After listening, the CEO or chairman would seek an opportunity to speak directly to the plaintiffs (in the presence of their lawyers and the neutral) and would communicate, gently, the following messages and proposals.

He would begin by telling the plaintiffs how sorry he and his company were about what had happened to them. Then he would say that he really doesn't understand what the causes were of these tragedies — but that he wants to. He would explain that the scientists who advise him do not think that chemicals from his operations reached the wells or caused the illnesses, and he would emphasize that he and his staff never would have permitted the operations to proceed if he had known that they would cause such effects. But he would concede that no one knows enough about the sources of these kinds of illnesses to be completely sure — so one of his goals will be to support the effort to learn from these tragedies.

He would propose doing that in two ways. One would be to cooperate fully with the EPA and all other governmental agencies who are investigating these matters. He would promise that his company would open its records and provide the authorities promptly with all the information and other forms of assistance they might seek. The second way his company (along with the other defendants) would support the search for answers would be to contribute several million dollars directly to support research into the possibility that there are environmental causes of leukemia.

In making these proposals, the spokesman for the company would emphasize that many of the company's valued and longtime employees live here — so it is partly on their behalf that he wants to help find out why this happened. But the spokesman also would emphasize that the company wants to be a responsible and valued member of this community — and thus wants to identify with certainty any aspects of its operations that might cause harm to any other members of the community.

Next, the CEO or chairman would commit the company to contribute its full fair share to the cost of cleaning up the contaminated area. He would say that even though it is not clear that the contamination that has been found caused the cancer, it is clear that the contamination is a legitimate source of concern and must be removed. So the company, the spokesman would say, stands ready to pay (toward the cost of the cleanup) whatever share the government scientists conclude is appropriate. The company representative also would say that the company would do everything it can to speed up the process of making that determination and to press for completion of the cleanup work on as fast a timetable as possible.

To evidence the company's good faith, the representative then would say that none of the commitments just described are contingent on the case settling. The company intends to go forward with them — including the commitment to support the cancer research, even if the parties cannot reach an agreement that would end the litigation.

Finally, the spokesman, on behalf of the defendants as a group, would offer money to help the plaintiffs meet the needs they face. The spokesman would start by acknowledging that no amount of money could adequately compensate for the personal losses that have been suffered — but also that the tragedies have had real and damaging consequences that require resources. The defendants collectively would like to provide some of those resources — and toward that end they are offering the plaintiffs, as a group, $10 million.

Making a package of proposals like this early in the pretrial period would have encouraged a perception that defendants were sincerely sorry about the plaintiffs' losses and wanted not only to act responsibly, but also as real members of a shared community. The likelihood that the plaintiffs would not have responded positively to such an offer is quite small. Good lawyers for them would have encouraged acceptance.

With acceptance of this offer, the defendants would have saved considerable money. They also would have generated considerable positive press and good will — and avoided the years of bad press (to say nothing of the criminal indictment) that accompanied the protracted litigation. Moreover, they would have distinguished themselves from their competitors — encouraging investors to perceive them as possessing especially acute business judgment — and so worthy of investment confidence.

It is clear that there is a very real chance that a scenario like the one described here could have occurred. That real possibility demonstrates, contrary to a high visibility suggestion to the contrary, that statesmanship actually can have a great deal to do with good lawyering. Breadth of solution-vision can be an essential tool even in pursuing narrow client interests. And a lawyer who cannot help his or her client explore problem-solving solutions simply cannot be considered a wise counselor.

Questions

13. Do you think Judge Brazil's admonitions are realistic? What barriers might there be — on the defendants' side, the plaintiffs' side, or elsewhere — to successfully executing the scenario he contemplates?

14. Was the outcome a bad result for the defendants? Despite the high cost of trial and negative press, the remaining defendants paid only about $3 million in settlement following trial, compared to more than $400 million demanded by the plaintiffs in the early hotel scene. Was this a lose-lose outcome, as implied by Judge Brazil, or a lose-win outcome in favor of the defendants?

15. How do Judge Brazil's comments and proposed conduct relate to ADR?

CHAPTER
13

Mediating for Negotiation Advantage

A. Introduction

Lawyers earn fees by offering something of value to clients. The value added in negotiations is the expertise and skill to help clients fulfill their needs and obtain their goals. When obstacles to a negotiated agreement get in the way of fulfilling a client's needs, lawyers, as we saw in the last chapter, may turn to mediation. The lawyer's role in mediation continues to be adding value by helping to fulfill the needs of clients and obtaining their goal. Now the lawyer is enlisting the mediator to reach an agreement favorable to his client.

Mediators of legal disputes have significant power, whether or not they decide to use it. Although mediators cannot compel parties to settle, they can greatly influence the *process* of bargaining, opening opportunities for advocates to mold the process to their clients' needs. Lawyers can use the mediation process to their advantage by approaching it actively and keeping in mind its special characteristics.

Modern mediation has been shaped by the concepts of principled negotiation and problem solving. Advocacy, advantage, and winning are words not usually associated with these concepts. However, people would not rationally choose to mediate if they did not feel that it would be to their advantage compared to the alternatives. So, attorneys must be proactive throughout the mediation process to help it work to their clients' advantage. Advocacy in mediation may look and feel different than it does in some forms of direct negotiation or trial, but it is nonetheless advocacy to fulfill your client's interests.

The first important issue to decide is what goal your client wants to achieve in mediation. Is the client seeking the best possible monetary outcome? An imaginative solution? Repair of a relationship? The desired goal will strongly influence the approach you take to the mediation process and how you relate to the mediator.

An organization that advocates the use of ADR in business disputes stresses that, "Mediation provides a framework for parties to . . . achieve remedies that may be outside the scope of the judicial process . . . maintain privacy . . . preserve or minimize damage to relationships and reduce the costs and delay of dispute resolution" (CPR Institute 1999). By contrast, a prominent tort lawyer, exemplifying a more traditional approach, describes mediation as "an opportunity — a time for you, as the legal representative of your client, to avoid putting your client through the litigation 'mill' . . . and get results. . . . It is a means of essentially 'selling' your client's lawsuit to a buyer, who buys off the expense and exposure of an ongoing lawsuit. The client has the money to begin the life restructuring process and has avoided the pressures and uncertainties of litigation . . ." (Kornblum, 2004).

If you see your objective as solving a problem or repairing a relationship, you will be inclined to treat the mediator almost as a member of your team, revealing your interests and soliciting the neutral's advice about how to achieve them. If the focus is on relationship repair, both lawyer and mediator may gradually withdraw as the process progresses to give the parties an opportunity to relearn how to communicate directly and positively. If, however, your goal is to obtain the best possible monetary settlement, your relationship with the mediator will be different. You can continue to take advantage of the neutral's knowledge, for example, by asking about hidden negotiation obstacles, and if you employ principled bargaining techniques you will be able to work together cooperatively. However, at the point that you begin to compete with the other side for the best possible terms, your goal and that of the neutral may diverge, because the mediator cannot take sides. Indeed, competitive bargainers talk about "spinning" a mediator to advance their client's objectives. They also see themselves as bargaining not simply with the other side, but also with the mediator, in a three-sided process. Attorneys bargain with neutrals, for example, over what the mediator will say about their offers to their opponent, what she will tell them about the attitudes of persons in the other camp, and whether and how the mediator will employ impasse-breaking tactics such as evaluation or a mediator's proposal.

There is another potential advantage of using mediation to assist in negotiating a good outcome. As a lawyer you may recognize that your client's unrealistic evaluation or intractable attitude is part of the problem and a barrier to a reasonable settlement. Not wanting to alienate or lose your client, you may enlist the mediator to help persuade a "difficult" or "unrealistic" client to look at the case from a different perspective. This is not inconsistent with acting in your client's best interests; you, in effect, are recruiting the mediator to become an ally in getting the best for your client. In doing so, you are taking advantage of the mediator's neutrality and allowing the mediator to be an advocate for settlement.

B. Initial Strategy

1. General Advice

We first consider the role of advocacy in mediation and how to take advantage of the opportunities offered by the process. What constitutes a "winning" strategy in mediation, and is it possible that the other advocate could play a role in achieving it? Consider this advice from an experienced commercial mediator.

❖ **Jeffrey G. Kichaven,** *HOW ADVOCACY FITS IN EFFECTIVE MEDIATION*

17 Alternatives 60 (1999)

Clients and attorneys generally have one of two conceptions of what it means to win in mediation. Some define winning as "clobbering the other side." Others see it as "the satisfaction of our own needs," regardless of whether the other side suffers along the way. In the litigation context, and in many others, clients often start out in a "clobbering" mode. They may believe they have been "done wrong," and want revenge. And more revenge. And more.

This is a serious problem for lawyers. Such a client is almost never satisfied with the result, with the process, or with counsel's performance, because the other side, no matter how badly clobbered, rarely has suffered enough. A vengeful client . . . has a hard time planning, in advance, the specific result to be achieved or the goal against which success or failure will be measured. No matter what happens to the other side, it could always have been worse! These clients believe that their attorneys have failed them. Yet the lawyers have done all that they can. Far better is the situation in which the client focuses on the satisfaction of his or her own needs. This client is better able to give clear instructions and if the client's own goals are satisfied, it doesn't matter very much whether the other side suffers a lot, a little, or even at all.

Mediation has an important role in the pursuit of this second concept of the win . . . In the hands of skilled mediators and counsel, the process can be designed to minimize the incentives to clobber and enhance the likelihood that the parties will engage in goal-oriented, client-satisfying negotiation.

In mediation after mediation, clients and lawyers come to change their negotiating tune. The desire for revenge is trumped by a desire for finality: A desire to eliminate the newly perceived enhanced risks of continued litigation; to eliminate the certainty of the mental, emotional and financial drains of conflict; and to get on with one's career and life with a "bird in the hand" settlement. . . . The key to all this, however, is profoundly counterintuitive. In mediation, your effectiveness as an advocate will vary in direct proportion to that of opposing counsel, not the inverse proportion you might expect in the generally "clobbering" mode of traditional litigation.

In this sense, you and opposing counsel have become each other's best friends. You have given each other's clients what you often cannot give your own: The means by which one can achieve a balanced perspective . . . with the craving to clobber taking a back seat. Let's face it: It's tough for a lawyer to break bad news to his or her own client. It's tough on clients, too, to go beyond denial, even when that bad news is broken with candor and compassion. Yet in virtually every unsettled case, bad news needs to be broken and accepted. In some cases, it's the other side that needs it. In others, it's your side. In most cases, there's plenty of bad news to go around.

In mediation, you and opposing counsel have found uniquely qualified messengers to deliver this essential communication — each other. The mediator works along with you to make sure that the bad news is not only delivered to your client, but also received. Effective mediation advocates, therefore, must be able to hold both conceptions of "the win" in mind simultaneously, side by side, each in its appropriate place, each conception taking the forefront when appropriate.

Although the following reading lists common problems in mediation strategy, the list provides a clear message about what lawyers can do to be effective in mediation.

❖ **Tom Arnold,** *Twenty Common Errors in Mediation Advocacy*

13 Alternatives 69 (1995)

Trial lawyers who are unaccustomed to being mediation advocates often miss important opportunities. Here are twenty common errors, and ways to correct them.

Problem: Wrong Client in the Room

CEOs settle more cases than vice presidents, house counsel, or other agents. Why? For one thing, they don't need to worry about criticism back at the office. Any lesser agent, even with explicit "authority," typically must please a constituency which was not a participant in the give and take of the mediation. That makes it hard to settle cases.

A client's personality also can be a factor. A "Rambo" who is highly self-confident, aggressive, critical, unforgiving, or self-righteous doesn't tend to be conciliatory. The best peace-makers show patience, creativity and sometimes tolerance for the mistakes of others. Of course, it also helps to know the subject.

Problem: Wrong Lawyer in the Room

Many capable trial lawyers are so confident that they can persuade a jury of anything (after all, they've done it before) that they discount the importance of preserving relationships, as well as the common exorbitant costs and emotional drain of litigation. They can smell a "win" in the court room, and so approach mediation with a measure of ambivalence. Transactional lawyers, in contrast, having less confidence in their trial outcome, sometimes are better mediation counsel. At a minimum, parties should look for sensitive, flexible, understanding people who will do their homework, no matter what their job experience. Good preparation makes for more and better settlements. A lawyer who won't prepare is the wrong lawyer. Good mediation lawyers also should be good risk evaluators and not averse to making reasonable risk assumptions.

Problem: Wrong Mediator in the Room

Some mediators are generous about lending their conference rooms, but bring nothing to the table. Some of them determine their view of the case and like an arbitrator urge the parties to accept that view without exploring likely win-win alternatives. The best mediators can work within a range of styles described by Leonard L. Riskin. As Mr. Riskin described them, these styles fall along a continuum from being totally facilitative, to offering an evaluation of the case, to being highly directive and adjudicative. Ideally, mediators should fit the mediation style to the case and the parties before them, often moving from style to style as a mediation progresses, relatively more facilitative at the beginning and more instructive or directive as the end comes into view. Masters of the questioning process can render valuable services whether or not they have relevant substantive expertise.

When do the parties need an expert? When do they want an evaluative mediator, or someone of relevant technical experience who can cast meaningful lights and shadows on the merits of the case and alternative settlements? It may not always be possible to know and evaluate a mediator and fit the choice of mediator to your case. But the wrong mediator may fail to get a settlement another mediator might have finessed.

Problem: Wrong Case

Almost every type of case, from antitrust or patent infringement to unfair competition and employment disputes, is a likely candidate for mediation. Occasionally, cases don't fit the mold, not because of the substance of the dispute, but because one or both parties want to set a precedent. For example, a franchisor that needs a legal precedent construing a key clause that is found in 3,000 franchise agreements might not want to submit the case to mediation. Likewise, an infringement suit early in the life of an uncertain patent might be better resolved in court; getting the Federal Circuit stamp of validity could generate industry respect not obtainable from ADR.

Problem: Omitting Client Preparation

Lawyers should educate their clients about the process and the likely questions the mediator will ask. At the same time, they need to understand that the other party (rather than the mediator) should be the focus of each side's presentation.

Problem: Not Letting a Client Open for Herself

At least as often as not, letting the properly coached client do most or even all of the opening, and tell the story in her own words, works much better than lengthy openings by the lawyer.

Problem: Addressing the Mediator Instead of the Other Side

Most lawyers open the mediation with a statement directed at the mediator, comparable to opening statements to a judge or jury. Highly adversarial in tone, it overlooks the interests of the other side that gave rise to the dispute. Why is this strategy a mistake? The "judge" or "jury" you should be trying to persuade in mediation is not so much the mediator as the adversary. If you want to make the other party sympathetic to your cause, most often at least it is best not to hurt him. For the same reason, plenary sessions should demonstrate your client's humanity, respect, warmth, apologies, and sympathy. Stay away from inflammatory issues, which are better addressed by the mediator in private caucuses with the other side.

Problem: Making the Lawyer the Center of the Process

Unless the client is highly unappealing or inarticulate, the client should be the center of the process. The company representative for the other side may not have attended depositions, so is unaware of the impact your client could have on a judge or jury if the mediation fails. People pay more attention to appealing plaintiffs, so show them off.

Prepare the client to speak and be spoken to by the mediator and the adversary. He should be able to explain why he feels the way he does, why he is or is not responsible, and why any damages he caused are great or only peanuts. But he should also consider extending empathy to the other party.

Problem: Failure to Use Advocacy Tools Effectively

You'll want to prepare your materials for maximum persuasive impact. Exhibits, charts, and copies of relevant cases or contracts with key phrases highlighted can be valuable visual aids. A ninety-second video showing one or more key witnesses in depositions making important admissions, followed by a readable-sized copy of an important document with some relevant language underlined, can pack a punch.

Problem: Timing Mistakes

Get and give critical discovery, but don't spend exorbitant time or sums in discovery and trial prep before seeking mediation. Mediation can identify what's truly necessary discovery and avoid unnecessary discovery.

One of my own war stories: With a mediation under way and both parties relying on their perception of the views of a certain neutral vice president who had no interest in the case, I leaned over, picked up the phone, called the vice president, introduced myself as the mediator, and asked whether he could give us a deposition the following morning. "No," said he, "I've got a board meeting at 10:00." "How about 7:30 A.M., with a one-hour limit?" I asked. "It really is pretty important that this decision not be delayed." The parties took the deposition and settled the case before the 10:00 board meeting.

Problem: Failure to Listen to the Other Side

Many lawyers and clients seem incapable of giving open-minded attention to what the other side is saying. That could cost a settlement.

Problem: Failure to Identify Perceptions and Motivations

Seek first to understand, only then to be understood. [B]rainstorm to determine the other party's motivations and perceptions. Prepare a chart summarizing how your adversary sees the issues: Part of preparing for mediation is to understand your adversary's perceptions and motivations, perhaps even listing them in chart form. Here is an example, taken from a recent technology dispute:

Plaintiff's Perceptions:	*Defendant's Perceptions:*
Defendant entered the business because of my sound analysis of the market, my good judgment and convictions about the technology.	I entered the business based on my own independent analysis of the market and the appropriate technology that was different from plaintiff's. . . .
Defendant used me by pretending to be interested in doing business with me.	Plaintiff misled me with exaggerated claims that turned out to be false.
Defendant made a low-ball offer for my valuable technology. Another company paid me my asking price.	I made plaintiff a fair offer; I later paid less for alternative technology that was better.

Problem: Hurting, Humiliating, Threatening, or Commanding

Don't poison the well from which you must drink to get a settlement. That means you don't hurt, humiliate, or ridicule the other folks. Avoid pejoratives like "malingerer," "fraud," "cheat," "crook," or "liar." You can be strong on what your evidence will be and still be a decent human being. All settlements are based upon trust to some degree. If you anger the other side, they won't trust you. This inhibits settlement.

The same can be said for threats, like a threat to get the other lawyer's license revoked for pursuing such a frivolous cause, or for his grossly inaccurate pleadings. Ultimatums destroy the process and destroy credibility. Yes, there is a time in mediation to walk out — whether or not you plan to return. But a series of ultimatums, or even one ultimatum, most often is counterproductive.

Problem: The Backwards Step

A party who offered to pay $300,000 before the mediation, but comes to the mediation table willing to offer only $200,000, injures its own credibility and engenders bad feelings from the other side. Without some clear and dramatic reasons for the reduction in the offer, it can be hard to overcome the damage done. The backwards step is a powerful card to play at the right time — a walk away without yet walking out. But powerful devices are also dangerous. There are few productive occasions to use this one, and they tend to come late in a mediation. A rule of thumb: Unless you're an expert negotiator, don't do it.

Problem: Too Many People

Advisors — people to whom the decision-maker must display respect and courtesy, people who feel that since they are there they must put in their two bits worth — all delay mediation immeasurably. A caucus that with only one lawyer and vice president would take twenty minutes, with five people could take an hour and twenty minutes. What could have been a one-day mediation stretches to two or three.

This is one context in which I use the "one martini lunch." Once I think that everyone present understands all the issues, I will send principals who have been respectful out to negotiate alone. Most come back within three hours with an oral expression of settlement. Of course, the next step is to brush up on details they overlooked, draw up a written agreement and get it signed. But usually those finishing touches don't ruin the deal.

Problem: Closing Too Fast

A party who opens at $1 million and moves immediately to $500,000 gives the impression of having more to give. Rightly or wrongly, the other side probably will not accept the $500,000 offer because they expect more give. By contrast, moving from $1 million to $750,000, $600,000, $575,000, $560,000, $550,000, sends no message of yield below $500,000, and may induce a $500,000 proposal that can be accepted. The "dance" is part of communication. Skip the dance, lose the communication, and risk losing settlement at your own figure.

Problem: Failure to Truly Close

Unless parties have strong reasons to "sleep on" their agreement, to further evaluate the deal, or to check on possibly forgotten details, it is better to get some sort of enforceable contract written and signed before the parties separate. Too often, when left to think overnight and draft tomorrow, the parties think of new ideas that delay or prevent closing.

Problem: Breaching Confidentiality

Sometimes parties to mediation unthinkingly, or irresponsibly, disclose in open court information revealed confidentially in a mediation. When information is highly sensitive, consider keeping it confidential with the mediator. Or if revealed to the adversary in a mediation where the case did not settle, consider moving before the trial begins for an order in limine to bind both sides to the confidentiality agreement.

Problem: Lack of Patience and Perseverance

The mediation "dance" takes time. Good mediation advocates have patience and perseverance.

Problem: Misunderstanding Conflict

A dispute is a problem to be solved together, not a combat to be won.

Questions

1. Most attorneys using commercial mediation are trial lawyers, who generally view claims and litigation as a competition for dollars. Do you think Arnold's list of problems applies to all lawyers, or just to competitive advocates?
2. Can you recast Arnold's list of problems as positive statements about how to be effective in mediation?

Next, Professor Abramson picks up on Tom Arnold's last point about a dispute being a problem to solve and explains how to represent clients in mediation as a zealous, problem-solving advocate.

❖ **Harold Abramson,** *MEDIATION REPRESENTATION:*
ADVOCATING IN A PROBLEM-SOLVING PROCESS

1 (NITA, 2004)

The mediation process is indisputably different from other dispute resolution processes. Therefore, the strategies and techniques that have proven so effective in settlement conferences, arbitrations, and judicial trials do not work optimally in mediation. You need a different representation approach. . . . Instead of advocating as a zealous adversary, you should advocate as a zealous problem-solver. . . .

[I]n mediation there is no third party decisionmaker, only a third party facilitator. The third party is not even the primary audience. The primary audience is the other side, who is surely not neutral and can often be quite hostile. In this different representational setting, the adversarial approach is less effective, if not self-defeating. Many sophisticated and experienced litigators realize that mediation calls for a different approach, but they still muddle through mediation sessions. They are learning on the job. . . .

As a problem-solver . . . you do more than just try to settle the dispute. You creatively search for solutions that go beyond the traditional ones based on rights, obligations, and precedent. Rather than settling for win-lose outcomes, you search for solutions that can benefit both sides. To creatively problem-solve in mediation, you develop a collaborative relationship with the other side and the mediator, and participate throughout the mediation process in a way that is likely to result in solutions that are enduring as well as inventive. . . .

You should be a constant problem-solver. It is relatively easy to engage in simple problem-solving moves such as responding to a demand with the question "why?" in order to bring to the surface the other party's interests. But it is much more difficult to stick to this approach throughout the mediation process, especially when faced with an adversarial, positional opponent. Trust the problem-solving approach. And, when the other side engages in adversarial tactics — a frequent occurrence in practice — you should react with problem-solving responses, responses that might even convert the other side into a problem-solver.

Also strive to create a problem-solving process when your mediator does not. Your mediator may fail to follow this approach (even though he professes to foster one) because he lacks the depth of experience or training to tenaciously maintain a consistent approach throughout the mediation process. Or, your mediator may candidly disclose his practice of deliberately switching tactics based on the needs of the parties — a philosophy that . . . undermines the problem-solving approach.

Finally, for the skeptics who think that problem-solving does not work for most legal cases because they are primarily about money, I offer three responses. First, the endless debate about whether or not legal disputes are primarily about money is distracting. Whether a dispute is largely about money varies from case to case. You have little chance of discovering whether your client's dispute is about more than money if you approach the dispute as if it is only about money. Such a preconceived view, backed by a narrowly focused adversarial strategy, will likely blind you to other parties' needs and inventive solutions. . . .

Second, if the dispute or any remaining issues at the end of the day turn out to be predominately about money, then at least you will have followed a representation approach that may have created a hospitable environment for dealing with the money issues. A hospitable environment can even be beneficial when there is no expectation of a continuing relationship between the disputing parties. Third, the problem-solving approach provides a framework for resolving money issues. . . .

In short, the problem-solving approach provides a comprehensive and coherent approach to representation that can guide you throughout the mediation process. By sticking to this approach, you will be prepared to deal with the myriad of unanticipated challenges that inevitably arise as mediation unfolds.

---

2. When to Mediate

Assuming that mediation is appropriate for your client's needs, when is the right time to undertake it? Sometimes there is no choice: Parties may be required to mediate by a contract clause or court order, and in such circumstances the issue of timing is academic. If a disputant does have a choice, however, the issue is an important one. To answer the question you and your client must again consider your goals for the process. If your primary objective is to solve a problem or restore a relationship, it is usually best to mediate as soon as possible. If not, the parties' positions are likely to harden and one of them may replace the relationship with a new one, making a repair nearly impossible.

If relationships are not a priority, then the issue of timing is more complex. By delaying mediation an advocate may be able to improve his client's bargaining position, for instance, by winning a round in court. But in doing so the client will incur costs, and its opponent may react in kind. As we know, the American legal system does not ordinarily allow litigants to recover their legal expenses and makes no provision for the non-legal costs of conflict. As a result, parties must "swallow" any expenses that they incur in an effort to improve their bargaining position. The phenomenon of loss aversion then becomes an even greater obstacle to agreement.

Disputants tend to enter legal mediation at particular points along the litigation continuum, in particular when they face either a sharp increase in cost or the risk of a significant loss in adjudication. Natural points for mediation are before a legal case is filed, before the start of costly discovery, before a significant court ruling, and just before trial.

Before a Formal Legal Action Is Filed.   A supplier and customer involved in a dispute over the quality of goods supplied under a contract, for example, may opt to mediate in order to minimize the damage to a profitable relationship and avoid the expense of hiring outside law firms. Or a discharged employee may decide to mediate before filing a charge of discrimination with a state agency, in order to avoid the inflamed feelings that often result from such a step. Whenever disputants decide to enter mediation before filing a lawsuit they accept a trade-off: Each side has less information about the case, but also has avoided the cost of litigating to obtain it. Business clients appear to be electing to enter mediation before filing suit with increasing frequency. However, most plaintiff's lawyers believe they will get more serious attention to their client's claim and more leverage if they file a lawsuit first.

After Preliminary Discovery. Parties may file suit and undertake some discovery, for example, an exchange of documents, but enter mediation at the point when they face more costly and adversarial processes such as depositions. In essence, the parties' common wish to avoid a higher level of conflict serves as a "settlement event." Thus Jeffrey Senger of the U.S. Justice Department has written that:

> One approach . . . is to follow the 80-20 rule: 80 percent of the relevant information that parties learn from discovery often comes from the first 20 percent of the money they spend. Tracking down the last, difficult-to-obtain data is the most expensive part of discovery. . . . If parties conduct initial core discovery, they may find all they need to know in order to resolve the case appropriately. Following this approach, parties can agree to take abbreviated depositions of the key witnesses and then proceed to ADR. If necessary, they also may serve certain essential interrogatories and requests for production of vital documents. Often this will give them everything they need to determine their negotiation position with reasonable accuracy. . . . (Senger 2004)

"In the Shadow" of a Significant Ruling. Parties sometimes elect to mediate when they are approaching a significant stage in the court process, such as a motion for summary judgment. In such situations, each side knows that its bargaining position will either improve or deteriorate, depending on the court's decision. One might think that if one side were willing to mediate because it fears a loss, its opponent would refuse in hope of obtaining a gain. As we have seen, however, humans are generally much more sensitive to losing than to winning, and as a result both parties in a case are often motivated to mediate at the point they face the risk of a significant loss in adjudication.

Shortly Before Trial. This has been the traditional point at which to pursue settlement, either through direct bargaining or mediation, for several reasons. First, as trial approaches, attorneys must prepare intensively, imposing higher costs on them or their clients. Second, trial represents the ultimate win-or-lose event, triggering feelings of loss aversion. Finally, there are cultural assumptions about the "right" time to broach settlement: In the legal community, this used to mean that mentioning mediation early in a case was considered a sign of weakness, while raising the issue on the eve of trial was acceptable, an assumption that no longer appears to be true.

3. How to Initiate the Process

In the past, lawyers were often reluctant to propose mediation, out of concern that an adversary would see it as a sign of weakness. That attitude has largely disappeared. In some parts of the United States, many lawyers now find it easier to propose mediation than to suggest direct negotiation. Lawyers have several options for initiating the process.

Point Out That Settlement Discussions Are Inevitable. Given the phenomenon of the "vanishing" civil trial, settlement discussions are nearly inevitable at some point. You like to litigate — it's what you do for a living. But given that the parties will be talking settlement sooner or later in any event, why not do it now and save everyone the distraction and expense of litigation?

Rely on a Policy. If a lawyer represents an organization that has a uniform policy of exploring ADR early in every dispute, she can cite the policy as the reason for suggesting mediation. The most prominent example is the "CPR Pledge," which appears at *www.cpradr.org.* More than 4,000 companies have signed this pledge, and 1,500 law firms have signed a similar commitment to explore ADR with their clients in appropriate cases.

Cite a Rule. Some court systems require counsel to discuss ADR or to make a good-faith effort at settlement in every case. Even if no judicial mandate exists, lawyers may consider contacting an ADR administrator or clerk of court, and ask that the judge in the case suggest mediation to both sides.

Invite a Third Party to Do It. Another way to have a third party play "match-maker" is to ask a private neutral to approach an adversary and advocate mediation. Although the opponent will probably know that opposing counsel initiated the contact, this allows lawyers to avoid the burden of "selling" the process to a reluctant adversary.

So far we have assumed that the issue is to persuade one's opponent to mediate. In some situations, though, the major obstacle is one's own client. In the words of one litigator:

> There are no hard and fast rules as to when that perfect moment has arrived to mediate, [but] one point is clear. Before you begin, recognize that the first obstacle to starting the dialogue early may well be your own client, particularly if you have not represented him in the past. He may wonder if you lack confidence in yourself or the case if you push for settlement too early. On the other hand, if you don't mention settlement to the more sophisticated client, he may well wonder whether you are looking to "milk" a case that will likely never be tried. As such, begin with the adversary only after you have reached a consensus with your own client. . . .
> (Stern 1998)

C. Structuring the Mediation

How mediation is structured is often crucial to its success. In each case an advocate must think about the following issues.

1. Selecting a Mediator

The most important issue in arranging for mediation, apart perhaps from agreeing on who will attend the process, is to select the right neutral. We have seen that mediators vary in characteristics such as the breadth or narrowness of their approach, substantive expertise, and willingness to use facilitative or evaluative techniques. When selecting a legal mediator you will typically be able to choose among former or practicing litigators, transactional lawyers, and ex-judges, as well as professionals in fields ranging from psychotherapy to civil engineering. Your goal should be to select a neutral with qualities that match the needs of your case.

One approach is to think about what barriers are making it difficult to negotiate directly with the other side. The answer will give you an insight into what qualities a neutral will need to help you overcome them. If, for example, the key problem is that your opponent has an abrasive or insulting manner, then a mediator with strong process skills may be the best choice. If your own client needs "cover" to justify a compromise to an outside constituency, then an evaluative neutral may be helpful. If the parties are very angry or need to repair their relationship, then a neutral with skills in counseling may be what is called for. In many situations more than one barrier exists, calling for a mediator with a blend of abilities.

❖ **David S. Ross,** *Strategic Considerations in*
Choosing a Mediator: A Mediator's Perspective

2 J. Alt. Disp. Resol. in Emp. 7 (Spring 2000)

Because the mediation process is only as effective as the mediator who manages it, choosing the right mediator is critical. The mediator selection process demands a thoughtful balancing of many criteria, including:

- Mediation experience
- Mediation process skills
- Substantive expertise
- Reputation for neutrality
- Creativity
- Strong interpersonal skills and an ability to connect with people, and
- The ability to help parties reach agreement

Since every case is different, it makes sense to prioritize these criteria based on the needs of the case and parties. . . .

Substantive Expertise.   People often ask whether they should choose a mediator with substantive expertise or one with strong process skills. A short answer is "both." A longer answer is that in most employment disputes, process skills count as much or more than substantive expertise. However, more mediators are specializing in specific substantive areas [such as] employment law, so parties now can more easily choose a mediator with both substantive expertise and process skills.

References.   Participants should take the time to speak directly with individuals — ideally both lawyers and principals — who have worked with a proposed mediator to learn their candid assessment of the mediator's strengths and weaknesses, mediation style, and overall effectiveness. Most mediators provide references upon request. If they do not, then press the mediator to do so.

Opposing Counsel's Recommendations.   What should you do if opposing counsel proposes a mediator? There may be a strong instinct to reject such a proposal. My experience suggests that sophisticated lawyers should seriously consider mediators proposed by opposing counsel, honestly hashing out the advantages and disadvantages of various candidates. . . .

Attorneys should consult with their clients when choosing a mediator . . . Encouraging client participation in the mediator selection process empowers clients. Finally, and perhaps most importantly, it builds trust in the attorney-client relationship and in the mediation process, promoting a sense of shared responsibility in making mediation work.

Assuming you have identified the skills you want in a mediator, how can you determine whether a particular candidate possesses them? Common sources of information about mediators include recommendations from colleagues, references, and the opposing party's suggestions. In addition, companies and law firms that engage regularly in mediation sometimes create private data banks with information about their experience with various neutrals.

Some organizations and government agencies develop rosters of mediators who are approved to handle their cases. Mediators and ADR provider organizations also provide prospective clients with information and mediator bios. Such documents typically emphasize the neutral's qualifications, but advocates may be able to read between the lines to determine suitability or identify potential bias. In addition, most mediators are willing to talk informally with attorneys who express interest in hiring them or have case managers who can provide more information.

Questions

3. What might be the advantage of selecting a transactional lawyer rather than a litigator as your mediator? What might be the advantage of selecting a litigator rather than a transactional lawyer as your mediator?
4. When generally would a retired judge be a good person to have as a mediator?
5. Under what circumstances might it be to your client's advantage to allow the other side to select a mediator who knows the opposing attorney well and may have engaged in a similar type of law practice as the opposing attorney? For example, if you represent a defendant insurance company, when might you allow a personal injury plaintiff's lawyer to choose another experienced plaintiff's lawyer as the mediator?
6. If you wished to propose a mediator with whom you had worked repeatedly, what would be the best way to do so?
7. Assume you have agreed to mediate one of the role-play cases you were previously assigned by your teacher to negotiate in this course and are now in the process of selecting a neutral. What qualities and experience would you look for in a mediator for that particular case? Would your opponent, if strategic, prefer a mediator with the same qualities and experience? If you can obtain biographies of mediators in your area, review some and prioritize the candidates. You can also find biographies online at *http:// www.jamsadr.com.*

2. Ensuring the Presence of Necessary Participants

We know that mediation is an intensely personal process. Therefore, the presence of the right people is a critical factor in its success. Who these people are in a particular case will depend again on your objectives.

- If the primary goal is to repair a personal relationship, then the presence of the principals themselves, to talk out their problems and regain the ability to relate productively with each other, is usually essential.
- If the parties' relationship is attenuated, as, for example, in the case of a rent dispute between a corporate landlord and a former commercial tenant, the presence of principals may be less important.
- If the objective is to work out an imaginative solution, then it is important that the participants be capable of thinking "outside the box" and know enough about the parties' interests to identify and flesh out useful options.
- Working out a novel solution to a business dispute, for instance, may require the presence of executives who know the business.
- If the only goal is to settle a legal claim on the best possible monetary terms, as is true in many negligence cases, then the primary concern is probably that the bargainers arrive at the table with sufficient settlement authority.

❖ **Jerry Spolter, *A Mediator's Tip: Talk to Me!***

The Recorder 4 (Mar. 8, 2000)

This may come as a surprise to even the most seasoned mediation participants, but there is nothing wrong with communicating ex parte with a mediator or prospective mediator. In fact, it's usually the smart and right thing to do to secure the best result for your client. So don't be bashful. Talk to your mediator.

A recent mediation session I conducted highlights what can happen when you leave your mediator in the dark. Everything went great for about five hours. . . . The joint session was textbook material, with lots of helpful information exchanged; the private caucuses peeled away postured "positions" to reveal the parties' real interests. And then it happened: Although the physician accused of malpractice was in the room, the doc wouldn't make a move until his personal attorney gave the OK.

Unfortunately, the personal attorney was on a chairlift in the Sierra with a dead battery in her cell phone. And since this was a malpractice case requiring the doc's consent, "my" mediation was suddenly in trouble. To make matters worse, the doc's insurance representative had to consult two "invisible-hierarchy" decision-makers to discuss increasing authority.

If only I had received a "heads up" beforehand, we could have resolved the authority problems in advance and taken advantage of the momentum we had generated that day to settle the case. (Instead, the parties are now scurrying around trying to acquire the necessary authority to put Humpty Dumpty back together again.)

There is a good deal that lawyers can do beforehand to ensure that the right people are at a mediation.

Parties. If the parties are individuals, then they should be personally present. Corporations and other organizations, however, must act through agents. Some corporate representatives are positively harmful to the settlement process; an example is an executive who has a personal stake in defending the decision at issue in the dispute. Others may lack the right kind of expertise: An outside litigator, for instance, might be a good representative in a process that turns on the trial value of a claim, but wrong for a mediation focused on resolving an employee's grievance and bringing him back to work.

When parties are represented by agents, and especially when a nonparty such as an insurer is involved, advocates face a challenge to ensure that the people who come to the table have the authority to make the decisions needed to resolve the case. Negotiators routinely claim to have "full authority," but in practice their ability to agree is usually limited. Bargainers may arrive at mediation with

- "Best-case" authority (the ability to accept the terms their side believes that their opponent *ought to accept*),
- "Reasonable" authority (their estimate of what the opponent at the end of the day *will agree to*), or

- "Worst-case" authority (the ability to agree, if necessary, to an outcome very close to the other side's *current offer* going into mediation).

In practice, disputants usually conceal or misrepresent their authority, for fear that it will be taken as their "bottom line." It is often useful, however, to touch on the issue with an opposing negotiator, and perhaps to ask about his role in the organization, in order to estimate his ability to make decisions.

Advisors and Stakeholders. People other than parties may also play key roles in decision making at mediation. A husband, for instance, may look to his wife for advice, or a company may be unable to make a deal without permission from its insurer. There is no easy way to resolve this issue. Anyone who has the power to sabotage the agreement should be at the table. Wise lawyers know that they may need to bargain for the presence of the right person, and that the mediator can help with the process. In asking a neutral for assistance in securing the presence of key decision makers, lawyers benefit from several forces. First, having agreed to mediate, disputants usually feel an interest in establishing a good relationship with the mediator. Mediators, too, acquire a stake in the process, and have a bias toward inclusion. Better, a typical legal mediator will think to ask for the presence of a person who later proves unnecessary rather than find herself lacking a key decision maker at crunch time. Advocates can take advantage of their opponent's wish to humor a mediator and the neutral's own investment in the process by agreeing to mediate, and then enlisting the neutral's help to shape the field of bargaining.

3. Influencing the Format

Mediation can occur in a wide variety of formats. The parties, for example, can choose to meet entirely in joint session or rely heavily on caucusing. They can bargain with each other directly or through attorneys. The best format for a particular case again depends on your overall goal.

- In a case focused on relationship repair, you will probably want the clients to have as much opportunity as possible to communicate directly. It may make sense, for instance, to arrange for the principals, at some point in the mediation, to talk without counsel present, or perhaps to remain in joint session throughout the process.
- In a highly emotional case, it may be important for a party to meet with the mediator ahead of time to begin venting, and for the mediator to carefully structure the party's interactions with the other side. Some relationships are so charged that the parties should never be in the same room together. If there is any history of physical intimidation or violence, scheduling separate mediation meetings at different times may be necessary.
- In factually complex cases, it may be necessary to arrange for enough time for each side to present a lengthy opening statement, perhaps supported by computerized exhibits or comments from an expert.

It is important to bear in mind that experienced advocates often ask for changes in the usual format of commercial mediation. If you see a reason to vary the format, you should alert the mediator to this before the process begins.

4. Planning for Court-Connected Mediation

The discussion to this point has assumed that you have the freedom to design an effective mediation process in conjunction with the mediator and the other party. Sometimes, however, your client may be required to engage in mediation by a contract clause. More often the court in which your case is pending will require litigants to go through mediation as a precondition to trial. Many state and federal courts have mandatory mediation programs. They are most prevalent in family disputes but have become common in general civil litigation as well. States such as Florida, Texas, and California require most civil cases filed in their courts to go through mediation.

Courts may order mediation but leave process choices to the parties, with court rules available only as a default mechanism. Many jurisdictions, however, channel cases into court-connected programs, assign mediators, require principals to attend, and impose other significant restrictions on the process. Litigants may have the option to opt out of restrictions by agreement, but in the context of adversarial litigation this can be difficult to accomplish.

If you have a case that is subject to mandatory mediation, whether by contract or court rule, you should consider the following questions, in addition to the general issues that arise in planning for any mediation. The most important are:

- Is the mandated mediation process adequate?
- If not, how should you respond to it?
- Is it in your client's interest to pay for a noncourt process, if permitted?

In considering the adequacy of the process, several issues are likely to arise that are peculiar to mandatory programs.

- Will you have a role in choosing the neutral? Some programs require parties to select a mediator from panels that consist of attorney-mediators with varying levels of experience. Others assign a mediator, sometimes a full-time court employee, to each case. Some programs and clauses give parties the option to select a private mediator. And contract clauses sometimes designate a named individual as the neutral.
- Who will be required to be present at the session? Many courts require each party to send a representative with "full settlement authority." This can create serious problems for organizations that have large numbers of cases pending in different court systems.
- Will you have an opportunity to brief the mediator in advance? Some programs have no restrictions, while others seek to reduce costs by barring parties from submitting statements or talking with neutrals in advance.
- Will you be required to pay for the process? Some programs are free, relying on volunteer attorney-mediators; others use private neutrals who charge

market prices; and still others require parties to pay mediators, but at below-market rates.

- Will you be required to mediate within a specific time frame? Court processes can range from a one-hour process, with the option to extend the time by agreement, to a full-day commitment. If the process is time-limited, the mediator is likely to feel pressure to produce progress quickly, leading him to forego interest-oriented questioning in favor of "cutting to the chase" and soliciting offers.
- What confidentiality guarantees does the program offer?
- Can you change the structure of the process by agreement with the other side? If so, will the other side agree to the changes you seek?

If you do not want to mediate, or conclude that the mandated process is not adequate, you should consider these questions:

- Is it possible to opt out of the process, for example, by applying for an exemption?
- If not, what is the minimum you have to do to comply with the mandate? Some programs, for example, require parties to participate in "good faith," which can be difficult to define.
- Are there penalties for nonparticipation or noncompliance? For example, if you fail to send a representative with settlement authority, will the court impose costs or attorneys' fees? Will the mediator report to the court about your cooperation? Will the mediator give the court a recommendation as to how the court should rule on unresolved issues, as is true of some divorce mediation programs?

In order to obtain information about these issues you may wish to:

- Talk with colleagues or a local lawyer who has participated in the program.
- Review the program brochure and rules.
- Talk with the program administrator.
- Talk with opposing counsel.

D. Preparing to Mediate

Once advocates have agreed on an overall structure for mediation, they should focus on how they will participate in the process. This requires planning not only what the lawyer will do, but also the roles of the client and other members of the team. Preparation includes at least three areas: developing a negotiation plan, exchanging information, and coaching clients about what to do and say.

1. Developing a Negotiating Plan

Lawyers usually make an opening statement at the outset of the process, which is a form of advocacy, but the rest of the mediation is typically taken up with discussions and bargaining. You should therefore plan for mediation in much the same way that you would for a direct negotiation. The points made in Chapter 5 about preparation for negotiation thus apply here as well. You will wish, for example, to consider each side's alternatives to agreement, principles that you can cite and those that your opponent will rely on, the parties' underlying interests, and potential options for settlement. If your primary goal is to obtain the best possible monetary outcome, your plan will be similar to that of a competitive bargainer, complete with a concession strategy. If you see the purpose of the process as solving a common problem, then you are likely to focus on the parties' interests and cooperate in finding ways to address them. Whatever your goal, however, you will need to modify your approach to bargaining to take advantage of the special aspects of mediation and what develops in the process.

2. Exchanging Information

One of the key aspects of any negotiation is exchanging information, and one of mediation's effects is to enhance the flow of data between the parties. This process often begins well before disputants actually meet to mediate. As an advocate, you will have to think about two types of information:

- What data does your client need to make a good settlement decision?
- What information will help get your adversary to agree to the outcome you are seeking?

If necessary, you should be prepared to enlist the mediator's help in persuading the other side to provide you with data. The neutral may also be able to help you explain to your own client why in this context it is a good idea to give an opponent some "free discovery."

What information is relevant depends again on your goals. If the process turns on money, then legal evidence and arguments are likely to be key. If your purpose is to repair a relationship, knowing the "why" behind a disputed action will be important. If the objective is to create a new business arrangement, then financial data may be more useful. As a rule, negotiations that focus on imaginative options require a broader base of information than discussions that revolve solely around money.

a. Exchanging Data with the Other Party

Disputants usually need less information to mediate effectively than they would require to try the same case. Still, especially if parties mediate early in a dispute, one side may lack information that is necessary to make an informed decision. The party may not be able to assess the value of its litigation alternative or determine whether an imaginative option is viable. An insurance adjuster, for example, may not be able to obtain the authority needed to settle a claim without documents verifying the plaintiff's medical expenses, while a plaintiff lawyer might be unable to accept a reasonable settlement offer without assurances that there is no "smoking gun" in the defendant's files.

In litigation there is ordinarily no reason for a party to show its hand to an adversary, but in mediation disputants know that providing information will increase their chances of reaping a good settlement. Equally important, they know that the mediator is present to help ensure that the exchange will be mutual. As a result, parties in mediation often provide each other with surprising amounts of information.

Questions

8. What types of data gathered before mediation might help an advocate avoid the "twenty common errors" described earlier by Tom Arnold?
9. Assume that you are the lawyer in a negotiation role-play previously assigned by your teacher in this class and you are now representing your client in mediation. What additional information, beyond the facts stated in the role-play instructions, would help you mediate well? What data might the other attorney ask you for?

b. Educating the Mediator

In small cases and court-connected programs, neutrals sometimes arrive at mediation knowing almost nothing about the dispute. In privately conducted mediations, however, lawyers typically make an effort to orient, and begin to persuade, the neutral in advance. Pre-mediation communications can take at least three forms: written statements, joint meetings, and private conversations.

Written Statements

Parties commonly give a mediator written statements, sometimes called mediation "briefs" or "submissions," to read in advance. As they prepare their statements, advocates should consider the following:

- Is it better to prepare a statement, or use an existing document? A customized document has obvious advantages, but particularly in smaller cases it is appropriate to use an existing document or pleading that summarizes the party's views.
- Is it preferable to submit the statement on an ex parte basis, or exchange it with opposing counsel? Mediators usually prefer that lawyers exchange statements, so that they are free to discuss the points one side makes with the other. In addition, it is the other side that you have to convince. Even if you exchange statements, however, you are ordinarily free to write or call the neutral to discuss sensitive issues privately.

What should be in the mediation statement? A mediator is likely to be interested in knowing, among other points:

- How did the dispute arise?
- What are the key factual and legal issues?

- What nonlegal concerns are present?
- What barriers have made direct bargaining difficult? Are there personal or emotional issues?
- What is the status of any legal proceedings? Is there a history of bargaining?
- Who are the key decision makers in the dispute?

Organizational Discussions

In complex cases, mediators often schedule joint meetings with counsel to discuss organizational questions, such as who will be present at the mediation. Such meetings usually occur by conference call, but they are sometimes convened in person. Organizational meetings are typically limited to lawyers, but clients and experts may occasionally participate as well.

Private Conversations

Mediators sometimes take the initiative to talk with advocates before a mediation session. Such conversations typically occur over the telephone but may occur in person. Mediators use these private conversations to ask about hidden obstacles, fill factual gaps, or simply listen to disputants vent.

Attorneys often do not ask for a pre-mediation conversation with the neutral, or if they do, they devote it primarily to repeating legal points made in their written statements. This is usually a mistake. Apart from the fact that the mediator may already have read the briefs, lawyers will have a chance to make their legal arguments during the process itself. At this stage many mediators want to know about issues that typically do not appear in the briefs, such as nonlegal obstacles, what the participants are like, and potential options to resolve the case. Pre-mediation private conversations provide an exceptional opportunity for advocates to shape a mediator's "take" on a dispute.

Another alternative is for a lawyer and client to meet personally with the neutral before the "formal" process begins. An advocate might seek out a meeting for these reasons, among others:

- To build a relationship with the neutral.
- To permit a client to begin the process of working through his emotions or to allow the client to get to know the mediator.
- To present sensitive data or proposals.
- To allow the mediator to meet with a key witness or decision maker who will not be present at the mediation itself.

3. Preparing the Client

As we have noted, mediation is in essence a process of negotiation, but one that varies in significant ways from direct bargaining, requiring different preparation of clients. Attorneys usually conduct direct negotiations outside their clients' presence, often without even meeting face-to-face. In mediation, by contrast, both clients are ordinarily physically present and the mediator has direct conversations with them. In addition, in the typical caucus-based mediation, disputants spend much of their time isolated from each other, interacting through the neutral rather than directly. Because of these structural differences, lawyers should cover the following topics, in addition to the issues they would address when preparing a client for a direct negotiation:

- How the mediation process will differ from negotiations to which the client is accustomed.
  — The background, personality, and likely approach of the mediator, including the potential for changes in style, for example, from an empathic to an evaluative approach.
  — The likely format of the process and potential variations in it, for instance, the possibility that the client will be invited to meet privately with the other principal.
  — The confidentiality rules that will apply to the process, as well as possible gaps and exceptions in them.
- What role the client should play in the process. In particular,
  — What questions the client should expect from the mediator.
  — What the client should be prepared to say, and when the client should remain silent.
  — What the other side may say and do.
  — How the lawyer and client should coordinate. The client should know, for instance, that it is entirely permissible for the client or the lawyer to ask the mediator to leave the room so that they can talk privately.
- What role the lawyer will play in the process. An advocate should be sure that the client understands that while their overall goal — getting the best possible outcome — will remain the same, she will adapt her tactics to the special nature of mediation. In particular,
  — The attorney will probably take a different tone than she would in a courtroom or direct bargaining session. In particular, the presence of the mediator may call for a more conciliatory stance.
  — The lawyer may also "pull punches" in order not to antagonize the other side while they explore a possible deal.
  — The lawyer may not mention certain key evidence in order to save it for trial.

E. Representing Clients During the Process

We now turn to the point in the mediation process at which the parties and mediator convene together to talk and bargain. This is what many lawyers think of as the "actual" mediation, although by now you know that effective advocacy begins well before the parties meet in person. We have seen that commercial mediation tends to follow a joint-session-plus-caucusing format, while family and problem-solving mediators are much more likely to keep disputants together.

Problem

You represent a company that vacated commercial space because of dissatisfaction with the condition of the building. Your client is being sued by a corporate landlord for rent due under the lease. Both sides have agreed to mediate. Apart from the basic issue of liability, which you see as a 50-50 proposition, you believe that the landlord ignored its responsibility to maintain the building and as a result would not be awarded much even if it did establish a technical violation of the lease.

1. How can you best use the opening session to make the landlord aware of its risk at trial?
2. Can you think of any type of dispute in which an initial joint meeting is likely to be counterproductive?
3. What format would you advocate using instead?

---

1. *Joint Meetings*

a. The Opening Session

Should There Be an Opening Session?

Many mediators prefer to begin the process with an opening session attended by all the disputants. Lawyers, however, regularly suggest to mediators that the parties dispense with the opening stage and go directly into caucuses. Each side already knows the other's arguments, they say; what benefit could there be to repeating them? Or, they warn, the session will simply inflame their clients. Moreover, time is limited; why not get to the bargaining?

There is often some truth to each of these concerns. No matter how repetitive or uncomfortable an opening session may appear, you should be extremely reluctant to ask that it be omitted entirely. An adversary's comments may offend your client (and vice versa), but the experience of speaking directly to an opponent often helps disputants to let go of emotions that would otherwise impair their decision making later in the process. Allowing a party to listen directly to an adversary's evidence and arguments can also help to bring reality to later discussions, giving each side a better appreciation and assessment of what they will face if the case does not settle. And after a time, even angry listeners usually become more calm. Mediators find that it is almost always useful to hold at least one joint meeting early in the process.

If you do have a reason for avoiding a joint meeting, raise this with your mediator in advance. Before doing so, however, carefully examine the pros and cons. Remember that you have the option to request that an opening session be restructured, and consider options that fall between cancellation and the "usual format." You might, for example, ask that the session be limited to presentations by experts or comments by executives.

What Role Will You Take in the Session?

You can have a variety of goals for a joint meeting. Even if your objective is solely to get the best possible monetary outcome, you will usually not want to exchange offers during the opening session. Too often, offers made directly by one side to another are reactively devalued. Instead, your strategy should be to create the conditions for successful bargaining later in the process. You can do this in several ways.

Foster a Working Relationship. Advocates and clients can use an opening session, and perhaps also the casual conversation that sometimes occurs as people assemble, to foster a better working relationship with an opponent. This does not necessarily mean repairing a past connection, although that might be desirable. Instead the goal is typically more modest — to create a basis for the parties to bargain effectively later on. Disputants can do this, for example, by demonstrating that they are serious about settlement and are willing to make principled compromises to reach one. Alternatively, a lawyer can use an opening session to help an emotional or angry participant work through difficult feelings.

Gather Information. Lawyers can also use the opening session to gather information. In a joint meeting, unlike discovery or court proceedings, disputants can talk informally with each other. Attorneys and clients also have the opportunity to observe the lawyer and witnesses for the other side, and perhaps also the chance to speak directly with the opposing principal. (The other side, of course, will have the same opportunity to "size up" you and your client.)

Focus the Discussion on Key Issues. Skilled lawyers use the opening session to focus discussion on the issues that are most helpful to their case or that create a platform for effective bargaining. If, for example, an advocate wants to emphasize the evidence (or lack of it) supporting the damage claims in a case, she can alert the mediator beforehand that this issue is significant to her client and then focus attention on it through her comments. If the attorney's primary goal is to explore an interest-based solution, she can use the opening session to send signals about this as well — or prime the mediator to raise the issue as his own idea. Neither side can control the agenda of an opening session, but attorneys who take the initiative can influence the content of such discussions significantly.

Persuade an Opponent. Finally, lawyers use the opening session to persuade their opponents to compromise. They focus their advocacy on the opposing decision maker, knowing that they will have other chances to talk with the mediator, but the opening session may be their only opportunity to speak directly to the other party. The goal will usually be to convince the other side that it is in its own best interest to compromise. Opponents are more likely to do so if they believe that:

- You are serious about seeking a settlement.
- You are open to options that will advance their interests.
- If discussions fail, you have a good alternative to settlement.

- You are willing to compromise, but will accept impasse sooner than agree to an unfair result.

What Role Will Your Client Take?

Most lawyers are inclined to take the lead in the opening session, treating it as a kind of informal pretrial hearing. As we have already noted, however, clients can play crucial roles in these meetings as well.

Should the Client Speak in the Opening Session?   As a general rule, clients should be active in joint meetings. Opponents tend to "tune out" what an opposing attorney says, but they are usually very interested in hearing from the opposing principal. Mediators also seek a connection with parties and therefore pay especially close attention to what they say. For these reasons, statements from principals are likely to have a greater impact than the same words spoken by an attorney. By participating effectively in a joint session, parties can significantly affect how opponents view them as witnesses, future partners, or negotiators.

- In personal injury and employment cases, in which the plaintiff's pain and suffering or emotional distress is often an important element of the claim, a plaintiff who can persuasively describe how he has suffered increases the settlement value of the claim. In general, whenever a person is likely to be a significant witness in a future adjudication, his presentation in mediation will affect the other side's estimate of the value of the case.
- When parties wish to repair a relationship, as in some business cases, or the principals cannot avoid a continuing relationship, as is true of many family cases involving children, one party's participation in mediation can significantly affect the other side's willingness to settle on terms that maintain a working relationship. Again, statements made by one party directly to another almost always have greater impact than comments made through a lawyer or mediator — for better or worse.
- Parties can often articulate their interests more persuasively if they speak themselves.
- If one side doubts an opponent's commitment to settling, the opponent may be able to dispel those concerns in the opening session.

All this assumes, of course, that a client presents himself positively. If a party is obnoxious, inarticulate, or repulsive, then his participation will lower an opponent's opinion of his case and hurt his bargaining objectives. In such situations the client should remain silent if possible.

b. Other Joint Formats

We have seen that commercial mediation typically relies on extensive private caucusing. The caucus format can be useful, but it also imposes significant limitations. Advocates should not let themselves fall into caucusing as a matter of routine without thinking about whether other formats might be more effective. Caucusing is most useful when disputants want to focus primarily on legal issues and monetary offers, or when they are too emotional, inarticulate, or unskilled in bargaining to interact effectively.

If, however, parties wish to repair a relationship or work out inventive solutions, direct discussions, perhaps moderated by the mediator, are often more effective because they allow the people who are most concerned or knowledgeable about a situation to talk directly with each other. Even when a case is "only about money," it may be useful for representatives of each side to talk directly to resolve emotional issues, address complex factual issues, or deal with misunderstandings. The flexible nature of mediation allows participants to change its structure on an ad hoc basis, including requesting joint sessions after or in between caucusing with the mediator. Joint sessions may also occur during a mediation just between the lawyers or with only clients present. This flexibility creates opportunities for sophisticated counsel to use the process to advantage. They understand that mediation is inherently a fluid process, and that mediators are working for the parties, not the other way around.

2. Caucusing

Because caucusing is so common in civil mediation outside the family law area, attorneys and mediators whom you encounter in practice are likely to expect to spend most of the time in caucuses. As a result, you will need either to take action in advance to obtain modifications in the caucus format or plan to reap the greatest advantage from using it.

To make the best use of caucuses, you will have to prepare in two ways. First, you will have to adapt your direct bargaining tactics to the special structure of caucusing, and second, you should deal with the mediator differently from the way you respond to opponents. If, for example, opposing counsel asks your client a question, you would ordinarily feel free to cut him off or step in and answer the question yourself. But if a mediator asks your client the same question in the privacy of a caucus, the considerations are different. You may be more willing to have your client answer a mediator's question because you can insist the mediator treat the answer as confidential, and you may be more reluctant to offend the neutral than opposing counsel. The nature of caucusing typically changes over the course of a mediation, and we therefore discuss early and later caucusing separately.

a. Early Caucuses

Exchanging Information and Arguments

Sophisticated negotiators often spend a good deal of time exchanging information and feeling each other out before making explicit offers. Because legal mediation is at heart a process of negotiation, it is not surprising that good advocates and mediators use caucusing to facilitate the flow of information prior to exchanging demands and offers. A lawyer might, for example, tell a mediator what she wishes the neutral to stress to an opponent as well as questions that she needs answered.

Neutrals, for their part, understand that disputants often come to mediation without data that they need to make settlement decisions, and that good lawyers will work to get points across to an adversary through them. Indeed, to the extent that a party's "questions" are implicit arguments, mediators are often willing to transmit them to encourage the listener to reassess the value of his case.

Initiating Bargaining

Depending on the circumstances, an advocate in mediation may decide to focus either on money bargaining or creative solutions. The format allows lawyers to advance either of these goals.

Interest-Based Bargaining.   Most mediators will urge interest-based bargaining. One practical problem for advocates, however, is that even when they wish to explore nonmonetary terms, they are often reluctant to do so for fear of signaling that their client is not committed to its monetary position. This is particularly true of plaintiffs because they are typically the ones seeking damages. Defense lawyers, by contrast, tend to be receptive to imaginative terms, because they see them as a substitute for paying money.

Mediation can allow a lawyer to have it both ways. He can press "publicly" — in communications sent through the mediator or made in joint session — for the best possible money outcome, while asking the neutral "privately" — through a pre-mediation talk or caucus discussion — to explore nonmonetary options.

A "Hard" Bargaining Strategy.   One rarely mentioned aspect of mediation is that it offers protection to parties who opt for a competitive approach, as well as to negotiators pursuing creative solutions. Indeed, the mediation process allows counsel to take tougher stands than would be possible in direct negotiation. Because mediation is more complicated and expensive to arrange than an ordinary bargaining session, participants are more reluctant to walk out in response to an "insulting" proposal. More important, a mediator will work to "scrape the other side off the ceiling" when they erupt at an opponent's stubbornness. Lawyers sometimes take advantage of this dynamic to play "tough cop," knowing that good mediators will instinctively take on a "good cop" role to keep the process alive.

As knowledgeable counsel you can use mediation to enhance both cooperative and competitive bargaining strategies. You can privately encourage the mediator to raise creative options while adhering to a monetary demand, or pursue a genuinely competitive strategy secure in the knowledge that the mediator will work to keep the process from falling apart. As an advocate, you should also keep in mind that the mediator will be interpreting your position and viewpoint to the other side, and you can offer suggestions to the neutral about what you would like him to say in the other room about your current position and thinking.

b. Later Caucuses

As caucusing progresses, the tactics of the disputants and the mediator are likely to evolve. Advocates will continue to probe for information, explore interests, and argue the merits, but as the process continues these aspects usually become less dominant. For one thing, the parties will return to the issues repeatedly, making continued discussion seem repetitive. As a result, during the later stages of a mediation that emphasizes monetary demands, caucuses are likely to become progressively shorter as both sides focus on bargaining. In a creative process, parties often shift their attention gradually from identifying and communicating interests to devising options to satisfy them. In this kind of process caucuses are likely to remain relatively long, but their focus is likely to be on crafting terms to produce the best possible fit of the parties' concerns.

Mediators are also more likely to express opinions as mediation continues. In part this is because as neutrals gather more information, they become increasingly confident about their assessment of the participants and the obstacles to agreement. Parties also typically become more receptive to a mediator's advice; they come to appreciate that the mediator has genuinely listened to their concerns, and from the answers she brings back after each round of caucusing, they know that the mediator has communicated their views clearly to the other side. Competitive bargainers in particular are likely to become more receptive to a mediator's advice when they realize that their positional tactics are likely to lead to an impasse. As mediators become more active in the process, advocates should consider modifying their own tactics in response.

Facilitating Bargaining

One option is to ask the mediator to assess the emotional "temperature" in the other room, or predict how a counterpart is likely to react to a proposal. Lawyers can also seek to take advantage of the mediator's special status to enhance the effectiveness of their offers.

Obtaining Information. One of the paradoxes of mediation is how mediators are expected to treat information that they gather during private caucuses. On the one hand, caucus discussions are confidential. On the other hand, one of mediation's key purposes is to foster better communication, and as long as the parties are separated in caucuses, this can only happen if the mediator conveys information between them. How can an advocate take advantage of this seeming contradiction?

In practice most lawyers in mediation designate very few facts as confidential from the other side, and they appear to expect a mediator to reveal at least some of what they say in private caucus. For example, a plaintiff lawyer might tell a mediator, "$500,000 is as low as we'll go at this point. You can tell them 500." The attorney knows that the neutral will interpret this to mean that he can tell the other side that the plaintiff is reducing his demand to $500,000, and also that the plaintiff will probably be willing to go further ("at this point") if the defendant makes an appropriate response.

Experienced lawyers know, in other words, that while mediators will not report sensitive data to the other camp, they will usually feel some license to go beyond simply repeating what a party says, to interpret its general intentions. Unless instructed otherwise, a mediator will convey this information as his own impression, not attributing it to the speaker. The result resembles the way government officials sometimes float trial balloons to the press on a "background" basis. This approach has two advantages. First, the listener may be left a bit unsure what signal has been given, giving the sender leeway to either reinforce or back away from its message in light of the response. Second, the fact that the mediator is the one making the interpretation makes it appear less manipulative, and therefore less subject to reactive devaluation, than if the lawyer had given the signal directly. Advocates should therefore consider what they want a mediator to say about their attitude and offer in the other room, and state their wishes to the neutral. If you want something you or your client say in mediation to truly remain confidential, clearly inform the mediator not to reveal it.

Advocates should also consider whether to ask the mediator about the other side's state of mind. If, for instance, a plaintiff seems agitated during an opening session, defense counsel might later ask the mediator, "Has Smith calmed down?" or "If his lawyer recommends a deal, do you think he'll listen?" Alternatively, a lawyer might ask a mediator to collect specific information, such as whether the other side has retained an expert. These requests for information should be reasonable and in aid of settlement. Lawyers can also ask mediators to explore an adversary's reaction to a potential deal without disclosing their own interest in it.

Questions about what the other side is thinking pose tricky ethical and practical issues for mediators because of the paradox mentioned above. But that does not mean that counsel should not ask them. Lawyers should be aware, however, that if they ask a mediator for information about their opponent, the mediator, as a neutral, may interpret this as permission to provide the other side with the same kind of data about the questioner. As in direct bargaining, in other words, information exchange is a two-way street. That does not mean, however, that asking questions is not helpful, and mediation can amplify the effectiveness of doing so. To take advantage of the mediator's ability to gather and convey information during the caucusing process:

- Ask the mediator questions about the other side's current attitude and intentions.
- Discuss with the mediator what he will say to your opponent about you.
- Use the mediator as a sounding board about how a potential offer will be received.

Using a Mediator's Neutrality. As we have seen, mediators have a key advantage that is not available even to the best advocate: the simple fact that they are seen by disputants as neutral. Although the phenomenon of reactive devaluation makes humans instinctively suspect anything that is proposed by an opponent, mediators can potentially deliver bargainers from its impact. Take, for example, a situation in which a defendant is stubbornly clinging to an offer of $75,000. The mediator could say to the plaintiff, "You know, I think that if we could ever get them up to $100,000, it would be worth serious consideration. . . . What do you think?" By phrasing the issue in this way, the neutral has done two things. First, she has presented the offer as hypothetical — it is not yet "cursed" by the fact that the defendant is actually willing to make it. Second, she has tentatively endorsed its reasonableness. If the plaintiff buys into the potential offer, the mediator will have partially "inoculated" it against being devalued if it materializes. Counsel can take advantage of a mediator's neutrality by:

- Asking a mediator to deliver unwelcome information to the other side.
- Suggesting that a mediator offer a party's proposal or argument as his own.
- Requesting a neutral to certify the fairness of a proposal, either to the other side or to an outside constituency, like a board of directors.

Using a Mediator to Carry Out Uncomfortable Tasks. Mediators are freer to use unorthodox tactics to solve bargaining impasses because they needn't worry about maintaining a judge's reserve or showing a litigator's resolve. Attorneys can take advantage of this by asking mediators to take on difficult tasks.

Mediators can take on a wide variety of unusual roles to support the settlement process. They might range from counseling a distraught litigant, to delivering a "hard sell" to a stubborn executive, to acting as the scapegoat for a difficult compromise. If a mediator does not see the need or seems reluctant to take on such a role, however, counsel should take the initiative to ask.

Impasse-Breaking Techniques

Each of the techniques described previously can help you achieve more than might be possible through direct negotiation. Suppose, however, that despite your best efforts the bargaining process hits an impasse. The reasons can be complex. Negotiations may become stalled because of a process issue such as lack of authority, psychological factors such as loss aversion, merits-based problems like misevaluation of the chances of winning in court, or other obstacles. Impasses occur most frequently when negotiators focus narrowly on monetary solutions, but they are possible even during interest-based bargaining. Two parties may agree, for example, that it would be desirable to restore their business relationship, but reach a stalemate trying to decide how to share the costs and rewards of the new arrangement. When an impasse does occur, you can often take advantage of a mediator's assistance to resolve it.

Problem

You are in the late afternoon of a mediation of a commercial contract dispute. You and your client, the plaintiff, have become very frustrated with the slow pace of the bargaining and the defendant's lack of realism. You began with a demand of $5 million, and your most recent proposal was $2.75 million; your client has a final "bottom-line" target of $1.9 million. The defense opened with an offer of $200,000 and has been inching up, their last move being only from $650,000 to $700,000. In a private conversation while the mediator is out of the room, your client tells you that he is willing to drop the demand to $2.5 million, but that unless the defendant's next offer "hits seven figures" (i.e., $1 million) he's inclined to pack up and leave. How might the mediator help you here? What should you and/or your client say to the neutral?

1. Assume that the mediator comes back 30 minutes later with a defense offer of $900,000. What should you do now?
2. Is there any reason that you as an advocate would feel reluctant to ask a mediator to take the kinds of initiatives described above?

Ask the Mediator for Advice. Mediators are experienced negotiators. More important, they have a unique opportunity to observe and talk candidly with both sides and, at least until the end of the process, are not under pressure to express an opinion themselves. As the process goes on, they often acquire a great deal of information about each party's state of mind, approach to bargaining, and priorities for settlement. A mediator will not help one side obtain an advantage over an opponent, and settlement-oriented neutrals do have an interest in seeing each side compromise as much as possible. But when the negotiation process bogs down, advocates should consider asking the mediator for advice about how to restart it. Lawyers can also use a mediator to educate an unsophisticated or emotional client, or to present difficult truths about what is achievable and what it is not.

Make a Hypothetical Offer. Counsel who will not make a unilateral concession will sometimes authorize a mediator to make an offer in a hypothetical, or "if . . . then," format. This is also refered to as "bracketing." The motivation can be to test the waters, probe the other side's flexibility, and/or ensure that a potential move will be reciprocated. For instance, a lawyer might say to the mediator, "Given the other side's refusal to go below 250, I cannot see us going beyond 100. However, you could tell them that you think you could get us to 125 if they would respond by breaking 200."

The hypothetical formula gains added impact if it is presented as a final resolution of the case rather than simply as a new move. By proposing an actual settlement, bargainers take advantage of the "certainty effect" — the fact that disputants will often make a special effort if they can achieve complete peace. An advocate wishing to take this approach might say, "You can tell them that if they could only get to 150, you have some optimism that you could convince my client to go there — but only if it would settle the case, once and for all." Such hypotheticals can sometimes short-circuit impasses caused by positional bargaining.

Ask the Mediator to Intervene. If other steps are not effective, lawyers can ask a mediator to intervene directly in the process. Good mediators will delay doing so for as long as possible, knowing that disputants may be alienated by the perception that the neutral is "taking over" the process, or because the mediator wants to avoid asserting control for philosophical reasons. Still, many commercial mediators will intervene actively in a case when the bargaining process appears to be seriously stalled.

If an advocate wants a mediator to adopt a restrained role in the face of impasse, she should make her preference known early in the process. Alternatively, if a lawyer wants the neutral to become more active, she should say that. We discuss below three of the most common interventions used by mediators to resolve impasses — confidential listener, evaluation of the merits, and a mediator's proposal. We also suggest ways in which lawyers can use each tactic to best advantage.

Confidential Listener. Sometimes each side in mediation will refuse to move to a reasonable position until its adversary has done so. The result is an "After you, Alphonse. . . . No you, Gaston . . ." effect in which both sides remain stuck, but the mediator is fairly sure that each would be willing to compromise further. In such situations a mediator may offer to play "confidential listener." This involves asking each side to disclose to him privately, either orally or with a number on a piece of paper, how far it would go to settle the case. The mediator can then make a judgment about the real gap between the parties.

At one time participants in mediation tended to assume that unless the parties' confidential positions were identical or very close, the mediation would end. This put considerable pressure on each party to give the mediator its "last and best offer." In current practice, however, both lawyers and mediators are likely to assume that the purpose of the confidential listener technique is for the neutral to form a better estimate of the actual gap between the parties. People now appear to approach confidential listener on the assumption that the mediator will not end the process even in the face of a large gap.

Mediators usually do not expect the tactic to settle a case, although they would be delighted if it did. Rather, their goal is to get a more realistic offer from each side. Once both sides have given their response, the neutral usually gives the litigants an assessment of the situation; for example, "You're still a considerable distance apart, but I think it's worth continuing." On occasion, some neutrals will ask both parties for permission to disclose their confidential responses on a mutual basis, so that both can form a better estimate of the distance between them.

What should you as an advocate tell a mediator who is playing confidential listener? Unless you are in a situation in which a mediator you trust completely states explicitly that she wants each side's true bottom-line number *and* you believe that she really means it — that unless the parties' positions either touch or come very close, the mediator will terminate the mediation — it is not wise to give your client's actual final terms. Doing so will place you at a disadvantage in the next stage of the process, in which the parties are asked to continue to bargain, and may lead your client to dig into an unrealistic position prematurely. For these reasons, experienced mediators often avoid asking litigants for a bottom-line number at all. Some mediators, for instance, ask disputants instead for their "next-to-last number"; this sends a signal that the mediators do not want them to commit to a "final" offer.

For a competitive bargainer, the challenge in the confidential listener process is to make an offer high or low enough to set up a favorable compromise, but realistic enough to motivate the other participants to continue. A cooperative negotiator will be inclined to answer the mediator honestly, but may also leave some room to move, and might consult with the neutral about steps to keep the process alive.

Evaluation.   If shuttle diplomacy fails, lawyers often ask mediators to evaluate the legal merits of a case. As we have seen, evaluation is a controversial technique, at least among academics, but can be useful not only with opponents but also with clients. Whenever, for example, an advocate stops a mediator in the hall and suggests that he give the client his "thoughts" about the case, the neutral knows that he is being enlisted in the difficult task of client education and management.

In the large majority of situations, evaluations will be delivered in caucus and will focus on a specific issue, like the strength of a key factual matter, who is likely to prevail on liability, the strength of an affirmative defense, or what the damages are likely to be. It is possible, however, to have a mediator evaluate other issues as well. If, for example, a disputant is suspicious that its adversary will not carry out a proposed settlement, the mediator could assess the risk on the basis of his discussions with the opponent or his experience in other cases.

Before requesting a mediator's evaluation, you should ask yourself two basic questions. First, is the primary obstacle to settling this case really a disagreement about the outcome in court, or some other issue that evaluation can address? As we have seen, the real barriers to settlement often lie in issues other than the legal merits. Second, if a mediator does evaluate the merits, are you confident that the result will be helpful — that is, will you get the opinion you want?

Once you have decided to seek an evaluation, the next issue is how to structure it so as to maximize the chances of a helpful result. The first issue is what data the mediator will consider. Bear in mind that a mediator's views about a case are usually based solely on the briefs and documents he sees, augmented by personal observations of the people present at the mediation. This has two implications:

- Like trial, mediation has a "primacy" effect: Evidence and people whom the mediator actually observes tend to be more vivid, and thus have more impact on her decision making, than data that the neutral merely hears about. Actual documents and face-to-face encounters with potential witnesses are thus likely to have much more impact on a mediator's opinion, and on a judge or jury, than evidence summarized in a brief.
- There is also a "melding" effect: When a mediator cannot personally observe a witness, he must place the person in a category ("nurse," "retired accountant," etc.), then make an assumption about how a fact finder would react to a typical member of that group.

If you want a mediator to give full weight to a witness or a piece of evidence, you should make a special effort to place it directly in front of the neutral. In a construction case, for example, you might ask the mediator to visit the site so that he has a vivid image of the project when he evaluates legal claims arising from it. You may also want to have a mediator meet a key witness. In mediation, unlike a court proceeding, you can arrange for a private meeting without incurring an obligation to expose the witness to your opponent, provided the opponent consents to this arrangement.

A second crucial question is what, exactly, you want evaluated. Don't simply say "the case." In the past mediators routinely provided global opinions about the likely outcome if a dispute were adjudicated. Increasingly, however, mediators think of evaluation simply as a means to jump-start a stalled negotiation — more like filling a "pothole" in which the "settlement bus" has gotten stuck than building a road to a predetermined destination. Often a prediction limited to a single issue is enough to put the parties back on the path to settlement. The question then is: What specific aspect of the case do you want evaluated?

Finally, you should not expect most evaluations to take the form of an explicit opinion. Good mediators see evaluation as a spectrum of interventions rather than a single event. They rely on pointed questions, raised eyebrows, and other "shadow" techniques, much more than explicit statements, to nudge negotiations back on track. When an advocate hears a mediator make such comments, he should realize that the evaluation process is under way, but in a form less likely to provoke resentment than an explicit conclusion.

Mediator's Proposal. In this method the neutral suggests a set of terms, usually in writing, to all parties under the ground rule that each litigant must tell the mediator privately whether it will agree to the proposal if the other parties do(a variation is that each litigant will respond directly to the mediator within a set deadline). If all say yes, there is a settlement. But if any party rejects the proposal, it never learns whether its opponent was willing to agree. Parties thus know that they can achieve complete peace by saying yes, but that if the effort fails to receive a "yes" from all parties, the mediator will not reveal if there were any "yeses," their bargaining position will not be compromised.

In formulating a proposal, mediators typically try to "balance the pain" that each party will have to bear in order to accept it. In other words, the proposed number is the amount he thinks is most likely to be accepted by all sides, not necessarilyhis estimate of the likely outcome in court. One concern is that mediator's proposals have a take-it-or-leave-it quality: Once made, a proposal will tend to "set in cement," in the sense that both parties will resist agreeing to terms less favorable than the neutral has recommended. As a result, if a mediator proposes terms that are even minimally acceptable to a party in light of the costs of litigation, it will feel significant pressure to accept it.

A mediator's proposal has some major advantages. For one thing, it allows a party to test a potential settlement without indicating to the other side that it is willing to compromise. The technique often works — parties often stretch to accept a proposal at the end of the mediation, when the alternative is impasse, because it holds out the promise of settling the dispute, while at the same time protecting their bargaining position if it does not. You might first clarify with the mediator about what standard he will use in making a proposal: balancing the pain that each side must suffer to settle, predicting the outcome in court, or something else.

Problem

You represent the plaintiff in an employment dispute. It is five in the afternoon and you have been mediating for nearly eight hours. You began with a demand of $1.5 million, and in response the defendant offered $25,000. After laborious bargaining, you have dropped to $400,000. Your client's bottom line is $350,000 in a cash only settlement, but would conceivably go to $200,000 if your client were offered a good job back at the company. Unfortunately, the defendant is only at $100,000, having moved there from a prior offer of $85,000. Your client is feeling very frustrated and has told the mediator this. The mediator has gone back to the defense and returned:

1. Should you share with the mediator your client's all cash bottom line and the reemployment alternative? What should you tell the mediator?
2. Assume that the defense suggests a "mediator's proposal." Should you agree? Why or why not?

If the Mediation Session Ends Without Agreement.   If a case does not settle at the mediation session, a good mediator will keep working for settlement and follow-up by phone or e-mail until the parties tell him unequivocally to stop, and he sees no plausible way to change anyone's mind. If a neutral does not appear ready to take the initiative, a good advocate can prod him to do so. Neutrals' spirits, like those of other humans, occasionally flag, and some have a narrow conception of their role. A polite reminder that you are counting on a mediator to pull a settlement out of his hat will often encourage the neutral to make further efforts.

If Negotiations Fail.   Sometimes settlement is genuinely unachievable. Even in such situations, a mediator can be of use by helping counsel to design an efficient process of adjudication. A mediator might, for example, facilitate negotiations over a discovery plan. Or the neutral could broker an agreement on an expedited form of arbitration.

How should an advocate leave an unsuccessful mediation process? Litigator David Stern offers the following advice:

> At some point, hours or days after you have started, the mediation process will end. If it ends with an agreement, that is fine. But if you can't reach agreement, accept that as well. Parties and lawyers often get desperate as the mediation nears conclusion, but the dispute remains unsettled. It is possible, but exceedingly unlikely, that the mediation is the last chance to settle the case. More likely, there will be multiple opportunities — at deposition, at court-ordered settlement conferences, before trial, during trial, even after trial and appeal — to settle. As such, do not despair or let your client despair if you walk away without a deal. . . . Search for partial agreements if feasible, or part company respectfully, so that the possibility of future negotiation remains open. In all likelihood, settlement will eventually occur and both you and your client will benefit if you keep that probability in mind.

F. Conclusion

Too often attorneys treat the mediation process simply as a safe place in which to conduct positional bargaining, trading arguments and offers until they reach impasse. At that point mediators take over the process by making settlement recommendations or offering evaluations. We hope you appreciate that whatever approach you take to bargaining, the mediation process can assist you in negotiation. Lawyers who approach mediation actively as advocates for favorable settlement, looking at the mediator as a trusted consultant, resource, and potential ally, can use the process to advantage and are able to obtain optimal outcomes for their clients.

CHAPTER

14

Negotiated Settlement Policy and Limits

A. Is Settlement Desirable?

In this last chapter we come full circle back to where we started. At the beginning of this text we stated, "A law student reading only casebooks might not know that the vast majority of disputes in which lawyers are involved are negotiated to a settlement without trial." Our legal education norms are premised on disputes being resolved by a judgment following a trial. Most people formulating an impression of lawyers based on popular literature and film have an image of lawyers in court, trying cases. This is consistent with our central notion that justice and rights depend on access to courts to resolve disputes according to law.

However, as you now know, negotiation, whether direct or assisted, is the way most legal disputes are concluded. Negotiation is a consensual process in which the parties may reach an agreement based on any standard or principle they choose. Negotiation is informal, lacks the checks and balances of a trial, and does not set legal precedent. Parties may settle because they get what they want by settling, or because one or both lack the resources necessary to litigate. Settlement may also be the result of imbalances of power, risk aversion, or other psychological factors. Rarely is an individually negotiated, civil settlement agreement reviewed by a court for fairness.

The increased interest in negotiation in the early 1980s, either evidenced or led by the popularity of *Getting to YES*, published in 1981, and the greater use and encouragement of mediation in the 1980s, prompted academic questions about negotiated settlements. Court policies and rules pushing settlements through court ADR programs raised issues about access to justice and fairness. These issues have not been fully addressed, and many of the questions persist. The most influential and often-cited critique of policies encouraging settlement of lawsuits is offered below.

❖ Owen M. Fiss, AGAINST SETTLEMENT

93 Yale L.J. 1073 (1984)

In a recent report to the Harvard Overseers, Derek Bok [then President of Harvard University; former dean of Harvard Law School] called for a new direction in legal education. He decried "the familiar tilt in the law curriculum toward preparing students for legal combat," and asked instead that law schools train their students "for the gentler arts of reconciliation and accommodation." He sought to turn our attention from the courts to "new voluntary mechanisms" for resolving disputes. In doing so, Bok echoed themes that have long been associated with the Chief Justice and that have become a rallying point for the organized bar and the source of a new movement in the law. This movement is the subject of a new professional journal, a newly formed section of the American Association of Law Schools, and several well-funded institutes. It has even received its own acronym — ADR (Alternative Dispute Resolution).

The movement promises to reduce the amount of litigation initiated, and accordingly the bulk of its proposals are devoted to negotiation and mediation prior to suit. But the interest in the so-called "gentler arts" has not been so confined. It extends to ongoing litigation as well, and the advocates of ADR have sought new ways to facilitate and perhaps even pressure parties into settling pending cases. . . .

The advocates of ADR are led to support such measures and to exalt the idea of settlement more generally because they view adjudication as a process to resolve disputes. They act as though courts arose to resolve quarrels between neighbors who had reached an impasse and turned to a stranger for help. Courts are seen as an institutionalization of the stranger and adjudication is viewed as the process by which the stranger exercises power. The very fact that the neighbors have turned to someone else to resolve their dispute signifies a breakdown in their social relations; the advocates of ADR acknowledge this, but nonetheless hope that the neighbors will be able to reach agreement before the stranger renders judgment. Settlement is that agreement. It is a truce more than a true reconciliation, but it seems preferable to judgment because it rests on the consent of both parties and avoids the cost of a lengthy trial.

In my view, however, this account of adjudication and the case for settlement rest on questionable premises. I do not believe that settlement as a generic practice is preferable to judgment or should be institutionalized on a wholesale and indiscriminate basis. It should be treated instead as a highly problematic technique for streamlining dockets. Settlement is for me the civil analogue of plea bargaining: Consent is often coerced; the bargain may be struck by someone without authority; the absence of a trial and judgment renders subsequent judicial involvement troublesome; and although dockets are trimmed, justice may not be done. Like plea bargaining, settlement is a capitulation to the conditions of mass society and should be neither encouraged nor praised.

The Imbalance of Power

By viewing the lawsuit as a quarrel between two neighbors, the dispute-resolution story that underlies ADR implicitly asks us to assume a rough equality between the contending parties. It treats settlement as the anticipation of the outcome of trial and assumes that the terms of settlement are simply a product of the parties' predictions of that outcome. In truth, however, settlement is also a function of the resources available to each party to finance the litigation, and those resources are frequently distributed unequally.

Many lawsuits do not involve a property dispute between two neighbors, or between [a major corporation] and the government . . . , but rather concern a struggle between a member of a racial minority and a municipal police department over alleged brutality, or a claim by a worker against a large corporation over work-related injuries. In these cases, the distribution of financial resources, or the ability of one party to pass along its costs, will invariably infect the bargaining process, and the settlement will be at odds with a conception of justice that seeks to make the wealth of the parties irrelevant.

The disparities in resources between the parties can influence the settlement in three ways. First, the poorer party may be less able to amass and analyze the information needed to predict the outcome of the litigation, and thus be disadvantaged in the bargaining process. Second, he may need the damages he seeks immediately and thus be induced to settle as a way of accelerating payment, even though he realizes he would get less now than he might if he awaited judgment. All plaintiffs want their damages immediately, but an indigent plaintiff may be exploited by a rich defendant because his need is so great that the defendant can force him to accept a sum that is less than the ordinary present value of the judgment. Third, the poorer party might be forced to settle because he does not have the resources to finance the litigation, to cover either his own projected expenses, such as his lawyer's time, or the expenses his opponent can impose through the manipulation of procedural mechanisms such as discovery. It might seem that settlement benefits the plaintiff by allowing him to avoid the costs of litigation, but this is not so. The defendant can anticipate the plaintiff's costs if the case were to be tried fully and decrease his offer by that amount. The indigent plaintiff is a victim of the costs of litigation even if he settles.

There are exceptions. Seemingly rich defendants may sometimes be subject to financial pressures that make them as anxious to settle as indigent plaintiffs. But I doubt that these circumstances occur with any great frequency. I also doubt that institutional arrangements such as contingent fees or the provision of legal services to the poor will in fact equalize resources between contending parties. . . .

Of course, imbalances of power can distort judgment as well: Resources influence the quality of presentation, which in turn has an important bearing on who wins and the terms of victory. We count, however, on the guiding presence of the judge, who can employ a number of measures to lessen the impact of distributional inequalities. He can, for example, supplement the parties' presentations by asking questions, calling his own witnesses, and inviting other persons and institutions to participate as amici. These measures are likely to make only a small contribution toward moderating the influence of distributional inequalities, but should not be ignored for that reason. Not even these small steps are possible with settlement. There is, moreover, a critical difference between a process like settlement, which is based on bargaining and accepts inequalities of wealth as an integral and legitimate component of the process, and a process like judgment, which knowingly struggles against those inequalities. Judgment aspires to an autonomy from distributional inequalities, and it gathers much of its appeal from this aspiration. . . .

The Lack of a Foundation for Continuing Judicial Involvement

The dispute-resolution story trivializes the remedial dimensions of lawsuits and mistakenly assumes judgment to be the end of the process. It supposes that the judge's duty is to declare which neighbor is right and which wrong, and that this declaration will end the judge's involvement. . . . Under these assumptions, settlement appears as an almost perfect substitute for judgment, for it too can declare the parties' rights. Often, however, judgment is not the end of a lawsuit but only the beginning. The involvement of the court may continue almost indefinitely. In these cases, settlement cannot provide an adequate basis for that necessary continuing involvement, and thus is no substitute for judgment.

The parties may sometimes be locked in combat with one another and view the lawsuit as only one phase in a long continuing struggle. The entry of judgment will then not end the struggle, but rather change its terms and the balance of power. One of the parties will invariably return to the court and again ask for its assistance, not so much because conditions have changed, but because the conditions that preceded the lawsuit have unfortunately not changed. This often occurs in domestic-relations cases, where the divorce decree represents only the opening salvo in an endless series of skirmishes over custody and support.

The structural reform cases that play such a prominent role on the federal docket provide another occasion for continuing judicial involvement. In these cases, courts seek to safeguard public values by restructuring large-scale bureaucratic organizations. . . .

The drive for settlement knows no bounds and can result in a consent decree even in the kinds of cases I have just mentioned, that is, even when a court finds itself embroiled in a continuing struggle between the parties or must reform a bureaucratic organization. The parties may be ignorant of the difficulties ahead or optimistic about the future, or they may simply believe that they can get more favorable terms through a bargained-for agreement. Soon, however, the inevitable happens: One party returns to court and asks the judge to modify the decree, either to make it more effective or less stringent. . . .

Justice Rather Than Peace

The dispute-resolution story makes settlement appear as a perfect substitute for judgment, as we just saw, by trivializing the remedial dimensions of a lawsuit, and also by reducing the social function of the lawsuit to one of resolving private disputes. In that story, settlement appears to achieve exactly the same purpose as judgment — peace between the parties — but at considerably less expense to society. The two quarreling neighbors turn to a court in order to resolve their dispute, and society makes courts available because it wants to aid in the achievement of their private ends or to secure the peace.

In my view, however, the purpose of adjudication should be understood in broader terms. Adjudication uses public resources, and employs not strangers chosen by the parties but officials chosen by a process in which the public participates. These officials, like members of the legislative and executive branches, possess a power that has been defined and conferred by public law, not by private agreement. Their job is not to maximize the ends of private parties, nor simply to secure the peace, but to explicate and give force to the values embodied in authoritative texts such as the Constitution and statutes; to interpret those values and to bring reality into accord with them. This duty is not discharged when the parties settle.

In our political system, courts are reactive institutions. They do not search out interpretive occasions, but instead wait for others to bring matters to their attention. They also rely for the most part on others to investigate and present the law and facts. A settlement will thereby deprive a court of the occasion, and perhaps even the ability, to render an interpretation. A court cannot proceed (or not proceed very far) in the face of a settlement. To be against settlement is not to urge that parties be "forced" to litigate, since that would interfere with their autonomy and distort the adjudicative process; the parties will be inclined to make the court believe that their bargain is justice. To be against settlement is only to suggest that when the parties settle, society gets less than what appears, and for a price it does not know it is paying. Parties might settle while leaving justice undone. The settlement of a school suit might secure the peace, but not racial equality. . . .

The Real Divide

To all this, one can readily imagine a simple response by way of confession and avoidance: We are not talking about *those* lawsuits. Advocates of ADR might insist that my account of adjudication, in contrast to the one implied by the dispute-resolution story, focuses on a rather narrow category of lawsuits. They could argue that while settlement may have only the most limited appeal with respect to those cases, I have not spoken to the "typical" case. My response is twofold.

First, even as a purely quantitative matter, I doubt that the number of cases I am referring to is trivial. My universe includes those cases in which there are significant distributional inequalities; those in which it is difficult to generate authoritative consent because organizations or social groups are parties or because the power to settle is vested in autonomous agents; those in which the court must continue to supervise the parties after judgment; and those in which justice needs to be done, or to put it more modestly, where there is a genuine social need for an authoritative interpretation of law. I imagine that the number of cases that satisfy one of these four criteria is considerable; in contrast to the kind of case portrayed in the dispute-resolution story, they probably dominate the docket of a modern court system.

Second, it demands a certain kind of myopia to be concerned only with the number of cases, as though all cases are equal simply because the clerk of the court assigns each a single docket number. All cases are not equal. The Los Angeles desegregation case, to take one example, is not equal to the allegedly more typical suit involving a property dispute or an automobile accident. The desegregation suit consumes more resources, affects more people, and provokes far greater challenges to the judicial power. The settlement movement must introduce a qualitative perspective; it must speak to these more "significant" cases, and demonstrate the propriety of settling them. Otherwise it will soon be seen as an irrelevance, dealing with trivia rather than responding to the very conditions that give the movement its greatest sway and saliency. . . .

[In] fact, most ADR advocates make no effort to distinguish between different types of cases or to suggest that "the gentler arts of reconciliation and accommodation" might be particularly appropriate for one type of case but not for another. They lump all cases together. This suggests that what divides me from the partisans of ADR is not that we are concerned with different universes of cases, that Derek Bok, for example, focuses on boundary quarrels while I see only desegregation suits. I suspect instead that what divides us is much deeper and stems from our understanding of the purpose of the civil lawsuit and its place in society. It is a difference in outlook.

Someone like Bok sees adjudication in essentially private terms: The purpose of lawsuits and the civil courts is to resolve disputes, and the amount of litigation we encounter is evidence of the needlessly combative and quarrelsome character of Americans. Or as Bok put it, using a more diplomatic idiom: "At bottom, ours is a society built on individualism, competition, and success." I, on the other hand, see adjudication in more public terms: Civil litigation is an institutional arrangement for using state power to bring a recalcitrant reality closer to our chosen ideals. We turn to the courts because we need to, not because of some quirk in our personalities. We train our students in the tougher arts so that they may help secure all that the law promises, not because we want them to become gladiators or because we take a special pleasure in combat. To conceive of the civil lawsuit in public terms as America does might be unique. I am willing to assume that no other country—including Japan, Bok's new paradigm—has a case like *Brown v. Board of Education* in which the judicial power is used to eradicate the caste structure. I am willing to assume that no other country conceives of law and uses law in quite the way we do. But this should be a source of pride rather than shame. What is unique is not the problem, that we live short of our ideals, but that we alone among the nations of the world seem willing to do something about it. Adjudication American-style is not a reflection of our combativeness but rather a tribute to our inventiveness and perhaps even more to our commitment.

Questions

1. In what types of cases, other than racial discrimination, does it seem most likely that the concerns about settlement set out by Professor Fiss may arise?
2. Are there categories of disputes, other than between neighbors, in which these concerns are unlikely to materialize?
3. Other than the cite to *Brown v. Board of Education*, is there any support for Fiss's arguments?
4. Does Fiss define what he means by justice or a just result? In the context of settlement, how would you define justice?
5. Based on what you have read and learned in this course and in your other studies, do you think Fiss's concerns, as stated in 1984, have been borne out or proven not to be problematic?
6. Fiss refers to "domestic-relations cases, where the divorce decree represents only the opening salvo in an endless series of skirmishes over custody and support." Does his statement that these cases return again and again to court for adjudication argue for or against negotiation/mediation of parental conflict? Can courts resolve these issues better and with more finality than the divorcing parties? (See Folberg et al. 2004)

Professor Fiss's article provoked considerable debate and a number of responses in defense of settlement. (See, e.g., Lieberman & Henry, *Lessons from the Alternative Dispute Resolution Movement*, 53 U. Chi. L. Rev. 424, 1986; Menkel-Meadow, *Whose Dispute Is It Anyway? A Philosophical Defense of Settlement (In Some Cases)*, 83 Geo. L.J. 2663, 1995.)

Marc Galanter and Mia Cahill view settlement negotiation versus litigation as a false choice. In a frequently cited article, they refer to negotiation and litigation as one process that they label "litigotiation." They believe that settlements are not intrinsically good or bad and argue that courts and policy-makers should approach settlement with a more critical eye, distinguishing "good" settlements from less desirable ones. (See *"Most Cases Settle": Judicial Promotion and Regulation of Settlement*, 46 Stan. L. Rev. 1339, 1994.)

Twenty-five years after the publication of *Against Settlement*, a symposium was held in New York City to revisit the theme of Fiss's article in light of new developments and thinking. An entire issue of the *Fordham Law Review* was dedcated to the topic. Professor Michael Moffitt's article, excerpted below, critiques Fiss's view and some of his assumptions, noting that settlement and litigation are co-dependant and exist in one another's shadow.

❖ Michael Moffitt, *THREE THINGS TO BE AGAINST ("SETTLEMENT" NOT INCLUDED)*

78 Fordham L. Rev. 1203 (2009)

Owen Fiss chose a great title for his article, *Against Settlement*.

Without even reading the associated article, most readers are provoked into immediate sympathy or antipathy. I blame (or credit) the word "settlement." "Settlement" has a Rorschach quality, conjuring different images and associations for different viewers. Perhaps we might even be able to derive some understanding of a person's experiences and values based on the meaning he or she makes of the idea of "settlement."

On one end of a definitional spectrum, we might imagine the reactions of some of the people one scholar has labeled "litigation romanticists." For many with this thorough devotion to the ideals of litigation, the word "settlement" has a distinctly negative set of implications. "Settlement" is viewed as synonymous with "compromise," or even "selling out." . . . On the other end of a definitional spectrum, we might imagine the reactions of some of the people who are so thoroughly devoted to the ideals of alternative dispute resolution (ADR) that one could fairly label them "ADR evangelists." For many with this view of the world, settlement" is an almost unquestioned positive. . . .

I. For Settlement and for Litigation

Both litigation and settlement are worthy of celebration, and both are worthy of critical examination. Litigation and settlement do not merely coexist. Instead, litigation and settlement have come to depend on each other in order to function properly.

Treating litigation and settlement as though they were entirely distinct processes is, of course, an oversimplification. In practice, the two are intertwined. The fundamental rules and structure of each clearly acknowledge the importance of the other. Modern civil procedure is structured to facilitate the interaction between litigation and settlement. . . . Similarly, settlement takes place within the confines of the parameters established by the prospect of litigation. . . . [D]isputants compare what they might receive through a settlement with what they expect might happen in litigation. Furthermore, each disputant's settlement behavior is bounded by the prospect of post settlement litigation. In this manner, private law concepts like fraud, unconscionability, and duress affect negotiators' behaviors precisely because litigation exists as a possible adjunct to settlement negotiations. The prospect of litigation shapes settlement behaviors and settlement outcomes.

A. What Litigation Gives to Settlement

. . . Within our common-law system, the court's role in articulating the law has an obvious contribution to settlement dynamics. Put most simply, courts clarify legal rules not only for the disputants in one case, but also for other disputants or prospective disputants who may be similarly situated. . . .

The other feature of litigation that has a profoundly supportive effect on settlement is the fact that courts have the ability to enforce their decisions. . . . This promise of enforcement affects and largely supports settlement in at least two ways. The first, and probably most conspicuous, way is that courts can be called upon to give effect to settlement agreements. In the event disputants decide voluntarily to resolve a matter, and subsequently one disputant reneges on the terms of that agreement, courts are available to give effect to the private settlement. . . .

Enforcement has an even bigger impact on the large-scale cases Fiss might label as "significant." Consider a mass tort, a widespread consumer fraud case, or an institutional reform action. Now consider how unlikely either the plaintiffs or the defendants would be to contemplate voluntary settlement in any of those cases if the court were unable to guarantee that the terms of the settlement would take effect. Without the court's power to enforce contracts, without consent decrees, and without the preclusion doctrines, neither side in any significant case would see an incentive to settle.

The second way the prospect of litigation shapes settlement stems from its effect on the way in which settlement *negotiations* take place. Courts are available, through litigation, to hear post-settlement complaints about any bargaining misbehavior that took place on the road to settlement. If courts were not available to hear such complaints, I strongly suspect that we would encounter more bargaining misbehavior, more expensive bargaining, or both. . . .

Settlement works today, in part, because courts articulate legal rules, establish at least some clarity around legal entitlements, enforce private settlements, and stand ready to audit settlement behavior after an agreement is reached.

B. What Settlement Gives to Litigation

Just as settlement benefits from certain features of modern litigation, litigation benefits from certain features of modern settlement. To illustrate this point, I highlight below two of the things settlement offers to litigation: docket clearance and selective case filtering.

The most conspicuous of settlement's contributions to modern litigation is its capacity to reduce the number of cases demanding judicial resources and attention. Fiss appears to imagine that docket lightening is, in fact, settlement's only contribution to our judicial system. Likening settlement to plea bargaining, he declares both of them to be undeserving of praise. . . . But Fiss's objection is not that all parties would prefer litigation and that many are somehow being prevented from litigating. His argument is that adjudication is superior when viewed from a societal level. The suggestion that the disputants in question might prefer to settle is, apparently, of little interest to Fiss. . . . But there are some kinds of disputes for which litigation is not particularly well suited, and if litigation need not contend with these disputes, it can do a better job of addressing the ones for which it is well designed.

Three different features of settlement make this selective filtering process possible. First, settlement offers the prospect of value creation. Litigation is necessarily backward looking, focused on binary entitlements, and framed in win/lose terms. Courts allocate or reallocate resources in a zero-sum manner. But in at least some disputes, the possible solution set is broader than the litigation model suggests. More than merely splitting the difference between probabilistically adjusted expected values, settlement outcomes can make parties better off, individually and in the aggregate.

Private disputants frequently discover these opportunities. Intellectual property disputes, for example, routinely culminate not in litigation, but rather in licenses or cross-licenses. Companies in disputes over the terms of supply contracts routinely renegotiate and extend contract terms. Divorcing couples routinely allocate child support and alimony in ways that minimize tax implications. Employees routinely return to work for employers with whom they have been in disputes. Private disputants often find ways to convert disputes into deal-making opportunities in which the total benefit for all parties is greater than could be achieved in litigation. . . .

Second, settlement offers the prospect of addressing nonfinancial, and even nonlegal, issues. Being in a dispute is an emotional experience. . . . Litigation operates within an adversarial structure, and whatever else we might say about it, litigation is not well-suited for relationship building. Settlement can help to filter some of these cases in which emotional concerns or relationship interests coexist with — or even overshadow — legally cognizable interests, and, as a result, litigation can reasonably concern itself more exclusively to the narrow purpose for which it is crafted.

Third, settlement offers the prospect of more fluid problem definition than litigation. Many of the most challenging and important cases of the modern world are ones in which litigation's rigid, and often narrow, joinder and standing rules risk excluding people who will be fundamentally affected by the case's outcome. I do not suggest that joinder and standing rules are necessarily too restrictive. Instead, I merely point out that these rules exist in their current form because they focus on the prospect of litigation. They are, to state the obvious, rules of litigation. Not everyone can, or should, be at the litigation table. But we should acknowledge the cost of excluding people from the table. . . .

II. Things to Be Against

. . . The three things I list below are inspired by the central concerns I understand to have motivated Fiss's declaration that he is against settlement. Each describes an aspect of a regrettable present reality. Each also presents a frame through which to observe not only settlement, but also litigation. None of them, however, presents a basis for opposing settlement.

A. Power Imbalances

Disputants do not always have identical "power," however one constructs the concept of power. And in some circumstances, one disputant has vastly more power than the other disputant. At some level, this is inevitable. No mechanism exists for assuring that I will only commit torts against people within my own tax bracket. We want large corporations to enter commercial or employment relationships with individuals. We need the government to engage with individuals, groups of people, and other governments. As long as these kinds of interactions take place, we must assume that disputes will arise. We must assume, therefore, that now and forevermore, power imbalances will mark at least some disputes. . . .

In its idealized form, litigation provides protections aimed against having outcomes determined by the resources of the disputants. A cash register appears nowhere in the traditional image of blind justice, holding the scales aloft, weighing the merits of each circumstance against the relevant law. . . . Litigation, in its perfect form, dispenses justice without reference to disputants' resources. These protections fail often enough, however, that we should not imagine that litigation has "solved" the power imbalance problem. . . . In short, no reasonable observer would suggest that a disputant's resources are actually irrelevant to the outcome that disputant can expect to get in court.

In its idealized form, private settlement occurs without the influence of power imbalances. A significant portion of the law of contracts aims to protect against the injustices that would arise from enforcing agreements struck under inappropriate conditions. . . . Settlement, in its perfect form, is the vehicle through which parties can arrive at mutually preferred outcomes, regardless of their resources. Settlement in practice, like litigation, too often also fails to protect against the possibility that power imbalances will skew the result in ways that deviate from settlement's underlying ideals. . . .

Power imbalances create problems in the real world. The on-the-ground practices of litigation and of settlement present pictures of sloppy, imperfect efforts at overcoming the worst aspects of power imbalances. We might reasonably compare the ideals of each process — ideals that largely assume away the persistence of power imbalances. We might also compare the sloppy reality of litigation with the sloppy reality of settlement.

The one thing we cannot responsibly do is compare the idealized vision of one practice against the sloppy reality of the other. Proponents of litigation must not present the question as, "*Which is better, (a) having a judge protect the powerless litigant through the promotion of public values as articulated by the law, or (b) sending that powerless litigant alone into the hallway to compromise away her rights?*" Proponents of settlement must not present the question as, "*Which is better, (a) employing fully inclusive deliberative discourse to reach an elegant, fair, and creative resolution, or (b) sending disputants into a formalistic process navigable only by the rich?*" The idealized visions of both processes are beautiful. The practices of both processes are flawed. If power imbalances skew one process, they skew the other, even if perhaps they do so in different ways. . . .

B. Agency Costs

. . . Agents [lawyers] sometimes negotiate settlements with which their clients are disappointed. In an ideal world, agents would understand and represent fully their principals' views of the relevant interests, parameters, tradeoffs, and opportunities. In practice, agents do not always understand their clients' priorities and underlying interests. In practice, agents sometimes have incentives at least partially at odds with some of their clients' interests. And, as a practical matter, agents cannot always bring every decision back to their clients for a new round of consultation. People do not merely hire agents for the agents' skill sets. Sometimes, a client hires an agent because the client does not have the bandwidth to do everything himself or herself. With the delegation of a task to an agent comes the risk that the agent will behave differently than the client would prefer. . . .

Unfortunately, agency costs are unavoidable in litigation as well. For example, every structure for attorneys' fees is fraught with the prospect of mismatching incentives. Few clients have the capacity to monitor attorneys' behavior in any meaningful way, both because of the cost associated with such monitoring and because of asymmetries in information and expertise. Even if a client were to monitor an attorney's actions, and even if a client were to detect behavior of which the client disapproves, the client's options are limited and unattractive. Firing an attorney is enormously costly, because the client would then need to pay another attorney to get up to speed. Filing a malpractice action against an attorney is possible, but malpractice actions are successful only in the most egregious cases. Courts are hesitant to second-guess an attorney's strategic decisions about how to craft the complaint, how to navigate joinder, whether and how to file a dispositive motion, how to navigate various trial decisions, or whether to file a particular sort of appeal. . . .

Just as attorneys risk settling in ways that clients subsequently dislike, attorneys risk litigating in ways that clients subsequently dislike. In the most egregious cases of each, the attorney's behavior may be the product of malpractice. An attorney may exceed the boundaries of the settlement authority a client has given, or an attorney may make litigation decisions so at odds with industry standards that the attorney risks professional sanction. Most of the time, however, an attorney's behavior — even behavior that may be self-interested — is de facto shielded from review or sanction. In short, the risk of agency problems plague both settlement and litigation.

C. Barriers to Court Access

Because courts are purely reactive, they function properly only if disputants have access to the courthouse. In an idealized vision of litigation, any aggrieved person would not only know his or her rights, but also would understand and have access to the state machinery designed to give effect to those rights. In practice, modern disputants encounter a number of different barriers to court access. The most conspicuous reason disputants might not perceive themselves to have access to the courthouse stems from financial concerns. In short, litigation is expensive, and many accurately perceive litigation's justice as beyond their price range. Litigation can also be costly in terms of time, reputation, and emotion. Even those who can afford its financial costs may perceive other litigation costs to be prohibitively high. In short, litigation's ideal assumes that disputants have unfettered and costless access to the courts — a level of access no disputants currently enjoy in practice. . . .

III. Questions to Keep Asking

. . . Owen Fiss's *Against Settlement* continues to be required reading in law school courses across the country not because it presents the final word on

whether we ought to celebrate settlement. . . . *Against Settlement* has an enduring quality because it demands that we wrestle with important questions. In this
final Part, I suggest that Fiss presented readers with at least three separate
categories of questions: about the practice of settlement, about the ideals of
settlement, and about the implications of all of this on legal education. . . . My
suggestion is that, while we are exploring these aspects of settlement, we also
ask the same questions of litigation. Litigation and settlement are linked in
practice. The values they seek to promote are often linked. And they are linked,
at least in part, in the challenges they present. Our understanding of each will
be richer for understanding the other, and these three lenses provide useful
perspectives on each. . . .

Conclusion

Against Settlement deserves robust praise and gratitude from those who care
about settlement and about litigation. This essay helpfully suggested at least
three perspectives from which to examine each of those processes. It focused
attention on power imbalances and their potentially destructive effects. It
raised questions about the pitfalls of agency dynamics, particularly in cases
involving significant numbers of disputants. It demanded that we wrestle with
what it means for people to have access to the court system and to the justice it
promises. All three of these perspectives remain at least as vital today as they
were in 1984.

Against Settlement deserves robust opposition to the extent it suggests a binary
choice between settlement and litigation. If Fiss urges such a choice, the
question he poses is not merely a "Which of your children do you love most?"
kind of question. Instead, it is one for which neither answer could possibly be
adequate: "Which is better, food or water?" Perhaps it is a misreading of Fiss to
think that he demands a binary choice. Perhaps he was merely urging us to
dampen our enthusiasm for settlement, in the face of what he perceived to be
important shortcomings in its implementation at that time and in that context.
Certainly, many commentators have re-read Fiss to be suggesting that we ought
to be asking more nuanced questions.

Many, for example, have suggested that Fiss merely urges us to think hard
before necessarily embracing settlement in all cases. Such a thesis would find
many modern supporters, both among those whose primary focus is litigation
and among those whose primary focus is settlement. But the title Fiss chose and
the language he uses in his article make more nuanced readings like these
difficult. If *Against Settlement* means what its language implies — that one could
do away with settlement, retain litigation, and be better off for the change —
then the article's thesis is flawed both as a theoretical and as a practical matter.

We should celebrate the beauty in each process's internal narrative of justice,
of truth, of efficiency, of predictability, and even of morality. Proponents of
settlement believe not merely in settlement's efficiency, but also in its ability to
bring justice, to discover truth(s), and to provide stability. Proponents of
litigation embrace the same values. We might usefully engage the empirical
question of whether one process or the other does a better job of promoting
each of these values. Both settlement and litigation fail on each of these
measures with some reliability, and both processes continue to undergo reforms
aimed at improving their performances as measured by these values. But to
characterize either as unconcerned with any one of these values is simply false.

If we set out to compare settlement with litigation, we should do so responsibly. We should compare the idealized vision of settlement with the idealized vision of litigation. Or we should compare the sloppy reality of settlement in practice with the sloppy reality of litigation in practice. But more than anything, we should recognize that settlement and litigation are no longer separate — in practice or in theory. Because settlement and litigation are coevolved, symbiotic processes, to stand against one is to stand against the other. I choose, instead, to be for litigation and for settlement.

Questions

7. What does Fiss mean when he refers to the danger of preferring peace over fairness? Is one exclusive of the other? How might Moffitt respond to this question?
8. Other articles in the twenty-fifth anniversary symposium point to the increased cost of litigation, the increased complexity of cases, and the proportionate decrease in court funding as reasons to reexamine Fiss's objections to settlement. How do these changes impact the arguments for and against settlement?

B. Should You Always Negotiate?

Apart from the sociological question of whether settlement is generally preferable over litigation, there is a more personal question of whether you should always negotiate, rather than go to court or battle. Even if you generally favor negotiation, by what criteria do you carve out exceptions? Consider the following situation.

Problem — Family War

An immigrant laborer in the 1950s, Casey, worked at construction sites as a mason's assistant. Mixing cement and mortar on site by hand was slow and labor intensive. Casey improvised various mixing devices driven by small motors, which saved time and labor as well as resulting in a better quality mortar mix. With financial backing from a contractor for whom he worked, Casey eventually obtained several patents for his portable mixers and created a company that manufactured the mixers. The company succeeded and grew. In time, it was a closely held corporation that supported the families of Casey's four adult children, a brother, Sean, and sister, Patty, and three adult nephews. Following Casey's death in 2008, the company, which produced sales in excess of $20 million a year, was managed by Sean as CEO, and Patty as CFO. Sean had extensive management experience and had been close to his deceased brother. Patty was a CPA. Each of the nine family members had equal corporate shares and a seat on the corporate board.

The Casey children believed that Sean and Patty received salaries beyond industry norms and incurred excessive expenses. Dividend payments had not increased as sales grew, which the Casey children attributed to high executive salaries and lavish expenses. Outside acquisition offers for the company had been opposed by management, and the rejection decisions were confirmed by one-vote margins on the Board of Directors, with Casey's four children voting as a block in favor of selling the company. They were upset by the rejection of the acquisition offers and felt that Sean's and Patty's resistance was a result of their desire to retain their positions and company perks. Sean and Patty cited Casey's wish that the company remain independent and family-owned. Palpable tension existed between Casey's children on the one side, with Sean and Patty and their three children on the other side. The two sides did not talk together. Casey's oldest son, Marty, was particularly vocal about his objection to management and made statements at corporate meetings and by e-mail accusing Uncle Sean and Aunt Patty of mismanagement, theft, and company exploitation. Marty's brother and sisters chimed in with other accusations and indicated that, under the circumstances, Casey would have sold the company to the highest bidder.

Casey's four children brought a minority shareholders' action to force a sale of the company and for repayment of excess compensation. Sean and Patty crossclaimed for damages based on libel and slander. Each side invoked the wishes and spirit of Casey in support of their positions. Neither side seems interested in reconciling or compromising.

As lawyer for the Casey children, would you recommend negotiation? Why or why not? Might mediation be appropriate?

There will be times in your representation of clients and in your personal life when you will face the decision of whether you should bargain with a "devil": A law firm partner betrays you by taking your clients as his and then demands a new, better compensation arrangement; a client's spouse, who instigates a divorce, makes extortionist demands knowing your client values peace over contentious divorce proceedings involving the children; a CEO of a small high-tech company you represent learns that his joint-venture partner, a big foreign corporation, has been secretly using the company's technology secrets under a license agreement and not reporting or sharing profits. In each instance, emotions run deep and you or your client feel wronged or threatened. You don't want to give in, be perceived as weak, or legitimize your nemeses' conduct by proposing to bargain with them. You want to be vindicated or get revenge.

Robert Mnookin, in the excerpt from his book that follows, warns that emotional traps can lock us into bad choices unless you and your client carefully examine your thinking process. In addition to the above scenarios, Professor Mnookin also examines decisions to negotiate or not made in infamous conflicts with evil regimes, where lives and liberty were at stake. He analyzes Winston Churchill's fateful choice in May 1940 — Britain's darkest hour — to reject negotiations with Adolf Hitler and to carry on World War Two. Nelson Mandela's decision to initiate negotiations with the South Africa apartheid government that had imprisoned him for life is compared with the imprisoned

Soviet dissident Natan Sharansky's decision not to negotiate with the KGB for his freedom. He also evaluates the willingness of Rudolf Kasztner, a Hungarian Jew, to negotiate with Adolf Eichmann in the hope of saving Jewish lives.

❖ **Robert Mnookin,** BARGAINING WITH THE DEVIL: WHEN TO NEGOTIATE, WHEN TO FIGHT

1 (Simon & Schuster, 2010)

Should you bargain with the Devil?

In an age of terror, our national leaders face this sort of question every day. Should we negotiate with the Taliban? Iran? North Korea? What about terrorist groups holding hostages?

In private disputes, you may face devils of your own. . . . You are furious. Your gut tells you to fight it out in court. To negotiate with this person would give him something he *wants*. It would reward him for bad behavior. You want your rights vindicated, and the thought of negotiating with your adversary seems wrong . . . .

A disputant must decide: Should I bargain with the Devil, or resist? By "bargain" I mean attempt to make a deal — try to resolve the conflict through negotiation — rather than fighting it out. By "Devil," I mean an enemy who has intentionally harmed you in the past or appears willing to harm you in the future. Someone you don't trust. An adversary whose behavior you may even see as evil.

My question, and this book, have their roots in September 11. In the fall of 2001, less than a month after the attacks, Harvard Law School's Program on Negotiation sponsored a public debate at Harvard on whether President Bush should be prepared to negotiate with the Taliban. This debate led me to begin thinking about a more general question: In any particular conflict, how should you decide whether or not it makes sense to negotiate? . . .

My colleague Roger Fisher and I were invited to discuss how Bush should respond to this offer [to negotiate with the Taliban]. Roger Fisher is probably the best-known negotiation guru in the world. He is the leading proponent of what is called interest-based or "win-win" negotiation. His seminal book, *Getting to Yes*, has sold over three million copies. I am his successor as chair of Harvard's Program on Negotiation. . . .

Essentially, Roger supports the categorical notion — prevalent in the field of dispute resolution — that you should *always* be willing to negotiate.

The core argument behind this notion is straightforward and appleaing. Before you resort to coercive measures — such as warfare or litigation — you should try to resolve the problem. To negotiate doesn't mean you must give up all that is important to you. It only requires that you be willing to sit down with your adversary and see whether you can make a deal that serves your interests better than your best alternative does. People and regimes are capable of change. You can't hope to make peace with enemies unless you are willing to negotiate.

You've also heard the categorical answer on the other side. The Faustian parable suggests you must *never* negotiate with the Devil. He's clever and unscrupulous. He will tempt you by promising something that you desperately want. But no matter how seductive the possible benefits, negotiating with evil is simply wrong; it would violate your integrity and pollute your soul.

I must confess a natural aversion to categorical claims of "always" or "never." There are usually examples that can puncture such arguments. In my debate with Roger, I explained that my two greatest political heroes of the twentieth century are Winston Churchill and Nelson Mandela. Each had to decide whether to negotiate with an oppressive and evil enemy. In May 1940, Churchill refused to negotiate with Adolf Hitler, even though Nazi forces had overrun Europe and were about to attach a weakened Britain. In 1985, on the other hand, Nelson Mandela chose to initiate negotiations with a white government that had erected and enforced a racist regime. . . .

"Should you bargain with the Devil?" If I were pressed to proved a one-sentence answer to this question, it would be: "Not always, but more often than you feel like it."

"Not always" because I reject categorical claims that you should always be willing to negotiate. "More often than you feel like it" for two different sorts of reasons. First, the negative traps and strong emotions may make you feel like fighting when clearheaded analysis would demonstrate that you should negotiate. The second relates to morality. You may feel that choosing to negotiate would violate a moral principle you hold dear, or be inconsistent with your sense of self. In the very hardest cases, you may feel deeply torn between the "principled" choice and the "pragmatic" one. When one is forced to choose between the two, I lean heavily in favor of pragmatism, but I want to acknowledge how painful that choice can be.

Why is it painful? Because you may feel that justice requires more than just a pragmatic resolution — it requires condemnation. In your eyes, the enemy has committed an act for which they should be *punished*, not rewarded. Your honor and integrity demand that you resist. This impulse can be just as powerful in business and family disputes as in international conflicts — perhaps even more so.

I have empathy for this desire to punish those who have wronged us. I share it. When we are caught between the demands of principle and pragmatism, what we really need to ask ourselves is, To what extent should we look backward and to what extent should we focus on the future? There's often an inescapable tension between achieving justice for *past* wrongs and the need for resolution. It is another aspect of the Faustian bargain. If you want to resolve the conflict and move forward, yo may have to give the devil something you feel *he doesn't deserve*. This is a bitter pill to swallow. . . .

But drawing on my framework and these stories, I can suggest four general guidelines.

1. Systematically Compare the Expected Costs and Benefits.

When we *feel* like fighting, we may jump to the conclusion that negotiating a satisfactory resolution is simply out of the question. The best antidote to that kind of knee-jerk impulse and the negative traps is to go through Spock's five questions carefully. [Spock is a fictional, pragmatic advisor.]

- Who are the parties and what are their interests?
- What are each side's alternatives to negotiation?
- What are the costs of negotiation for each side?

- Are there any potential negotiated agreements that might better serve the interests of both sides than their best alternatives away from the table?
- If such a deal is reached, what is the likelihood that it will be implemented? (In other words, can you trust the other side to live up to it? If not, can it be enforced anyway?)

I am the first to acknowledge that asking these questions will not necessarily lead to a single right answer. This isn't a mechanical exercise, like balancing your checkbook. This is tedious, it's hard, and it requires you to make predictions about future behavior in a context of uncertainty. It isn't value-free. Judgments about values and priorities — what's "good" and "bad," what counts as a benefit and what counts as a cost — will of course be included in your analysis. For example, when evaluating costs, one might ask, "Will a deal here encourage more evil in the future?" Reasonable people assessing the same alternatives may reach different conclusions. . . .

I am not suggesting you ignore your emotions or your intuitions. Instead I'm advising you to probe them. They may be traps, or they may be valuable insights. Ask yourself, What may have triggered this reaction? Is there evidence to support it? Evidence that would point in the opposite direction?

A second criticism of cost-benefit analysis is that it values pragmatic concerns over moral categorical principles. This goes to one of the most profound issues in philosophy: Is it proper to judge the morality of an act only on an assessment of its consequences? Cost-benefit analysis is consequentialist at its core — one makes choices among alternative course of action solely by evaluating and comparing the consequences of those actions. Some philosophers would argue that this is an incomplete and inadequate form of moral reasoning, and many ordinary people would intuitively agree. There are well-known philosophical puzzles that expose its limitations. Consequentialism doesn't explicitly leave room for philosophical and religious traditions that emphasize categorical principles for human conduct. So why do I still insist, at least as a first step, that you assess costs and benefits? To prevent you from relying *solely* on intuition or unarticulated moral claims, and to be suspicious of those who do. Conduct the analysis first. If you are still conflicted, you must make the difficult decision whether your moral principle is so absolute that you cannot negotiate, even under these extenuating circumstances.

2. Get Advice from Others in Evaluating the Alternatives: Don't Do the Analysis Alone.

Like Churchill, you should be willing to expose your reasoning to rigorous questioning by people you respect. When they ask how you reached your decision about whether to negotiate, "I just know it in my gut, I can't explain it" is not an adequate response. . . .

In our own lives, particularly in conflicts that involve demonization, there are times when we all need a War Cabinet. Talk with at least one person who's less emotionally involved. It may be a lawyer. It may be a trusted friend. It may be a group of advisors whose perspectives are different from yours. It may be a mediator who can help all the disputants understand the trade-offs. The point is, let other people help you weed out the traps.

In assessing the costs and benefits of the alternatives, members of your team may disagree. They may be making different trade-offs and predictions, or different value judgments about what counts as a benefit and what counts as a cost. Exposing these differences is helpful, for it will better ensure a considered decision.

3. Have a Presumption in Favor of Negotiation, but Make it Rebuttable.

Suppose your advisors disagree. Suppose that after thinking it through carefully, your mind is in equipoise — you think the costs and benefits of negotiating are roughly equal to those of not negotiating. In case of such a "tie," I would apply a presumption in favor of negotion.

Now the obvious question is: Why tip the scales in *favor* of bargaining with the Devil? Why not be neutral, or even have a presumption *against* negotiation? After all, this is the Devil we're talking about!

The Reason for the presumption is to provide an additional safeguard against the negative traps: Tribalism, Demonization, Dehumanization, Moralism, Zero-Sum Thinking, the Impulse to Fight or Flee, and the Call to Battle. As we've seen, these traps can distort clear thinking. And their effect can be subtle. You may think you're engaging in pure Spockian analysis, but you may be fooling yourself. The traps may already have sprung. You may be starting with your conclusion — having already intuitively decided what to do — and selectively looking for evidence to justify it. My presumption can mitigate this risk. . . .

Note that my presumption is not a flat rule. It is simply a guideline — and it is rebuttable. If you think the situation through and decide you are better off refusing to negotiate, the presumption is overcome. We've seen several examples in this book.

4. When Deciding on Behalf of Others, Don't Allow Your Own Moral Intuitions to Override a Pragmatic Assessment.

When it comes to making decisions that involve a perceived "devil," there is a difference between individuals acting solely on their own behalf and those acting in a representative capacity — deciding on behalf of others. For an individual, a decision to override a pragmatic assessment based on moral intuitions may be virtuous, courageous, and even wise — as long as that individual alone bears the risks of carrying on the fight. This is not true for a business executive deciding on behalf of a corporation, a union representative acting on behalf of a union, or political leader acting on behalf of his nation. Perhaps not even for parent acting on behalf of a child.

A person acting in a representative capacity not only must carefully and rationally assess the expected consequences of alternative courses of action, but also should be guided by that assessment. If cost-benefit assessment favors negotiation, I think it is improper for the representatives to decide nonetheless to go to battle based on his personal moral intuitions.

Questions

9. Does Mnookin trivialize the gravity of Hitler's intentions by analyzing whether or not Winston Churchill should have bargained with Hitler? What purpose is served by focusing on a situation where the folly and consequences of negotiating with Hitler are so obvious?
10. If you do negotiate with the devil, or your personal nemesis, should your bargaining style or approach be different? If so, how? (See Barbara Gray, *Negotiating with Your Nemisis*, 19 Negot. J. 299, 2003)
11. Some consider trials to represent a failure of attorneys to negotiate a settlement. Do you view trials as a failure? (See Gross & Kent 1991.)

C. Judicial Encouragement of Settlement

Much of the early impetus for encouraging settlement of cases filed in court came from judges concerned about overloaded dockets. It is not surprising, therefore, that courts throughout the United States established early settlement and ADR programs. Legislators have supported court-sponsored settlement programs; Congress, for example, has required every federal district court in the nation to implement a dispute resolution program (ADR Act of 1998, 28 U.S.C. § 651(b)). Settlement programs are most common at the trial level but exist, more and more, in appellate courts as well. Although some court programs offer litigants a choice of settlement processes, mediation has become by far the most popular form of court-connected dispute resolution.

Although the primary motivation is usually to reduce backlogs, courts encourage settlement for other reasons as well. Some cases involve complex technical issues that do not seem well-suited to the limitations of trial presentations. Other cases center on continuing relationships and evoke deep emotions, such as disputes between parents over the custody and visitation rights to their children. Adjudication is often ineffective to resolve such disputes, because it focuses on the past rather than the future and addresses only the presenting problem rather than underlying conflicts. Courts also sometimes promote settlement to divert cases that judges do not want to hear and that court personnel may feel they cannot adequately process. Asbestos-related claims and homeowners' association construction defect cases, for example, can consume vast court resources and can seem to court staff to be without end.

Judicial efforts to promote settlement and reduce trials raise important policy issues, which involve designing programs not simply to yield the greatest benefit to the system, but also to ensure court access and fairness for participants. Fairness and quality concerns arise most pointedly in the context of court-sponsored settlement programs, especially when courts require litigants to engage in the process.

Many courts, impressed with the value of pretrial settlement programs, have gone beyond encouragement and made participation in the process mandatory. Mandatory settlement conferences, as well as mandated mediation, raise issues of the court's authority to compel participation and the constitutionality of creating procedural barriers to trial.

The First Circuit Court of Appeals, in *In re Atlantic Pipe Corp.*, 304 F.3d 135 (1st Cir. 2002), confronted the issue of whether a federal district court may use its inherent powers to order a party in a civil case to participate in and pay for mediation. The case involved a complex construction dispute with many parties. The Court of Appeals confirmed the inherent power of a trial judge to order mediation over a party's objection, to require the objector to pay part of the cost of the process, and to name as a mediator a private neutral nominated by one of the parties. The court expressed concern, however, over the lack of any restriction over the extent of the process, particularly in light of the mediator's quoted rate of $9,000 per day, and remanded the case to the trial court for further orders.

Some state appellate courts have upheld judicial settlement conference and mediation mandates against arguments that they violate constitutional rights (See Golann 68 Or. L. Rev. 487, 1989.) Other courts have held that a party can not be compelled to participate in private mediation or pay the fee of the mediator. (See Jeld-Wen Inc. v. Superior Court, 146 Cal. App. 4th 536, 543, 53 Cal. Rptr. 3d 115, 2007.)

Even though most courts have held that mandating settlement negotiations is constitutional, that does not mean that a particular court has the authority to order participation in any case. Courts ordinarily derive their authority from specific sources, such as constitutional provisions and statutes. Many federal courts, for example, base orders compelling litigants to mediate on court rules adopted pursuant to the Civil Justice Reform Act of 1990, 28 U.S.C. §§471-482, or the ADR Act of 1998, 28 U.S.C. §§651-658. Can a federal court that has not adopted a rule pursuant to these statutes nevertheless order parties to participate in settlement conferences as a matter of "inherent judicial power"? On the one hand, the Seventh Circuit Court of Appeals has ruled that a federal court can use its inherent power to force parties to attend a pretrial settlement conference. (See Heileman Brewing Co. v. Joseph Oat Corp., 871 F.2d 648, 650 (7th Cir. 1989, en banc).) On the other hand, both the Sixth and Seventh Circuits have ruled that federal courts cannot rely on inherent powers to force litigants to engage in "summary jury trials," an ADR process that involves an abbreviated trial to a jury with a nonbinding verdict, usually followed by intensive negotiation. (See In re NLO, Inc., 5 F.3d 154, 6th Cir. 1993; Strandell v. Jackson County, 838 F.2d 884, 7th Cir. 1987).

Basic questions regarding mandated settlement processes are who should participate and who should pay for the service. It was a long-standing tradition in many courts that lawyers met with the judge prior to trial to discuss settlement, without clients present. Lawyer "control" of their clients and of the settlement process was a hallmark of the attorney-client relationship in litigation. This tradition has given way to a more client-centered approach, which recognizes the importance of client involvement in the settlement process. However, settlement conferences conducted without clients continue in some jurisdictions, and clients sometimes prefer, for strategic or economic reasons, not to be present.

The *Heileman Brewing* case, cited above, held that federal courts do have inherent power to order the attendance at a settlement conference of a party or corporate representative having full authority to settle. The appellate court found that, in the circumstances of that case, the trial court did not abuse its authority in ordering a represented corporation to send a corporate officer to a pretrial settlement conference and properly imposed sanctions for failing to do so. Judge Posner, dissenting, expressed concern "that in their zeal to settle cases judges may ignore the value of other people's time." Judge Easterbrook, also dissenting, took issue with the necessity to have a client present when the lawyer could adequately represent the client in settlement negotiations. He argued that lawyers adequately negotiate in collective bargaining and merger talks and are no less suited to negotiate in a settlement conference. (See Riskin, *The Represented Client in a Settlement Conference; The Lessons of* G. Heileman Brewing Co. v. Joseph Oat Corp, 69 Wash. U. L.Q. 1059, 1991.)

Note — Compelled Participation and Good-Faith Bargaining

If a court has the power to order disputants to participate in settlement conferences or mediate, should it require them to satisfy a minimum standard of negotiation conduct? If the adoption of court rules is any guide, the answer is yes. Professor John Lande has found that at least 22 states have "good-faith bargaining" requirements for mediation, and that 21 or more federal district courts and 17 state courts have local rules imposing such duties on disputants, usually in connection with a court ADR program. The problem is that virtually none of these rules defines what constitutes "good faith" or its absence. According to Professor Lande, the reported cases on good-faith obligations break down as follows:

- Failure to attend mediation at all.
- Failure to send a representative with adequate settlement authority.
- Failure to submit required memoranda or documents.
- Failure to make a suitable offer or otherwise participate in bargaining.
- Failure to sign an agreement.

In practice, courts have found it easiest to sanction objective conduct, such as a party's failure to appear or file a statement. Judges have found it much more difficult to determine whether a party has made a "suitable offer" or sent a representative with "adequate settlement authority." There are only a few cases in which sanctions based on subjective conclusions about misconduct in settlement programs have been upheld on appeal. (Lande 2002.)

Attempts to regulate parties' conduct during compelled settlement discussions raise difficult issues. To begin with, a court would have to define what it meant by "good faith." In many cases the court would also have to take evidence about what had been said or done during the mediation process itself, raising serious issues of confidentiality. Assuming that enforcement were feasible, many argue that good-faith bargaining requirements are in conflict with the concept of self determination, a central value of mediation. Standard I of the Model Standards of Conduct for Mediators (2005) states, "Parties may exercise self-determination at any stage of a mediation, including mediator selection, process design, participation in or withdrawal from the process, and outcomes." If parties have the unfettered right to make their own decisions about mediating, however, how can any specific level of participation in the process be required? At the same time, if parties are ordered to mediation by a court and one party expends substantial resources to comply, should its adversary be permitted to nullify the process by failing to prepare or refusing to bargain?

In response to the difficulty of defining and enforcing "good faith" requirements, some have argued that such rules should be discarded. Professor Lande, for example, proposes that courts limit themselves to enforcing objective standards of conduct, such as a requirement that parties appear at mediation for a minimum period of time.

The most bizarre story about "good-faith' participation begins in Panama City Beach, Florida, during Spring Break 2003, where Joseph Francis filmed an episode in his series of *Girls Gone Wild*. As alleged in the complaint filed by unidentified minor girls and their parents, Francis enticed, with the help of alcohol, underage girls to engage in various sexual acts, in front of the cameras. A civil action, Doe v. Francis, No. 5:03cv260 (FL ND), was filed about the same time as a parallel criminal charges were brought against Francis. A federal judge ordered Francis to participate in mediation, for which he arrived, via his private plane, four hours late.

As recounted in an article by Michael D. Young ("Mediation Gone Wild," 25 Alternatives 103, June 2007),

> Francis was wearing sweat shorts, a backwards baseball cap, and was barefoot. He was playing on his electronic devise. As [plaintiffs' counsel] began his presentation, Francis put his bare, dirty feet up on the table, facing plaintiffs' counsel. [Plaintiffs' counsel] said four words, "Plaintiffs were minor girls," when Francis barked, "Are the girls minors now?" Continuing, [Plaintiffs' counsel] said, "Plaintiffs are minor girls who were severely harmed by Defendant." Francis then erupted. "Don't expect to get a f . . . dime — not one f . . . dime!" This was Francis' mantra which he repeated, about fifteen times, during his tantrum that ensued. "I hold the purse strings. I will not settle this case, at all. I am only here because the court is making me be here!" Francis shouted. Seeing there was to be no mediation in "good faith," plaintiffs' attorneys got up to leave the room. Less than three minutes had passed, almost completely taken up by Francis' outburst. As plaintiffs' attorneys were leaving, Francis' threats escalated. "We will bury you and your clients!" Francis threatened. Francis then got up and faced off with [Plaintiffs' counsel]. Right in [Plaintiffs' counsel's] face, Francis barked, "I'm going to ruin you, your clients, and all of your ambulance chasing partners!" . . . Francis then made the only offer he was to make that day, "suck my d . . . ," Francis shouted repeatedly, as plaintiffs' counsel left the mediation room.
>
> The Judge's contempt order stated, "Coercive incarceration is an appropriate sanction for this situation. Mr. Francis can cure his contempt and have this sanction of incarceration removed upon his proper participation in mediation." The court then ordered the parties to participate in another mediation session, instructing them to arrive the night before. It insisted that Francis "will be dressed and groomed appropriately, i.e., business suit and tie, business shoes and socks." The court further ruled that "This mediation is ordered as an activity of this Court." Finally, the court ruled that Francis would be released from incarceration "when the mediator certifies in person to the court that Mr. Francis has fully complied with this order and has participated in the mediation in good faith."

Questions

12. Assuming mediation communications are considerd to be confidential in Florida, how is it that Francis's comments came before the judge and are reported on the court's record and then appear in articles about the mediation?

13. Assume you are a law clerk to the trial judge in the *Atlantic Pipe* case. What conditions might you suggest adding to the mediation order to meet the First Circuit's concerns?

14. In a first caucus meeting with the mediator, the plaintiff's lawyer says that while its previously communicated $750K demand is "negotiable," it will not make any concessions until the defense puts a "significant offer" on the table. The defense lawyer informs the neutral that she will not make any offer at this point because the plaintiff is "on another planet." She tells the mediator that it's his job first to bring the plaintiff into a zone of reality, and that the $750K demand is not it. The court's ADR rules require the parties to "engage in good-faith bargaining." Is either the plaintiff or the defendant violating its obligation?

15. Assume that in the above mandatory mediation, counsel for the defendant offered $10,000 in response to the plaintiff lowering its demand from $750,000 to $450,000. If applicable rules require that the parties "bargain in good faith," has the defense complied?

16. Consider the situation of defense counsel in the following California case: A court-appointed master ordered the parties to engage in a five-day mediation process of a complex construction defect claim. Knowing that such claims necessarily involve expert testimony, the neutral instructed each side to bring its experts to the process. The neutral's charges and the plaintiff's cost for assembling its experts for mediation totaled nearly $25,000. Defense counsel, however, arrived 30 minutes late for the first session and appeared alone. Asked about his failure to bring his client or his experts, he said, "I'm here, you can talk to me." (See Foxgate Homeowner's Association, Inc. v. Bramlea California, Inc., et al., 25 P.3d 1117 (Cal. 2001).)

    (a) Did the defense counsel's actions in this mediation constitute bad faith?

    (b) The mediator in *Foxgate* reported to the court that defense counsel took this approach because he believed that his pending motion for partial summary judgment would substantially reduce the value of the plaintiff's claims. Does this justify the lawyer's strategy?

    (c) The neutral also reported that, in his opinion, the defendant had sufficient time to present the motion before the mediation but had not done so. Does this change your opinion?

17. Can a court require a representative of an insurer, who is not a party, to attend a settlement conference and participate in good faith? (See *In re Novak*, 932 F. 2d 1397, 11th Cir. (1991).)

D. Court Approval of Negotiated Settlements

At the beginning of this chapter, it was stated that "Rarely is an individually negotiated, civil settlement agreement reviewed by a court for fairness." However, when class representatives purport to negotiate a settlement for absent class members, FRCP 23, and similar state provisions, requires court review and approval for fairness to the class. Although lawyers representing corporate defendants and class plaintiffs may start the case as true opponents, perhaps viewed by one another as "devils" for purposes of negotiation, if a settlement is reached they become united in interest because they each see the bargained-for-result as the best outcome to satisfy their needs. The former opponents become united in seeking required court approval for the deal they have negotiated. The role of the court under Rule 23 and its progeny is to determine if the negotiated settlement is fair to absent class members and not just a collusive convenience favorable to those at the table.

This issue was before a federal trial court in a 2007 national wage and hour class action against Oracle Corporation seeking a maximum recovery of $52.7 million. The class had not yet been certified or the pleadings finalized when the lawyers for the three named class representatives and Oracle reached a universal settlement agreement. The settlement would have extinguished the potential claims of 1,500 putative class members residing in 35 states by creating an exclusive claims procedure with total payout limited to $9 million.

The court, in denying approval of the settlement, stated,

> By expressly obligating itself only on a "claims-made" approach, Oracle would pay only those who submit claims up to a total of nine million dollars less all fees and expenses. Counsel wants $2.25 million in attorney's fees and $75,000 in expenses. In addition to their own shares of the settlement, $45,000 total would be paid to the three named plaintiffs as "incentive payments." Costs of administration would also be deducted. Because it will be a "claims-made" settlement, there will be no residue. All unclaimed amounts will revert to Oracle. . . . Class actions are ideally suited to the efficient resolution of numerous parallel claims in a single proceeding and to encourage the pooling of small claims against a common target. They are an engine of justice in our federal courts. But they can also lend themselves to abuse. One form of abuse is collusive settlement. Once the named parties reach a settlement in a purported class action, they are always solidly in favor of their own proposal. . . .
>
> It is also no answer to say that a private mediator helped frame the proposal. Such a mediator is paid to help the immediate parties reach a deal. Mediators do not adjudicate the merits. They are masters in the art of what is negotiable. It matters little to the mediator whether a deal is collusive as long as a deal is reached. Such a mediator has no fiduciary duty to anyone, much less those not at the table. Plaintiffs' counsel has the fiduciary duty. It cannot be delegated to a private mediator. (Judge William Alsup, Madhav Kakani, et al. v. Oracle, No. C 06-06493 WHA, USDCNC (June 19, 2007).)

Note — Class Settlement Fairness and Objectors

In the above case, the judge rejected the proposed settlement prior to notice being sent to class members that a settlement was pending. Had Judge Alsup given preliminary approval, the notice then given to the class would have allowed class members to object if any thought the proposed settlement terms were not fair to the class, including the maximum amount available for claims, the amount deducted for attorneys' fees, and the adequacy of notice. Because the defendant and plaintiff class counsel are now on the same side in supporting the settlement they negotiated, objectors can provide the only form of adversarial testing that a proposed settlement will have. The prospect of possible objections plays an important role as a safeguard in protecting the interests of absent class members, tending to sharpen the scrutiny of the court in promoting fairness and preventing collusive negotiations. If an objector raises points that refine the settlement or cause it to be disapproved, the objector can be awarded attorneys' fees and costs.

Plaintff class lawyers and some corporate defense attorneys have labeled lawyers who file objections "professional objectors — attorneys who make a living by serially objecting to any class action settlement, regardless of merit." Class lawyers accuse repeat objectors of being "hold-up artists" and "extortionists." If objectors are unsuccessful in the approving trial court they have a right to appeal, which can delay the settlement and payment of class counsel fees for years. The potential delay provides objectors with leverage to negotiate with both class counsel and the original defendant for payment (and perhaps refinement of the class settlement) in exchange for dismissal of the objections. This leads class counsel to state, "the delay inherent in appellate review allows professional objectors to hold class counsel's fees hostage by demanding a 'fee' for the release of those fees. . . . Many class counsel have resigned themselves to the reality of professional objectors, simply seeing them as a 'tax' imposed on class action counsel." Kabateck & Torrijos, *The Rise of Professional Objectors in Class Action Settlements*, 5 Daily Journal, July 8, 2010. (See also Kullar v. Foot Locker Retail, Inc and Crystal Echeverria, et al., Objectors, 168 Cal. App. 4th 116 (2008).)

Questions

18. Do you agree with Judge Alsup that a mediator does not care if a settlement deal is collusive and has no duty regarding fairness for class members not at the table?
19. Given the role of objectors in keeping class action settlement negotiations honest, can you suggest any ways that abuse of the objector mechanisim can be prevented?

E. A New Role for Lawyers — Settlement Counsel

Experienced trial lawyers totally invest themselves in preparation for a court-room contest. They are similar to athletes getting ready for a big game or soldiers going to battle. To do well in a competitive situation, they have to focus on winning; they get "psyched up," and they cannot "back down." The clients they represent, who in non-contingent fee cases will pay the tab for the trial, incur "sunk" costs for this preparation. They must get more to recoup their expenses and make the time spent worthwhile. Attorney and client create for themselves an image of victory over an opponent, who, as trial approaches, is seen as the enemy to be defeated. The "demonization" of the enemy becomes a self-fulfilling prophecy based on selected observations of the opponent's be-havior, who is also preparing for battle. The trial attorney develops a personal interest in proceeding and justifying the expense of preparation, as well as making good on the advice given and predictions of success at trial. This scenario is mirrored on the other side. The motivation and the interests of the trial attorneys may be in conflict with pursuit of settlement.

Is there a way to insulate the role of the trial attorney, so she can do her job in preparing to win at trial while a settlement is negotiated? In England, solicitors traditionally handle settlement negotiations and "quarterback" the case, calling in a barrister as needed for pleadings, arguments, and trial. This allows the solicitor and the barrister to focus on their separately defined roles of negotiation and trial, much like a Secretary of State and a Secretary of War. In the United States the same division of roles can be achieved by separately retained settlement counsel and trial counsel. (See Coyne, *The Case for Settlement Counsel*, 14 Ohio St. J. Disp. Resol. 367, 1999.) The next and final reading proposes greater use of settlement counsel in business disputes by combining the concept with "collaborative law," which you read about in Chapter 10.

❖ **Kathy A. Bryan,** *WHY SHOULD BUSINESSES HIRE SETTLEMENT COUNSEL?*

195 J. Disp. Resol. 195 (2008)

I. Introduction

As a former in-house litigation manager, I hired separate settlement counsel in only a few cases and with varying results. With responsibilities for hiring and managing a large portfolio of outside firms, I was loath to increase case-staffing ranks for many reasons — and cost was only one factor. Internal resources must oversee litigation, and having another set of outside lawyer relationships on the same case generally seemed duplicative. Worse, it demanded more of my scarce time to manage both the relationship and the primary litigation firm. In addition, I viewed in-house counsel's role as akin to settlement counsel — coordinating with the litigation team but reaching agreements separately in many cases. In-house attorneys generally tend to share this bias against settle-ment counsel.

Today, with a greater understanding of the sea change that Collaborative Law has had in family law, I want to reconsider that conclusion and explore whether using separate settlement counsel, and borrowing other techniques from the Collaborative Law movement, enhances and increases the potential to resolve business disputes.

II. Collaborative Law and Collaborative Law Techniques

With humble beginnings in Minnesota family courts in the early 1990s, Collaborative Law (CL) has grown swiftly to include groups in thirty-three states in the United States and in most Canadian provinces, as well as professional associations, law school courses, and even ethical codes. An essential CL element has come to be the disqualification provision, or "Participation Agreement," where the lawyers for both sides agree in writing to work toward a negotiated resolution and, if the case proceeds to court, clients must engage other counsel. Another CL hallmark is the "four-way meeting," in which the parties and counsel participate. Parties also agree to good-faith negotiation, cooperative information exchange, and to consider jointly hiring neutral experts.

This non-adversarial approach promotes resolution that is fundamentally different from the traditional negotiation occurring in the context of a lawsuit. . . . While U.S. businesses and their in-house counsel have come to embrace mediation as a settlement mechanism, relatively few have adopted CL techniques into their day-to-day practices. Instead, most prefer using positional bargaining and court-oriented solutions, most likely resulting in a settlement after a long discovery process, heavy motion practice, and, rarely, trial. CL techniques should be added to the business dispute resolution toolbox. This article examines the types of cases where CL techniques may be appropriate. It also discusses the potential benefits of using settlement counsel in particular.

III. Advantages

A. Preserving Relationships

An often-cited factor for the CL movement's success in family law is the need to preserve relationships in the interests of children, which overrides the parents' openly adversarial mode. Clearly, relationships can be equally critical in business conflict. Companies that create a culture focused on building and enhancing relationships tend to flourish. True, there are competitive situations where all-out legalistic war seems more appropriate, but much of U.S. companies' litigation portfolios concern employees, customers, vendors, suppliers, contractual partners, etc., where continuing relationships are paramount — especially when conflict erupts. In fact, when surveyed, corporate counsel describe the need to preserve relationships as one of the top reasons for using mediation.

Collaborative practices create an environment where relationships can be repaired and healed — as opposed to litigation, arbitration and, sometimes even mediation, with winners and losers often defaulting to a "zero-sum" approach. Claims of personal harm in medical error, employment, and torts all hold promise for benefits from using CL or settlement counsel. Particularly when the dispute involves systemic harm, solutions to a common problem rather than finding fault should be explored at the outset.

B. Reducing Cost and Time to Resolution

Collaborative Law processes can significantly reduce the time to resolution. In family law, the CL process makes it harder for the parties to end the negotiations. It also creates an incentive to keep the parties working to avoid impasse. In particular, the disqualification provision gives the lawyers substantial financial incentive to negotiate a resolution. Many describe this as an "essential feature" of CL. CL is thus an extremely powerful tool to promote early settlement.

For commercial cases where protracted litigation seriously threatens business interests, using a pure form of CL at the outset has real potential. Putting aside for the moment the challenge of convincing the opposing party to use CL, (which is discussed more below) imagine the power of an early four-way meeting with the parties and their lawyers, all taking time out from the oppositional conflict dialogue to engage in structured discussions focused on interests and solutions.

Several other CL techniques hold additional promise for cost savings. Jointly hired neutral experts and truncated information exchange could drastically reduce time and cost. Corporate counsel recognize that the most significant cost savings occurs when the matter is resolved at the earliest possible stage, preferably before expending the costs of discovery and motion practice. When time is critical, and if relationship building overcomes the tendency to maximize adversarial advantage, CL offers an unmatched tool to explore solutions and reach early resolution.

C. Overcoming Adversarial Bias

Adversarial bias — essentially the human tendency to need "to be right" in a dispute — affects everything in litigation. As lawyers, our adversarial training becomes a part of our intellectual DNA. We are so accustomed to positional thinking that we define the dispute in legal terms and forget problem solving in the heat of the conflict. By the time a suit is filed, the parties' relationship has become so strained, and the trust so broken, that both sides are in full riot gear. Worse yet, we don't even recognize it. As Malcolm Gladwell described in his thoughtful book, *Blink*, bias tends to be unconscious.

One reason that CL has grown so quickly in family law probably is that its techniques overcome unconscious adversarial bias and actually create new resolution possibilities. CL acts as a sort of an imposed cooling-off period, allowing parties, and especially their lawyers, to think more clearly and creatively. What does this mean for business disputes? By the time lawyers become involved in the dispute, conflict is usually entrenched and the role of the lawyer is to define the legal position and begin the legal process. The typical question put to the lawyer is, "How strong is our legal claim?" In addition to the answer to that question, the most innovative counsel also concentrates on an interest-based analysis.

. In-house counsel generally keep business issues front and center better than outside counsel, who quite naturally view their role as a zealous advocate. Nevertheless, it is difficult for the same lawyer to maintain both mindsets at the same time. Having a set of lawyers solely devoted to overcoming the culture of adversarial negotiation presents the best opportunity to find interest-based solutions.

IV. Overcoming Barriers

A. Opponents' Acceptance

When mediation was in its infancy, it was common to hear the concern that hiring a mediator would be interpreted as weakness by the opposing counsel. Thanks to the broader use and acceptance of mediation, court direction, and in no small measure the International Institute of Conflict Prevention and Resolution's "CPR Pledge©," that refrain is heard less often. CL seems to be in the same nascent stage. As is typical in adversarial situations, the concern is with losing leverage. Several techniques can be employed to lessen this impression. First and foremost, in-house counsel's demand for CL or settlement counsel has the most power to diffuse an unintended signal of weakness. Providing the neutral statement that it is the business policy, or otherwise the standard practice, removes the impression that CL is needed because of factual or legal weakness in the matter at hand. Additionally, the in-house lawyer is uniquely positioned to emphasize the importance of cooperation and good-faith negotiation, which could ring hollow when coming from outside counsel engaged to "defend" the matter. Finally, the in-house counsel can commit to have the right business executives present and can demand the opponent do the same.

Another reasonable approach is to expressly designate in-house lawyers as settlement counsel. While the implicit strength of the disqualification agreement would not apply, in-house lawyers could use the other interest-based negotiating techniques to reduce the effect of ego, open up communication, and broaden the potential resolution options. CL practitioners have found that early focus on interests reduces parties' tendency to become entrenched in their positions. Second, pointing to an established protocol, practice guidance, or pledge helps define the process, provides legitimacy, and, again, takes the focus away from the particular case to a broader company-wide approach. A newly formed CPR Institute committee is developing a business-oriented process to address this need in the commercial context.

Third, when settlement counsel are deployed, it can be done in conjunction with and complementing an aggressive litigation track. For example, settlement counsel need not break off communications just because one side or the other decides to commence litigation. It is difficult for the litigator to say convincingly, "We filed suit this morning, but we still want to talk this afternoon." Settlement counsel can say, "The litigation team started suit this morning, but my job is still to continue to talk settlement this afternoon."

In situations where the potential for good-faith negotiation is low, a dualtrack approach has less risk, although clearly it also is more costly and potentially time consuming.

B. Lack of Sufficient Information

Throughout my career, I have heard litigation lawyers explain that they cannot evaluate a case's strengths and weaknesses, complete a reasonable budget, negotiate a resolution, or recommend mediation, until they have sufficient information about the facts and the law. It is certainly true that information is needed, but today this attitude has become a slippery slope into a rabbit hole of endless discovery.

In the majority of cases, probably more than 80% of the most relevant information is obvious in the first month of a case evaluation, and most of the trial documents already are identified and analyzed. In the business world, significant decisions are routinely made with much less information, and the "80/20 rule" is often invoked. How much more certainty is enough in the legal context? How much "hiding the ball" actually benefits the clients?

In comparison, CL agreements typically provide for "complete and honest" information exchange. In the context of family law disputes, the universe of relevant information may be reasonably defined. The opposite is true in commercial litigation. The mediator's toolbox provides some guidance because mediators sometimes request categories of information after the parties have outlined the issues. These requests are far from the typical discovery request. They are tailored to disclose information helpful to identifying interests and developing mutual gain.

Settlement counsel similarly can define a reasonable information exchange process shielded from disclosure in litigation. Document exchange shrinks significantly when information exchange is designed to identify business interests, rather than strengthen legal claims, and when it is focused on what is needed to evaluate settlement proposals. Therefore, it is possible to exchange documents and engage in the equivalent of the four-way meeting much earlier in the process.

C. Lack of Trust

Today, most commercial litigation is conducted in an atmosphere of mutual distrust, not an atmosphere of trust and good-faith negotiation, to say the least. In many business disputes such as class actions, claims between competitors, failed business ventures, patent infringement actions, etc., there is little likelihood that negotiations can proceed on the basis of mutual trust. In some cases involving longstanding relationships, however, trust can and should be built. How can trust be built in those cases where the potential exists, and how can those cases be identified? Or, alternatively, do we need trust to conduct good-faith negotiation, or just a different mindset?

Since the legal system and legal training is based on the adversarial model, it may be more important to change our mode of thinking than to require trust be present. Just as civil procedure rules were defined in the context of the adversarial system, CL practices are being defined in the context of interest-based negotiation. As these practices evolve and become more refined, it is possible to simply redefine the procedure, without the need to develop trust at the outset. Good-faith negotiation will follow that process.

V. Ideas and Proposals for Future Direction

Reflecting on the development of U.S. mediation practices, there appear to be a number of parallels with the current perspective on CL techniques and the use of settlement counsel in commercial disputes. Both began with understandable skepticism. Both require significant hands-on experience with the tools to shape them to fit the business context. Modifications and adaptations are necessary and should be encouraged.

CL in family law arose as a lawyer-led movement. If CL is to be adopted in commercial matters, it must be client or corporate counsel driven. The economic incentives in law firms simply do not encourage CL or settlement counsel practices. Just as with mediation, it will take demand by general counsel or the judiciary before widespread acceptance by law firms.

A broader dialogue supporting the use of CL techniques in business should include the following:

1. A range of options allowing flexibility in the process, such as borrowing from Leonard Riskin's "grid" concept to refine the range of CL options.
2. Exploring the importance of the disqualification provision in the commercial context, including ethical considerations.
3. More settlement counsel practitioners who are trained in interest-based negotiation and mediation advocacy skills.
4. The use of tiered dispute resolution clauses with an initial step that includes some CL elements, such as the equivalent of a four-way meeting with settlement counsel before the next step, which could be mediation, arbitration, or filing suit.
5. Using different techniques with settlement counsel such as:
   a. For a range of matters within a business. Often settlement counsel can see patterns among classes or types of cases that allow them to maximize settlement opportunities.
   b. Unilaterally. When opposing counsel refuses to engage parallel settlement counsel, even one side's settlement counsel can effectively negotiate directly with litigation counsel.
   c. With and without the disqualification provision. The "pure" form of CL is not always necessary.
   d. With alternative fee arrangements and other economic incentives. Many settlement counsel are adept at using creative fee arrangements with incentives since they are confident that the overall transaction cost will be lower with early and effective settlements.
   e. Designating and developing a modified settlement counsel position, where appropriate, on in-house legal staffs. In-house counsel frequently view themselves as settlement counsel and, when they can be objective about the matter, can be highly effective in that role.
6. More defined information exchange procedures applicable to business settings.
7. Client education on preventive legal counseling and interest-based negotiation.
8. Continuing to increase awareness about educational institutions' tendency to emphasize adversarial training.
9. Promoting graduate legal and business curriculums on problem solving and collaborative methods of dealing with conflict.

VI. Conclusion

There is natural resistance to radical new ideas. Given the rapid growth and stunning impact of CL in family law, it is time to experiment with CL concepts in the business setting. Corporate counsel should take the lead and experiment with using separate settlement counsel and with more pure forms of CL. If successful, CL will begin to take root.

Questions

20. Is there any reason why a law firm or a corporate law department could not have a trial component and a settlement or ADR specialist?

21. Is there any distinction between the British legal system and the American one that might undermine the usefulness of the solicitor/barrister role models for purposes of settlement? Is the fact that in England the roles of barrister and solicitor are becoming less rigidly defined likely to increase the use of mediation and other assisted negotiation, which was slower to take hold in England?

22. Is trial experience essential to serve as settlement counsel? What are the best qualifications to be an effective settlement counsel? It is said that, "He who is good with a hammer thinks everything is a nail." Is a lawyer who is good at trial more likely to think every dispute needs to be tried?

APPENDIX

The appendix to this book is entirely Web based and is shared with Resolving Disputes: Theory, Practice, and Law, Second Edition. This makes it possible for students and teachers to have access to more resources and download and edit materials to meet their individual needs. To access the combined Appendix, enter the following URL:

www.aspenlawschool.com/books/folberg_resolvingdisputes

The contents of the Appendix, which will be updated from time to time, include the following:

Negotiation

- Ethical Guidelines for Settlement Negotiations (ABA)
- Federal Rule of Civil Procedure 68
- Model Rules of Professional Conduct (ABA)

Mediation

- Legislation
  - ADR Act of 1998
  - Uniform Mediation Act (NCCUSL)
- Rules
  - Commercial Mediation Procedures (AAA)
  - CPR Mediation Procedure (CPR)
  - Ethics 2000 ("E2K") Report (ABA)
  - Model Rule of Professional Conduct for the Lawyer as Third-Party Neutral (CPR-Georgetown)
  - 2005 Model Standards for Mediators (AAA, ABA, and ACR)
  - Model Standards of Practice for Family and Divorce Mediators (ACR)
  - Sample Mediation Agreements

Arbitration

- Legislation
  - Federal Arbitration Act
  - Convention on the Recognition and Enforcement of Foreign Arbitral Awards

- Model Legislation for Potential State Adoption
  - Uniform Arbitration Act (1956)
  - Revised Uniform Arbitration Act (2000)
  - Revised Uniform Arbitration Act with Commentary
- Rules
  - Code of Ethics for Arbitrators in Commercial Disputes (AAA and ABA)
  - Commercial Arbitration Rules and Mediation Procedures (AAA)
  - Arbitration Appeal Procedure (CPR)
  - Comprehensive Arbitration Rules (JAMS)
  - Optional Appeal Procedure (JAMS)
  - Principles for ADR Provider Organizations (CPR-Georgetown)
  - Rules for Non-Administered Arbitration (CPR)
  - Rules of Arbitration (ICC)
  - Streamlined Arbitration Rules (JAMS)
- Protocols
  - Consumer Due Process Protocol (AAA)
  - Consumer Arbitration Minimum Standards (JAMS)
  - Employment Minimum Standards (JAMS)

BIBLIOGRAPHY AND REFERENCES

The titles of books are in italics and the titles of articles are in quotes.

Aaron, Marjorie Corman (1995) "The Value of Decision Analysis in Mediation Practice," 11 *Negot. J.* 123.

Aaron, Marjorie Corman (2002) "At First Glance: Maximizing The Mediator's Initial Contact," 20 *Alternatives* 167.

Aaron, Marjorie Corman (2005) "Do's and Don'ts of Mediation Practice," 11 *Disp. Resol. Mag.* 19 (Winter).

Aaron, Marjorie Corman, & David P. Hoffer (1996) "Decision Analysis as a Method of Evaluating the Trial Alternative," in D. Golann, *Mediating Legal Disputes* 307. Boston: Aspen Publishing.

ABA Sub-Committee on Alternative Means of Dispute Resolution (1986) "The Effectiveness of the Mini-Trial," in *Resolving Complex Commercial Disputes: A Survey.* Chicago: American Bar Association.

Abramson, Harold I. (2004) *Mediation Representation: Advocating in a Problem-Solving Process.* Notre Dame, IN: NITA.

Abramson, Harold I. (2004) "Problem-Solving Advocacy in Mediation," 59 *Disp. Resol. J.* 56.

Adamowicz, Viktor L., et al (1999) "Experiments on the Difference Between Willingness to Pay and Willingness to Accept," 69 *Land Econ.* 86.

Adler, Robert S. (2005) "Flawed Thinking: Addressing Decision Biases In Negotiation," 20 Ohio St. J. on Dispute Reol. 683.

Adler, Robert S., & Elliot M. Silverstein (2000) "When David Meets Goliath: Dealing with Power Differentials in Negotiations," 5 *Harv. Negot. L. Rev.* 1 (Spring).

Albrecht, Karl & Steve Albrecht (1993) *Added Value Negotiating: The Breakthrough Method for Building Balanced Deals.* Homewood, Ill.: Irwin.

Alexander, Janet Cooper (1991) "Do the Merits Matter? A Study of Settlements in Securities Class Actions," 43 Stan. L. Rev. 497.

Alexander, Nadja (2004) "Mediation on Trial: Ten Verdicts on Court-Related ADR," 22 *Law in Context* 8.

Alfini, James J. (2001) "Ethics 2000 Leaves Mediation in Ethics 'Black Hole,'" 7 *Disp. Resol. Mag.* 3 (Spring).

Alfini, James J. (1999) "Settlement Ethics and Lawyering in ADR Proceedings: A Proposal to Revise Rule 4.1," 19 *N. Ill. Univ. L. Rev.* 255.

Alfini, James J., & Eric R. Galton, eds. (1998) *ADR Personalities and Practice Tips.* Washington, D.C.: ABA Section of Dispute Resolution.

Arnold, Tom (1995) "Twenty Common Errors in Mediation Advocacy," 13 *Alternatives* 69.

Arnold, Tom (1999) "Client Preparation for Mediation," 15 *Corporate Counsel's Q.* 52 (April).

Arrow, Kenneth J. et al., eds. (1995) *Barriers to Conflict Resolution.* New York: W.W. Norton.

Austin, Elizabeth and Leslie Whitaker (2001) *The Good Girl's Guide to Negotiating: How to Get What You Want at the Bargaining Table.* Boston: Little, Brown.

Axelrod, Robert M. (1984) *The Evolution of Cooperation.* New York: Basic Books.

Austin, William (1980) "Friendship and Fairness: Effects of Type of Relationship and Task Performance on Choice of Distribution Rules," 6 *Pers. & Soc. Psychol. Bull.* 402.

Ayres, Ian (1995) "Further Evidence of Discrimination in New Car Negotiations and Estimates of Its Cause," 94 *Michigan L. Rev.* 109.

Ayres, Ian (1991) "Fair Driving: Gender and Race Discrimination in Retail Car Negotiations," 104 *Harv. L. Rev.* 817.

Ayres, Ian, & Barry J. Nalebuff (1997) "Common Knowledge as a Barrier to Negotiation," 44 *U.C.L.A. L. Rev.* 1631.

Ayres, Ian, & Barry J. Nalebuff (1995) "The Role of Fairness Considerations and Relationships in a Judgmental Perspective of Negotiation," Kenneth Arrow, et al., eds. *Barriers to Conflict Resolution.* New York: W.W. Norton.

Babcock, Linda, & Sara Laschever (2003) *Women Don't Ask: Negotiation and the Gender Divide.* Princeton, N.J.: Princeton University Press.

Bahadoran, Sina (2000) "A Red Flag: Mediator Cultural Bias in Divorce," 18 *Mass. Fam. L. J.* 69.

Baird, Douglas G., Robert H. Gertner, & Randal C. Picker (2002) *Game Theory and the Law,* Cambridge, Mass.: Harvard University Press.

Bartos, Otomar (1978) "Simple Model of Negotiation," William Zartman, ed. *The Negotiation Process.* Thousand Oaks: Sage.

Baruch Bush, Robert A. (1984) "Dispute Resolution Alternatives and the Goals of Civil Justice: Jurisdictional Principles for Process Choice," 1984 *Wis. L. Rev.* 893.

Bazerman, Max H., & Margaret A. Neale (1992) *Negotiating Rationally.* Free Press.

Belhorn, Scott R. (2005) "Settling Beyond the Shadow of the Law: How Mediation Can Make the Most of Social Norms," 20 *Ohio St. J. on Disp. Resol.* 981.

Benoliel, Michael (2005) *Done Deal: Insights from Interviews with the World's Best Negotiators.* Avon, MA: Platinm Press.

Bennett, Mark D., & Scott Hughes (2005) *The Art of Mediation* (2nd *ed*). Notre Dame, IN: NITA.

Bentham, Jeremy (1996) *An Introduction to the Principles of Morals and Legislation.* Oxford: Oxford University Press.

Bercovitch, Jacob (2002) *Studies in International Mediation.* New York: Palgrave Macmillan.

Berger, Vivian (2003) "Employment Mediation in the Twenty-First Century: Challenges in a Changing Environment," 5 *U. Pa. J. Lab. & Empl. L.* 487 (Spring).

Bernard, Phyllis, & Bryant Garth, eds. (2002) *Dispute Resolution Ethics: A Comprehensive Guide.* Washington, D.C.: ABA Section of Dispute Resolution.

Berryman-Fink, Cynthia, & Claire C. Brunner (1985) "The Effects of Sex of Source and Target on Interpersonal Conflict Management Styles," 53 *S. Speech Comm. J.* 38.

Bingham, Gail (2002) "The Environment in the Balance: Mediators Are Making a Difference," 2 *AC Resolution* 21 (Summer).

Bingham, Lisa (2002) "REDRESSTM at the USPS: A Breakthrough Mediation Program," 1 *AC Resolution* 34 (Spring).

Birke, Richard (1999) "Reconciling Loss Aversion and Guilty Pleas," 1999 *Utah L. Rev.* 205.

Birke, Richard, & Craig R. Fox (1999) "Psychological Principles in Negotiating Civil Settlements," 4 *Harv. Negot. L. Rev.* 1 (Spring).

Birke, Richard (2000) "Settlement Psychology: When Decision-Making Processes Fail," 18 *Alternatives* 203 (December).

Birke, Richard (2010) "Neuroscience and Settlement: An Examination of Scientific Innovations and Practical Applications," 25 Ohio St. J. on D.R. 477.

Birkoff, Juliana, & Robert Rack, with Judith M. Filner (2001) "Points of View: Is Mediation Really a Profession?" 8 *Disp. Res. Mag.* 10 (Fall).

Boettger, Ulrich (2004) "Efficiency Versus Party Empowerment — Against a Good-Faith Requirement in Mandatory Mediation," 23 *Rev. Litig.* 1.

Bohnet, Iris, & Bruno S. Frey (1999) "The Sound of Silence in Prisoner's Dilemma and Dictator Games," 38 *J. Econ. Behav. & Org.* 43.

Bone, Robert G. "To Encourage Settlement: Rule 68, Offers of Judgment, and the History of the Federal Rules of Civil Procedure," 102 *Nw. U. L. Rev.* 1551 (2008).

Bordone, Robert C. (1998) "Electronic On-line Dispute Resolution: A Systems Approach — Potential, Problems, and a Proposal," 3 *Harv. Negot. L. Rev.* 175

Bowling, Daniel, & David Hoffman, eds. (2003) *Bringing Peace into the Room.* San Francisco: Jossey-Bass.

Bowling, Daniel, & David Hoffman (2000) "Bringing Peace into the Room: The Personal Qualities of the Mediator and Their Impact on the Mediation," 16 *Negot. J.* 5.

Brams, Steven J., & Alan D. Taylor (2000) *The Win-Win Solution: Guaranteeing Fair Share to Everybody.* New York: W.W. Norton.

Brams, Steven J. & Alan D. Taylor (1996) *Fair Division: From Cake-Cutting to Dispute Resolution.* Cambridge, England: Cambridge University Press.

Braz, Avi (2004) "Out of Joint: Replacing Joint Representation with Lawyer Mediation in Friendly Divorces," 78 *S. Cal. L. Rev.* 323.

Brazil, Wayne (January 2001) "A Judge's Perspective on Lawyering and ADR," 19 *Alternatives* 44.

Brazil, Wayne D. (1998) "Why Should Courts Offer Non-binding ADR Services?" 16 *Alternatives* 65.

Brazil, Wayne D. (1988) *Effective Approaches to Settlement: A Handbook for Lawyers and Judges.* Clifton, NJ: Prentice-Hall Law and Business.

Brazil, Wayne D. (1984) "Setting Civil Cases: What Lawyers Want from Judges," 1984 *Judges' J.* 14 (Summer).

Breslin, J. William, & Jeffrey Z. Rubin, eds. (1991) *Negotiation Theory and Practice.* Cambridge, Mass.: Program on Negotiation.

Brett, Jeanne M. (2000) "Culture and Negotiation," 35 *Intl. J. Psychol.* 97, 273, Collected References.

Brett, Jeanne M., Zoe I. Barsness, & Stephen B. Goldberg (1996) "The Effectiveness of Mediation: An Independent Analysis of Cases Handled by Four Major Service Providers," 12 *Negot. J.* 259 (July).

Brown, Jennifer Gerarda (1997) "The Role of Hope in Negotiation," 44 *U.C.L.A. L. Rev.* 1661 Buhring-Uhle, Christian (1996) *Arbitration and Mediation in International Business.* The Hague: Kluwer Law International.

Bunker, Barbara Benedict, & Jeffrey Z. Rubin, eds. (1995) *Conflict Cooperation & Justice: Essays Inspired by the Work of Morton Deutsch.* San Francisco: Jossey-Bass.

Burton, Lloyd et al. (1991) "Feminist Theory, Professional Ethics, and Gender Related Distinctions in Attorney Negotiation Styles, 1991 *J. Disp. Resol.* 199.

Bush, Robert A. Baruch, & Joseph P. Folger (2004) *The Promise of Mediation: The Transformative Approach to Conflict.* San Francisco: Jossey-Bass.

Bush, Robert A. Baruch (1996) "What Do We Need a Mediator For?: Mediation's 'Value-Added' for Negotiators," 12 *Ohio St. J. on Disp. Resol.* 1.

Bush, Robert A. Baruch, & Sally Ganong Pope (2004) "Transformative Mediation: Principles and Practice in Divorce Mediation," in J. Folberg, et al., eds., *Divorce and Family Mediation.* New York: Guilford Press.

Camp, Jim (2007) *No: The Only Negotiating System You Need for Work and Home*. New York: Crown Business.

Carroll, Eileen, & Karl Mackie (2000) *International Mediation — The Art of Business Diplomacy*. The Hague: Kluwer Law International.

Carter, Jimmy (1982) *Keeping Faith: Memoirs of a President*. New York: Bantam Books. Carter, Jimmy (2003) *Negotiation: The Alternative to Hostility*. Macon, GA: Mercer Univ. Press.

Chester, Ronald (1999) "Less Law, But More Justice?: Jury Trials and Mediation as Means of Resolving Will Contests," 37 *Duq. L. Rev.* 173 (Winter).

Chew, Pat K., ed. (2001) *The Conflict & Culture Reader*. New York: New York University Press.

Cialdini, Robert B. (2001) *Influence: Science and Practice* (4th. ed.). Allyn & Bacon.

Cialdini, Robert B. (2001) "Persuasion," 284 *Scientific American* 76.

Cloke, Kenneth (2000) *Mediating Dangerously*. San Francisco: Jossey-Bass.

Cobb, Sarah, & Janet Rifkin (1991) "Practice and Paradox: Deconstructing Neutrality in Mediation," 16 *Law & Soc. Inquiry* 35.

Coben, James, & Harley Penelope (2004) "Intentional Conversations About Restorative Justice, Mediation and the Practice of Law," 25 *Hamline J. Pub. L. & Pol'y* 235.

Cohen, Herb (2003) *Negotiate This!: By Caring, But Not That Much*. New York: Warner Business Books.

Cohen, Jonathan R. (1999) "Advising Clients to Apologize," 72 *S. Cal. L. Rev.* 1009.

Cohen, Jonathan R. (2000) "Apologizing for Errors," *Disp. Res. Mag.* (Summer).

Cohen, Jonathan (2001) "When People are the Means: Negotiating with Respect," 14 *Geo. J. Legal Ethics* 739.

Cohen, Raymond (1999) *Negotiating Across Cultures: International Communication in an Interdependent World*. Washington, D.C.: United States Institute of Peace.

Cole, Sarah Rudolph (2000) "Managerial Litigants? The Overlooked Problem of Party Autonomy in Dispute Resolution," 51 *Hastings L.J.* 1199.

Cole, Sarah R., Craig McEwen, & Nancy H. Rogers (2001) *Mediation: Law, Policy & Practice*. St. Paul, MN: West Publishing.

Colosi, Thomas R. (2001) *On and Off the Record: Colosi on Negotiation* (2d. ed.). New York: American Arbitration Association.

Condlin, Robert J. (1992) "Bargaining in the Dark: The Normative Incoherence of Lawyer Dispute Bargaining Role, 51 *Md. L. Rev.* 1.

Contuzzi, Peter (2000) "Should Parties Tell Mediators Their Bottom Line?" 8 *Disp. Res. Mag.* 30 (Spring).

Cooley, John W. (2000) *The Mediator's Handbook*. Notre Dame, IN: NITA.

Cooley, John W. (1997) "Mediation Magic: Its Use and Abuse," 29 *Loy. L. Rev.* 1 (Fall).

Cooley, John W. (2002) *Mediation Advocacy*. Notre Dame, IN: NITA.

Cooley, John W. (2004) "Defining the Ethical Limits of Acceptable Deception in Mediation," 4 *Pepperdine Disp. Resol. L. J.* 263.

Cooper, Christopher (2000) "Police Mediators: Rethinking the Role of Law Enforcement in the New Millennium," 7 *Disp. Res. Mag.* 17 (Fall).

Cooter, Robert, et al. (1982) "Bargaining in the Shadow of the Law: A Testable Model of Strategic Behavior," 11 *J. Legal Stud.* 225.

Coylewright, Jeremy (2004) "New Strategies for Prisoner Rehabilitation in the American Criminal Justice System: Prisoner Facilitated Mediation," 7 *J. Health Care L. & Pol'y* 395.

CPR Institute of Dispute Resolution (2001) *Into the 21st Century: Thought Pieces on Lawyering, Problem Solving, and ADR*. New York: CPR Institute.

Craver, Charles B. (1997) "Negotiation Ethics: How to Be Deceptive Without Being Dishonest/ How to Be Assertive Without Being Offensive," 38 *Tex. L. Rev.* 713.

Craver, Charles B., & David W. Barnes (1999) "Gender, Risk Taking, and Negotiation Performance," 5 *Mich. J. Gender & L.* 299.

Craver, Charles B. (2001) *Effective Legal Negotiation and Settlement* (5th. ed.). Newark: LEXIS.

Cronin-Harris, Catherine (1997) *Building ADR into the Corporate Law Department: ADR Systems Design*. New York: CPR Institute.

Croson, Rachel, & Nancy Buchan (1999) "Gender and Culture: International Experimental Evidence from Trust Games," 89 *Am. Econ. Rev.* 386.

Crystal, Nathan M. (1998) "The Lawyer's Duty to Disclose Material Facts in Contract or Settlement Negotiations," 87 *Ky. L.J.* 1055.

Curtis, Dana (1998) "Reconciliation and the Role of Empathy," in J. Alfini & E. Galton, eds., *ADR Personalities and Practice Tips*. Washington, D.C.: ABA Section of Dispute Resolution.

Curtis, Dana, & John Toker (December 2000) "Representing Clients in Appellate Mediation: The Last Frontier," 1 *JAMS Alert No. 3* 1.

Dauer, Edward A. (1994) *Manual of Dispute Resolution*. San Francisco: Shepard's/McGraw-Hill.

Dauer, Edward A. (2005) "Apology in the Aftermath of Injury: Colorado's 'I'm Sorry' Law, "34 *COLAW* 47.

Dauer, Edward A. (2000) "Justice Irrelevant: Speculations on the Causes of ADR," 74 *So Cal. L. Rev.* 83.

Davis, Benjamin G. (2005) "International Commercial Online and Offline Dispute Resolution: Addressing Primacism and Universalism," 4 *J. Amer. Arb.* 79.

Davis, Morton D. (1997) *Game Theory: A Nontechnical Introduction*. Mineola, N.Y.: Dover.

Dawson, Roger (2001) *Secrets of Power Negotiating* (2d. ed.). Franklin Lakes, N.J.: Career Press.

Deason, Ellen E. (2001) "Enforcing Mediated Settlement Agreements: Contract Law Collides with Confidentiality," 35 *U.C. Davis L. Rev.* 33 (November).

Deason, Ellen E. (2002) "Predictable Mediation Confidentiality in the U.S. Federal System," 17 *Ohio. St. J. on Disp. Resol.* 239.

Deason, Ellen E. (2005) "Procedural Rules for Complementary Systems of Litigation and Mediation — Worldwide," 80 *Notre Dame L. Rev.* 553.

Deaux, Kay (1976) *The Behavior of Women and Men* Monterey, CA: Brooks/Cole Publishing.

Delgado, Richard (1988) "ADR and the Dispossessed: Recent Books About the Deformalization Movement," 13 *Law & Soc. Inquiry* 145.

Deutsch, Morton (1973) *The Resolution of Conflict*. New Haven, CT.: Yale University Press.

Deutsch, Morton, & Peter T. Coleman, eds. (2000) *The Handbook of Conflict Resolution*. San Francisco: Jossey-Bass.

Dixit, Avinash K., & Barry J. Nalebuff (1991) *Thinking Strategically: The Competitive Edge in Business, Politics, and Everyday Life*. New York: W.W. Norton & Co.

Donahey, M. Scott (1995) "The Asian Concept of Conciliator/Arbitrator: Is It Translatable to the Western World?" 10 *Foreign Inv. L. J.* 120.

Dore, Laurie Krath (1999) "Secrecy by Consent: The Use and Limits of Confidentiality in the Pursuit of Settlement," 74 *N.D. L. Rev.* 283.

Dunnigan, Alana (2003) "Comment — Restoring Power to the Powerless: The Need to Reform California's Mandatory Mediation for Victims of Domestic Violence," 37 *U.S.F. L. Rev.* 1031.

Eckel, Catherine, & Philip Grossman (1998) "Are Women Less Selfish Than Men?: Evidence from Dictator Experiments," 108 *Econ. J.* 726.

Eckel, Catherine & Philip Grossman (1996) "The Relative Price of Fairness: Gender Differences in a Punishment Game," 30 *J. Econ. Behav. & Org.* 143.

Edwards, Harry, & James J. White (1977) *The Lawyer as Negotiator*. St. Paul: West.

Edwards, T. Harry (1986) "Alternative Dispute Resolution: Panacea or Anathema?" 99 *Harv. L. Rev.* 668 (January).

Epstein, Lynn A. (1997) "Post-Settlement Malpractice: Undoing the Done Deal," 43 *Cath. U. L. Rev.* 459 (Winter).

Erickson, Stephen K., & Marilyn S. McKnight (2001) *The Practitioner's Guide to Mediation: A Client Centered Approach*. San Francisco: Jossey-Bass.

Fairhurst, Gail T., & Robert A. Sarr (1996) *The Art of Framing*. San Francisco: Jossey-Bass.

Fazzi, Cindy (2005) "The Five Golden Rules of Dispute Resolution: Gain the Edge!" 59 Disp. Resol. J. 88.

Fehr, Ernst, & Simon Gachter (2000) "Fairness and Retaliation: The Economics of Reciprocity," 14 *J. Econ. Persp.* 159.

Felder, Raoul (2004) *Bare-Knuckle Negotiation*. Hoboken, N.J.: John Wiley & Sons.

Fisher, Roger (1991) "Negotiating Power: Getting and Using Influence," William J. Breslin, & Jeffrey Z. Rubin, eds. *Negotiation Theory and Practice*.

Fisher, Roger, et al. (1994) *Beyond Machiavelli: Tools for Coping with Conflict*. Cambridge, Mass.: Harvard University Press.

Fisher, Roger, & Danny Ertel (1995) *Getting Ready to Negotiate: The Getting to Yes Workbook*. New York: Penguin.

Fisher, Roger, & Scott Brown (1988) *Getting Together: Building a Relationship that Gets to Yes*. Boston: Houghton Mifflin.

Fisher, Roger, & Daniel Shapiro (2005) *Beyond Reason*. New York: Viking.

Fisher, Roger, & William J. Ury, with Bruce Patton (1991) *Getting to Yes* (2d ed.). New York: Penguin.

Fisher, Tom (2001) "Advice by Any Other Name," 29 *Conflict Resol. Q.* 107.

Fiss, Owen, (1984) "Against Settlement," 93 *Yale L.J.* 1073.

Fobia, Cynthia S., & Jay J. Christensen-Szalanski (1993) "Ambiguity and Liability Negotiations: The Effects of the Negotiator's Role and the Sensitivity Zone," 54 *Org. Behav. & Hum. Decision Proc.* 277.

Folberg, Jay (1982) "Divorce Mediation: The Emerging American Model," paper presented at the Fourth Ann. Conf. of the Int'l Socy. for Family Law, Harv. U (June).

Folberg, Jay (1985) "Mediation of Child Custody Disputes," 19 *Colum. J. L. Soc. Probs.* 413.

Folberg, Jay (1996) "Certification of Mediators in California: An Introduction," 30 *U.S.F. L. Rev.* 609 (Spring).

Folberg, Jay (2003) "The Continuing History of Conflict Resolution Practice," *ACR Res*.

Folberg, Jay, & Alison Taylor (1984) *Mediation: A Comprehensive Guide to Resolving Conflicts Without Litigation*. San Francisco: Jossey-Bass.

Folberg, Jay, Ann L. Milne, & Peter Salem (eds.) (2004) *Divorce and Family Mediation — Models, Techniques and Applications*. New York: Guilford Press.

Folberg, Jay, Joshua Rosenberg & Robert Barrett (1992) "Use of ADR in California Courts: Findings and Proposals," 26 *U.S.F. L. Rev.* 343.

Frascogna, Jr., X.M., & H. Lee Hetherington (2001) *The Lawyer's Guide to Negotiation: A Strategic Approach to Better Contracts and Settlements*. Chicago: ABA.

Freund, James C. (1992) *Smart Negotiating: How to Make Good Deals in the Real World*. New York: Simon & Schuster.

Freedman, Lawrence R., & Michael L. Prigoff (1986) "Confidentiality in Mediation: The Need for Protection," 2 *Ohio St. J. on Disp. Resol.* 37.

Freshman, Clark, Adele Hayes & Greg Feldman (2002) "The Lawyer-Negotiator as Mood Scientist: What We Know and Don't Know About How Mood Relates to Successful Negotiation," 2002 *J. Disp. Resol.* 1.Friedman, Gary J., & Jack Himmelstein (2008) *Challenging Conflict: Mediation Through Understanding*. Chicago: ABA.

Fuller, Lon (1971) "Mediation: Its Forms and Functions," 44 *S. Cal. L. Rev.* 305 (February).

Fuller, Lon (1978) "The Forms and Limits of Adjudication," 92 *Harv. L. Rev.* 353.

Galanter, Marc (1983) "Reading the Landscape of Disputes: What We Know And Don't Know (And Think We Know) About Our Allegedly Contentious and Litigious Society," 31 *U.C.L.A. L. Rev.* 4.

Galanter, Marc, & Joel Rogers (1991) *The Transformation of American Business Disputing: Some Preliminary Observation*. Madison, WI: University of Wisconsin Law School.

Galanter, Marc & Mia Cahill (1994) "Most Cases Settle: Judicial Promotion and Regulation of Settlements," 46 *Stan. L. Rev.* 1339.

Galton, Eric (1994) *Representing Clients in Mediation*. Dallas, TX: American Lawyer Mediation.

Gelfand, Michele J., & Sophia Christakopoulou (1999) "Culture and Negotiator Cognition: Judgment Accuracy and Negotiation Processes in Individualistic and Collectivistic Cultures," 79 *Org. Behav. & Hum. Decision Proc.* 248.

Geronemus, David (2001) "The Changing Face of Commercial Mediation," 19 *Alternatives* 38 (January).

Gifford, Donald G. (1989) *Legal Negotiation: Theory and Applications*. St. Paul: West.

Gilligan, Carol (1982) *In a Different Voice: Psychological Theory and Women's Development*. Cambridge: Harvard University Press

Gilson, Ronald J. (1984) "Value Creation by Business Lawyers: Legal Skills and Asset Pricing," 94 *Yale L. J.* 239.

Gilson, Ronald J., & Robert H. Mnookin (1995) "Disputing Through Agents: Cooperation and Conflict Between Lawyers in Litigation," 94 *Colum. L. Rev.* 509.

Goh, Bee Chen (1998) "Sino-Western Negotiating Styles," 7 Canterbury L. Rev. 82.

Golann, Dwight (1989) "Making Alternative Dispute Resolution Mandatory: The Constitutional Issues," 68 *Or. L. Rev.* 487.

Golann, Dwight (2000) "Variations in Style: How — and Why — Legal Mediators Change Style in the Course of a Case," 2000 *J. Disp. Resol.* 40.

Golann, Dwight (2001) "Cognitive Barriers to Effective Negotiation, 6 *ADR Currents* 6 (September).

Golann, Dwight (2002) "Is Legal Mediation a Process of Reconciliation — Or Separation? An Empirical Study, and Its Implications," 7 *Harv. Negot. L. Rev.* 301.

Golann, Dwight (2004) "Death of a Claim: The Impact of Loss Reactions on Bargaining," 20 *Negot. J.* 539.

Golann, Dwight (2004) "How to Borrow a Mediator's Powers," 30 *Litig.* 41 (Spring).

Golann, Dwight (2009) *Mediating Legal Disputes: Effective Strategies for Lawyers and Mediators*. Chicago: American Bar Association.

Golann, Helaine, & Dwight Golann (2003) "Why Is It Hard for Lawyers to Deal with Emotional Issues?" 9 *Disp. Res. Mag.* 26 (Winter).

Goldberg, Stephen B. (2005) "How Interest-based, Grievance Mediation Performs Over the Long Term," 59 *J. Disp. Resol.* 8.

Goldman, Barry (2008) *The Science of Settlement: Ideas for Negotiators*. Philadelphia: ALI-ABA.

Goleman, Daniel (1996) *Emotional Intelligence*. Vancouver: Raincoast.

Goodpaster, Gary (1993) "Rational Decision-Making in Problem-Solving Negotiation: Compromise, Interest-Valuation, and Cognitive Error," 8 *Ohio St. J. on Disp. Res.* 299.

Goodpaster, Gary (1997) *A Guide to Negotiation and Mediation*. Irvington-on-Hudson, N.Y.: Transnational.

Grant, Malcolm J., & Vello Sermat (1969) "Status and Sex of Other as Determinants of Behavior in a Mixed-Motive Game," 12 *J. Personality & Soc. Psych.* 151.

Green, Eric (1986) "A Heretical View of the Mediation Privilege," 2 *Ohio St. J. on Disp. Resol.* 1.

Green, Stuart (2005) "Theft by Coercion: Extortion, Blackmail, and Hard Bargaining," 44 *Washburn L. J.* 553.

Grillo, Trina (1991) "The Mediation Alternative: Process Dangers for Women," 100 *Yale L.J.* 1545.

Gross, Samuel R., & Kent D. Syverud (1991) "Getting to No: A Study of Settlement Negotiations and the Selection of Cases for Trial," 90 *Mich. L. Rev.* 319.

Guernsey, Thomas F. (1982) "Truthfulness in Negotiation," 17 Univ. Rich. L. Rev. 99.

Guernsey, Thomas F. (1996) *A Practical Guide to Negotiation*. South Bend, In.: NITA.

Guthrie, Chris (2003) "Panacea or Pandora's Box?: The Costs of Options in Negotiation." 88 *Iowa L. Rev.* 601.

Guthrie, Chris, & James Levin (1998) "A 'Party Satisfaction' Perspective on a Comprehensive

Mediation Statute," 13 *Ohio St. J. on Disp. Resol.* 885.

Hall, Lavinia, ed. (1993) *Negotiation: Strategies for Mutual Gain*, Newbury Park, Ca.: Sage.

Halpern, Richard G. (1998) "Settlement Negotiations: Taking Control," 34 *Trial* 64 (February).

Hammond, John S. (1999). Ralph L. Kenney, &

Howard Raiffa, *Smart Choices: A Practical Guide to Making Better Decisions*. Cambridge, Mass.: Harvard University Business School.

Hartman, Raymond S., et al. (1991) "Consumer Rationality and the Status Quo," 106 *Q. J. Econ.* 141.

Hartwell, Steven, et al. (1992) "Women Negotiating: Assertiveness and Relatedness," Linda A.M. Perry, et al., *Constructing and Reconstructing Gender*. Albany, NY: State University of New York Press.

Haydock, Roger S., et al (1996) *Lawyering: Practice and Planning*. St. Paul: West.

Haynes, John (1989) *Mediating Divorce: Casebook of Strategies for Successful Family Negotiations*. San Francisco: Jossey-Bass.

Hazard, Geoffrey (1981) "The Lawyer's Obligation to Be Trustworthy When Dealing With Opposing Parties," 33 *S.C. L. Rev.* 181.

Hensler, Deborah R. (2003) "Our Courts, Ourselves: How the Alternative Dispute Resolution Movement is Reshaping Our Legal System," 108 *Penn St. L. Rev.* 165.

Herman, G. Nicholas (2005) "10 Tools for Mediation Cases," 41 *Trial* 66.

Hermann, Michele (1994) "New Mexico Research Examines Impact of Gender and Ethnicity in Mediation," 1 *Disp. Res. Mag.* 10 (Fall).

Herring, Victoria L. (2004) "Creative Advocacy in Voluntary Alternative Dispute Resolution," 40 *Trial* 40.

Hetherington, H. Lee (2001) "The Wizard and Dorothy, Patton and Rommel: Negotiation Parables in Fiction and Fact," 28 *Pepperdine L. Rev.* 289.

Hindrey, Leo, & Leslie Cauley (2003) *The Biggest Game of All: The Inside Strategies, Tactics, and Temperaments that Make Great Dealmakers Great*. New York: Free Press.

Hirshleifer, Jack (2001) "Game-Theoretic Interpretations of Commitment," Randolph Nesse, ed., *Evolution and the Capacity for Commitment*. New York: Russell Sage Foundation Publications.

Hodges, Ann C. "Mediation and the Transformation of American Labor Unions," 69 *Mo. L. Rev.* 365.

Hoffman, Elizabeth, et al. (1994) "Preferences, Property Rights, and Anonymity in Bargaining Games," 7 *Games & Econ. Behav.* 346.

Hoffman, Elizabeth & Matthew L. Spitzer (1985) "Entitlements, Rights, and Fairness: An Experimental Examination of Subjects' Concepts of Distributive Justice," 14 *J. Legal Stud.* 259.

Honeyman, Christopher (1990) "On Evaluating Mediators," 6 *Negot. J.* 23.

Honeyman, Christopher, James Coben & Giuseppe DePalo (2009) *Rethinking Negotiation Teaching Innovations for Context and Culture*. Minneapolis: Dispute Resolution Institute.

Hughes, Scott H. (1998) "A Closer Look: The Case for a Mediation Confidentiality Privilege Still Has Not Been Made," 5 *Disp. Res. Mag.* 14 (Winter).

Hyman, Jonathan M. (2004) "Swimming in the Deep End: Dealing With Justice in Mediation," 6 *Cardozo J. of Conflict Res.* 19.

Issacs, William (1999) *Dialogue and the Art of Thinking Together*. New York: Doubleday.

Izumi, Carol L., & Homer C. La Rue (2003) "Prohibiting 'Good Faith' Reports Under the Uniform Mediation Act: Keeping the Adjudication Camel Out of the Mediation Tent," 2003 *J. Disp. Resol.* 67. Jandt, Fred E., with Paul Gillette (1985) *Win-Win Negotiating: Turning Conflict Into Agreement*. New York: John Wiley & Sons.

Johnston, Jason S. & Joel Waldfogel (2002) "Does Repeat Play Elicit Cooperation? Evidence From Federal Civil Litigation," 31 *J. Legal Stud.* 39.

Kahneman, Daniel & Amos Tversky (1979) "Prospect Theory: An Analysis of a Decision Under Risk," 47 *Econometrica* 263.

Kahneman, Daniel, Paul Sovic, & Amos Tversky (1982) *Judgment under Uncertainty: Heuristics and Biases*. Cambridge: Cambridge University Press.

Kahneman, Daniel, & Amos Tversky (1984) "Choices, Values, and Frames" 39 *Am. Pyschologist* 341.

Kahneman, Daniel, & Dale T. Miller (1986) "Norm Theory: Comparing Reality to Its Alternatives," 93 *Psychol. Rev.* 136.

Kahneman, Daniel, Jack L. Knetsch, & Richard H. Thaler (1990) "Experimental Tests of the Endowment Effect and the Coase Theorem," 98 *J. Pol. Econ.* 1325.

Kakalik, James, et al. (1996) *An Evaluation of Mediation and Early Neutral Evaluation Under the Civil Justice Reform Act*. Santa Monica, Calif.: RAND Corp.

Kaplow, Louis, & Steven Shavell (2004) *Decision Analysis, Game Theory, and Information*. New York: Foundation Press.

Katsh, Ethan, & Janet Rivkin (2001) *Online Dispute Resolution — Resolving Conflicts in Cyberspace*. San Francisco: Jossey-Bass.

Keating, Michael (1996) "Mediating in the Dance For Dollars," 14 *Alternatives* 71 (September).

Kennedy, Gavin (1994) *Field Guide to Negotiation: A Glossary of Essential Tools and Concepts for Today's Manager*. Boston: Harvard Business School Press.

Kheel, Theodore W. (1999) *The Keys to Conflic Resolution: Proven Methods of Settling Disputes Voluntarily*. New York: Four Walls Eight Windows.

Kichaven, Jeffrey G. (1999) "How Advocacy Fits in Effective Mediation," 17 *Alternatives* 60.

Kimmel, Melvin J., et al. (1980) "Effects of Trust, Aspiration and Gender on Negotiating Tactics," 38 *J. Pers. & Soc. Psychol.* 9.

Kimmel, Paul R. (1994) "Cultural Perspectives on International Negotiations," 50 *J. Soc. Issues* 179.

Kirtley, Alan (1995) "The Mediation Privilege's Transition from Theory to Implementation: Designing a Mediation Privilege Standard to Protect Mediation Participants, the Process and the Public Interest," 1995 *J. Disp. Resol.* 1.

Kiser, Randall, et al. (2008) "Let's Not Make A Deal: An Empirical Study Of Decision Making In Unsuccessful Settlement Negotiations, " 5 *Journal of Empirical Studies* 451.

Kiser, Randall (2010) Beyond Right and Wrong: The Power of Effective Decision Making for Attorneys and Clients. Heidelberg: Springer

Kloppenberg, Lisa A. (2002) "Implementation of Court-Annexed Environmental Mediation: The District of Oregon Pilot Project," 17 *Ohio St. J. on Disp. Resol.* 559.

Knetsch, Jack L., & J.A. Sinden (1984) "Willingness to Pay and Compensation Demanded: Experimental Evidence of an Unexpected Disparity in Measures of Value," 99 *Q. J. Econ.* 507.

Koh, Hea Jin (2004) "Yet I Shall Temper So Justice with Mercy: Procedural Justice in Mediation and Litigation," 28 *Law & Psychol. Rev.* 169.

Krolb, Deborah M. & Gloria Coolidge (1991) "Her Place at the Table: A Consideration of Gender Issues in Negotiation," in J. William Breslin & Jeffrey Z. Rubin, eds., *Negotiation, Theory and Practice*. Cambridge, MA: Program on Negotiation.

Kolb, Deborah M. & Judith Williams (2003) *Everyday Negotiation: Navigating the Hidden Agendas in Bargaining*. San Francisco: Jossey-Bass.

Kolb, Deborah M & Judith Williams (2000) *The Shadow Negotiation: How Women Can Master the Hidden Agendas that Determine Bargaining Success*. New York: Simon & Schuster.

Kolb, Deborah M. et. al. (1994) *When Talk Works — Profiles of Mediators*. San Francisco: Jossey-Bass.

Korobkin, Russell (2008) "Against Integrative Bargaining," 58 Case Western L. Rev. 1323.

Korobkin, Russell (2002) *Negotiation Theory and Strategy*. New York: Aspen.

Korobkin, Russell (2002) "Aspirations and Settlement," 88 *Corn L. Rev.* 1.

Korobkin, Russell (1998) "Inertia and Preference in Contract Negotiation: The Psychological Power of Default Rules and Form Terms," 51 *Vand. L. Rev.* 1583.

Korobkin, Russell (2000) "A Positive Theory of Legal Negotiation," 88 *Geo. L. J.* 1789.

Korobkin, Russell, & Chris Guthrie (1994) "Psychological Barriers to Litigation Settlement: An Experimental Approach," 93 *Mich. L. Rev.* 107.

Korobkin, Russell, & Chris Guthrie (1994) "Opening Offers and Out of Court Settlement: A Little Moderation Might Not Go a Long Way," 10 *Ohio St. J. on Disp. Res.* 1.

Korobkin, Ruseell, & Chris Guthrie (1997) "Psychology, Economics, and Settlement: A New Look at the Role of the Lawyer," 76 *Tex. L. Rev.* 77.

Korobkin, Russell, Michael Moffett, & Nancy Welch (2004) "The Law of Bargaining" 87 *Marq. L. Rev.* 839.

Kovach, Kimberlee K. (1997) "Good Faith in Mediation — Requested, Recommended, or Required? A New Ethic," 38 *S. Tex. L. Rev.* 38.

Kovach, Kimberlee K., & Lela P. Love (1998) "Mapping Mediation: The Risks of Riskin's Grid," 3 *Harv. Negot. L. Rev.* 71.

Kramer, Roderick M., et al. (1993) "Self-Enhancement Biases and Negotiator Judgment: Effects of Self-Esteem and Mood," 56 *Org. Behav. & Human Dec. Proc.* 110.

Kremenyuk, Victor A., ed. (1991) *International Negotiation: Analysis, Approaches, Issues*. San Francisco: Jossey-Bass.

Kressel, Kenneth, & Dean G. Pruitt (eds.) (1989) *Mediation Research: The Power and Effectiveness of Third-Party Intervention*. San Francisco: Jossey-Bass.

Kritek, Phyllis Beck (2002) *Negotiating at an Uneven Table: Developing Moral Courage in Resolving Our Conflicts* (2d ed.). San Francisco: Jossey-Bass.

Kritzer, Herbert M. (1991) *Let's Make a Deal: Understanding the Negotiation Process in Ordinary Litigation*. Madison: University of Wisconsin Press.

Kritzer, Herbert M., "Fee Arrangements and Negotiation," 21 *L. & Soc. Rev.* 341 (1987)

Krivis, Jeffrey (2006) *Improvisational Negotiation*. San Francisco: Jossey-Bass.

Laborde, Genie Z. (1987) *Influencing with Integrity*. Palo Alto, Ca.: Syntony.

Laflin, James, & Robert Werth (2001) "Unfinished Business: Another Look at the Microsoft

Mediation," 12 *California Tort Reporter No. 3*, 88 (May).

Lande, John (2002) "Using Dispute Systems Design Methods to Promote Good-Faith Participation in Court-Connected Mediation Programs," 50 *UCLA Law Rev.* 69 (October).

Lang, Michael D., & Alison Taylor (2000) *The Making of a Mediator: Developing Artistry in Practice*. San Francisco: Jossey-Bass.

Lawrence, James K.L. (2003) "Collaborative Lawyering: A New Development in Conflict Resolution," 17 *Ohio St. J. on Disp. Res.* 431.

Lax, David A., & James K. Sebenius (1986) *The Manager as Negotiator: Bargaining for Cooperation and Competitive Gain*. New York: Free Press.

Lax, David & James Sebenius (1992) "Thinking Coalitionally: Party Arithmetic, Process Opportunism, and Strategic Sequencing," H. Peyton Young, ed., *Negotiation Analysis*. UMP.

Levi, Deborah (1997) "The Role of Apology in Mediation," 72 *N.Y.U. L. Rev.* 1165.

Levinson, Jay Conrad, Mark S. A. Smith, & Orvel Ray Wilson (1999) *Guerilla Negotiating: Unconventional Weapons and Tactics to Get What You Want*. New York: John Wiley & Sons.

Lewicki, Roy J., et. al. (2004) *Essentials of Negotiation* (3d. ed.). Chicago: Irwin.

Lewicki, Roy J., et. al. (2003) *Negotiation: Readings, Exercises, and Cases* (4th. ed.). New York: McGraw-Hill Higher Education.

Lewicki, Roy J., David M. Saunders, & John W. Minton (2006) *Negotiation* (5th. ed.). New York: McGraw-Hill/Irwin.

Lewis, Michael (1995) "Advocacy in Mediation: One Mediator's View," 2 *Disp. Res. Mag.* 7 (Fall).

Liebman, Carol B. & Chris S. Hyman (2004) "A Mediation Skills Model to Manage Disclosure of Errors and Adverse Events to Patients," 23 *Health Affairs* 22.

Lieberman, Jethro K. (1991) *The Litigious Society*. New York: Basic Books.

Lieberman, Jethro K., & James F. Henry (1986) "Lessons from the Alternative Dispute Resolution Movement," 53 *U. Chi. L. Rev.* 424.

Lipsky, David B., & Ronald L. Seeber (1998) *The Appropriate Resolution of Corporate Disputes: A Report on the Growing Use of ADR by U.S. Corporations*. Ithaca, NY: Cornell/PERC Institute on Conflict Resolution.

Lipsky, David B., & Ronald L. Seeber (1999) "Patterns of ADR Use in Corporate Disputes," 54 *Disp. Res. J.* 66 (February).

Locke, Edwin A, & Gary P. Latham (1990) *A Theory of Goal Setting and Task Performance*. Englewood Cliffs, N.J.: Prentice-Hall.

Loder, Reed Elizabeth (1994) "Moral Truthseeking and the Virtuous Negotiator," 8 *Geo. J. Legal Ethics* 45.

Loewenstein, George F., et al. (1989) "Social Utility and Decision Making in Interpersonal Contexts," 57 *J. Pers. & Soc. Psychol.* 426.

Loewenstein, George, et al. (1993) "Self-Serving Assessments of Fairness and Pretrial Bargaining," 22 *J. Legal Stud.* 135.

Longan, Patrick (2001) "Ethics in Settlement Negotiations: Foreward," 52 *Mercer L. Rev.* 810.

Love, Lela P. (1997) "The Top Ten Reasons Why Mediators Should Not Evaluate," 24 *Fla. St. U. L. Rev.* 937.

Lowry, L. Randolph (1997) "To Evaluate or Not — That Is Not the Question!" 2 *Resolutions* 2 (Pepperdine Univ.).

Lubet, Steven (1996) "Notes on the Bedouin Horse Trade or 'Why Won't the Market Clear, Daddy?'" 74 *Tex. L. Rev.* 1039.

Luce, R. Duncan, & Howard Raiffa (1989) *Games and Decisions: Introduction and Critical Survey*. Mineola, NY: Dover Publications.

Luskin, Frederic, & Dana Curtis (2000) "The Power of Forgiveness," *Cal. Lawyer* (December).

Lynch, Hon. Eugene F., et al. (1992) *California Negotiation and Settlement Handbook*. Rochester, NY: Lawyers Co-operative.

Maccoby, Eleanor Emmons, & Carol Jacklin (1974) *The Psychology of Sex Differences*. Palo Alto: Stanford University Press.

Madoff, Ray D. (2002) "Lurking in the Shadow: The Unseen Hand of Doctrine in Dispute Resolution," 76 *S. Cal. L. Rev.* 161.

Douglas S. Malan, "A Numbers Game," *Connecticut Law Tribune*, 36, No. 4, 2010

Malhotra, Deepax & Max H. Bazerman (2007) *Negotiation Genius*, 27, New York: Bantam Books.

Matz, David E. (1999) "Ignorance and Interests," 4 *Harv. Negot. L. Rev.* 59.

Max, Rodney A. (1999) "Multiparty Mediation," 23 *Am. J. Trial Advoc.* 269.

Mayer, Bernard (2009) *Staying with Conflict: A Strategic Approach to Ongoing Disputes*. San Francisco: Jossey-Bass.

McCarthy, William (1985) "The Role of Power and Principle in Getting to Yes," 1 *Negot. J.* 59

McEwen, Craig (1998) "Managing Corporate Disputing: Overcoming Barriers to the Effective Use of Mediation for Reducing the Cost and Time of Litigation," 14 *Ohio St. J. on Disp. Resol.* 1

McGuire, James E. (2004) "Certification: An Idea Whose Time Has Come," 10 *Disp. Res. Mag.* 22 (Summer).

McKean, David, & Douglas Frantz (1995) *Friends in High Places: The Rise and Fall of Clark Clifford*. Boston : Little, Brown & Co.

Menkel-Meadow, Carrie (1984) "Toward Another View of Legal Negotiation: The Structure of Problem-Solving," 31 *U.C.L.A. L. Rev.* 754.

Menkel-Meadow, Carrie (1991) "Pursuing Settlement in an Adversary Culture: A Tale of Innovation Co-Opted of 'the Law of ADR,'" 19 *Fla. St. U. L. Rev.* 1.

Menkel-Meadow, Carrie (1999) "Do the 'Haves' Come out Ahead in Alternative Judicial Systems?: Repeat Players in ADR," 15 *Ohio St. J. on Disp. Resol.* 19.

Menkel-Meadow, Carrie (2001) "Ethics in ADR: The Many 'Cs' of Professional Responsibility and Dispute Resolution," 28 *Fordham Urban L. J.* 979.

Menkel-Meadow, Carrie (2000a) "Teaching About Gender and Negotiation, Sex., Truth, and Videotape," 16 *Negot. J.* 357.

Menkel-Meadow, Carrie (2000b) "When Winning Isn't Everything: The Lawyer as Problem Solver," 28 *Hofstra L. Rev.* 905.

Menkel-Meadow, Carrie (2003) *Dispute Processing and Conflict Resolution.* Burlington, VT.: Ashgate.

Menkel-Meadow, Carrie, & Elizabeth Plapinger (1999) "Model Rules Would Clarify Lawyer Conduct When Serving as a Neutral," 6 *Disp. Res. Mag.* 20 (Summer).

Menkel-Meadow, Carrie, & Michael Wheeler, eds. (2004) *What's Fair: Ethics for Negotiators.* San Francisco: Jossey-Bass.

Miller, Geoffrey P. (1987) "Some Agency Problems in Settlement," 16 *J. Legal Stud.* 189.

Miller, Lee E.,& Jessical Miller (2002) *A Woman's Guide to Successful Negotiating:How to Convince, Collaborate, & Create Your Way to Agreement.* New York: McGraw-Hill.

Milne, Ann L. (2004) "Mediation and Domestic Abuse," in J. Folberg, et al., eds., *Divorce and Family Mediation.* New York: Guilford Press.

Mnookin, Robert (2010) *Bargaining with the Devil.* New York: Simon & Schuster.

Mnookin, Robert H. (2003) "Strategic Barriers to Dispute Resolution: A Comparison of Bilateral and Multilateral Negotiations," *8 Harv. Negot. L. Rev. 1.* (Spring).

Mnookin, Robert H. (1993) "Why Negotiations Fail: An Exploration of Barriers to the Resolution of Conflict," 8 *Ohio St. J. on Disp. Res.* 235.

Mnookin, Robert H., & Lawrence E. Susskind, eds. (1999) *Negotiating on Behalf of Others.* Thousand Oaks: Sage.

Mnookin, Robert H., & Lewis Kornhauser (1979) "Bargaining the in Shadow of the Law: The Case for Divorce," 88 *Yale L. J.* 950.

Mnookin, Robert H., & Ronald J. Gilson (1994) "Disputing Through Agents: Cooperation and Conflict Between Lawyers in Litigation," 94 *Colum. L. Rev.* 509.

Mnookin, Robert H., Scott R. Peppet, & Andrew S. Tulumello (2000) *Beyond Winning: Negotiating to Create Value in Deals and Disputes.* Cambridge, Mass.: Harvard University Press.

Mnookin, Robert H., Scott R. Peppet, & Andrew S. Tulumello (1996) "The Tension Between Empathy and Assertiveness," 12 *Negot. J.* 217.

Moffit, Michael (2003) "Suing Mediators," 83 *B.U. L. Rev.* 147.

Moffit, Michael (2003) "Ten Ways to Get Sued: A Guide for Mediators," 8 *Harv. Negot. L. Rev.* 81.

Moffitt, Michael L. & Robert C. Bordone, eds. (2005) *The Handbook of Dispute Resolution,* San Francisco: Jossey-Bass.

Moffit, Michael (2009) "Three Things to Be Against ("Settlement" Not Included)," 78 *Fordham L. Rev.* 1203.

Moore, Christopher (2004) *The Mediation Process: Practical Strategies for Resolving Conflict.* San Francisco: Jossey-Bass.

Mosten, Forrest S. (1996) *The Complete Guide to Mediation: The Cutting-Edge Approach to Family Law Practice.* Chicago: ABA Section of Family Law.

Murnighan, J. Keith (1992) *Bargaining Games.* New York: W. Morrow.

Murray, John S. (1986) "Understanding Competing Theories of Negotiation," 2 *Negot. J.* 179.

Nadler, Janice (2001) "In Practice: Electronically Mediated Dispute Resolution and E-Commerce," 17 *Negot. J.* 333.

Nelken, Melissa L. (2007) *Understanding Negotiation.* Cincinnati: Anderson.

Niemic, Robert J., Donna Stienstra, & Randall E. Ravitz (2001) *Guide to Judicial Management of Cases in ADR.* Washington, D.C.: Federal Judicial Center.

Nierenberg, Gerald I. (1981) *The Art of Negotiating* New York: Pocket Books.

Nolan-Haley, Jacqueline (1996) "Court Mediation and the Search for Justice Through Law," 74 *Wash. Univ. L. Q.* 47.

Nolan-Haley, Jacqueline (1998) "Lawyers, Clients, and Mediation," 73 *Notre Dame L. Rev.* 1369.

Ochs, Jack, & Alvin E. Roth (1989) "An Experimental Study of Sequential Bargaining," 79 *Am. Econ. Rev.* 335.

O'Connor, Kathleen M., & Peter J. Carnevale (1997) "A Nasty but Effective Negotiation Strategy: Misrepresentation of a Common-Value Issue," 23 *Personality & Soc. Psychol. Bull.* 504.

O'Hara, Erin Anne, & Douglas Yarn (2002) "On Apology and Concilience," 77 *Wash. L. Rev.* 1121.

Olson, Walter (1991) *The Litigation Explosion.* New York: Penguin Books.

Ordover, Abraham P., & Andrea Doneff (2002) *Alternatives to Litigation: Mediation, Arbitration, and the Art of Dispute Resolution.* Notre Dame, IN: NITA.

Owen, Rebecca M. (2005) "In re Uncertainty: A Uniform and Confidential Treatment of Evidentiary and Advocatory Materials Used in Mediation," 20 *Ohio St. J. on Disp. Resol.* 911.

Parks, McLean, et al. (1996) "Distributing Adventitious Outcomes: Social Norms, Egocentric Martyrs, and the Effects of Future Relationships," 67 *Org. Behav. & Human Decision Proc.* 181.

Peppet, Scott R. (2002) "Mindfulness in the Law and ADR: Can Saints Negotiate?" 7 *Harv. Negot. L. Rev.* 83 (Spring).

Peppet, Scott R. (2004) "Contract Formation in Imperfect Markets: Should We Use Mediators in Deals?" 38 *Ohio St. J. on Disp. Resol.* 283.

Perry, Linda A.M., et al., eds. (1992) *Constructing and Reconstructing Gender.* Albany, NY: State University of New York Press.

Perschbacher, Rex R. (1985) "Regulating Lawyers' Negotiations," 27 *Ariz. L. Rev.* 75.

Peters, Geoffrey M. (1987) "The Use of Lies in Negotiation," 48 *Ohio St. L. J.* 1.

Picker, Bennett G. (1999) "New Roles: Problem Solving ADR: New Challenges, New Roles, and New Opportunities," 72 *Temple L. Rev.* 883 (Winter).

Picker, Bennett G. (2003) *Mediation Practice Guide: A Handbook for Resolving Business Disputes.* Washington, D.C.: ABA Section of Dispute Resolution.

Picker, Bennett G. (2008) "Navigating Relationships: The Invisible Barriers to Resolution," 2 *Amer. J. of Mediation* 41.

Pinkley, Robin L., et al., "The Impact of Alternatives to Settlement in Dyadic Negotiation," 57 Org. Behav. & Human Decision Proc. 97 (1994)

Plant, David W. (2008) *We Must Talk Because We Can.* Paris: International Chamber of Commerce.

Polythress, Norman G. (1994) "Procedural Preferences, Perceptions of Fairness and Compliance with Outcomes: A Study of Alternatives to the Standard Adversary Trial Procedure," 18 *L. & Hum. Behav.* 361.

Polzer, Jeffrey T., et al. (1993) "The Effects of Relationship and Justification in an Interdependent Allocation," 2 *Group Decision & Negot.* 135.

Press, Sharon (1998) "Florida's Court-Connected State Mediation Program," in Edward J. Bergman & John G. Bickerman, eds., *Court-Annexed Mediation: Critical Perspectives on State and Federal Programs.* Washington, D.C.: ABA Section of Dispute Resolution.

Price, Marty (2000) "Personalizing Crime: Mediation Produces Restorative Justice for Victims and Offenders," 7 *Disp. Res. Mag.* 8 (Fall).

Priest, George, & Benjamin Klein (1984) "The Selection of Disputes for Litigation," 13 *J. Legal Stud.* 1.

Rachlinski, Jeffrey J. (1996) "Gains, Losses, and the Psychology of Litigation," 70 *S. Cal. L. Rev.* 113.

Raiffa, Howard (2002) *Negotiation Analysis: The Science and Art of Collaborative Decision Making.* Cambridge, Mass.: Harvard University Press.

Raiffa, Howard (1985) "Post-Settlement Settlements," 1 *Negot. J.* 9.

Raiffa, Howard (1982) *The Art and Science of Negotiation.* Cambridge, Mass.: Harvard University Press.

Raitt, Susan E., Jay Folberg, Joshua Rosenberg & Robert Barrett (1993) "The Use of Mediation in Small Claims Courts," 9 *Ohio St. J. Disp. Res.* 55.

Reichert, Klaus (2005) "Confidentiality in International Mediation," 59 *J. Disp. Resol.* 60.

Reno, Janet (2001) "Promoting Problem Solving and Peacemaking as Enduring Values in Our Society," 19 *Alternatives* 16.

Resnik, Judith (1995) "Many Doors? Closing Doors? Alternative Dispute Resolution and Adjudication," 10 *Ohio St. J. on Disp. Res.* 211.

Riskin, Leonard (1993) "Mediator Orientations, Strategies and Techniques," 12 *Alternatives* 111.

Riskin, Leonard (1996) "Understanding Mediator's Orientations, Strategies, and Techniques: A Grid for the Perplexed," 1 *Harv. Negot. L. Rev.* 7 (Spring).

Riskin, Leonard (2003) "Decision-Making in Mediation: The New Old Grid and the New New Grid System," 79 *Notre Dame L. Rev.* 1 (December).

Riskin, Leonard (2003) "Retiring and Replacing the Grid of Mediator Orientations," 21 *Alternatives* 69.

Riskin, Leonard L. & James E. Westbrook (1998) *Dispute Resolution and Lawyers* (2d ed.). St. Paul, MN: West.

Robbennolt, Jennifer K. (2003) "Apologies and Legal Settlement: An Eumirical Examination," 102 *Michigan L. Rev.* 460.

Robinson, Peter (1998) "Contending with Wolves in Sheep's Clothing: A Cautiously Cooperative Approach to Mediation Advocacy," 50 *Baylor L. Rev.* 963.

Robinson, Robert J. (1995) "Defusing the Exploding Offer: The Farpoint Gambit," 11 *Negot. J.* 277.

Rogers, Joshua S. (2004) "Riner v. Newbraugh: The Role of Mediator Testimony in the Enforcement of Mediated Agreements," 107 *W. Va. L. Rev.* 329.

Rose, Carol (1995) "Bargaining and Gender," 18 *Harv. J. L. & Pub. Pol'y.* 547.

Rosenberg, Joshua D., & Jay Folberg (1994) "Alternative Dispute Resolution: An Empirical Analysis," 46 *Stan. L. Rev.* 1487.

Rosengard, Lee A. (2004) "Learning From Law Firms: Using Co-Mediation to Train New Mediators," 59 *Disp. Resol. J.* 16.

Ross, David (2000) "Strategic Considerations in Choosing a Mediator: A Mediator's Perspective," 2 *J. Alt. Disp. Res. in Empl.* 7 (Spring).

Ross, Lee (1995) "Reactive Devaluation in Negotiation and Conflict Resolution," Kenneth Arrow, et al., eds., *Barriers to Conflict Resolution*. New York: W.W. Norton.

Ross, Lee, & Andrew Ward (1995) "Psychological Barriers to Dispute Resolution," 27 *Advances Experimental Soc. Psychol.* 255.

Roth, Bette J., Randall W. Wulff & Charles A. Cooper (1993) *The Alternative Dispute Resolution Practice Guide*. Scarborough: Carswell.

Rubin, Jeffrey Z. (1993) "*Conflict From a Psychological Perspective*," in Laviria Hall, ed., Negotiation Strategies for Mutual Gain. Newbury Parle, CA: Sage.

Rubin, Jeffrey Z. (1991) "Some Wise and Mistaken Assumptions About Conflict and Negotiation," William J. Breslin & Jeffrey Z. Rubin, eds., *Negotiation Theory and Practice*. Cambridge, MA: Program on Negotiation.

Rubin, Jeffrey Z., & Bert R. Brown (1975) *The Social Psychology of Bargaining and Negotiation*. New York: Academic Press.

Rubin, Jeffrey Z., & Frank E.A. Sander (1991) "Culture, Negotiation, and the Eye of the Beholder," 7 *Negot. J.* 249.

Rubin, Michael H. (1995) "The Ethics of Negotiation: Are There Any?" 56 *La. L. Rev.* 447.

Rule, Colin (2002) *Online Dispute Resolution for Business: B2B, Ecommerce, Consumer, Employment, Insurance, and Other Commercial Conflicts* San Francisco: Jossey-Bass.

Rummel, R.J. (1991) *The Conflict Helix*. New Brunswick, NJ: Transaction.

Salacuse, Jeswald W. (1988) "Making Deals in Strange Places: A Beginner's Guide to International Business Negotiations," 4 *Negot. J.* 5.

Salacuse, Jeswald W. (1998) "Ten Ways That Culture Affects Negotiating Style: Some Survey Results," 14 *Negot. J.* 221.

Salacuse, Jeswald (2002) "Mediation in International Business," in J. Bercovitch, ed., *Studies in International Mediation*. New York: Palgrave Macmillan.

Salacuse, Jeswald W. (2003) *The Global Negotiator: Making, Managing, and Mending Deals Around the World in the Twenty-First Century*. Hampshire, UK: Palgrave Macmillan.

Salem, Richard (2003) "The Benefits of Empathic Listening," Conflict Research Consortium, University of Colorado, *http://www.crinfo.org*.

Scanlon, Kathleen, ed. (1999) *Mediator's Deskbook*. New York: CPR Institute.

Schelling, Thomas C. (1960) *The Strategy of Conflict*. Cambridge, Mass.: Harvard University Press.

Schneider, Andrea Kupfer (2000) "Perceptions, Reputation and Reality: An Empirical Study of Negotiation Styles," 6 *ABA Disp Res. Mag.* 24 (Summer).

Schneider, Andrea Kupfer (2002) "Shattering Negotiation Myths: Empirical Evidence on the Effectiveness of Negotiation Style," 7 *Harv. Negot. L. Rev.*, 143 (Spring).

Schon, Donald (1983) *The Reflective Practitioner*. New York: Basic Books.

Sebenius, James K. (2002) "Caveats for Cross-Border Negotiations," 18 *Negot. J.* 122.

Senger, Jeffrey M. (2004) *Federal Dispute Resolution: Using Alternative Dispute Resolution with the United States Government*. San Francisco: Jossey-Bass.

Senger, Jeffrey M. (2002) "In Practice: Tales of the Bazaar — Interest-Based Negotiation Across Cultures," 18 *Negot. J.* 233 (July).

Seul, Jeffrey R. (1999) "How Transformative Is Transformative Mediation?: A Constructive-Developmental Assessment," 15 *Ohio St. J. on Disp. Resol.* 135.

Shapiro, Ronald M., & Mark A. Jankowski, with James Dale (2001) *The Power of Nice* (2d. ed.). New York: John Wiley & Sons.

Shell, G. Richard (1988) "Substituting Ethical Standards for Common Law Rules in Commercial Cases: An Emerging Statutory Trend," 82 *Nw. Univ. L. Rev.* 1198.

Shell, G. Richard (1991) "Opportunism and Trust in Negotiation of Commercial Contracts: Toward a New Cause of Action," 44 *Vand. L. Rev.* 221 (1991)

Shell, G. Richard (2006) *Bargaining for Advantage: Negotiation Strategies for Reasonable People*. New York: Viking.

Sherman, Edward F. (1988) " From 'Loser Pays' to Modified Offer of Judgment Rules: Reconciling Incentives to Settle with Access to Justice," 76 *Tex. L. Rev.* 1863.

Silbey, Susan S. (2002) "The Emperor's New Clothes: Mediation Mythology and Markets," 2002 *J. Disp. Resol.* 171.

Simon, William H. (1988) "Ethical Discretion in Lawyering," 101 *Harv. L. Rev.* 1083.

Singh, J. P. (2008) *Negotiation and the Global Information Economy*. New York: Cambridge

Singer, Linda (1994) *Settling Disputes: Conflict Resolution in Business, Families, and the Legal System*. Boulder, CO: Westview.

Sjostedt, Gunnar (2003) *Professional Cultures in International Negotiation: Bridge or Rift?* Lanham, MD: Lexington Books.

Slaikeu, Karl A. (1996) *When Push Comes to Shove: A Practical Guide to Mediating Disputes*. San Francisco: Jossey-Bass.

Slavitt, Evan (2006) "Using Risk Analysis as a Mediation Tool," 2006 *Disp. Resol. J.* 18.

Smith, Robert M. (2000) "Advocacy in Mediation: A Dozen Suggestions," 26 *S.F. Att'y* 14.

Spegel, Nadja M., Bernadette Rogers, Ross P. Buckley (1998) *Negotiation: Theory and Techniques*.

Sydney, Australia: Butterworths.

Sperber, Philip (1985) *Attorney's Practice Guide to Negotiations*. Wilmette, Ill.: Callaghan & Co.

Spolter, Jerry (2000) "A Mediator's Tip: Talk to Me!" *The Recorder* 4 (March 8).

Stallworth, Lamont E., et al. (2001) "Discrimination in the Workplace: How Mediation Can Help," *Disp. Res. J.* 35.

Starr, V. Hale (1999) "The Simple Math of Negotiating," 22 *Trial L.* 5 (January — February)

Stempel, Jeffrey W. (1997) "Beyond Formalism and False Dichotomies: The Need for Institutionalizing a Flexible Concept of the Mediator's Role," 24 *Fla. St. U. L. Rev.* 949.

Stern, David M. (1998) "Mediation: An Old Dog with Some New Tricks," 24 *Litigation* 31.

Sternberg, Robert J., & Diane M. Dobson (1987) "Resolving Interpersonal Conflicts: An Analysis of Stylistic Consistency," 52 *J. Pers. & Soc. Psychol.* 794.

Sternberg, Robert J., & Lawrence J. Soriano (1984) "Styles of Conflict Resolution," 47 *J. Pers. & Soc. Psychol.* 115.

Sternlight, Jean R. & Jennifer Robbennolt (2008) "Good Lawyers Should Be Good Psychologists: Insights for Interviewing and Counseling Clients" 3 *Ohio State Journal on Dispute Resolution Vol.* 23

Stienstra, Donna (1998) "Demonstrating the Possibilities of Providing Mediation Early and by Court Staff: The Western District of Missouri's Early Assessment Program," *Court-Annexed Mediation: Critical Perspectives on State and Federal Programs* 251.

Stienstra, Donna, Molly Johnson, & Patricia Lombard (1997) "Report to the Judicial Conference Committee on Court Administration and Case Management: A Study of the Five Demonstration Programs Established Under the Civil Justice Reform Act of 1990." Washington, D.C.: Federal Judicial Center.

Stipanowich, Thomas J. (1998) "The Multi-Door Contract and Other Possibilities," 13 *Ohio St. J. on Disp. Resol.* 3.

Stipanowich, Thomas J. (2001) "Contracts Symposium: Contract and Conflict Managment," 2001 *Wis. L. Rev.* 831.

Stipanowich, Thomas J. (2004) "ADR and 'The Vanishing Trial': What We Know–and What We Don't," *Disp. Res. Mag.* (Summer).

Stone, Douglas, Bruce Patton, & Sheila Heen (1999) *Difficult Conversations: How to Discuss What Matters Most*. New York: Penguin Books.

Stone, Katharine V.W. (2000) *Private Justice: The Law of Alternative Dispute Resolution*. New York:

Foundation Press. Strudler, Alan (1998) "Incommensurable Goods, Rightful Lies, and the Wrongness of Fraud," 146 *U. Pa. L. Rev.* 1529.

Stulberg, Joseph (1981) "The Theory and Practice of Mediation: A Reply to Professor Susskind," 6 *Vt. L. Rev.* 85.

Stulberg, Joseph (1997) "Facilitative Versus Evaluative Mediator Orientations: Piercing the 'Grid' Lock," 24 *Fla. St. U. L. Rev.* 985.

Sumner, Anna Aven (2003) "Is the Gummy Rule of Today Truly Better Than the Toothy Rule of Tomorrow? How Federal Rule 68 Should be Modified," 52 Duke L. J. 1055.

Sullivan, Jay (2003) "Lawyers and Technology: A Crash Course in Writing Effective E-Mails," 229 *N.Y.L.J.* 5, Feb. 2003.

Susskind, Lawrence (1981) "Environmental Mediation and the Accountability Problem," 6 *Vt. L. Rev.* 1.

Susskind, Lawrence, Sarah McKearnan, & Jennifer Thomas Larmer (eds.) (1999) *The Consensus Building Handbook: A Comprehensive Guide to Reaching Agreement*. Thousand Oaks, CA: Sage.

Symposium (2001) "ADR and the Professional Responsibility of Lawyers," 28 *Ford. Urb. L. J.* No. 4. Taft, Lee (2000) "Apology Subverted: The Commodification of Apology," 109 *Yale L. J.* 1155.

Taleb, Nassim (2007) *The Black Swan*. New York: Random House.

Temkin, Barry R. (2004) "Misrepresentation by Omission in Settlement Negotiations: Should there Be a Silent Safe Harbor?" 18 Geo. J. Legal Ethics 179.

Tesler, Pauline H. (2003) "Collaborative Law Neutrals Produce Better Resolution," 21 *Alternatives* 1.

Tesler, Pauline H. (2001) *Collaborative Law*. Chicago: ABA Section on Family Law.

Thaler, Richard H. (1988) "Anomalies: The Ultimatum Game," 2 *J. Econ. Persp.* 195.

Thompson, Leigh (2001) *The Mind and Heart of the Negotiator* (2d. ed.). Upper Saddle River, N.J.: Prentice-Hall.

Thompson, Leigh L., et al. (1999) "Some Life it Hot: The Case for the Emotional Negotiator," Leigh L. Thompson, et al. *Shared Cognition in Organizations: The Management of Knowledge*. Mahwah, NJ: LEA.

Thompson, Leigh & Reid Hastie (1990) "Social Perception in Negotiation," 47 Org. *Beh. & Human Dec. Processes* 98.

Thompson, Leigh, & Janice Nadler (2002) "Negotiating Via Information Technology: Theory and Application," 58 *J. Soc. Issues* 109.

Thompson, Peter (2004) "Enforcing Rights Generated in Court-Connected Mediation — Tension Between the Aspirations of a Private Facilitative Process and the Reality of Public

Adversarial Justice," 19 *Ohio St. J.Disp. Resol.* 509.

Trachte-Huber, E. Wendy & Stephen K. Huber (1999) *Mediation and Negotiation: Reaching Agreement.* Cincinnati: Anderson. Tversky, Amos, & Daniel Kahneman (1992 "Advances in Prospect Theory: Cumulative Representation of Uncertainty," 5 *J. Risk & Uncertainty* 297.

Uelmen, Gerald F. (1990) "Playing 'Godfather' in Settlement Negotiations: The Ethics of Using Threats," *Cal. Litigation* 3 (Fall).

Ury, William (1993) *Getting Past No: Negotiating Your Way From Confrontation to Cooperation.* New York: Bantam Books.

van Dijk, Eric, & Daan van Knippenberg (1996) "Buying and Selling Exchange Goods: Loss Aversion and the Endowment Effect," 17 *J. Econ. Psych.* 517.

Wade, John (2004) "Representing Clients Effectively in Negotiation, Conciliation and Mediation of Family Disputes," 18 *Austl. J. Fam. L.* 283.

Waldman, Ellen A. (2004) "Healing Hearts or Righting Wrongs?: A Mediation on the Goals of 'Restorative Justice,'" 25 *Hamline J. Pub. L. & Pol'y* 355.

Walton, Richard E., Joel E, Cutcher-Gershenfeld, & Robert B. McKersie (2000) *Strategic Negotiations: A Theory of Change in Labor-Management Relations.* Ithaca: Cornell University Press.

Wangerin, Paul T. (1994) "The Political and Economic Roots of the 'Adversary System' of Justice and Alternative Dispute Resolution," 9 *Ohio St. J. on Disp. Res.* 203.

Ware, Stephen J. (2001) *Alternative Dispute Resolution.* St. Paul: West.

Ware, Stephen J. & Sarah Rudolph Cole (2000) "Introduction: ADR in Cyberspace," 15 *Ohio St. J. on Disp. Res.* 589.

Watkins, Michael, & Susan Rosengrant (2001) *Breakthrough International Negotiations.* San Francisco: Jossey-Bass.

Watkins, Normal J. (1999) "Negotiating the Complex Case," 41 *For the Defense* 36 (July).

Watson, Carol (1994) "Gender versus Power as a Predictor of Negotiation Behavior and Outcome," 10 *Negot. J.* 117.

Weinstein, John (1996) "Advocacy in Mediation," 32 *Trial* 31.

Welsh, Nancy A. (2001) "Making Deals in Court-Connected Mediation: What's Justice Got to Do
With It?," 79 *Wash. Univ. L.Q.* 787 (Fall).

Welsh, Nancy A. (2004) "Remembering the Role of Justice in Resolution: Insights from Procedural and Social Justice Theories," 54 *J. Legal. Educ.* 49.

Wetlaufer, Gerald B. (1990) "The Ethics of Lying in Negotiation," 76 *Iowa L. Rev.* 1219.

Wetlaufer, Gerald B. (1996) "The Limits of Integrative Bargaining," 85 *Geo. L. J.* 369.

White, James J. (1984) "Essay Review: The Pros and Cons of 'Getting to Yes;'" Roger Fisher, "Comments on White's Review," 34 *J. of Legal Educ.* 115.

White, James J. (1980) "Machiavelli and the Bar: Ethical Limitation on Lying in Negotiation," 1980 *Am. Bar. Found. Res. J.* 926.

Wilkinson, John H., ed. (1990 and annual supplements) *Donovan Leisure Newton & Irvine ADR Practice Book.* New York: Wiley Law Pulbications.

Williams, Gerald R. (2007) *Legal Negotiation.* St. Paul: West Publishing.

Williams, Gerald R. (1996) "Negotiation as a Healing Process," *J. of Disp. Res.* 33.

Wissler, Roselle L. (2001) "To Evaluate or Facilitate? Parties' Perceptions of Mediation Affected by Mediator Style," 7 *Disp. Res. Mag.* 35 (Winter).

Wissler, Roselle L. (2002) "Court-Connected Mediation in General Civil Cases: What We Know from Empirical Research," 17 *Ohio St. J. on Disp. Resol.* 641.

Wittenberg, Carol, Susan Mackenzie, & Margaret Shaw (1996) "Employment Disputes,"
in D. Golann, ed., *Mediating Legal Disputes: Effective Strategies for Lawyers and Mediators.* Boston: Little, Brown.

Wood, Robert W. (2007) "Taxing Matters in Settling Cases," 27 *California Lawyer* 41.

Young, Michael D. (2007) "Mediation Gone Wild," 25 Alternatives 103.

Zitrin, Richard A. (1999) "The Case Against Secret Settlements'' 2 *J. Inst. For Study of Legal Ethics* 115.

Zitrin, Richard, & Carol M. Langford (1999) *The Moral Compass of the American Lawyer.* New York: Ballantine Books.

WEB SITES

Alternative Dispute Resolution Section of the Association of American Law Schools, http://www.law.missouri.edu/aalsadr/index.htm.

American Bar Association Section of Dispute Resolution, http://www.abanet.org/dispute

Art of Negotiating, http://www.projectkickstart.com.

The Association for Conflict Resolution, http://www.acrnet.org (2003).

Center for Analysis of Alternative Dispute Resolution Systems, http://www.caadrs.org

Center for Dispute Resolution, Williamette University College of Law, http://www.willamette.edu/law/wlo/dis-res.

The Center for Information Technology and Dispute Resolution, http://www.odr.info.

Center for the Study of Dispute Resolution, University of Missouri, http:// www.law.missouri .edu/csdr/adr

Centre for Effective Dispute Resolution, http:// www.cedr.co.uk

Court ADR Resource Center, http://courtadr. org/.

Collaborative Practice, http://www.collaborative practice.com.

Conflict Research Consortium, A Comprehensive Gateway to the Websites of the University of Colorado Conflict Research Consortium, http://conflict.colorado.edu.

Conflict Resolution Information Source, Conflict Research Consortium, University of Colorado, http://www.crinfo.com (1999).

CPR Institute of Dispute Resolution, http:// www.cpradr.org

Dispute Resolution Channel, http://mediate .com.

Federal ADR Network, http://www.adr.af.mil

Indiana Conflict Resolution Institute, http:// www.spea.indiana.edu/icri/condataexp.htm (1999).

JAMS (The Resolution Experts), http:// www.jamsadr.com.

The Negotiator Assistant, ddruckman@gmu .edu.

Negotiator Pro, http://www.negotiatorpro.com.

Treeage Software, Software for Decision Analysis, Cost Effectiveness, Decision Trees, Markov Models, Influence Diagrams, and Monte Carlo Simulation, http://www.treeage.com (2004).

Win Squared: Simple Software for Power Persuasion, http://www.arcadiansoftware.com (2002).

CASES

Abbot Ford, Inc. v. The Superior Court of Los Angeles County; Ford Motor Co., 43 Cal.3d 858 (1987).

Alcala Co., Inc. v. Sup. Ct.,
57 Cal.2d 349 (1996).

Puder v. Buechel, 183 N.J. 428 (2005).

BMW of North America, Inc. v. Krathen, 471 So.2d 585 (1985).

Evans v. Jeff D., 475 U.S. 717 (1986).

KentuckyBarAss'nv.Geisler,938S.W.578 (KY.1997).

Marek v. Chesny, 473 U.S. 105 (1985).

Muhammad v. Strassburger et al., 528 Pa. 345 (1991).

Nicolet Instrument Corp. v. Lindquest & Vennum, 34 F.3d 453 (7th Cir. 1994).

Sumeral. v. Goodyear Tire & Rubber Co., Colo. App., May 27, 2009.

Ziegelheim v. Apollo, 128 N.J. 250 (1992).

TABLE OF CASES

Principal cases are indicated by italics.

INDEX